T0299064

Japan's Network Economy

Japan's economy has long been described as organized around or embedded in networks. In times past, the web of stable, reciprocated relations among Japanese banks, firms, and ministries was thought to play an important role in Japan's ability to navigate smoothly around economic shocks. Now those networks are widely blamed for Japan's faltering competitiveness. This book applies the perspective of structural sociology to a study of how the form and functioning of the Japanese network economy has evolved from the pre-war era to the late 1990s. It asks in particular whether, in the face of deregulation, globalization, and financial disintermediation, Japan's corporate networks – the keiretsu groupings in particular – have withered away in terms both of lost cohesion and their historical function of supporting member firms in hard times. Based on detailed quantitative and qualitative analysis, the book's answer is a qualified "yes." Relationships remain central to the Japanese way of business, but they are much more subordinated to the competitive strategy of the enterprise than was true of the network economy of the past.

James R. Lincoln is Warren E. and Carol Spieker Professor in the Organizational Behavior and Industrial Relations group at the Walter A. Haas School of Business at the University of California at Berkeley. He is the author (with Arne Kalleberg) of *Culture, Control, and Commitment: A Study of Work Organizations and Work Attitudes in the U.S. and Japan* (Cambridge University Press, 1990).

Michael L. Gerlach is an associate professor at the Walter A. Haas School of Business, University of California at Berkeley. He has previously published a major book on Japan, *Alliance Capitalism: The Social Organization of Japanese Business* (University of California Press, 1992), as well as numerous articles and book chapters on business in Japan.

Structural Analysis in the Social Sciences

Mark Granovetter, editor

The series Structural Analysis in the Social Sciences presents approaches that explain social behavior and institutions by reference to relations among such concrete entities as persons and organizations. This contrasts with at least four other popular strategies: (a) reductionist attempts to explain by a focus on individuals alone; (b) explanations stressing the casual primacy of such abstract concepts as ideas, values, mental harmonies, and cognitive maps (thus, "structuralism" on the Continent should be distinguished from structural analysis in the present sense); (c) technological and material determination; (d) explanation using "variables" as the main analytic concepts (as in the "structural equation" models that dominated much of the sociology of the 1970s), where structure is that connecting variables rather that actual social entities.

The social network approach is an important example of the strategy of structural analysis; the series also draws on social science theory and research that is not framed explicitly in network terms, but stresses the importance of relations rather than the atomization of reduction or the determination of ideas, technology, or material conditions. Though the structural perspective has become extremely popular and influential in all the social sciences, it does not have a coherent identity, and no series yet pulls together such work under a single rubric. By bringing the achievements of structurally oriented scholars to a wider public, the Structural Analysis series hopes to encourage the use of this very fruitful approach.

Mark Granovetter

Other Books in the Series:

1. Mark S. Mizruchi and Michael Schwartz, eds., *Intercorporate Relations: The Structural Analysis of Business*
2. Barry Wellman and S. D. Berkowitz, eds., *Social Structures: A Network Approach*
3. Ronald L. Breiger, ed., *Social Mobility and Social Structure*
4. David Knoke, *Political Networks: The Structural Perspective*
5. John L. Campbell, J. Rogers Hollingsworth, and Leon N. Lindberg, eds., *Governance of the American Economy*
6. Kyriakos Kontopoulos, *The Logics of Social Structure*
7. Philippa Pattison, *Algebraic Models for Social Networks*
8. Stanley Wasserman and Katherine Faust, *Social Network Analysis: Methods and Applications*
9. Gary Herrigel, *Industrial Constructions: The Sources of German Industrial Power*
10. Philipe Bourgois, *In Search of Respect: Selling Crack in El Barrio*
11. Per Hage and Frank Harary, *Island Networks: Communication, Kinship, and Classification Structures in Oceania*
12. Thomas Schweizer and Douglas R. White, eds., *Kinship, Networks and Exchange*
13. Noah E. Friedkin, *A Structural Theory of Social Influence*
14. David Wank, *Commodifying Communism: Business, Trust, and Politics in a Chinese City*
15. Rebecca Adams and Graham Allan, *Placing Friendship in Context*

Japan's Network Economy

Structure, Persistence, and Change

JAMES R. LINCOLN
University of California, Berkeley

MICHAEL L. GERLACH
University of California, Berkeley

 CAMBRIDGE
UNIVERSITY PRESS

CAMBRIDGE
UNIVERSITY PRESS

32 Avenue of the Americas, New York NY 10013-2473, USA

Cambridge University Press is part of the University of Cambridge.

It furthers the University's mission by disseminating knowledge in the pursuit of education, learning and research at the highest international levels of excellence.

www.cambridge.org
Information on this title: www.cambridge.org/9780521453042

© Cambridge University Press 2004

First published 2004
First paperback edition 2007

A catalogue record for this publication is available from the British Library

Library of Congress Cataloguing in Publication data

Lincoln, James R.
Japan's network economy : structure, persistence, and change / James R. Lincoln and Michael L. Gerlach.
    p.   cm. – (Structural analysis in the social sciences)
Includes bibliographical references and index.
ISBN 0-521-45304-6
1. Business networks – Japan.   2. Strategic alliances (Business) – Japan.
3. Organizational change – Japan.   4. Industrial organization – Japan.
I. Gerlach, Michael L.   II. Title.   III. Series.
HD69.S8L553   2004
338.8'7 – dc22   2003065167

ISBN 978-0-521-45304-2 Hardback
ISBN 978-0-521-71189-0 Paperback

To our families

Contents

Figures

Tables

xiii

Acknowledgments

This book has been longer in the making than we care to admit. Academic careers have their twists and turns, and both of us took some detours on the road to completion of the project. So it is altogether fitting that we begin with an expression of gratitude to Mark Granovetter, editor of the Cambridge Series on Structural Analysis in the Social Sciences, and to Cambridge University Press Social Science Editor Alia Winters for their patience and support over the course of a project that extended well beyond the contractually agreed-upon completion date. We are also grateful to Mark for his thoughtful comments on successive drafts of the manuscript.

The research of professors invariably in part reflects the efforts of their students, and our work here is no exception. We are much indebted to a group of talented and dedicated Berkeley graduate students, who served not just as research assistants, but often as colleagues and collaborators as well. Topping the list is Christina Ahmadjian, now on the faculty of the Graduate School of International Corporate Strategy at Hitotsubashi University and an established Japan business scholar in her own right. Chris was a full partner in much of the work discussed in these pages, doing interviews, gathering data, designing and conducting analyses, coauthoring papers, and sharing her experience, theoretical and methodological acumen, and clear sense for what was going on in Japan. Didier Guillot, another Berkeley doctoral student (now on the faculty of INSEAD), contributed importantly in the late stages of the project to the management and analysis of data, the interviewing, and the writing and preparation of papers. Eliot Mason's expert data analytic skills and helpful thoughts on organization and network issues are much appreciated, as is Mike Thayer's conquest of the daunting data management challenges posed by Chapter 3's dyad analysis. In an early phase of our work, Berkeley doctoral students Joan Boothe, Frank Freitas, Ha Hoang, and Peggy Takahashi supplied us with able research assistance. We further acknowledge the cheerful diligence of our undergraduate coders who put in hour after hour at the Institute of Industrial Relations (IIR) translating and transcribing Japanese-language materials. We are grateful, too, to IIR and Haas staff members Olivia Armstrong, Deborah Huoy, and Lorraine Seiji, among others, who supplied us with efficient and capable administrative assistance.

We owe a considerable debt to a number of Japanese scholars. At the start of the project, Ikujiro Nonaka arranged a productive and stimulating year for the two of us at the Institute of Innovation Research at Hitotsubashi University. He also opened doors to companies and enlightened us with his firm grasp of the philosophical underpinnings of Japanese business practice. Another senior Hitotsubashi figure at the time, Ken-ichi Imai, arranged interviews with top firms and trade associations, directed us to data sources, and otherwise helped get our work off the ground. His own influential network theory of the Japanese economy was of particular value as we struggled to formulate the structuralist perspective that frames this volume. Other prominent Hitotsubashi scholars whose help we gratefully acknowledge are Tsuyoshi Tsuru and Konosuke Odaka, who invited Jim Lincoln to spend four months in 2001 in the vibrant intellectual setting of Hitotsubashi's Institute of Economic Research (IER). Lunch discussions with Akira Goto, Hideshi Itoh, Toshi Nishiguchi, and other resident faculty made our Hitotsubashi stays all the more stimulating and edifying. Two joint conferences between Hitotsubashi's IER and Berkeley's Institute of Industrial Relations provided further opportunities to hash through some intriguing issues in Japanese business and labor practice with a group of distinguished American and Japanese scholars.

Several faculty at Kyoto University were also quite instrumental in the progress of our work. Masahiro Shimotani of the Economics Department has long been a friend, supporter, and collaborator. His deep understanding of corporate governance and organization issues was immensely helpful in giving us a fix on what was happening in turbulent late 1990s Japan. Until the sad event of his premature death in 1996, Banri Asanuma, another eminent Kyoto University economist, enlightened us on several occasions with his analysis of the organization of Japanese electronics and auto industry supply networks. A third Kyodai scholar, Hiroshi Shiomi, assisted with interviews and opened our eyes to a number of important issues in auto industry subcontracting and distribution.

A very special debt is owed Yoshi Nakata, a long-time friend and the founding dean of the new Management School at Doshisha University. On multiple occasions Yoshi paved the way for Jim Lincoln to teach and study in that nicest of Japanese cities – Kyoto – and in Doshisha's supportive academic environment. Yoshi also helped with company interviews, data access, research assistance, and a multitude of other tasks. Other

Doshisha colleagues, most notably Mitsuo Ishida and Hugh Whittaker, provided stimulating company and now and then guidance on how to navigate the instructional and administrative landscape at Doshisha. Having Hugh, formerly of Cambridge and a major figure in Japanese management studies, as a Doshisha colleague in 2002–03 was a particular treat. Still other friends, colleagues, and students at Japanese universities provided assistance, advice, and insight along the way.

We are further indebted to the Center for Global Communications (Glocom) and the Institute for Social Research at the University of Tokyo where Michael Gerlach spent time as a visiting scholar in 2000 and 2001. Special thanks are owed to Shumpei Kumon of Glocom, who helped provide contacts for interviews and other logistical support through his organization.

We also gratefully acknowledge the generous funding support of a number of agencies and foundations, specifically the Japan Society for the Promotion of Science, the National Science Foundation (grant SES 891 2498), the Social Science Research Council, the U.S.–Japan Friendship Commission, the University of California Education Abroad and Pacific Rim Programs, the Warren E. and Carol Spieker Chair, and the Center for International Business and Policy and the Institute for Management, Innovation, and Organization of the Haas School of Business. We are also grateful to Haas for the summer support and leave time that made possible lengthy stays in Japan and to Berkeley's Institutes of Industrial Relations and East Asian Studies, which supported us with research and administrative assistance, travel funds, and office space.

Some of the material in these chapters saw life in earlier published work. Parts of Chapter 1 draw on Gerlach and Lincoln (1998). Chapter 2 appeared in early form in Gerlach (1997). Chapters 4 and 5 build on two *American Sociological Review* articles coauthored with then-students Christina Ahmadjian and Peggy Takahashi (Lincoln, Gerlach, and Takahashi, 1992; Lincoln, Gerlach, and Ahmadjian, 1996). A section of Chapter 6 draws on Guillot and Lincoln (2001). Other passages here and there take material from Lincoln and Ahmadjian (2001); Lincoln and Nakata (1997); and Lincoln, Gerlach, and Ahmadjian (1998).

More people than we can fairly give credit to offered useful commentary on our work over the years, among them Clair Brown, Ron Burt, Glenn Carroll, Jerry Davis, Ron Dore, David Flath, Mark Fruin, Gary Hamilton, Leonard Lynn, Mark Mizruchi, Masao Nakamura, Hugh Patrick, Charles Perrow, John Ries, Tom Roehl, Ulrike Schaede, Paul Sheard, Chuck Weathers, Harrison White, and Oliver Williamson. Berkeley colleague and eminent Japan scholar, Bob Cole, provided support in more ways than we can fairly acknowledge. David Vogel's persistent queries as to when the book would be finished and why it was taking so long were a nontrivial spur to completion. Berkeley friends Neil Fligstein and Trond Peterson provided general moral support, insightful commentary on business networks in Europe, and a sympathetic ear to gripes and frustrations. Our work also benefited significantly from the commentary of seminar and workshop participants at Berkeley, British Columbia, Carnegie Mellon, Dartmouth, Davis, the Hong Kong University of Science and Technology, Kobe University, Kyoto University, Marburg, Northwestern, Osaka University, Ritsumeikan, Stanford, the Stockholm School of Economics, UCLA, the University of Tokyo, and Yale. The PRISM (Pacific Roundtable on Industry, Strategy, and Management) group organized by Michael Gerlach and Mark Fruin was for years a stimulating forum for friendly and relaxed, if not always gentle, criticism from a group of accomplished West Coast Japan scholars.

Last but by no means least, we are deeply grateful for the patient and loving support of our families, who put up with far too many weekends and evenings when Dad was busy writing or, worse, not even in the country but off in Japan on research.

Introduction

In Japan...zaibatsu and other affiliations link industrial, commercial, and financial firms in a thick and complex skein of relations matched in no other industrial country.

Caves and Uekusa, 1976:59

Networks and the Japanese "Miracle"

Japan is by all accounts the advanced capitalist society whose market transactions have been most intertwined or embedded in social relations, as Caves and Uekusa suggest in the quote above. The most conspicuous form of network organization in the Japanese economy is keiretsu, a term referring to clusters of interlinked firms that, in the late 1980s, sounded exotic and intimidating given the competitive might of Japanese business at the time, but in the early 2000s smacks of third world crony capitalism, the rigidities of an overly managed economy, and anachronism.

Thus, how Japan's forms of business organization are seen fluctuates with the country's economic fortunes. From the 1950s until the early 1970s, when Japan was growing rapidly but on most development criteria still lagged behind Europe and the United States, a dominant view was that Japan's distinctive economic institutions were cultural anomalies, and the nation's economic advancement was proceeding *in spite*, not because, of them.[1] In the 1980s, with Japan emerging as the equal, if not the superior, of the West in an array of business and technological endeavors, while retaining, even leveraging, its exotic network forms, the flavor of the commentary changed. Japan's peculiar patterns of industrial organization were then claimed to have evolved in ways that enabled the performance with considerable efficiency of the critical functions of a modern market

---

[1] See, e.g., Abegglen (1958).

1

2 *Japan's Network Economy*

economy. Its complex network structures looked to be evolutionary advances on Anglo-American style labor, capital, and product markets. Keiretsu ties, main bank monitoring, stable shareholders, and active industrial policy were no longer the residues of Japanese feudalism but were recast as worldwide best practice.

New bodies of economic and management theory argued the merits of Japanese-style corporate governance arrangements, not only in Japan, but in the West as well.[2] Scholars and policy makers concerned with the inability of American shareholders to obtain complete information from and exercise real control over the salaried managers who ran corporations looked to the Japanese system of main bank ties and concentrated and stable shareholding for lessons in the design of corporate monitoring and disciplining systems. Managers, consultants, and policy makers concerned with the quality declines and falling competitiveness of U.S. manufacturing saw a model to emulate in the Japanese vertical keiretsu network, in which a major assembler maintained close, trusting, and reciprocal relations with a relatively small cadre of dedicated suppliers and subcontractors.

Japan in the 2000s: The Collapse of Crony Capitalism?

What a difference a decade can make. The perception is now strong that, battered by global competition, technological change, and (in rapid succession) boom and recession, Japan's network forms of organization – long seen as central to the economy if not the Japanese way of life – are unraveling, leaving Japanese business more market oriented, transparent, arm's length, and geared to the short term. With the bursting of the asset-price bubble in 1991 and the country's plunge into ten years (and counting) of recession and stagnation, the scholars, journalists, and practitioners who had bought the paradigm of Japan as vanguard economy have struggled mightily to find an explanation for what was going on. The easy one, advanced enthusiastically – even jingoistically at times – by hard partisans for the U.S. brand of capitalism, was simply that Japan's chickens had come home to roost. In the Japanese economic crisis – and that of Asia more generally – the long-overdue comeuppance of network or crony capitalism was at hand. Broadly shared again is the sense that Japan succeeded in the past only because it overcame the inherent limitations of its network institutions. Their continued persistence, however, explains the downward spiral of the economy in the 1990s. Critics see the structure

---

[2] Aoki (1988); Dore (1983); Ouchi (1986); Lazear (1979); Sheard (1989a); Womack, Jones, and Roos (1990).

and functioning of Japan's network economy behind an assortment of contemporary ills – from complacency and uncompetitiveness rooted in inbred trade and investment practices to the protection of the corporate unfit and the spread of *moral hazard* due to widespread subsidies and easy bailouts.[3]

Thus, in the global competition of economic paradigms, it appeared by the end of the twentieth century that the American way – with its distinctive mix of large corporations, efficient markets, legal contracting, "tooth and claw" competition, and weak employment relationships – had triumphed.[4] Despite their short-lived posturing as serious alternatives, the continental European and East Asian models were exposed as inefficient and unsustainable, and the United States was once again the global icon of market rationality. The seeming virtues of patient capital, long-termism, the subordination of profit seeking to growth and scale, relationship investing, and stakeholder capitalism had proved hollow and fleeting. Only a decade or so ago such practices were extolled by American academic luminaries such as Lester Thurow, whose book *Head to Head* argued the superiority of German and Japanese "communitarian capitalism."[5] Now, cozy and reciprocal relationships among stable business partners are judged to misallocate capital and distort corporate goals and strategies, all to the deep and lasting detriment of the economy as a whole.

After more than thirty years of relative stability, much evidence backs the conclusion that, however halting and uneven the process, Japan is shedding its "networkness." Under pressure to raise liquidity and dispose of underperforming assets, banks are writing off problem loans and selling "stable" shares, thereby canceling implicit insurance contracts with long-term clients. Manufacturers have responded to pressure from international trading partners to purchase more from foreign vendors. Pressed to cut costs in high-wage Japan, they have also reduced their commitments to domestic suppliers by shifting production offshore, sourcing online, and entering into pacts with one another to design and produce components.[6] Rising concerns over health, working hours, and family life

---

[3] On the role of the Japanese main bank and *convoy* systems in breeding moral hazard, see, for example, Spiegel (2000).

[4] As a *Wall Street Journal* article documented (Murray, 2001), the popular notion that big firms had gone the way of the dinosaur in the new American economy was largely myth. "By 1999, the average annual revenue of the 50 largest public companies in the U.S., about $50.8 billion, was 70% higher than it had been just 15 years earlier, even taking inflation into account. More than 50 public companies currently employ more than 100,000 workers; in the mid-1980s, only 18 did." For a scholarly treatment of small firms in the United States that reaches similar conclusions, see Harrison (1994). On small firms in Japan, see Friedman (1988) and Whittaker (1997).

[5] Thurow (1993).

[6] Ahmadjian and Lincoln (2001).

(e.g., Japan's low fertility rate) have further eroded business networks as managers and officials spend less time in boozy evening social gatherings (*tsukiai*) cultivating interpersonal ties (*jinmyaku*).

Do Japan's network structures deserve the blame now heaped upon them for the country's chronic country travails? Is their wholesale elimination the harsh medicine the economy needs in order to stage a return to steady growth? Many observers who concede that the keiretsu and other network structures played a useful role in the catch-up, high-growth phase of Japanese economic development (1950–73) now feel those forms have long outlived their usefulness. Japan is no longer playing catch-up – it needs to lead, not follow – and the global rules of economic play have changed in fundamental ways.

However, while Japan has stumbled badly, a case can be made that much of the cause lies with the peculiar mix of conditions associated with the late 1980s bubble, a time when Japanese business, caught up in a wave of "irrational exuberance" (to use Alan Greenspan's colorful phrase), embraced what looked more like the style and values of American business than those the world had come to associate with Japan. As one scholar noted:[7]

> sustained by the liberalization of finance, Japanese corporations began to shift away from their real businesses to financial speculation. When the world praised Japanese corporations for their long-term thinking in business strategy in the 1980's, Japanese corporations had begun to turn to short-term profits earned at a rapid rate.

In the bubble years, leading industrial corporations such as Toyota, Sony, and Honda, much admired for their manufacturing capabilities, were making 40–60 percent of their pretax profits from financial machinations or *zaitech*. In 1990, a prominent Tokyo consultant told us, it was very difficult to get a Japanese bank to invest in a manufacturing venture that might take years to produce a return when that same money put into real estate would yield a superior gain in a matter of weeks. An array of forces in the late eighties – the growth of equity financing by large firms, the shift of bank finance to small and medium sized firms, excess household savings, the government's expansionary fiscal and monetary policy, the sharp escalation of the yen a few years before, and widespread construction industry subsidies, not to mention a certain national chutzpah borne of global manufacturing success – conspired to drive stock and real estate prices to astronomical levels. The explosion in wealth also

---

[7] Gao (2001:169).

spawned vast overinvestment in production capacity, setting the stage for steep cutbacks in the wake of the bubble's 1991 collapse.

Moreover, while we will show that the major keiretsu groupings were weakened by the bubble, there is no denying that the speculative fever of the times was both the offspring of and exacerbated by the system of sticky business ties. Cross-shareholdings within the "big-six" horizontal groups (Mitsubishi, Sumitomo, Mitsui, Dai-Ichi Kangyo (DKB), Fuyo, and Sanwa) enabled companies to issue huge volumes of new shares and find ready buyers yet not risk takeover. More important, a far-flung corporate safety net, woven largely of reciprocated keiretsu commitments but also of an array of government supports, spawned an epidemic of moral hazard – the taking of excessive risks on the presumption that someone else would bear the downside. Firms threw money at risky ventures in full confidence that if the bottom did fall out, a main bank or keiretsu bailout would surely be forthcoming.

Finally, in the superheated business climate and brimming overconfidence of the times, the monitoring mechanisms that had in the past afforded some protection against moral hazard broke down. The growth of equity financing in the 1980s undercut the main bank relationship. Indeed, keiretsu relations, instead of monitoring and constraining risky and opportunistic behavior, often fueled it. Large banks and blue-chip corporations used affiliated firms as fronts for dubious real estate and stock deals.[8] Other players, quick to note the heavy hitters lined up to back such ventures, assumed that an investment in trading company Itoman (for example) was a de facto bet on its patron, Sumitomo Bank.[9] While Western policy makers and economic critics such as Richard Katz and Taggart Murphy see the economic gloom of the 1990s as a case of chickens coming home to roost – the accumulated failings of the network economy overwhelming Japan's manufacturing strengths – many in Japan hold to a very different view. In the heated internal debates over what went wrong, one prominent school of thought has it that Japan's travails in the 1990s are the bubble's doing pure and simple. Perhaps the bubble was, as the Western critics suggest, the inevitable outcome of the

---

[8] An amusing anecdote along these lines is the story of the Osaka restaurateur and stock speculator Nui Onoue, chronicled in Kerr (2001). Onoue possessed a ceramic toad, which, she claimed and many bankers and stockbrokers believed, gave her the powers to divine the movements of the stock market. "At its peak in 1990," writes Kerr, "the toad controlled more than $10 billion in financial instruments, making its owner the world's largest individual stock investor."

[9] Itoman was an Osaka trading company that became involved in a number of extravagant but highly shady art and property deals. Itoman received some ¥600 billion in loans from Sumitomo Bank for this purpose. Its collapse and the exposure of the underworld-linked ventures severely sullied Sumitomo's reputation, cost its chairman his job, and later contributed to the resignation of Ichiro Isoda, the bank's prominent president.

system's built-in flaws – that sooner or later it was *bound* to happen – but that is not an easy thing to prove. Japan, after all, had navigated quite successfully around a host of macroeconomic shocks and hazards in the past. Many of the economy's network trappings – large insider boards, keiretsu obligations, main bank ties, tight-knit trade associations, guidance by regulators – seemed to function well in the days when Japanese business was all about investing for the long term, honoring obligations to patient stakeholders, making quality products, and growing the firm. But they generated calamitous results when Japanese business abruptly switched its energies to financial wheeling and dealing. Had the bubble never happened, the Japanese economy, its deep-set network institutions included, might still be going strong – or at least stronger than it has – and the country would have been spared the trauma of the "lost decade." In this reasoning, the bubble was utterly destructive of Japanese economic vitality because it was such a radical departure from the fundamentals of the post-war business system.

In any case, the negative fallout from the bubble has been extraordinarily hard to expunge. Some twelve years after the Nikkei Index lost half its value in the space of two years (from 38,000 in 1990 to 15,000 in 1992), the index as of this writing, is below 8,000. Land prices in six major metropolitan areas are 30 percent of what they were in 1990. Japan remains in trouble, much of it the direct or indirect hangover of the unsustainable business practices of the bubble era.

A principal finding of the research we report in this book is that, as far as the keiretsu are concerned, the bubble *was* to some degree anomalous – during it, ties frayed markedly but with its passing some facets of the network regime were restored. Others, however, seemed to be gone for good. Cross-shareholding – the signature tie from which the keiretsu were woven – lost much of its macro-network character. The banks' positions in the network, already weakened by financial deregulation and disintermediation, deteriorated further in the bubble and did not recover in its wake. The strongest keiretsu groupings – those descended from the pre-war zaibatsu – regained much of the cohesion they surrendered in the bubble, but the weaker clusters – the bank-centered groups – did not.

Then in the mid-1990s, under the pressure of continued economic decline, a further "regime shift," to use Pemple's apt characterization, took place.[10] The institutional framework for Japanese network capitalism was assaulted from every side. Regulatory adjustments eroded the foundation for keiretsu. Revisions to bankruptcy law made legal filing easier and raised the profile of the courts in business restructurings, thus sidelining

[10] Pempel (1998).

banks and keiretsu partners. The lifting of the Occupation-era ban on holding companies returned to managers the device for coordinating a diverse set of businesses on which the pre-war zaibatsu had been built and the absence of which in the post-war era brought the keiretsu into being. New corporate governance guidelines shrank boards and separated director and executive roles in ways that limited keiretsu involvement in the decision making of member firms. Accounting rule changes forced companies to disclose how their finances meshed with those of their affiliates. Next came a wave of consolidations and alliances, first of banks and then of their industrial clients. New exchanges such as NASDAQ Japan and the Mothers section of the Tokyo Stock Exchange were established to spur the founding and growth of new business, and, indeed, a number of new firms grew to prominence on the strength of innovative business models (e.g., Internet sales). New government entities – the Financial Services Agency, Financial Reconstruction Commission, and, most recently, the Industrial Revitalization Corporation – exposed the shadier of keiretsu practices and preempted the role of the bank-keiretsu convoys in industrial adjustment and corporate rehabilitation.

In sum, the institutional rug was being pulled out from under the Japanese network economy. As we suggest in Chapter 6, no one such change taken on its own merits necessarily had great import, but in combination they reshaped the Japanese business landscape in ways that made the received relational configurations much harder to sustain. The old networks are by no means entirely withered away. Much of the evidence we review in these chapters shows them persisting in various forms and sectors, even as their legitimacy fades and the legal and normative pillars supporting them topple. They still have their advocates in business, government, and the press. Even without them, the roots of network capitalism run so deep in Japan that they are not easily dislodged. Sometimes they resurface in new and unexpected ways, such as the move in 2003 (to loud condemnation by the Western business press) by Toyota to rescue failing trading company Tomen. Some recent upticks in the economy's performance, coupled with the dramatic collapse of the U.S. Internet economy bubble, have evoked in Japan a surge of support for traditional ways. More than a few Japanese are unsold on the virtues of the American "market-individualist" model, as Ronald Dore (1973) called it, and quite a few took satisfaction in its humiliating fall from grace in the corporate scandals of 2001–02. While acceptance of the need for market-oriented reform remains broad, many Japanese, like many Europeans, still see value in the network economy and wish to preserve some measure of it.[11]

---

[11] Dore (2000); Lincoln and Nakata (1997); Orru, Biggart, and Hamilton (1997).

The Agenda: A Structural Analysis of Japan's
Network Economy

Our work has been a long time in the making, and over the years we were
interviewing, coding, and analyzing data and writing, Japan was not sit-
ting still. Any research addressed to recent events faces similar problems,
but the study of the Japanese political economy of the 1990s is particularly challenging in this regard. From the 1960s until the late 1980s, the
foundation of the Japanese business system evolved in various ways – for
example, in the shift on the part of large corporations from bank to equity
finance in the 1980s – but the system's core stayed largely the same. As the
economy expanded, Japan became rich, powerful, and a global business
and technology leader, but the network character of its political economy
held firm. A tight hierarchical social order within firms and bureaus and
a thick tapestry of relations among them were its distinguishing features.

In Chapter 6 we devote considerable space to these and other changes,
but the core of our quantitative analysis falls within the "old" network paradigm of Japan. That stability is evident in the persistence
of the large financials and industrials at the economy's core. Neither
merger/acquisition activity nor entry by new firms appreciably altered
the rank ordering of the largest Japanese companies over the thirty-year
period we observe. Without such stability, much of our longitudinal analysis, which follows the largest 259 (as of 1980) financials, industrials,
and trading companies, could not have been done. By the same token, the
changes of the late 1990s and early 2000s preclude taking our quantitative
inquiry right up to the present.

Our subject is business networks in Japan – chiefly the horizontally
and vertically organized groups or keiretsu. We study how they arose
and were structured, how they evolved from the 1960s to the 1990s, and
how they functioned – particularly in terms of the support of weak firms
at the expense of strong ones. Keiretsu is a fascinating organizational
form, for, unlike the centralized business groups of Korea, India, and
elsewhere in the global economy, the keiretsu are true *network organizations*. In Lockwood's (1968:503) words, they are "webs with no spider" –
no holding company or home office or family of owners sits at the top and
pulls the strings.[12] They do have leaders – the banks and trading companies of the horizontal groups and the parent manufacturers in the vertical
keiretsu – but the minority equity stakes and periodic personnel dispatches
that link firms together are not sufficient to give any one corporate actor

---

[12] On the question of what organizational forms are encompassed by the term *business
group*, see Granovetter (2003).

group-wide control. The cohesion and definition of the groups derive from webs of relatively thin and weak ties.

As the keiretsu are bona fide networks, they are apt candidates for a study making use of the methods and perspectives of sociological network or structural analysis. Structural analysis is a powerful paradigm, comprising an array of tools for analyzing social ties, whether of individuals or groups. It also boasts a set of rich relational concepts – such as density, connectivity, multiplexity, and reciprocity – and propositions relating them to social and economic action. The field of economics has developed its own conceptual and methodological apparatus for studying business and organizational forms. These – principal–agent theory and transaction cost economics in particular – have been quite influential in the social sciences. They differ from the sociological perspectives in that (1) they are more mechanistic in their assumptions of an efficiency imperative and hyperrational self-interested actors, and (2) in their focus on the dyad – the transacting pair – as unit of analysis to the general neglect of the broader network in which that pair is likely to be embedded. As Oliver Williamson put it: "Transaction cost economics is preoccupied with dyadic relations, so that network relations are given short shrift."[13] However, at many junctures the lessons offered by the economics models are either similar to or complement the sociological views. The reader will see in the chapters to follow that, while we favor a sociological story, we are eclectic in how we draw upon theory in our attempts to understand the evolving structure and functioning of Japan's network economy.

[13] Williamson (1994).

1

The Structural Analysis of the Network Economy

The network idea has become a central metaphor in our daily lives. We talk of *networking* as a way to advance a career or gain political leverage. We refer to the breadth, density, and connectivity of someone's network as *social capital* that has real productive value and can be cultivated and deployed. With the fusion of computer and communications technology in the Internet have come significant new forms of social and economic organization as organizational and geographic boundaries dissolve in unbounded cyberspace. The drift toward network thinking has also broadly shaped the business world, as companies everywhere are forced to rethink not only their own relationships with suppliers, customers, banks, shareholders, and other stakeholders, but the relations among these as well. In some industries, firms are forging alliances with competitors and across industries in order to exploit market opportunities offered by new technologies. In others, the scale and scope of business activities has grown so broad that no firm can handle all the steps of the production process and firms cooperate simply to survive.

Nowhere is the importance of network thinking more evident than in Japan. As an emerging social science literature contends, the constitutive tissue of Japanese society is the formal and informal relationships that span all walks of daily life, from local community to political arena to economic sphere. Whether the relations at issue are those of bureaucrat and executive, manufacturer and supplier, or among coworkers within a firm, these take the form of complex, durable, and socially significant ties compared to the impersonal, arm's-length transactions of textbook economic theory.

Our goal in this chapter is to link these concerns: network organization as a general social and economic phenomenon and its specific manifestation in Japan.[1] In the first section, we discuss in broad terms the network character of the Japanese political economy. The quintessential Japanese network form is, of course, the keiretsu – still a topic of controversy among scholars, policy makers, and executives. We consider some defining features of keiretsu networks and review some debates regarding their structure and functioning. The problem in understanding Japanese economic organization, in our view, is the lack of deep analysis of its fundamental *network* character. Japanese business is no mere dance of dyads: a bank and its borrower, a subcontractor and its customer, and so on. Such pairs are embedded in complex, multilayered webs. In the second section, we give an overview of structural analysis as a methodology for the analysis of networks and suggest ways that it can aid in the understanding of economic organization. We briefly contrast a structural approach with the perspectives and methods of economics, noting that for all its analytical power and depth, most economics slights the role of networks in economic organization and thus discounts a fundamental part of economic reality. Finally, we suggest that there are limits to the explanatory power of a purely structural approach, and we address some ways it may be modified and augmented through consideration of the institutional forces that create and constrain network structures.

Network Organization in Japan

The concept of network lies at the core of much sociological and anthropological work on Japanese society.[2] Japan is widely described as a society in which personal, obligatory, and diffuse relations permeate and dominate walks of life, while the "legal-rational" institutions of competitive markets, court-ordered contracts, and the like have been less prevalent and consequential than in the West.[3] To an extraordinary degree the Japanese have molded human relations to the requirements of political, economic, and community affairs and count on trust and reciprocity to ensure the credibility and sustainability of commitments. Murphy (1996:46) offers a representative viewpoint:

---

[1] For a collection of writings on the network organization of Asian economies generally, see Fruin (1997). Some of this chapter follows the discussion in Gerlach and Lincoln's contribution to that volume.

[2] Nakane (1970).

[3] See, e.g., Imai and Itami (1984); Johnson (1982); Kawashima (1963); Kondo (1990).

What really matters for the Japanese company are the strength and credibility of its network. Its "capital" consists less of yen than the number and quality of its relationships. Such relationships would begin with the bureaucracy, with other firms in the same keiretsu – the large business alliances that dominate the Japanese economy – and with the industrial associations. But they would also include lines of access to Japan's oligopolistic advertising industry, ties to important politicians who can run interference with the bureaucracy and help land big contracts, and contacts with university professors, ensuring a stream of quality recruits. They would certainly comprise banking and brokerage house relationships. They can even include ties to organized crime, especially *sokaiya*, racketeers who disrupt shareholder meetings or, who paid off, keep others from doing so. Network capitalism tells us that it is the quality of these links that really constitutes a Japanese firm's capital.

The strong social networks within the Japanese workplace have drawn special scrutiny from scholars and business practitioners eager to unlock the mysteries of the tight coordination of the Japanese manufacturing firm and the fabled discipline of Japanese labor. The classic studies of Japanese work organization document the informal vertical and horizontal bonds that Japanese companies strive to nurture and that seem to figure centrally in the commitment and cooperation for which the Japanese workforce is renowned.[4] A telling example is Cole's (1971) finding from a participant observation study of Japanese factories that workers in neighboring plants of different companies had little contact; their relations were largely confined to the boundaries of their respective firms. Lincoln and Kalleberg's (1990:88) survey of over 100 manufacturing plants and 8,000 employees in Japan and the United States provided survey evidence of the same: a higher density and depth of coworker ties within the Japanese factories. Besides a greater incidence of quality circles and other team activities in the Japanese plants, the Japanese employees they surveyed reported more than twice the number of coworker friends than the Americans had and three times the likelihood of getting together informally after hours with workers and supervisors. As we argue below, the Japanese firm is much less a unitary entity than is the American firm from the standpoint of ownership, control, and legal definition. But in terms of the cohesion of its internal networks and the commitment, loyalty, and identification toward the company employees display, it is paradoxically much more so.

---

[4] See Cole (1971); Dore (1973); Rohlen (1974).

Similar to and overlapping with Japan's workplace and business networks is an intricate web of political connections. Political power is directly proportional to the scope of a politician's or ministry's networks and the strength of the obligations (*giri*) implied in those relations. As van Wolferen (1989) put it in his best-selling critique of power in Japanese society:

> In the upper levels of society, the *kone* (connections) multiply to form whole networks of special relationships. These may derive from one-time favours, school ties or shared experiences, or may involve intricate mutual back-scratching deals. They are referred to as *jinmyaku* – *jin* meaning "personal" and *myaku* a "vein" such as is found in mineral deposits, so that *jinmyaku* means a vein, or web, of personal connections running through the fabric of society. *Jinmyaku* are much more widespread, and of incomparably greater importance, than old-boy networks in the West.... The actual power of a highly placed Japanese depends on his *jinmyaku*. A bureaucrat without a good *jinmyaku* cannot climb to great heights. A minister without an elaborate *jinmyaku* is worthless to his ministry and his clique within the LDP. The power of Japan's top politicians is derived from a large complex of intermeshing *jinmyaku* forged with favours, money, marriage ties and political acumen.

The Japanese state has not been very large by any measure. The Ministry of International Trade and Industry (MITI) for decades ran Japan's international and industrial policy making with a staff of about 2,500 people and a small budget. It furthermore lacks backing in a strong, formal authority codified in law, operating instead through an informal process of *administrative guidance* (*gyosei shido*) rather than through direct orders or explicit sanctions applied to firms.[5]

The image of a powerful state exercising strong guidance runs through much commentary on the post-war Japanese political economy. The reasons, we believe, have to do with the ministries' positions as central nodes in the bureaucratic-corporate network. They enjoy *positional rents* by virtue of their command of critical resources – information, expertise, patents, licenses, regulatory exceptions, tax breaks, control over exports and imports, and subsidies for research and development. As van Wolferen observes, they leverage their *jinmyaku* – the old-boy networks rooted in an alignment of interests with the business community and cultivated through many rounds of wining and dining *tsukiai* (socializing). Finally,

[5] Johnson (1982).

they exploit effectively the network configurations within the private sector economy, in particular the keiretsu pyramids of cascading ties from financial institutions to large manufacturers to the ends of supply and distribution chains. Policies judiciously applied at one level ripple up and down the pyramid to affect all others.

There is a genuine network, as opposed to dyadic, logic to the guidance the Japanese state exercises over the economy. The Japanese society of organizations is such that cooperation or tension between a ministry and a company in its regulatory sphere is never a purely bilateral matter. Either the ministry has as backing for its position the consensus and support of most firms in the industry – in which case a recalcitrant firm is subject to a tsunami of pressure from its business partners and competitors – or, as in the case of MITI's failed attempt in the 1960s to cartelize the Japanese auto industry, it is the ministry that is isolated by the closing of ranks within the business community.

Thus, the Japanese state is best viewed as merely one more network actor in the political economy, a major one to be sure, but one whose resource base and influence strategies do not set it fundamentally apart from the private sector players. As William Lockwood (1968:503) famously put it:

> The metaphor that comes to mind is a typical Japanese web of influences and pressures interweaving through government and business, rather than a streamlined pyramid of authoritarian control.... A web it may be, but a web with no spider.... The industrial bureaus of MITI proliferate sectoral targets and plans; they confer, they tinker, they exhort. This is "economics by admonition" to a degree inconceivable in Washington or London. Business makes few major decisions without consulting the appropriate governmental authority; the same is true in reverse.

A "web with no spider," of course, is precisely what networks represent – or, perhaps more accurately, a web with *many* spiders, none of them dominant.

It is via this well-spun web of connections that the Japanese government has managed simultaneously to be a *minimalist state* in its day-to-day operations and an *interventionist state* when market processes lead the economy off the designated course.[6] MITI and the Ministry of Finance (MOF) may lack the legal authority to dictate to industry or otherwise mandate solutions autocratically, but a company that ignores an explicit guidance from the bureaucracy does so at its peril. As Okimoto wrote of

[6] Okimoto (1989:151).

MITI, it makes up in savvy and network position what it lacks in size and resources to remain "perhaps the single most effective institution for industrial policy-making among all the major states in the Organization for Economic Cooperation and Development (OECD)."[7]

The focal industries of MITI's (now METI the Ministry of Economy, Trade and Industry) policy making have changed significantly over time,[8] yet close business–state relations remain the norm. Indeed, the critical role of these reciprocal, face-to-face relations between bureaucrats and corporate managers is a major factor in the continuing migration of business headquarter activity to Tokyo. Longtime Osaka and Nagoya firms such as Toyota and Matsushita have recently established Tokyo offices to better tap the political, financial, and media networks concentrated in the capital. A Sumitomo Corporation executive complained to us in an interview of the disadvantage that his and other Kansai-area companies were put to by virtue of their limited day-by-day access to the political-industrial "keiretsu" (his phrase) centered in Tokyo.

Keiretsu: The Quintessential Network Form

The most distinctive form of network organization in Japan – and the most critical to understanding its economy – is the clusters of industrial, commercial, and financial corporations known as keiretsu. While this term conjures up images of closed markets and opaque insider deals, such images caricature a more complex and interesting reality. The keiretsu label has been applied to a variety of Japanese network forms. As a general definition, we view them as clusters of independently managed firms maintaining close and stable business ties, cemented by governance mechanisms such as presidents' councils, partial cross-ownership, and interlocking directorates.

Within this broad definition lie several distinctive structural variations. The horizontal, or intermarket, keiretsu (also known as *kigyo shudan* or enterprise groups) are diversified constellations of major corporations, each firm typically representing a separate industry sector, including, perhaps most important, financial services. Vertical supply keiretsu are pyramids of large manufacturers, their suppliers, and their suppliers'

---

[7] Okimoto (1989:144–45).

[8] On January 6, 2001, MITI was reborn as METI. During the early post-war period, MITI's main industrial focus was economic reconstruction. In the high-growth era of the 1950s and 1960s, it shifted to the building of various heavy industries. In the post-oil shock 1970s and 1980s, MITI's attention turned to providing adjustment aid to mature industries in which Japan was no longer competitive (Komiya, Okuno, and Suzumura, 1988). Most recently, the ministry's concern has been with promoting the knowledge-intensive (high-tech) industries.

suppliers. Distribution keiretsu are the dedicated retail networks of large manufacturers such as Matsushita, Shiseido, and Fuji Photo Film. Other intercorporate networks that have been given the keiretsu label are department stores linked with railroads and amusement parks, large firms and spun-off affiliates in new industries, and bank–nonbank financial clusters.

Six principal horizontal groups ("the big six") have dominated the postwar Japanese economy. Three are direct descendents of the former *zaibatsu* – Mitsui, Mitsubishi, and Sumitomo.[9] In the pre-war period, these were centrally administered by holding companies controlled by prominent families close to the Japanese state. The other three are the post-war bank-centered groups, so called because their main structural feature is dependence on a major money center city bank: Dai-Ichi Kangyo, Fuyo, and Sanwa. Estimates of the overall importance of the big six for Japan's economy vary substantially from one source to another: Ito (1992:188), for example, estimates that the big-six groups account for 5 percent of the Japanese labor force and 16 percent of total sales, while Pempel (1998:70) estimates that they comprise 0.1 percent of all Japanese companies but 25 percent of post-war gross national product (GNP) and 75 percent of the value of shares on the Tokyo Stock Exchange. These numbers, however, miss the point: there are no hard and fast boundaries to Japan's network economy that unequivocally divide one group from another or from unaffiliated firms. In contrast with the Korean *chaebol* and other business groups around the world – most having a well-defined holding company or headquarters function at their core – the horizontal or intermarket keiretsu represent fluid, overlapping networks, not discrete and bounded groups at all.[10]

The one formal structure associated with the horizontal keiretsu is the shacho-kai, or presidents' council, a regularly convening association of the presidents (*shacho*) of member firms. While lists of big-six presidents' council members are readily available, the deliberations of the shacho-kai

---

[9] Gerlach (1992a); Morikawa (1993).

[10] On business groups in countries other than Japan see Feenstra, Huang, and Hamilton (1997); Ghemawat and Khanna (1998); Guillen (2000, 2001); and Orru et al. (1997). Granovetter (2003) gives a definition of a business group that subsumes both true network organizations of the keiretsu sort and imperatively coordinated entities such as the *chaebol*. "'Business groups' are sets of legally separate firms bound together in persistent formal and/or informal ways. The level of binding is intermediate between, and should be contrasted to, two extremes that are not business groups: sets of firms linked merely by short-term strategic alliances, and those legally consolidated into a single entity." Lawrence (1991), too, highlights the network character of the vertical and horizontal keiretsu. Keister (2001) suggests that the new business groups forming in China resemble the vertical keiretsu: vertically linked equity and trade networks of legally independent firms centered on a large manufacturer.

are less transparent to outsiders. Minutes of shacho-kai meetings are not made public, and participants claim that meetings are essentially social gatherings or, at the very most, a forum for the discussion of broad economic issues rather than a device for coordinating group action or monitoring individual firms. However, council membership does bear strongly on a company's network position and financial performance, as subsequent chapters show. Here we see the central paradox of the keiretsu phenomenon: while there is ample evidence of coordinated action, there is a lack of centralized control – member firms are operationally independent. As Chapter 2 discusses, this mix of strategic centralization and operational decentralization was key to the evolution of Japan's network economy in the pre-war period.

The list of presidents' council members as of 1992 appears in Table 1.1. The table illustrates another distinctive feature of the horizontal keiretsu: the *one-set principle (wan-setto shugi)*. Groups typically have one, and only one, member from each major industry segment. Each group has a cement company, a steel maker, a real estate company, and so on. This membership standard is better maintained by the three former zaibatsu than by the bank groups. It has also been more faithfully followed within the membership of the presidents' council itself than among the much larger universe of firms maintaining loose affiliations with a group.[11]

Although the big six are referred to as horizontal groups, based on the translation from the Japanese terminology (*yoko keiretsu*), this is a misleading label. In common economics parlance *horizontal* refers to relations among rivals within the same industry.[12] As noted, the horizontal groups are quite diverse in industry makeup. Price-fixing cartels they are not, as the one-set principle promotes inter- rather than intraindustry ties. Rather, it is the social quality of the relationship (an important consideration in Japan) that is considered horizontal. In contrast to the hierarchical distinctions that characterize the vertical keiretsu, the big-six groups are in principle communities of equals.

Still, while interfirm relations within the horizontal groups are not formally hierarchical, neither are they symmetric: each group features

---

[11] Gerlach (1992a: Chap. 5).

[12] On this point, Sheard (1997) notes, "from an industrial organization viewpoint, the relations observed in all three forms of keiretsu are not horizontal. Firms associated with supplier or distribution keiretsu are firms that are linked in vertical input-ouput supply relations. Firms associated with financial keiretsu are either linked in vertical relations (including factor inputs in the case of bank-firm ties) or operate in different intermediate or final product markets. Firms in a given keiretsu, generally speaking, are not direct competitors in a given market." Because of the ambiguity of horizontal, Gerlach (1992a) refers to the big six as *intermarket* groups, a term that underscores the industrial diversity of the member firms.

Table 1.1. List of Member Companies of Presidents' Councils (shacho-kai) of Six Major Horizontal Keiretsu Groups (as of 31 March 1993)

	Mitsui group (Nimoku-kai): 1980 = 24 firms; 1993 = 26 firms)	Mitsubishi group (Kinyo-kai): 1980 = 28 firms; 1991 = 29 firms)	Sumitomo group (Hakusui-kai): 1980 = 21 firms; 1991 = 20 firms)	Fuyo group (Fuyo-kai = 29 firms)	Sanwa group (Sansui-kai): 1980 = 40 firms; 1991 = 44 firms)	DKB group (Sankin-kai): 1980 = 43 firms; 1991 = 45 firms; 1993 = 46 firms)
Industry						
Finance and Commerce	Mitsui Bank Mitsui Trust Mitsui Mutual Life Taisho Marine & Fire Mitsui & Co. Mitsukoshi Dept. Store	Mitsubishi Bank Mitsubishi Trust *Meiji Mutual Life* Tokio Marine & Fire Mitsubishi Corp.	Sumitomo Bank Sumitomo Trust Sumitomo Mutual Life Sumitomo Marine & Fire Sumitomo	Fuji Bank Yasuda Trust Yasuda Mutual Life Yasuda Fire & Marine Marubeni	Sanwa Bank Toyo Trust *Nippon Life* Nichimen Nissho Iwai *Iwatani International* Takashimaya	Dai-Ichi Kangyo Bank Asahi Mutual Life Fukoku Mutual Life Nissan Fire & Marine Taisei Fire & Marine Nippon Kangyo Kakumaru Securities Itochu Nissho Iwai Kanematsu Kawasho Seibu Department Store *Itoki (post 91)*
Forestry			Sumitomo Forestry			
Mining	Mitsui Mining Hokkaido Colliery & Steamship		Sumitomo Coal Mining			
Construction	Mitsui Construction Sanki Engineering	*Mitsubishi Construction*	Sumitomo Construction	Taisei	*Obayashi* Toyo Construction *Zenitaka (post 1980)* *Sekisui House*	Shimizu
Foodstuffs and beverages	Nippon Flour Mills	Kirin Brewery		Nissin Flour Milling Sapporo Breweries Nichirei	Itoham Foods *Suntory (post 1980)*	

Textile products				Nisshinbo Industries Toho Rayon Sanyo-Kokusaku Pulp	*Unitika*	
Paper and pulp	Oji Paper					Honshu Paper
Chemical products	Mitsui Toatsu Mitsui Petrochemical Toray Industries *Denki Kagaku Kogyo (post 91)*	Mitsubishi Kasei Mitsubishi Gas Chemical Mitsubishi Petrochemical *Mitsubishi Monsanto* Mitsubishi Plastics Mitsubishi Rayon	Sumitomo Chemical Sumitomo Bakelite	Showa Denko K K Kureha Chemical Nippon Oil & Fats	Teijin Tokuyama Soda Sekisui Chemical Ube Industries Hitachi Chemical Tanabe Seiyaku Fujisawa Pharmaceutical Kansai Paint	Denki Kagaku Kogyo Kyowa Hakko Kogyo Nippon Zeon Asahi Denka Kogyo Sankyo Shiseido Lion Asahi Chemical
Petroleum refining		Mitsubishi Oil		Toden	Cosmo Oil	Showa Shell Sekiyu
Rubber products					Toyo Tire & Rubber	Yokohama Rubber
Ceramic, stone, clay	Onoda Cement	Mitsubishi Mining & Cement Asahi Glass	Nippon Sheet Glass	Nihon Cement	*Osaka Cement*	Chichibu Cement
Rubber products					Toyo Tire & Rubber	Yokohama Rubber
Ceramic, stone, clay and glass products	Onoda Cement	Mitsubishi Mining & Cement Asahi Glass	Nippon Sheet Glass Sumitomo Cement	Nihon Cement	*Osaka Cement* *Kyocera*	Chichibu Cement
Iron and steel	Japan Steel Works	*Mitsubishi Steel Mfg*	Sumitomo Metal	NKK	Kobe Steel Nisshin Steel Nakayama Steel Works Hitachi Metals	Kobe Steel Kawasaki Steel Japan Metals & Chemicals
Nonferrous metals	Mitsui Mining & Smelting	Mitsubishi Metal *Mitsubishi Aluminum* *Mitsubishi Cable*	Sumitomo Metal Mining Sumitomo Light Metal Sumitomo Electric		Hitachi Cable	Nippon Light Metal Furukawa Furukawa Electric
General machinery and apparatus		*Mitsubishi Kakoki* *Mitsubishi Kakoki*	Sumitomo Heavy Industries	Kubota Nippon Seiko K K	NTN	Niigata Engineering Iseki Ebara

(continued)

Table 1.1 (*continued*)

Industry	Mitsui group (Nimoku-kai: 1980 = 24 firms; 1993 = 26 firms)	Mitsubishi group (Kinyo-kai: 1980 = 28 firms; 1991 = 29 firms)	Sumitomo group (Hakusui-kai: 1980 = 21 firms; 1991 = 20 firms)	Fuyo group (Fuyo-kai = 29 firms)	Sanwa group (Sansui-kai: 1980 = 40 firms; 1991 = 44 firms)	DKB group (Sankin-kai: 1980 = 43 firms; 1991 = 45 firms; 1993 = 46 firms)
Electric machinery and apparatus	Toshiba	Mitsubishi Electric	NEC	Hitachi Oki Electric Industry Yokogawa Electric	Hitachi *Iwatsu Electric* Sharp *Nitto Electric*	Hitachi Fuji Electric *Yasukawa Electric* Fujitsu *Nippon Columbia*
Transportation and equipment	Toyota Motor *Mitsui Engineer Ishikawajima-Harima & Shipbuilding (post 91)*	Mitsubishi Heavy *Mitsubishi Motors*		Nissan Motor	Hitachi Zosen *Shin Meiwa Industry* Daihatsu Motor	Kawasaki Heavy Ishikawajima-Harima Isuzu Motors
Precision machinery		Nikon		Canon	*Hoya (post 80)*	Asahi Optical
Real estate	*Mitsui Real Estate Development*	Mitsubishi Estate	*Sumitomo Realty & Development*	Tokyo Tatemono		
Railways and road transport				Tobu Railway Keihin Electric Express	*Hankyu* *Nippon Express*	
Water transport	*Mitsui O S K Lines*	Nippon Yusen		Showa Line	*Navix Line*	*Kawasaki Kisen*
Warehouse	*Mitsui Warehouse*	*Mitsubishi Warehouse*	*Sumitomo Warehouse*			*Shibusawa Warehouse*
Services					*Orix*	*Orient Co. (post 80)*
Other					*Nittsu (pre 1991)*	*Korakuen Stadium Co.* *Nittsu (pre 1991)*

Note: Italicized firms are *not* in the present sample.
Source: Fair Trade Commission (1992).

a leading city bank as nerve center and acknowledged leader.[13] The bank typically hosts the monthly presidents' council meeting and provides some coordination of the member firms through its lending, cross-shareholding, and board connections. In the past, the large trading companies (*sogo shosha*) were similarly key actors in the coordination of keiretsu activities, but as their role as broker of global commercial transactions declined, so has their leadership of group affairs.[14]

The second major keiretsu form is the manufacturing or supply chain groups: suppliers, subcontractors, and distributors organized in a vertical division of labor around a large industrial firm such as Hitachi, Toyota, or Matsushita. Much research on vertical keiretsu in Japanese manufacturing suggests that the close, cooperative, yet flexible relations typical of these networks facilitate responsiveness, coordination, and learning on the part of affiliated firms. The team-style participation of suppliers in the design and development of products, parts, and processes is a familiar example.[15] The supply chain keiretsu have been widely praised as a model of manufacturing best practice. Although an older school of dual economy thought held that the parent manufacturers in such systems exploited the smaller up- and downstream firms as risk buffers, recent scholarship views the partnership between the supplier and the assembler as one of risk sharing: each party supports the other by absorbing some of its costs and risks.[16]

The vertical and horizontal keiretsu are often portrayed as quite distinct phenomena.[17] In fact, the two are highly intertwined, as depicted in Figure 1.1. The Toyota group is a vertical keiretsu linked mainly to the Mitsui horizontal keiretsu, as is Nissan within Fuyo, NEC in Sumitomo, Furukawa in DKB, and so forth. By the same token, where vertical keiretsu span horizontal groups, they thereby tether them together. Toyota is a Mitsui *Nimoku-kai* member, and most Toyota group companies deal with Toyota's primary banks, Mitsui and Tokai. Daihatsu, however, is a Toyota affiliate that uses Sanwa as its main bank and maintains a seat on the Sanwa *Sansui-kai*. Prior to a bailout by Toyota in the 1960s, Daihatsu was a separate automaker aligned with the Sanwa group.[18]

---

[13] Sheard (1989a).
[14] Gerlach (1992a: Chap. 4); Yoshino and Lifson (1986).
[15] See, inter alia, Ahmadjian and Lincoln (2001); Dyer (1996a); Dyer and Ouchi (1993); Helper and Sako (1995); Imai et al. (1985); Liker et al. (1996); Nishiguchi (1994); Womack et al. (1990).
[16] See Aoki (1988); Asanuma and Kikutani (1992); Broadbridge (1966); Nishiguchi (1994); Kawasaki and McMillan (1987).
[17] Miyashita and Russell (1994).
[18] Ahmadjian and Lincoln (2001).

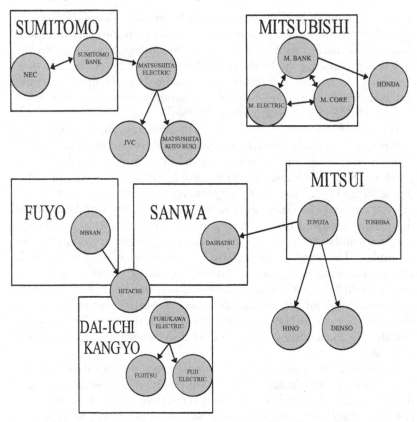

Figure 1.1. How horizontal and vertical keiretsu interconnect.
Note: Firms within a rectangle are shacho-kai members.

Keiretsu as Network Organizations: A Structural Overview

How networks "act" – what forces give them direction and coordination –
is a challenging but intriguing question. When business networks take the
place of vertically integrated and divisionalized corporations, there is a
problem of attributing agency, identity, and goals. In the vertical supply
and distribution keiretsu, some leadership and control emanates from
the parent firm position in the network. Similarly, as noted, Japan's chief
commercial banks have played leadership roles in the horizontal groups,
although their influence is by no means the equal of the peak firm in
a vertical group. Some see the keiretsu are functional equivalents to the
diversified and divisionalized *M-form* corporation.[19] While there are some

[19] The relative rarity and apparent ineffectiveness of the M-form in Japan provide a measure of support for the view that the keiretsu is a functional alternative. Yoshihara
et al. (1981) replicated on a sample of Japanese firms Rumelt's (1974) pioneering study

parallels there, the keiretsu are nonetheless genuine network organizations with a number of distinctive structural features, requiring a distinctively structural assessment. Among those features are the following.

Vague and Permeable Boundaries

Some observers criticize the indiscriminate use of the term keiretsu and argue for limiting its application to a particular network form – usually the vertical nets of satellite suppliers and distributors in which a large manufacturer holds equity stakes. However, a broad use of the label is justified by the fact that the main keiretsu types (vertical and horizontal) are not mutually exclusive. They are overlapping and interpenetrating webs of affiliations. The placement of boundaries is largely arbitrary.

To take an example, NEC is a member of the Sumitomo *Hakusui-kai*, maintaining close strategic and capital links with that big-six group since the start of the twentieth century. However, NEC has maintained its vertical network of suppliers and distributors, some of which were spun off as legally distinct enterprises, while others were founded independently and moved toward the group over time. The NEC group is also a member of the family of suppliers to NTT, Japan's dominant telecommunications carrier. And finally, as with other high-tech electronics firms, NEC maintains an elaborate network of strategic alliances with direct competitors in its own industry, including Mitsubishi Electric from its archrival group, and a variety of computer companies overseas. While these diverse relations vary in the extent and character of their significance to NEC, they are also intertwined in important ways. NEC's own banks, for example, have been the leading source of debt financing for most of its vertical affiliates and also serve as major lenders to NTT. In this way, seemingly clean distinctions, such as those between vertical and horizontal keiretsu, are blurred by the location of key firms (e.g., Hitachi, NEC, Toyota) at the interstices of multiple groups.

Continuous vs. Categorical Membership

Related to the issue of permeable boundaries is the observation that firms vary by degrees in their keiretsu alignments. The Mitsubishi affiliations of Tokyo Mitsubishi Bank, Mitsubishi Motors, and Mitsubishi Electric are easy to discern. That Kirin Beer is a Mitsubishi *Kinyo-kai* member is less obvious, as it lacks the Mitsubishi name. Less transparent yet is

of diversification and divisionalization in U.S. corporations. Their work produced two noteworthy results: (a) compared to U.S. firms, the Japanese companies were less diversified and divisionalized and more likely to use the functionally departmentalized form (although M-form adoption was rising); (b) also at odds with Rumelt's and other U.S.-based results, the functionally organized firms in Yoshihara's sample outperformed the product-divisional firms (see also Cable and Yasuki, 1985; Goto, 1981; Itoh, 2003).

Honda's weaker but still real Mitsubishi tilt. The same is true of the Mitsui leanings of Toyota, Fuji Photo Film, and more distantly, Sony. With the one exception of shacho-kai, the dimensions on which linkage may be evaluated – commercial trade, lending ties, cross-shareholding, and director interlocks – are continuous. Any sharp line separating members from nonmembers necessarily ignores the shades of gray that color the keiretsu landscape. Thus, while categorical indicators of group affiliation such as presidents' council membership or main bank affiliation are useful roadmaps in the tracing of relations, they should not blind the observer to the array of less discrete, more graduated dimensions along which firms are closely or loosely tied.

Multiplexity
The ties that bind Japanese companies satisfy a third criterion for a network: multiplexity.[20] No one has critical importance; it is the pattern they weave in common that counts. Thus – and this is key to structural analysis – content matters less than form. The degree to which diverse corporate ties map the same underlying relations and have similar consequences for corporate behavior and performance is a core theme of this book. Much past keiretsu research ignores such multidimensionality, relying either on single measures of affiliation (e.g., shacho-kai) or subjective classifications that obscure the criteria whereby firms are assigned to groups. Presidents' council membership gives a clear and concise picture of group membership, but it is a misleading one. Only a fraction of the firms oriented to the big six occupy shacho-kai seats; many more connect to the group through the diverse ties of equity ownership, interlocking directorates, loans from group banks, goods and services trade, and a slew of harder-to-measure relations. Network data and analysis allow us to map the aggregate of such relations.

The Quality of Ties: Trust and Reciprocity
Fourth, it is axiomatic to the concept of keiretsu and that of network organization more generally that the ties relating firms are often – if by no means exclusively – informal, imbued with sentiment, and governed by norms of obligation, trust, and reciprocity.[21] Simple human interactions are the elementary building blocks from which far-flung corporate networks arise. The strong ties between suppliers and assemblers in industries such as autos, for example, often rest on the personal, face-to-face

---

[20] Such structural properties as multiplexity, reciprocity, and connectivity are often taken as indicators of the more diffuse concept of *embeddedness* (see, e.g., Uzzi and Gillespie, 2002).
[21] Dore (1983); Gouldner (1960).

relations that purchasing managers develop (e.g., through late-night get-togethers) with suppliers' representatives.

Ronald Dore (1983) has argued that the Japanese take this farther than most societies do. He points to the critical role in Japanese market processes of goodwill, or "the sentiments of friendship and the sense of diffuse personal obligation which accrue between individuals engaged in recurring contractual economic exchange":

> "It is not," said Adam Smith, "from the benevolence of the butcher, the brewer, or the baker, that we expect our dinner, but from their regard to their own interest." The trouble with the Japanese is that they have never really caught up with Adam Smith. They don't believe in the invisible hand. The butcher and the brewer have got to be benevolent. They need to have a conscience about the quality of the meat and the beer they supply. They need to care.

That such qualities of benevolence and reciprocity figure importantly in keiretsu transactions is shown in the description of a *Kigyo Denki* manager's description of his efforts, as a *shukko'd* (transferred) employee, to make *Nihon Shohin* profitable, a supplier in which *Kigyo Denki* held a 20 percent stake.[22] The manager was pouring time into this, not merely because it was a good business venture, but because he felt a moral obligation to assist Shohin and its employees. Shohin had served *Kigyo Denki* well in the past, so *Kigyo Denki* was bound to reciprocate:

> Once *Kigyo Denki* makes an investment in a company, we have a very important social responsibility. *Nihon Shohin* has 800 people and I see the faces of all of these people and their families. I will do everything I can to make *Nihon Shohin* an excellent company. The employees of this company made a very nice contribution during the bubble years, so we are not going to cut them loose during a downturn. The ultimate goal is to make *Nihon Shohin* employees happy.

In general, when business networks are multiplex, reciprocal, and embedded – for example, when financial and commercial transactions entwine with equity stakes, personnel transfers, shared values, and mutual trust – self-interest cannot fully account for actors' motives. Kigyo Denki managers said that when suppliers are 100 percent dependent, they feel a strong sense of obligation to them. An equity relationship increases that

---

[22] Lincoln and Ahmadjian (2001). Both names are pseudonyms. Kigyo Denki is one of Japan's major electronics firms.

obligation. In this, they said, lies the distinctive "wetness" of Japanese economic relations. It is hard for a Japanese company to tell a long-term supplier that it can offer it no more business. This *kimochi* (mood, sentiment) rests on personal relations of *giri* and *ninjo* (obligation and human feeling).

Japan, as Dore suggests, may be an outlier in the degree to which economic exchange is imbued with such cultural norms and sentiments but it is by no means unique in this respect. Inspired in some measure by the attention given the Japanese case, the claim that benevolence, trust, and reciprocity are essential to the smooth functioning of even so efficient a market economy as the United States has gained wide adherence in recent years.[23] Podolny and Page (1998), reviewing research on the topic, agree that network organization implies a distinctive set of norms and motives and that these permit a degree of "flexibility and adaptability" in exchange relations that formal contracts do not:

> To be sure, it is probably true that a "moral community" or "spirit of goodwill" is not a functional necessity for a network form of organization to exist. If two economic actors wish to enter into an enduring relation and lack a legitimate authority to resolve disputes, they may enter into a long-term contract.... However, an exchange relation governed by a contract with provisions only for anticipated changes will generally be less flexible than an exchange governed by a norm of reciprocity. Moreover, a contract allowing for recontracting at a later date based on unanticipated changes to circumstance requires some level of trust that the other party will act in good faith at the time of recontracting. In short, while a long-term contract may represent a substitute for what some have identified as a moral community, spirit of goodwill, or norm of reciprocity, such a contract is not likely to allow for the same flexibility and adaptability as these ethics of exchange.

Severing ties and switching partners to realize a short-term cost reduction or competitive advantage are rational economic behaviors only on the assumption that nothing binds the parties beyond the economic value to be realized from the exchange. In many real-world transactions, as George Akerlof (1982) has pointed out, what one party offers the other may be less the selling of a good or service at a market price than a gift, tailored to the relationship and bestowed as an expression of commitment and reciprocity.

[23] Heimer (1992); Sako and Helper (1998); Uzzi (1996).

Connectivity: The Role of Indirect Ties

A fifth respect in which Japanese business groups can be cast as networks concerns the importance to their organization of indirect ties.[24] Implicit in the idea of a network economy is that transactions and the social and political relations among economic actors that accompany them are not strictly dyadic but weave together large numbers of companies in a thick fabric of relations.[25] Such interrelatedness need not involve close, dense, or frequent interactions between every pair of actors (networks vary in these respects), but it does imply a high degree of *connectivity*. That is, actors are generally accessible to one another through a chain of intermediaries. A network marked by high connectivity is thoroughly integrated; information and resources diffuse quickly and far. While most networks have dense patches, bridged by sparse or intermittent links, a well-connected network has few, perhaps no, complete breaks isolating one such patch from another. Keiretsu firms link directly to one another through equity stakes, personnel transfers, interlocking directorates, presidents' councils and cooperative associations, bank loans, and the preferential buying and selling of goods and services. In a network of high connectivity, every tie serves to link each firm to the web as a whole, giving it access to many others. Lincoln, Gerlach, and Takahashi (1992:574) showed that cross-shareholding ties in 1980 occurred in no more than 2.2 percent of the pairings of Japan's 250 largest banks and industrial firms. The density of direct *and indirect* connections, however, was much greater at 29 percent.

What Keiretsu Do: Performance Consequences

What, if any, are the effects of keiretsu networks on the contemporary Japanese economy? And do those effects stem from conscious, strategic action to achieve group-wide goals or are they better seen as unintended consequences? The possibility that keiretsu might matter to an understanding of Japanese economic organization – as opposed to being curious but otherwise unimportant historical legacies – drew increased attention from social scientists in the 1980s. A range of viewpoints has been offered

---

[24] Standard economic modeling, exemplified, say, by game theory, generally portrays economic relations as bilateral or dyadic patterns of negotiation and exchange, abstracted from and unaffected by the long chains of relations that in the real world link each player to the economy. In their context-specific applications to corporate governance and organizational form, transaction cost and agency theory relax the assumption of transactions in a vacuum, while holding to the premise that little matters beyond the pair at hand (Granovetter, 1985).

[25] Lincoln (1982); White, Boorman, and Breiger (1976).

on the question of keiretsu effects. Most such thinking can be sorted into the following four categories.

Keiretsu as Ceremonial

One stock set of answers has been regularly given over the years by Japanese managers and officials grown defensive in the face of U.S. and European criticism of the role of keiretsu in Japan's imbalanced trade and hard-to-penetrate markets. The horizontal groups, they claim, have no real economic significance. Whereas in earlier phases of Japanese economic development the big-six clusters played useful roles, they have since become dinosaurs – that is, atavistic survivals.[26] They persist from institutional inertia and a certain nostalgia among the member firms for the history, name, and logo of the group. They may sponsor exhibitions (e.g., the Osaka Flower Exhibition) or decide on uses of the group's name (e.g., for marketing purposes), but otherwise stay aloof from strategic or operational decision making. In keeping with this allegedly marginal role, managers we interviewed in shacho-kai companies stressed the traditions and symbolism of a group. In the unsubtle terms in which the Japanese tend to characterize their culture, one executive put it simply: "The Japanese are a group-oriented people. I feel comfortable being in a (keiretsu) group."

Keiretsu as Oligopolies

However often the dinosaur mantra is chanted, the evidence shows the economic consequences of the horizontal groups to be nontrivial. Early treatments by industrial organization economists, examining the problem through a conventional antitrust lens, cast the big six as colluding oligopolists, bent on the extraction of monopoly rents from firms outside the network. In Caves and Uekusa's version of this story, the groups practice efficient pricing (i.e., in line with opportunity costs) in their dealings with one another, but with outsiders they profit-maximize by leveraging the membership's dominance across an array of markets.[27] That theory foundered, however, on strong evidence that firms affiliated with the big six were in fact *less* profitable than were comparable independent firms.[28]

Keiretsu as Efficient Organizational Forms

Like such other distinctive institutions of Japanese economic society as lifetime employment and strong industrial policy, the keiretsu have been

---

[26] Fair Trade Commission (1992).
[27] Caves and Uekusa (1976); Hadley (1970).
[28] See Caves and Uekusa (1976); Cable and Yasuki (1985); Gerlach (1992a:190); Lincoln et al. (1996); Nakatani (1984); Roehl (1983a); Weinstein and Yafeh (1995).

credited with conferring competitive, even unfair, advantage on Japan in world markets. The groups are claimed to facilitate communication and ensure trust and reliability in the execution of business transactions, thereby reducing cost and risk for member firms.[29]

Organizational economists of the principal–agent persuasion have seen in the keiretsu – the main bank relation in particular – a solution to the problems of asymmetric information and incentive misalignment that routinely led U.S. management teams to neglect the interests of stockholders.[30] By concentrating ownership and investment in the hands of a few close business partners, the keiretsu system seemed to provide superior monitoring and governance at lower transaction cost (owing, e.g., to reduced need for lawyers, accountants, and consultants). Moreover, their internal capital market function filled gaps in Japan's weak and inefficient equity and bond markets.[31] Their risk-pooling role enabled member firms to pursue a distinctive and for a time successful competitive strategy: subordinate profit making to the single-minded pursuit of growth.[32] The groups also relieved Japanese corporations of the pressures to maximize near-term share-price appreciation, the standard of performance to which Wall Street held U.S. firms. A company's keiretsu banks and stockholders could be counted on to behave as patient capital, staying loyal (resisting acquisition) and taking a long view of corporate success.

Unfortunately for many of these arguments, the hard evidence for efficiency gains to keiretsu organization has been less than compelling. The well-documented tendency for sales growth and profitability to be lower in big-six affiliates than in unaligned firms does not sit easily with claims that the horizontal groupings economize on information and transaction costs. If networks lower costs, why do they not increase profits?[33]

Moreover, even the most ardent defenders of Japan's economic institutions have been reluctant to claim that the distribution keiretsu – as dense and enduring a thatch of stable and reciprocal interorganizational commitments as anywhere exists – economize on much of anything. Their chief economic function, it would seem, is the absorption of surplus labor. The case for an efficiency rationale is prima facie greatest in regard to the vertical manufacturing keiretsu, although even there doubts are sometimes voiced. Still debated in some circles is whether such networks generate genuine efficiencies or whether the advantages they afford to

---

[29] Aoki (1988); Dore (1986); Imai and Itami (1984); Sheard (1991b); Smitka (1991).
[30] Goto (1982); Hoshi, Kashyap, and Scharfstein (1991a); Sheard (1994b).
[31] Aoki and Patrick (1994).
[32] Odagiri (1992).
[33] Aoki (1988); Caves and Uekusa (1976); Nakatani (1984).

parent firms such as Matsushita or Toyota come at the expense of the profits, growth rates, and wages of suppliers.

Even were the Toyota production network the model of efficiency so often claimed, it is by no means the only or even the prevailing model for how the Japanese manufacturing economy is organized. As Asanuma (1989) notes, the Japanese electronics industry conforms less well to the network model in which suppliers and customers bind to one another through the sharing of assets such as know-how and technology and the joint pursuit of cost savings, product design, and innovation. Within the Japanese car industry itself, the Toyota network has been an extreme case, unmatched by other automakers.[34] Some research by Christina Ahmadjian (1997) shows that, consistent with Toyota's own reliable standing as one of Japan's most profitable corporations, Toyota *kyoryoku-kai* (cooperative association) suppliers are likewise more profitable than the industry average. But the Toyota effect is unique; similar gains are not evident among other carmakers' *kyoryoku-kai* members. Much of the faith in the efficiency of the vertical keiretsu form would seem to rest on scholars' and journalists' fascination with the Toyota case.

Keiretsu as Risk-Pooling Mechanisms

If the case for the efficiency of Japan's keiretsu groupings is dubious, a solid body of evidence nonetheless testifies to another set of economic effects. Both quantitative and case studies find that the low profitability of big-six firms masks important variations in how keiretsu shape corporate fortunes. Specifically, keiretsu affiliation is a very useful thing to have when a company finds itself in dire financial straits. What Japan's business groups seem to do is manage terms of trade and lending to advance the long-term fortunes of the membership in accordance with group norms governing the distribution of risk, returns, and resources. In a word, groups *share* the burdens and benefits of economic activity. The degree to which the group is committed to any given company is proportionate to the strength of its tie to that company in terms of business (trade and lending) and governance (ownership and board representation) relations.

The most dramatic and visible evidence for this intervention and redistribution process is the bailouts and turnarounds that groups launch to rescue financially distressed or otherwise troubled members.[35] However, there is evidence as well of intervention at the high end of the performance distribution. As a function of the strength of their keiretsu alignments, strong performing firms display a subsequent tendency to drop back,

[34] Ahmadjian (1997); Fruin and Nishiguchi (1992); Nishiguchi and Beaudet (1998); Smitka (1991).
[35] Gerlach (1992a:111); Hoshi et al. (1991a); Sheard (1994a).

reporting lower profitability one or two years hence.[36] It is hard to determine whether these processes of bolstering weaklings and reining in high fliers are directly linked – that is, through the strongest firms paying the premium on the implicit insurance contract that buffers all against the risk of failure – or whether they are distinct – that is, groups restrain profiteering or simply claim the right to redistribute excess returns. It does appear, however, that the *same pattern* of intervention and redistribution describes both the big-six keiretsu and at least some of the vertical supply networks in the Japanese electronics and automobile industries.[37] In any case, the general phenomenon of risk and return sharing is consistent with our perspective on interfirm networks as *communities* that strive to limit inequality and opportunism while affording protection and support to the network as a whole.

At a more macro level, the groups played key roles in the restructuring of declining industries. One of the real strengths of the Japanese economy in the post-war era has been its capacity for fast adaptation to macroeconomic shock (e.g., the 1974 oil crisis, the 1986 *endaka* revaluation of the yen) and smooth transitions from stagnant or declining industries (e.g., shipbuilding, steel) to sectors in which Japan's competitive potential remained high. These structural adjustments were by and large carried out without the labor unrest, government subsidy, and business failures troubling the Western economies that moved down similar paths. While Japan's peculiar labor market institutions (permanent employment, employee transfers or *shukko*, enterprise unions, early mandatory retirement) facilitated these shifts, it is also true that large-scale cooperative pacts among keiretsu partners, encouraged and abetted by the state, provided the infrastructure wherein these changes could be handled in a deliberative and cooperative manner.[38]

Other close observers of Japan offer a much less sanguine portrait of the keiretsu risk-sharing and redistribution function. Indeed, the *convoy system*, as such activity is sometimes called, was much criticized in the recessionary 1990s for its role in maintaining unfit firms, dragging down strong firms, and weakening the financial system – since the bad debt problem at the root of the chronic financial crisis is largely one of banks and healthy firms keeping "deadbeat" or "zombie" firms on life support.[39] Katz (1998:171) writes:

> In Japan … [i]n the name of egalitarianism … the bigger or stronger firms were sometimes pressured to take [a] … cut … [t]o

---

[36] Lincoln et al. (1996, 1998).
[37] Ahmadjian (1997).
[38] Dore (1986, 2000); Taira and Levine (1985); Sheard (1991b).
[39] Hoshi (2002); Spiegel (2000).

help out the weakest. . . . The Japanese call this a "convoy" system in which the whole convoy can move no faster than the slowest ship.

Again, whether the keiretsu phenomenon is admired as a device for managed structural adjustment or attacked as an impediment to market efficiency seems to depend on how well Japan is doing and how effective the particular intervention is perceived to be. Pascale and Rohlen's (1983) tale of the Sumitomo bailout of Mazda (updated by Hoshi and Kashyap, 2000); Kester's (1991) account of the Mitsubishi rescue of Akai Electric; Nishiguchi and Beaudet's (1998) description of the Toyota group's quick action to avert a supply chain crisis triggered by a fire in one plant; and Sheard's (1991b) treatment of the Sumitomo group's role in the restructuring of the aluminum industry all exude admiration for the smooth orchestration of private sector efforts that worked to head off crisis and revamp individual firms and whole sectors while averting the litigation, shutdowns, layoffs, and other disruption that such adjustments have engendered in the West.[40]

However, with the bursting of the bubble, Japan – its ministries, leading banks, and keiretsu groupings – appeared to lose the magic touch that enabled the country to adjust to tough times and so impressed a previous generation of Western observers. Nothing then seemed to work to turn the economy around, so there was a natural inclination on the part of American observers to view the convoy system and other tools of risk-sharing as doing much more harm than good. We devote Chapter 5 to a detailed empirical study of keiretsu redistributive interventions. Our analyses, of course, cannot directly tackle the question of whether over the long term it has been a good or a bad thing for the economy as a whole. Given the breadth of the question, it is doubtful that any serious research can provide a satisfying answer. However, we do see our effort

---

[40] Williamson's (1975:145) comments on the merits and demerits of financial reallocations in the decentralized and divisionalized corporation recall the pros and cons of risk- and return-sharing in the keiretsu: "If the holding company serves as a collection agency for unabsorbed cash flows and uses these to shore up the ailing parts of the enterprise, the resulting insularity may encourage systematic distortions . . . among the divisional managements. Being shielded from the effects of adversity in their individual product markets, slack behavior sets in." Yet, he goes on to say, this is because the general office is lax in its monitoring and management responsibilities: "It might scrutinize reinvestment decisions every bit as well as the unassisted capital market could. Indeed, because it enjoys an internal relationship to the divisions, with all of the constitutional powers that this affords, the general management might be prepared to assume risks that an external investor ought properly to decline. Thus, the general management can ordinarily detect distortions and replace the divisional management at lower cost than can an external control agent similarly detect and change the management of a comparable, free standing business entity."

as a fine-grained empirical inquiry into a problem that has often drawn more heat than light.

The Structuralist Perspective

Our discussion above of the defining properties of keiretsu groupings gives a flavor for the kind of conceptualization and reasoning typical of structural analysis, a perspective that we generally adhere to throughout this book. In this section, we further flesh that perspective out. Structural analysis operates from a set of premises that distinguishes it from more established approaches to social and economic organization. Most basic is the theoretical and methodological emphasis on networks as an organizing principle. As one theorist described it, "The metaphorical use of the idea of the social network emphasizes that the social links of individuals in any given society ramify through that society. The analytical use of the idea of social network seeks to specify how this ramification influences the behavior of the people involved in the network."[41] This has several implications for how we approach our subject.

Ties as Elementary Units of Analysis
Structural analysis is forthrightly preoccupied with relations. Its elementary datum is the tie between a pair of actors, typically represented in binary – present or absent – form. In a study of complex economic structures and processes such as our own, many market processes, whether lending and borrowing, buying and selling, owning and investing, or personnel exchanges, are recast as ties. The binary representation has both methodological and substantive virtues. The methodological one is easy scalability: the analyst may span levels of analysis while preserving essential meanings. In Chapter 3, for example, we analyze patterns of change in such structural properties of the Japanese large-firm network as density and connectivity. Then in Chapter 4, the unit of observation becomes the dyad, a single pair of firms. Such multilevel conceptualization enables a more thoroughgoing assessment of the causality in systems of business relations than a single-level treatment makes possible. At the network level, we can ask, for example, how macroeconomic business cycle fluctuations and such exogenous shocks as exchange rate or regulatory shifts shape the cohesion and form of the network. At the dyad level, the question is how the probability of an equity or director interlock varies with the volume and reciprocity of business between a pair of firms

[41] Mitchell (1974).

34   *Japan's Network Economy*

and such attributes of firms as size, shacho-kai membership, industry, and region.

As a substantive matter, a focus on the presence or absence of a tie centers attention on whether or not a direct relationship simply *exists* between a pair of companies, as opposed to how strong or weak or frequent it is. Much attention has shifted recently, for example, to Japanese banks and corporations' selling-off ("unwinding") of cross-held shares, a trend indicative, it would seem, of the dissolution of business networks. Our data in Chapter 3 show, however, that the density of equity ties (the ratio of observed to potential ties in the corporate population) actually edged up through the eighties and nineties. A bank may reduce the volume of its lending to a client firm, or an assembler may cut its stake in a supplier, but in either case the tie persists. It is altogether consistent with the rules of keiretsu affiliation that a company's business with or governance tie to a group may vary in magnitude with the business cycle or the fortunes of the individual firm. The wholesale elimination of a tie – that is, the permanent severing of a supply relationship or the complete divestiture of an ownership stake in a trading partner – is a quite different action with farther-reaching implications for the structure and solidarity of the group.

The Locus of Causation Resides in Network Position Rather Than Actor Attributes

A focus on ties is also key to the etiology or causal reasoning peculiar to the structuralist mode of explanation. Structuralism abhors the reductionism of much contemporary social science inquiry, which locates the causes of social action – whether the actors are persons, firms, agencies, or institutions – solely in the attributes and motives of individual persons, be they the hard incentives that economics assigns to human decision makers' utility functions or the internalized values and rules stressed by cultural determinists in anthropology and sociology.[42] Structuralist inquiry may thus seem out of step with the times in its demurral from the fashionable view that large-scale institutions flow smoothly from the aggregation of individuals' choices. At the core of structuralist explanation is an assumption that causality lies with the constraints imposed by networks of relations. Leifer and White (1987:85) put it well:

> Structural analysis focuses upon the patterns of relationships among social actors. This emphasis rests on the often unspoken postulate that these patterns – independent of the content of ties – are themselves central to individual action. Moreover, structural

---

[42] Heimer (1992).

analysis posits that the constraints associated with positions in a network of relationships are frequently more important in determining individual action than either the information or attitudes people hold.

In a similar vein, structural analysis resists the prevalent tendency in much social science to accept at face value common-sense or formalistic labels for the objects of study. Most organizational research reflexively uses legal ownership or physical location to operationally identify the unit of analysis, even in today's globally integrated economy where such criteria have less real-world validity than in the past. Structural analysis begins with relations and classifies actors (e.g., firms) not on the basis of attributes (e.g., company size or industry), but in terms of positions (e.g., centrality or peripherality) in a matrix of ties to and from shareholders, banks, suppliers, technology partners, and so forth.[43]

The problems with the categoric approach are well-profiled in much extant research on the keiretsu. Group affiliation may be indexed by a single indicator (shacho-kai membership) or some combination of indicators (shacho-kai plus main bank relationship) or simply an investigator's "inside dope" or "common knowledge."[44] In our diverse analyses of keiretsu, we use such nominal indicators as well, but in much of our analysis – Chapter 3 in particular – we forego these and infer keiretsu clusterings from the degree to which firms have structurally equivalent relations with the network as a whole. This method of beginning with ties and inferring group boundaries from the empirical breaks and ripples in the network has the added virtue of enabling us to weigh the importance of the keiretsu principle against such alternative principles of clustering as industry or region.

Analysis Relies on Concrete (Relational) Data

The structuralist paradigm is also distinctive in its insistence on the systematic collection and analysis of empirical data on real social and economic action and relations. In the best structuralist inquiry, theory interacts with data in a series of iterative cycles. Network concepts (e.g., centrality, density, structural equivalence, diffusion) convert readily into operational procedures and the information yield from those operations lays the groundwork for the next round of theorizing.

The challenge, of course, is that appropriate network data are not easily obtained – leading to continued reliance on abstract and problematic proxies. Much essential information on corporate business networks is

---

[43] For a clear-cut example of structuralist inquiry, see Burt (1992).
[44] See, e.g., Career Development Center (2002); Miyashita and Russell (1994).

proprietary and is thus excluded from public-domain sources. Interorganizational network research would be greatly facilitated, for example, were companies mandated to report the names of their trading partners and the volumes of their commercial transactions. But such information is obviously sensitive and unlikely ever to be available for large and diverse populations of firms.[45] Consequently, students of business networks often resort to the expedient of proxying firm-level business relationships – that is, with highly aggregated industry-level input–output flows.[46]

It is a matter of good fortune (and no accident) that Japan, the economy that in recent years has garnered the greatest interest and closest scrutiny for the density, complexity, and even efficacy of its corporate networks, also makes widely available some of the richest relational data. An array of published government and private sources offer detailed, micro-level information on creditors, stockholders, trading partners, subsidiaries, and affiliates for publicly listed firms and for a large number of unlisted firms. Fine-grained information on boards of directors and management teams from directories such as *Kaisha nenkan* make possible inquiries into how corporate hierarchies interlock either contemporaneously through joint incumbency or sequentially via managerial career paths. Since the transfer or dispatch of management personnel from one company to another is pervasive practice in Japan, contributing much to the economy's network character, such data are extraordinarily useful. Sources such as the *Jinji koshin roku* (various years) provide details for management personnel on educational history, family members, leisure interests, and early careers, thereby enabling assessments to be made of corporate linkages based on schooling (*gakubatsu*) or marriage (*kekkonbatsu*) ties.

Finally, the quasi-formal enterprise groupings – the big-six horizontal groups in particular (see below) – are researched and described in exhaustive detail in sources such as Dodwell, *Keiretsu no kenkyu*, and *Kigyo keiretsu soran*. These identify the member companies of the shacho-kai and map the specific business and governance relations that account for group coherence.[47] In some industries (e.g., steel and autos) it is also possible to get detailed information on specific trading relations between firms,

[45] See Burt (1983); Flath (1993); Mintz and Schwartz (1985); Mizruchi (1996).

[46] Direct survey methods offer an alternative means of obtaining information on flows and ties not recorded in archival sources, and some investigators have measured through questionnaires and interviews supply relations and other concrete ties (Kelley and Brooks, 1991; Sako and Helper, 1998). But the obstacles to the use of survey methods to generate longitudinal data on large samples of corporations are formidable.

[47] The Ministry of Finance requires that all publicly traded corporations provide in their annual securities reports (*Yuka shoken hokokusho*) detailed information on their borrowing positions with major lenders and lists of major shareholders.

while general lists of major trading partners are available across Japanese industry. This range of data enables the determination of multiplex network structures based on the diverse interests companies have in one another, and it points up the array of problems to which such data can be applied.[48]

The reason for the relatively much greater availability of data on the Japanese economy's network organization is clear. It is not so much that regulators and information-gathering agencies are more enlightened than in other countries as to the intrinsic importance of business relationships and so are more supportive of network research. As in the West, apart from the information compiled by government ministries, which are generally circumspect about the disclosure of identities, the credit-rating agencies and investor services that offer such data are responding to demand. In Japan, more so than in the West, information on a corporation or financial institution's network of creditors, suppliers, customers, stockholders, affiliates, government agencies, and the like is considered essential for judging its credit-worthiness and soundness as an investment. Japanese corporate governance is much criticized by Westerners for the weakness of financial disclosure rules and the nontransparency of accounting practices. Yet Japanese firms are in many respects more open than their Western counterparts about their business networks and the backgrounds of their management teams.

Thus, structural analysis offers a lens on economic organization in a world where networks have become the fabric of economic life. This is arguably true of advanced economies in general, but it is especially true of Japan – the archetypal network economy. Yet few self-consciously structuralist attempts have been made to trace the structure and functioning of these networks out, and none, we believe, with the breadth and depth of data and method used here.[49]

Structural and Economic Analysis

It is no small intellectual irony that the most complete paradigm in the social sciences – the neoclassical framework within economics – still holds

---

[48] Much of these data have been readily available in directory form but not computer-readable form. Indeed, some years ago, in attempting to obtain tapes on directors in Tokyo Stock Exchange listed companies, we were informed by the publisher of the source that they were destroyed after the current year, since investors would have no interest in the information from prior years.

[49] For other examples of structural analysis using Japanese data, see Hoshi and Ito (1992), Knoke et al. (1996), Scott (1986). Of these two, the Scott study more closely approximates our own, since it focuses on intercorporate networks, while the Knoke study addresses networks in the public policy sphere.

sway over economic inquiry at a time when its underlying premises have never seemed less realistic and tenable. In early twenty-first century societies, the vast majority of important economic decisions are made by social collectives of various kinds (corporations, government agencies, etc.), rather than by isolated individuals. Capital investment is heavily mediated by banks and other major institutions; product markets are dominated by large manufacturing enterprises; labor markets are internalized within firms, occupations, and industries; and so on. When small numbers of large companies linked in long-term relationships with one another set prices and quantities, the identities and behaviors of transaction partners are factored into each firm's strategic decision making. Thus, market variables – prices, competition, terms of trade – are actively managed, bearing scant resemblance to the abstract and impersonal forces of mainstream economic theory. Clearly, this is truer of some national economies than others. In comparison especially with Japan but also with Europe, the United States has been a bastion of few-holds-barred competition in many sectors: capital, labor, intermediate products, and end-user goods and services.

It is also true that in recent years economists have taken a strong interest in problems of organization, and several of the most active new areas of economic inquiry, such as agency theory and transaction cost economics, take as their *explananda* managed relations within and between firms. Moreover, while contributors to this literature may not use the language, they nonetheless address the ties of control, communication, even dependence, trust, and reciprocity that are the natural domain of structuralist inquiry. How such flows and ties surround and regulate the exchange of goods and services to economize on information and transaction costs is key to such theory. They are thus not greatly different in substance from such sociological perspectives as exchange or resource dependence, which focus on how firms forge ties ("bridge") to one another via, for example, director interlocks, in managing dependence and uncertainty. Nor are they fundamentally at odds with embeddedness/ social capital theory, which attends to the inextricable fusing of economic and social relations.[50]

Two noteworthy differences between the economic and structuralist approaches, however, are (a) the narrower range of relations that economists consider relevant to economic activity, and (b) the optimizing assumptions and equilibrium calculus that seeks an efficiency explanation for any stable pattern of behavior. The "thick skein of relations" through which Caves and Uekusa saw Japanese economic activity carried out has been fair game for economic models only in the short period since Western economic

---

[50] Coleman (1986); Granovetter (1985); Pfeffer and Salancik (1978).

science began conceding the superiority of certain Japanese ways and entertaining the possibility that Japan's distinctive network forms might play some part in that superiority. The agency-theoretic role of banks as monitors in extracting information from and disciplining incumbent managements is nowhere better realized than in the Japanese "main bank" relation chronicled in the case studies by Sheard (1989a, 1994a) and other scholars. Moreover, the transaction cost ideas of *relational contracting* and *hybrid forms*, which blend elements of market contracting with the bureaucratic devices of authority and formal rules, were quickly picked up by students of the Japanese economy who saw in the country's thick business networks clear realizations of these phenomena.[51]

This view of economic exchange as inextricable from the broader web of social relations is generally resisted by mainstream economic inquiry if for no other reason than the sacrifice in parsimony that it entails. But there is no gainsaying its realism. Even Frank Hahn, one of the founding fathers of modern equilibrium theory, admitted late in his life to the need for economics examine more of the complexity and specificity of the real social world: "there is something scandalous in the spectacle of so many people refining the analysis of economic states which they have no reason to believe will ever, or have ever, come about."[52] An analogy might be drawn with the shift toward behavioral perspectives on managerial decision making in the study of organizations. Herbert Simon, James March, and other representatives of the Carnegie School argued that the human behavior of managers cannot be excluded from a theory of the firm. If, for example, bounded rationality and opportunism are basic to the cognition and motivation of human actors, then these must be incorporated in models of decision making. Similarly, we contend that if economic actors approach transactions, not as abstracted and isolated economic processes but as socially embedded, broadly interdependent relations infused with qualities such as trust and reciprocity, then the study of economic action requires a network-analytic framework.

The structuralist paradigm is thus generally at odds with the working assumption of much economics that models of market processes gain in parsimony by discounting social relations and give up little in explanatory power. A host of new claims for the flexibility, equity, and efficiency of network organization assert not merely that transactions abstracted from social structure cannot be fully understood. They further claim that forms of economic organization that in the real world conform to the abstract polarities of legal-rational bureaucracy and atomized, arm's-length

[51] Goto (1982); Imai and Itami (1984).
[52] Quoted in Loasby (1976: 226).

market exchange are fast being superceded by network forms that feature personal ties, reciprocal commitment, and permeable boundaries.[53]

Structuralism and Institutional Analysis

We have argued for a distinctively structural or network approach to the study of Japanese economic organization. Much of the analysis in this book uses the formalistic concepts and quantitative methods of mainstream structural analysis. However, there are limits to what a full-blown structural inquiry can accomplish, and at such limits complementary perspectives and methods must be invoked. Strong-form arguments for the power of structural analysis contend that an actor's position in the social structure suffices to explain that actor's behavior.[54] We believe, in contrast, that structural inquiry must be supplemented by analysis of the institutional constraints that frame networks and give them form and substance. These constraints will reflect these effects of history and culture in creating taken for granted modes of behavior that are neither codifiable in pure network terms nor fully explicable in terms of rational individual action.

Business environments may change rapidly, yet firms can be slow to respond. When they do, the courses of action they follow are often guided by idiosyncratic, outdated, and even inappropriate models. Managers have a finite set of organizational options from which to choose, and the optimal choices at any given point in time may lie outside the set. The range of options is constrained by the institutional environment, for example, the political and legal setting, the values and expectations of key constituencies, and the inherited legacies of decisions long past. All these arise from complex historical processes, and history is not something actors get to choose.

Our investigation of Japan's evolving business networks considers three major types of institutional constraint: institutional coevolution, institutional inertia, and institutional isomorphism.

Institutional Inertia
For a host of reasons – vested interests, persistent legitimacy, regulatory requirements, and sunk costs – organizational forms may continue long after they have ceased to perform useful functions in any technical or economic sense. This is a common take on the zaibatsu and keiretsu forms: that,

---

53 Miles and Snow (1987); Gerlach and Lincoln (1992); Lincoln et al. (1992); Piore and Sabel (1984); Powell (1990); Uzzi (1996).
54 See, e.g., Burt (1992); White (1992); Wolff (1950).

while they were key to Japan's early industrialization, they have outlived their usefulness and survive only because they remain an entrenched and legitimated feature of Japanese economic organization. Like a complex software program that resists deinstalling, they have so worked themselves into the recesses of the economic system that they are very hard to expunge.

Beyond the simple persistence of obsolete organizational forms, inertial forces cause evolutionary trajectories to be *path dependent*, bound to courses of development that early choices or events set in motion and so are unresponsive to current conditions. A considerable stream of research shows organizations bearing the imprint of environmental circumstances prevalent in the formative years of their industry. Examples from Japan abound. The concerns in Japan's Meiji era political economy with technological catch-up as a national security strategy have persisted, albeit in revised form, to the present day. Similarly, fears of foreign domination prompted a variety of formal controls over foreign direct investment that continued, in revised form, into this century. Such fears were also the impetus for more subtle, covert barriers to foreign penetration (which the U.S. Structural Impediments Initiative (SII) of the early 1990s sought to bring down).[55] Despite their breakup by the U.S. Occupation, the pre-war zaibatsu conglomerates provided the template on which the post-war keiretsu networks were forged. Another path-dependent process is the deeply ingrained practice of risk-sharing and redistributive intervention – the support of weak firms for bailout and turnaround by strong firms, banks, and ministries. Critics see the practice as the root cause of Japan's present bad-loan crisis and lagging competitiveness, but it retains a hold on public policy and corporate strategy. Although the organizational apparatus for interventions is shifting (see Chapter 6), the impetus behind them persists.

Institutional Coevolution
A second set of constraints arises from institutional coevolution. A country's socioeconomic organizational systems coevolve and complement one another in mutually reinforcing ways. Institutional fields such as government, law, education systems, and market organization are of necessity tightly coupled. The development of each thus drives the sequencing and patterning of others. Late developers such as Japan may have some advantage here, as they can shop for best practices, picking and choosing attractive institutions while foregoing some of the encumbrances of their

---

[55] Chief among such covert barriers targeted by the SII were the keiretsu themselves. See Imai (1990).

historical legacies. Getting the adopted systems to work in combination and with those of local origin, however, may demand considerable innovative adjustment.[56]

Institutional theorists have directed particular attention to constraints on economic organization imposed by the state. Government shapes the economy and the strategies and structures of individual firms in myriad ways.[57] Indeed, in the writings of Chalmers Johnson (1982) and others, the state bears responsibility for many of the distinctive institutional features of the modern Japanese economy. Chapter 2 shows how the Japanese wartime state contributed importantly to the fashioning of Japan's vertical and horizontal networks. But the role of the state goes farther back. Such modern industries as the railroads were owned and managed by the government during the early Meiji years.[58] When the nationalized industries were later sold off to private investors, the latter maintained close links to the organs of government and continued to profit from government largesse. Meiji entrepreneurs such as Yataro Iwasaki, founder of Mitsubishi, cultivated ties with the finance minister and thereby secured direct and indirect government subsidies to his shipping line. He later leveraged these same ties in expanding into warehousing and insurance. Similarly, Eiichi Shibusawa, the founder of present-day Toshiba, made effective use of his political acquaintances in founding an array of businesses in the banking, paper, textile, and brewing industries. Clark (1979) writes:

> In the early years of Japanese industrialization, private enterprise, while remaining private, was underwritten by the state in a manner quite without parallel in England, where the Industrial Revolution took place almost without government help, or the United States, where the distrust of central government and the size of the country precluded government interference in private business.

Japan's late-developing legal system also contributed to the shaping of its business networks. Modern property and contract law was slow to emerge, so that recourse to the courts as a means of dispute resolution was not generally an option. *Private ordering* within clusters of enterprises served as a substitute mechanism for ensuring reliable performance by business partners. Even in present-day Japan, the relatively low profile

---

[56] Japan's wedding of American statistical quality control techniques with Japanese-style small group activities is a familiar example (Cole, 1989). Westney's (1987) historical study shows how Meiji Japan modeled its police, military, education, government, and other national organizational systems on the developed nations of the day.

[57] See, e.g., Baron, Dobbin, and Jennings (1986); Fligstein (1990); Jacoby (1985).

[58] The Meiji Restoration of 1868 deposed the Tokugawa Shogunate, restored the Emperor as head of state, and launched the country on a program of rapid modernization.

of lawyers and the courts in economic affairs has spawned extraordinary reliance on alternative, extra-legal mechanisms for ensuring contract compliance and punishing malfeasance.[59] Such maneuvers, moreover, have been largely unregulated. Antitrust laws were generally absent until after the war and then remained weak and ineffective. Core firms had wide discretion in their management of affiliates – whether through board seats, stock voting, or their power as monopoly buyers and sellers. In sharp contrast, legal restrictions on merger and acquisition rendered these near-impossible without the incumbent management's consent.

The distinctive form taken by the Japanese financial system is another example of institutional coevolution, with profound implications for the growth of Japan's business networks. Unlike the United States and United Kingdom, where corporate equity and bond markets emerged early as a means of funneling capital to firms, finance in fast-industrializing Japan was largely grounded in nonmarket mechanisms – wealthy entrepreneurs, zaibatsu families, and commercial banks who (aided and prodded by the government) maintained tight, supportive relations with their principal client firms. Japan's banking system developed rapidly in the 1870s and 1880s and prior to most other major industries.[60] Decades later, banks aligned with merchant houses and large manufacturers took advantage of a wave of bank consolidations to create the concentrated financial centers that persist today. Reinforcing such bank–corporate ties were lax securities regulation and opaque accounting systems that made Japanese securities markets, until the post-war period, an arena for unsavory speculation as opposed to an efficient vehicle for distributing capital to productive uses.

Japan's modern network economy was also molded by developments in enterprise governance imposed, first, by the Japanese state and then by the U.S. Occupation. Wartime regulation and heightened political and cultural pressure to subordinate profit seeking to nationalist goals shifted the legitimate conception of the firm from a specialized instrument for the creation of shareholder wealth to a social institution in which employees and the community at large were dominant stakeholders. This focus continued after the war, as labor–management tensions encouraged as a democratizing force by the U.S. Occupation gave way to accommodations based on long-term employment guarantees, internal promotion, and enterprise-based unions.[61] The internal labor markets that thus materialized in large firms prompted wide use of subcontractors to buffer the core workforce from fluctuations in labor and product

---

[59] Hadley (1984).
[60] Nakamura (1983).
[61] Cole (1971); Shirai (1983).

market demand. It also required stable shareholders willing to overlook near-term performance shortfalls for the sake of long-term business growth.

Institutional Isomorphism

The third set of institutional constraints informing our analysis is what in organizational sociology is known as institutional isomorphism.[62] As economies mature, some organizational forms are identified as best or standard practice. They may represent the careful distillation of accumulated know-how and experience, or they may owe their legitimacy to unconscious and untested cultural assumptions about how the world works. When organizational fields gain wide acceptance as normal and legitimate, they display *isomorphism* – that is, take on similar observable features whatever the variations in the historical paths or local conditions.

Built into contemporary Japanese network structure are various assumptions about the nature of the firm, its relations with others, and its relations with the state that are widely shared within the Japanese business community. Although differing substantially in their formative histories – some emerging out of mining and manufacturing, others out of trade, and still others out of finance – the post-war horizontal keiretsu adopted many of the same organizational features. All used councils of executives (shacho-kai) to identify core membership, share information, and build collective purpose. All used minority equity stakes to reinforce business relationships. And all had at their center a triumvirate of a large commercial bank, general trading company, and heavy industry manufacturer.

Thus, institutional forces operate to create, configure, and maintain organizational forms and foster isomorphism or consistency in organizational fields. An institutional perspective thus helps to explain not only the strong and distinctive patterning of the Japanese economy itself, but also the differences between it and the rest of the industrial world. What is true of Japan is of course also true for other nations, for while Japan embarked on an ambitious program of nation-building, the rest of the world was changing as well. Because the working rules of network construction vary significantly from setting to setting, we see multiple solutions emerging to similar economic problems in diverse countries, industries, and periods. While increased functional requirements (e.g., efficiency, productivity, innovativeness) do of course bring on institutional change, the adjustment process is slow and halting, so that at any point in time economic systems will be out of equilibrium – less than perfectly tailored in an instrumental sense to extant conditions. As we see in later chapters, such

---

[62] DiMaggio and Powell (1983).

considerations are salient to recent debates in Japan over how and how much to restructure the country's troubled economy.

Conclusion

Post-war Japanese capitalism has been administered, relational capitalism to an extraordinary degree. However, it is not easy to discern who is doing the managing or whence the control derives.[63] For those in search of a single authoritative institution that holds the reins and snaps the whip, there is little satisfaction in the notion that the order in Japanese economic relations flows from strong but pliant social networks that enmesh corporations, banks, and ministries in a fabric of dependencies and obligations that has no one player in control. The perplexing reality of Japanese network capitalism is that it lacks a center. Reducing one's focus to a single institution, therefore, while perhaps an analytic convenience, is likely to lead the analyst astray.

Japan is not unique in this. As popular and scholarly writing on organizations and work life has highlighted over the past decade, rich, multiplex networks are a pervasive and salient feature of the modern business world. That is not to say that the degree and form of "networkness" is invariant across countries. Notwithstanding the conventional wisdom on system convergence, there are marked national differences, traceable to cultural, historical, and other forces, in the network textures of whole economies. Component parts tend to cluster in ways that are both internally coherent (e.g., the joining of durable employment, capital, and supplier relations in Japan) and distinguish one economy from another. This will come as no surprise to any business practitioner with experience in Japan and elsewhere around the globe. But it is a lesson that the scholarly study of economic organization does well to keep in mind.

An Overview of the Book

The chapters that follow take a self-consciously structuralist approach to the study of Japan's network economy. We analyze relationships among firms; how these aggregate to form large and complex networks; how individual firms connect to those networks; and how degrees of connectedness condition the performance of those firms. Chapter 2 is qualitative, using historical case materials to trace the structural evolution of

---

[63] For interesting treatment of this problem, see Kogut (2000).

the Sumitomo and Furukawa groups and to show how the interactions and obligations of individual managers mold interorganizational politics and outcomes. It documents how the rapid expansion of the Japanese economy was tied to the growth and diversification strategies of major companies, which, in turn, laid the foundation for the creation of Japan's distinctive network organizations. Specifically, the zaibatsu combined centralized resource allocation with decentralization of operational decisions through a process of nurturing new business and then spinning it off in the form of quasi-autonomous satellite enterprises. Second, the chapter shows how the wartime Japanese state and then the post-war Allied Occupation reconfigured the institutional environment of Japanese business to spawn a host of network forms. Finally, the chapter offers two short case studies, one of the struggle among Sumitomo group companies to determine which company would represent the group in the aluminum industry and the second the failed attempt in the late 1960s to merge Mitsubishi Bank and Dai-Ichi Bank. Both cases demonstrate the network politics – as opposed to pure market mechanisms – through which the processes of industry growth and corporate consolidation and restructuring have unfolded in Japan.

Chapters 3, 4, and 5 report quantitative analyses of a panel data set on Japan's largest 200 industrials, 50 financials, and 9 trading companies. The focus is structure and performance. Chapters 3 and 4 address problems of structure and use techniques of network analysis that will be familiar to the network cognoscenti, while hopefully, given our exposition, comprehensible to newcomers to the paradigm. Chapter 3 examines the global structural properties of the large firm network – how the density, cohesion, and clustering of lending, trade, equity, and director networks have been evolving over time. In its use of a well-established clustering algorithm, CONCOR, this chapter provides the most direct attack on the problem of change in the structure of the network economy. A striking finding is that the *density* of equity ties spiraled up across our period of observation, but *connectivity* – the tendency for partial ownership relations to enmesh firms in long and interwoven chains – peaked in the mid-1980s and has since trended down. Thus, cross-shareholdings, while remaining *the* signature tie on which the Japanese corporate network is constructed, have changed in form and function. They are now much more the instruments of individual firms' competitive strategies and less the threads from which a macro-network web is spun. The cause, it seems clear, is the decline of the keiretsu. Absent the groups' role in aggregating and shaping ties, one firm's equity stake in another reduces either to the firm-level process of an investment aimed at realizing a return or to the dyad-level process of two firms credibly committing to a bilateral pact.

Chapter 3 also looks in a fine-grained way at the evolution of particular horizontal and vertical keiretsu. Despite its format as a series of snapshots of a continuously changing network, the picture from this analysis is a clear one. In 1978, the beginning of our series, the keiretsu clusters were sharply profiled. Both horizontal and vertical groups correspond to well-defined blocks. Never again are the keiretsu contours of the network so vividly on display. The late 1980s bubble years are a nadir for the keiretsu, in terms of both group cohesion *and* (as Chapter 5 shows) interventionist bent. Yet in the 1990s, the former zaibatsu and such vertical groups as Matsushita and Toyota stage comebacks, recovering much of the cohesion they lost in the bubble. But the dissolution of the bank-centered groups continues, such that, by mid-decade, they can hardly be said to exist. Apart from these broad trends, we find that groups wax and wane with the business cycle – retrenching in bad times (circling the wagons) while loosening in good times as member firms, unsurprisingly, drift away.

Chapter 4 takes a different tack. We address a hypothesis posed by Banri Asanuma that the issue of keiretsu reduces to the control or governance that transacting firms adopt or exploit, whether consciously or in an evolutionary way, to manage transactions. This proposition is at the heart of such strong traditions of interorganizational theory as the "embeddedness" and resource dependence perspectives of organizational sociology and the transaction cost and principal–agent perspectives of organizational economics. While Chapter 3 takes equity, director, lending, and trade ties as alternative but equally valid and reliable indicators of a single multiplex network, Chapter 4 casts equity and director interlocks as the governance structures whereby firms organize financial and commercial exchange. As in Chapter 3, the question of change is key. We find a general decline in the reciprocity of equity and director ties, again interpreted as erosion of the macro-network logic of Japanese intercorporate ties and its replacement by strategic, firm-specific rationale. A simple rendering of the Asanuma hypothesis, however, proves wrong: with the economic exchange between the pair statistically netted out, strong effects of keiretsu remain, although these weaken in the bubble and ensuing years.

So the keiretsu effect on the structuring of Japanese business networks is real – equity and director ties, in particular, have a group solidarity rationale that is distinct from – if not to the exclusion of – any role they play in the management of exchange. Even so, equity and director ties do function to control or govern bilateral transactions. Both lending–borrowing and selling–buying transactions are powerful drivers of these ties. Lenders control borrowers more than vice versa. On the transaction cost–resource dependence assumption that banks seek control of clients in order to monitor their use of borrowed assets, this was expected. Based on images of the vertical keiretsu that have long framed research on Japanese purchase–supply relations, we assumed commercial exchange to be broadly asymmetric as well – that net of size, age, and the like, customers control suppliers more than the reverse. The data, however, reveal general symmetry in the control (equity and director) ties between suppliers and customers, although in some industries, autos in particular, customers clearly dominate. The control flowing from banks is in excess of their lending relations, but that wielded by trading companies is in line with the volume of their trade. Another finding consistent with the Asanuma worldview is a strong negative effect of trade reciprocity on control ties. This supports the influential idea that trust and mutuality substitute for hard governance in economic exchange.

Chapter 5 shifts the focus to performance – how a company's sales growth and profit margins are conditioned on its involvement in a keiretsu network. The hypothesis explored is key to much discussion of the keiretsu and other networks in the Japanese political economy: that groups act to maintain balance in their ranks and ensure the survival of all members by supporting their weak at the expense of their strong. The evidence for the intervention hypothesis is substantial, although it varies: (directly) with the size of the target firm; the cohesion of the group; the performance outcome – greater for ROA than for sales growth; and with the keiretsu tie – greater for shacho-kai, lending, and equity than for trade partnerships and director dispatch. We also observe a pattern of differences among industries that is somewhat supportive of the idea that keiretsu interventions are more prevalent in the less competitive, domestic sectors than in the leading export sectors of autos and electronics. Like the groups themselves, the intervention pattern fluctuates with the times but by the end of our data series has largely faded away. It all but disappears in the 1986–1991 endaka-bubble era. It then resurfaces in some if not all forms (e.g., not bank-based) but generally as a pale shadow of the prebubble pattern. This striving to keep the corporate community intact and afloat – even if it means pumping life into unsalvageable "zombie" firms – is seen as the source of many of Japan's current difficulties – bad loans, deflated stock market, and weak growth. However, in rosier times such keiretsu-engineered adjustments elicited broad praise for their seemingly graceful execution and low direct public cost. In both Chapters 5 and 6, we give some consideration to the implications of redistributive interventions for the health of the economy as a whole.

Chapter 6, the concluding chapter, also dwells on change, but the mode of inquiry is for the most part qualitative. We give an overview of some recent developments in the Japanese network economy – the major consolidations that have reconfigured the financial services industry (e.g., the formation of the Mizuho group from Dai-Ichi Kangyo, Fuji Bank, Industrial Bank of Japan (IBJ)), a number of mergers of industrial firms, regulatory changes in accounting practice (e.g., tightening of consolidated reporting requirements) and corporate governance (the lifting of the holding company ban), the rise of a new breed of entrepreneurial firm (e.g., Softbank) and the creation of institutions (e.g., new stock exchanges) for breeding more, the forging of innovative strategic alliances and the role of keiretsu in shaping them, and the decline of the keiretsu system of behind-the-scenes redistributive intervention and its replacement by a new convoy of public and private organizations aimed at rehabilitating failing companies in a more above-board and policy-directed way. As for the implications of these developments for Japan's legacy networks, we acknowledge that the pace and depth and scope of change is unprecedented in the post-war period. Perhaps business journalists can now claim as they have so often in the past that Japan has been altered in fundamental ways and history will judge this to be a fair assessment.

The network structure of the Japanese economy as a whole and the organization and action of the keiretsu clusterings within it figured critically in Japan's economic evolution. The keiretsu played a huge part in Japan's pre-war development and in the post-war economic miracle – the fifteen-year spell of double-digit gross domestic product (GDP) growth that catapulted the country from wartime devastation to its present standing as the second largest economic power in the world. Keiretsu networks were also key to the competitive superiority of Japanese manufacturing and to Japan's distinctive – and on some dimensions still effective – corporate governance system. In recent years, business groups as a global economic phenomenon have received increased scholarly attention. The keiretsu by any standard represent the most successful deployment of this distinctive organizational form in the development process, a point often loss in the harsh assessments of their role in the Japanese economy of today. Russia, China, Brazil, India, Korea, and other still-developing nations whose economies feature business groups as a conspicuous institution look to Japan as the foremost historical example of how to do groups right. Japan itself, however, is a modern and mature economy, and, consistent with all development theory, its keiretsu groupings, while persisting to some degree in some forms, are giving way and have been since the late 1980s.

We close by noting the continuing discussions in Japanese business, policy, and academic circles over the form of capitalism best suited to twenty-first-century Japan, a debate intensified recently by the collapse of the U.S. Internet economy and the wave of corporate scandals that, for a time at least, put a damper on American claims to be the global standard-bearer of economic transparency and efficiency. Japan's network economy has been transformed in significant ways since the bursting of the late

1980s bubble, but offsetting and legitimating the change is a new conservatism among Japanese business elites – a commitment, amid all the talk of reform, to preserving some of the distinctive features of the country's post-war economic organization such as long-term commitments to employees and business partners and a conception of the corporation as a social institution beholden to a host of broad constituencies, something other than a specialized contrivance for the creation of shareholder wealth.

2

The Origins of Japanese Network Structures

The organization of Japanese and Western industry was probably more similar in 1910 than in 1970.

Rodney Clark, 1979:258

Introduction

As the first non-Western country to industrialize, Japan is an important test case for alternative models of economic development. While knowledgeable observers may disagree on the specifics, most will concur with the premise that Japan's development was not simply the product of convergent modernization – its economic, political, and social institutions reflect distinctive features of Japan's own history, not merely the re-creation of their Western counterparts. Indeed, as Clark suggests in the introductory quote, the general trend through much of this century may have been toward divergence away from Western (or at least American) assumptions about how development takes place.

This chapter considers the issue of Japan's economic development from an institutionally informed network perspective by exploring the organizational and industrial arrangements that have underpinned it. Our methodology, unlike the quantitative analyses in chapters to follow, is qualitative and historical, covering a period of roughly a century from the early years of Japan's modernization in the late 1800s to the miracle years of the 1950s to 1980s. Our treatment is focused and analytical rather than exhaustive and descriptive. A few underlying principles explain much of what we see today, even if the specifics have varied by time period, industry, and company.

We divide the evolution of Japanese network organization into three phases of development. The first phase, beginning in Meiji and continuing through the 1920s, witnessed the emergence and gradual evolution of the zaibatsu, the predecessors of the keiretsu. During the early years of its industrialization, Japan faced the problems of any developing economy. Critical resources, notably capital and technical know-how, were in scarce supply and required efficient allocation to the economically and strategically important industries. As late-developer theories often advocate, these allocation decisions could in principle be turned over to a small cadre of state agencies and privileged industrialists to ensure centralized control over the process. But that course of action risked creation of unwieldy bureaucracies and alienating the managers whose skills and commitment were needed to build and run the actual plants and enterprises. Using the growth and diversification strategies pursued by the Sumitomo and Furukawa groups as empirical anchor, we see how the division of growing businesses into clusters of more or less loosely networked enterprises was Japan's organizational solution to this tension.

The second phase of development, during wartime, transformed Japan's economic system and its network structures in fundamental ways. The basic relationship between state and industry changed dramatically during this period, as new forms of centralized controls over resource allocation were implemented. By 1940, Japanese industry was a planned economy, structured around vertical production systems controlled by state institutions at the top, operating through key first-tier corporations and industrial associations in the middle, and extending to medium- and small-sized enterprises at the bottom.

The third phase of development came with Japan's defeat in World War II. Although the first few years of the Occupation witnessed the implementation of economic reforms intended to democratize Japan, this agenda soon gave way to the more pressing need to rebuild the economy as a bulwark against communist expansion. The period from the late 1940s to the 1980s saw not so much the elimination of network structures as their evolution and expansion as a core component in an integrated business system comprising lifetime employment, main bank relationships, subcontracting relations, and industrial policy-making. The success of this revised system, as measured by Japan's high growth rates, ensured that it would continue in basic form over the next three decades. The system's very success, however, also ensured that companies had to accept stringent rules on business transactions, even when these were not in their interests. Two case studies that conclude the chapter, of the Sumitomo and Dai-Ichi Kangyo groups, demonstrate how the institutionalization of the post-war system played itself out, as network structures emerged as powerful sources of strategic constraint over companies' primary business activities.

The result by the end of this century was an institutionalized pattern of relations substantially different than the one with which Japan had started, but also one in which evolving network structures were built on top of preexisting arrangements. This fusing of historical legacy and contemporary Japan-specific circumstance gave rise to a distinctive form of capitalism – one based in ownership by strategic business partners rather than independent financiers – and also a distinctive system of production and innovation, based in networks of suppliers and distributors arrayed vertically around large manufacturers. It was rather different from the systems of capitalism and production that Japan's trading partners (at least the United States) were accustomed to. But it was also a business network configuration that accomplished much in the intervening years.

Emergence of Network Structures: From Meiji through Pre-War

The first phase in this development of Japan's modern industrial architecture began after the Meiji Restoration in 1868 and continued through the pre-war era, one marked by the tremendous transformations that came in the wake of Japan's opening to the outside world and subsequent rapid modernization. The half-century period from the late 1800s through the 1920s witnessed considerable economic change and entrepreneurial initiative, as thousands of new companies were founded and whole new industries created. As evidence of this, one need look no farther than our own core sample of 259 large Japanese firms (see Chapter 3): the vast majority of these companies got their start during these decades, while only a small fraction were founded during or after the war years.

The dynamic technological and geopolitical conditions that distinguished Japan's early modern history are critical to an understanding of the network structures that came to dominate Japanese economic life. In order to see just how, one must understand how times of rapid change shape basic organizational processes. As Schumpeter (1955) first noted, economic organization under conditions of industrial change varies substantially from that found under stable conditions. Dynamic conditions are particularly prevalent in industries at the frontiers of global technology, but they exist within any rapidly developing economy, including Japan's during these years. Japanese firms were continually innovating – crafting combinations that differ substantially from preexisting arrangements – even if they benefited from the ability to borrow technologies, production processes, and organizational models from other countries.

Growth and diversification, especially at Japan's technological frontier, were a driving force behind the organizational shifts that Japanese firms underwent in the decades leading up to World War II. Representative of how these processes gave rise to inchoate network structures were the zaibatsu. As is well known, zaibatsu-affiliated firms were instrumental in developing Japan's frontier industries – from the introduction of new metal and chemical manufacturing processes to the development of an electrical machinery industry to the expansion into overseas markets.[1] By the 1930s, companies linked either to the old, family-based zaibatsu (e.g., Mitsui, Mitsubishi, and Sumitomo) or to the new, industrial zaibatsu (e.g., the Nissan group) were involved in most major industries in Japan and held leading positions in many.[2]

This growth and diversification, we argue, reflected the balancing of strategic advantages enjoyed by the zaibatsu as a centralized resource allocator with a continual process of decentralizing operational decisions through formation of new and partially autonomous enterprises. Among the most important of the head office's centralized resources were capital reserves made possible by successful mines, profitable landholdings, exclusive licenses for the development of new regions, and so forth. These operations served as cash cows, the excess from which could be funneled into promising new ventures. Another important strategic resource was management talent and experience, which could be allocated to promising ventures through information sharing and the dispatch of trained personnel. A third was political connections, as the zaibatsu leadership used relations to politicians and bureaucrats to gain exclusive business licenses, subsidies, and government contracts.

Balancing these centralizing forces was an equally powerful set of decentralizing forces. Managerial aggressiveness and entrepreneurial initiative reflected the extraordinary investment opportunities made possible by new technologies, industries, and markets offered by Japan's opening to the West. The zaibatsu and their affiliates were by far the heaviest investors in developing overseas branch offices to handle imports and exports, in the licensing of the latest technologies from Europe and the United States, and in other risky investments. But in order to harness these investments within their increasingly far-flung empires, they also had to grant freedoms to enterprise managers not necessary in earlier years.

Growth and Diversification in the Sumitomo and Furukawa Groups

In the case of the Sumitomo and Furukawa groups, analyzed here, we observe the forces of strategic centralization and operational decentralization at work, but we also see important differences resulting from

---

[1] Lockwood (1968); Ohkawa and Rosovsky (1973).

[2] One important exception to this generalization is cotton spinning. Most companies in this industry operated relatively independently of both banks and the state. Funding came primarily through direct finance, especially from affluent individuals who, in comparison with the zaibatsu holding companies, were far more interested in immediate profitability than long-term growth and high dividends over capital reinvestment (Okazaki, 1993).

MINING → REFINED METALS → WIRE PRODUCTION → ELECT. MACHINERY

→ CHEMICALS (Sumitomo only)

→ IRON AND STEEL (Sumitomo only)

Figure 2.1. Sumitomo techno-organizational chain.

their distinctive evolutionary paths. Both companies diversified out of a core base in copper mining operations – the Besshi mine in the case of Sumitomo and the Ashio mine in the case of Furukawa. These highly productive operations (the two largest in Japan) became an important source of investment capital during the rapid-growth years beginning in the late 1800s. They also provided an important source of accumulated know-how that could be used in new fields – both related (where the know-how was technology or industry specific) and unrelated (where the know-how was generic).

Both Sumitomo and Furukawa used their capital reserves and knowledge base to expand aggressively into related industries in serial fashion, at each point creating a new satellite organization to handle the responsibilities. One such techno-organizational chain connected mining, refined metal, wire production, electrical machinery, chemicals, and iron and steel, as depicted in Figure 2.1. In both groups, the most important chain ran from the copper mining operations through copper refining and wire production to electrical machinery production. In the case of Sumitomo, this led to the formation of Sumitomo Electric, Sumitomo Machinery, and the later adoption of Nippon Electric (NEC) as major affiliate. In the case of Furukawa, the chain of satellites ran from Furukawa Electric to the Fuji Electric joint venture with Siemens to Fujitsu, a later spinoff from Fuji Electric.

Of the two groups, Sumitomo was by far the more aggressive and successful diversifier overall, into both related and unrelated areas. Sumitomo's full-scale diversification out of mining began with the establishment of Sumitomo Bank in 1895, which within ten years of founding had become the third largest bank in Japan (after Mitsui and Dai-Ichi). Sumitomo also diversified at the turn of the century into the iron and steel industry, with the establishment of Japan's first cast steel mill and open hearth furnace, an operation that later was incorporated as part of Sumitomo Metal Industries, one of Japan's steel giants. Although both groups sought to diversify into chemicals from the Taisho period on, only Sumitomo's effort was fully successful, resulting in the creation of Sumitomo Chemical, then and now one of Japan's largest chemical companies.

Diversification in Furukawa's case was more limited and proceeded more slowly. Although, as Japan's largest copper producer, it had amassed a substantial storehouse of capital, it concentrated on copper-related operations until well into the Taisho period (1912–26). In the late 1800s and early 1900s, at a time when Mitsui, Mitsubishi, and Sumitomo were moving rapidly into unrelated businesses, Furukawa continued to focus on vertical and horizontal integration – purchasing and expanding mines, producing copper and electric wire, mining coal used to run its refineries, and expanding refinery operations themselves. As a result, it never grew into the kind of group that could rival the other three.[3]

How do we explain these differences? An important reason lies in Sumitomo's early effort to expand into banking, which provided the group with a strategic core of support operations for its broad diversification during the rapid expansion in the interwar period. After its founding, the Sumitomo Bank grew quickly, resulting in a bank that ranked among Japan's top five by the early 1900s and served as an important source of capital for affiliated enterprises throughout the remainder of the century. In contrast, Furukawa did not finally move into banking until 1917, with the founding of Tokyo Furukawa. But its late start kept it small relative to its counterpart in Sumitomo. At the time of founding, it comprised only ¥5 million in share capital (compared to ¥30 million); ¥13.5 million in deposits (compared to ¥187.6 million); and ¥15.3 million in loans (compared to ¥120.1 million).[4]

A second reason can be located in the effects of Furukawa's failure to develop strategic support operations in overseas commerce. Mitsui dominated this area for much of the pre-war period, controlling roughly one-third of all Japan's international trade and using these operations to promote its affiliated businesses. Furukawa attempted to expand its international operations by spinning off its marketing arm as Furukawa Trading in 1917. This operated as a successful operation for a number of years, but speculative grain transactions in its Dalian branch led to about ¥58 million in losses and led to its later bankruptcy. This event reinforced Furukawa's conservatism about expansion out of its mining and machinery core and prevented it from developing the kind of international and overseas support network that might have compensated for its small financial core.

The net result of these differences is evident in subsequent group evolution. By the 1930s, Sumitomo had an elaborate network of affiliates involved in a wide range of industries, while Furukawa's activities remained limited to a few operations centered on mining, metals, and machinery. The Sumitomo zaibatsu, as seen in Figure 2.2, was organized within a

---

[3] Although Furukawa did not develop on its own into a broader zaibatsu, it did consolidate important ties that it had maintained since the late 1800s with the Dai-Ichi Bank and its affiliates to create during the post-war period the core of what is now the DKB group.

[4] Morikawa (1993: 137–138).

Figure 2.2. Illustration of the organization of the Sumitomo Concern (approximately 1930). ● indicates that Sumitomo's control (over a company) is defined. Unmarked indicates that Sumitomo's control is less than the above. ❖ indicates that Sumitomo's control is not classified as either one of the above two.

Source: *Nihon no zaibatsu* Miyamoto and Nakagawa (1976:61).

multisatellite structure of directly and indirectly related enterprises, often referred to (borrowing from the German) as a "konzern." In this structure, the head office typically controlled a substantial share of each venture's total equity and retained a number of seats on its board, it maintained strong claims on the revenue stream the venture company created, and in some cases it also managed the affiliate's top-level personnel decisions. But balanced against this central strategic function, as we see below, was a recognition of an important degree of enterprise autonomy.

Sectoral Variations in Organizational Growth

Additional evidence for the importance of the dual processes of strategic centralization and operational decentralization comes from a detailed analysis of the patterns of organizational growth and diversification at the level of individual enterprises within the zaibatsu – sectoral variations that began before the war but have continued into the present and exist across Japanese industry. As Figures 2.3 and 2.4 demonstrate, the predominant growth pattern within Japan's largest financial institutions (represented here by Sumitomo Bank and Dai-Ichi Kangyo Bank) has been one of strategic consolidation: moving over time from multiple banks (left-hand side of the figures) to a single bank (right-hand side of the figures) through a chain of mergers and acquisitions. Although some city banks (including Sumitomo) began the splitting off of financial operations from the original zaibatsu family enterprises, they grew largely through acquisitions in the late Taisho and early Showa periods (1920s and 1930s). That is, once the basic division from the head office was established, the financial institution continued to expand without significant further division.

In sharp contrast, as evidenced in the organizational trees for NEC and Fujitsu, industrial firms at Japan's technological frontier have tended to grow through an atomizing process of satellite formation.[5] This process, depicted in Figures 2.5 and 2.6, involved both spin-offs from the core operation and strategic alliances with other firms. NEC and Fujitsu both began as strategic partnerships with foreign companies (Western Electric and Siemens, respectively), but their effort to expand after the war through segmentation was largely through internal spin-offs. This led to the development of their own satellite networks – the primary member of which is now Fujitsu Fanuc, separated from Fujitsu in 1972

---

[5] This is not to say that mergers and acquisitions are never used by these firms. But it is to say that their distinctive significance comes in the ways in which their growth through satellite formation has dominated new venture creation in Japan.

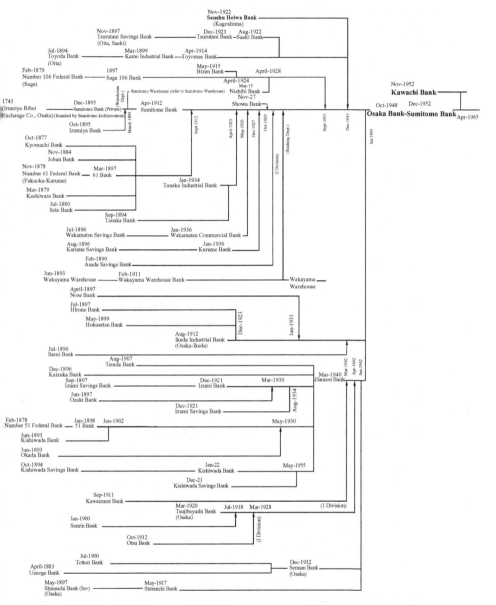

Figure 2.3. Sumitomo Bank.
Sources: Sumitomo Bank (1926:240; 1955a:182; 1955b:405; 1955c:34; 1965:298; 1979:14).

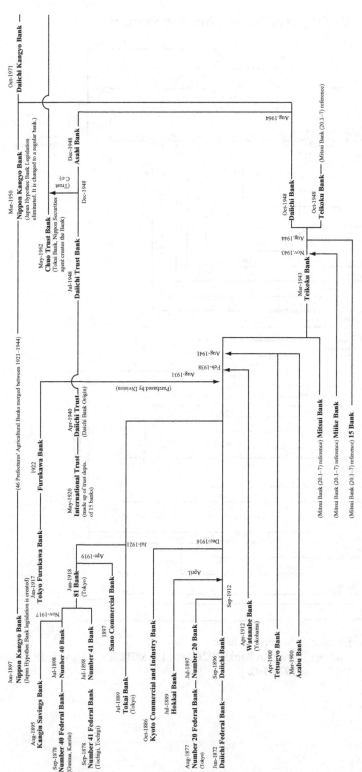

Figure 2.4. Dai-Ichi Kangyo (Hypothec) Bank (DKB).

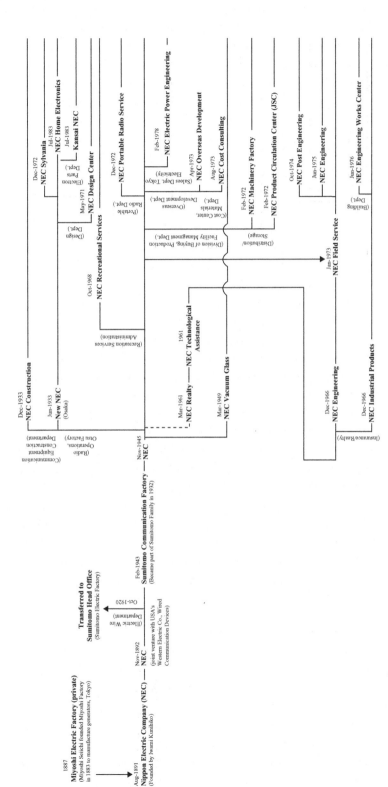

Figure 2.5. Nippon Electric Company (NEC).
Sources: NEC (1958a: 63), NEC (1958b:598), NEC (1969:79).

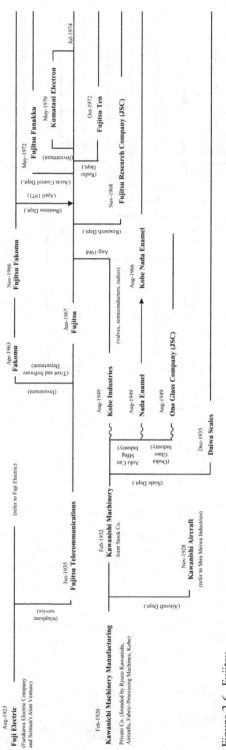

Figure 2.6. Fujitsu.
Sources: Fujitsu (1964:206; 1976:203).

and now Japan's largest robotics and numerically controlled machine tool company.

One of the important consequences of these sectoral variations has been divergent levels of industrial concentration. Japan's financial sector became substantially more concentrated throughout the years leading up to the war. According to Nakamura (1983:207), the share of total deposits held by the five largest banks increased from 20.7 percent in 1901 to 24.1 percent in 1925 to 41.8 percent in 1940, while their share of loans went up even faster, from 12.0 to 18.4 to 57.1 percent. In contrast, he finds, industrial concentration in nearly all sectors actually declined during the rapid diversification of the 1920s and 1930s.

A second consequence of these contrasting growth patterns is that the development of the zaibatsu as a whole was asymmetric. The strategic core was marked by internal growth among a few key players closely tied to the head office – several major financial institutions and a major trading company were the extent of this core in even the largest groups. In contrast, the operational frontier was marked by the continual expansion into new fields through ongoing satellite formation. For this reason, by far the most important source of growth in business activities and in the formation of affiliated companies came from the decentralized expansion and diversification of venture businesses intended to exploit new technologies and markets.

Consider the process of organizational growth of the group. At present, it encompasses twenty core companies, as indexed by membership in the group presidents' council, the *Hakusui-kai*. More detailed analysis of the foundings of these companies reveals two important facts. First, new firms were formed primarily through spinoffs from the core operation, with all but seven of the twenty resulting from intentional spin-offs, either from the head office or from other satellite firms. Among the seven that were not spin-offs, three (Sumitomo Bakelight, NEC, and Nippon Sheet Glass) started independently but built ties to Sumitomo during the pre-war period and an additional two (Sumitomo Forestry and Sumitomo Realty) were created out of the remains of the head office after the post-war zaibatsu dissolution. Second, all of the industrial spin-offs (Sumitomo Coal Mining, Sumitomo Metal Mining, Sumitomo Construction, Sumitomo Chemical, Sumitomo Electric, Sumitomo Metal Industries, Sumitomo Heavy Industries, and Sumitomo Light Metals) were the direct or indirect result of Sumitomo's operations in a small number of interrelated industries – mining operations during the Meiji period and chemical, metal, and machinery businesses later. It was these sectors that were the leading edge of Sumitomo's business and the primary source of new member firms during its pre-war diversification.

The Advantages to Satellite Organization

These divergent processes of growth pose a fundamental question as to the logic of the zaibatsu: Why grow through fragmentation of the core staff? The reasons begin in the complex and dynamic technical and market conditions structured into frontier industries. These conditions imposed considerable demands on the resource and administrative core of the zaibatsu. Owing to high rates of growth in many key sectors and the importance of establishing early entry to gain competitive advantage, capital investment requirements were enormous. At the same time, head office employees generally had little experience in the technical and market requirements of emerging industries and were often more adept at managing financial and strategic affairs (monitoring subsidiary accounts, cultivating political relationships, etc.) than they were at handling local operations.

By segregating activities, the head office could accomplish two important objectives. First, it provided greater autonomy for localized decisions and incentives to operate and thus fostered a more entrepreneurial environment in the satellite business. Second, by creating an independent location in which to concentrate partner-related activities, it facilitated strategic partnering. Emerging out of this was a natural division of labor between (1) a decentralized network of industrial firms focused on the complex logistics of managing diverse technological and industrial activities, and (2) a head office taking on the functions of overall strategic planning and resource allocation.

Building in Independence and Flexibility
A dysfunctional side effect of large-scale organizational systems structured in terms of standardized and formalized processes is that employees focus on the observance of rules and procedures rather than acting independently or entrepreneurially. Whereas that might be an advantage in a stable setting, where reliability and cost containment are primary goals, it works against the organization's ability to respond to rapid technological and industrial change. A partial solution is to decentralize those operations in frontier areas by segregating them from the core operation, granting them a degree of autonomy to develop new and more appropriate procedures to follow, and providing strong managerial incentives toward venture growth. A degree of control is no doubt given up by the head office, but the underlying logic is that the agency costs produced by a weakened administrative control structure are oftentimes less important than the organizational flexibility and entrepreneurial initiative gained.

This process of satellite formation in the zaibatsu unfolded as a dynamic series of cycles. As new ventures gained experience – developing their own business relations and training their own workers – they acquired a corresponding degree of independence from the core firm. Several stages were typical: The venture would first establish its identity as an internal division of the head office or one of its satellites. As new markets and technologies generated business opportunities outside the core firm's basic lines of business, the strategy shifted toward segregating the operation as an independent entity, leading eventually to full-scale incorporation. Such segregation typically involved the spinning off of whole self-contained units, either divisions or factories. Thus, complementing the differentiation of the venture from the core firm were steps to ensure the former's internal coherence. As it succeeded and grew, its ties to the parent (in both a control and a resource sense) weakened and its own satellite network took form.

Managers in the head office increasingly removed themselves from the day-to-day running of subsidiary operations – especially those unrelated to its strategic and cash-cow operations. By the 1930s, less than half the top management in most satellites came from the head office; internally promoted managing directors were put in charge of day-to-day administration. For example, Tomozumi Sumitomo withdrew from his position as president of Sumitomo Steel Mill and Sumitomo Electric Wire, serving only as president of the group's bank, warehouse, and trust bank. As a Sumitomo executive explained in 1928: "Each branch operation has its own authority to pursue actively business activities. Under our decentralized organization, these operations can be flexible. The head office must support the affiliates, but it cannot ultimately regulate or control them."[6]

To be sure, the loss of core firm control due to the segregating and spinning off of operations was an ever-present danger. In Morikawa's (1980) detailed discussion of Mitsui's trading operations during the Taisho period, for example, we find a continuing tension between the head office and the local branch managers over personnel matters, the kind of products to be promoted, and other important business decisions. But this account also makes clear that Mitsui's loss of central control was countered by a corresponding set of advantages in terms of increased entrepreneurial initiative and organizational flexibility. As did other successful groups, Mitsui managed this tension by loosening control of its expanding empire.

This logic is reinforced by two examples involving the Furukawa group. The rapidly expanding operations of Furukawa Electric in the early 1920s continued to be held back by the lack of financial and strategic support from a conservative head office that was still trying to recover from its losses in the trading business and from the recession that followed World

---

[6] Translated from Miyamoto and Sakudo (1979:356).

War I. Although Siemens of Germany had agreed to enter a broad-ranging technical tie-up with Furukawa, the parent firm head office backed out at the last minute. Rather than abandon the project, the top management of Furukawa Electric agreed *independently* to sign the contract, leading to the establishment of a new enterprise, Fuji Electric, in 1925. Of the original capitalization of ¥10 million, 3 million came from Siemens and an additional 4 million from Furukawa-related companies, but none from the head office. It was not until the end of 1928, several years later, that the parent firm bought any shares in the new company. The venture also sought additional capital through loans from outside financial institutions (Dai-Ichi Bank, Mitsui Bank, Mitsubishi Bank, and Mitsui Trust Bank), rather than relying on the limited resources of the Furukawa Bank. And in terms of management, the new venture's first president was brought in not from the head office, but from a textile company outside the group.

Another example of Furukawa Electric's independent initiative is found in its diversification into the aluminum business. Beginning in 1919, Furukawa had been working in a technical partnership with British Aluminum for the production of aluminum cables. As the business expanded, the top management of Furukawa Electric proposed to the head office of Furukawa that it build an aluminum refinery with which to supply the venture. Once again, the Furukawa head office opposed the move, expressing concern about the financial liabilities it might entail. On the surface, Furukawa Electric complied. It discontinued research it had underway in collaboration with a syndicate of several other Japanese firms. But on its own it moved to expand the project by bringing in funding from the Mitsui, Mitsubishi, and Taiwan Electric Power company. In 1935, Japan Aluminum Corporation (Nihon Arumi Kabushiki Gaisha) was established and soon became one of Japan's major producers.[7]

Facilitating Strategic Partnering

A second major advantage of satellite-based growth was that of building a network of relations outside the group. By segregating and decentralizing operations, the zaibatsu created an array of distinct organizational nodes with which localized strategic alliances could be forged with other companies. The partner's material and other resource contributions could be directed at a limited and well-defined set of activities. This protected the core firm from undue intrusions on its turf by the partner, while enabling the latter to pursue new markets and customers (including those who, due to strategic conflicts, were reluctant to deal directly with the parent firm).

The history of Japan's technological development is a history of strategic partnering, both domestic and international. Among Japan's leading

[7] Morikawa (1980:130–132).

C&C (computers and communications) firms, for example, most can trace their history to partnerships with foreign firms. One producer, NEC, was founded in 1899 as a joint venture between Western Electric and a small Tokyo-based broadcasting equipment manufacturer by the name of Nippon Denki. A second, Fujitsu, maintained close connections to Siemens through Fujitsu's parent company, Fuji Electric, which was itself a joint venture between Siemens and Furukawa Electric (as noted above). Two other companies, Toshiba and Mitsubishi Electric, received substantial technical assistance and capital investment from foreign partners (General Electric and Westinghouse, respectively).

Also important were strategic partnerships with domestic firms, as the growth of Sumitomo Chemical illustrates. During the pre-war period, Japan Dyestuffs (Nihon Senryo) had maintained a close association with Sumitomo Chemical, which used the former company's tar products in the construction of coke ovens. Sumitomo Chemical gradually increased its shares in Nihon Senryo and by 1937 controlled half of it. Sumitomo dispatched a general director from its head office to take over as director of the Nihon Senryo board of governors and chief administrator.

Thus, the historical evidence makes clear that business relations among zaibatsu-affiliated enterprises were by no means exclusive. Wray's (1984) study of the evolution of the Mitsubishi group's flagship company, Nippon Yusen Kaisha (NYK), for example, demonstrates that from its beginning, NYK consciously balanced the interests of the larger zaibatsu with its own strategic concerns. A number of its shareholders and creditors (Mitsui, Yasuda, and Dai-Ichi banks) hailed from outside the group. And in the pre-war period, it took the very independent step of terminating contracts held with Mitsubishi Shipbuilding. Indeed, Wray attributes much of the success of NYK during its early years to the strategic relations it pursued beyond the Mitsui zaibatsu. Of these alliances with importers, trading companies, shipping firms, industrial producers, and banks, he writes, "The company's major innovation prior to World War I, the opening of the lightly subsidized Calcutta line, demonstrated the key to further expansion to be the business alliances in which the N.Y.K. joined with other Japanese firms in quest of their corporate goals" (p. 516).

A very fine-grained analysis of the independent business ties formed through strategic partnering exists for the Fuji Electric joint venture between Siemens and Furukawa Electric. In the first volume of its company history, Fuji Electric provides an unusually detailed listing of unit sales of major products (power generators, turbines engines, etc.) from the 1920s through the early post-war period. As seen in the figures reported in Table 2.1, it is clear that Fuji Electric sold the vast majority of its output outside the Furukawa group throughout these decades, its leading purchasers being power utility companies.

Table 2.1. *Fuji Electric's Sales to Furukawa Group and Other Firms*

Customer	1924–45		1946–56	
	No.	%	No.	%
Affiliated companies				
Furukawa Co.	14	5.6	4	1.4
Furukawa Electric	0	0.0	1	0.4
Other firms in the present-day DKB group	8	3.2	34	12.1
SUBTOTAL	22	8.7	39	13.8
Unaffiliated companies				
Firms in one of the other 5 bank groups[a]	30	11.9	51	18.1
All others (e.g. public utilities)	200	79.4	192	68.1
SUBTOTAL	230	91.3	243	86.2
TOTAL	252		282	

[a] These groups are Mitsui, Mitsubishi, Sumitomo, Fuyo, and Sanwa.
Note: Numbers represent total units sold of large-scale industrial products (power generators, turbine engines, etc.).
Source: Fuji Electric (1973).

In summary, the spinning-off of business units to form a network of satellites served as an important means of accomplishing several strategic objectives of the zaibatsu. By limiting the size and scope of the firm as it entered new fields, the network fostered more managerial autonomy and organizational flexibility than would otherwise have existed. It also bred strategic partnering skills, facilitating movement into new markets with the aid of unaffiliated enterprises. The fact that this process was most common among industrial firms at Japan's technological and market frontier is no surprise. These were the fields in which conditions were changing fastest (thus requiring flexible responses) and where know-how and markets were most dispersed (requiring strategic linkages across an array of firms and industries).

Transformation of Network Structures: The Wartime Economy

The requirements of Japan's wartime economy – a period beginning in the early 1930s and extending to Japan's defeat in 1945 – wrought important changes in the Japanese political economy. The relationship between state and industry was fundamentally altered, as Japanese policy makers found it increasingly necessary to manage an industrial production system for their rapidly expanding colonial empire. Not surprisingly, this also proved to be a critical juncture in the evolution of Japan's business networks, as enterprise relations were transformed in ways that have persisted to the present. Executives' earlier concerns with their own enterprises – including managing the tension between strategic centralization and operational decentralization discussed earlier – gave way to new worries over how to meet military requirements within a centrally controlled system of industrial production.

Beginning with the Manchurian Incident in 1931, companies in sectors such as steel, machinery, shipbuilding, banking, and international trade found themselves responding to increased demand for their products and services and by the new systems of state planning. The expanded need for military-oriented industrial production came at a time that access to foreign suppliers was being dramatically curtailed because of the Western blockade. The solution to these changed conditions in the 1930s involved two critical steps. The first was the creation of a stable core of enterprise groups that could be presumed to have both the broad capabilities necessary to make complex expansion projects work and the reliability and trustworthiness necessary to carry them out. The second was to organize those enterprises themselves into horizontal and vertical networks that could be counted on to follow state production plans.

In creating a stable enterprise core, Japanese labor and capital markets were transformed and the nature of the corporation itself fundamentally altered. Representative of the changes was the Industrial Relations Adjustment Measure (*Roshi kankei chosei hosaku*) of March 1938. Describing industry as "an organic organization whereby employers and employees are bound together in their respective functions," it marked the creation of a new doctrine on the firm.[8] Meanwhile, the Ministry of Welfare, with jurisdiction over labor matters, advocated institutionalizing a system in which the long-term stakeholders of management and labor should have priority over short-term shareholders, one consequence of which was the distribution of profits among administrative staff and company employees. In August 1938, the deputy ministers of Public Welfare and Domestic Affairs passed the Circular Concerning the Implementation of the Industrial Relations Adjustment Policy, which acknowledged the class of white-collar and blue-collar workers as the chief constituency of the firm. This was reinforced by the formation of unitary patriotic societies in all business establishments, which also served as forums for discussing worker concerns, improving efficiency, and the like.

Supporting these changes was the implementation of Article 11 of the National Mobilization Act (*Kokka sodoin ho*), which imposed new restrictions on corporate capital markets. Firms with dividend rates of over 10 percent seeking to change their rates were required to obtain a special permit from the Ministry of Finance, while those with rates over 6 percent

---

[8] Okazaki (1993:362).

needed a permit for dividend increases over 2 percent. In this way, corporate capital was reallocated to internal use rather than distributed back to shareholders – a sharp contrast with the shareholder-first philosophy that guided many nonzaibatsu firms in the pre-war period.

In addition, the Savings Promotion Committee announced in July 1938 that the bulk of the population was required to participate in the movement for more savings to help fund the expanding war effort in China. This was based on a standard saving rate corresponding to the income level of the individual in terms of salary and bonuses and was especially directed at those managers and workers in flourishing war-related industries. Significantly, most of these savings were channeled indirectly through banks rather than directly through the stock market, further diminishing the role of stockholders. Between 1939 and 1941, securities-related investments dropped from 27.9 to 14.2 percent while indirect investing through financial institutions (banks, postal savings, etc.) rose from 72.2 to 82.5 percent. As a result, banks increasingly came to perform the external financing function not only for zaibatsu firms but also for the economy as a whole.

The overall effect of these changes was to reshape the nature of the Japanese corporation itself, as the planners in Japan's wartime machine found that stabilizing industrial relations and internalizing capital markets made it easier to control strategic enterprises than was the case under a more market-like system. Wartime changes greatly weakened the part played by individual shareholders in the finance and control of nonzaibatsu enterprise, thus freeing managers to pursue aggressive growth to help promote the wartime agenda. (Zaibatsu subsidiaries already enjoyed this freedom from outside interference since their ownership and financing lay within the group.) Similarly, the organic organization that had linked management and companies in the zaibatsu enterprises was extended to other companies, becoming a formal part of Japanese corporate regulation. What had been characteristic organizational features of zaibatsu-affiliated enterprise became the model on which the remainder of the economy would be run.

Once this reconception of the corporation was embraced, the next step in the wartime transformation process was to organize companies themselves into a tightly structured web of associations in order to take on the job of supporting wartime production plans. Japanese wartime planners were impressed by and hoped to emulate Soviet central planning, which had produced impressive growth over the twenty-year period following the Bolshevik Revolution. In addition, the government faced a sudden rise in international raw material prices due to Japan's economic isolation and further worried that social and labor unrest might result from escalating inflation and the ongoing diversion of resources from consumption to production. This led it (in 1937) to freeze prices of all domestic goods and rewrite the basic price system, replacing market-based supply and demand with a flow of quantitative orders within a state-led quasi-hierarchy.

In order to accomplish this, enterprises themselves were organized under well-defined horizontal and vertical networks. Horizontally, within-industry trade associations became critical nodes between state and private sectors. Representative of this role was the reliance placed by the planning board (*kikakuin*) on the control association (*toseikai*) in each industry. As Okazaki (1993:191) explains:

> The sectoral organization which constituted the middle layer of the model carried out the role of (a) taking part in the formation of the plan, and (b) implementing the plans decided by the government by allocating them to the firms involved. As an embodiment of such organization, a *toseikai* (control association) was established in each industry and participated in the iteration process to draw up plans.

In addition to the forging of these intraindustry ties was the strengthening of vertical ties between elite or core firms of the Japanese dual economy and the periphery. Three points of linkage were key. First, the designated financial institution system formalized main bank relationships by mandating the assignment of city banks to specific client companies.[9] Second, international commerce was channeled through a small number of general trading companies (*sogo shosha*). Finally, medium- and small-scale industrial producers were organized as subcontractors under large-scale industrial enterprises, which became their representative parent companies in dealings with national production plans.[10]

Institutionalization of Network Structures: The Post-War Economy

The third phase in the evolution of Japan's network economy began with Japan's defeat in 1945 and the round of subsequent reforms initiated by the Allied Occupation. This period saw the rationalization and modernization of the country's business networks but not the elimination of the densely connected hierarchical system already in place. Indeed, one of the ironies of post-war Japanese history is that, despite the Occupation's goal of quashing the zaibatsu, the post-war period actually saw the extension of tightly organized network forms throughout the Japanese economy. By

---

[9] Hoshi, Kashyap, and Loveman (1993).
[10] Nishiguchi (1994).

1955, ten years after Japan's defeat, the main features of an integrated business system were already in place and with it the institutional underpinnings of the two decades of high growth that comprised Japan's economic miracle.

The primary aim of the Occupation, led by the General Headquarters of the Supreme Commander for the Allied Powers (GHQ), was to obliterate Japan's war-making capacity and to democratize the more feudalistic elements of the Japanese political economy. As a first step, the GHQ sought to cut the ties that held together zaibatsu families, holding companies, and subsidiaries. Approximately 2,000 former executives were purged from management positions over the first several years after the war. Replacing them were salaried managers who had served in the subsidiaries, so that a kind of instant managerial revolution took place as traditional owner-managers were forced to cede authority to professional salaried executives.[11]

The GHQ also dissolved concentrated ownership by zaibatsu families and other large-scale shareholders through the forced selling of shares and the imposition of steeply progressive asset taxes. In order to increase the role of individual shareholders, strict priority rules were established for the liquidation of stocks, with first priority in transferring stockholdings going to a firm's employees and second to residents of the area in which the company operated. No single individual was allowed to purchase more than 1 percent of a given company's shares. Significantly, financial institutions and manufacturing companies with zaibatsu association were prohibited from buying shares in other affiliated firms. Owing to these reforms, the number of individual shareholders in Japan more than doubled during the first five years after the war, and by 1950 nearly 70 percent of all corporate shares were held by individuals.

The GHQ also attempted to weaken the large corporations that had profited from the wartime economy. To block munitions firms from any further gains from wartime activities, the Occupation ordered the government to suspend payments of wartime indemnities, greatly reducing the cash flow to these companies in the early post-war period. In addition, the GHQ sought to reduce concentration and to weaken Japan's ability to remilitarize by breaking up 325 large companies under newly formulated antimonopoly laws in 1947.

Despite these efforts, Occupation reforms proved in the end to be a good deal less than the universal overhaul of the Japanese economy that its formulators had intended. Of the 325 targeted companies, for example, only 18 were in fact dissolved. Banks themselves were exempted from dissolution, both because the financial sector was perceived as less concentrated

---

[11] Miyajima (1994).

and because of worries about the stability of the financial system.[12] More-over, the GHQ's small staff was heavily dependent on its Japanese coun-terparts in agencies such as the Ministry of Commerce and Industry (fore-runner of MITI) to draft and implement the reforms. Not only did these bureaucrats lack familiarity with the concepts of antimonopoly law that the United States was introducing, but they were also less than enthusiastic about seeing them successfully implemented.

Perhaps the greatest shortcoming of the democratization process was its short duration. By the late 1940s, the Occupation's priorities had shifted from eliminating Japan's war potential to promoting rapid economic re-covery as a means of keeping Japan firmly in the Western sphere of influ-ence amid an intensifying Cold War.[13] The so-called Dodge Line of 1949, which established a fixed exchange rate and suspended new loans from the Reconstruction Financing Bank, imposed severe liquidity constraints on Japanese companies in a period when their finances were already highly precarious. Firms found themselves unable to raise new capital in the stock markets precisely as growth prospects, owing largely to the Korean War, were starting to improve.

As a result, Occupation authorities reevaluated a number of reform policies. Revisions to early post-war banking laws helped to reorganize long-term financial institutions and allowed them once again to become primary lenders to client companies and to arrange loan syndicates with other banks. These banks were also assigned the role of "special manager of a firm" under corporate reorganizations, giving them privileged access to information about their clients, continuing the practice of the wartime designated financial institution.[14]

The GHQ also gave up on the objective of creating strong capital mar-kets dominated by small shareholders: depressed share prices and exces-sive speculation led it to relax restrictions on large institutional holdings. An amendment to the antimonopoly law in 1949 made it possible once again for manufacturing companies to cross-hold one another's stocks, as long as competition was not obviously reduced. Further amendments in 1951 and 1953 raised the ceiling on bank ownership in companies from 5 to 10 percent.[15]

With the signing of the peace treaties in 1952 the government recov-ered full political autonomy, effectively stopping the reform process in its tracks. Even as the most rigid trappings of the state economic planning apparatus were eliminated by defeat, the Japanese government continued

---

[12] The exception was Teikoku Bank, formed from a merger of Mitsui and Dai-Ichi banks.
[13] Hadley (1970).
[14] Miyajima (1994).
[15] This ceiling was reduced again to 5 percent in 1987.

to find network structures useful in executing industrial production plans. As one example, MITI helped rebuild the trading companies by issuing laws that authorized tax write-offs for the costs of opening foreign branches and for contingency funds against bad debt and trade contracts. Meanwhile, its powerful Industrial Rationalization Council called for the "keiretsu-ization" of trading companies and manufacturers. As Johnson (1982:206) writes:

> This meant, in practice, that MITI would assign an enterprise to a trading company if it did not already have an affiliation. Through its licensing powers and ability to supply preferential financing, MITI ultimately winnowed about 2,800 trading companies that existed after the Occupation down to around 20 big ones, each serving a bank keiretsu or a cartel of smaller producers.

The Ministry of Finance and MITI were both involved in promoting stable cross-shareholdings within keiretsu networks, as wartime concerns over strategic control of resource mobilization were replaced in the post-war period by concerns over capital liberalization and foreign takeover of Japanese industry. Quoting Johnson (1982:276) again:

> The very thought of capital liberalization struck terror in the hearts of MITI officials and Japanese industrial leaders.... The issue, of course, was nationalistic rather than economic – the belief on the part of some Japanese that the United States had for all intents and purposes "bought" Western Europe – and was about to buy Japan as well.

Japan had witnessed firsthand the technological and industrial superiority of its Western conquerors. The ministries overseeing the wartime economy had found a stable core of elite enterprises essential to carrying out industrial planning and minimizing confusion in the market.[16] If market-oriented reform destabilized those enterprises, it had to go. By 1953, only one year after the departure of the GHQ, the shacho-kai members in the Sumitomo and Mitsubishi groups held an estimated 12 percent of the shares of other member companies.[17]

Even where ministerial policies were not specifically designed to buttress network structures, they often in practice had that effect. Controls on insurance premia and bank deposit interest rates, for example, promoted preferential transactions within the reemerging banking groups. Since product characteristics varied little if at all from firm to firm, and regulation ruled out price competition, "it require[d] only a little subtle

---

[16] The term *konran*, or confusion, is a popular one among Japanese policy leaders. For a discussion in the context of the Ministry of Finance and MITI, see Sheard (1991a).
[17] Miyajima (1994).

pressure (or group orientation) to convince corporate and individual customers in group firms to choose to purchase from their group's affiliated insurance company (or bank)" (Ito, 1992:193).

Vertical relationships between manufacturers and suppliers also tightened in the 1950s, as Japan's rapidly growing economy led industrial producers to rely more heavily on subcontractors to help meet demand. Parent companies provided capital, equipment, and raw materials to these ancillary firms and organized them into cooperative factories (*kyoryoku kojo*) – underscoring the more integral part of production operations that they would be playing. Rapid growth put similar pressures on subcontractors themselves, leading them to depend increasingly on secondary subcontractors and resulting in the elaborate, multitier interfirm structure that persists in industries such as motor vehicles and machinery. The keiretsu terminology itself came into being during this period, beginning sometime in the early 1950s.[18]

In the 1960s, as these companies began to produce for export and as Japan faced new pressures to open its markets to foreign rivals, demands for international competitiveness increased. Parent companies felt strong pressure to bring costs down and quality up, leading to greater rationalization of outside ordering. Producers became pickier about what they would accept and put pressure on subcontractors, who passed this along to the second-level subcontractors and sometimes became specialized parts makers supplying multiple companies. Parent companies concentrated orders on subcontractors they wanted to commit themselves to, while other suppliers were turned into second- and third-level subcontractors. Computer systems were linked and investments in a limited number of the best suppliers were increased. They also developed and expanded the system of target pricing (*mokuhyo genka*), wherein the parent considered basic costs to each subcontractor and used these to set prices.

The 1970s exposed Japan to a new regime of rapidly rising oil prices and additional pressures toward rationalization. Parent companies responded by continuing to merge suppliers, limiting their number and concentrating ordering, coordinating the production domains of each subcontractor, and so forth. There was also serious talk in this period of bringing more operations in-house to use up idle capacity, but in the end most parent companies relied instead on structural changes: asking each subcontractor to cut 10 or 15 percent off of prices while dropping those that could not. Prime contractors demanded subcontractors open their books, continuously reduce prices, and improve quality – in return for which the parent company would guarantee long-term relationships. These firms borrowed value analysis techniques originally developed by General Electric

---

[18] Nakamura (1983) attributes the first use of the term to a textile producer, Toyoran, circa 1952.

in the United States, so that an increasingly complex cost structure could be decomposed into smaller parts and cost-sensitive elements could be identified item by item.[19] To further strengthen relationships to remaining suppliers, *kanban* and similar systems of inventory control were expanded, and parent companies also dispatched additional personnel to key suppliers (*haken yakuin*).

The post-war period also witnessed the rapid expansion of downstream distribution networks, as large manufacturers and wholesalers brought retail outlets into exclusive, long-term relations. Large parent companies in the 1950s began introducing brand naming, dividing up market territories among distributors, and offering preferential rebates based on sales volume. In addition, they extended capital and managerial assistance to many retail outlets, including sending salespeople and providing training programs and equipment. A leading driver of these changes was the electrical appliance industry, as companies such as Hitachi, Matsushita, and Sanyo began establishing chain stores around Japan in the late 1950s. Firms in other consumer industries soon followed, including Shiseido in cosmetics and – to the chagrin of Kodak – Fuji Photo Film in the packaged film industry.

In summary, the post-war period from the late 1940s on witnessed the institutionalization of what came to be known as the Japanese business system. Internal labor markets, main banks, cross-shareholding, and vertical supply and distribution relationships evolved together, each a necessary component in making the others work: cross-shareholding freed managers to focus on company and employee interests and helped reinforce ties to suppliers; internal labor markets ensured continuity in personal relationships underpinning ties to banks and other affiliates; subcontracting allowed the parent company to remain small enough that it could provide employment guarantees to its core workers; and so on.[20] Over succeeding decades, these became taken-for-granted features of the Japanese economic landscape capable of surviving Japan's changing industrial structure and a variety of reform programs.

Institutionalized Networks as Constraints: Two Case Studies

The process of institutionalization described above is important because it testifies that relationships take on a life of their own and come to constrain

---

[19] Nishiguchi (1994).
[20] See Aoki (1988) for an economic interpretation of these connections and Dore (1986) for a mixed economic and sociological interpretation.

managerial behavior in powerful and unanticipated ways. While Japanese network structures first emerged as a means of marshalling scarce resources for technological development in the period of early industrialization and were later reshaped to serve the interests of wartime expansion, by the time that Japan's era of rapid growth was in full force these relationships had evolved into enduring features of Japan's industrial architecture. This is not to say that they were unamenable to strategic manipulation, but rather that they had become routinized in the sense of Samuels' (1987:260) description of Japanese business–state relations: conflict among actors was managed less through consensus than through an iterative process of negotiation among various interests "within an environment of unusually stable elites and extraordinarily durable institutions."

To help see the process in action, we consider two cases of strategic conflict, involving the Sumitomo and DKB groups. The first case, featuring several major Sumitomo group players, concerns corporate diversification into new industrial fields. Our focus is the operational-level conflicts that surrounded the negotiation of investments in a newly formed spin-off operation. The second case, involving DKB's predecessor institution, the Dai-Ichi Bank, focuses on the group bank's efforts to expand. The conflicts here are mainly at the strategic level, across groups, and centered on a process of full-scale integration through merger.

More important than the differences, however, are several common features in the cases and what they tell us about the constraints imposed by Japan's post-war network structures. As in our pre-war analysis, the creation of enterprise is a critical driver in the group-formation process. Only here the pursuit of expansion bumps up against a set of institutionalized roles, which constrained executive action in ways that the entrepreneurial founders of the zaibatsu never faced. These roles play out through the interaction of intracompany, intercompany, and business–state interests. No one set of interests prevails and mutual accommodation ultimately results.

The Sumitomo Aluminum War

The Sumitomo group has long been known for tight unity. It has the smallest presidents' council and various measures place it, along with Mitsubishi, as the most cohesive of the big-six intermarket groups (see Chapter 3). But cohesion was noticeably lacking in the early 1970s, when several member companies battled over who would participate in Japan's aluminum industry in what came to be called the Sumitomo Aluminum War. The principals in the battle were two core group members, Sumitomo

Chemical and Sumitomo Metal Industries (SMI), plus a satellite of SMI, Sumitomo Light Metals.

In keeping with its roots in the mining business, Sumitomo had been involved in the aluminum business since the late 1800s. Sumitomo Chemical had traditionally done the upstream smelting of aluminum while Sumitomo Metal Industries did the downstream processing for industrial applications. This division of labor continued after 1959, when SMI (whose primary business was steel) spun off its aluminum rolling and copper rolling division to form Light Metals. SMI retained a substantial ownership position in its satellite firm.

Battle lines were drawn, however, when in September 1971 Sumitomo Light Metals announced its intention to go into aluminum smelting as well, a vertical integration step that would give it some control over raw material supply. Sumitomo Chemical, facing the prospect of competing with a group member (in violation of the one-set principle), strongly objected, claiming that increased production of aluminum would create confusion (*konran*) in the industry. Sumitomo Light Metals, along with its parent SMI, insisted that such an integration of facilities was essential to its business and refused to abandon the project.

Into the fray stepped the chairman of Sumitomo Bank, Shozo Hotta, who was asked to mediate at the behest of the minister of MITI at the time, Kakuei Tanaka. The mediation was a failure, however, as neither side was willing to compromise, forcing MITI into the negotiations. MITI's basic policy at the time regarding the aluminum business was threefold: (1) promote an increase in domestic capacity in anticipation of shortages expected by the end of 1976; (2) encourage vertical integration across smelting, rolling, and fabrication, consistent with the practice of foreign producers; and (3) limit entry into any stage of the aluminum business to existing manufacturers. Since Sumitomo Light Metal's plan was consistent with these goals, MITI was favorably disposed, but it also recognized that there would have to be some compromises made. In June 1972, Tanaka called in the presidents of Sumitomo Chemical and Sumitomo Light Metals and presented the government's ruling (*saitei*). The basic plans would be approved, he said, but the two companies would have to cooperate in establishing the new company and the scale of the operations and starting date had to be coordinated with new facilities being planned by Sumitomo Chemical.

At this point, negotiations shifted back to the group level where the details were to be worked out. One issue was how much aluminum base would be purchased from Sumitomo Chemical. Sumitomo Chemical's position was that Sumitomo Light Metals should buy 30 percent of the total base to use in its rolling production. Sumitomo Light Metals' position was that it would maintain a high level of sourcing (even if this meant reducing its procurement from foreign sources), but it would not make a formal promise to do so. A second issue was ownership of the new venture. Sumitomo Chemical initially insisted on holding 50 percent of the shares of the new venture, making it an equal partner. Sumitomo Light Metals opposed this but did agree to sell additional shares of its own stock to Sumitomo Chemical. A third issue was timing. Sumitomo Chemical sought to postpone the start-up of production until 1978 to avoid creating excess capacity in the industry, while Sumitomo Light Metals maintained that high growth forecasts for rolled aluminum, plus its commitments to the regional government that had been facilitating the project, demanded an earlier starting date.

Other group companies were brought into the process to help with the negotiations: Hotta from Sumitomo Bank; Hosai Hyuga, president of SMI; Norishige Hasegawa, president of Sumitomo Chemical; and Sueo Tanaka, president of Sumitomo Light Metals. The negotiations themselves were once again mediated by Hotta and were held at the head offices of Sumitomo Bank. Finally, in February 1993, the four executives announced a compromise agreement: (1) the new company would be a joint venture of the four companies with Sumitomo Light Metals being the principal stockholder; (2) aluminum smelting and rolling production would begin in 1977; (3) smelting technology for the operation would be introduced from Sumitomo Chemical; and (4) raw materials would be purchased from Sumitomo Chemical, the details of which would be worked out in the immediate future.

Initially capitalized at ¥2 billion (about $5.6 million at the time), the new venture was given the name Sumikei Aluminum Kogyo. An estimated 2,700 employees were expected to produce about 180,000 tons a year at the smelter and 350,000 tons a year at the rolling plant. Equity ownership in the venture was carefully crafted to reflect the anticipated contributions of each partner firm. Sumitomo Light Metals held the largest share, 40 percent, which was less than the majority position it had originally sought. Sumitomo Chemical held the second largest share, 30 percent, less than the one-half stake it wanted. Sumitomo Metal Industries held 15 percent, which, when added to the shares of its satellite, Light Metals, gave the two companies effective control of the venture. The remaining 15 percent of the shares were split evenly between three other Sumitomo companies that were expected to provide additional financing and handle sales and distribution: Sumitomo Bank, Sumitomo Trust and Banking, and Sumitomo Corporation (the group trading firm).

The Failed Dai-Ichi–Mitsubishi Bank Merger

Dai-Ichi Bank was Japan's first modern bank (the name itself means "number one"). From its founding in the 1870s, it had been known as relatively independent, less closely linked to industrial clients than were the *organ banks* that had sprung up later from the zaibatsu. Thus, it had not yet formed a presidents' council, although other banks were doing so in the 1950s and 1960s. But it did have a set of long-term clients for which it was the main bank, the most important being affiliates of the old-line industrial groups, Kawasaki and Furukawa. These clients proved decisive in shaping Dai-Ichi's corporate strategy as the 1960s drew to a close.

Plans for a merger between Dai-Ichi Bank and Mitsubishi Bank quietly took form in 1968 and hit the news as an exclusive story in the Yomi-uri newspaper on 1 January 1969. The Ministry of Finance had for some time been encouraging bank mergers as a means of improving their financial strength, efficiency, and profitability, as well as creating a bulwark against foreign banks once liberalization in financial markets took place. The president of Dai-Ichi at the time, Juzaburo Hasegawa, was sympathetic to this view, having been quoted as saying, "In entering an era of internationalization, when industrial reorganization is necessary, those adhering to a small-group framework will be left behind the times."

In choosing Mitsubishi as the merger partner, however, Hasegawa appears to have relied primarily on personal relationships rather than an objective analysis of strategic complementarities. Hasegawa had known the president of Mitsubishi Bank, Wataru Tajitsu, since before the war. These ties extended to their families, as Hasegawa's eldest son had gone to work at Mitsubishi Bank and Tajitsu's wife had acted as Hasegawa's marriage go-between. In addition, Hasegawa was a friend of the Minister of Finance from his days at Tokyo University, so he was certain that the merger would be approved by both the government and the Bank of Japan.[21]

Hasegawa's mistake lay in assuming that these personal bonds would suffice to overcome whatever opposition to the merger might take place. While negotiating the merger, he kept nearly everyone else in the dark about his plans, both within and outside of Dai-Ichi.[22] When Dai-Ichi's own chairman, Inoue Kaoru, learned of the proposed merger, he was furious, and immediately set about to ensure that it would not take place. He formed an ad hoc group named the *Dai-ichi ginko o mamoru kai* (Dai-Ichi Bank Preservation Association).

Three days after the news story broke, Inoue held a press conference to outline the reasons for his opposition: While he did not oppose the idea of merging Dai-Ichi with another bank, he said, he was adamantly

---

[21] Further increasing the probabilities of approval was the fact that the governor of the Bank of Japan, Usami Makoto, had been the president of Mitsubishi Bank when Tajitsu was vice president.

[22] At Mitsubishi Bank, the situation was just the opposite, as Tajitsu had told all his directors in advance and faced no opposition.

opposed to a merger with the much larger, more profitable, and better capitalized Mitsubishi Bank, for it would not be a merger of equals. This meant that Dai-Ichi's affiliated companies, as well as its own employees, would be put at a disadvantage relative to those of its larger partner. Inoue was also concerned that the leading shareholders after the merger would be Mitsubishi group companies rather than Dai-Ichi's own affiliates.

Compounding the disparities in size was Mitsubishi's tendency to follow the one-set principle more closely than did Dai-Ichi. This created a potential problem for those Dai-Ichi affiliates that competed directly with Mitsubishi Bank's client firms should the newly merged entity favor the Mitsubishi side. The Japanese economy was growing rapidly and large industrial clients were borrowing heavily from their main banks on advantageous terms. Among the companies at greatest risk of becoming second-tier clients were such core group members as Fuji Electric and Fujitsu (competitors of the larger Mitsubishi Electric), Kawasaki Heavy Industries (one-third the size of its chief competitor, Mitsubishi Heavy Industries), and Asahi Mutual Life (a competitor of the Mitsubishi group's Meiji Mutual Life, and, not incidentally, the top shareholder in Dai-Ichi Bank).

To round up support, Inoue conferred with the heads of Dai-Ichi's clients and major stockholders. He attended special sessions of the shacho-kai of the Kawasaki group companies, the *Mutsu-kai* (Harmony Council), and the Furukawa group's *Sansui-kai* (Third Wednesday Council). Comments leaked from those meetings made clear that there was substantial opposition to the proposed merger. Those within the Kawasaki group went so far as to indicate that it might not continue its customer relations with the new bank following the merger, despite ties to Dai-Ichi that went back decades.

Opposition outside and inside of the bank intensified to the point that, on 13 January 1969, less than two weeks after the original announcement, Dai-Ichi declared that it was aborting the proposed merger. A week later, Hasegawa took responsibility for the fiasco and resigned from his position, as did a half-dozen of his internal board supporters. Inoue was restored to his former position as president of the company (a more important position in Japan than chairman). As a final indignity, Hasegawa was called upon to make the formal request to Inoue.

Two years later, Dai-Ichi merged successfully with another bank, Nippon Kangyo, to form the present-day Dai-Ichi-Kangyo Bank. This time there was no significant opposition to the merger. Nippon Kangyo was of similar size and had a client base with few competitive overlaps with Dai-Ichi's own base. Leading the merger and becoming the chairman of the newly formed entity was Inoue himself.

Lessons from the Cases

One finds in these two cases neither the impersonal markets and unfet-tered rational action of orthodox economic theory, nor the conflict-free cooperation typical of culturalist views of Japanese business. What we see is something closer to *network politics* – actors maneuvering within institutionalized role positions in mutually constrained interactions at the firm, group, and state level. Corporate managers sought to expand and diversify their operations, much as they had in the pre-war period. But their strategic moves collided with those of partner organizations, cre-ating conflict. Resolving these conflicts was itself a problematic process, as each executive exploited the elasticity of the network to maximum advantage. Factionalism, political maneuvering, and strategic manipula-tion were all apparent. Equally important, however, were the ways the conflict was tempered through highly routinized mechanisms of dispute resolution.

The intercorporate conflicts in these cases evidenced both structural and institutional features, as did their resolution. Structurally, group rela-tionships were not simply dyadic, as multiple actors were involved in each and conflict resolution took place at the network level. Sumitomo Light Metals was backed in its battle with Sumitomo Chemical by its parent, Sumitomo Metal Industries, while other leading companies in the group got involved in negotiations and later investments. In the failed merger of Dai-Ichi and Mitsubishi Banks, it was Dai-Ichi's client firms outside the initial negotiations who played the role of spoiler.

Institutionally, relations based in long-term intercorporate histories and ongoing business ties proved more powerful than the personal networks among the individual managers. The conflict among Sumitomo compa-nies was resolved not by reliance on the goodwill of the principals or a sense of mutual trust but rather through a carefully crafted compromise in which the disputants negotiated precise quantities of material supplies, amounts that each would invest as equity capital, and starting dates for the new venture. In the Dai-Ichi case, the close friendship and family con-nections between the presidents of the Dai-Ichi and Mitsubishi banks were ineffective against the institutionalized interests of Dai-Ichi and its client companies. (We note here that the importance of institutional, as opposed to purely personal, ties is a key difference between the Japanese form of network capitalism and the kinship-based forms prevalent elsewhere in East Asia.)

The interaction of structure and institutions defined the role position of each player in the drama. The state played one key role – directly in the case of Sumitomo (regulating market entry and forcing the disputants to negotiate) and indirectly in the case of Dai-Ichi (providing overall justification for bank consolidation). Banks played another important role, one consistent with their position as central group financier, information conduit, and mediator. Subgroup cliques also showed up in the Dai-Ichi case, as did the presidents' councils of Furukawa and Kawasaki. The active involvement of these councils in ending the merger showed them to be something more than a social club of golfing buddies, as they are sometimes presented. (Shortly after Dai-Ichi's later merger with Nippon Kangyo Bank, an integrated shacho-kai was formed subsuming these and other subgroups.)

Especially important in defining roles in both cases was the one-set principle. The Sumitomo Aluminum War could have been avoided entirely had the traditional separation of business activities among group companies continued to be followed. That it was not demonstrates that role constraints built into these networks are far from absolute. But their existence is demonstrated by the resolution of the conflict through joint investment in a new operation – a less than ideal compromise for either partner – rather than via unrestricted entry into new industries. One-settism is also key to understanding the failure of the Dai-Ichi–Mitsubishi merger. Each industrial company wanted to be the primary client of its main bank, and each worried that the superior power of Mitsubishi Bank would translate into preferential treatment of Mitsubishi group companies.

Despite a good deal of recent attention to intragroup conflict as claimed testimony to keiretsu breakdown, such conflict is nothing new in the Japanese network economy. While it is usually hidden behind the facade of harmony that the Japanese like to call *tatemae* (surface appearance), occasionally it becomes apparent to outsiders. In this way, rational self-interest-seeking at the firm level works to shape Japan's business networks. But as those networks have over the post-war period become structured in institutionalized roles, so too have the constraints on self-interested corporate action. Whereas the entrepreneurial leaders in Japan's early modern development (people like Iwasaki and Shibaura) were able to move relatively freely in seizing new opportunities, this was much less the case for Japan's post-war business leadership.

Conclusion

Japan's network structures have undergone significant evolution over time, from Meiji-led modernization to wartime transformation to post-war institutionalization. Each phase represents an attempt to adapt to the prevailing conditions of the time, but each also built on top of preexisting structures of relations. In this sense, the underlying evolutionary process has been path dependent rather than discontinuous. The continuing debate among economic historians over whether the wartime or post-war periods were more decisive in shaping the contemporary Japanese economy miss the point that both were important junctions in a larger process of development and both built on an organizational logic that began much earlier and persists today.[23]

From the opening of Japan following the Meiji Restoration after centuries of isolation into the 1920s came the emergence of an extraordinary set of new entrepreneurial opportunities. During this early developmental phase, Japan's inchoate networks were driven primarily by two competing organizational dynamics. One dynamic, strategic centralization, was evident in the integrated decision making and resource allocation provided by the zaibatsu head office and key supporting institutions (banks and trading companies). In this way, major decisions were made by a strategically and financially savvy, as well as a politically well-connected, cadre of head office executives. Equally important, however, were the forces of operational decentralization through satellite formation, the attendant advantages being entrepreneurial initiative, organizational flexibility, and stable ties to strategic partners.

While this dual dynamic was most apparent in the zaibatsu, where the tensions of managing vast and diverse business empires were greatest, it has played out more generally in the Japanese economy from Meiji to the present. This is evident in the variations in overall growth patterns that exist among Japanese firms across different sectors. On the one hand, financial institutions have tended to grow primarily through mergers with and acquisition of other operations – continuing today, as we see in the final chapter, in the creation of such new entities as Mizuho Bank (formed out of the core banks of Fuji, DKB, and IBJ). Such expansion of scale has been practical in this sector because technologies were simple and industrial conditions relatively stable. In addition, business consolidation meant that banks were well positioned to act as the powerful and concentrated strategic core of the interfirm group.

On the other hand, industrial firms have faced conditions that have produced a very different growth dynamic. Those firms that developed new technologies and entered fast-growing markets relied far more heavily on the formation of more loosely organized satellite groupings – either through spin-offs from the core firm or through strategic partnerships with other firms. Again, this pattern continues at Japan's technological frontier, as firms in sectors such as information technology expand through

---

[23] For proponents of the view that present-day Japan reflects primarily wartime legacies, see Noguchi (1998) and Okazaki (1993). For a view that emphasizes post-war reforms, see Miyajima (1994).

extended families of legally independent but densely meshed enterprises. Indeed, as we see in the final chapter, one of Japan's most innovative new companies, Softbank, calls itself a zaibatsu, in deference to these organizational legacies.

This organizational logic is only part of the story, however, as the larger institutional environment in which network structures emerged has changed. The second phase of network evolution occurred during the wartime period, from 1931–1945. The system that then arose was a significant departure from the model of the 1920s, when internal labor markets were uncommon and independent shareholders had real clout. Much of what we now think of as the core features of the Japanese network economy took root then, as the architects of Japan's wartime machine found that stabilizing industrial relations and internalizing capital markets made it easier to control strategic enterprises than a market-like system allowed. Well-defined horizontal (intraindustry) and vertical (banking and subcontracting) networks were organized to manage relations among these enterprises in the interests of overall production efficiency.

The institutional environment changed once again after Japan's wartime defeat, ushering in a third phase of network evolution. In breaking up the zaibatsu and important industrial combines, as well as outlawing holding companies, the Occupation put in motion a process that helped to reduce concentration at the very top of the economy. The support of the GHQ for a strong labor movement as a democratizing force similarly accelerated the adoption of such "traditional" labor market institutions as lifetime employment, which expanded from a handful of very large companies to a much broader section of Japanese industry. Meanwhile the weakness of Japanese capital markets in the early post-war years shifted emphasis away from individual shareholding to the stabilization of markets and the channeling of capital to cash-starved companies. The large city banks that had already taken on important financing functions during the latter half of the war once again were called on to assume this function. Finally, with the departure of the Occupation and as Japan entered its high-growth era in the 1950s, companies began rapidly expanding their networks of suppliers and distributors in seeking new ways to rationalize production chains. This gave rise to the vertical keiretsu still prevalent today.

As networks of enterprises became an increasingly institutionalized feature of Japan's industrial architecture, they also constrained managerial action in the ways that the two case studies concluding the chapter illustrate. As we discuss in Chapter 6, Japan's economic troubles in the 1990s may stem from changes in the business environment that make these institutionalized constraints more problematic than in the past and so require new network forms. At the same time, Japan's reluctance to give up on close-knit networks altogether, even after more than a decade of uninspired economic performance, is a testimony to the continuing reality of institutional inertia and path dependency. It is not easy to reform economic systems – particularly ones whose roots go back many decades and have become a highly legitimate part of business life.

3

The Evolution of a Corporate Network

A Longitudinal Network Analysis of 259 Large Firms

> *The network metaphor has become increasingly popular with social scientists; it has even penetrated the conservative precincts of economics. . . . [A]ttempts to develop the metaphor into operational concepts have taken two directions. One has emphasized the paths or "threads" in a single network: the manner in which long chains of contact wind their way through large social systems. . . . The second has emphasized the "knittedness" of interconnections within a network and the overlaps between multiple (many-stranded) types of networks for a given population.*
>
> White, Boorman, and Breiger, 1976:730

Introduction

Some 25 years after the publication of White, Boorman, and Breiger's classic paper on blockmodeling, most uses of the network idea in economic and organizational research remain metaphoric. They convey a quality of fluidity, permeability, even embeddedness in a set of relationships, but are typically silent on how one might measure and analyze such properties in testing hypotheses about network causes and consequences. This chapter offers a quantitative analysis of structural change in Japan's corporate network. We use some well-known methods of formal network analysis to map the evolution of business networks in Japan from longitudinal data on the country's largest financial institutions, trading companies, and industrial corporations. We will see that, to an extraordinary degree, Japanese economic organization in a network sense was built around keiretsu clusterings. Second, consistent with much recent commentary, this structure has eroded over time. Yet the decline has not been even or continuous. The cohesion of the keiretsu and that of the large-firm network as a whole have fluctuated over the period we examine in response to cyclical and to systemic economic shifts. The late 1980s asset bubble, in particular, was a watershed event in the evolution of Japan's network economy.[1] All but one (Mitsui) of the horizontal groups lost cohesion during it. While former zaibatsu Mitsubishi and Sumitomo regained much of their prebubble coherence, the bank-centered groups continued to founder. Similar patterns hold for the vertical manufacturing keiretsu. The Toyota and Matsushita groups both weakened in the bubble period but pulled together in its wake. In step with their faltering competitiveness in Japan and abroad, the Nippon Steel and Nissan groups, on the other hand, saw their positions in the network steadily erode.

The chapter is organized as follows. First, we discuss alternative theoretical hypotheses for how the cohesion of the Japanese corporate network might be changing over time. We then test those hypotheses by examining variations in the density and connectivity of corporate relations over a thirty-year period. We do this both for our entire population of 259 firms and within the memberships of the big-six keiretsu groupings. We then turn to a different analysis – blockmodeling – whose signature algorithm – CONCOR – detects clusterings of the network based on industry, keiretsu, and other commonalities.

Models of Network Change

Consider three models of change in Japan's network economy. The first posits more or less continuous decline. Owing to the end of the high-growth era, the maturation of Japan's economic institutions, and the country's growing global integration, it argues that Japan's corporate networks have been unraveling for decades. The second model – institutional persistence – argues the opposite: that the country's business networks in general and keiretsu groupings in particular have been quite resilient.[2] They persist to some degree today, despite (in the view of many) having lost most of their functionality as an economic form. The third model is one of cyclical change. It portrays the cohesion of the network as a whole and within the keiretsu groupings as rising and falling in response to business cycle fluctuations, regulatory shifts, and exchange rate and asset price volatility.

Modernization Theory and the Hypothesis of Linear Decline

The "Japanese model" that we see today is not, as some have suggested, a different kind of capitalism. It is rather a holdover

---

[1] Cargill, Hutchison, and Ito (1997).
[2] See, for example, Hamilton and Biggart (1988).

from an earlier stage of capitalism. It is the spectacle of a country vainly trying to carry into maturity economic patterns better suited to its adolescence. (Katz, 1998:6)

Steady decay in the strength and breadth of Japanese business networks is the prediction of the familiar modernization or convergence perspective on Japan's economic development. It casts the country's distinctive economic institutions as the legacy of an era when the country was tradition-bound and isolated from the world.[3] As Japan advanced to the front ranks of industrial nations, this theory held, it would shed the residues of feudalism and the strategies of catch-up, while taking on the trappings of modernity. In network terms, this means substitution of *weak* (single-stranded, unembedded, fleeting, arm's-length, and asymmetric) for *strong* ties (dense, trusting, multiplex, lasting, reciprocated, etc.).

Whether of old or new vintage, adherents to the modernization paradigm see the United States as world icon of economic maturity and efficiency. With its distinctive mix of strong markets and weak networks, the U.S. economy is cast as the end state toward which the laws of economic evolution have the rest of the world inexorably headed. There is, as Chapter 1 notes, a maverick strain of modernization thought portraying Anglo-American "market individualism," to use Dore's (1973) term, as behind the global curve and a political-economic regime in decline.[4] Such theories gained ground in the 1980s, when strong competition from Germany and Japan fueled the perception in and outside the United States that U.S. corporations had grown bloated and complacent, run by managers who were more preoccupied with financial deals than with the core strategy and competency of the enterprise, no longer able to produce high quality goods and services. With the onset of recession and stagnation in the early 1990s, however, and a gathering sense that Japan was falling ever farther behind in the global economic sweepstakes, such claims lost credence. In the late 1990s, even the Japanese, angst-ridden over the "disappearance of Japan" (*Nihon ga kieru*), piled on the "America is No. 1" bandwagon.

Two nations will of course converge if each changes in ways that make it more similar to the other. U.S. and European manufacturing in the past 20 years has moved strongly toward the Japanese model of longer-term and deeper (i.e., trust-infused) procurement relations, while Japan has weakened such relations and opened its production networks to suppliers and vendors worldwide.[5] Our focus on Japan keeps us from saying much

---

[3] Abegglen (1958); Dore (1973); Inkeles and Smith (1974); Kerr (1960); Marsh and Mannari (1976).
[4] Dore (2000); Piore and Sabel (1984).
[5] Helper and Sako (1995).

that is substantial on the topic of whether other economies have edged in its direction, although the prima facie case for that is strong. Our concern is with the evolving organization of the Japanese corporate network. If, as now appears, such institutions as permanent employment and keiretsu are being shed as the outworn garb of a fading economic adolescence, it would seem that the (neo)classical modernization thesis as applied to Japan has prevailed in the end.

A standard view is that keiretsu clusterings and main bank relations were a rational adaptation to the high-growth catch-up economy of the 1950s and 1960s, but with the slowing of growth in the 1970s such network forms lost their usefulness.[6] A compelling take on business groups around the world – whether in East Asia (China, Indonesia, Japan, South Korea, Taiwan) or elsewhere (Latin America, Russia, India) – is that they play vital economic roles in allocating capital and structuring supply chains, which in more developed economies efficient markets perform.[7] The strategic emphasis of Japanese firms in the catch-up era – on fierce price competition and rapid capacity expansion to capture global market share – demanded tight relationships with banks and government ministries.[8] The supply and distribution transactions among the companies of the group, typically brokered by the general trading companies (sogo shosha), were useful in ramping up production and achieving economies of scale. As Japanese capital and product markets matured, there was less call for these functions.[9]

Moreover, the winding down of the high growth economy coincided with a series of regulatory changes. Japan began deregulating capital markets in the mid-1970s, giving firms greater access to equity and bond financing, thereby reducing dependence on banks.[10] Another round of deregulation in the early 1980s further loosened strictures on corporate bond issuance.[11] A different policy shock was the 1985 Plaza Accord, which ended fixed exchange rates, thus doubling the yen against the dollar and triggering the wrenching but short-lived *endaka* (high yen) slowdown of 1986–87. Then followed the bubble economy boom from 1988 to 1991. In the superheated business climate of the period, asset values soared, driving banks and corporations to seek short-term gains in speculative ventures.

---

[6] Caves and Uekusa (1976); Gao (2001); Gerlach (1991); Goto (1982); Katz (1998); Roehl (1983a).
[7] Aoki and Patrick (1994); Guillen (2000); Khanna and Pelepu (2000); Leff (1978).
[8] Porter (1990).
[9] Gerlach (1992a:140–143).
[10] Aoki (1988).
[11] Hoshi and Kashyap (2000); Kobayashi, Endo, and Ogishima (1993); Morck and Nakamura (1999).

The bubble's burst in 1991 ushered in the era of stagnation and recession from which Japan has yet to extricate itself. Much journalistic opinion has it that this troubled phase in Japanese economic history, like the boom preceding it, hastened the pace of keiretsu decline. To contend with weak operating earnings and new regulations requiring the reporting of consolidated (including keiretsu) income and assets at market (versus book) value, firms have sold off ("unwound") cross-shareholdings. Banks' bad debt loads and diminished capital reserves (due to deflated domestic stock and real estate prices) curtailed their ability to lend, thereby straining main bank ties.[12] Even the vertical keiretsu appear to be unraveling as manufacturers absorb affiliates as majority-owned subsidiaries (in the cases of Matsushita and Toyota) or impose control through the newly legal holding company form (e.g., Mizuho Holdings). Further fraying vertical ties are manufacturers' efforts to cut costs by simplifying and standardizing models and parts and shift sourcing (recently via online exchanges) to larger, often foreign, vendors.[13] Such developments have forced small suppliers to broaden their customer base or face failure.[14]

Further changes have weakened the interlocking directorates and other personnel transfers (e.g., *shukko*) key to the organization of keiretsu. Revised rules of corporate governance, if by no means ending executive dispatches (*haken yakuin*), have made them harder to execute. Companies are shrinking boards and moving to separate the roles of directors and executives.[15] The combination of large boards and inside (managerial) directors, long typical of Japanese corporate governance, was tailor-made to the accommodation of dispatched directors from lending and trading partners and government ministries as well. The board was always expandable, and the incoming director's operating duties ensured that his organization of origin had a direct communication link to and leverage over the management of the receiving firm.

H3.1: *The cohesion of the corporate network has been declining since the 1970s.*

H3.2: *The coherence and cohesion of the principal keiretsu groupings have been declining since the 1970s.*

---

[12] Dodwell Marketing Consultants (various years); Aoki and Patrick (1994); Orru, Hamilton, and Suzuki (1989).

[13] Ahmadjian and Lincoln (2001). Under the control of Renault, Nissan has eliminated most of its equity ties to affiliated suppliers, dealers, and even banks such as the Industrial Bank of Japan in which Nissan halved its stake in 2001. Associated Press, 17 May 2001.

[14] Whittaker (1997).

[15] Ahmadjian (2003); Clark (1979).

An Institutional Perspective on the Persistence of Japan's Network Forms

The message of the institutional perspective is that organizational forms lacking a clear functional (e.g., efficiency) rationale may nonetheless persist, even expand and diffuse, sometimes in the process prevailing over better (economically) adapted alternatives. The chief mechanism of such persistence and diffusion is *legitimacy*: by dint of longevity and pervasiveness, business practices take on cultural meanings and become cherished traditions.[16] In Selznick's (1949) classic definition of the institutionalization process, they are "infused with value beyond the technical requirements of the task at hand."

The Japanese corporation has long been described as a social institution whose mission extends well beyond mere profit- or share-price maximization.[17] The roots of such institutionalization lie in part with Japan's state-spearheaded late development and use of economic growth as a tool in the attainment of political ends. Another is the post-war campaign by Japanese managers and policy makers to legitimize work routines and authority relations through appeals to traditional values.[18] In the 1970s and 1980s, Japanese firms were described by Western scholars and consultants as enterprise communities that bound employees to them in reciprocal lifetime commitments.[19] Even today, Japanese managers extol the spiritual (*seishin*) and "wet" (*uetto*) qualities of Japanese management as against the emotionally dry (*dorai*) and calculative flavor of Western management styles. The core constituencies of the Japanese firm – labor, local communities, government bureaucrats, and partner companies in a keiretsu network – are more diverse and hold corporations accountable on a greater range of performance criteria than do the stockholders to whom the modern U.S. corporation is mostly beholden.[20]

Corporate restructurings serve a signaling function – they convey to target audiences information on shifts in a company's strategy and goals. Recent calls for such restructurings in Japan are often tailored to satisfy opposing legitimacy constraints. To signal forward-looking adaptation to the new and harsh realities of a volatile business environment, firms proclaim that once-sacrosanct ways – permanent employment, seniority promotion, loyalty to customers and suppliers – are costly anachronisms and with some fanfare introduce reforms that look to be dramatic breaks

---

[16] Berglof and Perotti (1994).
[17] Abegglen (1958); Fruin (1983); Lincoln (1990); Rohlen (1974).
[18] Cole (1979); Gordon (1985).
[19] Dore (1973); Lincoln and Kalleberg (1990); Ouchi (1981).
[20] Dore (2000); Kester (1997); Roe (1994); Useem (1996).

with the past. On closer scrutiny, however, these often prove to be cautious and incremental.

Key to grasping the legitimacy-preserving nature of Japanese corporate change is whether the alterations made are fundamental and structural – accounting for the demise of core institutions and their replacement by new ones – or cyclical and transitory, kept within the limits of the current system and designed to give way to tradition once economic momentum is regained. Japan has gone through cycles of boom and recession before. The antecedents of earlier downturns – currency appreciation, heightened competition, capital shortages, and muddled policy response – are operative again today. They were handled in the past by adjustments that may have been wrenching but were not greatly at odds with the established institutional framework. So the case might be made that Japan's present malaise is by no means novel and that it, too, will pass, leaving intact both the fundamentals of the Japanese business system and its underlying legitimacy and consensus.

Thus, Japan's corporate network has been evolving in significant ways, as marked changes in the economic environment rend the fabric of keiretsu, while at the same time sewing the seeds of new alliance forms. Yet the new forms are emerging within an institutional framework whose parameters were set by the old. Japan remains a society that resists radical and discontinuous change, even in times of economic stress. The logic of institutional inertia explains why such distinctive trappings of the keiretsu system as cross-shareholdings and risk-sharing interventions are enduring even as the economic environment has markedly changed.[21]

An interview in the spring of 2001 with a major company closely tied to Mitsui but not a *Nimoku-kai* member underscores the ongoing value and meaning of keiretsu commitments to Japanese businesspeople, even at a time when the functionality and public legitimacy of the form are in doubt.[22] We spoke with two managers, an older fellow nearing retirement and his younger, seemingly more westernized, counterpart. Asked their views on the future of keiretsu in general and, in particular, their firm's alignment with the Mitsui group, the senior executive did not hesitate. He thought keiretsu had declined in importance, but he still felt some obligation to Mitsui companies and identification with the "culture" (his term) of the group. The younger manager was at first skeptical of the idea that keiretsu retained any significance at all, saying that he rarely gave the matter much thought. Noting the generation gap between them,

[21] As Chapter 6 discusses, the tarnishing of the American corporate governance and accounting model by Enron and other scandals of 2001–02 were a boon to Japanese conservatives who cling to Japan's business traditions and resist reform and restructuring along Anglo-American lines.
[22] Interview on 29 March 2001.

he distanced himself from the views of his colleague. But, pressed on the issue and warming to the discussion, he acknowledged some sensitivity to keiretsu alignments, conceding that it was always a little easier to do business with another Mitsui firm. The group connection imbued negotiations with a degree of trust and goodwill. Keiretsu would never be a first or even second consideration in a business decision to contract with another company, he said. But if "everything else were equal," he, like his colleague, might favor a Mitsui firm.

H3.3: *The corporate network as a whole and those of the individual keiretsu groupings have remained cohesive.*

H3.4: *The former zaibatsu have remained more cohesive than the bank-centered horizontal groups.*

The Hypothesis of Countercyclical Change

Between the neo-modernization argument that Japan's network forms are fast dissolving and the institutionalist claim that they persist, there is the possibility that the network expands and contracts with the ebb and flow of business conditions and the fortunes of member firms. We devote considerable attention in Chapter 5 to keiretsu interventions in affiliates' affairs for the purpose of sharing risks and redistributing returns. One might suppose that interventionism to buffer firms from business fluctuations comes and goes while the networks that support it stay the same, yet the ties that bind firms to groups are not mere *channels* through which assistance and control flow. The creation or reinforcement of a tie is itself a means of inducing a distressed or wayward company to get its house in order.[23] As our own case studies document, the taking of an equity stake or the dispatch of a director may be integral to the process of bailout and restructuring. When Mazda fell on hard times in the 1970s, Sumitomo Bank hiked its stake in the Hiroshima automaker, supplied it with new loans, and seconded executives to its board. Daihatsu was brought into the Toyota vertical keiretsu during a brush with bankruptcy in the 1960s. Toyota launched a rescue, taking an equity stake and dispatching several directors to Daihatsu's board. Similar events played out in countless reenactments of the corporate rescue scenario in Japan.

Thus, a plausible hypothesis is that keiretsu wither in good times when firms have little need of them and rebound in slumps when they do need

[23] For example, a bank might arrange a debt–equity swap with a troubled borrower, forgiving the debt in exchange for an ownership stake.

them.[24] Casual observers of Japanese economic trends often claim the opposite: that downturns weaken business networks, as companies cannot then afford the gift exchange of cross-held shares and other reciprocated commitments.[25] But the selling-off of cross-shareholdings to cope with financial distress generally has the sanction of the group. At an interview at Yasuda Trust – a *Fuyo-kai* member – we queried managers on the purpose of equity ties. They said that protection from acquisition – the early post-war rationale – had become less important, as so many other barriers to takeover had arisen in Japan.[26] (Many of these are now falling due to recent corporate governance and accounting rule changes.) The chief function of equity ties, our Yasuda informants averred, was insurance. To offset weak earnings, one member of a group might sell down its stake in another, yet count on still others to buy up the shares. Toyota's recent move to hike its holdings in affiliates Denso, Hino, Kanto Auto Works, and Aisin Seiki illustrates.[27] Because of poor performing loans and other problems, the Toyota group's main banks, Mitsui and Sanwa, were reducing their equity stakes in Toyota group firms.[28] Toyota bought up the shares the banks were unloading in order to maintain the price while keeping predators at bay. Another way keiretsu ease companies through downturns is by absorbing their redundant workers. Under Japan's permanent employment system, large-scale layoffs generally remain taboo, so the transfer of surplus people, usually from larger to smaller firms, is one of few options available to managers for reducing headcount.[29]

H3.5: *The cohesion of the Japanese corporate network as a whole and of the horizontal and vertical keiretsu fluctuates against the business cycle: tightening in bad times, loosening in good times.*

A variant on the cyclical model is that the period from 1986 to 1991 – beginning with the *endaka* contraction, through the bubble expansion, and terminating with the crash of stock prices in 1991 – was anomalous in the changes it wrought in the Japanese network economy. A number of findings reported in our book support the idea that the bubble was an odd

---

[24] Of course, similar patterns exist beyond Japan. Davis and Mizruchi (1999) document the countercyclical fluctuations in U.S. firms' dependence on bank borrowing. In upswings, corporations finance investment with retained earnings, stock and corporate bond issues, and the like. In slumps, when these pools dry up, they turn to banks.
[25] Akerlof (1982).
[26] See, for example, Clark (1979); Kester (1991).
[27] Interview with Toyota's chief corporate auditor, 7 December 1998.
[28] The sell-off of Toyota group shares by its erstwhile main banks has continued. The now-merged Sumitomo–Mitsui Banking Corporation sold 65 million shares in Toyota Motor in the fall of 2002. Sumitomo–Mitsui's stake in Toyota is now 115.62 million shares, or 3.2 percent, down from its presale stake of 5 percent. *Nikkei Net Interactive*, 16 November 2002.
[29] Lincoln and Nakata (1997); Lincoln and Ahmadjian (2001).

blip in the country's economic trajectory. With the bubble's collapse, some return to normalcy (i.e., keiretsu alignments and main bank relations) took place. There is now a lively debate in Japanese policy circles over whether the bad debt and price deflation problems of the last twelve years are wholly a legacy of the bubble, which, many argue, was a time of reckless abandonment of the mainstay Japanese business principles of patient capital, trusted partnerships, long-term strategies, and the like. The resolution to this question has obvious implications for the degree and type of restructuring the Japanese economy needs today.[30]

H3.6: *The cohesion of the Japanese corporate network declined in the bubble period (1988–90) but rose thereafter.*

Methods

Network Analysis

We use formal network methods to study the changing structure of interfirm relations in Japan. While an abundant scholarly and popular literature discusses the decline of the large integrated corporation and its replacement by loosely linked networks of small- and medium-sized firms, it does so mainly with case studies and historical analysis, not hard data and quantitative method.[31] The network metaphor in such writing is rich and evocative but defies operational definition in quantitative terms. By contrast, structural or network analysis is an abstract and arcane field, given to quantitative measurement and modeling.[32] To be sure, technical network analysts do address important substantive problems in organizational and economic research. Still, few studies in a network analytic vein have engaged the large and timely issues of changing corporate, regional, and national economic structure that concern theorists of network capitalism in the *flexible specialization* and related traditions.[33] In its use of formal network methods to study the evolving structure of the Japanese large-firm network economy, we see the present chapter as an effort to fill this void.

Network analysis invokes a simple image of a network: a set of points or *nodes* (individuals, firms, industries) and the lines or *arcs* that connect

---

[30] Personal communication from Akira Goto of Hitotsubashi University, a member of various METI panels on Japan's economic restructuring.

[31] Chesbrough and Teece (1996); Miles and Snow (1987); Perrow (1992); Powell (1990); Piore and Sabel (1984); Saxenian (1996).

[32] See, for example, Burt (1980); Knoke and Kuklinski (1982); Lincoln (1982); Wasserman and Galaskiewicz (1994); Wellman and Berkowitz (1987).

[33] But see Keister (2001); Walker, Kogut, and Shan (1997).

them. In social science applications, the points are human actors (individual or collective) and the lines are relations. If the tie is asymmetric or directional (selling, ownership), the lines are arrows. The same information can be rendered in matrix form where the rows and columns are nodes (e.g., rows as senders; columns as receivers), and the presence and absence of relations are indicated as 1's and 0's. This binary representation loses much information on the strength and other attributes of ties, but it enables matrix manipulations that can reveal subtle and interesting patterns.

We apply two kinds of network methods to longitudinal network data on the largest 259 firms in the Japanese economy as of 1980. First, we use elementary graph theoretic measures to analyze change in *global* (the network as a whole) as well as *local* cohesion (within the big-six horizontal groups). Second, we use blockmodel techniques in portraying the Japanese network economy as a matrix of keiretsu groupings and mapping its change over time.[34] A canonical method of network analysis, blockmodeling sorts nodes into mutually exclusive clusters or *blocks* by a structural equivalence criterion: the degree of similarity of relations to others. This methodology is useful in an investigation of how the keiretsu structure the Japanese economy, for it grapples at once with the composition of groups, their ties to one another, and the pull they exert on unaffiliated firms.

Data and Sample

The population of Japanese firms we study is the 50 largest (in 1980) financials (banks, trust banks, securities firms, and insurance companies), 200 largest industrials, and 9 largest trading companies (see Tables 3.1–3.6). We have data on four ties – lending, trade, shareholding, and director dispatch – among these 259 firms for a series of years. Each tie is dichotomized as present or absent; i.e., whether *I* is a top ten lender to *J*, whether *I* is a top ten shareholder in *J*, whether *I* is a major vendor to *J* (or *J* a major customer to *I*), and whether a member of *J*'s board transferred in from *I*. A final tie is whether *I* and *J* are represented on the same shacho-kai. Since this last is the hardest and most stable indicator of a firm's link to a group, we treat it not as one more tie, but as a validity check and interpretive guide.

Again, this treatment of relations as simply present or absent is standard network analytic practice. Most of its trademark concepts and

---

[34] White et al. (1976).

methods – for example, the graph-theoretic density and connectivity con-structs – require it. But the simple binary representation also has sub-stantive meaning. It focuses research attention on the occurrence (at the firm or dyad level) and distribution (at the population level) of *relation-ships*, rather than, say, the volume or value of goods, services, and capital flowing between firms or sectors.

The industries represented are of three main sorts: (1) financials ("city" – major money center – banks, regional banks, *sogo* – mutual – banks, trust banks, insurance companies, and securities firms); (2) in-dustrials (manufacturing and extractive industry – oil, mining, and fish-eries); and (3) the nine major trading companies (*sogo shosha*). Other than the shosha, retail and wholesale trade and nonfinancial services are excluded.

Aside from the odd coding error and the limitation of our archival sources to top ten debt and equity holders, the lending, shareholding, and director data have high reliability.[35] The trade data, on the other hand, derive from each company's voluntary citation of its major trading partners and thus are more subjective and fallible.[36] We take either the seller or the buyer's citation as a sufficient signal that a trading partnership exists. If one company reports another as a major customer or vendor, that is very likely true. The error comes in nonreport: big firms have so many partners that they overlook the smaller ones. Small firms have fewer partners, so they are better informants of the same ties.

A problem for any panel analysis – in which the same set of firms is observed over a significant span of time – is that of change in the target population. It appears here in three respects. First, is the list of Japan's largest firms in 1980 of any relevance today? Fortunately for our research design, we deal with Japan, not the United States, and the stability of the firm size distribution in the Japanese economy is remarkable. The difference between our sample of firms (the largest in assets in 1980) and a list of the largest 259 in 1993 is only 15 firms. A second and related problem is how to deal with mergers and acquisitions. Again, the variety of large firm mergers in post-war Japan makes this less troublesome than

---

[35] The archives from which we obtained the director information list the names of all mem-bers of each selected company's board. Note, however, that directors are only the highest level employees transferred from one firm to another. Nondirector managers, technical people, and rank-and-file production workers add to the personnel flow (Lincoln and Ahmadjian, 2001).

[36] Our data were coded from a variety of Japanese archival sources, including Dod-well Marketing Consultants (various years); *Jinji koshin roku* (various years); *Kaisha nenkan* (various years); *Kigyo keiretsu soran* (various years); Nikkei Databank Bu-reau (various years); *Keiretsu no kenkyu* (various years); Japan Development Bank (2000).

in a comparable U.S. study. In recent years, however, rates of mergers and acquisitions and bankruptcy in Japan have risen sharply. Among the firms in our data set, seven mergers occurred within the period we observe.[37] The final potential issue of this sort is that of firms leaving or joining the big-six shacho-kai. Here again, however, the stability of membership is so great that no problem is posed (see Table 1.1).

Analysis I. Cohesion Trends in the Large Firm Network

Cohesion Dimensions: Density and Connectivity

Cohesion is a colloquial concept that lends itself to fairly precise measurement in network terms. It translates into two operational definitions: density and connectivity.[38] *Density* is the ratio of direct ties to potential ties, a potential tie being an ordered pair of nodes (e.g., I, J as distinct from J, I). Alternatively, density is the probability of a tie. *Connectivity* is the ratio of direct *and* indirect ties to potential relations. Two firms, I and J, may have no direct exchange, but if each trades with K, goods, information, and other resources may pass between I and J via this third party tie.

Connectivity has little distinct meaning when density is high. In the limiting case of density = 1.0, every node (e.g., firm) links directly to every other, so that connectivity = density. But a network of low density and high connectivity has a noteworthy structure. It is efficient in the sense that few ties connect most nodes. Take the extreme case in which each node links to every other in two-step chains through a single peak coordinator.[39] Here, density = $N - 1$ and connectivity = $N(N - 1)$. Brokered networks in which one or two nodes relay most relations have this structure.[40] In Japan, large commercial banks, trading companies, and lead manufacturers play such brokerage roles in the corporate network and thus contribute disproportionately to its cohesion.

The modernization hypothesis predicts gradual disintegration of the web of corporate ties. Market transactions, it argues, are becoming less relational, more arm's length and atomized. In operational terms, this

---

[37] The mergers we record are the following: Mitsubishi Mining and Cement and Mitsubishi Metals became Mitsubishi Materials in 1990; Sanyo Electric and Tokyo Sanyo Electric became Sanyo Electric in 1989; Daikyo Oil and Cosmo Oil became Cosmo Oil in 1991; Mitsui Bank and Taiyo Kobe Bank became Sakura Bank in 1992; Saitama Bank and Kyowa Bank became Asahi Bank in 1991; Sanyo Kokusaku Pulp and Jujo Pulp became Nippon Paper in 1993.

[38] Harary, Cartwright, and Norman (1965).

[39] Guetzkow (1965); Lincoln (1982); Williamson (1970).

[40] Gould and Fernandez (1989).

implies lower density – fewer ties for the same set of nodes. It may also mean less connectivity – fewer indirect links. The decline we report in the connectivity of the equity networks relative to its density suggests that corporate ties in Japan are acquiring a more dyadic, less macro-network, rationale.

Figure 3.1 plots the densities and connectivities of the 259 × 259 firm network by tie and year. The debt and equity measurements begin in the 1960s and continue at varying intervals until 1997. The director and trade data are available for shorter series, 1972 to 1997 (trade) and 1978 to 1997 (directors). Connectivities for debt are not given. Since financials lend to commercial and industrial firms, which do not lend, indirect debt relations are nonexistent. Commercial ties, again, are different, for long supply chains link up companies that have no direct transactions with each another. The figure shows connectivity to be highest in the trade network. By contrast, both density and connectivity of director ties are low. An implication is that Japanese director interlocks are fundamentally dyadic, having less to do with the macro-network fabric of keiretsu than with the means whereby one firm establishes control over another.[41]

The Changing Cohesion of the Network

How has the cohesion of the large firm network changed with time? Has it declined as modernization theory (and the conventional wisdom) suggests? By some indicators, yes. By others, however, we find period-to-period fluctuation and on one key dimension – the density of cross-shareholdings – a steadily rising trend.

Consider first the lender–borrower network. Its cohesion follows the slowing of GDP growth and the "disintermediation" of Japanese corporate finance.[42] From a high in 1972, the last high-growth year, debt density fell linearly until 1982, held relatively steady until the bubble, climbed to a peak in 1995 (the one strong period in an otherwise dismal decade), and, finally, with the economy in tatters amid the Asian financial crisis, plummeted in 1997–98, a thirty-year nadir.

For the other networks, we have two measures of cohesion: besides density (the relative frequency of direct ties), there is connectivity (the relative frequency of direct *and* indirect ties). Of particular importance to an understanding of the evolving structure of these networks is the gap or *spread* between the two. The density–connectivity spread varies with

[41] Kaplan and Minton (1994); Lincoln et al. (1992).
[42] Aoki (1988).

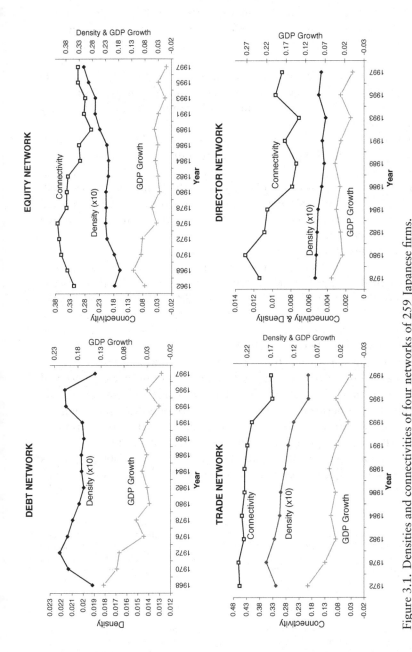

Figure 3.1. Densities and connectivities of four networks of 259 Japanese firms.

Note: Plotted values are "density" (the proportion of pairs of firms in which a *direct* tie is present); "connectivity" (the proportion of pairs of firms in which a *direct or indirect* tie is present); and the proportion change in nominal gross domestic product over the previous year.

101

the tie.[43] In the trade network, the spread is large: fewer than 2 percent of all the pairings of our 209 industrial firms involve an "important" trading partnership, but some 35–45 percent are connected through a chain (in graph theory terms, directed path) of partnerships. However, the trade network spread is also very stable: density and connectivity fall mostly in tandem through this period, accelerating postbubble (1991) but flattening toward the end of the series. The global expansion and integration of Japanese supply chains that began in the 1980s very likely figured in this trend.[44]

In sharp contrast with the trade case, the changes in the equity network's spread suggest a pre- and postbubble regime shift in the structure and role of cross-shareholdings. By either indicator, cohesion peaked in the mid-1970s. From there, density held steady until 1984 and connectivity fell. In the bubble year of 1989, density turned up while connectivity turned down. Thereafter, the spread between them greatly diminished, the two ascended in lockstep.

With densities of around .5 percent and connectivities twice that, the director network is easily the sparsest of the four. There is, however, a difference in the shape of the two curves and thus the dynamics of the spread. From a peak in 1980 to a trough in 1989, both fell monotonically, connectivity more steeply so. In the 1990s, they rose to a peak in the growth year of 1995 and then reversed course. Thus, the spread bottomed out in the prime bubble year of 1989.

Extrapolating across the four ties and two cohesion indices, what lessons can be drawn? The cohesion of the corporate network peaked in the 1970s, and the pattern since has been one of general decline. This suits the modernization model – that networks fray and fragment as economies mature.[45] Also supporting that model is the shrinking connectivity–density spread in the director and, most notably, equity networks. The narrowing in the equity case in 1989, the bubble, warrants special attention. Aggressive stock buying by financial institutions and corporations was occurring, not to cement long-term relations, but to realize

---

[43] We have placed the actual year to which the data pertain as two years prior to the date of the publication. In fact, the data overlap calendar years: the debt and equity data pertain to the prior fiscal year – April 1 to March 31. *Kigyo keiretsu soran* – our primary source for the director and trade data – states that the information on directors is valid until June of the subsequent year and that for trade until July. Thus, we used 1999 sources (*Kigyo keiretsu soran* and the Japan Development Bank *Corporate Finance Data Bank*) to code information on what we indicate here is the 1997 calendar year. In fact, the data refer to a period from the first third to half of 1997 to the same interval of 1998.

[44] Ahmadjian and Lincoln (2001).

[45] The 1970s and early 1980s were the heyday of main bank relations, keiretsu, and ministry guidance. The mid- to late 1980s began an important transition period due to capital market deregulation and expansion, globalization of production and distribution, *endaka* shock, and, most of all, the bubble economy.

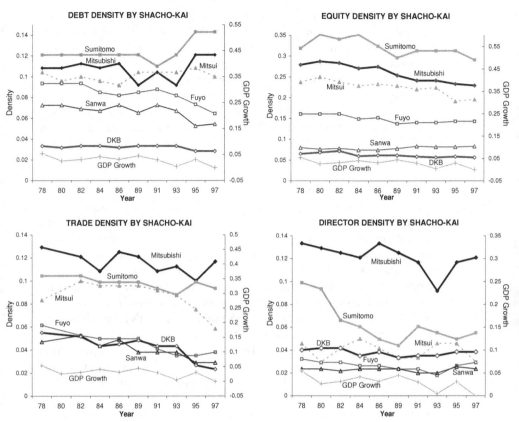

Figure 3.2. Network densities by shacho-kai.
Note: Plotted values are densities of ties within shacho-kai and GDP
growth.

capital gains in a white-hot market. When the market cratered and the
bubble burst, cross-shareholding resumed to some degree its prebubble
governance role as a bridge to or bond with business partners. But the logic
behind such ties had changed. Business ties in Japan over most of the past
half-century served to cement and symbolize the stable macro-structural
commitments that keiretsu represent. They thus presented themselves to
firms as fixed constraints on business dealings. The postbubble network
is different: more micro-strategic – that is, firm- and dyad-specific – and
less macro-keiretsu. The upward trend in density says that large Japanese
firms were adding equity relations – most of which were outside keiretsu
groups (see Figures 3.2 and 6.2). These were dyadic and direct, unlike the
expansive cross-shareholding networks of the past.

Evidence from key industries, such as autos and electronics, shows Japanese corporations in the 1990s and 2000s taking keiretsu commitments less for granted and moving to jettison the less productive ones.[46] To be sure, alliances retain great value in the new Japanese economy – but they are scrutinized for cost-effectiveness and strategic utility more than before.[47] At the same time – and despite the routine pronouncements of keiretsu demise – many of the strategic partnerships formed among Japanese firms in the 1990s retain some grounding in keiretsu ties.[48] That, as we later show in Chapter 6, is less true of alliances aimed at research and development.

Is Cohesion Countercyclical?

Our treatment of the dynamics of cohesion to this point is roughly compatible both with the institutional theory of pattern persistence and with the modernization hypothesis that the networks at the core of the Japanese economy are atrophying as well as undergoing change in form. Our third model of network evolution is the countercyclical one. The cohesion of the corporate network is sensitive to shifts in business conditions and other macroeconomic shocks. As noted, the business press sees downturns (e.g., the *endaka* shock in 1986) hastening the decay of Japan's network organizations. Our suggestion, however, is that networks tighten in downturns and loosen in upturns. Thus, in business cycle troughs, Japanese firms retreat to the security of the keiretsu fold, but in rebounds, when opportunity and capital abroad, they go it alone, disdaining groups as useless baggage.

Our limited and unevenly spaced observations preclude a fine-grained treatment of cyclical change. When the economy alters course between measurements, the effect on cohesion is not observed. However, if our relatively crude eyeballing of the data turns up some credible indications of cyclical change, we may assume that better data and analysis will reveal even more. We index the business cycle with the annual rate of growth in GDP. Other economic indicators (e.g., yearly sales growth of publicly listed (1,000–1,200 firms)) yield a similar picture.

The pattern is imperfect, varying with the tie and period, but some countercyclical fluctuation can be seen. Periods of strong trending – 1972–82

---

[46] Miwa and Ramseyer (2000).

[47] An example is Nippon Steel. A decade ago, the steelmaker held shares in sixty-seven banks. Now its equity ties are down to the four megabanking groups (Mizuho, Sumitomo–Mitsui, Tokyo–Mitsubishi, and UFJ) and the major trust banks. "We hardly have any shares left that we are able to sell given our business relationships," Tetsuo Seki, a vice president of Nippon Steel was quoted by the Nikkei as saying. "We have to continue to hold bank shares even if valuation losses emerge." *Nikkei Net Interactive*, 10 April 2002.

[48] Cole and Rtischev (2003); Gerlach (1992a); Guillot and Lincoln (2001).

for debt or 1962–76 for equity – imply little short-term macroeconomic volatility, so at those junctures the evidence for countercyclicality is slim. Thus, the debt network seemed impervious to a succession of macroeconomic events in the second half of the 1970s: the first oil shock (1974–76) and recovery (1976–78), and the second oil shock (1978–80) and recovery (1980–84). Bear in mind that we ignore in this analysis shifts in the *volume* of loans between a lender and a borrower. Our data pertain only to the presence or absence of ties. The steep first oil shock downturn in 1976 registers no change in debt or equity ties. Thereafter, equity cohesion displays a series of countercyclical bumps: down in the rebound from the first oil shock (1978), up (or at least stabilized) in the second oil shock slump, down in the 1980–84 recovery, up in the 1986 *endaka* slump, down in the bubble (1989), and up in its recessionary aftermath. Strong trending may again explain the lack of equity network response to the GDP surge in 1995–96.

We might expect trade to be the network least apt to move countercyclically, since the density of buying and selling relationships – whatever it says about cohesion – is also a sign of the economy's health. With the puzzling exception of the declines in cohesion in the 1995 business upswing, that appears true. We shall see, however, quite a bit of countercyclicality in the trading ties within the horizontal groups.

On the assumption that director interlocks form when firms are in trouble and partners dispatch executives to bail them out, the cohesion of the director network should move countercylically and, indeed, the evidence for that – the hourglass traced by the connectivity and GDP curves – is fairly strong.

In sum, our data on the large firm network as a whole offer degrees of support for all three paradigms of change. Save for equity density and the postbubble upturn in debt ties, the general picture is the one of disintegration that modernization theory paints. However, in line with institutional theory, the declines are neither steep nor consistent. Finally, the evidence of countercylicality is considerable, if hardly complete: Japan's networks strengthen in bad times and weaken in good times.

Analysis II: The Keiretsu Structuring of the Network

In the section above, we speculated on the role of keiretsu in cohesion changes in the corporate network (e.g., in the narrowing of the equity network spread) but did not consider the keiretsu issue directly. Our focus now shifts to the groups. The strategy is two-pronged. First, hewing to the graph-theoretic perspective of the last section, we look at the shacho-kai of the big-six horizontal groups. We then broaden our investigation by examining via a blockmodel analysis the changing horizontal and vertical keiretsu leanings of the set of 259 firms.

Cohesion Analysis: Density Trends within the Shacho-kai

Recall again our three models of change: (1) modernization theory's theme of network decline; (2) institutional theory's claim of structural persistence; and, finally, (3) the hypothesis of countercyclical change. Beyond the general assertion that groups persist – whatever their deficits in efficiency – institutional reasoning ascribes more cohesion to the zaibatsu than to the bank-centered groups. The former have longer and richer histories, including strong pre-war links to the state.

Figure 3.2 plots the densities by shacho-kai and time. Given the small numbers in these networks, the connectivities add little information and are omitted.

Group Differences
The ordering of groups by coherence is consistent with our expectations and with past research. From high to low, it is (1) Mitsubishi and Sumitomo, (2) Mitsui, (3) Fuyo, (4) Sanwa, and (5) Dai-Ichi Kangyo.[49] Mitsubishi edges Sumitomo in trade and, most conspicuously, director ties, but Sumitomo leads in debt and equity relations.[50] Mitsui is a close third in equity, debt, and trade ties but its director network puts it with the bank-centered groups. Fuyo, a post-war bank group with a partial zaibatsu history, ranks fourth in debt and equity density but last in directors and trade. The DKB and Sanwa councils are in general the least cohesive.[51] However, DKB's director network is on a par with Mitsui's and denser than Fuyo's or Sanwa's, a pattern Appendix 3.1 examines in detail.

[49] Hoshi and Ito (1992), using a somewhat different graph-theoretic methodology, also report an ordering of the horizontal groups by cohesion in which Mitsubishi and Sumitomo are at the top and Fuyo, Mitsui, and Sanwa are in the middle (and essentially similar), with DKB the least cohesive of the groups.

[50] Our data (see also Appendix 3.1) accord with the Mitsubishi group's reputation for preferential trade. *Business Week* notes, for example, that Mitsubishi affiliates buy a third of Mitsubishi Motors' trucks and buses. Moreover, "a third of the keiretsu's employees own Mitsubishi cars. Group companies also buy 30% of their own fleets from Mitsubishi Motors.... The beer routinely served at Mitsubishi gatherings is Kirin, another Kinyo-kai member" (Bremner and Thornton, 1999). The Fair Trade Commission (1992) report on the horizontal groups shows Mitsubishi and Sumitomo tied for first place in intragroup sales and purchases, Fuyo and Mitsui tied for second, and DKB and Sanwa last.

[51] In general, larger populations have lower network densities, so this ordering of groups by density is also one of keiretsu size. We do not see this as a matter of misinterpretation. Size, along with pre-war versus post-war founding, is a reason groups differ in cohesion.

Long-Term Trends

The shacho-kai nets have become less cohesive with time. The equity densities are the most stable, but even they trend down. The other three ties have messier patterns, more volatile and group-specific, particularly in the latter 1990s. The debt densities, for example, were stable up to the bubble (1989) and much less so thereafter. They also differ by group: up in the zaibatsu, down in the bank-centered groups. The same is roughly true of trade, save that Mitsui's disintegrating trade network fits the bank-centered pattern. The decline in the density of the director network – steep for Mitsubishi and Sumitomo – shows some reversal in the 1990s.

Cyclical Change

The countercyclical model – that networks expand and contract, respectively, as the economy waxes and wanes – is arguably better applied to keiretsu groups than to the corporate network as a whole. It is their members, after all, who circle the wagons to support one another in hard times. Alternatively, the shacho-kai might be so tight-knit in terms of dense and stable business relations that they are impervious to the business cycle's twists and turns.

However, the countercyclical hypothesis gets a degree of support. Indeed, the cohesion of one network – trade – whose movements were mostly procyclical in the corporate population at large looks countercyclical within the shacho-kai.

More generally, the 1980 second oil shock slump sparked upticks in most groups' equity ties. The relatively strong 1982 and 1984 years, by contrast, saw declining equity, trade, and debt densities. The 1986–87 *endaka* downturn occasioned upturns in cohesion, while the bubble brought declines. Most networks tightened in the postbubble recession (1991 to 1993), with some, not all, loosening again in the growth spurt of 1995. The year 1997 was another bad year that produced upticks for some groups and ties but not others.

Shacho-kai Cohesion: Conclusions

Thus, the horizontal groups were less cohesive in 1997 than they were in 1978. More important, through this period their ties, like the corporate network as a whole, were buffeted by macroeconomic change. First, group cohesion tended to ebb and flow against the business cycle. Second – and perhaps more important – the one–two punch delivered by the *endaka*-bubble caused a systemic shift. Most (except equity) look more stable and orderly before the turbulent late 1980s than during or after. These three themes – the long-term trend, the short-term volatility, and the pre- and postbubble regime shift – will occupy much of our inquiry from this point on.

Blockmodeling the Network

We now extend our investigation with an analysis that clusters firms into groups or positions by multiple criteria of network proximity. While cluster analyses of Japanese corporate networks have been done before, no prior study has analyzed a population of firms on the scale of the 259 we study.[52] Nor have earlier inquiries used these techniques to address what seems the paramount question in contemporary keiretsu research: how much have the groups disintegrated before the powerful forces that have reconfigured the Japanese economy in the last 20 years, among them *kudoka* (hollowing out due to offshore production), *endaka* (the high yen), *gaiatsu* (external pressure, e.g., to open markets), regulatory change, and the rapid-fire shocks of boom and recession.

Previous attempts to construct a keiretsu taxonomy or classification began with shacho-kai lists. They then proceeded to use data on other ties – for example, lending, trade, equity, and director interlocks – to assign affiliate status to some noncouncil firms.[53] Such assignments often hinged on a researcher's judgment that an independent firm did sufficient business with the financials, manufacturers, and trading companies on a shacho-kai that assignment to membership status was justified. Many such taxonomies are therefore arbitrary and overly inclusive and have been criticized as such.[54]

The course we follow is to turn the task of clustering over to a computer algorithm able to digest large quantities of raw network data. In the technical network literature, two perspectives on clustering govern the choice of algorithm. These have important implications for the substantive problem of identifying keiretsu groups. Viewed one way, groups are *cohesive cliques*. A clique comprises closely or densely connected nodes (firms).[55] Some network theories ("homophily") see cliques forming among *similar* nodes. Others, such as the resource dependence and transaction cost perspectives that dominate the study of interorganizational exchange, see

[52] Gerlach (1992b); Scott (1986).
[53] Career Development Center (2002); Fair Trade Commission (1992); Dodwell Marketing Consultants (various years); Miyashita and Russell (1994); Nakatani (1984); Orru et al. (1997).
[54] See, e.g., Hadley's (1984) critique of Nakatani's (1984) influential study of the economic consequences of the big-six horizontal groups.
[55] Mizruchi (1993).

difference – that is, complementarity of resource needs – motivating ties.[56] The one-set principle on which Japan's pre-war zaibatsu were erected assumes cohesion through differentiation and interdependence: each group includes one major firm from each industry sector.[57]

Positions (Blocks) in the Network: Industry vs. Keiretsu
A second relational perspective on groups views them not as cliques, but as *positions* in a social structure.[58] Two actors (firms) are structurally equivalent and thus occupy a single position if their role relations with others are the same. The method of *blockmodeling* aggregates network nodes into positions or blocks by the criterion of structural equivalence – similarity in relations to and from others. Casual observation, as we suggest above, typically regards keiretsu as cohesive cliques. Closer scrutiny, however, reveals two respects in which both horizontal and vertical keiretsu are better cast as positions. First, the defining criterion for the group is less the linkage among the members themselves than their role relations as a set with one or two network-defining positions. The Toyota or Nissan vertical keiretsu are defined much more by the suppliers' ties to the lead manufacturers than by their ties to one another. The same is true of the Matsushita or NEC downstream distribution keiretsu. Among the big-six horizontal groups, the defining ties issue from the core of the network – the principal banks, trading companies, and heavy industrials – to a broad periphery. Our data matrices reveal large variations in the volume of ties sent. Major financial institutions (city banks and trust banks) and commercial firms (trading companies and leading manufacturers) produce the lion's share of structure in these networks through the business they do with, the ownership stakes they maintain in, and the managers they dispatch to a broad spectrum of lesser firms.

Second, keiretsu are defined by how the member firms relate to the economy as a whole. The lines of competition and cooperation in the Japanese economy are etched by keiretsu boundaries. A Toyota supplier such as Denso or Aisin Seiki might sell to Honda, Mazda, or Isuzu but never to Nissan, nor would Toyota purchase electronic components from Nissan affiliate Hitachi.[59] Who companies compete with, contract with, or borrow from are thus heavily shaped by keiretsu affiliations. A study

---

[56] Burt (1983); Lincoln and McBride (1985); Pfeffer and Salancik (1978); Williamson (1985).
[57] See Gerlach (1992a); Morikawa (1993).
[58] Burt (1987); White et al. (1976).
[59] At a 19 August 1997 interview at Toyota's Hirose Plant – a facility specializing in automotive electronics – we asked engineers why Toyota could not source electronics from Hitachi in order to reduce its dependence on Toyota group member Denso. "Hitachi is in the Nissan group," they said. We can't buy from them." See Ahmadjian and Lincoln (2001); Lincoln, Ahmadjian, and Mason (1998); Nishiguchi (1994).

that examines the density or connectivity of ties within groups but ignores ties to the broader corporate community cannot fully grasp how keiretsu configure the network economy.

Finally, as Borgatti and Everett (1992) point out, the distinction between structural equivalence and cohesion or position and clique is often over-drawn. "As a general rule, nodes cannot be structurally equivalent if they are more than two links apart. Hence, cohesion/proximity is part and parcel of the notion of structural equivalence."[60] Thus, while the CONCOR algorithm, which we use here, is a device for blocking a network by the structural equivalence criterion, the clusters it detects typically display high cohesion as well.

Industry, on the face of things more than keiretsu, is a pure realization of the structural equivalence principle. An industry is definable as a collection of firms distinguished by similarity of their exchange relations with a set of other firms. Burt (1983:532) puts it thus:

> Firms producing similar types of goods are structurally equivalent and so jointly occupy a single "position" in the economy. The economic transactions between individual firms therefore can be aggregated into relations between groups of structurally equivalent firms.... These ... constitute "sectors" ... or "industries" in the economy.

Indeed, a baseline assumption of much industrial organization research is that firms within a (narrowly drawn) industry do *not* exchange or otherwise link to one another. The firewalls between competing firms are in some respects higher in Japan than in the United States and in others lower. Keiretsu boundaries constrain the degree to which a company's suppliers and distributors serve its competition. On the other hand, strong trade associations and R&D consortia, plus the administrative guidance of ministries such as MITI, have been powerful vehicles for aligning and coordinating otherwise competing firms.[61]

Do industry and keiretsu, then, represent opposing principles of network organization? It depends on the keiretsu type. The vertical groups – Matsushita, Toyota, Nippon Steel, Nissan, and the like – are generally organized within one sector such as electronics, autos, or steel. Thus, a subpartition of the macro-position occupied by the automotive industry is the micro-position held by the Toyota keiretsu. In the horizontal groups, however, these structural principles are at odds. Horizontal keiretsu cannot, by definition, occur within industries or vice versa.[62]

H3.7: *Over time, the positions (in a structural equivalence sense) in the Japanese economy have become decreasingly keiretsu based and increasingly industry based.*

Thus, competition within an industry is a centrifugal force repelling horizontal groups. Conversely, cooperation within an industry, e.g., along a supply chain, is a centripetal or cohesive force. Toyota's vertical keiretsu is a subnet of the Mitsui group, as is Nissan's within Fuyo, NEC's in Sumitomo, Furukawa's in DKB, and so forth. Conversely, when vertical keiretsu bridge horizontal groups, as we earlier noted, they pull them together. Toyota is a Mitsui *Nimoku-kai* member but it also has ties to the Sanwa group, one being Toyota affiliate Daihatsu's seat on the Sanwa *Sansui-kai*. Similarly, Nissan is a *Fuyo-kai* member tied vertically to Hitachi, which sits on the Fuyo, Sanwa, and DKB councils.[63] Moreover, straddling of boundaries by vertical keiretsu is one reason that the Mitsui, Fuyo, Sanwa, and DKB horizontal groups appear as less distinct and bounded than are the Mitsubishi and Sumitomo networks. Vertical and horizontal keiretsu are often portrayed as separate phenomena.[64] In fact, the two configure the Japanese economy in highly overlapping ways, as Figure 1.1 depicts.

Applying CONCOR
Blockmodeling is a useful method for detecting structure in networks, but it requires some hard decisions up front. The CONCOR algorithm sorts firms into blocks by the criterion of structural equivalence. But the way the raw network data are delivered to CONCOR conditions the results. "Garbage in," as the saying goes, "garbage out." A first decision is whether to construct a separate blockmodel for each tie versus applying the algorithm simultaneously to all observed ties. We noted the fallacy in treating shacho-kai as a sufficient measure of keiretsu affiliation. Similarly,

---

[62] Reflecting the one-set principle, Japan's auto firms, for example, are spread rather evenly across groups: Toyota in Mitsui, Mitsubishi Motors, Mazda in Sumitomo, Nissan in Fuyo, Daihatsu in Sanwa, and Isuzu in DKB. Mazda is not a Sumitomo *Hakusui-kai* member but its relationship with that group, reinforced by Sumitomo's bailout of Mazda in the 1970s (Pascale and Rohlen, 1983), has been strong. Honda, the youngest and most independent of the Japanese car markers, utilizes Mitsubishi as its main bank, and Fuji Heavy (Subaru) is linked to the Fuyo group chiefly through its affiliation with Nissan. See Gerlach (1992a); Miyashita and Russell (1994).

[63] Hitachi is one of five companies to hold seats on multiple councils. Hitachi and Kobe Steel are on the Fuyo and Sanwa councils, and Nissho Iwai is on the DKB and Sanwa councils. Since 1991, DKB *Sansui-kai* members Ishikawajima-Harima (DKB) and Denki Kagaku Kogyo have joined the Mitsui *Nimoku-kai* (see Table 1.1).

[64] See, e.g., Miyashita and Russell (1994).

the other ties we study – equity holding, director, lending–borrowing, and trade – are correlated but imperfectly; that is, the network is not fully multiplex. Firms bunched by similarity or proximity on one tie may well be distant on another. Yet it is at least implicit in the concept of keiretsu that the implicated firms relate to one another in *multiple* ways. We thus need a method for extracting one set of clusters from four observed networks. Such multiple-network clustering is standard blockmodel procedure and is consistent with the evidence to be presented in Chapter 5 that diverse keiretsu ties have similar corporate performance consequences.[65]

CONCOR is a disaggregative clustering algorithm: like the splitting of a cell, it iteratively partitions a population into more and smaller sets. The analyst decides when to halt the process and commit to a final set of clusters. Partitions beyond a certain stage must (a) yield clusters too numerous or trivial to consider, and (b) be substantively uninterpretable. At the same time, a proper grasp of CONCOR output requires attention to where the process has been and where it is going; that is, to map the nesting of late stage clusters within early stage clusters and so on up the iterative tree. The branching of CONCOR is a progression from coarse- to fine-grained structural equivalence. A virtue of the blockmodeling strategy of keiretsu classification is that, unlike other taxonomies, it makes explicit that *any* assignment of firms to groups is a simplifying heuristic. Companies differ by degrees in their positions in the network. Firms separated by late-stage iterations are closer in network space than firms separated earlier. For the most part, we examine blocks produced by four CONCOR iterations. Since every iteration splits each prior cluster in two, this rule yields sixteen partitions (two, four, eight, sixteen).[66] However, we do present and discuss several cases in which higher iterations produced important and interesting subdivisions. Also – and probably symptomatic of the recent transformation of the Japanese corporate network – our 1995 and 1997 blockmodels required more iterations to reveal keiretsu groupings.[67]

---

[65] Lincoln et al. (1996); White et al. (1976).

[66] The tables presenting the CONCOR results for each of the three years (Table 3.1–3.6) indicate the location of each cluster of firms in the CONCOR tree by a four-character alphanumeric index. Thus, the first partitioning divides the 259 firms into *1* and *2*; the second into *1A*, *1B*, *2A*, *2B*; and the third into *1A1*, *1A2*, *1B1*, *1B2*, *2A1*, *2A2*, *2B1*, *2B2*. The fourth partition produces the sixteen-fold partitioning shown in the tables: *1A1a*, *1A1b*, ..., *2B2a*, *2B2b*.

[67] CONCOR iteratively correlates the columns of a matrix. The input to the first iteration is the raw binary matrix of 0's and 1's, capturing the presence and absence of ties to and from N nodes. This gives an $N \times N$ correlation matrix indexing the degree of structural equivalence of every pair of nodes. In our setup, a row holds information on the ties sent by a firm to others in the network, whereas a column reports on ties received. To cluster firms both on ties sent and received, we transformed the matrix, X' (i.e., reversed the rows and columns). The columns of the two matrices are then concatenated – producing a matrix, Xc, of order $2N \times N$. Next the columns of Xc are iteratively correlated via CONCOR to yield a clustering based simultaneously on equivalence of ties sent *and* received. This

The 2072 × 259 matrix is input to CONCOR in each of six years: 1978, 1986, 1989, 1993, 1995, and 1997. These years span a critical interval in Japanese post-war economic history. The year 1978 was a time of relative stability and moderate growth during which keiretsu were institutional fixtures of the Japanese corporate terrain. The year 1986 marked the *endaka* recession, and the mid-eighties high water mark for deregulation and restructuring, which set the stage for the bubble acceleration. The year 1989 was the bubble's peak; 1993–94 was the first trough of the postbubble slump; in 1995 the Japanese economy grew 3.6 percent, its best performance of the 1990s; and 1997–98, reflecting the Asian financial crisis, was the low point.[68]

Industry Blocks

The 1-block: Financials. Our baseline assumption – that industry is the bedrock of structural equivalence in any system of economic exchange – is validated in that CONCOR's first iteration in each year of data splits the population of firms into financials and industrials. Tables 3.1–3.6 present the clusterings generated by the application of the algorithm to the eight tie matrices for the 259 firms at each of six time points.[69]

Consider first the financial 1-block. The partitioning of the network is revealed in the functional subdivision of financial services firms: city banks, trust banks, regional and *sogo* banks, insurance companies, and brokerages. This ordering is also a status ranking – from the city and trust banks to the regional and *sogo* banks – which is fairly stable over time. The first block in the CONCOR taxonomy, *1A1* (both *a* and *b* partitions), contains the major city, trust, and long-term credit banks with one exception: Mitsui (Sakura after 1990), which occupies the *1A2* block in every year save the last, 1997, where it appears in *1A1a*, close to Sumitomo, its soon-to-be merger partner (see Chapter 6).[70]

---

operation also is used to aggregate over substantive relations. We concatenate the columns of 0's and 1's for different types of relations, giving a $KN \times N$ matrix, where K is the number of distinct relations. We use four relations among 259 large Japanese firms: lending, trade, equity, and director dispatch. Since, as noted, we also take the transpose of each matrix to tap the equivalence of sending and receiving ties, we have an $8N \times N$ or 2072×259 matrix.

[68] *Wall Street Journal*, 29 January 2001.

[69] We handled the mergers by equating the rows and columns in the data matrices subsequent to the merger. The CONCOR runs thus put all merged pairs in the same block. Because we have reordered firms within blocks by group and by industry, these pairs are not always adjacent.

[70] Mitsui/Sakura has been one of the weakest of the city banks, and its bad loan problems after the bursting of the bubble required it to accept the largest amount of government bailout money in spring of 1999. In October 1999, Mitsui merged with Sumitomo. Although the merger was claimed to be a marriage of equals, Sumitomo was clearly the stronger partner, thus giving the merger the appearance of a bailout and takeover. See Landers (2000a, 2000b, 2000c; 2002) and Chapter 6.

Table 3.1. CONCOR Partitioning of 259 Japanese Firms, 1978

1 A & B

1 A 1 a — DKB & REGIONALS

Firm		Industry
DAI-ICHI KANGYO	Dk	Banking
KYOWA	In	Banking
BANK YOKOHAMA	In	Banking
TAIYO KOBE	In	Banking
TOKAI	In	Banking
BANK OF TOKYO	In	Banking
DAIWA	In	Banking
SAITAMA	In	Banking

1 A 1 b — CITY & TRUST BANKS

Firm		Industry
YASUDA TRUST	Fu	Banking
FUJI	Fu	Banking
MITSUBISHI TRUST	Mb	Banking
MITSUBISHI	Mb	Banking
MITSUI TRUST	Mi	Banking
SANWA	Sa	Banking
SUMITOMO	Su	Banking
SUMITOMO TRUST	Su	Banking
CHUO TRUST	In	Banking
INT'L BANK JAPAN	In	Banking
NIPPON CREDIT	In	Banking
LTCREDIT	In	Banking

INSURANCE & REGIONAL BANKS

1 A 2 a

Firm		Industry
TAISHO MARINE & FIRE	Mi	Banking
MITSUI	In	Banking
BANK FUKUOKA	In	Banking

1 A 2 b

Firm		Industry
TOKIO MARINE & FIRE	Mb	Insurance
SUMITOMO MARINE & FIRE	Su	Insurance
NIPPON FIRE & MARINE	In	Insurance

1 B 1 a

Firm		Industry
HOKURIKU	In	Banking
HOKKAIDO TAKUSHOKU	In	Banking

1 B 1 b

Firm		Industry
YASUDA FIRE & MARINE	Fu	Insurance
TOYOTA MOTOR	Mi	Automobile
CHIYODA FIRE & MARINE	In	Insurance
NICHIDO FIRE & MARINE	In	Insurance

1 B 2 a

Firm		Industry
SHIZUOKA	In	Banking
ASHIKAGA	In	Banking
JOYO	In	Banking
CHIBA	In	Banking

2 A 1

2 A 1 a — MATSUSHITA GROUP

Firm		Industry
NIKKO SECURITIES	In	Securities
DAI-TOKYO FIRE & MARINE	In	Insurance
YAMAHA CORP.	In	Gen. manuf.
PIONEER ELECTRONIC	In	Electronics
TOTO	In	Ceramics
MATSUSHITA DENKO	In	Electronics
VICTOR COMPANY OF JAPAN	In	Electronics
MATSUSHITA-KOTOBUKI	In	Electronics
MATSUSHITA REGRIGERATION	In	Electronics
MATSUSHITA COMMUNICATION	In	Electronics

2 A 1 b — SOGO SHOSHA

Firm		Industry
KANEMATSU GOSHO	Dk	Trade
SHISEIDO	Dk	Chemicals
ITOCHU (C. Itoh)	Dk	Trade
MITSUBISHI ELECTRIC	Mb	Electronics
MITSUBISHI CORP	Mb	Trade
MITSUI & CO.	Mi	Trade
NICHIMEN	Sa	Textile
GUNZE	In	Textile
NGK INSULATORS	In	Ceramics
YAMAHA MOTOR	In	Automobile

2 A 2

2 A 2 a — TOYOTA GROUP

Firm		Industry
DAIHATSU MOTOR	Sa	Automobile
NISSHO IWAI	Sa	Trade
FUJI FIRE & MARINE	In	Banking
KANTO AUTO WORKS	In	Automobile
NIPPONDENSO	In	Electronics
AISIN SEIKI	In	Machinery
TOYOTA AUTO BODY	In	Automobile
TOYODA AUTOMATIC LOOM	In	Machinery
AICHI STEEL WORKS	In	Heavy metal
HINO MOTORS	In	Automobile
NOMURA SECURITIES	In	Banking

2 A 2 b — MITSUI GROUP

Firm		Industry
ISEKI	Dk	Machinery
SANKYO	Dk	Pharm.
CANON	Fu	Prec. equip
(CHICHIBU) ONODA CEMENT	Mi	Ceramics
MITSUI TOATSU CHEMICALS	Mi	Chemicals
MITSUI PETROCHEMICAL	Mi	Chemicals
TOSHIBA	Mi	Electronics
THE JAPAN STEEL WORKS	Mi	Heavy metal
MITSUI MINING & SMELTING	Mi	Light metal
MITSUI MINING	Mi	Mining
OJI PAPER	Mi	Paper
DAIKYO OIL	Mi	Oil
MITSUI ENGIN & SHIPBLDG	Mi	Shipyard
DAICEL CHEMICAL	In	Chemicals
CENTRAL GLASS	In	Chemicals
FUJI PHOTO FILM	In	Chemicals
ALPS ELECTRIC	In	Electronics
OMRON TATEISI	In	Electronics
SONY	In	Electronics
KYOKUYO	In	Fishing
MORINAGA MILK	In	Food
PRIMA MEAT PACKERS	In	Food
TOPPAN PRINTING	In	Gen. manuf.
FUJIKURA	In	Light metal
TOYO SEIKAN KAISHA	In	Light metal
BROTHER INDUSTRIES	In	Machinery
ARABIAN OIL	In	Oil
NIPPON OIL	In	Oil
KOA OIL	In	Oil
NIPPON (JUJO) PAPER	In	Paper

2 B 1

2 B 1 a — SUMITOMO GROUP

Firm		Industry
COSMO OIL	Sa	Oil
SUMITOMO CORP	Sa	Trade
SUMITOMO CHEMICAL	Su	Chemicals
SUMITOMO METAL INDUSTRIES	Su	Heavy metal
SUMITOMO METAL MINING	Su	Light metal
SUMITOMO HEAVY INDUSTRIES	Su	Light metal
SUMITOMO LIGHT METAL	Su	Light metal
NIPPON SHEET GLASS	Su	Ceramics
NEC	Su	Electronics
SUMITOMO ELECTRIC	Su	Light metal
SUMITOMO (OSAKA) CEMENT	Su	Ceramics
DAIWA SECURITIES	In	Banking
KOKUYO	In	Gen. manuf.
SHIONOGI	In	Pharm.
KOMATSU	In	Machinery
DAIKEN TRADE & INDUSTRY	In	Gen. manuf.
TOKYO SANYO ELECTRIC	In	Electronics
DAIKIN INDUSTRIES	In	Machinery
ASAHI BREWERIES	In	Food
NIPPON ALUMINUM	In	Light metal
MARUDAI FOOD	In	Food
RENGO	In	Paper
MAZDA MOTOR	In	Automobile
DAIKYO OIL	In	Oil
DAISHOWA PAPER	In	Paper
TOMEN (TOYO MENKA)	In	Trade
EZAKI GLICO	In	Food
TDK	In	Electronics
HOUSE FOOD INDUSTRIAL	In	Food
MATSUSHITA ELECTRIC	In	Electronics
SANYO ELECTRIC	In	Electronics
SUZUKI MOTOR	In	Automobile
KOYO SEIKO	In	Machinery

2 B 2

2 B 2 a (1) — FUYO GROUP (NISSAN)

Firm		Industry
NIHON CEMENT	Fu	Ceramics
SAPPORO BREWERIES	Fu	Food
OKI ELECTRIC	Fu	Electronics
TOA NENRYO KOGYO	Fu	Oil
NIPPON REIZO	Fu	Food
MARUBENI	Fu	Trade
NISSAN MOTOR	Fu	Automobile
SANYO-KOKUSAKU PULP	Fu	Paper
NIPPON SEIKO	Fu	Machinery
YAMAICHI SECURITIES	In	Banking
RICOH	In	Prec. equip
SNOW BRAND MILK	In	Food
YAMAZAKI BAKING	In	Food
SHOWA ALUMINUM	In	Light metal
TOPY INDUSTRIES	In	Transport
FUJIYA	In	Food
NISSAN DIESEL MOTOR	In	Automobile
ZEXEL (DIESEL KIKI)	In	Machinery
AICHI MACHINE	In	Automobile
TAKEDA CHEMICAL	In	Pharm.
DAI NIPPON PRINTING	In	Gen. manuf.

2 B 2 a (2) — SANWA GROUP (HITACHI)

Firm		Industry
NIPPON ZEON	Dk	Chemicals
FUJI ELECTRIC	Dk	Electronics
NIIGATA ENGINEERING	Dk	Machinery
SHOWA DENKO	Fu	Chemicals
HITACHI	Fu	Electronics
NISSHINBO INDUSTRIES	Fu	Textile
HITACHI CHEMICAL	Sa	Chemicals
TOKUYAMA SODA	Sa	Chemicals
SEKISUI CHEMICAL	Sa	Chemicals
SHARP	Sa	Electronics
ITOHAM FOODS	Sa	Food
HITACHI METALS	Sa	Heavy metal
KOBE STEEL	Sa	Heavy metal
NTN TOYO BEARING	Sa	Light metal
TANABE SEIYAKU	Sa	Pharm.
HITACHI ZOSEN	Sa	Shipyard
TEIGIN	Sa	Textile
NISSAN CHEMICAL	In	Chemicals
JAPAN SYNTHETIC RUBBER	In	Chemicals
NIPPON SUISAN KAISHA	In	Fishing
TOSHIN STEEL	In	Heavy metal
YODOGAWA STEEL WORKS	In	Heavy metal
NIPPON MINING	In	Light metal
DOWA MINING	In	Light metal
KURABO INDUSTRIES	In	Textile
DAIWABO	In	Textile

SOGO BANKS

1 B 2 b

Firm	Keiretsu	Industry
NISSAN FIRE & MARINE	Dk	Banking
BANK HIROSHIMA	In	Banking
GUNMA	In	Banking
HYOGO SOGO	In	Banking
NISHI-NIPPON SOGO	In	Banking
KINKI SOGO	In	Banking
TOKYO SOGO	In	Banking
NAGOYA SOGO	In	Banking

DKB & SANWA GROUPS (NIPPON STEEL)

2 B 1 b

Firm	Keiretsu	Industry
DENKI KAGAKU KOGYO	Dk	Chemicals
HONSHU PAPER	Dk	Paper
KAWASAKI HEAVY	Dk	Shipyard
ISHIK.-HARIMA HEAVY	Dk	Shipyard
ASAHI CHEMICAL	Dk	Textile
KUBOTA	Fu	Machinery
FUJI HEAVY	In	Automobile
KAO	In	Chemicals
TOSOH	In	Chemicals
KANEKA (KANEGAFUCHI)	In	Chemicals
NIPPON STEEL	In	Heavy metal
TOKYO STEEL	In	Heavy metal
TOYO KOHAN	In	Heavy metal
DAIDO STEEL	In	Heavy metal
FUJI KOSAN	In	Oil
BRIDGESTONE	In	Rubber
KANEBO	In	Textile
TOYOBO	In	Textile
KURARAY	In	Textile
NITTO BOSEKI	In	Textile
TOKYU CAR	In	Transport
NIPPON FLOUR MILLS	Mi	Food
TORAY INDUSTRIES	Mi	Textile
UBE INDUSTRIES	Sa	Chemicals
NISSHIN STEEL	Sa	Heavy metal
NAKAYAMA STEEL WORKS	Sa	Heavy metal
UNITIKA	Sa	Textile

DKB GROUP

2 B 2 b (1)

Firm	Keiretsu	Industry
YOKOHAMA RUBBER	Dk	Rubber
SHOWA SHELL SEKIYU	Dk	Oil
EBARA	Dk	Machinery
FURUKAWA ELECTRIC	Dk	Light metal
NIPPON LIGHT METAL	Dk	Light metal
KAWASAKI STEEL	Dk	Heavy metal
FUJITSU	Dk	Electronics
KYOWA HAKKO KOGYO	Dk	Pharm.
ISUZU MOTORS	Dk	Automobile
LION	Dk	Pharm.
NISSHIN FLOUR MILLING	Fu	Food
FUJISAWA PHARMACEUTICAL	Sa	Pharm.

MITSUBISHI GROUP

2 B 2 b (2)

Firm	Keiretsu	Industry
MITSUBISHI RAYON	Mb	Textile
MITSUBISHI HEAVY INDUSTRIES	Mb	Shipyard
MITSUBISHI PAPER MILLS	Mb	Paper
MITSUBISHI OIL	Mb	Oil
MITSUBISHI MATERIALS (METAL)	Mb	Light metal
KIRIN BREWERY	Mb	Food
MITSUBISHI PETROCHEMICAL	Mb	Chemicals
MITSUBISHI GAS CHEMICAL	Mb	Chemicals
MITSUBISHI CHEMICAL	Mb	Chemicals
MITSUBISHI MINING & CEMENT	Mb	Ceramics
ASAHI GLASS	Mb	Ceramics
TOYO TIRE & RUBBER	Sa	Rubber
NIPPON MEAT PACKERS	In	Food
MORINAGA & CO.	In	Food
KIKKOMAN	In	Food
AJINOMOTO	In	Food
NIHON NOSAN KOGYO	In	Food
NISSHIN OIL MILLS	In	Food
NISSHIN FOOD PRODUCTS	In	Food
SHOWA SANGYO	In	Food
MEIJI MILK	In	Food
MEIJI SEIKA KAISHA	In	Food
Q. P. CORP.	In	Food
NICHIRO GYOGYO KAISHA	In	Fishing
MARUHA (TAIYO FISHERY)	In	Fishing
DAINIPPON INK & CHEMICALS	In	Chemicals
SHIN-ETSU CHEMICAL	In	Chemicals
KONISHIROKU PHOTO	In	Chemicals
TOYO INK MFG	In	Chemicals
HONDA MOTOR	In	Automobile
KAYABA INDUSTRY	In	Automobile

Note: Each panel is a cluster of firms identified by a given CONCOR iteration. The alphanumeric label (1A, etc.) indicates the iteration that produced the cluster; i.e., iteration 1: 1, 2; iteration 2: 1A, 1B, 2A, 2B; iteration 3: 1A1, 1A2,..., 2B1, 2B2; iteration 4: 1A1a,..., 2B2b; iteration 5: 1A1a(1),... 2B2b(2); iteration 6: 1A1a(1b),..., 2B2b(2b). Keiretsu identifiers are Mi = Mitsui, Mb = Mitsubishi, Su = Sumitomo, Fu = Fuyo, Sa = Sanwa, Dk = DKB, In = shacho-kai independent. Vertical keiretsu names are in parentheses (e.g., Hitachi).

Table 3.2. CONCOR Partitioning of 259 Japanese Firms, 1986

Column 1A & B — CITY, TRUST, & MAJOR REGIONAL BANKS / INSURANCE / REGIONAL & SOGO BANKS

1A1a
Firm		
DAI-ICHI KANGYO	Dk	Banking
FUJI	Fu	Banking
MITSUBISHI TRUST	Mb	Banking
MITSUBISHI	Mb	Banking
DAIWA SECURITIES	Mb	Banking
SUMITOMO	Su	Banking
SUMITOMO TRUST	Su	Banking
BANK OF TOKYO	In	Banking
TOKAI	In	Banking
TAIYO KOBE	In	Banking
KYOWA	In	Banking
SAITAMA	In	Banking
BANK YOKOHAMA	In	Banking

1A1b
Firm		
YASUDA TRUST	Fu	Banking
MITSUI (Sakura)	Mi	Banking
MITSUI TRUST	Mi	Banking
TOYO TRUST	Sa	Banking
DAIWA	In	Banking
INT'L BANK JAPAN	In	Banking
LTCREDIT	In	Banking
NIPPON CREDIT	In	Banking

1A2a
Firm		
HOKKAIDO TAKUSHOKU	In	Banking
HOKURIKU	In	Banking

1A2b
Firm		
YASUDA FIRE & MARINE	Fu	Insurance
TOKIO MARINE & FIRE	Mb	Insurance
SUMITOMO MARINE & FIRE	Su	Insurance
NIPPON FIRE & MARINE	In	Insurance

1B1a
Firm		
SHIZUOKA	In	Banking
GUNMA	In	Banking
CHIBA	In	Banking
JOYO	In	Banking
ASHIKAGA	In	Banking
BANK FUKUOKA	In	Banking
BANK HIROSHIMA	In	Banking
NIKKO SECURITIES	In	Banking
HYOGO SOGO	In	Banking
NISH-NIPPON SOGO	In	Banking
TOKYO SOGO	In	Banking
SANYO ELECTRIC	In	Electronics

Column 2A1 — INDEPENDENTS / SUMITOMO GROUP

2A1a
Firm		
CANON	Fu	Prec. equip.
MATSUSHITA COMMUNICATION	In	Electronics
FUJI FIRE & MARINE	In	Insurance
DAIWA SECURITIES	In	Securities
TOKYO SANYO ELECTRIC	In	Electronics
SONY	In	Electronics
PIONEER ELECTRONIC	In	Electronics
KOKUYO	In	Gen. manuf.
TAKEDA CHEMICAL	In	Pharm.
SHIONOGI &	In	Pharm.
KAO CORP.	In	Chemicals
KOYO SEIKO	In	Machinery
HOUSE FOOD INDUSTRIAL	In	Food
YAMAHA CORP.	In	Gen. manuf.
TOYO SEIKAN KAISHA	In	Light metal
BROTHER INDUSTRIES	In	Machinery
ALPS ELECTRIC	In	Electronics

2A1b
Firm		
SUMITOMO METAL MINING	Su	Heavy metal
SUMITOMO METAL INDUSTRIES	Su	Light metal
SUMITOMO LIGHT METAL	Su	Light metal
SUMITOMO HEAVY INDUSTRIES	Su	Heavy metal
SUMITOMO CORP	Su	Trade
SUMITOMO CHEMICAL	Su	Chemicals
SUMITOMO (OSAKA) CEMENT	Su	Ceramics
NIPPON SHEET GLASS	Su	Ceramics
NEC	Su	Electronics
TOYO KOHAN	In	Light metal
TOMEN (TOYO MENKA)	In	Trade
TOKYO STEEL	In	Automobile
TDK CORP.	In	Electronics
SANKYO ALUMINUM	In	Light metal
RENGO	In	Paper
MAZDA MOTOR	In	Automobile
MARUDAI FOOD	In	Food
KAYABA INDUSTRY	In	Machinery
EZAKI GLICO	In	Food
DAIKYO OIL	In	Oil
DAIKIN INDUSTRIES	In	Gen. Manu.
DAIKEN TRADE & INDUSTRY	In	Heavy metal
ASAHI BREWERIES	In	Food

Column 2A2 — MITSUBISHI GROUP

2A2a
Firm		
LION	Dk	Chemicals
MITSUBISHI HEAVY INDUSTRIES	Mb	Shipyard
MITSUBISHI GAS CHEMICAL	Mb	Chemicals
MITSUBISHI MATERIALS (METAL)	Mb	Light metal
MITSUBISHI CHEMICAL	Mb	Chemical
MITSUBISHI OIL	Mb	Oil
MITSUBISHI PAPER MILLS	Mb	Paper
MITSUBISHI RAYON	Mb	Textile
MITSUBISHI PETROCHEMICAL	Mb	Chemicals
MITSUBISHI MINING & CEMENT	Mb	Ceramics
TOTO	In	Ceramics
KONISHIROKU PHOTO	In	Chemicals
HONDA MOTOR	In	Automobile
FUJI PHOTO FILM	In	Chemicals
RICOH	In	Prec. equip
NISSHIN FOOD PRODUCTS	In	Food

2A2b
Firm		
SHOWA SHELL SEKIYU	Dk	Oil
NISSHIN FLOUR MILLING	Fu	Food
MITSUBISHI CORP	Mb	Electronics
ASAHI GLASS	Mb	Ceramics
KIRIN BREWERY	Mb	Food
NGK INSULATORS	In	Ceramics
MEIJI SEIKA KAISHA	In	Food
MEIJI MILK	In	Food
MORINAGA & CO.	In	Food
KOA OIL	In	Oil
KIKKOMAN	In	Food
OMRON TATEISI ELECTRONICS	In	Electronics
GUNZE	In	Textile
SHIN-ETSU CHEMICAL	In	Chemicals
Q. P. CORP.	In	Food
TOYOBO	In	Textile
NICHIRO GYOGYO KAISHA	In	Fishing
NIHON NOSAN KOGYO.	In	Food
NISSHIN OIL MILLS	In	Food
YAMAZAKI BAKING	In	Food

Column 2B1 — FUYO GROUP (NISSAN)

2B1a
Firm		
FUJI ELECTRIC	Dk	Electronics
NIPPON ZEON	Dk	Chemicals
YOKOHAMA RUBBER	Dk	Rubber
TOA NENRYO KOGYO	Fu	Oil
HITACHI	Fu	Electronics
SAPPORO BREWERIES	Fu	Food
NIHON CEMENT	Fu	Ceramics
NIPPON REIZO	Fu	Food
NIPPON KOKAN	Fu	Heavy metal
SHOWA DENKO	Fu	Chemicals
MARUBENI	Fu	Trade
NIPPON SEIKO	Fu	Machinery
OKI ELECTRIC	Fu	Electronics
NISSHINBO INDUSTRIES	Fu	Textile
SANYO-KOKUSAKU PULP	Fu	Paper
NISSAN MOTOR	Fu	Automobile
YAMAICHI SECURITIES	Sa	Banking
HITACHI CHEMICAL	In	Chemicals
TOKYU CAR CORP.	In	Transport
TOSHIN STEEL	In	Heavy metal
TOPY IDUSTRIES	In	Heavy metal
YODOGAWA STEEL WORKS	In	Light metal
SHOWA ALUMINUM	In	Light metal
DAI NIPPON PRINTING	In	Heavy metal
NIPPON STEEL	In	Heavy metal
NISSAN SHATAI	In	Automobile
NISSAN CHEMICAL	In	Chemicals
TOSOH	In	Chemicals
NISSAN DIESEL MOTOR	In	Automobile
DAISHOWA PAPER	In	Paper
KOMATSU	In	Machinery
FUJI HEAVY	In	Automobile
AICHI MACHINE	In	Automobile
ZEXEL (DIESEL KIKI)	In	Machinery
FUJIYA	In	Food
NIPPON SUISAN KAISHA	In	Fishing
SNOW BRAND MILK	In	Food

Column 2B2 — DKB, MITSUI, & SANWA GROUPS / MITSUI AND SANWA GROUPS

2B2a
Firm		
SHISEIDO	Dk	Chemicals
FURUKAWA ELECTRIC	Dk	Light metal
FUJITSU	Dk	Electronics
NIIGATA ENGINEERING	Dk	Machinery
ISEKI	Dk	Machinery
ITOCHU (C. Itoh)	Dk	Trade
OJI PAPER	Mi	Paper
MITSUI & CO.	Mi	Trade
NTN TOYO BEARING	Sa	Machinery
NISSHO IWAI	Sa	Trade
NIPPON OIL	In	Oil
HINO MOTORS	In	Automobile
BRIDGESTONE	In	Rubber
PRIMA MEAT PACKERS	In	Food

2B2b
Firm		
DENKI KAGAKU KOGYO	Dk	Chemicals
HONSHU PAPER	Dk	Paper
SANKYO	Dk	Pharm.
KYOWA HAKKO KOGYO	Mi	Chemicals
TOSHIBA	Mi	Electronics
MITSUI MINING & SMELTING	Mi	Light metal
THE JAPAN STEEL WORKS	Mi	Heavy metal
MITSUI TOATSU CHEMICALS	Mi	Chemicals
MITSUI PETROCHEMICAL	Mi	Chemicals
MITSUI MINING	Mi	Mining
MITSUI ENGIN. & SHIPBLDG	Mi	Shipyard
TORAY INDUSTRIES	Sa	Textile
NIPPON FLOUR MILLS	Sa	Food
CENTRAL GLASS	In	Chemicals
DAICEL CHEMICAL	In	Chemicals
MORINAGA MILK	In	Food
KYOKUYO	Dk	Fishing
FUJIKURA	In	Light metal
NIPPON MINING	In	Light metal
DAIDO STEEL	In	Heavy metal
DAINIPPON INK & CHEMICALS	In	Chemicals
NITTO BOSEKI	In	Textile
DOWA MINING	In	Mining
KANEKA (KANEGAFUCHI CHEM.)	In	Chemicals
KANEBO	In	Textile
NIPPON MEAT PACKERS	In	Food
TOYODA AUTOMATIC LOOM	In	Machinery
KURABO INDUSTRIES	In	Textile
NIPPON (JUJO) PAPER	In	Paper

1 B 1 b

MIXED FINANCIALS

NISSAN FIRE & MARINE	Dk	Insurance
CHUO TRUST	In	Banking
NICHIDO FIRE & MARINE	In	Insurance
KINKI SOGO	In	Banking
NAGOYA SOGO	In	Banking
DAI-TOKYO FIRE & MARINE	In	Insurance
NOMURA SECURITIES	In	Securities
TOPPAN PRINTING	In	Gen. manuf

1 B 2 a

TOYOTA GROUP

TAISHO MARINE & FIRE	Mi	Insurance
TOYOTA MOTOR	Mi	Automobile
CHIYODA FIRE & MARINE	In	Banking
NIPPONDENSO	In	Electronics
AISIN SEIKI	In	Automobile
KANTO AUTO WORKS	In	Automobile
AICHI STEEL WORKS	In	Heavy metal
TOYOTA AUTO BODY	In	Automobile

1 B 2 b

MATSUSHITA

MATSUSHITA ELECTRIC	In	Electronics
MATSUSHITA DENKO	In	Electronics
VICTOR COMPANY OF JAPAN	In	Electronics
MATSUSHITA-KOTOBUKI ELEC.	In	Electronics
MATSUSHITA REGRIGERATION	In	Electronics

2 B 1 b

SANWA AND D K B GROUPS

KAWASAKI HEAVY	Dk	Shipyard
KAWASAKI STEEL	Dk	Heavy metal
KANEMATSU GOSHO	Dk	Trade
ISUZU MOTORS	Dk	Automobile
NIPPON LIGHT METAL	Dk	Light metal
EBARA	Dk	Machinery
ASAHI CHEMICAL	Dk	Textile
KUBOTA	Fu	Machinery
NICHIMEN	Sa	Trade
SHARP	Sa	Electronics
ITOHAM FOODS	Sa	Food
DAIHATSU MOTOR	Sa	Automobile
KOBE STEEL	Sa	Heavy metal
UBE INDUSTRIES	Sa	Chemicals
SEKISUI CHEMICAL	Sa	Chemicals
COSMO OIL	Sa	Oil
NAKAYAMA STEEL WORKS	Sa	Heavy metal
TOKUYAMA SODA	Sa	Chemicals
NISSHIN STEEL	Sa	Heavy metal
UNITIKA	Sa	Textile
TOYO TIRE & RUBBER	Sa	Rubber
TEIGIN	Sa	Textile
FUJISAWA PHARMACEUTICAL	Sa	Pharm.
HITACHI ZOSEN	Sa	Shipyard
HITACHI metals	Sa	Heavy metal
HITACHI CABLE	Sa	Light metal
TANABE SEIYAKU	Sa	Pharm.
FUJI KOSAN	In	Oil
ARABIAN OIL	In	Mining
SUZUKI MOTOR	In	Automobile
MARUHA (TAIYO FISHERY)	In	Fishing
JAPAN SYNTHETIC RUBBER	In	Chemicals
SHOWA SANGYO	In	Food
DAIWABO CO.	In	Textile
TOYO INK MFG	In	Chemicals

Table 3.3. CONCOR Partitioning of 259 Japanese Firms, 1989

1 A & B

1 A 1 a — CITY & REGIONAL BANKS

Firm		Sector
DAI-ICHI KANGYO	Dk	Banking
MITSUBISHI	Mb	Banking
SANWA	Sa	Banking
TAIYO KOBE	In	Banking
TOKAI	In	Banking
LTCREDIT	In	Banking
INT'L BANK JAPAN	In	Banking
NIPPON CREDIT	In	Banking
HOKURIKU	In	Banking
BANK OF TOKYO	In	Banking

1 A 1 b

Firm		Sector
FUJI	Fu	Banking
SUMITOMO	Su	Banking
BANK YOKOHAMA	In	Banking
KYOWA	In	Banking
SAITAMA	In	Banking

1 A 2 a — TRUST BANKS

Firm		Sector
YASUDA TRUST	Fu	Banking
MITSUBISHI TRUST	Mb	Banking
MITSUI (SAKURA)	Mi	Banking
MITSUI TRUST	Mi	Banking
TOYO TRUST	Sa	Banking
SUMITOMO TRUST	Su	Banking
DAIWA	In	Banking
CHUO TRUST	In	Banking

2 A 1

2 A 1 a (1) — SANWA, DKB, FUYO

Firm		Sector
LION	Dk	Chemicals
YASUDA FIRE & MARINE	Fu	Insurance
SEKISUI CHEMICAL	Sa	Chemicals
TANABE SEIYAKU	In	Pharm.
TAKEDA CHEMICAL	In	Pharm.
NIPPON MINING	In	Light metal
TOSHIN STEEL	In	Heavy metal
KAO CORP.	In	Chemicals
EZAKI GLICO	In	Food

2 A 1 a (2) — MITSUBISHI GROUP

Firm		Sector
KIRIN BREWERY	Mb	Food
MITSUBISHI MATERIALS	Mb	Light metal
MITSUBISHI OIL	Mb	Oil
MITSUBISHI MINING & CEMENT	Mb	Ceramics
DAI NIPPON PRINTING	In	Gen. manuf.
KIKKOMAN	In	Food
NGK INSULATORS	In	Ceramics
TOTO	In	Ceramics
GUNZE	In	Textile
TDK CORP.	In	Electrics
RICOH	In	Electrics
PIONEER ELECTRONIC	In	Electrics
TOYO INK MFG	In	Chemicals

2 A 1 b — SUMITOMO GROUP (MATSUSHITA)

Firm		Sector
SUMITOMO MARINE & FIRE	Su	Insurance
MATSUSHITA REGRIG.	In	Electrics
MATSUSHITA COMMUNICATION	In	Electrics
ASAHI BREWERIES	In	Food
TOKYO STEEL	In	Heavy metal
HOUSE FOOD INDUSTRIAL	In	Food
DAIKIN INDUSTRIES	In	Machinery
MARUDAI FOOD	In	Food
DAIWA SECURITIES	In	Securities
SANYO ELECTRIC	In	Electrics
TOKYO SANYO ELECTRIC	In	Electrics
MATSUSHITA ELECTRIC	In	Electrics
MATSUSHITA DENKO	In	Electrics

2 A 2

2 A 2 a (1) — MITSUI GROUP

Firm		Sector
TAISHO MARINE & FIRE	Mi	Insurance
SONY	In	Electrics
FUJI PHOTO FILM	In	Chemicals
TOPPAN PRINTING	In	Gen. manuf.
OMRON TATEISI ELECTRONICS	In	Electrics
NISSHIN FOOD PRODUCTS	In	Food

2 A 2 a (2) — TOYOTA GROUP

Firm		Sector
KOYO SEIKO	In	Machinery
CHIYODA FIRE & MARINE	In	Insurance
AISIN SEIKI	In	Automobile
NIPPONDENSO	In	Electrics
KANTO AUTO WORKS	In	Automobile
AICHI STEEL WORKS	In	Heavy metal

2 A 2 b — DKB & FUYO & FINANCIALS

Firm		Sector
SHISEIDO	Dk	Chemicals
SANKYO	Dk	Pharm.
NIPPON REIZO	Fu	Food
NIHON CEMENT	Fu	Ceramics
DAI-TOKYO FIRE & MARINE	In	Insurance
NOMURA SECURITIES	In	Securities
FUJI FIRE & MARINE	In	Insurance
NIKKO SECURITIES	In	Securities
YAMAICHI SECURITIES	In	Securities
BROTHER INDUSTRIES	In	Machinery
YAMAHA MOTOR	In	Automobile
YAMAHA CORP.	In	Gen. manuf.
FUJIKURA	In	Light metal
NIPPON OIL	In	Oil

2 B 1

2 B 1 a (1) — FUYO GROUP (NISSAN)

Firm		Sector
NIPPON KOKAN	Fu	Heavy metal
NISSAN MOTOR	Fu	Automobile
TOA NENRYO KOGYO	Fu	Oil
NIPPON SEIKO	Fu	Machinery
MARUBENI	Fu	Trade
SHOWA DENKO	Fu	Chemicals
SAPPORO BREWERIES	Fu	Food
OKI ELECTRIC	Fu	Electrics
NIPPON STEEL	In	Heavy metal
KURARAY	In	Textile
YODOGAWA STEEL	In	Heavy metal
DAISHOWA PAPER	In	Paper
SHOWA ALUMINUM	In	Light metal
TOPY INDUSTRIES	In	Transport

2 B 1 a (2) — DKB GROUP (NISSAN)

Firm		Sector
KYOWA HAKKO KOGYO	Dk	Chemicals
NIPPON LIGHT METAL	Dk	Light metal
FUJI ELECTRIC	Dk	Electrics
NIPPON ZEON	Dk	Chemicals
SANYO-KOKUSAKU PULP	Fu	Paper
HITACHI METALS	In	Heavy metal
KAYABA INDUSTRY	In	Automobile
NISSAN DIESEL MOTOR	In	Automobile
NITTO BOSEKI	In	Textile
KANEBO	In	Textile
FUJI HEAVY	In	Automobile
NISSAN CHEMICAL	In	Chemicals
CENTRAL GLASS	In	Chemicals
DOWA MINING	In	Light metal
AICHI MACHINE	In	Automobile
NISSAN SHATAI	In	Automobile
ZEXEL (DIESEL KIKI)	In	Machinery
DAIDO STEEL	In	Heavy metal
FUJI KOSAN	In	Oil

2 B 2

2 B 2 a (1) — MITSUBISHI GROUP

Firm		Sector
YOKOHAMA RUBBER	Dk	Rubber
MITSUBISHI HEAVY INDUSTRIES	Mb	Shipyard
MITSUBISHI RAYON	Mb	Textile
MITSUBISHI PAPER MILLS	Mb	Paper
MITSUBISHI GAS CHEMICAL	Mb	Chemicals
MITSUBISHI CHEMICAL	Mb	Chemicals
MITSUBISHI PETROCHEMICAL	Mb	Chemicals
MITSUBISHI CORP	Mb	Trade
MITSUBISHI ELECTRIC	Mb	Electrics
ASAHI GLASS	Mb	Ceramics
NIHON NOSAN KOGYO	In	Food
KONISHIROKU PHOTO	In	Chemicals
HONDA MOTOR	In	Automobile
MORINAGA & Co.	In	Food
NICHIRO GYOGYO KAISHA	In	Fishing
AJINOMOTO	In	Food
NISSHIN OIL MILLS	In	Food
TOYOBO	In	Textile
SHIN-ETSU CHEMICAL	In	Chemicals
DAINIPPON INK & CHEMICALS	In	Chemicals

2 B 2 a (2) — SANWA, SUMITOMO, & DKB GROUPS

Firm		Sector
ITOCHU	Dk	Trade
SHOWA SHELL SEKIYU	Dk	Oil
ISUZU MOTORS	Dk	Automobile
UBE INDUSTRIES	Sa	Chemicals
KOBE STEEL	Sa	Heavy metal
UNITIKA	Sa	Textile
NISSHIN STEEL	Sa	Heavy metal
NAKAYAMA STEEL WORKS	Sa	Heavy metal
COSMO OIL	Sa	Oil
TOKUYAMA SODA	Sa	Chemicals
TOYO TIRE & RUBBER	Sa	Rubber
NTN TOYO BEARING	Sa	Machinery
NISSHO IWAI	Sa	Trade
NICHIMEN	Sa	Trade
SUMITOMO METAL	Su	Heavy metal
SUMITOMO ELECTRIC	Su	Light metal
SUMITOMO METAL MINING	Su	Light metal
SUMITOMO HEAVY	Su	Machinery
SUMITOMO CORP	Su	Trade
MAZDA MOTOR	Su	Automobile
RENGO	In	Paper
SHOWA SANGYO	In	Food
JAPAN SYNTHETIC RUBBER	In	Chemicals
DAIKYO OIL	In	Oil
MARUHA (TAIYO FISHERY)	In	Fishing

118

REGIONAL & MUTUAL BANKS, & INSURANCE

1 A 2 b
TOKIO MARINE & FIRE	Mb	Insurance
NIPPON FIRE & MARINE	In	Insurance

1 B 1 a
HOKKAIDO TAKUSHOKU	In	Banking
JOYO	In	Banking
SHIZUOKA	In	Banking

1 B 1 b
CHIBA	In	Banking
GUNMA	In	Banking
HYOGO SOGO	In	Banking
ASHIKAGA	In	Banking
BANK HIROSHIMA	In	Banking
BANK FUKUOKA	In	Banking
TOKYO SOGO	In	Banking

1 B 2 a
NISSAN FIRE & MARINE	Dk	Insurance
NICHIDO FIRE & MARINE	In	Insurance
KINKI SOGO	In	Banking
NISHI-NIPPON SOGO	In	Banking
NAGOYA SOGO	In	Banking

TOYOTA

1 B 2 b
TOYOTA MOTOR	Mi	Automobile
TOYOTA AUTO BODY	In	Automobile
VICTOR COMPANY OF JAPAN	In	Electrics

SANWA & FUYO GROUPS (NISSAN)

2 B 1 b (1)
NIIGATA ENGINEERING	Dk	Machinery
HITACHI	Fu	Electrics
CANON	Fu	Prec.equip
KUBOTA	Fu	Machinery
NISSHINBO INDUSTRIES	Fu	Textile
HITACHI ZOSEN	Sa	Shipyard
HITACHI CABLE	Sa	Light metal
FUJISAWA PHARM.	Sa	Pharm.
HITACHI CHEMICAL	Sa	Chemicals
TEIJIN	Sa	Textile
ITOHAM FOODS	Sa	Food
SNOW BRAND MILK	In	Food
KOMATSU	In	Machinery
NIPPON SUISAN KAISHA	In	Fishing
NIPPON (JUJO) PAPER	In	Paper
YAMAZAKI BAKING	In	Food
BRIDGESTONE	In	Rubber
KOKUYO	In	Gen. manuf.
SHIONOGI &	In	Pharm.
KURABO INDUSTRIES	In	Textile
DAIWABO	In	Textile

TOYOTA GROUP

2 B 1 b (2)
TOSHIBA	Mi	Electrics
DAIHATSU MOTOR	Sa	Automobile
SHARP	Sa	Electrics
HINO MOTORS	In	Automobile
TOYOTA AUTOMATIC LOOM	In	Machinery
KANEKA (KANEGAFUCHI)	In	Chemicals
FUJIYA	In	Food
TOMEN (TOYO MENKA)	In	Trade
SUZUKI MOTOR	In	Automobile

DKB & SUMITOMO GROUPS

2 B 2 b (1)
FURUKAWA ELECTRIC	Dk	Light metal
KAWASAKI STEEL	Dk	Heavy metal
ISEKI	Dk	Machinery
FUJITSU	Dk	Electrics
EBARA	Dk	Machinery
ISHIK.-HARIMA HEAVY	Dk	Shipyard
KAWASAKI HEAVY	Dk	Shipyard
ASAHI CHEMICAL	Dk	Textile
NISSHIN FLOUR MILLING	Fu	Food
NIPPON SHEET GLASS	Su	Ceramics
NEC	Su	Electrics
SUMITOMO LIGHT METAL	Su	Light metal
SUMITOMO CHEMICAL	Su	Chemicals
MEIJI SEIKA KAISHA	In	Food
MEIJI MILK	In	Food
Q. P. CORP.	In	Food
TOKYU CAR CORP.	In	Transport
PRIMA MEAT PACKERS	In	Food
TOYO KOHAN	In	Heavy metal
ARABIAN OIL	In	Mining
DAIKEN TRADE & INDUSTRY	In	Gen. manuf.
SANKYO ALUMINUM	In	Light metal

MITSUI & DKB GROUPS

2 B 2 b (2)
DENKI KAGAKU KOGYO	Dk	Chemicals
HONSHU PAPER	Dk	Paper
KANEMATSU GOSHO	Dk	Trade
TORAY INDUSTRIES	Mi	Light metal
MITSUI MINING & SMELTING	Mi	Textile
MITSUI MINING	Mi	Mining
MITSUI TOATSU CHEMICALS	Mi	Chemicals
MITSUI PETROCHEMICAL	Mi	Chemicals
NIPPON FLOUR MILLS	Mi	Food
MITSUI ENGIN. & SHIPBLDG	Mi	Shipyard
OJI PAPER	Mi	Paper
(CHICHIBU) ONODA CEMENT	Mi	Ceramics
THE JAPAN STEEL WORKS	Mi	Heavy metal
MITSUI & CO	Mi	Trade
SUMITOMO (OSAKA) CEMENT	Su	Ceramics
KOA OIL	In	Oil
MORINAGA MILK	In	Food
TOYO SEIKAN KAISHA	In	Light metal
NIPPON MEAT PACKERS	In	Food
KYOKUYO	In	Fishing
ALPS ELECTRIC	In	Electrics
DAICEL CHEMICAL	In	Chemicals
TOSOH	In	Chemicals

119

Table 3.4. CONCOR Partitioning of 259 Japanese Firms, 1993

1 A & B

CITY & TRUST BANKS

1 A 1 a

Firm		Sector
DAI-ICHI KANGYO	Dk	Banking
FUJI	Fu	Banking
YASUDA TRUST	Fu	Banking
MITSUI TRUST	Mi	Banking
TOYO TRUST	Sa	Banking
SANWA	Sa	Banking
SUMITOMO	Su	Banking
CHUO TRUST	In	Banking
INT'L BANK JAPAN	In	Banking

1 A 1 b

Firm		Sector
TOKIO MARINE & FIRE	Mb	Insurance
MITSUBISHI	Mb	Banking
MITSUBISHI TRUST	Mb	Banking
SUMITOMO TRUST	Su	Banking

REGIONAL BANKS

1 A 2 a

Firm		Sector
MITSUI (Sakura)	Mi	Banking
TAISHO MARINE & FIRE	Mi	Insurance
LTCREDIT	In	Banking
NIPPON CREDIT	In	Banking
BANK OF TOKYO	In	Banking
HOKKAIDO TAKUSHOKU	In	Banking
TOKAI	In	Banking
DAIWA	In	Banking
TAIYO KOBE	In	Banking

1 A 2 b

Firm		Sector
SAITAMA	In	Banking
KYOWA	In	Banking
BANK YOKOHAMA	In	Banking

1 B 1 a

Firm		Sector
NISSAN FIRE & MARINE	Dk	Insurance
HOKURIKU	In	Banking

2 A 1

(NISSAN) FUYO

2 A 1 a

Firm		Sector
SHISEIDO	Dk	Chemicals
YASUDA FIRE & MARINE	Fu	Insurance
NISSAN MOTOR	Fu	Automobile
CHIYODA FIRE & MARINE	In	Insurance
NIKKO SECURITIES	In	Securities
RICOH	In	Prec. equip.
NISSAN SHATAI	In	Automobile
FUJI FIRE & MARINE	In	Insurance
YAMAHA MOTOR	In	Automobile
YAMAHA CORP.	In	Gen. manuf.
DAIWA SECURITIES	In	Securities
DAI NIPPON PRINTING	In	Gen. manuf.
KAO CORP.	In	Chemicals
TAKEDA CHEMICAL	In	Pharm.
HOUSE FOOD INDUSTRIAL	In	Food
YAMAICHI SECURITIES	In	Securities
KOMATSU	In	Machinery

MATSUSHITA GROUP

2 A 1 b

Firm		Sector
SUMITOMO MARINE & FIRE	Su	Insurance
MARUDAI FOOD	In	Food
TOKYO SANYO ELECTRIC	In	Electronics
SANYO ELECTRIC	In	Electronics
MATSUSHITA DENKO	In	Electronics
TDK	In	Electronics
MATSUSHITA ELECTRIC	In	Electronics
VICTOR COMPANY OF JAPAN	In	Electronics
MATSUSHITA-KOTOBUKI	In	Electronics
MATSUSHITA COMMUNICATION	In	Electronics
MATSUSHITA REGRIGERATION	In	Electronics

2 A 2

SANWA & FUYO (HITACHI & NIPPON STEEL)

2 A 2 a (1)

Firm		Sector
ASAHI CHEMICAL	Dk	Textile
KUBOTA	Fu	Machinery
NIPPON KOKAN	Fu	Heavy metal
HITACHI	Fu	Electronics
NIPPON SEIKO	Fu	Machinery
NIPPON REIZO	Fu	Food
HITACHI CHEMICAL	Sa	Chemicals
HITACHI METALS	Sa	Heavy metal
HITACHI ZOSEN	Sa	Shipyard
TEIGIN	Sa	Textile
COSMO OIL	Sa	Oil
NAKAYAMA STEEL WORKS	Sa	Heavy metal
NISSHIN STEEL	Sa	Heavy metal
NICHIMEN	Sa	Trade
FUJISAWA PHARMACEUTICAL	Sa	Pharm.
SNOW BRAND MILK	Sa	Food
DAIKYO OIL	In	Oil
TOSOH	In	Chemicals
EZAKI GLICO	In	Food
TOKYO STEEL	In	Heavy metal
NIPPON STEEL	In	Heavy metal
KURARAY	In	Textile

SUMITOMO GROUP

2 A 2 a (2)

Firm		Sector
ITOCHU (C. Itoh)	Dk	Trade
SUMITOMO CHEMICAL	Su	Chemicals
SUMITOMO METAL INDUSTRIES	Su	Heavy metal
SUMITOMO LIGHT METAL	Su	Light metal
SUMITOMO METAL MINING	Su	Light metal
NEC	Su	Electronics
SUMITOMO HEAVY INDUSTRIES	Su	Machinery
SUMITOMO ELECTRIC	Su	Light metal
SUMITOMO (OSAKA) CEMENT	Su	Ceramics
SUMITOMO CORP	Su	Trade
MAZDA MOTOR	In	Automobile
RENGO	In	Paper
SANKYO ALUMINUM	In	Light metal
DAIKIN INDUSTRIES	In	Machinery
SHIONOGI & CO.	In	Pharm.
AICHI MACHINE	In	Automobile

2 B 1

INDEPENDENTS

2 B 1 a (1)

Firm		Sector
ITOHAM FOODS	Sa	Food
NICHIDO FIRE & MARINE	In	Banking
NISSHIN FOOD PRODUCTS	In	Food
NIPPON MEAT PACKERS	In	Food
NOMURA SECURITIES	In	Banking
PIONEER ELECTRONIC	In	Electronics
FUJI PHOTO FILM	In	Chemicals
TOPPAN PRINTING	In	Gen. manuf.

TOYOTA GROUP

2 B 1 a (2)

Firm		Sector
DAIHATSU MOTOR	Sa	Automobile
AISIN SEIKI	In	Automobile
AICHI STEEL WORKS	In	Heavy metal
KANTO AUTO WORKS	In	Machinery
KOYO SEIKO	In	Machinery
TOYOTA AUTO BODY	In	Automobile
TOYOTA AUTOMATIC LOOM	In	Machinery

2 B 2

DKB & FUYO GROUPS

2 B 2 a

Firm		Sector
ISHIK.-HARIMA HEAVY	Dk	Shipyard
FURUKAWA ELECTRIC	Dk	Light metal
NIIGATA ENGINEERING	Dk	Machinery
KYOWA HAKKO KOGYO	Dk	Chemicals
ISEKI	Fu	Machinery
SAPPORO BREWERIES	Fu	Food
MARUBENI	Fu	Trade
NISSHIN FLOUR MILLING	Fu	Food
SHOWA DENKO	Fu	Chemicals
OKI ELECTRIC	Fu	Electronics
SHARP	Sa	Electronics
DAI-TOKYO FIRE & MARINE	In	Banking
DOWA MINING	In	Light metal
TOKYU CAR CORP.	In	Transport
SUZUKI MOTOR	In	Automobile
YAMAZAKI BAKING	In	Food
NIPPON OIL	In	Oil
DAINIPPON INK & CHEMICALS	In	Chemicals
FUJI HEAVY	In	Automobile
NISSAN DIESEL MOTOR	In	Automobile
KAYABA INDUSTRY	In	Automobile
NISSAN CHEMICAL	In	Chemicals
SHOWA ALUMINUM	In	Light metal
TOPY INDUSTRIES	In	Transport
YODOGAWA STEEL WORKS	In	Heavy metal
DAISHOWA PAPER	In	Paper
TOSHIN STEEL	In	Heavy metal

DKB & FUYO GROUP

1 B 1 b — TOYOTA

TOYOTA MOTOR	Mi	Auto
NIPPON FIRE & MARINE	In	Banking
NAGOYA SOGO	In	Banking

1 B 2 a — REGIONALS

SHIZUOKA	In	Banking
GUNMA	In	Banking
JOYO	In	Banking
ASHIKAGA	In	Banking
CHIBA	In	Banking

1 B 2 b — MUTUAL BANKS

TOKYO SOGO	In	Banking
BANK HIROSHIMA	In	Banking
BANK FUKUOKA	In	Banking
KINKI SOGO	In	Banking
NISHI-NIPPON SOGO	In	Banking
HYOGO SOGO	In	Banking

2 A 2 b — MITSUBISHI GROUP

LION	Dk	Chemicals
SHOWA SHELL SEKIYU	Dk	Oil
NISSHINBO INDUSTRIES	Fu	Textile
MITSUBISHI HEAVY INDUSTRIES	Mb	Shipyard
MITSUBISHI GAS CHEMICAL	Mb	Chemicals
MITSUBISHI CHEMICAL	Mb	Chemicals
MITSUBISHI OIL	Mb	Oil
MITSUBISHI PAPER MILLS	Mb	Paper
ASAHI GLASS	Mb	Ceramics
KIRIN BREWERY	Mb	Food
MITSUBISHI MINING & CEMENT	Mb	Ceramics
MITSUBISHI MATERIALS	Mb	Light metal
NIHON NOSAN KOGYO	In	Food
KONISHIROKU PHOTO	In	Chemicals
TOTO	In	Ceramics
SHIN-ETSU CHEMICAL	In	Chemicals
KIKKOMAN	In	Food
NISSHIN OIL MILLS	In	Food
TOYO INK MFG	In	Chemicals
AJINOMOTO	In	Food
TOYOBO	In	Textile
MARUHA (TAIYO FISHERY)	In	Fishing
MEIJI MILK	In	Food
MORINAGA & CO.	In	Food

2 B 1 b — MITSUI, DKB & SANWA GROUPS

SANKYO	Dk	Pharm.
KAWASAKI STEEL	Dk	Heavy metal
KANEMATSU GOSHO	Dk	Trade
DENKI KAGAKU KOGYO	Dk	Chemicals
HONSHU PAPER	Dk	Paper
SANYO-KOKUSAKU PULP	Fu	Paper
TOSHIBA	Mi	Electronics
(CHICHIBU) ONODA CEMENT	Mi	Ceramics
MITSUI & CO	Mi	Trade
NIPPON FLOUR MILLS	Mi	Food
MITSUI ENGIN. & SHIPBUILDG	Mi	Shipyard
MITSUI PETROCHEMICAL	Mi	Chemicals
MITSUI MINING	Mi	Mining
MITSUI TOATSU CHEMICALS	Mi	Chemicals
MITSUI MINING & SMELTING	Mi	Light metal
TORAY INDUSTRIES	Mi	Textile
OJI PAPER	Mi	Paper
THE JAPAN STEEL WORKS	Mi	Heavy metal
UNITIKA	Sa	Textile
UBE INDUSTRIES	Sa	Chemicals
SEKISUI CHEMICAL	Sa	Chemicals
NIPPON SHEET GLASS	Su	Ceramics
TOMEN (TOYO MENKA)	In	Trade
NIPPON MINING	In	Light metal
DAICEL CHEMICAL	In	Chemicals
CENTRAL GLASS	In	Chemicals
KANEKA (KANEGAFUCHI)	In	Chemicals
TOYO SEIKAN KAISHA	In	Light metal
ASAHI BREWERIES	In	Food
FUJIKURA	In	Light metal
KANEBO	In	Textile
NITTO BOSEKI	In	Textile
KURABO INDUSTRIES	In	Textile
KYOKUYO	In	Fishing
BROTHER INDUSTRIES	In	Machinery
HINO MOTORS	In	Automobile
KOA OIL	In	Oil
ALPS ELECTRIC	In	Electronics
OMRON TATEISI ELECTRONICS	In	Electronics

2 B 2 b — DKB, SANWA, MITSUBISHI & FUYO GROUPS

NIPPON LIGHT METAL	Dk	Light metal
FUJITSU	Dk	Electronics
EBARA	Dk	Machinery
FUJI ELECTRIC	Dk	Electronics
NIPPON ZEON	Dk	Chemicals
YOKOHAMA RUBBER	Dk	Rubber
KAWASAKI HEAVY	Dk	Shipyard
ISUZU MOTORS	Dk	Automobile
NIHON CEMENT	Fu	Ceramics
CANON	Fu	Prec. equip.
TOA NENRYO KOGYO	Fu	Oil
MITSUBISHI ELECTRIC	Mb	Electronics
MITSUBISHI RAYON	Mb	Textile
MITSUBISHI PETROCHEMICAL	Mb	Chemicals
MITSUBISHI CORP	Mb	Trade
KOBE STEEL	Sa	Heavy metal
NTN TOYO BEARING	Sa	Machinery
'TANABE SEIYAKU	Sa	Pharm.
HITACHI CABLE	Sa	Light metal
TOYO TIRE & RUBBER	Sa	Rubber
NISSHO IWAI	Sa	Trade
GUNZE	In	Textile
SONY	In	Electronics
BRIDGESTONE	In	Rubber
MEIJI SEIKA KAISHA	In	Food
Q. P. CORP.	In	Food
TOYO KOHAN	In	Heavy metal
KOKUYO	In	Gen. manuf.
ARABIAN OIL	In	Mining
DAIDO STEEL	In	Heavy metal
JAPAN SYNTHETIC RUBBER	In	Chemicals
MORINAGA MILK	In	Food
ZEXEL (DIESEL KIKI)	In	Machinery
SHOWA SANGYO	In	Food
PRIMA MEAT PACKERS	In	Food
DAIKEN TRADE & INDUSTRY	In	Gen. manuf.
DAIWABO	In	Textile
HONDA MOTOR	In	Automobile
NGK INSULATORS	In	Ceramics
FUJI KOSAN	In	Oil

Table 3.5. CONCOR Partitioning of 259 Japanese Firms, 1995

1 A & B

CITY & TRUST BANKS

1 A 1 a

Firm		
DAI-ICHI KANGYO	Dk	Banking
MITSUBISHI	Mb	Banking
MITSUBISHI TRUST	Mb	Banking
TOKIO MARINE & FIRE	Mb	Banking
SUMITOMO	Su	Banking
SUMITOMO TRUST	Su	Banking
BANK OF TOKYO	In	Banking
INTL BANK JAPAN	In	Banking

1 A 1 b

Firm		
FUJI	Fu	Banking
YASUDA TRUST	Fu	Banking
MITSUI (SAKURA)	Mi	Banking
MITSUI TRUST	Mi	Banking
SANWA	Sa	Banking
TOYO TRUST	Sa	Banking
KYOWA	In	Banking
SAITAMA	In	Banking
TOKAI	In	Banking
DAIWA	In	Banking
CHUO TRUST	In	Banking
LTCREDIT	In	Banking
NIPPON CREDIT	In	Banking
TAIYO KOBE	In	Banking

REGIONAL BANKS

1 A 2 a

Firm		
HOKKAIDO TAKUSHOKU	In	Banking
HOKURIKU	In	Banking
NIPPON FIRE & MARINE	In	Banking

1 A 2 b

Firm		
BANK YOKOHAMA	In	Banking
JOYO	In	Banking
SHIZUOKA	In	Banking
BANK FUKUOKA	In	Banking

1 B 1 a

Firm		
NISSAN FIRE & MARINE	Dk	Banking
CHIBA	In	Banking
ASHIKAGA	In	Banking
BANK HIROSHIMA	In	Banking

2 A 1

FUYO GROUP

2 A 1 a (1)

Firm		
ASAHI CHEMICAL	Dk	Textile
HITACHI	Fu	Electronics
NIPPON KOKAN	Fu	Heavy metal
TOA NENRYO KOGYO	Fu	Oil
NISSAN MOTOR	Fu	Automobile
SHOWA DENKO	Fu	Chemicals
SAPPORO BREWERIES	Fu	Food
NIHON CEMENT	Fu	Ceramics
TEIGIN	Sa	Textile
NIPPON STEEL	In	Heavy metal
YAMAHA MOTOR	In	Automobile
YAMAHA CORP.	In	Gen. manuf.
TOSOH	In	Chemicals
TOPY INDUSTRIES	In	Transport
SHOWA ALUMINUM	In	Light metal
KAYABA INDUSTRY	In	Automobile

DKB & SANWA GROUPS

2 A 1 a (2)

Firm		
NIPPON ZEON	Dk	Chemicals
NIPPON LIGHT METAL	Dk	Light metal
FUJI ELECTRIC	Dk	Electronics
HITACHI ZOSEN	Sa	Shipyard
HITACHI CHEMICAL	Sa	Chemicals
HITACHI METALS	Sa	Heavy metal
UNITIKA	Sa	Textile
KOMATSU	In	Machinery
NIPPON SUISAN	In	Fishing
NISSAN DIESEL	In	Automobile
AICHI MACHINE	In	Automobile
NISSAN CHEMICAL	In	Chemicals
DOWA MINING	In	Light metal
BRIDGESTONE	In	Rubber
KURARAY	In	Textile
SHOWA SANGYO	In	Food
ZEXEL (DIESEL KIKI)	In	Machinery

2 A 2

MITSUI GROUP

2 A 2 a (1)

Firm		
HONSHU PAPER	Dk	Paper
TORAY INDUSTRIES	Mi	Textile
MITSUI TOATSU	Mi	Chemicals
MITSUI MINING	Mi	Mining
MITSUI ENGIN. & SHIPBLDG	Mi	Shipyard
MITSUI PETROCHEMICAL	Mi	Chemicals
MITSUI MINING & SMELTING	Mi	Light metal
MITSUI & CO	Mi	Trade
TOSHIBA	Mi	Electronics
JAPAN STEEL	Mi	Heavy metal
NIPPON FLOUR	Mi	Food
NIPPON OIL	In	Oil
KURABO INDUSTRIES	In	Textile
FUJIKURA	In	Light metal
TOMEN (TOYO MENKA)	In	Trade
KANEKA (KANEGAFUCHI)	In	Chemicals
DAICEL CHEMICAL	In	Chemicals
NITTO BOSEKI	In	Textile
ALPS ELECTRIC	In	Electronics

TOYOTA GROUP

2 A 2 a (2)

Firm		
MARUBENI	Fu	Trade
TANABE SEIYAKU	Sa	Pharm.
DAIHATSU MOTOR	Sa	Automobile
TOYOTA AUTO BODY	In	Automobile
HINO MOTORS	In	Automobile
BROTHER INDUSTRIES	In	Machinery
KANTO AUTO	In	Automobile

2 B 1

FUYO, DKB, & SANWA GROUPS

2 B 1 a (1)

Firm		
MATSUSHITA ELECTRIC	In	Electronics
SANYO ELECTRIC	In	Electronics
TOKYO SANYO ELECTRIC	In	Electronics
SHIONOGI & CO.	In	Pharm.
MARUDAI FOOD	In	Food
MATSUSHITA DENKO	In	Electronics
MATSUSHITA COMMUNICATION	In	Electronics
MATSUSHITA KOTOBUKI	In	Electronics
MATSUSHITA REFRIGERATION	In	Electronics

2 B 1 a (2)

Firm		
EBARA	Dk	Machinery
KUBOTA	Fu	Machinery
CANON	Fu	Prec. equip
NISSHINBO INDUSTRIES	Fu	Textile
HITACHI CABLE	Sa	Light metal
SNOW BRAND MILK	In	Food
DAI NIPPON PRINTING	In	Gen. manuf.
KAO CORP.	In	Chemicals
HOUSE FOOD INDUSTRIAL	In	Food
KOKUYO	In	Gen. manuf.
EZAKI GLICO	In	Food
TOSHIN STEEL	In	Heavy metal
YODOGAWA STEEL	In	Heavy metal
DAIWABO	In	Textile

2B1b(1a)

ITOHAM FOODS	Sa	Food
SONY	In	Electronics
FUJI PHOTO FILM	In	Chemicals
VICTOR COMPANY OF JAPAN	In	Light metal
PIONEER ELECTRONIC	In	Electronics

TOYOTA GRP

2 B 1 b (1b)

NIPPONDENSO	In	Electronics
AISIN SEIKI	In	Machinery
KOYO SEIKO	In	Machinery
TOYODA AUTOMATIC LOOM	In	Machinery
AICHI STEEL	In	Heavy metal

2 B 2

MITSUBISHI GROUP

2 B 2 a (1)

Firm		
KIRIN BREWERY	Mb	Food
ASAHI GLASS	Mb	Ceramics
MITSUBISHI CORP	Mb	Trade
GUNZE	In	Textile
MORINAGA & CO.	In	Food
TOTO	In	Ceramics
OMRON TATEISI ELEC.	In	Electronics
NGK INSULATORS	In	Ceramics
AJINOMOTO	In	Food
TOPPAN PRINTING	In	Gen. manuf.
RICOH	In	Prec.equip
SUZUKI MOTOR	In	Automobile
FUJI KOSAN	In	Oil

DKB & FUYO

2 B 2 a (2)

Firm		
KYOWA HAKKO KOGYO	Dk	Chemicals
SHISEIDO	Dk	Chemicals
LION	Fu	Machinery
NIPPON SEIKO	In	Machinery
NISSAN SHATAI	In	Automobile
TDK CORP.	In	Electronics

FOOD INDUSTRY

2 B 2 b

Firm		
NISSHIN FLOUR MILLING	Fu	Food
SUMITOMO FORESTRY	Su	Forestry
SUMITOMO CORP.	Su	Trade
TAKEDA CHEMICAL	In	Pharm.
KIKKOMAN	In	Food
Q. P. CORP.	In	Food
YAMAZAKI BAKING	In	Food
NISSHIN OIL MILLS	In	Food
NIPPON MEAT PACKERS	In	Food
NISSHIN FOOD	In	Food

FIRE & MAR. INS

1 B 1 b

YASUDA FIRE & MARINE	Fu	Banking
SUMITOMO MARINE & FIRE	Su	Banking
GUNMA	In	Banking
DAI-TOKYO FIRE & MARINE	In	Banking
FUJI FIRE & MARINE	In	Banking
CHIYODA FIRE & MARINE	In	Banking

MUTUAL BANKS & SECURITIES

1 B 2 a

TAISHO MARINE & FIRE	Mi	Banking
KINKI SOGO	In	Banking
TOKYO SOGO	In	Banking
HYOGO SOGO	In	Banking
NAGOYA SOGO	In	Banking
NIPPON MINING	In	Light metal
NOMURA SECURITIES	In	Banking
NIKKO SECURITIES	In	Banking
YAMAICHI SECURITIES	In	Banking
DAIWA SECURITIES	In	Banking

TOYOTA

1 B 2 b

TOYOTA MOTOR	Mi	Automobile
NICHIDO FIRE & MARINE	In	Banking
NISHI-NIPPON SOGO	In	Banking

MITSUBISHI GROUP

2 A 1 b (1a)

YOKOHAMA RUBBER	Dk	Rubber
MITSUBISHI HEAVY	Mb	Shipyard
MITSUBISHI ELECTRIC	Mb	Electronics
MITSUBISHI OIL	Mb	Oil
MITSUBISHI CHEMICAL	Mb	Chemicals
MITSUBISHI PETROCHEM.	Mb	Chemicals
MITSUBISHI MATERIALS (METAL)	Mb	Light metal
MITSUBISHI MINING & CEMENT	Mb	Ceramics
MITSUBISHI RAYON	Mb	Textile
MITSUBISHI GAS CHEMICAL	Mb	Chemicals
MITSUBISHI PAPER MILLS	Mb	Paper
DAINIPPON INK	In	Chemicals
MEIJI SEIKA KAISHA	In	Food
NIHON NOSAN KOGYO	In	Food
SHIN-ETSU CHEMICAL	In	Chemicals
MARUHA (TAIYO FISHERY)	In	Fishing
TOYOBO	In	Textile
NICHIRO GYOGYO	In	Fishing

SANWA GROUP

2 A 1 b (1b)

ISUZU MOTORS	Dk	Automobile
COSMO OIL	Sa	Oil
NISSHO IWAI	Sa	Trade
NISSHIN STEEL	Sa	Heavy metal
TOYO TIRE & RUBBER	Sa	Rubber
NICHIMEN	Sa	Trade
HONDA MOTOR	In	Automobile
DAIKYO OIL	In	Oil
DAIDO STEEL	In	Heavy metal
KONISHIROKU PHOTO	In	Chemicals
TOYO INK MFG	In	Chemicals

SUMITOMO GROUP

2 A 1 b (2)

SHOWA SHELL SEKIYU	Dk	Oil
KAWASAKI HEAVY	Dk	Shipyard
ITOCHU (C. Itoh)	Dk	Trade
UBE INDUSTRIES	Sa	Chemicals
TOKUYAMA SODA	Sa	Chemicals
NTN TOYO BEARING	Sa	Machinery
NAKAYAMA STEEL	Sa	Heavy metal
SUMITOMO METAL	Su	Heavy metal
SUMITOMO CHEMICAL	Su	Chemicals
SUMITOMO LIGHT METAL	Su	Light metal
SUMITOMO (OSAKA) CEMENT	Su	Ceramics
NEC	Su	Electronics
SUMITOMO HEAVY	Su	Machinery
SUMITOMO METAL MINING	Su	Light metal
NIPPON SHEET GLASS	Su	Ceramics
MAZDA MOTOR	In	Automobile
JAPAN SYNTHETIC RUBBER	In	Chemicals
RENGO	In	Paper
SANKYO ALUMINUM	In	Light metal
MEIJI MILK	In	Food
DAIKIN INDUSTRIES	In	Machinery
TOKYU CAR CORP.	In	Transport

DKB GROUP

2 A 2 b

KAWASAKI STEEL	Dk	Heavy metal
ISHIK.-HARIMA HEAVY	Dk	Shipyard
FURUKAWA ELECTRIC	Dk	Light metal
NIIGATA ENGINEERING	Dk	Machinery
FUJITSU	Dk	Electronics
KANEMATSU GOSHO	Dk	Trade
DENKI KAGAKU KOGYO	Dk	Chemicals
SANYO-KOKUSAKU PULP	Fu	Paper
OKI ELECTRIC	Fu	Electronics
OJI PAPER	Mi	Paper
(CHICHIBU) ONODA CEMENT	Mi	Ceramics
PRIMA MEAT PACKERS	In	Food
FUJIYA	In	Food
KANEBO	In	Textile
NIPPON (JUJO) PAPER	In	Paper
FUJI HEAVY	In	Automobile
KOA OIL	In	Oil
DAISHOWA PAPER	In	Paper
CENTRAL GLASS	In	Chemicals
DAIKEN TRADE & INDUSTRY	In	Gen. manuf.
ARABIAN OIL	In	Mining
ASAHI BREWERIES	In	Food
KYOKUYO	In	Fishing
TOYO KOHAN	In	Heavy metal
MORINAGA MILK	In	Food

DKB & SANWA

2 B 1 b (2)

SANKYO	Dk	Pharm.
ISEKI	Dk	Machinery
SHARP	Sa	Electronics
SEKISUI CHEMICAL	Sa	Chemicals
FUJISAWA PHARM.	Sa	Pharm.

123

Table 3.6. CONCOR Partitioning of 259 Japanese Firms, 1997

1 A & B — CITY & TRUST BANKS / REGIONAL BANKS & INSURANCE

1 A 1 a
DAI-ICHI KANGYO	Dk	Banking
MITSUBISHI	Mb	Banking
MITSUBISHI TRUST	Mb	Banking
SANWA	Sa	Banking
TOYO TRUST	Sa	Banking
INT'L BANK JAPAN	In	Banking
LTCREDIT	In	Banking
NIPPON CREDIT	In	Banking
BANK OF TOKYO	In	Banking

1 A 1 b
MITSUI (SAKURA)	Mi	Banking
MITSUI TRUST	Mi	Banking
TOKAI	In	Banking
TAIYO KOBE	In	Banking
SHIZUOKA	In	Banking
CHUO TRUST	In	Banking

1 A 2 a
FUJI	Fu	Banking
YASUDA TRUST	Fu	Banking
SUMITOMO	In	Banking
SUMITOMO TRUST	In	Banking

1 A 2 b
KYOWA	In	Banking
SAITAMA	In	Banking

1 B 1 a
NISSAN FIRE & FIRE	Dk	Banking
HOKKAIDO TAKUSHOKU	In	Banking
BANK YOKOHAMA	In	Banking
HOKURIKU	In	Banking
DAI-TOKYO FIRE & MARINE	In	Banking
FUJI FIRE & MARINE	In	Banking
CHIYODA FIRE & MARINE	In	Banking
CHIBA	In	Banking
BANK HIROSHIMA	In	Banking
GUNMA	In	Banking
NIPPON FIRE & MARINE	In	Banking

1 B 1 b
TOKIO MARINE & FIRE	Mb	Banking
YASUDA FIRE & MARINE	Fu	Banking
SUMITOMO MARINE & FIRE	Su	Banking
DAIWA	In	Banking

2 A 1 — SANWA GROUP / MITSUBISHI & DKB / MATSUSHITA GROUP

2 A 1 a (1)
EBARA	Dk	Machinery
NIPPON SEIKO	Fu	Machinery
SEKISUI CHEMICAL	Sa	Chemicals
FUJISAWA PHARMACEUTICAL	Sa	Pharm.
NTN TOYO BEARING	Sa	Machinery
JOYO	In	Banking
SUMITOMO FORESTRY	In	Forestry
KIKKOMAN	In	Food
TOTO	In	Ceramics
TOYO INK MFG	In	Chemicals
NGK INSULATORS	In	Ceramics
JAPAN SYNTHETIC RUBBER	In	Chemicals
DAIWABO	In	Textile

2 A 1 a (2)
LION	Dk	Chemicals
SHISEIDO	Dk	Chemicals
NISSHIN FLOUR MILLING	Fu	Food
MITSUBISHI CORP	Mb	Trade
ASAHI GLASS	Mb	Ceramics
BANK FUKUOKA	In	Banking
AJINOMOTO	In	Food
RICOH	In	Prec. equip
GUNZE	In	Textile
Q. P. CORP.	In	Food
SHIN-ETSU CHEMICAL	In	Chemicals
NISSHIN FOOD PRODUCTS	In	Food

2 A 1 b (1)
MATSUSHITA ELECTRIC	In	Electronics
MATSUSHITA DENKO	In	Electronics
SANYO ELECTRIC	In	Electronics
TOKYO SANYO ELECTRIC	In	Electronics
SHIONOGI & CO.	In	Pharm.
VICTOR COMPANY OF JAPAN	In	Electronics
MATSUSHITA REFRIGERATION	In	Electronics
MATSUSHITA COMMUNICATION	In	Electronics
MATSUSHITA-KOTOBUKI ELEC.	In	Electronics
MARUDAI FOOD	In	Food
EZAKI GLICO	In	Food
HOUSE FOOD INDUSTRIAL	In	Food
TOKYO STEEL	In	Heavy metal

2 A 2 — MITSUI GROUP / TOYOTA GROUP / SANWA & DKB GROUPS

2 A 2 a
SANKYO	Sa	Pharm.
MITSUI TOATSU CHEMICALS	Mi	Chemicals
SONY	In	Electronics
FUJI PHOTO FILM	In	Chemicals
NIPPON MEAT PACKERS	In	Food
TOPPAN PRINTING	In	Gen. manuf.
TOYO SEIKAN KAISHA	In	Light metal

2 A 2 b (1)
ITOHAM FOODS	Sa	Food
DAIHATSU MOTOR	In	Automobile
NIPPONDENSO	In	Electronics
AISIN SEIKI	In	Automobile
TOYOTA AUTO BODY	In	Automobile
KOYO SEIKO	In	Machinery
TOYODA AUTOMATIC LOOM	In	Machinery
AICHI STEEL WORKS	In	Heavy metal
HINO MOTORS	In	Automobile
PIONEER ELECTRONIC	In	Electronics
SUZUKI MOTOR	In	Automobile

2 A 2 b (2)
ISUZU MOTORS	In	Automobile
NIPPON ZEON	Dk	Chemicals
ASAHI CHEMICAL	Fu	Textile
SHOWA DENKO	Fu	Chemicals
COSMO OIL	Sa	Oil

2 B 1 — HITACHI / FUYO GROUP / SUMITOMO GROUP

2 B 1 a (1)
HITACHI	Fu	Electronics
TEIGIN	Sa	Textile
HITACHI ZOSEN	Sa	Shipyard
HITACHI METALS	Sa	Heavy metal
HITACHI CHEMICAL	Sa	Chemicals
KOMATSU	In	Machinery
DOWA MINING	In	Light metal

2 B 1 a (2)
NISSAN MOTOR	Fu	Automobile
NIPPON KOKAN	Fu	Heavy metal
NIPPON REIZO	Fu	Food
NIHON CEMENT	Fu	Ceramics
SAPPORO BREWERIES	Fu	Food
NISSAN DIESEL MOTOR	In	Automobile
DAISHOWA PAPER	In	Paper
TOPY INDUSTRIES	In	Transport
SHOWA ALUMINUM	In	Light metal
KAYABA INDUSTRY	In	Automobile
FUJI HEAVY	In	Automobile
ZEXEL (DIESEL KIKI)	In	Machinery
SNOW BRAND MILK	In	Food
NIPPON SUISAN KAISHA	In	Fishing
NISSAN CHEMICAL	In	Chemicals
YAMAHA CORP.	In	Gen. manuf.

2 B 1 b (1)
SUMITOMO METAL INDUSTRIES	Su	Heavy metal
SUMITOMO CHEMICAL	Su	Chemicals
SUMITOMO ELEC	Su	Light metal
SUMITOMO OSAKA CEMENT	Su	Ceramics
NEC	Su	Electronics
SUMITOMO HEAVY MINING	Su	Light metal
SUMITOMO METAL MINING	Su	Light metal
NIPPON SHEET GLASS	Su	Ceramics
SUMITOMO CORP	Su	Trade
DAIKIN INDUSTRIES	In	Machinery
SANKYO ALUMINUM	In	Light metal
MAZDA MOTOR	In	Automobile

2 B 2 — MITSUI GROUP / DKB & SANWA GROUPS

2 B 2 a (1)
HONSHU PAPER	Dk	Paper
DENKI KAGAKU KOGYO	Dk	Chemicals
OKI ELECTRIC	Fu	Electronics
TORAY INDUSTRIES	Mi	Textile
MITSUI ENG. & SHIPBLDG	Mi	Chemicals
OJI PAPER	Mi	Paper
(CHICHIBU) ONODA CEMENT	Mi	Ceramics
MITSUI PETROCHEMICAL	Mi	Chemicals
MITSUI &CO	Mi	Trade
MITSUI MINING & SMELTING	Mi	Light metal
JAPAN STEEL WORKS	Mi	Heavy metal
TOSHIBA	Mi	Electronics
MITSUI MINING	Mi	Mining
TANABE SEIYAKU	Sa	Pharm.
KURABO INDUSTRIES	In	Textile
KANEKA (KANEGAFUCHI)	In	Chemicals
CENTRAL GLASS	In	Chemicals
DAICEL CHEMICAL	In	Chemicals
KANEBO	In	Textile
KANTO AUTO WORKS	In	Automobile
FUJIKURA	In	Oil
NIPPON OIL	In	Oil
BROTHER INDUSTRIES	In	Machinery
ALPS ELECTRIC	In	Electronics
KOA OIL	In	Oil
TOMEN (TOYO MENKA)	In	Trade

2 B 2 a (2)
KAWASAKI STEEL	Dk	Heavy metal
FURUKAWA ELECTRIC	Dk	Machinery
NIIGATA ENGINEERING	Dk	Machinery
ISHIK-HARIMA HEAVY	Dk	Shipyard
NIPPON LIGHT METAL	Dk	Light metal
KOBE STEEL	Sa	Heavy metal
NISSHIN STEEL	Sa	Heavy metal
TOYO TIRE & RUBBER	Sa	Rubber
ARABIAN OIL	Sa	Oil
KYOKUYO	In	Fishing
YAMAZAKI BAKING	In	Food
FUJIYA	In	Food
PRIMA MEAT PACKERS	In	Food

DAIKEN TRADE & INDUSTRY	In	Gen. manuf.
ASAHI BREWERIES	In	Food
RENGO	In	Paper
TOYO KOHAN	In	Heavy metal

124

1 B 2 a — TOYOTA

TOYOTA MOTOR	Mi	Automobile
ASHIKAGA	In	Banking
NICHIDO FIRE & MARINE	In	Banking
NISHI-NIPPON SOGO	In	Banking

1 B 2 b (1) — MUTUAL BKS & SECURITIES

TAISHO MARINE & FIRE	Mi	Banking
NOMURA SECURITIES	In	Banking
KINKI SOGO	In	Banking
NAGOYA SOGO	In	Banking
TOKYO SOGO	In	Banking
HYOGO SOGO	In	Banking
NIKKO SECURITIES	In	Banking
DAIWA SECURITIES	In	Banking
YAMAICHI SECURITIES	In	Banking

1 B 2 b (2)

NIPPON MINING	In	Light metal

2 A 1 b (2) — FUYO & SANWA GROUPS

KYOWA HAKKO KOGYO	Dk	Chemicals
KUBOTA	Fu	Machinery
CANON	Fu	Prec equip
NISSHINBO INDUSTRIES	Fu	Textile
SHARP	Sa	Electronics
HITACHI CABLE	Sa	Light metal
YODOGAWA STEEL	In	Heavy metal
NISSAN SHATAI	In	Automobile
AICHI MACHINE	In	Automobile
BRIDGESTONE	In	Rubber
DAI NIPPON PRINTING	In	Gen. manuf.
YAMAHA MOTOR	In	Automobile
KAO CORP.	In	Chemicals
TOSHIN STEEL	In	Heavy metal
KOKUYO	In	Gen. manuf.

2 B 1 b (2) — DKB GROUP

FUJITSU	Dk	Electronics
FUJI ELECTRIC	Dk	Electronics
ISEKI	Dk	Machinery
YOKOHAMA RUBBER	Dk	Rubber
KAWASAKI HEAVY	Dk	Shipyard
SANYO-KOKUSAKU PULP	Fu	Paper
NIPPON FLOUR MILLS	Mi	Food
TOKUYAMA SODA	Sa	Chemicals
TOYOBO	In	Textile
KURARAY	In	Textile
NITTO BOSEKI	In	Fishing
NICHIRO GYOGYO KAISHA	In	Textile
SHOWA SANGYO	In	Food
MARUHA (TAIYO FISHERY)	In	Fishing
NIPPON (JUJO) PAPER	In	Paper

2 B 2 b (1) — MITSUBISHI GROUP

MITSUBISHI HEAVY INDUSTRIES	Mb	Shipyard
MITSUBISHI OIL	Mb	Oil
MITSUBISHI MATERIALS (METAL)	Mb	Light metal
MITSUBISHI MINING & CEMENT	Mb	Ceramics
MITSUBISHI RAYON	Mb	Textile
MITSUBISHI GAS CHEMICAL	Mb	Chemicals
MITSUBISHI PAPER MILLS	Mb	Paper
MITSUBISHI ELECTRIC	Mb	Electronics
MITSUBISHI CHEMICAL	Mb	Chemicals
MITSUBISHI PETROCHEMICAL	Mb	Chemicals
KIRIN BREWERY	Mb	Food
NICHIMEN	Sa	Trade
DAINIPPON INK & CHEMICALS	In	Chemicals
FUJI KOSAN	In	Oil
NISSHIN OIL MILLS	In	Food
MORINAGA & CO.	In	Food
OMRON TATEISI ELECTRONICS	In	Electronics
KONISHIROKU PHOTO	In	Chemicals

2 B 2 b (2) — TRADING COMPANIES

KANEMATSU GOSHO	Dk	Trade
SHOWA SHELL SEKIYU	Dk	Oil
ITOCHU (C. Itoh)	Dk	Trade
TOA NENRYO KOGYO	Fu	Oil
MARUBENI	Fu	Trade
NISSHO IWAI	Sa	Trade
HONDA MOTOR	In	Automobile
MEIJI MILK	In	Food
MEIJI SEIKA KAISHA	In	Food
TOKYU CAR CORP.	In	Transport
MORINAGA MILK	In	Food
NIHON NOSAN KOGYO	In	Food

125

The trust banks are generally assigned to the same blocks as the city banks, and, within them, to horizontal groups. The year 1989 is the one year this pattern does not hold. Then, *1A2a* is a trust bank cluster, and the city banks are grouped in *1A1*. The *sogo* banks form a cluster along with regional banks and insurance companies. Four regional institutions – Shizuoka, Gunma, Joyo, Ashikaga, and Chiba – are together in each year. Three prominent regionals – Kyowa, Saitama, and Yokohama – occupy the elite position in 1978, 1986, and 1989 but are later reduced to the company of other regionals and insurers.[71] In passing, we note that the *1A2a* block in 1993 consists of a number of banks soon to experience severe financial distress: Daiwa, Hokkaido Takushoku, Long-Term Credit, and Nippon Credit.

CONCOR's separation of financials and industrials blurs in the late 1980s. A recurrent theme in our work is that the bubble era was an anomaly in Japan's post-war economic evolution and that some return to fundamentals occurred in the 1990s. In 1978, 1993, 1995, and 1997 a single industrial corporation – one often in Japanese business circles labeled as a bank to its vertical keiretsu network – shows up in the financial 1-block. That firm is Toyota, clustered with such Toyota- or Mitsui-leaning financials as Chiyoda Fire and Marine, Nagoya Sogo, and Taisho Marine. In 1986 and 1989 more industrials join the 1-block. These are Sanyo Electric, Toppan Printing, and Toyota Motor along with several Toyota keiretsu firms, Matsushita Electric, and Matsushita affiliate JVC. We see this 1989 pattern, in particular, as indicative of a breakdown in the financial–industrial division of labor in a volatile period when companies were substituting equity and bond issues for bank debt. By 1993, however, Toyota is again the only industrial in the financial position.

Until 1995, a few financials – securities firms and insurance companies – appear in the 2-block. One reason CONCOR paints them as industrials is that none is a top ten lender to any of the 259. In the last two years of the series, 1995 and 1997, however, only industrials occupy the 2-block.

The 2-block: Industrials. Again, the 1-block (financials) is subdivided functionally. The keiretsu alignments are minor ones. The picture is very different in the 2-block. Here, the principal divisions are keiretsu-based.[72]

---

[71] Note, again, that Kyowa and Saitama Banks merged in 1991 to form Asahi Bank.

[72] Our highly aggregated industry classification may, of course, dilute the industry effects. A more detailed classification might reveal structural equivalences based on input–output flows of materials and semi-finished goods within a single supply chain. In a sense, Toyota Motor's role as a financial in our blockmodels reflects an industry or functional logic of equivalence within the automotive sector and within the Toyota group. Toyota purchases materials and components from Denso, Aisin Seiki, and Aichi Steel, while it contracts

That keiretsu has been a powerful organizing principle of the post-war Japanese economy needs no belaboring. It is nonetheless striking how sharply these data reveal the contours of this distinctive form, which has no real parallel in other advanced economies. As for how that principle shapes the network over time, we observe both linear and curvilinear trends. There is significant deterioration in the keiretsu patterning of the network as a whole and in the structural integrity (boundedness and coherence) of the horizontal and vertical groups. At the same time, there are indications that some keiretsu clusterings that blurred in the late 1980s reappear in the 1990s, most notably the Mitsubishi and Sumitomo zaibatsu-based groups.

Trading Companies (Sogo Shosha)
The exception to the rule that keiretsu – not industry – organizes the 2-block is that in 1978 only a distinct trading company position, *2A1b*, exists.[73] The decline in the economic role of the sogo shosha has been much discussed.[74] At one time, these distinctive businesses performed crucial functions on which Japanese manufacturers were dependent. They handled overseas procurement of raw materials and the distribution of finished goods. They provided essential financial, administrative, and legal services, which manufacturers, for reasons of language and cultural insularity, were ill-equipped to handle. This was particularly true of the flagship shosha of the big-six groups: Mitsubishi Corporation, Mitsui and Company, Sumitomo Corporation, Marubeni (Fuyo), Nichimen (Sanwa), and Itochu and Kanematsu Gosho of DKB. Along with a prominent commercial bank and heavy manufacturer, the general trading companies were the leaders of their respective groups, orchestrating joint ventures, monitoring members' behavior, and, on occasion, launching rescues and restructurings. As Japanese firms acquired experience at maneuvering in a global environment – and as the rising complexity of their products put marketing and after-service beyond the shoshas' reach – the shoshas' mediating function diminished, and they sought new lines of business. These tended to be less Japan-dependent and so involved fewer transactions with Japanese firms. In 1978, five of the nine shosha occupied a single block (*2A1b*) that was heterogeneous in keiretsu makeup. In later

out final assembly of Toyota models to affiliates Kanto Auto Works, Hino, and Toyoda Automatic Loom.
[73] In 1997 – the last blockmodel year – we find four shosha in *2B2b(a)*, a mixed block with some Mitsubishi fellow travelers (Honda, Meiji Milk) and some affiliates of bank-centered groups. This is not a shosha cluster, however, for the next partition [*2B2b(2a)*] does not "wall off" the trading companies; it divides them.
[74] See, e.g., Gerlach (1992a:140–43); Hirschmeier and Yui (1975); Roehl (1983b); Sheard (1989b); Yoshihara and Yonekawa (1987); Yoshino and Lifson (1986).

years, however, the shosha generally align with their respective groups. This restructuring of the shosha position was completed by 1986. The only difference between the 1986 and the 1993 blockings in this respect is that in 1986 Sanwa trader Nissho Iwai is in a DKB block. In 1989 and 1993, however, Nissho Iwai is in a Sanwa block. Mitsubishi Corporation, by contrast, is farther from the main Mitsubishi cluster in 1993 than in 1986 or 1989. It appears with three other Mitsubishi firms in a large and diverse cluster dominated by the bank-centered groups (DKB, Sanwa, and Fuyo).

The changing network position of the shosha is at odds with our hypothesis that industry has superceded keiretsu as a network organizing principle. After 1978, they appear closer in the network to their historical keiretsu allies.[75] The shift might in part be due to keiretsu risk-sharing activity. As uncertainty over the shosha's economic future deepened, their respective groups may have channeled more business their way. Also, in the stepped-up global competition of the 1980s and 1990s, several groups launched large international ventures in which the shosha played coordinating roles. An example is the broad-based tie-up between the Mitsubishi and Daimler groups in the early 1990s.

Horizontal Keiretsu
Our remaining discussion of the 2-block considers one at a time the positions corresponding to particular horizontal and vertical keiretsu. A strong indication of each cluster's coherence and identity as a keiretsu is the extent to which shacho-kai and other known affiliates appear in it. A second criterion is the extent to which firms on other shacho-kai are excluded. Correspondence between a block and a group is indicated when the block contains only one group's shacho-kai and known noncouncil affiliates.

1. Sumitomo. The Sumitomo group is thought to be the most cohesive of the big six, with Mitsubishi a close runner-up.[76] Our cohesion analysis of the *Hakusui-ka* (Figure 3.2) agreed, and CONCOR does as well. The blockings in 1978 and 1986 show almost perfect correspondence between block and shacho-kai. In 1978, 2*B1a* holds thirteen *Hakusui-kai*

---

[75] Whereas the stacked clustering generated a functional shosha block only in 1978, an application of CONCOR to the trade matrices puts all the shosha in one block in each year (see Appendix 3.1). Thus, in the network of selling and buying transactions, the shosha position persists. However, its significance in terms of financial links and control and governance of the network is diminished.

[76] Among the reasons are its pre-war zaibatsu origins, Osaka business culture (viewed in Japanese business circles as more hard-edged than Tokyo's), and the small size of its shacho-kai.

members – all but the financials, Sumitomo Bank and Sumitomo Trust (in *1A1b*). Even Sumitomo Corporation, the group's flagship shosha, is there, unlike most traders this year (in *2A1b*). Just one firm – Cosmo Oil – comes from another council (Sanwa). The others present are independents with known Sumitomo leanings: Matsushita Electric, Mazda, Sanyo Electric, Asahi Breweries, and Daiwa Securities. Sumitomo is also easily identifiable in 1986 as *2A1b*. Here, no other shacho-kai are present, although compared to 1978 fewer Sumitomo-leaning independents appear. Among the departures are Matsushita, Daiwa Securities, and Komatsu.

In 1989, the height of the bubble, Sumitomo disintegrates. Five *Hakusui-kai* members go to a DKB-led position, *2B2a(2)*. More are in *2B2b(1)*, also DKB-led. Still others are in *2A1b*, a Matsushita and electronics cluster, and *2B2b(2)*, a Mitsui block. The bubble, it seems, was a shock to the structural integrity of the Sumitomo group.

By 1993, however, Sumitomo is back, clearly identifiable as *2A2a* with ten *Hakusui-kai* firms and just one interloper, DKB trader Itochu. A single council member – Nippon Sheet Glass – has fled the 1989 cluster with some Sumitomo-leaning independents in tow (e.g., Asahi Breweries, Daishowa Paper). Also, the block has a new independent – Aichi Machine – a Nissan (hence Fuyo-leaning) subcontractor. Sanyo Electric, another Kansai area independent with Sumitomo ties, has also abandoned the block for the nearby Matsushita cluster (*2A1b*), which since 1986 has edged closer to Sumitomo in the network.

The period 1995–96 was Japan's best spell of GDP growth in an otherwise dismal decade, while 1997–98 was the worst. Our cohesion analysis found a pattern of loosening in good times and tightening in bad. The blockmodel portrait of Sumitomo concurs. The major Sumitomo block in 1995, *2A1b(2)*, holds four Sanwa and three DKB firms. Three other key *Hakusui-kai* members are in *2A1a(2)* and *2B1b*. In 1997, the group is much more tightly clustered as *2B1b(1)*. All ten nonfinancial *Hakusui-kai* members are here plus three independents of known Sumitomo orientation and no other shacho-kai. The historical closeness of Sumitomo and Matsushita is evident in neither 1995 or 1997.

2. Mitsubishi. The Mitsubishi group in 1978 materializes in a fifth iteration block, *2B2b(1)*. It holds eleven *Kinyo-kai* members; that is, apart from the financials (in the 1-block) and trading company (in the shosha block, *2A1b*), all but Mitsubishi Electric (also in *2A1b*). Eighteen independents are included, many (e.g., Ajinomoto, Honda, Kikkoman, Meiji Milk, Nissin Food) with known Mitsubishi leanings. As with Sumitomo, only one firm from a competing shacho-kai appears: Toyo Tire, a Sanwa *Sansui-kai* member.

Mitsubishi is also clearly etched in 1986 (the *endaka*). It dominates *2A2*. One partition, *2A2a*, has nine *Kinyo-kai* members and six independents. The other, *2A2b*, has the shosha (Mitsubishi Corporation), three *Kinyo-kai* industrials, sixteen independents, and two firms from other shacho-kai: one DKB and one Fuyo.

Mitsubishi fragments in the bubble (1989) but less than Sumitomo. The *Kinyo-kai* financials (Mitsubishi Bank, Mitsubishi Trust, and Tokio Marine) are more dispersed than previously between *2A1a(2)* and *2B2a(1)*. One firm from another shacho-kai (DKB) appears. The group rebounds in 1993, but again less than Sumitomo. The Mitsubishi financials tighten up (*1A1b*), but the industrials remain rather divided.[77]

The Mitsubishi cluster has about the same coherence in 1995. It is not a distinct block until the sixth iteration [*2A1b(1a)*], sharing *2A1b(1)* with several Sanwa firms. Other *Kinyo-kai* members (Kirin, Mitsubishi Corporation, Asahi Glass) and fellow travelers (Ajinomoto) are off in *2B2a(1)* In the recessionary period of 1997–98, however, Mitsubishi regroups: eleven *Kinyo-kai* members combine in *2B2b(1)* with one Sanwa firm and six independents. Its complement block, *2B2b(2)*, holds some Mitsubishi-leaning independents (e.g., Honda and Meiji Milk).

So, Mitsubishi does not recover from the bubble to the degree of Sumitomo, but otherwise it, too, disperses in good times and coalesces in bad. Moreover, judging by some recent statements by Mitsubishi executives, Mitsubishi's cohesion in 1997 is less a defensive "last gasp" than a proactive strategy:

> Mitsubishi Corp. Chairman Minoru Makihara sees this consolidation as Japan's logical response to the mega-mergers taking place in the United States and Europe. "I think due to global competition and the credit crunch, the ties will get stronger" among keiretsu, he said. "I've been saying in this time of global competition and economic difficulties, we should look again at the various companies within our own group, first of all, because it's the easiest way to do it, and see if we can join forces, provided it's not an exclusive kind of thing."[78]

3. Mitsui. In 1978, Mitsui, the third and final big three zaibatsu group to survive intact to the post-war period, is distinctly profiled (*2A2b*), if less so

---

[77] With nine *Kinyo-kai* members and known fellow travelers Ajinomoto and Kikkoman, *2A2b* is the main Mitsubishi block. Diluting the block's Mitsubishi identity, however, are two DKB *Sankin-kai* firms and one *Fuyo-kai* representative. Other Mitsubishi industrials are assigned to *2A2b*, a large and diverse block.

[78] Sugawara (1998).

than Mitsubishi and Sumitomo in that year. Nine *Nimoku-kai* members are included, plus two DKB members. Excluding the Mitsui financials (in the 1-block) and shosha (*2A1b*), only three *Nimoku-kai* are missing. Two are in *2B1b*, a DKB–Sanwa block. The third deviant case is a special one: Toyota Motor, positioned with the financials.

The complement block (*2A2a*) is the Toyota vertical keiretsu: Aichi Steel, Aisin Seiki, Daihatsu, Kanto Auto Works, Nippondenso, and Toyota Auto Body. In 1978 and 1993, it adjoins the Mitsui position. We discuss it further in a later section on vertical keiretsu.

Thus, more than fellow zaibatsu Mitsubishi and Sumitomo, the Mitsui block is diluted by competing shacho-kai, mainly from DKB and Sanwa. Moreover, higher iterations do not separate them out.

Mitsui does not fragment in the bubble as Sumitomo and Mitsubishi do. Eleven *Nimoku-kai* members hold *2B2b(2)*, the Mitsui position in 1989, and twelve are in its 1993 counterpart (*2B1b*). In no other 2-block position is there more than one *Nimoku-kai* firm. Still, the Mitsui constellation is less tight in 1986 and (especially) 1989 than earlier or later. In these years, it shares no boundary with the Toyota keiretsu.

Also at odds with the countercyclical model is that Mitsui tightens in 1995, a GDP growth year. Ten *Nimoku-kai* members cluster in *2A2a(1)* with one DKB firm and eight Mitsui-leaning independents. Its complement [*2A2a(2)*] is some Toyota-linked firms, suggesting resumption of the Mitsui–Toyota alignment. Not for long, however, for in 1997 the Mitsui block *2B2a(1)* is much the same, but the Toyota affiliates are gone.

Thus, in contrast to the bumpy trajectories of the Mitsubishi and Sumitomo groups, Mitsui resists the ups and downs of the business cycle. A possible reason, explored in Chapter 5, is that it is less given to risk-sharing interventions.

4. Fuyo. Fuyo is classed as a bank-centered group, for its post-war configuration is centered on Fuji Bank. The cohesion analysis revealed the bank-centered keiretsu as less cohesive than the former zaibatsu, probably due to shorter history, weaker economic integration, lack of common name, and larger size. They should thus be less clearly delineated as CONCOR blocks.

Yet because the Fuyo group absorbed the pre-war Yasuda zaibatsu, we expect it to form a tighter cluster than DKB and Sanwa.[79] It is in fact sharply profiled in 1978 as *2B2a(1)*. Nine of nineteen *Fuyo-kai* members are here with no competing shacho-kai. By the criterion of shacho-kai concentration, Fuyo is thus less crystallized than Mitsubishi and Sumitomo but comparable to Mitsui. Of the absent ten *Fuyo-kai* firms,

[79] Gerlach (1992a); Morikawa (1993).

three – Fuji Bank, Yasuda Trust, and Yasuda Fire & Marine – are financials in the 1-block. Four more are in *2B2a(2)*, a Sanwa block adjoining the Fuyo cluster. (One of these, Hitachi, holds a *Sansui-kai* seat as well.) The remaining three are widely dispersed.

What becomes of Fuyo in later years? In line with the countercylical hypothesis, its profile rises in 1986, the *endaka* year. Thirteen Fuyo firms then concentrate in *2B1a*.[80] In the bubble (1989), Fuyo, as did Sumitomo and Mitsubishi, comes unglued. *2B1a(1)* has eight *Fuyo-kai* members, and *2B1b(1)* has four but it is Sanwa-led. Two more are off in *2A2b*.

In recessionary 1993, Fuyo departs from the countercyclical script and all but disappears. Two *Fuyo-kai* members appear in a mix of mostly financials and manufacturers (*2A1a*). Five are in a Sanwa-dominated block, *2A2a(1)*, whose complement is the Hitachi keiretsu. Five more share *2B2a* with DKB. Finally, three *Fuyo-kai* members occupy a very diverse block (*2B2b*) with DKB, Sanwa, and Mitsubishi firms. Higher iterations do not distinguish the groups, and many industries are represented. Thus Fuyo in 1993 is a loose assortment of network shards, some of which are Fuyo-based vertical keiretsu such as Hitachi and Nissan.

Fuyo looks a bit more robust in 1995. *2A1a(1)* is a relatively pure Fuyo block. However, complemented by *2A1a(2)*, this again is mostly a Nissan–Hitachi cluster.

The year 1997 brings near-extinction to the Fuyo group. Its core is *2B1a(2)* with five *Fuyo-kai* members (Nissan included). Three more *Fuyo-kai* firms join with two Sanwa and two DKB firms in *2A1b(2)*. Thus, in this last year of our panel, Fuyo is effectively gone. Until the 1990s, it resembled Mitsubishi and Sumitomo: a well-bounded cluster of firms that further tightened in the *endaka* and loosened in the bubble. But while Mitsubishi and Sumitomo groups kept up this ebb and flow through the 1990s, Fuyo just decayed.

5. Sanwa. Like Fuyo, the Sanwa group is tightly clustered in the early years of our series, if less to the exclusion of other shacho-kai. Also similar to Fuyo is that, by the latter nineties, the Sanwa group has effectively disappeared. In 1978, the largest cluster of Sanwa firms (twelve) is *2B2a(2)*, also held by a considerable number of Fuyo and DKB firms. It includes the Hitachi group. Four more Sanwa firms are in the heterogeneous *2B1b* cluster, probably centered on Nippon Steel. Nichimen, a Sanwa trader, is with other shosha in *2A1b*. Two more *Sansui-kai* members (Daihatsu and Nissho Iwai) are with the Toyota keiretsu in *2A2a*. Sanwa Bank and Toyo, the Sanwa trust bank, are in the city–trust bank cluster *1A1b*.

---

[80] Ten of the *Fuyo-kai* plus Sanwa member Hitachi Chemical are separated at the fifth-iteration from three Fuyo (one being Nissan Motor) and three DKB firms.

In 1986, the *endaka* downturn, Sanwa (as did Fuyo) tightens up. Nineteen *Sansui-kai* are in *2B1b*, but so are seven DKB and one Fuyo firm as well. (Higher iterations do not separate out the two groups.) Sanwa's gravitational pull is sufficient in this year to draw in Sanwa shosha Nichimen and Toyota affiliate Daihatsu. At other times Daihatsu is firmly planted in the Toyota camp.

The year 1989, the bubble, brings fragmentation to Sanwa as it did to other groups. The large Sanwa cluster of 1986 splits into *2B1b(1)* with six *Sansui-kai* firms and *2B2a(2)* with eleven. Both have sizable numbers of DKB or Fuyo members as well as [in *2B2a(2)*] five Sumitomo firms. Some Sanwa, DKB, and Fuyo mixing occurs in all years, but the overlap with Sumitomo is unique to 1989 and highlights the bubble's adverse impact on both groups.

Whereas Fuyo further disintegrated in 1993, Sanwa regains some strength. The *2B2b(1)* block of 1989 becomes the *2A2a(1)* block of 1993: larger and with greater Sanwa representation but otherwise similar (e.g., in its inclusion of five *Fuyo-kai* firms). Handfuls of *Sansui-kai* firms are here and there around the network, but the largest remaining Sanwa clump is the six in *2B2b*, the diverse cluster of DKB, Sanwa, Mitsubishi, and Fuyo firms.

In 1995, Sanwa decomposes in a major way. The clearest cluster, with just five *Sansui-kai*, is *2A1b(1b)*. Four Sanwa firms occupy *2A1a(2)*, and four more *2A1b(2)*, but other shacho-kai are well represented, too. In 1997, the Sanwa membership is spread even more thinly across blocks, usually in the company of DKB and Fuyo, and sometimes Mitsui [e.g., *2A1b(2)* or *2A2b(2)*]. As with Fuyo, other Sanwa clusters are the Sanwa-leaning vertical groups, such as Toyota [*2A2b(1)*] or Hitachi [*2B1b(1)*].

While never quite as tight as Fuyo, then, the Sanwa group's path is similar: waxing and waning against the business cycle until the 1990s, then unraveling.

6. Dai-Ichi Kangyo. With twenty-two *Sankin-kai* members, DKB is usually described as the least cohesive of the big six.[81] Except that DKB's director network proved surprisingly tight-knit (see Appendix 3.1), our cohesion analysis (Figure 3.2) agreed. CONCOR's portrayal is similar. In all observation years, its members, more than any other group, are strewn across the network. The blocks with sizable DKB clusters incorporate numerous other shacho-kai. DKB's descent started earlier and proceeded faster than other groups, which in 1978 and 1986 were relatively well defined but by the bubble are less so. In 1978, a clean cluster of ten DKB members exists [*2B2b(1)*]. Smaller numbers of DKB firms combine with

---

[81] Gerlach (1992b); Hoshi and Ito (1992).

Sanwa to form *2B1b*, a heavy industry cluster, probably pivoting on Nippon Steel. Three more show up in *2B2a*, a Sanwa-led position.

DKB, like Mitsui, deviates from the pattern of heightened cohesion in 1986. It fragments more. Seven *Sankin-kai* firms are in *2B1b*, a Sanwa-dominated block. The DKB firms are in a heavy industry group centered on Kawasaki Heavy and Kawasaki Steel. The only block DKB leads in this year is a small and heterogeneous one, *2B2a*. The DKB-based Furukawa industrial keiretsu, whose history we charted in Chapter 2, is important here. Finally, five DKB firms are in the Mitsui block *2B2b*. (Higher iterations do not distinguish them from the Mitsui firms.)

Also like Mitsui but unlike the other groups, DKB is more coherent in 1989. Eight members (including the DKB-based Furukawa and Kawasaki vertical groups) dominate *2B2b(1)*. The cluster is peculiar in its inclusion of four Sumitomo firms, but this stems from Sumitomo's bubble-era disintegration. Four DKB firms lead *2B1a(2)*, the Nissan–Nippon Steel cluster, whose counterpart partition [*2B1a(1)*] is a Fuyo block. Two more are in the *2A2b* mix of financials and industrials.

By 1993, however, DKB's downward spiral matches Fuyo's (unlike other groups' rebound in this year). The *Sankin-kai* is the dominant council in the diverse DKB–Sanwa–Mitsubishi–Fuyo block, *2B2b*, but, as noted, there is little pattern to any group's assignment to this cluster, and higher iterations do not partition them. Five DKB firms appear in no particular order in the Mitsui block *2B1b*. The 1993 cluster that DKB may have the greatest hand in structuring is *2B2a*, where it and Fuyo have five shacho-kai members each. This is a heavy industry group with some Nissan representation (Nissan Diesel and Fuji Heavy). A fifth iteration does isolate the DKB firms.

The 1995 blocking reveals one clear DKB cluster: *2A2b*. In 1997, a small DKB clump is *2B1b(2)*. Another is *2B2A(2)*, shared by Sanwa. Otherwise DKB is widely dispersed across the space.

Thus, DKB's trajectory across this twenty-year period is one of almost continuous decline, unrelieved by the countercyclical fluctuations experienced by the other groups. DKB went from moderately crystallized in 1978, to fragmentation and intermingling with Fuyo, Sanwa, and Sumitomo in the *endaka*-bubble years, to fast dissolution in the nineties.

7. A Quantitative Metric. Our treatment of how the large-firm network is structured by the horizontal keiretsu over this twenty-year period is admittedly impressionistic. This is rather in the nature of blockmodeling: one eyeballs the data to make sense of blocks and their interrelations. Still, a simple quantitative metric may reinforce our qualitative assessment. To summarize the distribution of shacho-kai firms across blocks by years, Table 3.7 presents for each observation year the Herfindahl concentration

Table 3.7. *Herfindahl Measures of Concentration in the Distribution of Shacho-kai Firms over CONCOR Blocks by Year*

Shacho-kai	Year	Herfindahl
Mitsui	1978	0.359
	1986	0.438
	1989	0.500
	1993	0.586
	1995	0.430
	1997	0.422
Mitsubishi	1978	0.508
	1986	0.398
	1989	0.391
	1993	0.414
	1995	0.461
	1997	0.508
Sumitomo	1978	0.621
	1986	0.621
	1989	0.266
	1993	0.503
	1995	0.378
	1997	0.541
Fuyo	1978	0.291
	1986	0.485
	1989	0.247
	1993	0.191
	1995	0.197
	1997	0.136
Sanwa	1978	0.299
	1986	0.642
	1989	0.292
	1993	0.264
	1995	0.135
	1997	0.115
DKB	1978	0.238
	1986	0.197
	1989	0.171
	1993	0.197
	1995	0.142
	1997	0.13

Note: The Herfindahl is computed as $\Sigma_i P_i^2$ where p_i is the proportion of the shacho-kai membership in the ith block.

index (Σp^2), the sum of squared proportions. A Herfindahl of 1.0 says that 100 percent of a shacho-kai's membership is in one block and 0 percent is in others. This taps the degree to which the positions a council holds are shared with other councils. Thus, it measures the crowding of a shacho-kai into a narrow niche in network space.[82] The Herfindahl is calculated over all fifth-iteration blocks generated by CONCOR in each year. If, for example, *2A1b(1a)* in 1995 is mostly Mitsubishi and *2A1b(1b)* is mostly Sanwa, the two shacho-kai are intermingled in *2A1b(1)*. In such a case, the Herfindahl is lower than had we done the calculations on a six-iteration partitioning, but we need a consistent rule for calculating shacho-kai concentration across the year-by-year CONCOR runs.

What do these measurements show? First – and unsurprisingly – the former zaibatsu are better revealed than the bank groups; among them, Sumitomo and Mitsubishi are clearer-cut than Mitsui and Fuyo. The Herfindahls are higher in these cases.

What do they say about change? Our hypothesis (H3.4) is less decay of the zaibatsu groups. The Herfindahls agree. For the zaibatsu-based groups, no clear trend over twenty years is discernible. For the bank-centered groups, the trend is steep descent, accelerating in the nineties.

Finally, what of the countercylical hypothesis: do groups circle the wagons in lean times, parting company in fat times? If so, we should observe cohesion upswings in 1986, 1991–93, and 1997 and downswings in 1978, 1989, and 1995. The Herfindahls show Mitsui, Fuyo, and Sanwa tightening from 1978 to 1986; Sumitomo does not change, and Mitsubishi and DKB loosen slightly. All but Mitsui are less concentrated in 1989, the peak of the bubble. All but Fuyo and Sanwa coalesce in 1993. All but Mitsubishi and Fuyo loosen in 1995. The former zaibatsu and the bank-based groups react differently to 1997–98, a business cycle trough. Mitsubishi and Sumitomo regroup, while Mitsui is unchanged. Yet Fuyo, Sanwa, and DKB weaken more.

Thus, the Herfindahls by and large confirm the picture yielded by our finer-grained qualitative analysis: the zaibatsu groups persist, the bubble and some countercyclical fluctuations notwithstanding. However, the bank-centered groups failed to recover from the bubble but stayed on a downward trajectory, such that, by the latter nineties, very little "group" was left.

Vertical Keiretsu

We expect the vertical manufacturing keiretsu to decompose less over time than have the horizontal *kigyo-shudan*. There is a clear supply chain logic to their organization, which by most accounts has bolstered Japanese

---

[82] Our qualitative analysis used another criterion of group coherence: inclusion in the block of independent firms. This is hard to represent quantitatively, since the degree to which independents reinforce or dilute an identity of the position rests on our ex ante grasp of their histories vis-à-vis the keiretsu. Mazda, Matsushita, and Sankyo Aluminum should be close in CONCOR space to the Sumitomo *Hakusui-kai*, but there is no way to index that knowledge.

global competitiveness in industries such as autos and electronics. This reasoning, however, rests on a view of the vertical nets as self-contained cliques. It is as true of them as of the horizontal big six that their status as groups depends as much on their equivalence vis-à-vis the network at large as on the well-oiled relationships among the member firms. Take the case of Toyota and its former division and keiretsu supplier of automotive electronics, Denso. Toyota has maintained an approximate 25 percent stake in Denso, but much of their relationship is via third-party ties to a set of financials that own significant shares of both. These include Mitsui, Tokai, and Sanwa Banks, Mitsui Trust, Mitsui Fire and Marine, and Nippon Life.

In fact, the vertical networks' evolutionary paths parallel those of the horizontal groups. Some (e.g., Nippon Steel and to a lesser degree Nissan) have frayed more or less steadily with time. For others (Toyota and Matsushita), the change has been nonlinear: fragmenting in the late 1980s and regrouping in the 1990s.

1. Toyota. First we look at that stellar global performer and archetypal vertical keiretsu, the Toyota group. While Toyota's *shacho* or president sits on the Mitsui *Nimoku-kai* (as an "observer"), the heads of Toyota's principal affiliates do not.[83] The only such firm on any council – the Sanwa *Sansui-kai* – is Daihatsu. Interestingly, while Toyota Motor in 1978 is itself a "financial" in positional terms, the Toyota keiretsu is one part (*2A2a*) of a cluster whose complement is the Mitsui group (*2A2b*).

The coherence of the Toyota keiretsu varies with the period and hence the state of the economy. In 1986, as noted, it is far from the Mitsui sphere of influence, occupying *1B2a* with Toyota Motor, a block adjoining *1B2b*, the Matsushita group. *1B2* is thus an interesting configuration: two preeminent industrial keiretsu sharing a position that is equivalent structurally to the financial institutions. The bubble year 1989 brings fragmentation to the Toyota keiretsu. Toyota Auto Body joins Toyota Motor as another structural financial (*1B2b*), an all-Toyota cluster is *2A2a(2)*, and still other Toyota-linked firms – Daihatsu, Hino, Toyoda Loom, Suzuki – are in Sanwa-based *2B1b(2)*, owing presumably to Daihatsu's *Sansui-kai* membership and the Toyota group's history of dealings with Sanwa Bank.

Yet, as is true of Sumitomo and to some degree the Mitsubishi group, the Toyota keiretsu's slide is halted in the recessionary year of 1993. As in 1978, the Toyota firms in *2B1a(2)* abut the Mitsui group in *2B1b*. *2B1a(1)*

---

[83] As noted, Toyota has publicly minimized its commitment to the Mitsui group by being the only big-six shacho-kai firm to refer to its membership as that of "observer" (Miyashita and Russell, 1994). The Toyota keiretsu's stable alignment with Mitsui, however, suggests that there is more symbolism than substance to this posture.

is a set of Mitsui-leaning (e.g., Fuji Film) and Sanwa-leaning (e.g., Itoham Foods) firms.

In the growth year of 1995, the Toyota group splits. Four affiliates – Daihatsu, Hino, Kanto, and Toyota Auto Body – spin off to *2A2a(2)*, a chip off the main Mitsui block, *2A2a(1)*. The remainder is in *2B2b(1b)*, its complement [*2A2b(1)*], with Fuji Photo and Sony, a nonautomotive Mitsui–Sanwa cluster. This splitting of a position with a Mitsui block appears again in the recessionary trough of 1997–98, but by then the Toyota group has mostly reassembled. Only Kanto Motors – in the main Mitsui block – and Toyota itself – are absent. At this time, however, the distance between the Toyota and Mitsui clusters [*2B2a(1)*] is considerable.

Thus, as with the horizontal groups, the Toyota keiretsu frays in the growth years of 1989 and 1995 and then revamps in 1993 and 1997. But its Mitsui orientation is weaker in 1997 than in 1995.

2. Matsushita. The Matsushita group's network proximity to Sumitomo parallels the Toyota group's affinity for Mitsui. In 1978, the only other industrial in that position is Sanyo Electric, also an Osaka company normally inhabiting the Matsushita–Sumitomo region of the network. Another similarity is that, while the affiliates of these two vertical keiretsu constitute well-defined blocks in each year, the parent corporations, Matsushita Electric and Toyota Motor, are sometimes absent.[84] Further, in 1986, Matsushita joins Toyota in the financial 1-block. Moreover, like Toyota's Mitsui alignment, the Matsushita block is close to Sumitomo in 1978 and 1986, much more distant in 1989, closer again in 1993, but distant in 1995 and 1997.[85] Thus, in the late 1980s, both Matsushita and Toyota drifted from their principal big-six moorings but returned to the fold in the 1990s, if only temporarily in Matsushita's case. Moreover, the Matsushita group, like Toyota, is less cohesive in 1986 and 1989. In 1986, one Matsushita firm is outside the Matsushita block (*1B2b*). In 1989, the entire Matsushita group is together in *2A1b*, but so are various others, some with Sumitomo leanings (e.g., Sumitomo Marine, Asahi Breweries, Daiwa Securities, Sanyo Electric). Although 1993 is the last

---

[84] This structural division of labor between the lead firm of a vertical keiretsu and its satellite affiliates is akin to that of the financials and industrials among the horizontal groups. It underscores the conceptual and operational definition of a keiretsu as block or position versus clique. The basis for the cluster is less internal cohesion than equivalence in relation to others – in particular, such network-maker positions as main bank, trading company (at least in 1978), and heavy manufacturer.

[85] In 1978, Matsushita Electric is clustered with the Sumitomo group [*2B1a(2)*] but its affiliates in *2A1a* are in another region of the space. That changes in later years: Matsushita Electric shows up in the same block as its satellites (*1B2b* in 1978; *2A1b* in 1989 and 1993).

year of Matsushita–Sumitomo affinity, this pattern persists: the group is tighter knit in 1993 and 1995 but the 1997 block is looser – similar in size and composition to that of 1989. Thus, the Matsushita group gave up some coherence in the bubble, regained it in the early to mid-nineties, but by the decade's end had weakened again. As an update, in 2002 Matsushita Electric absorbed several of its keiretsu affiliates as wholly owned divisions. The stated reason was that lack of coordination within the group had produced an excess of overlapping and competing product lines.

3. Nippon Steel. Nippon Steel, Japan's largest steel corporation, has been the acknowledged leader of a major post-war industrial keiretsu. Given the general decline of the Japanese steel industry and Nippon Steel's slippage from the front ranks of corporate Japan, we expect and find the greatest evidence for a Nippon Steel block (*2B1b*) in 1978. It has no clear big-six identity, taking members from Sanwa, Mitsui, and Fuyo. The industry mix is steel, other heavy manufacturing, oil, and chemicals.

In 1986 and 1989, however, Nippon Steel appears in a larger, more industrially diversified block (*2B1a*), built on the thirteen-firm Fuyo core. There is similarly scant evidence of a Nippon Steel group in 1993. The company appears on the Fuyo and Sanwa side of *2A2a*, whose fifth iteration partition [*(2A2a(1)*] is the Sumitomo group. In 1995, Nippon Steel is in a smallish Fuyo cluster [*2A1a(1)*] that includes Nissan, and in 1997 it appears in a small Sanwa cluster [*2A2b(2)*] adjoining the Mitsubishi group.

4. Nissan. In 1978, a distinct Nissan cluster exists within the Fuyo block [*2B2a(1)*]. It includes Nissan Motor and such affiliates as Nissan Diesel, Diesel Kiki, Nissan Auto Body, Aichi Machine, and Nippon Seiko. These firms combine in a sixth partition subblock (not shown). Other Nissan satellites not in that subpartition are in adjacent blocks – Hitachi and Nissan Chemical in *2B2a(2)* and Fuji Heavy in *2B1b*. The Nissan group is similarly positioned in 1986, although the Fuyo block (*2B1a*) is larger then and more diverse. Expectedly, Nissan's keiretsu is less coherent in later years. Fewer known Nissan affiliates appear in or near the Nissan Motor block. This might reflect Nissan's declining strength in the Japanese auto market, but it could also signal the disintegration of the Fuyo group as a whole. Indeed, unlike the Toyota keiretsu, which fragmented in the bubble (1989), there is more Nissan togetherness in 1989 (*2B1a*) than in later years. In 1993, Nissan Motor and Nissan Auto Body are in *2A1a*, a mixed financial–industrial cluster, but Fuji Heavy, Nissan Diesel, and Nissan Chemical are in *2b2a*, the heavy industry DKB–Fuyo block. In 1995,

Nissan joins Nissan Diesel and Nissan Chemical in a smallish DKB–Fuyo block [2B1b(1a)] close to the Sumitomo group [2B1b(1b)]. However, in a Fuyo–Sanwa block some distance removed [2A2b], we find such Nissan affiliates as Hitachi, Aichi Machine, Nissan Shatai, and Fuji Heavy. In 1997, Fuji Heavy rejoins Nissan Motor in 2B2a(2), but other Nissan-related firms do not.

Like the Matsushita and Toyota cases, Nissan's affiliates are structurally equivalent in relation to Nissan Motor despite being removed in network space. Thus, Nissan, too, is a network maker: even at a distance it configures the positions of its keiretsu firms.

5. Hitachi. The Hitachi group holds up well over time. In 1978, every member – Hitachi Cable, Hitachi Chemical, Hitachi Zosen, and Hitachi Metals – is in the overwhelmingly Sanwa-based 2B2a(2), and subsequent years also show them close together. All the Hitachi firms are on the Sanwa *Sansui-kai*. This includes parent company Hitachi Electric, which has the unique distinction of holding three different shacho-kai seats. Like the bridge between the Mitsui and Sanwa groups constituted by the Toyota group (including *Sansui-kai* member Daihatsu), the Hitachi–Nissan network is the linchpin between the Fuyo and the Sanwa groups.

Summary and Conclusions

This chapter reports on an analysis of the changing network structure of Japan's large-firm economy. We entertained three theoretical perspectives on network change: (1) the modernization–convergence hypothesis that Japan's highly connected and multiplex networks have been withering away as the economy matured and globally integrated; (2) the institutional inertia hypothesis that Japan's network forms, whatever economic role they play, retain much legitimacy and are thus resistant to change; (3) the business cycle hypothesis that the cohesion of the network overall and within the keiretsu groupings rises and falls with macroeconomic circumstances – tightening in bad times and loosening in good.

We used two methodologies: (1) graph-theoretic cohesion analysis to assess structural change both in the large-firm network as a whole and within the big-six shacho-kai, and (2) blockmodeling techniques to address the roles of keiretsu and industry in structuring the transaction and control networks that have bound Japanese companies to one another from the 1960s to the late 1990s.

We found degrees of support for all three theories of network change. As regards the modernization hypothesis, the cohesion analysis revealed general, if not steep, declines in the densities and connectivities of the network as a whole and within the presidents' councils of the big-six horizontal groups. This was most dramatically true of the connectivity of the equity network. Moreover, the blockmodel analysis testified that by the end of the 1990s the bank-centered keiretsu had disintegrated to the point that they were no longer groups in any meaningful sense.

Yet institutional theory receives a measure of support in the remarkable continuance of the former zaibatsu groups, Mitsubishi, Sumitomo, and, to a lesser degree, Mitsui. Given their long histories, close ties to the state, key role in Japan's economic development, and the high legitimacy and charisma, so to speak, of their corporate names and logos, they are reasonably cast as much more institutionalized network organizations than is true of the bank-centered groups (DKB, Fuyo, Sanwa). Their relative stability over periods of significant economic change is thus in line with institutional theory. Finally, our data support the countercyclical hypothesis that Japan's corporate networks in general and keiretsu groups in particular have lost and gained cohesion and coherence with the ups and downs of the business cycle. In contrast with the modernization and institutional stories, the countercylical model assumes that Japan's corporate networks do indeed play an economic role, albeit now a controversial one: to provide member firms with support in hard times. Networks strengthen in downturns, because ties are vehicles for channeling resources to affiliates in need. In upturns, group firms have less need of one another and drift apart. The bubble era, while arguably no ordinary uptick in the business cycle but a systemic shift in the Japanese way of business, nonetheless illustrates the point. The cohesion of the corporate network and of the horizontal and vertical groups within it lapsed markedly then, but with the bubble's passing, some of the groups bounced back.

Beyond these general observations, we can summarize what we found.

1. Marked declines over a twenty- to thirty-year period in the *density* of four kinds of networks in this population of large Japanese firms are generally not conspicuous in our data. Indeed, in the important case of equity relations, the density trend is up. Densities of trade and director ties show small secular declines since the 1970s. The density of lender–borrower relations fell steadily from 1972 to 1981 and then fluctuated tightly around a flat trend until turning up post-1990.

2. Yet the *connectivity* of the equity and director networks has fallen markedly since the late 1970s. Our interpretation is as follows. Interfirm relations remain critical to the Japanese economy. Yet pairwise strategic partnerships and other micro-network patterns are replacing the integrated macro-network that had the keiretsu

system at its core. In the case of equity ties, it is also probable that they increasingly serve an investment function, less often the cementing or symbolizing of long-term relationships.

3. Within the horizontal group shacho-kai, gradual cohesion declines are apparent in most groups from the early 1980s until 1990 when the bubble burst and the economy slumped. The upward trend in equity tie density for the large-firm network as a whole does not exist within the keiretsu. With the exception of Sanwa, intragroup equity ties have declined since the early 1980s. Debt tie density rose postbubble in the Mitsubishi and Sumitomo groups, held steady in the Mitsui group, and declined in the bank-centered groups.

4. In each period, the former zaibatsu (Mitsubishi, Mitsui, Sumitomo) are more coherent and cohesive clusters than are the bank-centered *kigyo-shudan*. That is evident both from the density of shacho-kai data and from the blockmodeling analysis. But the blockmodeling methodology makes clear in a way that the cohesion analysis does not that, while all six groups weaken over time, the bank-centered groups were decomposing faster than the former zaibatsu. Indeed, by the end of our series in the second half of the 1990s, they no longer exist as structural positions in the network. Declining coherence indicated by the CONCOR blockings is also the fate of two notable vertical keiretsu: Nippon Steel and Nissan Motors. Such trends accord with their diminished roles in the economy of the 1990s.

5. However, other keiretsu nets, both vertical and horizontal, exhibit a different pattern of change. They decline in boundedness and cohesion, particularly in 1989, the peak of the bubble, only to firm up again in the 1990s. This description fits Sumitomo, Mitsubishi, and, to a smaller degree, Mitsui, DKB, and Sanwa (in the sense that it combines with Sumitomo in 1989), Matsushita, and Toyota. Given journalistic claims that the crisis-ridden and recessionary 1990s delivered the coup de grâce to an organizational form already crippled by the late-1980s bubble, this pattern is significant.

6. The cohesion of the network increases or stabilizes in bad times while trending down in good times. That pattern is very clear in the evolution of the lender–borrower network over twenty-five years. It is reasonably clear in how the connectivity, if not the density, of the equity and director networks moves with time. In the director case, the countercylical model describes the movement of connectivity since the bubble's onset in 1987, but earlier that

network moved in sync with the business cycle. In the trade network of all firms, the cohesion fluctuations are procyclical, but, *within* the shacho-kai, some countercylicality in trade cohesion is evident.

7. The blockmodels show the principal structural divide in the corporate network to be financial (1-block) versus industrial (2-block). That may not seem newsworthy, but it is a baseline fact that CONCOR's first pass lays out in bold relief. Moreover, it *is* newsworthy that some industrial firms – most consistently Toyota Motor (known colloquially in Japan as "Toyota Bank") – is equivalent structurally to the banks and insurance companies. Other industrials gravitate to the financial 1-block in 1986 and 1989, a time of change in the post-war financial–industrial division of labor. The 1993 blocking, however, redraws the boundary between the two. But for Toyota, the 1-block is all financials. The 2-block has all the industrials, plus a few financials as well, chiefly insurance companies and securities firms. Thus, the separation of financial and industrial positions in the network – so clear in 1978 – blurred in the late 1980s but sharpened in the 1990s.

8. Within the financial position (1-block), industry or functional differences are primary and keiretsu effects are secondary. Moreover, across time, we see increased functional and status differentiation (into city and trust banks, regional and *sogo* banks, and insurance) within the 1-block of financials and diminishing differentiation by keiretsu. Within the industrial position, keiretsu effects are primary and industry effects are secondary. Both functional (see point 9) and keiretsu differentiation of positions within the 2-block diminish with time.

9. A sogo shosha (trading company) block is identified by CONCOR only in 1978. In later periods, individual shosha are generally assigned to their respective horizontal groups or to industries in which their business is large. This decay in the shosha position is consistent with the declining functional role of these firms in the globalizing Japanese economy.

10. Both vertical keiretsu (Toyota, Matsushita, Nissan, Hitachi, Nippon Steel) and horizontal keiretsu (the big-six *kigyo-shudan*) organize the industrial (2-block) position and to a far lesser degree the financial (1-block) position. Vertical keiretsu appear as clusters within or adjacent to blocks defined by big-six groupings (Toyota and Mitsui; Matsushita and Sumitomo). However, where vertical keiretsu span *kigyo-shudan* boundaries (e.g., the Toyota

group's links to Mitsui and Sanwa; Nissan and Hitachi's vertical links to Fuyo and Sanwa), the result is overlap and boundary blurring of the horizontal groups.

Appendix

3.1. Unstacking the Blockmodel

In applying the CONCOR algorithm to the stack of eight matrices (four ties sent and received), we obscure how individual relations shape aggregate results. We have also done separate CONCOR runs for the four ties in 1978 and 1993 on the two-level stacks of sent and received matrices. For brevity's sake, we merely summarize that evidence in this Appendix, rather than present the eight CONCOR tables and the detailed analysis of them. The keiretsu structuring of the economy comes across much more clearly in the stacked than in the single-strand analysis. This validates our multiple-network clustering strategy: no one tie reveals all the contours of the network.

In general, the single-strand equity and debt blockmodels' portrayal of the network is similar to the stacked blocking. One difference in the debt case is that, in both years, we observe a large, structurally homogeneous (i.e., no higher-order partitions) block of financials that show up neither as creditors nor as debtors. It includes the casualty insurers, the *sogo* banks and securities firms, along with several industrials: in particular, Toyota and Matsushita affiliates. This block doubles in size by 1993, chiefly through the inclusion of substantially more industrial firms. Its growth is testimony, we believe, to the secular decline of bank financing (and the rise of equity and corporate debt alternatives) *and*, perhaps, to the recessionary conditions that were then depressing loan demand.

Cross-shareholding is the core tie on which the post-war horizontal and vertical keiretsu are based. The drift to keiretsu dissolution shown by the stacked blocking – for example, the virtual disappearance of the Fuyo and DKB groups in 1993 – is strongly evident in a comparison of the single-stranded 1978 and 1993 clusterings. The zaibatsu, however, are clearly revealed. Sumitomo is a distinct cluster in both years, close in network space to Matsushita in 1993 but not in 1978. Mitsubishi is also well-defined in both years. Mitsui is clearly profiled in 1978 but is much more amorphous in 1993. As before, Sanwa is a distinct position in both years: the blocks comprise some twenty firms, two-thirds of which are *Sansui-kai*.

The director-only blockmodel, as with that of debt, features a large and thoroughly homogeneous residual block of firms that neither send nor receive directors. That block shows little patterning by keiretsu in 1978, and it holds firms from the less cohesive groups: DKB, Fuyo, Sanwa, Mitsui, and independents. No Mitsubishi firms are here and only one Sumitomo member. It is similarly diverse in industry: banking, food, insurance, electronics, and so forth. Most noteworthy, as again is true of debt, is that this block doubles in size by 1993, although its keiretsu composition is essentially unchanged: Fuyo, DKB, a few Sanwa and Mitsui, and one Sumitomo firm are present, but no Mitsubishi *Kinyo-kai*.

Our earlier inference from the stacked and equity-only blockings – that DKB mostly ceased to be a "group" in the structural equivalence sense post-1978 – needs qualification in light of the director-only blockmodel. In both 1978 and 1993, it is a distinct block. (Recall Figure 3.2's evidence that director density within the *Sankin-kai* was the highest of the bank-centered groups.) Mitsubishi, too, is depicted in CONCOR's clustering of the director matrix as a very cohesive group in 1978 and 1993, a pattern also in line with Figure 3.2. The Toyota group is well-defined by director interlocks in both years, Toyota Motor included. Nissan is a tight cluster in 1978, less so in 1993 when it pulls in Nippon Steel and an assortment of nonautomotive (food, chemicals) firms. Sanwa is clearly outlined in 1978: of thirty-one firms in the Sanwa block, fourteen are *Sansui-kai*. But in 1993, the Sanwa block has shrunk to twenty-one, eight of which are *Sansui-kai*. Other Sanwa firms show up in vertical industry clusters such as a Hitachi. Defined by the director network, the Sumitomo group, too, is weaker in 1993, again consistent with Figure 3.2.

CONCOR's blocking of the trade matrix is much less influenced by the big six – and much more by industry – than is true of the other three ties. Almost no cross-industry keiretsu clusterings exist. Within industries small numbers of shacho-kai members cluster, but the general pattern is a marked departure from the blockings of other ties, whether done singly or in stacked fashion. This is one more sign that preferential trade is a weak defining criterion for the horizontal groups.[86] Also noteworthy is that CONCOR's application to the trade matrices puts all the sogo shosha in one block in both years, whereas the stacked models identified a functional shosha block in 1978 only. Thus, we should modify our conclusion on the demise of the shosha position: the shosha retained a position in the trade network, but their role in the financial and governance networks declined. Other industry-based clusters appear in the trade-specific blocking: the principal electronics firms – Matsushita, Sanyo, Canon, Sony Victor, Pioneer, Omron, Sanyo, Alps, and TDK – and textiles each form distinct blocks in every period. The auto firms by contrast, Toyota and Nissan in particular, are less industry-driven, shaped more by vertical keiretsu. The horizontal groups have a low profile in the trade blockmodels. Mitsubishi

---

[86] Gerlach (1992a); Fair Trade Commission (1992).

and Mitsui are clear clusters in 1978; and a few Sumitomo firms form a block, although most Sumitomo members do not occupy it. The bank groups do not cluster in either year. In 1993, a diversified industry block appears that is mostly Mitsubishi with a smattering of Fuyo, Sanwa, and DKB firms. Otherwise, aside from mini-positions holding two or three shacho-kai firms within an industry block, the big six add little to the structuring of the trade network.

4

Exchange and Control: Explaining Corporate Ties

A Longitudinal Dyad Analysis

> *Whereas the conventional view has tended to regard keiretsu affilia-tions and the subcontracting relationship as remnants of feudalistic re-lations or derivatives of the cultural peculiarities of the Japanese, the most important explanatory variable should be the kind and nature of the transaction of goods or services conducted beneath each of these relations.... [T]he fundamental link between a pair of firms should be located in...the resource flow...between them. To regulate this flow, a control apparatus is formed between the firms, the possible mode of which ranges from simple contract to a very complex and developed structure. The elaborateness of the control apparatus depends on the composition and the nature of the flow; the most developed type along this spectrum may have shareholding as its superstructure.*[1]
>
> Asanuma (1985)

Introduction

A criticism that might fairly be made of our network analysis in the last chapter is that it ignores the causality between lending and trade on the one hand and equity and director ties on the other. An alternative ap-proach is to draw on organizational theory to model the cause-and-effect relationships between exchange and control and between them and at-tributes of firms such as industry, size, and location. Such an analysis, as the quote from Asanuma suggests, might well reveal that the concept of "keiretsu" adds little to an understanding of how firms vary in their involvement in business networks.

Are cross-shareholding and director interlocks governance structures that pairs of Japanese firms rationally apply to the task of managing

---

[1] This passage was taken from a prepublication draft of Asanuma (1989).

147

bilateral financial and commercial exchange or are they, like preferential trading and lending, network devices for maintaining the macrosolidarity of the keiretsu grouping as a whole? Generally speaking, these are the questions we now address. Asanuma's passage nicely captures the exchange–control/governance perspective on corporate networks that guides what we do in this chapter. Our purpose is to inquire into the degree to which control relations between Japanese firms are driven by those firms' economic *transactions*. Using the *dyad* or pair of firms as unit of analysis – the elementary particle of a network – we attempt to determine with a fair amount of statistical precision why one firm might bind itself to another through executive transfers and equity stakes. We also remain very interested in the question of change: how such relations have evolved over a fifteen-year period in step with macroeconomic fluctuations, regulatory shifts, and other period-specific circumstances.

Interorganizational Theory and Business Networks in Japan

Much organizational theory engages the problem of how interfirm exchange is monitored, managed, or governed in various ways. Underlying otherwise diverse schools of thought on the topic is the idea that the commercial and financial transactions among the firms that comprise the market economy are typically encased in, overlaid with, or embedded in supportive infrastructure. Indeed, the theme that market exchange in capitalist economies is inextricably enmeshed in social networks has been orthodoxy for economic sociology and – perhaps surprisingly due to its sometime celebration of an invisible hand whereby unfettered markets self-manage and equilibrate – has won growing acceptance by economics as well.[2] A large interdisciplinary literature documents how interlocking directorates, cross-shareholdings, old boy networks, school ties, trade associations, political connections, common regional location, shared culture, and mutual trust make up the fabric of economic exchange.[3] No invisible hand, this network infrastructure is a palpably visible structure of control, channeling transactions along well-worn paths between transaction partners who not only know but often are committed and beholden to one another.

What, then, are the governance mechanisms and other forms of social infrastructure claimed by organizational theory to play a role in reducing uncertainty and dependence in economic exchange? Transaction cost economics highlights merger, acquisition, vertical integration, franchises,

---

[2] Teece (1986).
[3] Dore (1983, 1986); Imai and Itami (1984); Podolny and Page (1998); Richardson (1972).

and even sequential and relational contracts as alternative ways of placing administrative boundaries around transacting economic nodes in order to offset the failure of pure market mechanisms to thwart opportunism or free up information.[4] Agency theory approaches the same question less symmetrically in asking how *principals* – goal-seeking actors – contrive monitoring and disciplining devices to overcome the information and incentive asymmetries that invariably arise when they hire or otherwise contract with *agents* to implement those goals. More sociological in orientation but in many respects similar, exchange or resource dependence theory focuses on the bridging strategies firms employ to constrain or coopt one another and thereby manage and direct exchange.[5] Embeddedness theory stresses the rootedness of economic exchange in social relations and institutions, focusing, in particular, on the role of trust, commitment, and reciprocity in enabling market processes to operate.[6] These strategies manage transactional dependencies in adaptive, incremental ways, stopping well short of full integration within a hierarchically coordinated firm. In response to criticism that the markets and hierarchies framework is too stark a polarity, the transaction cost paradigm has been expanded to accommodate hybrid forms.[7] Presumed to forestall the failures both of markets and of formal administration, these represent a middle road between the anarchy of unfettered atomized exchange and the dead weight of bureaucratic control. Network forms such as keiretsu may be viewed as hybrids in this sense, although some argue that networks represent another distinct dimension of organization, not a point on the markets–hierarchies continuum.[8]

The governance forms that encompass market transactions in Japan are wondrously rich and diverse. Some are explicit and concrete; others informal and opaque. Examples of the first are the R&D consortia supported by key ministries such as the Ministry of International Trade and Industry, the trade associations and employers' groups such as *Keidanren* and *Nikkeiren*, and the shacho-kai where the CEOs of big-six group companies meet to discuss matters of group-wide concern.[9] These are matched in the vertical supply keiretsu by *kyoryoku-kai*, or cooperative associations of suppliers, organized around a large manufacturing firm such as Toyota or Matsushita.[10] In the middle is an array of equity participation arrangements – joint ventures, spun-off subsidiaries, and

---

[4] Williamson (1975, 1985).
[5] Burt (1983); Lincoln and McBride (1985); Pfeffer and Salancik (1978); Thompson (1967).
[6] Sako (1992); Uzzi (1996).
[7] Teece (1986); Williamson (1991).
[8] Powell (1990).
[9] Guillot, Mowery, and Spencer (2000); Schaede (2000); Sakakibara (1993).
[10] On Japanese supplier associations, see Ahmadjian (1997); Guillot and Lincoln (2003); and Sako (1996).

cross-shareholdings.[11] Least formal but perhaps most dense are the bonds forged by old-school ties (*gakubatsu*), regional loyalties, kinship, and most important, employee transfers (e.g., *shukko*) between companies.[12] Such transfers, which may involve management, technical personnel, or direct labor, fuse the interpersonal networks and corporate cultures of separate companies as the transferred employees maintain a dual commitment: to the firm of origin and of destination.

Severe obstacles to reliance on full internal organization as a governance mode figure prominently in the proliferation of network forms in the Japanese economy. Due to an array of legal and cultural barriers, the Japanese market for corporate control has been miniscule; that is, mergers and acquisitions, particularly of the hostile sort, were all but foreclosed.[13] Even in recent years, despite the apparent crumbling of many such barriers, Japanese firms have had ample defenses, most involving keiretsu mobilizations, against genuinely hostile takeover attempts.[14] Moreover, antitrust regulations and accounting standards are often vague and toothless, or, alternatively, tough-sounding but unenforced.[15] Collusive relationships among companies – operating to fix prices, advantage partners, and restrict competition – were rarely questioned by the state. On the contrary, regulatory agencies typically saw their role as that of offering guidance through networks to build cooperation and consensus within an industry or technology sector.[16]

The resource dependence perspective on interorganizational networks and its intellectual cousin the embeddedness paradigm, while lacking some of the rigor of the economics approaches, better attend to the softer social

---

[11] Fruin (1992); Gerlach (1992a).

[12] Imai (1984); Lincoln and Ahmadjian (2001).

[13] Kester (1991).

[14] In early 2000, a Japanese investor, Yoshiaki Murakami, failed in his attempt at a hostile takeover of Shoei Corporation, an electronics firm with attractive real estate holdings. Shoei's principal institutional shareholders – Canon, in particular – were affiliated with the Fuyo group, and, despite Murakami's offer of a 14 percent premium over the market price of the stock, refused to sell to him. Of particular note is that the Fuyo group's blockage of the takeover occurred after Fuji Bank had combined with Dai-Ichi Kangyo Bank and the International Bank of Japan to form Mizuho Bank, seen by some as the end of the Fuyo and DKB keiretsu (Landers, 2000a, 2000b, 2000c, 2002). More recently, Bank of America announced on 13 February 2003 that, because of poor business, it was moving most of its operations out of Tokyo. The decision comes on the heels of departures by a string of other Western financial services firms, including Merrill Lynch, Morgan Stanley, and JP Morgan Chase. High on the list of reasons, according to the *Financial Times*, was "extremely disappointing merger and acquisition activity, attributable to disappointing levels of corporate restructuring.... Total M&A volume last year was at its lowest level since 1998, driven by an absence of cross-border deals and mega-deals" (Ibison, 2003a, 2003b).

[15] Hadley (1970); von Mehren (1963); van Wolferen (1989).

[16] Johnson (1982); Okimoto (1989).

and cultural bonds on which business transactions routinely depend.[17] They have also been skeptical of the economist's assumption that hierarchical governance serves all parties' interests in systemic efficiency gains as contrasted with the more parochial interests of, say, the dominant partner to the exchange. Notwithstanding the role keiretsu played in the past in the efficiency and strength of the Japanese economy, asymmetries of power and dependence and an uneven distribution of economic benefits have been prominently featured in Japanese business relations.[18]

The differences in perspective notwithstanding, the sociological (resource dependence, network theory, and embeddedness theory) and economic (transaction cost and agency theory) theories share an assumption that an array of organizational structures serve to channel and control economic exchange to offset market uncertainties and the propensity for exchange partners to exploit dependence on a critical or relationship-specific resource and bargain opportunistically. A difference is how they view the causal ordering between exchange and control. With some exceptions, the economic models treat exchange as exogenous and organization as endogenous; that is, governance arrangements emerge as solutions to various processes (uncertainty, opportunism, information and incentive asymmetry) that operate to compromise the efficiency of the market mechanism. Some of the sociological theories – resource dependence in particular – agree on the cause-and-effect sequencing but dispute the optimizing logic behind economic reasoning. Much competitive strategy theory in a conventional industrial organization's mold concurs: cooperation, trust, and the formal institutions (e.g., cartels) that support these work to confer advantage on some players while barring others from the game. But a core assumption of most sociology and anthropology is that social structures and cultural patterns are exogenous – that is, received, given, even primordial – while economic exchange is rooted or embedded in social life.[19]

In the real world, social structures such as kinship, community, religion, and politics plainly shape the contours of markets. Once in place, however, market processes spawn new institutions, which in turn work to hold economic players to the rules of the game and thus avert the flaws and distortions with which unfettered markets are rife. Exchange relations inevitably give rise to asymmetries of information and power,[20] thus ensuring that, however level the initial field, subsequent rounds will favor some players over others. Still, from an evolutionary perspective, whether

[17] But see, e.g., Akerlof (1982); Eccles and Crane (1988); Geertz, Geertz, and Rosen (1979).
[18] Aoki (1988); Goto (1982); Nishiguchi (1994).
[19] Granovetter (1985); Polanyi (1944).
[20] Blau (1964); Lincoln and McBride (1985); Pfeffer and Salancik (1978).

social structures are exogenous or endogenous with respect to exchange may be moot.[21] If markets flourish because they happen to be embedded in an ethnic enclave, for example, or other high-trust, tight-knit community, one can still speak reasonably of the social structure as providing the solution to an economic problem.[22] Our general view, which underpins the statistical analysis we offer, is that exchange begets governance, not the other way around.

Our analysis, then, addresses whether the transactions of trade and lending among the firms we study account for equity and director interlocks. We further assume that director dispatch is contingent on equity ties. Only in rare circumstances should we expect to find one company seconding a director to another absent the leverage of an ownership stake.[23] It is the dispatcher's prerogative as major shareholder to participate in the governance of the receiving firm that empowers and legitimates the transfer. Thus, we model director dispatch as a consequence of equity, trade, and lending relations. Equity ties, in turn, are presumed to derive from trade and lending.

Methodology

Causal Ordering

The core assumption of our analysis is the Asanuma conjecture: control nets manage and channel financial and commercial exchange. The causality may well work the other way: control – including extant social networks and cultural patterns such as trust and obligation – conditions the form and volume of transactions. But without some stringent assumptions we cannot disentangle these causal possibilities. Thus, some of the effects we report may be inflated – others attenuated – by what the econometrics literature refers to as simultaneity bias. The causal ordering we posit derives from the various theories (e.g., resource dependence and transaction cost economics) that frame our inquiry: Organizations manage transactional uncertainties through the bridging and governance devices of shareholding and director dispatch. Some evidence agrees: A survey by the Japanese Fair Trade Commission (1987:9) of the top 200 industrial companies concluded:

> As it was said that stock holdings were acquired only after business relationships had existed for some time, it appears that

[21] Aldrich (1999); Hannan and Freeman (1989); Nelson (1995).
[22] Light (1972).
[23] Gerlach (1992a:134) discusses evidence that 86 percent of the firms dispatching directors to companies were among those companies' top ten shareholders.

stockholding is most frequently a result rather than a cause of long-term supplier relationships.

Whether control is determined by exchange or vice versa depends on the time frame and control device at issue. The shacho-kai is a governance structure, but with few exceptions (see Table 1.1), memberships have been stable over the past thirty years.[24] It thus makes little sense to model two firms' joint council membership as a function of the business they currently transact. Late additions to the council might be explained this way, but for long-standing members the causality necessarily runs the other way.

Moreover, while cross-shareholding is unlikely in the absence of a pre-existing exchange, once in place it may be used to extract more business from a partner. Banks pressure clients in which they have ownership stakes to increase deposits, and insurance companies actively market policies to employees of firms in which they hold shares.

Data

Our sample is the largest 50 financial corporations, 9 general trading companies, and 200 industrial firms in Japan as of 1980. We have measurements on this panel for each of the following years: 1978, 1982, 1986, 1989, 1991, 1993. Table 4.1 presents definitions and descriptive statistics for all variables in the analysis for each year.

As in Chapter 3, bilateral control (measured by cross-shareholding and director transfer) *and* exchange relations (lending and trade) are measured for each pair of firms in our sample. This time, however, we work with more closely spaced data, measuring the firms in our sample at approximate two-year intervals. The director and trade measures are binary variables, so the mean reported in Table 4.1 is the proportion of dyads with a tie present. This is the network *density* measure of Chapter 3. The lending and equity measures are the logs of the proportions of firm J's debt and equity contributed by firm I.

Previous studies of corporate interlock networks in the resource dependence and transaction cost traditions lacked the information on exchange partnerships that our debt and trade data afford. Some researchers used aggregate, industry-level measurements to proxy firm-level transactions.[25] Critics warned of aggregation bias – flows between sectors may be poor approximations to flows between firms.[26] The weakness of our firm-level trade data, on the other hand, is that they tell us only whether (= 1) or not (= 0) firm I sold goods to firm J in the past year such that either of the two firms reported the transaction as a major trading partnership.

---

[24] On the stability of shacho-kai memberships, see Gerlach (1992a:167–8).
[25] Burt (1983); Flath (1993); Pfeffer and Salancik (1978).
[26] Aldrich (1979); Useem (1984).

Table 4.1. Measures and Descriptive Statistics for 259 Firms and 66,822 Firm Dyads by Year

Variable	Definition	1978 Mean (SD)	1982 Mean (SD)	1984 Mean (SD)	1986 Mean (SD)	1989 Mean (SD)	1991 Mean (SD)	1993 Mean (SD)
Director I J[JI]	Manager from firm I(J) is on board of firm J(I); otherwise 0 (×100)	.00536 (.07305)	.00542 (.0735)	.00503 (.07075)	.00462 (.06782)	.00403 (.06335)	.00446 (.06653)	.00397 (.06287)
Equity I J[JI]	(Ln) percent of firm J(I)'s stock owned by firm I(J) if I(J) is one of J(I)'s top ten stockholders; otherwise 0	.00092 (.010)	.00081 (.13445)	.00085 (.00896)	.00088 (.00994)	.00094 (.00863)	.00098 (.00092)	.00092 (.0083)
Debt I J[JI]	(Ln) percent of firm J(I)'s debt lent by firm I(J) if firm I(J) is one of J(I)'s top ten lenders; otherwise 0	.00164 (.01386)	.00174 (.01458)	.00160 (.01428)	.001604 (.01444)	.00092 (.01265)	.00147 (.01357)	.00142 (.01297)
Trade I J[JI]	Firm I(J) sold goods to firm J(I); otherwise 0	.01818 (.13360)	.01842 (.13445)	.01526 (.12259)	.01506 (.12180)	.01408 (.11782)	.01375 (.11646)	.01248 (.11101)
I(J) is in Tokyo	Firm I(J) is headquartered in the Kanto (Tokyo) region; otherwise 0	.607 (.488)	.588 (.492)	.607 (.488)	.607 (.488)	.608 (.490)	.602 (.490)	.602 (.490)
I(J) is in Kansai	Firm I(J) is headquartered in the Kansai (Osaka) region; otherwise 0	.233 (.423)	.243 (.429)	.233 (.423)	.233 (.423)	.235 (.424)	.239 (.427)	.239 (.427)
I & J in same group	Firms I(J) and J(I) are on the same big-six shacho-kai = 1; otherwise = 0	.032 (.177)	.033 (.180)	.032 (.177)	.032 (.177)	.033 (.178)	.033 (.179)	.033 (.179)
I is independent (J)	Firm I(J) is not on a big-six shacho-kai = 1; is on a council = 0	.560 (.496)	.555 (.497)	.560 (.496)	.560 (.496)	.557 (.497)	.558 (.497)	.558 (.497)
I is financial	Firm I is a financial = 1; otherwise 0	.195 (.396)	.148 (.355)	.195 (.396)	.195 (.396)	.196 (.397)	.191 (.393)	.191 (.393)
I is trading co.	Firm I is a trading company = 1; otherwise 0	.035 (.184)	.037 (.189)	.035 (.184)	.035 (.183)	.035 (.185)	.036 (.186)	.036 (.186)
Assets of I(J)	(Ln) total assets of firm I(J)	12.590 (1.336)	12.920 (1.433)	13.046 (1.431)	13.153 (1.475)	13.405 (1.539)	13.575 (1.537)	13.582 (1.507)
Age of I(J)	Years since founding of firm I(J)	54.518 (22.155)	54.922 (22.489)	54.518 (22.155)	54.518 (22.155)	54.698 (22.128)	54.562 (22.014)	54.462 (22.014)
Director autoregression	See Appendix 4.1	.00535 (.00547)	.00526 (.07345)	.00502 (.00510)	.00462 (.00487)	.00404 (.00431)	.0045 (.0045)	.00408 (.004)
Equity autoregression	See Appendix 4.1	.00091 (.00076)	.00081 (.00924)	.00085 (.00072)	.00088 (.00075)	.00093 (.00092)	.00099 (.00091)	.00093 (.00089)

Appendix 4.1 discusses these issues in more detail, but some comment on methods is warranted here. The observation units are ordered pairings (I, J) of the 259 firms in our population, minus the diagonal (same-firm pairings). This rule yields $N^2 - N$ or 66,882 observations in each year. The ultimate outcome variable we model is whether firm I had a director on the board of J in the year of measurement. These are not event data: a director tie between firms I and J need not have originated in the year in question. We know only that in that year our source identifies a director on the board of J who had a career at I and may yet hold a management position there. The second outcome variable considered is the percentage of J's shareholder equity owned by I, conditioned on I being a top-ten shareholder in J. If I held stock in J but was not a top-ten owner of J, the dyad was coded as zero.

The dependent variables of equity ownership and director transfer are defined only for the pair; they have no meaning for individual firms. Other dyad-level variables are the measures of lending and trade relations. Measured at the level of the firm are size (the natural log of total corporate assets), age (the number of years since the founding of the firm), shacho-kai, region, and industry.

Regression Models
Table 4.2 presents the maximum likelihood estimates for our regressions of cross-equity and director transfer in each year. Under our causal assumptions, they form a recursive system: Debt and trade ties are explanatory (predetermined) in the equation for shareholding. Debt, trade, and shareholding are explanatory with respect to director dispatch. The director and shareholding regressions are calculated on the full set of 66,822 dyads. As the director variable is a simple dichotomy, we use probit regression. The equity and debt variables are limited-continuous (most observations are zero but the nonzero cases take a range of values), so tobit regression is the appropriate statistical tool.

As with Chapter 3's blockmodel analysis, we begin with the earliest observation year, 1978, and then proceed to later years in order to draw inferences about change. We deal first with the dependence of the director on equity ties; second, with the dependence of both such control relations on lending and trade; third, with the hypothesis that reciprocity operates as a governance mode; and fourth, with the firm attributes of size, age, and location. We also return to the question of groups, asking whether our modeling of the causality between control and exchange puts the keiretsu question to rest. We shall see that it does not. At odds with Asanuma's conjecture, our controls for exchange relations and firm attributes do not demolish the keiretsu effects on control ties in this population of firms. Throughout we also address the problem of change, searching for signs

Table 4.2. *Probit (Director) and Tobit (Equity) Regressions of Corporate Ties for Pairs of Japanese Firms by Year*

Explanatory variable	1978		1982		1984		1986		1989		1991		1993	
	Director IJ	Equity IJ	Director IJ	Equity IJ	Director IJ	Equity IJ	Director IJ	Equity IJ	Director IJ	Equity IJ	Director IJ	Equity IJ	Director IJ	Equity IJ
Director IJ	1.443***		1.323***		1.150***		1.363***		1.358***		1.134***		.288	
Equity IJ	26.732***		28.911***		29.408***		9.593***		17.026***		15.898***		21.354**	
Equity JI	−1.020	.257***	.661	.347***	.757	.344***	−.205	.240**	.599	.402***	.965	.304**	3.095**	.280***
Equity IJ* Equity JI	64.995		96.046		117.045		431.530*		238.092*		315.442*		28.394	
Debt IJ	5.686***	.667***	3.755***	.764	3.665***	.631***	6.968***	.628***	3.277**	.319***	6.448***	.496***	5.894***	.469***
Debt JI	−4.562	.434***	−2.261	.377***	.994	.273***	−5.674	.223***	−1.989	.120*	.345	.285***	−2.019	.253***
Trade IJ	.849***	.104***	.557***	.106***	.670***	.095***	.866***	.110***	.786***	.083***	.770***	.097***	.780***	.089***
Trade JI	.461*	.106***	.271	.105***	.356	.104***	.828***	.111***	.764***	.086***	1.105***	.101***	.768***	.101***
Trade IJ* Trade JI	−.799***	−.079***	−.075	−.096***	−.267	−.076***	−1.114***	−.081***	−.904*	−.058***	−.976***	−.067***	−.930***	−.064***
I is financial	−.177	.065***	−.466**	−.007	−.555***	.057***	−.579***	.061***	−.447**	.042**	−.607**	.050**	−.479***	.051***
I is trading co.	−.172	−.008	−.291	−.047**	−.395	−.012	−.387*	−.021	−.231	−.032*	−.294	−.031*	−.072	−.026
I in Tokyo and J in Tokyo	.220**	.015*	.188**	.008	.214*	.014*	.129*	.013*	.163*	.014**	.186*	.014*	.117	.011*
I in Tokyo and J in Kansai	.127	.004	.099	−.004	.179*	.005	.050	.004	.055	.008	.103	.005	.114	.006
I in Kansai and J in Kansai	.224	.024*	.226	.031**	.308*	.026*	.259*	.025*	.346*	.027**	.138	.023*	.153	.016*
I in Kansai and J in Tokyo	.007	−.003	−.024	.002	.014	−.001	−.159	−.001	−.097	.002	−.118	.000	−.013	−.002
I and J in same group	.831***	.077***	.726***	.080***	.775***	.080***	.988***	.080***	.837***	.068***	.795***	.058***	.823***	.054***
I is independent	.213*	−.014*	.273**	.003	.331***	−.006	.293***	−.011	.207**	−.013*	.195	−.012*	.146	−.016**
J is independent	.379***	.024***	.267***	.027***	.306***	.024***	.328***	.025***	.373***	.022***	.333***	.020***	.428***	.017***
Assets of I	.268***	.012***	.322***	.031***	.340***	.012***	.373***	.013***	.324***	.016***	.365***	.013***	.257***	.011***
Assets of J	−.023	−.005*	−.064*	−.003	−.056*	−.003	−.058	−.003	−.080**	−.006**	−.041	−.006*	−.012	−.005***
Age of I	.003*	.005	.001	−.018	.000	.002	.000	.005	.002	−.014	.002	−.020	.001	−.013
Age of J	−.003*	−.019*	−.002	−.024*	−.003	−.022*	−.003	.020**	−.003	−.007	−.004**	−.013+	−.001	−.010
Autoregression	6.637	17.202**	8.882	13.534*	8.593*	17.907**	1.720*	2.433**	21.893	18.238***	3.900	21.302***	15.143	18.904***
Constant	−6.937***	−.338***	−7.025***	−.615***	−7.371***	−.358***	−7.747***	−.396***	−7.063***	−.366***	−8.032***	−.316***	−7.076***	−.290***
Pseudo R^2	.573		.553		.549		.525		.492		.534		.513	

*** $p < .001$; ** $p < .01$; * $p < .05$; + $p < .10$. Standard errors are adjusted for clustering by firm.

Note: The units of observation are the (259^2-259) pairings of all firms in the sample. "IJ" refers to a directed relation from the first firm in the dyad ("I") to the second ("J"). "JI" refers to the reverse relation.

of cyclical and secular trends in how these networks have evolved across a critical phase of Japanese economic history.

Finally, we examine industry differences: does exchange shape control in the same way across industry sectors? There are theoretical reasons to suppose that industry matters, and, while the industry differences are generally not large, some notable ones are revealed.

Equity and Director Ties

To use Asanuma's language, we hypothesize that cross-ownership is a control apparatus that pairs of Japanese firms deploy in order to regulate the resource flows between them. A second, less prevalent, but no less important device is director dispatch.

The Equity Case

We identify two distinct perspectives on cross-shareholding. From the first, it is an investment one firm makes in another in order to realize a return. Such a transaction requires some form of governance, which for large investors is typically board representation.[27] Thus, one of the functions of the board of directors is that of governance structure designed to protect the interests of owners by enabling them to monitor the management of the firms in which they invest.

From the second perspective, an equity stake is itself a governance mechanism designed to manage an exchange. Concentrated share ownership – a single large shareholder or a consortium of large shareholders as in the horizontal keiretsu – is claimed to be a solution to the classical Berle and Means agency problem posed by the separation of corporate ownership and control.[28] A large shareholder, in part but not entirely owing to its ability to command seats on the board, is positioned to monitor and discipline incumbent management. When shares in a public corporation are widely dispersed across a multitude of small and unorganized owners, executives can be expected to pursue goals that advance their interests as a class (e.g., scale, stability, power, prestige) while forsaking those of the shareholder community (earnings growth and stock price appreciation).

Whether equity ownership is best seen as an investment or control device varies with the institutional setting. In the United States, where large investors are mostly pension funds, mutual funds, insurance companies,

---

[27] Indeed, Williamson (1985) argues that equity investors have a greater claim to representation on the board of directors than do creditors or suppliers.
[28] Berle and Means (1932); Jensen and Meckling (1976); Useem (1996).

and the like, the equity investment is the transaction and a board seat is the governance. In Japan and Germany, where equity markets have been weak, a firm's large investors are its principal banks and trading partners. Thus, the equity stake is better cast as monitoring infrastructure erected in support of a financial or commercial exchange.[29]

From the perspective of two firms in a bargaining situation, the purchase of a partner's stock is a credible and public commitment assuring each that the other will forego opportunism, divulge information, and otherwise maximize the shared value accruing to the exchange. Writing of the 19.2 percent stake that Toyota took in headlight manufacturer Koito, Murphy (1996:49) puts the issue well:

> Such an investment in the United States would suggest an impending take-over, a joint venture or a simple financial stake. In the absence of a formal equity relationship, two American firms could not enter into cozy marketing, pricing, or supply agreements without violating the law. But the stake Toyota took in Koito was fundamentally ceremonial in nature; it functioned as the seal of a done deal, an irrevocable announcement to the Japanese business community that Koito had become a Toyota group company. Once Koito joined the Toyota group, Toyota naturally began to supply much of Koito's senior management and to coordinate investment, financing, and R&D programs. Koito's current chairman, Matsuura Tako, is from Toyota. So are the president, Nagamura Yoshio, and much of the rest of the senior management. Toyota is, of course, Koito's principal customer.

Thus, an equity stake is the platform from which an intervention is launched. It gives the owning firm, in concert with other key stakeholders, rights to information about and participation in the management of the company owned. In general, though, it is safe to say that cross-shareholding in the Japanese economy came to represent a "credible way of formalizing commitment to a relationship while ensuring that a high percentage of a company's stock remains in safe hands."[30]

A natural assumption is that the firm taking the equity stake assumes a degree of control over the firm in which the stake is taken. Thus, banks

---

[29] Dore (2000:114) cites a survey of Japanese finance managers on the following question: "When reviewing your cross-holdings, how many and which of the following criteria do you use when deciding whether to keep them or not?" Sixty-four percent said "the business we do with the other firm," 10 percent said the dividend returns, and 21 percent said the capital value of the shares. Moreover, 95 percent said that the cross-shareholding system was either essential or, if not essential, had merit.

[30] Kester (1991); Gerlach (1992a).

acquire shares in client firms to constrain how the borrower uses the bank's capital.[31] An auto assembler takes stakes in its suppliers to gain leverage over their pricing and production processes. Large pension funds have a say in the governance of the corporations in their portfolios. However, the control in an equity tie may also flow the other way. Ballon and Tomita (1988:43–44) suggest that the stakes Japanese manufacturers hold in their suppliers come at the latter's behest:

> When the manufacturer and his first-tier or first- and second-tier contractors work closely together over a period of time, the contractor is often requested to participate in the ownership of his more important subcontractors; eventually the smaller company asks the larger one to buy its shares. Therefore, rather than the larger company simply buying out the smaller ones, acquisition is by mutual agreement.

The contractor, supplier, or distributor firm derives security from the equity relation, which formalizes and symbolizes its partnership with the parent. The more the satellite comes under the core firm's wing in this fashion, the greater its confidence that it will have a steady flow of orders and the better its reputation in the business community. In the rigid status system of corporate Japan, such positive reputation effects translate into more resources at reduced cost, owing to improved credit standing, access to the main bank and technical and managerial skills of the parent, enhanced attractiveness to labor, and so on.[32]

Director Dispatch (*Haken yakuin*)

Interlocking directorate networks are much researched by North American and European students of corporate governance and strategy. Unlike information on such interorganizational relations as lending, trade, and equity, firm-level data on these board ties are abundant, and various studies find them channeling information and influence between firms.[33] Less clear is whether interlocking boards function as a control mechanism in the fashion often claimed by organizational theory. Some research says

---

[31] Miwa and Ramseyer (2002).

[32] Flath (1993) notes that a firm that is owned (*J*) holds the owning firm (*I*) hostage in a commercial or lending transaction, for if *J*'s margins are too narrow, its share price may fall, thus reducing the value of *I*'s investment. At the same time, *I* has leverage over *J* in that *I* might threaten *J* with withdrawal of the investment. In Japan, where until recently cross-shareholding arrangements were very stable and stock prices were much less likely than in the United States to rise or fall with short-term earnings fluctuations, the power of these incentives is questionable.

[33] See, inter alia, Davis (1991); Haunschild and Beckman (1998); Mizruchi (1996).

they do. A number of studies find that the volume of trade between industries, for example, predicts the rate of interlocking between firms in those industries.[34] Other scholars doubt that board interlocking figures prominently in the control of interfirm exchange. Baker's (1990:618) careful study of market ties between U.S. investment banks and corporations found

> only partial support for the long-untested assumption that director interlocks network of overlay economic ties. Interlocks strongly embed market exchange in some cases, but generally interlocked firms do not tend to favor the investment banks on their boards.... [I]nterlocked firms give business to their board-represented banks less often than expected by chance alone.

From interviews with directors of large British and U.S. companies, Useem (1984) similarly concluded that overlapping boards were rarely forged or mobilized for the purpose of managing resource dependencies. His executive informants said their firms deliberately skirted board appointments that might link them to a trading partner or competitor (the latter being a violation of the Clayton Act of 1914).[35]

Evidence on broken interlocks in the United States also argues against a resource dependence interpretation.[36] The low replacement rate of interlocking board members who die, resign, or are removed is at odds with the hypothesis that board ties function as a stable governance structure for the coordination of exchange.[37]

In Japan, by contrast, ties overlapping board are less dense than in the United States but arguably much more instrumental in the management of exchange. Most interlocks are between companies with strong business ties, and when one forms – that is, firm *I* seconds a director-level executive to firm *J* – the dispatcher gains a degree of real control over the target. Since a Japanese company's directors are with very few exceptions insiders – that is, high-level operating executives – the influence gained may be considerable. Japanese boards have few outsiders in the Anglo-American sense – directors who stay aloof from day-to-day management and are rarely on-site. A far cry from the model of an independent body representing the interests of shareholders and other external constituencies,

---

[34] Burt (1983); Flath (1993); Palmer, Friedland, and Singh (1986); Pfeffer and Salancik (1978).
[35] Bacon and Brown (1978); Mace (1971).
[36] Palmer (1983); Ornstein (1984).
[37] See also Pennings (1980); Zajac (1988).

the Japanese board has been coterminous with the company's senior management.[38]

Miyashita and Russell (1994:183) quote the managing director of a major Japanese auto supplier on the significance of receiving a director dispatched by a major assembler:

> What does it mean to have such directors in your firm? At least in my experience, it means that every single thing discussed in your board room is relayed to your parent company and probably a lot of it to their main bank. The directors assigned from up above are responsible for reporting back on your operations, and they do.... [T]he big companies and the banks like to keep tabs on everything.

The system of director transfers creates some tensions within the Japanese company between two classes of managers whose formal rank and employment standing is the same: (1) true permanent employees who entered the firm in the traditional way immediately upon the completion of their schooling, and (2) managers who transferred in from a parent firm, bank, or other company. In the mid-1990s Toyota's relations with Denso – former division and keiretsu supplier of electronics parts – were strained over the automaker's decision to integrate vertically into electronic direct components and thus become a "second source" and competitor of Denso.[39] Observers close to both companies told us that the two Toyota directors on Denso's board were excluded from some executive meetings.

An argument for the rationality of large stakeholders such as the main bank or large manufacturers involving themselves in the management of a firm this way is that, owing to their lengthy history of dealings with it, they well understand its management and its problems. In the U.S. corporate governance system, a merger or takeover may ensconce in top leadership positions newcomers whose credentials for the task are suspect, for example, financiers like Carl Icahn whose poor performance at the

[38] A major goal of the current corporate governance reform movement in Japan has been to remove inside executives from corporate boards, replace them with bona fide outsiders, and reduce board size. For example, KDDI, Japan's largest international telecommunications carrier, announced plans to adopt a corporate officer system as a step toward shrinking the board and separating director and executive roles. "Corporate officers will not belong to the board of directors and will engage in day-to-day business activities instead of long-range planning. DDI, the surviving entity of a three-way merger of DDI, KDD Corp. and IDO Corp. in October, has a total of 53 directors from the three firms and major shareholders such as Kyocera Corp. and Toyota Motor Corp. but it intends to reduce the number to less than 15." *Nikkei Net Interactive*, 16 February 2001.

[39] Ahmadjian and Lincoln (2001).

helm of TWA was attributable to a lack of line management experience. In Japan, control shifts to a main bank and partner firms in possession of intimate knowledge of the troubled company.

In our interviews with high-level managers in large Japanese manufacturing firms, we posed the question of whether and why they took equity stakes and dispatched directors to suppliers and distributors. Often – as in Toyota's stakes in Daihatsu and Hino – the purpose of the transfer was rescue and restructuring. The equity stake shored up the finances of the target firm, while the incoming directors set about revamping its organizational structures and processes.[40] Managers, as Ballon and Tomita propose in the quote above, typically maintained in our interviews that they were responding to a request from a supplier or other business partner.[41] Both Toshiba, which does take equity stakes in suppliers, and Matsushita, which generally does not, said they were often pressured by suppliers to take stakes and send directors.[42]

Termed *cooptation*, the offer of a board seat to a potentially troublesome outsider is a proactive strategy of managing an interfirm dependency.[43] The co-opting organization reduces uncertainty by *absorbing* the external agent into its management hierarchy in hopes of gaining acquiescence to decisions already in place. First noted in Selznick's (1949) classic work on the Tennessee Valley Authority, cooptation is a common ritual in U.S. organizational life. By contrast with the Japanese case, the risk to the U.S. firm is low that such an outsider will divert its course, for its board is a distant oversight body and the coopted director is unlikely to be involved in line management.

In general, only major shareholders may legitimately claim seats on a company's board. Yet an equity stake provides no guarantee of a board seat, particularly if the company owned is a keiretsu member and the owner is an outsider or foreigner.[44] As noted, a notorious case in point

---

[40] An important point relevant to our work in the next chapter is that keiretsu rescues and bailouts – whether spearheaded by a main bank, trading company, or large customer – are unlikely unless the troubled party has some kind of preexisting business relationship with the group. As these examples testify, however, such interventions almost invariably result in stronger ties between the firm and the group.

[41] In the early 1990s, we conducted a series of interviews within a number of prominent corporations and financial institutions affiliated with the big-six horizontal keiretsu.

[42] On Toshiba's supplier relations, see Fruin (1997).

[43] Burt, Christman, and Kilburn (1980); Pfeffer and Salancik (1978); Selznick (1949); Thompson (1967).

[44] However, one firm may take an equity stake in the other for the express purpose of transferring managers. Consider the case of a small Kansai printing firm discussed by Lincoln and Ahmadjian (2001). The firm, which had a cash flow problem, was enticed into joining the keiretsu of a large financial institution. The financial firm thus made a sizable equity investment in the printing firm. The capital infusion helped solve the smaller firm's liquidity problem but at the cost of forcing upon it three high-level managers whose background ill-prepared them for the printing business. Clearly, the financial's

was American corporate raider T. Boone Pickens' failure as a 26 percent shareholder to secure a seat on the board of Toyota supplier, Koito, over the opposition of Toyota and other Toyota group firms.[45]

H4.1: *If firm I is a major shareholder in firm J, I will have a director on J's board.*

Equity and Director Ties: Results
Hypothesis 4.1 holds that an equity stake is a precondition for director dispatch. Specifically, a company *sends* directors in order to participate in the management of a firm it partially owns. Our empirical results, presented in Table 4.2, completely agree. Yet the pattern over time is puzzling. There is no change from 1978 to 1984. Then in 1986, the year of the *endaka* shock, the association ends. In 1989 and 1991 it resumes but below the pre-1986 level. Between 1986 and 1987 the maximum equity stake any Japanese bank could legally hold in a corporation fell from 10 percent to 5 percent.[46] Perhaps the regulatory change reduced the equity–director correlation by restricting the variance in equity ties.[47] The resumption of the effect in subsequent years supports this interpretation. As the initial shock recedes, the ordering of bank shareholders should be restored and along with it the historical pattern of director dispatch. Our

chief interest in adding the printing firm to its keiretsu was to find a suitable repository for redundant managers.

[45] The contrast with the U.S. case is interesting. Arguing against the notion that director ties mobilize the latent control of cross-shareholding, Mintz and Schwartz (1985:129) assert that "even if stockholder control were consistently traced by director interlocks, concentrated stockholding by nonfinancial firms . . . is not commonplace, while interlocks among the largest corporations are pervasive. Hence, only a very small proportion of total director exchanges would be indicative of these types of control relationships." However, one study demonstrates that cross-shareholding between pairs of U.S. firms, along with other types of formal coordination (joint ventures, etc.), is strongly predictive of director interlock persistence over time (Palmer et al., 1986).

[46] Aoki (1988:119) summarizes the regulatory limits on stockholding by industrial corporations in Japan as follows: "A large nonfinancial corporation may hold stocks of other corporations where the effect is not 'substantially to restrain competition,' and only to the extent that the acquisition value of those stocks does not exceed the value of its own assets. Even this limitation may be lifted in some cases, for example, when a joint venture is set up with a foreign company or when a company spins off a part of its business as a fully owned subsidiary."

[47] That is, in 1986, 5 percent of Firm *K* might be held by Bank *I* and 10 percent by Bank *J*. Bank's *J*'s larger stake would in that year signal a greater commitment to Firm *K* amid a consensus in the community of stakeholders in Firm *K* that Bank *J* was the firm's main bank and delegated monitor of its business affairs (Sheard, 1994b). By 1987, however, Bank *I* would have had to sell down by half its share in the firm, while Bank *J*'s share would remain unchanged at 5 percent. Presumably, the regulatory change would not have substantially reduced Bank *I*'s right to intervene in Firm *K* by dispatching a manager, but it would have eliminated an important piece of information about the two banks' monitoring and intervention rights, thus attenuating the correlation we observe between shareholding and director dispatch.

suggestion is that, net of this adjustment to the measurement of an equity tie, the correlation between directors and equity stakes has been stable over the observation period.

To test this hypothesis, we divided the set of dyads into bank–industrial pairs and industrial–industrial pairs. At odds with our conjecture, the effect of bank shareholding on the dispatch of bank directors to those same corporations was time invariant. By contrast, the sharp drop in the equity effect was clearly evident in the industry-to-industry subsample. There was in addition a notable dip in the overall mean of the director transfers from the pre- to post-1986 period (also evident in Figure 3.2). Just what took place in this interval to produce these results is unclear. We know the endaka was a time of broad restructuring of the Japanese corporate network, but we have no explanation for why it perturbed the association between equity and director ties in 1986.

What about the other side of the cross-shareholding relation? Do the firms that are held dispatch directors to the firms that hold them? We hypothesize that they do not. The transfer of a director gives the dispatching firm direct access to executive decision making and to high-level information on strategy and operations. The rights to such participation come with ownership. The one circumstance in which director transfer might occur in the absence of an equity relation is a group-orchestrated bailout. The group bank might be the shareholder in a troubled client firm, but the director sent is an operating manager from an affiliated manufacturer with no ownership stake in the target firm.[48]

What do the data say? The dyad regressions for director dispatch contain a term for the receiving firm's equity stake in the sending firm. Consistent with our reasoning, its coefficient lacks significance in all years but one: 1993.

Financial Exchange and the Flow of Control

We now examine how financial exchange shapes networks of control. Subsequently, we consider the effect of commercial transactions. It is well known that lenders – banks, trust banks, insurance companies, and the

---

[48] For example, in September of 2000, Kajima Corporation, a large construction firm, dispatched two directors to troubled midsize contractor Kumagai Gumi Co. as part of a restructuring and turnaround. Kajima had no existing capital stake in Kumagai Gumi and refused to take one, a stance, analysts noted, which dealt a blow to Kumagai's recovery hopes. Kajima was in fact acting as agent for the main bank and major stockholder in both firms, Sumitomo. As in the famous Mazda bailout, the Kajima rescue makes clear that equity and director ties are not strictly dyadic but have a broader network logic. *The Nikkei Weekly*, 25 September 2000.

like – bridge (own shares in and dispatch directors) to borrowers.[49] Borrowers may, in turn, take stakes and place people in lenders (e.g., Toyota's share in Tokai Bank or Nissan's in IBJ), but this is less common. Industrial firms depend on banks for debt financing – offering the lender a board seat is a co-optive strategy of managing the dependence. When committing large sums to uncertain ventures, banks expose themselves to risk and thus seek to monitor and intercede in the decision making of their clients.[50] Thus, high corporate debt/equity ratios and dependence on main banks go hand in hand with widespread bank shareholding, bank representation on corporate boards, and bank-led bailouts.[51]

H4.2: *Lenders own shares and place directors in borrowers.*

Have lenders' monitoring and control of borrowers shifted over time?[52] A plausible hypothesis is that they have declined in step with Japanese corporations' substitution of shareholder equity and corporate bonds for bank debt. Less dependence on borrowing from financial institutions should lower the leverage of those institutions over companies' affairs.

Aoki (1988:139) agrees: "De-intermediation ha[s] doubtlessly diminished the relative bargaining power of the bank vis-à-vis the *J*-firm and contributed to the reduction of overborrowing of the latter." In his view, the disintermediation process was substantially advanced by the mid-1970s, predating the period our chapter considers. Still, corporate dependence on bank debt fell additionally in the mid-1980s with the endaka shock and further rounds of deregulation of the corporate bond market. Hoshi and Kashyap (2000:11) observe that "between 1983 and 1989 the Japanese bond market blossomed, permitting many internationally known companies to tap the public debt markets for the first time. [This]... deregulation has permitted the largest Japanese firms to become almost as independent of banks as their US counterparts." Soaring equity prices in the bubble era further prompted corporations to reduce reliance on bank debt, and the banks, for their part, shifted a substantial portion of their lending to real estate and other inflating assets.

---

[49] Aoki and Patrick (1994).

[50] Horiuchi, Packer, and Fukuda (1988); Williamson (1985:307).

[51] Sheard (1986).

[52] The percentage of stocks owned by financial institutions in Japan peaked at 45.2 percent in 1990, declining to 36.1 percent in 1999. The percentage owned by nonfinancial corporations similarly peaked at 25.2 in 1990, declining to 23.7 in 1999. Individual ownership hit a trough at 23.1 percent in 1990, increasing to 26.4 percent in 1999. The biggest gains have come from foreign corporations and individuals, whose combined percentage was 4.2 percent in 1990, rising to 12.4 percent in 1999 (*Asahi Shimbun*, 2003).

Results: Financial Exchange and Control

Table 4.2 shows lenders' tendency to own borrowers to be roughly twice the tendency for borrowers to own lenders. Both effects are positive and significant in all years, but some year-to-year volatility is evident. First, until the bubble, 1989, the borrower effect fell annually while the lender effect held steady. In 1989, both shrink by half, rising again in the two years following (1991 and 1993) to less than the prebubble level. We draw two conclusions. In line with the last chapter's network analysis and the next chapter's performance analysis, we observe in the bubble years a decline in the part played by lending–borrowing transactions in the distribution of control ties. But with the bubble's demise, the earlier pattern was largely if not wholly restored. Second – and less anticipated on the assumption that corporations' dependence on banks had been declining since the 1970s – we see that the governance of financial transactions gradually became less symmetric until the postbubble era: that is, lenders' power over borrowers stayed the same but borrowers' control of lenders (in terms of equity holding and director dispatch) diminished.

As hypothesized, lenders also dispatch directors to borrowers, but there is no indication that borrowers place their people in lenders. This reinforces the picture from the equity analysis that, at least until the bubble, lenders controlled borrowers, not the other way around. These effects fluctuate temporally in a fashion similar to, if less consistently than, the equity case, but the pattern is less stable. The bubble's peak – 1989 – is the nadir of the lender effect. It is up again in the last two years of the series.[53]

Bank Control

We know that the flow of control in terms of equity and board ties is for the most part from financials to industrials; the flow from industrials to financials is much smaller.[54] A plausible hypothesis is that this flow exceeds what is strictly necessary to monitor transaction partners. Ramseyer (1994:253) argues that it does not:

> Japanese banks...monitor more extensively...than do American banks because they have lent more funds. If so, banks in Japan have more money at stake in the client firms and, all else equal, should monitor more heavily and rescue more frequently

---

[53] Pennings (1980) finds an association for U.S. industrial firms between debt dependence and interlocking *to* as well as *from* banks.
[54] Gerlach (1992a:79); Kuroki (2001).

for that reason alone. Japanese banks do not lend heavily, in other words, because they monitor or rescue extensively; they monitor and rescue extensively . . . because they lend so heavily.

The issue has important implications. If banks' monitoring and control of firms are commensurate with their lending to those firms, a transaction cost–resource dependence view – focused on the transacting pair or dyad – finds support. If, on the other, the control flow surpasses this threshold – if banks own and participate in the management of companies with whom they do no or little business – a rather different, more macro-network theory of the structural position and role of financials is endorsed. The bank control–hegemony models of critical political economy discussed by Mintz and Schwartz (1985) and Davis and Mizruchi (1999) qualify. So does Sheard's (1994b) perspective on main banks as "reciprocal delegated monitors," acting to monitor and discipline errant firms, not solely on the bank's own behalf, but on that of a community of debt holders and keiretsu partners.[55]

H4.3: *Net of lending–borrowing, financial firms send equity and director ties; industrials receive them.*

Bank Control: Results
Hypothesis 4.3 can be tested by including in our regressions a dummy variable for whether the sending firm is a financial. Table 4.2 shows the coefficient on this term to be positive and significant in the equity equation in every year but one – 1982. The one year seems anomalous. More believable is the smaller drop in 1989, consistent with our knowledge that bank dependence diminished in the bubble years.

The effect of the financial dummy on director dispatch, however, is *negative*. This is implausible, and we discount it as a collinearity symptom. A fair conclusion is that bank control in terms of equity, but not director, ties exceeds the level required to manage bilateral exchange.

Thus, in contrast to perspectives on bank monitoring and governance that take the transacting dyad as unit of analysis (transaction cost, resource dependence, principal–agent theory), our results – showcasing financials as structural leaders of the network (or *delegated monitors*) – testify to the need for a macro-network perspective on Japanese interfirm control.

---

[55] Aoki (1988:149) suggests that concerns with reputation motivate the bank to take a monitoring role disproportionate to its investment in a firm. See Scher (1997) for a critique of theories of main bank monitoring.

Commercial Exchange and the Flow of Control

The flow of control in a commercial exchange is harder to ascertain. Most research in the resource dependence and business strategy traditions lets the issue of whether suppliers bridge to customers or vice versa turn on which side of the exchange is the more concentrated or organized versus competitive or dispersed. Large firms and monopolistic or cartelized industries offer fewer alternatives and hence greater power and autonomy relative to exchange partners.[56]

Resource dependence reasoning would likely view the purchasing firm as the more dependent party to a transaction, since its production hinges directly on that of its suppliers, whereas the reverse need not be true.[57] From a transaction cost vantage point, Williamson (1985:307–8) argues that neither customers nor suppliers have the claim to board representation enjoyed by lenders and stockholders (whose assets when loaned or invested are in the control of another and hence exposed to risk), but the supplier's claim outweighs that of the customer:

> Whether or not suppliers of raw material and intermediate product have a stake in a firm depends on whether they have made substantial investments in durable assets that cannot be redeployed without sacrificing productive value if the relationship with the firm were to be terminated prematurely.

This is the familiar theory of *asset-* or *relation-specific* investment. It has widely advised the study of merger and acquisition, supply chain coordination, and strategic alliance. Yet Williamson's contention that only the supplier – not the customer – in a commercial transaction makes specific investments does not stand up to scrutiny. Japanese intermediate product markets appear to be distinctive in the degree to which customer and supplier alike make long-term relationship-specific investments.[58] Assemblers routinely transfer know-how, technology, and skilled personnel to suppliers in order to guarantee the quality and reliability of the materials they source. They thus dedicate assets and expose themselves to risk owing to such investments in the know-how and processes of their suppliers.

This postulate of symmetry in the interdependence of the partners to a commercial exchange suggests that the control/governance apparatus between supplier and purchaser is balanced, not favoring one over the other.

---

[56] Burt (1983); Ahmadjian and Robinson (2001); Thompson (1967).

[57] See, e.g., Thompson (1967) on sequential interdependence. Also, the greater the value added by the externally supplied input, the more critical the resource and the higher the dependence of the purchasing firm.

[58] Aoki (1988:209), too, notes that the power of a Japanese supplier depends on the technological expertise it brings to the exchange.

Yet the institutional makeup of Japanese supply networks has been such that most close observers see the preponderance of control flowing upstream – from customer to supplier. Japanese vertical keiretsu structures in manufacturing comprise a final, finished-goods assembler (e.g., Toyota, Hitachi, Toshiba) and its satellite subcontractors and suppliers. Size and concentration account for some of the power of assemblers but not all. The customer firm is apt to be older, better known, and higher in status. Status and reputation differentials among Japanese firms shape access to resources such as capital and labor to a greater degree than typically occurs in Western economies.[59] The literature on vertical supply keiretsu amply documents the dominance of final assembler firms and the dependence of satellite suppliers.[60] Customers control suppliers through equity stakes and personnel transfers, and the supplier firms, seeking stability via cooptation strategies, actively solicit such control.[61]

From these institutionalized asymmetries in Japanese industrial goods markets, we infer that control flows from customers to suppliers, not vice versa.

H 4.4: *The customer in a commercial exchange owns shares and places directors in the supplier, not vice versa.*

Results: Commercial Exchange and Control
There is a shift over time in the relative control exercised by buyers and sellers in commercial transactions. The evidence for the early years is that *sellers* (consistent with Williamson's reasoning) are more likely to dispatch directors to *buyers* than the reverse. In later years, however, the buyer effects increase in magnitude, while the seller effects stay the same, so that after 1986 the two are roughly equal.[62]

This pattern of change might reflect the declining role of trading companies, which as brokers of procurement relations among Japanese firms were major sellers of services, raw materials, and other inputs. We have controls for function – whether the firm is a financial, trading company, or manufacturer (the excluded baseline category). Such controls, however, adjust the means (or intercepts) of the outcome variable for type of firm, not the causal parameters (regression slopes) that interest us most. To

---

[59] Clark (1979). On the importance of status in interfirm transactions, see Podolny (1993).

[60] Odaka, Ono, and Adachi (1988); Nishiguchi (1994).

[61] Equally important, as suggested earlier, is that the supplier and subcontractor firms with closest ties to a large assembler such as Toyota or Matsushita are often spun-off divisions. Despite the spin-off's standing as an independently managed firm, its hierarchical relationship with the parent is for a number of purposes preserved (Gerlach and Lincoln, 2001).

[62] This pattern of change in the buying and selling effects is much stronger with the interaction term deleted from the regression.

address the possibility that the change we observe in the process whereby trade ties drive director dispatch stems from the declining role of the shosha, we deleted the shosha from the sample, decreasing its size from 259 to 250 and the maximum number of dyads from 66,822 to 62,500. However, this made little difference in our results.

By contrast, the effects of selling and buying transactions on equity ties are all but identical and remain so over time. Thus, while some change seems to have occurred in how sellers and buyers participate in the management of a partner, little corresponding change is evident in how they use equity stakes to formalize a commitment. We will see, however, that these findings for the full population of firms mask some interesting differences within particular industries.

Shosha Control

Are trading companies, as we found of banks, disproportionately prone to owning shares and placing directors in firms?[63] They, too, performed significant leadership roles in the horizontal groups and in the broader network, including the mounting of rescues and restructurings.[64] Their power was never the equal of the banks, however, and it has eroded more steeply with time. If the shosha's equity stakes and director transfers derive only from their selling and buying patterns, we should conclude that they hold no distinct position in the network.

Results: Shosha Control
In fact, the control exercised by financial institutions does not find a match in the trading company case. A declining shosha role in the Japanese corporate network was indicated by Chapter 3's blockmodel analysis. They comprised a well-formed block in 1978 but not in later years. The present dyad analysis reveals no difference between trading companies and industrial firms in rates of ownership and control. (We will see that in one industry only – metals – a unique shosha effect does exist.) Any part the shosha played in governance was strictly via the transactions they brokered. Not that this is trivial. We do not present analyses of trade and lending ties as outcome variables.[65] We have, however, performed

---

[63] Aside from this issue, a dummy variable for whether the sending or receiving firm is a financial or an industrial is an essential control in the shareholding and director regressions. It adjusts for the constraints on the debt and trade relations imposed by the structure of the data (financials lend almost exclusively to industrials; industrials trade only with industrials).

[64] Sheard (1989b).

[65] Our earlier paper on this topic, however, did present and discuss regression models for lending and trading relations. See Lincoln et al. (1992).

them, and they show the trading companies to be very central nodes. Their profile is particularly high as sellers, although in some years and for some industries they are above-average purchasers as well.[66] Since trading partnerships of both sorts convert into ownership of and directors sent to other firms, the shosha are revealed as powerful shapers of the network. But unlike banks and insurers, they play no particular part in governance beyond their commercial dealings with individual firms.

Reciprocity

Much has been made of the *reciprocity* in Japanese cross-shareholding, director interlocking, and trade and lending networks. It figures, in particular, in the portrait of keiretsu as exclusionary, mutually supportive cliques and has thus been a sensitive issue in Japan's international trade. Where customers and buyers or banks and clients reciprocate business, loops arise from which outsiders are excluded. As Dore (1986:248) put it, "Imports penetrate markets, and where there are no markets, only a network of established 'customer relationships,' it is hard for them to make headway."[67]

The norm of reciprocity is a fundamental organizing principle in any network of exchange.[68] It carries particular force in Japan, where the cultural stress on personal, trusting, and lasting relations fosters mutual obligation to a degree uncommon in the West.[69] Japanese social structural patterns such as *on-giri kankei* (benevolence-obligation relations) strongly

---

[66] Indeed, with the exception of the first year in our series,1980, the stability of the effects of the trading company dummy on selling relationships is striking. They are 0.284 (1980); 0.450 (1982); 0.449 (1984); 0.416 (1986); 0.435 (1989); 0.427 (1991); and 0.433 (1993), all significant beyond the .001 level.

[67] Orru et al. (1997) cite Hiroshi Okumura, a leading Japanese expert on keiretsu, on reciprocal commercial exchanges in Japan. "The role played by trading companies within each intermarket group and outside it reiterates the networking features of large groups in Japan. Within intermarket groups, the trading company facilitates the reciprocal exchange of goods. In some cases, the trading firm acts only as intermediary in the reciprocal exchange of goods between two group firms; in other instances, however, such reciprocity is created by the trading co. Okumura observes that a trading firm can contrive a reciprocal deal where only a unilateral deal would otherwise be possible. Mitsubishi Heavy might sell ships to Nippon Yusen but Yusen would have nothing to sell to Mitsubishi Heavy. Mitsubishi Corp, however, has a reciprocal relation with both; it sells steel to and purchases ships from Mitsubishi Heavy and sells these ships to New York and relies on its services for the transportation of goods.... Trading companies also promote intergroup exchanges. Outside firms which sell their products to group firms are obliged to purchase goods from these companies. The reciprocity of the transaction is made possible by the mediation of the general trading company." See also Gerlach (1992a:148).

[68] Gouldner (1960).

[69] Dore (1983); Nakane (1970); Sako and Helper (1998).

encourage reciprocal commitments of the "you scratch my back and I'll scratch yours" sort.

Reciprocity of Control

The concept of cross-shareholding – so common to the usual portraits of the Japanese corporate network – conveys a strong sense of mutuality or reciprocity (*kabushiki mochiai*) in Japanese business networks. The NLI Research Institute finds that nearly 15 percent of shareholdings among firms listed on Japanese stock exchanges are reciprocated (Kuroki, 2001).[70] What purpose does reciprocal stock ownership serve? The prime rationale for interlocking ownership in the early post-war Japanese economy was that of takeover defense. If one firm sold the shares it held in another, the latter was thereby released from its obligation to the first, exposing both to takeover risk. The web of cross-shareholdings removed most stock from active trading, thus insulating the participating firms from acquisition. Further, as earlier observed, an equity tie is a form of gift exchange, publicly announcing each party's commitment to the other.[71] Reciprocity of equity ties is key to the risk pooling function of Japanese corporate networks: *I* is unlikely to take a stake in and thus credibly commit to the welfare of *J* unless *J* is willing to commit similarly to *I*.

Thus, reciprocal cross-shareholding signals a pair of firms' mutual obligations and provides a basis for active intervention (e.g., the transfer of managers), all the while keeping much of a company's stock in stable, friendly hands.

H4.5: *Reciprocity in equity ties has been high but declining.*

We expect less, perhaps even *negative*, reciprocity in the director transfer network, that is, a tie from *I* to *J* *dampens* the probability of a tie from *J* to *I*. Interlocking directorate research often finds such ties to be symmetric or reciprocated. But director dispatch in Japan, as noted, is different: it is a much more intrusive and consequential involvement by one firm in the management of another. It is often the instrument whereby a large manufacturer, main bank, or keiretsu grouping rescues, restructures, or disciplines a troubled partner. It seems inherently less symmetric than cross-shareholding. A possible parallel exists with the dependence of equity and director relations on financial transactions studied earlier: lenders and borrowers own stakes in one another, but lenders dispatch directors to borrowers, not vice versa.

---

[70] See also Gerlach (1992a:77–78); Lincoln et al. (1992:577).
[71] Akerlof (1982).

H4.6: *Reciprocity in director dispatch is absent or negative.*

Results: Reciprocity of Control
The idea of reciprocity is used widely but metaphorically to convey a sense of trust, obligation, and exclusiveness in a network of relationships.[72] Absent careful measurement, its importance as a distinctive structural property cannot be assessed. Moreover, it is important to distinguish between reciprocity as a descriptive *attribute* of a network – for example, the NLI study that 15 percent of interfirm shareholdings are reciprocated – and as *causal* process – for example, the propensity of one actor to return a favor bestowed by another.[73] Firm I might own a stake in J because I is J's main bank and the source of much of its debt. Suppose, in addition, that J owns shares in I because I is a large manufacturer and J is main bank to most of I's supply chain. Thus, I owns J and vice versa but the observed reciprocity is not causal but reflects the business I and J do with each other and with a set of third-party firms.

In formal network analysis, however, reciprocity is modeled as a distinct causal parameter. In a dyad regression of the sort this chapter uses, the reciprocity effect is β in the equation $E_{ij} = \alpha + \beta E_{ji} + \Sigma_k x_k + \varepsilon_{ij}$ where E_{ij} is the equity tie from firm I to J, E_{ji} is the equity tie from J to I, $\Sigma_k x_k$ are other dyad- and firm-level explanatory variables, and ε_{ij} is the usual stochastic error term (see Appendix 4.1). $\beta > 0$ in this example implies *positive* reciprocity of shareholding: I is more likely to own J if J owns I. $\beta < 0$ implies *negative* reciprocity: I is *less* likely to own J if J owns I.

What do we find? Our hypotheses hold that shareholding reciprocity is greater than director reciprocity; indeed, that the latter might even be negative. In fact, the data in Table 4.2 say it is the other way around. In most years we observe positive and significant reciprocity effects on equity and director ties alike. But the reciprocity in equity ties is consistently the weaker of the two.

Reciprocity and Size
The relatively weak reciprocity in equity ties evident in our entire set of firms might be due to the fact that cross-shareholding is predominantly a large-firm phenomenon.[74] To test this hypothesis, we split the sample of 259 companies at the median of size (log of total assets). This yields a greatly reduced set of dyads: 16,384 as opposed to 66,882. To save space, we do not present these regressions, but merely comment on them in the

---

[72] Powell (1990); Uzzi (1996).
[73] Akerlof (1982); Blau (1964); Gouldner (1960); Schelling (1978).
[74] See also Gerlach (1992a:77).

text. The picture in regard to director dispatch is unchanged: In 1980, for instance, the reciprocity coefficient shifts only slightly from 1.5 in the full population to 1.8 in the large-firm subsample. But the reciprocity in equity ties more than doubles: from 0.192 in the full set to 0.510 in the large firm subset. The lending and trade effects are correspondingly reduced. Thus, the pattern is what we surmised: reciprocity of ownership is high when the firms involved are large. When either or both are small, there is much less of it.

Is Reciprocity Fading Away?

A reasonable assumption is that business reciprocity has been declining in Japan. Like the connectivity studied in the previous chapter, reciprocity is a socially embedded structural property of the network economy that appears to be withering away as companies cast off received obligations and seek partnerships more strategically tailored to business goals and competitive markets. Indeed, a drop in reciprocity would in part explain the downward trending connectivity of the equity network so conspicuously apparent in Chapter 3's cohesion analysis. For a simple example, compare the case of A $\Rightarrow$ B $\Rightarrow$ C with A $\Leftrightarrow$ B $\Leftrightarrow$ C. In the first case (no reciprocity), connectivity = 0.5. In the second case (perfect reciprocity), connectivity = 1.0. The evidence for the hypothesis of reciprocity decline varies with the relation. With respect to director ties, it is solid. From 1978 and 1986, the reciprocity effect on directors is significant and stable, but in 1993 it vanishes. On the other hand, reciprocity in equity relations is significant in every observation year, and the year-to-year differences are small. Contrary to expectations, it ticks up discernibly in the bubble year, 1989. Recall from Chapter 3 that the *density* of the equity network rose from 1986 to 1989, while *connectivity* declined. Our interpretation there was twofold: (a) upwardly spiraling stock values were motivating companies to view stock purchases much more as investments than commitments; (b) where equity ties had a governance rationale, it was strategic and dyadic rather than obligatory and macro-network (i.e., keiretsu).

Reciprocity Economizes on "Hard" Governance

To the many contemporary critics of Japanese crony capitalism, reciprocity is a cancer on the country's body economic that obstructs the path to modernization and reform. An interesting strain of mainstream interorganizational theory, on the other hand, sees reciprocity as a governance device serving to avert information asymmetries and opportunistic behavior and thus otherwise support and stabilize an exchange. Williamson (1985:191–3) held that reciprocity in customer–supply transactions lowers the downside risk of investments in specialized assets. A supplier will commit productive resources to the specialized needs of a single corporate customer if that customer in turn dedicates production to the input needs of the supplier. Such reciprocity, in his language, constitutes an "exchange of hostages," which commits each party to long-term business dealings with the other.[75] Resource dependence theory similarly holds that reciprocity balances the power in an exchange and will thus be sought by the weaker party as a means of managing its dependence.[76] Such reasoning parallels arguments that sentiments of trust, commitment, or benevolence smooth exchange relations and economize on "hard" governance. Sako and Helper (1998), for example, argue that reciprocity of information exchange between customers and suppliers in intermediate product markets fosters trust. Gulati (1995) finds that partner firms with a history of strategic alliances are less inclined to formalize new ones with an equity stake, because, he believes, the buildup of trust renders it unnecessary. Important as they may well be, the sentiments of trust and benevolence are hard to measure. Reciprocity, on the other hand, is a concrete and observable network property whose effects can be measured and modeled with some precision.[77]

H4.7: *Trade reciprocity reduces equity and director ties.*

Although we are not aware of scholarly literature explicitly addressed to the issue, similar reasoning might apply to the relationship between equity and director ties. When cross-shareholding is *reciprocated*, its efficacy as a governance device is arguably bolstered, thus reducing the need for additional layers of control.[78]

H4.8: *Equity tie reciprocity reduces director ties.*

Results: Reciprocity as Governance
We measure the *effect* of reciprocity – e.g., that of trade reciprocity on equity ties – with an interaction term: the product of "sells to" and "buys

---

[75] Caves and Uekusa (1976:61), however, offer an explanation for commercial reciprocity that is supported by, not in lieu of, cross-shareholding. In a producer goods market characterized by some monopolization, such that list prices exceed marginal costs, a customer confers a rent upon its chosen supplier. If the customer in addition has an equity stake in that supplier, part of the rent returns to the customer in the form of a dividend payment.

[76] Pfeffer and Salancik (1978:149).

[77] Kogut (1989) also notes the association between the trust concept and the observables of continuance and reciprocity in an economic exchange. For a recent experimental treatment of the trust-reciprocity relationship in a cooperative game-theory framework, see McCabe, Rigdon, and Smith (2003).

[78] Sheard (1994b) makes the interesting argument that diligence and honesty in performing the Japanese main bank monitoring role is enforced, not by a written contract or formal governance procedure, but by a similar set of reciprocal obligations among all the lenders to a given firm.

from." A positive coefficient means that the likelihood that I sells to (buys from) J is higher if J sells to (buys from) I.

We do not present regressions for commercial and financial relations – only for equity and director ties. We have, however, run them, and they reveal substantial reciprocity in firms' selection of trading partners.[79] The question for us now is whether trade reciprocity attenuates governance ties as our hypotheses contend. The results are clear-cut. In the regressions for equity ties, the interaction term takes a negative and significant coefficient in every year. It is stable over time, save for some postbubble (after 1989) weakening. Reciprocity in trade also dampens director linkage in all years but 1982 and 1984. In particular, the effect intensifies from 1986 (the endaka year) on. (Recall that the lending–borrowing effect on directors also rose in this year.)

Thus, as much recent theory and research suggests, reciprocity of exchange (with its various implications of trust, benevolence, and obligation) enables firms to economize on formal governance.

On the other hand, H4.8 – that reciprocity in cross-shareholding enables a pair of firms to economize on director exchange – gets no support. To the contrary, this effect (the equity tie interaction), while nonsignificant in most years, is *positive*. This pattern is consistent with the postulate of *multiplexity* in Japanese corporate networks key to the blockmodel analysis in Chapter 3: rather than strong ties of one sort (e.g., reciprocated cross-shareholding) economizing on or reducing the need for strong ties of another sort (director dispatch), firms bound one way to one another are generally bound other ways as well. Thus, reciprocity in commercial exchange, as transaction cost and resource dependence theories suggest, seems to substitute for formal governance. Reciprocated equity ties, however, are reinforced with director interlocks.

Attributes of Firms

Our analysis considers three firm-level attributes as potential explanatory variables. By evaluating the contributions of firm size, age, and financial/industrial sector to the shaping interfirm ties, we glean further insight into exchange and control asymmetries in Japanese corporate networks.

Size and Age

The extent to which networks of trade, lending, shareholding, and director transfers are balanced and reciprocated versus asymmetric and

---

[79] Lincoln et al. (1992).

hierarchical turns in part on the relative scale of the transacting firms. The Japanese economy has long been characterized as dualistic (*niju kozo*), meaning that small firms are subject to the control of large firms and to general discrimination in capital, labor, and product markets.[80] While still figuring prominently in critical and journalistic commentary, dualist theory has been challenged in recent years by considerable evidence that the relationship between the two sectors is in fact one of *risk-sharing*.[81] Large firms (including financial institutions and major manufacturers) do take advantage of small ones as product and labor market buffers (e.g., by off-loading redundant employees in a downturn or taking production in-house). But they in turn insulate smaller partners from risk by guaranteeing markets, access to capital and skills, and rescue in the event of crisis. Even so, the flow of control in the network is predominantly from large firm core to smaller firm periphery.

Early founding is typical of the core of the Japanese economy, while younger and smaller companies populate the periphery. The "liability of newness" much discussed in organizational ecology, operates with particular force in Japan as the established business networks pose severe barriers to entry by entrepreneurial firms.[82] Moreover, the reputation and status conferred by longevity determine a company's fortunes in labor and capital markets. The oldest and most established firms in the Japanese economy are often big-six shacho-kai members. The zaibatsu groups (Mitsui, Mitsubishi, and Sumitomo) have long pre-war histories. Post-war companies such as Honda, Sony, and Kyocera are not on shacho-kai, and all had difficulty overcoming keiretsu barriers to their participation in supply and distribution networks.[83] Their success stemmed from their overseas competitiveness. In trade networks, purchasing firms are typically older than suppliers and consequently enjoy an advantage in legitimacy and reputation. Two reasons for the age disparity are (1) attachment as a parts supplier to a larger, more experienced firm gives a start-up access to scarce know-how and capital; (2) affiliated suppliers are often spun-off divisions of the parent firm.[84]

H4.9: *Larger and older firms send equity and directors to other companies; smaller and younger firms receive them.*

---

[80] Ito (1992); Nishiguchi (1994); Whittaker (1997).
[81] Aoki (1984); Asanuma and Kikutani (1992); Kawasaki and McMillan (1987).
[82] Freeman, Carroll, and Hannan (1983).
[83] Managers we interviewed at Kyocera Corporation in 1996 made this point emphatically. Had President Inamori, the founding chief executive, not aggressively sought business in the United States, they said, Kyocera could not have survived.
[84] On the Japanese corporate practice of spinning-off businesses as keiretsu affiliates, see Gerlach and Lincoln (2001); Ito (1995); Takahashi (1995).

Results: Size and Age

The support for H4.9 is strong. Table 4.2 shows the predicted pattern in the equity case holding in most years: positive size and age effects of owning firm and negative size and age effects of the firm owned. The director results are less clear-cut: the size and age effects of the dispatching firm are large and positive. They are less consistent predictors of director receipt: negative in all years, as hypothesized, but often nonsignificant.

Groups Again

Homophily

The blockmodel inquiry gave a fairly clear and interpretable picture of how function (industry) and group (keiretsu) organize the large-firm network and how that network has changed over time. Our conclusion was that keiretsu as a principle of economic organization has been hugely important – among industrials more so than among financials. The power of that principle has diminished, but much more markedly in regard to the bank-centered groups than the former *zaibatsu*. Our evidence thus addressed the nature and evolution of the keiretsu form but it could not speak to what we are calling Asanuma's problem: whether keiretsu effects are cultural or historical in nature as opposed to having an economic and managerial rationale.

We extract from Asanuma's passage two propositions. The first, with which he is clearly at odds, is the assumption on which the blockmodeling rests: that the four exchange and control ties are substitutable indicators of how firms affiliate with groups. The working hypothesis here is that the intercorrelations among them are due not to the causality relating one to another, but to the underlying power, first, of keiretsu and, second, of industry in weaving an array of interorganizational linkages into structurally equivalent sets.

The contrasting view, favored by Asanuma, is that any claim to independent causal status for keiretsu is just wrong. Clusterings of Japanese firms based on tight or similar relations of governance and exchange may well exist. But they are explicable as outcomes of routine operations of economic institutions that have close parallels in the West: the monitoring or governance of regularized financial and commercial exchange. For historical reasons Japan failed to evolve certain institutional arrangements key to the operations of the U.S. or British economies – for example, an active merger and acquisition market or a system of independent auditing or true outside directors. But it produced parallel structures – for example, the main bank system – that functioned similarly in monitoring transactions and disciplining management teams who strayed too far from the straight and narrow path of earnings growth and share price maximization.

Our rendering of the Asanuma hypothesis is that keiretsu makes no unique contribution to the shaping of equity and director networks. While such ties may appear to be means of maintaining the cohesion of the group, they exist only to coordinate the market transactions of member firms.[85] Asanuma thus seems to allow for the possibility of keiretsu homophily in trade and lending – that firms within groups favor one another's business over that of outsiders – but rule it out in the equity and director nets.

We respectfully disagree. There are too many indications that equity and director ties are forged merely to maintain and protect the group – for example, from hostile takeovers or as a way of assisting member firms. If we detect tendencies, net of debt and trading partnerships within groups, for firms in the same groups to link to one another via equity and director ties, we conclude that Asanuma is wrong and that a cohesion–maintenance rationale accounts for groups' use of governance ties.[86]

H4.10: *Big-six homophily: Equity and director ties are most prevalent within groups. This fluctuates with the business cycle but has declined over time.*

Results: Group Homophily
We use a single measure of whether a pair of companies is in the same horizontal group. The alternatives are as follows: (1) the pair spans

---

[85] The one form of governance associated with keiretsu for which this claim is not easily made is that of the shacho-kai, which, as elsewhere noted, is the only truly formal administrative manifestation of big-six affiliation. Moreover, shacho-kai membership is by definition group-wide, not bilateral in the sense of a control structure evolved to manage the business exchange of a given pair of firms. Indeed, while the shacho-kai do occasionally deal with the business dealings of the group firms – for example, the early 1990s tie-ups of several Mitsubishi firms with Daimler Benz, the Sumitomo *Hakusui-kai*'s involvement in the 1996 Sumitomo Shoji copper trading scandal, the Mitsui *Nimoku-kai*'s handling of the "Mitsukoshi incident" (Gerlach, 1992a:111) – active business planning by the councils is circumscribed by Japan's antimonopoly law and risks the ire of the Fair Trade Commission.

[86] Caution is required in using statistical evidence to reach this conclusion. There is a risk of attributing cultural effects to residual differences between countries, regions, or, in this case, business groupings (Hauser, 1970; Lincoln, Olson, and Hanada, 1978). The principal concern is that the researcher may not have measured and controlled the composition of the group on other causal factors. There are, of course, only two forms of economic exchange – financial and commercial – and we have data on both. Yet our ability to control them is only as strong as our measurement. In the case of lending, that is not a problem – we have excellent information on the identities of major lenders to every corporation in our sample and the volume of their loans. But the trade data are much less complete. We only know that one firm names another as an "important" seller or buyer of goods, nothing about the volume of the sale. Moreover, the definition of "important" or "major" is up to the firm to interpret.

different groups; (2) one is in a group and the other is independent; or
(3) both are independent. To separate these possibilities, we include two
dummy variables for whether firm I (the sending firm) or firm J (the
receiving firm) is independent (= 1) versus shacho-kai (= 0). This combination of measures enables us to address an important distinction. Big-six
corporations, as Chapter 3 showed, may be more inclined to trade within
groups than between them. At the same time, however, given their central
position in the network, we expect transactions and control to issue from
the big six as a set, with noncouncil firms the targets.

There is indeed positive homophily (a propensity to forge within-group
ties) in the equity and director networks in all years. This is at odds with
the Asanuma conjecture, construed here to mean that the keiretsu question
devolves to how pairs of firms use governance ties to manage bilateral
exchange. Even with debt and trade held constant, marked tendencies
remain for firms to send equity and directors within groups. The big-six
molding of the director network warrants special note, since this is net,
not only of lending and trade, but also of cross-shareholding.

Do the homophily effects show a secular decline, some business cycle
fluctuations notwithstanding? The shifts in how group firms use control
ties are conspicuous, interesting, and hinge on the tie in question. In the
equity case, 1989 – the bubble's peak – is a watershed year. The group
effect, stable over the preceding interval, is cut by a quarter in 1989 and
declines more in the remaining two years. A look back at the group-
specific equity densities in Figure 3.2 shows Mitsubishi, Sumitomo, and
Fuyo following this kind of trend.

The most notable change in how the big six mold the contours of the
director network is the large increase in homophily in 1986. This was
a time of marked restructuring within the big six – a scaling down of
old industries and a transfer of resources and personnel to new ones.[87]
Another glance at Figure 3.2 shows a sharp rise in the director density of
the Mitsubishi group, a smaller one in the case of DKB, and no discernible
change in the other groups.

Group Centrality

Beyond the homophily effects just documented and discussed, the horizontal groups mold the corporate network in another way – through centrality effects. Specifically, shacho-kai members are centrally positioned
in the network of corporate control; independents occupy the periphery.
In financial exchange, for example, control relations issue from big-six
banks and insurers to all firms, whether shacho-kai or not. Likewise, in

[87] Dore (1986); Taira and Levine (1985).

commercial exchange, big-six manufacturers take stakes in and send directors to off-council suppliers and distributors. This, as discussed earlier and illustrated in Figure 1.1, is the interface between the horizontal and vertical keiretsu. The final-assembly firms at the top of the vertical groups are shacho-kai members; their satellite suppliers are not. Through such hierarchically ordered networks, then, the group extends control from the core to the periphery of the corporate economy.

H 4.11: *Big-six centrality: shacho-kai firms send equity and directors; independent firms receive them.*

Results: Big-Six Centrality
Applied to the equity network, the hypothesis of shacho-kai centrality finds clear confirmation. Group firms are likely to be owners and independent firms are likely to be owned, although the second pattern decays with time. The directors' case, however, differs. Independents both send and receive more directors. We thought this result might be spurious, induced by collinearity among the many terms in the regression and aggravated by the sparseness of the director matrix, hence the extremely low variance of the dependent variable. We reran the director regressions, omitting the equity terms. It changed things not a whit: independents remained more likely to dispatch directors, albeit less so than their propensity to receive them. There is thus a difference in how groups shape director and equity interlock networks; that is, the homophily constraint on director ties is greater. Netting out the tendency for shacho-kai members to second executives to one another, independents both send and receive at higher rates. Group firms dispatch within the group and independents dispatch to independents. Note, however, that the tendency of independents to send directors is time dependent: peaking in 1984 then fading to nonsignificance in 1991 and 1993. By contrast, independents' propensity to receive directors is strong in all periods.

Region

Distance and location are also powerful forces in the structuring of corporate networks. Indeed, the primary cliques of companies identified in U.S. studies are regionally based, centered on local banking institutions.[88] While Japan has no equivalent to U.S.-style regulatory strictures on interstate banking, its financial and commercial networks do display a good deal of regional differentiation. The distinctive cultures and competitive

---

[88] Kono et al. (1998); Levine (1972); Lincoln (1978); Mintz and Schwartz (1985); Pred (1977).

rivalries of the Kansai (Kobe, Kyoto, Osaka) and Kanto (Tokyo basin) areas contribute importantly to this localization of networks. The powerful strains toward interpersonal, face-to-face interaction in Japanese business contribute as well. Yet in recent years, Tokyo's centripetal pull has grown, notwithstanding efforts of other regions – Kansai in particular – to raise their profiles in the national economy through a variety of expensive development plans, the most significant of which was the new Kansai International Airport that opened in 1994.

Defining an industrial district as a "great number of enterprises geographically close to each other engaged in industrial production with a division of labor, which also functions as the core of the regional economy," a report by the Japan Small Business Research Institute (1999:17) notes the strongly hierarchical form such districts frequently assume. The reason is their organization around a spatially concentrated vertical keiretsu:

> Castle town districts... consist of companies belonging to specific industries such as electrical machinery, motor vehicles and steel. The industrial district in Hitachi City, for example, is a typical castle town type district where Hitachi... [is] at its apex and subcontractors for lower layers that serve Hitachi. These are relations based on coexistence and co-prosperity between the parent company and subcontract enterprises nurtured through many years of steady transactions.

The best known case of vertical keiretsu concentration in one region, however, is the Toyota group, much of it situated in Aichi Prefecture, which includes Nagoya. The network's high site-specificity gave Toyota suppliers easy access to one another and to the headquarters and assembly plants of the parent firm. It has thus figured importantly in the vaunted efficiency of the Toyota supply chain. Toyota's strategy since the mid-1980s of dispersing production both within (e.g., to the southernmost island of Kyushu) and outside Japan has sped the erosion of the traditional system of tightly cooperative supply relations.[89]

The interface between regional loyalties and keiretsu ties is nicely highlighted in a recent *Financial Times* article on a series of recent actions (discussed further in Chapter 6) by Toyota Motor Corporation to rescue and rehabilitate ailing affiliates.[90] The piece is sufficiently revealing that it is worth quoting at length.

> The decision by Dai Nippon Construction to file a rehabilitation plan with the Tokyo Courts, after out of control debts prompted

[89] Ahmadjian and Lincoln (2001).
[90] Ibison (2003a, 2003b).

its collapse, attracted scant attention. But, although low key, the deal symbolized a troubling recent development: the growing use of traditional business relationships by two of the country's banks to help replenish their capital base. Dai Nippon's main lender was Gifu Bank, a small regional bank, which had received financial support in 2001 from Tokai Bank, one of the banks that was merged to create UFJ Bank. Gifu Bank needed additional financial assistance to cover its exposure to Dai Nippon and turned to UFJ, which, despite its own huge portfolio of non-performing loans, agreed to transfer some of its healthy loans to the regional lender. But UFJ was also exposed to Tomen, a struggling general trading company, and succeeded in getting Toyota to make a ¥1 billion [$85m] capital injection into Tomen with a view to rolling it under the wing of Toyota Tsusho, its own trading company. In addition, UFJ asked Toyota to provide it with an additional ¥30bn in direct financial support by subscribing to preferred UFJ shares it plans to issue. *The link between Dai Nippon Construction, Gifu Bank, Tokai Bank, UFJ and Toyota is the industrial city of Nagoya. The city is effectively Toyota's home town. It had a longstanding relationship with Nagoya-based Tokai Bank before it became UFJ. Gifu Bank is also located in the next prefecture and shares a number of borrowers with Tokai, most of whom are manufacturers in and around the Nagoya area. Brian Waterhouse, analyst at HSBC Securities, pointed out that Nagoya's banks and companies maintain notoriously tight links. He said lenders, including Tokyo city banks, were forced to pull out of the area as none of the Nagoya companies would use non-Nagoya banks.* The Dai Nippon experience reveals that geography and history are being used to dictate lending decisions and financial support between companies in a manner redolent of the keiretsu links between various business groupings, famous from the pre-bubble days. (Our italics.)

Spatial concentration has been notably characteristic of the horizontal groups as well, particularly the two most cohesive former zaibatsu: Mitsubishi, where the *honsha* or headquarters of most member companies sit cheek-to-jowl in the Marunouchi district of Tokyo. The headquarters of core Sumitomo group firms are similarly concentrated in Osaka. Some of Sumitomo's insularity and cohesion as a group is attributed to its Kansai location and its business commitments to other locally headquartered firms such as Matsushita and Sanyo.

Casual discourse in Japanese business circles routinely alludes to the contrasts in style and values that mark companies and practices in different regions. Kansai firms have a long-standing reputation for hard business dealings and a strong bottom-line orientation. Toyota corporate culture is widely perceived as Nagoya-based: stodgy and provincial, never flashy or off the beaten path. Our blockmodel analysis in the previous chapter highlighted the regional component in keiretsu alignments: Kansai and other Western Japan companies often have Sumitomo or Sanwa Bank leanings, as both banks are Osaka-based.

We thus expect regional homophily to structure the corporate network: companies do business with and make commitments to one another within regions and somewhat less so between regions. Yet there is also a distinct hierarchy of regions in terms of centrality in the economy as a whole. Tokyo (Kanto) is the paramount metropolitan region, the center of government, media, finance, business and professional services, and trade association activity. In distant second place but still enormously significant as a hub of economic activity is the Kansai area, including the cities of Osaka, Kobe, and Kyoto. The trend through the 1990s was one of greater concentration of corporate activity in Tokyo, due in large measure to a perception on the part of non-Kanto companies that they were disadvantaged in the competition for government attention. In Chapter 1, we noted the lament of a Sumitomo Bank executive regarding the Tokyo-based "keiretsu" of politicians, bureaucrats, and business interests. Sumitomo's solution, as well as other Western-headquartered firms such as Matsushita, Sanwa Bank, and Toyota, was to establish a Tokyo headquarters in addition to its historical base in Osaka.

We hypothesize a greater flow of interorganizational control from Tokyo to Kansai than in the reverse direction. Moreover, we expect this asymmetry in the regional structuring of business networks to increase over time.

H4.12: *Regional homophily: Equity and director ties are greatest within the Kansai and Kanto regions.*

H4.13: *Regional centrality: Kanto (Tokyo) firms send equity and directors; firms in other regions receive them.*

Region Results

We do find some regional homophily in director and equity networks: both are denser within the Kanto (Tokyo) and Kansai (Osaka) regions than between them. Indexed by the regression slopes, the degree of regional homophily is about the same in Tokyo and Kansai. Because more of our firms are headquartered in Tokyo, however, fewer of the Kansai effects are statistically significant. Also, Kansai homophily has diminished with time. The first part of H4.13 – the centrality hypothesis – is weakly confirmed: Tokyo firms wield more control over Kansai firms than vice versa. However, that pattern has not increased with time. Combined with the signs of falling homophily, it appears that Kanto and Kansai firms have been stepping up their equity and executive transfers to the rest of the country. This, of course, is consistent with our knowledge that domestic manufacturing has been migrating to less populated and costly regions of Japan.

An Industry-Specific Analysis

To this point, our inquiry rested on the implicit assumption that the processes whereby Japanese firms are networked to one another through exchange and control relations are industry invariant. Clearly, however, industry matters. However, we are not equipped to undertake more than an exploratory treatment of industry differences. Our population of large Japanese firms is not representative of major industries, and even were it so, we have insufficient firms for a rigorous within-industry analysis. Our main purpose here is to gain some assurance that the aggregate results examined thus far do not mask patterns unique to individual industries. We shall see that, for the most part, the industry differences are not large, yet some are noteworthy and warrant attention. We begin by laying out several theories for how industries might differ in network organization.

A Transaction Cost Perspective

From a transaction cost perspective, networks constitute a hybrid organizational form, intermediate between arm's-length markets and top-down bureaucratic control. Whether particular industries rely more or less on network forms should vary with the economies realizable from locating production stages within the boundaries of a single firm as opposed to distributing them across a set of networked firms. Asanuma (1985) and Ahmadjian and Lincoln (2001) see a transaction cost logic behind the rather different modes of organizing exchange in the Japanese automobile and electronic industries. The close and cooperative keiretsu-based customer–supplier relations that have drawn so much attention are much more distinctive of automobile than electronics manufacturing. Transaction cost reasoning says this is due to the intermediate level of asset specificity typical of parts and subassemblies. Components (engines, transmissions, wiring harnesses, brake systems, electronic components) are produced in clearly separable stages but may require substantial customization by vehicle type and model. Thus, Japanese automakers tended to specialize in design and assembly, leaving the production of key parts to suppliers and subcontractors. The nonstandard nature of many such inputs, however, required that suppliers bind with manufacturers and with one another in stable, cooperative relationships.

In electronics, on the other hand, fast development times, short product life cycles, and close integration of components demand such tight coupling of production stages that the kind of flexible outsourcing to and partnering with suppliers typical of autos has been the exception rather than the rule.[91] Thus, electronics makers internalized the design, manufacture, and assembly of high-value electronic parts and assemblies, contracting out for highly standardized and low value-added materials and parts such as moldings, casings, packaging, and the like. These could be bought off the shelf from external vendors or fabricated by the supplier from a manufacturer's blueprint without extensive coordination or communication between the two. Thus, Japan's large electronics firms have been more vertically integrated than the country's auto producers, have rather more arm's length relations with suppliers, and were less likely to manage supply transactions with equity stakes, personnel transfers, and the like. They also have been less prone to risk-sharing interventions.[92]

Consequently, Japanese automakers – Toyota being the best-known case – evolved a highly distinctive model of production and supply chain organization. Compact firms with narrow product lines (e.g., passenger sedans) specialized in design and assembly, while relying on an array of partners both to supply them with components and to fill out product offerings on a consignment or original equipment manufacturer (OEM) basis.[93] Japan's major electronics corporations, on the other hand, have broad product lines, decentralized divisional structures, are vertically integrated into parts making and subassemblies, and deal at relative arm's length with a larger base of suppliers who are relatively uninvolved in design and development.[94]

Supply Chain Stage
A more general hypothesis in a TCE vein rests on the observation that whole industries differ in their approximate stage in the supply or value chain from raw materials to finished products delivered to an end user. Autos and electronics run the gamut: from production of early-stage components and subassemblies used in downstream manufacture to finished consumer products. Chemicals, which in our coding includes pharmaceuticals

---

[91] Asanuma (1989); Guillot and Lincoln (2001).
[92] Our observations on the Japanese electronics industry are based on a series of interviews between 1994 and 1997 with Matsushita, Sanyo, and Mitsubishi Electric. See Guillot and Lincoln (2003); Lincoln et al. (1998).
[93] Fruin and Nishiguchi (1992), Nishiguchi (1994); Shioji (1995).
[94] Beer and Spector (1981); Shimotani (1998).

and petrochemicals, is also a mix. Much of the industry's production is sold as inputs to other sectors, but a great deal of it is also purchased by end users. However, machinery and metals are industries that for the most part are high in the supply chain: their customers are other manufacturers, not individual consumers.

A classification of industries by supply chain stage signifies multiple things, but particularly important for a network study such as our own is its implications for the specificity of assets and hence the interdependence of exchange partners. Consumer goods approximates the economic ideal of an efficient spot market. The number of customers is large, and little specialization of customer to producer exists. Switching costs are low. Customers do develop loyalties to brands or companies, and companies tailor marketing and product offerings to customer types and market segments. But on the whole these markets better fit the neoclassical ideal than do industrial goods markets.

The transaction cost hypothesis is that industries marked by asset- and relation-specific transactions display more complex governance forms. In our terms, this means greater reciprocity and stronger statistical associations between the magnitude or frequency of financial or commercial exchange and the overlaying of exchange with cross-shareholdings and interlocking boards.

H4.14: *Relative to industries low in the supply chain (e.g., autos and electronics), industries high in the supply chain (e.g., metals and machinery) embed exchange in complex governance relations (cross-shareholding, director transfer, reciprocity).*

An Institutional Perspective

Viewed through a sociological lens, industries constitute distinct institutional environments for their constituent firms.[95] The managerial practices and modes of organization common to the industry acquire a taken-for-granted legitimacy, making them models that later generations of firms will reflexively emulate. Such differences in environment come about in a variety of ways: the age of the industry, the state of the world when it came into being, its defining technological and entrepreneurial innovations, the past or present dominance of a lead company, or its particular relations with regulators, banks, unions, and other critical parties. These are just a few of the founding and development forces driving industries down sharply divergent paths.[96]

---

[95] Hirsch (1975); Scott and Meyer (1994).
[96] Hannan and Freeman (1989); Stinchcombe (1965).

The Japanese automobile industry illustrates. Why this sector was con-figured in keiretsu networks of quasi-independent suppliers and manu-facturers while its U.S. counterpart was organized much more in terms of integrated and diversified firms was, in the eyes of the economic histo-rians who studied the issue, a matter of later development, weak capital markets, fragmented supply networks, and strong bank control.[97] Similar tales can be told about other industries, since each has its own history and thus to some degree a unique institutional environment.

Industry Age
A specific hypothesis drawn from institutional theory is that of *imprint-ing*: older industries are encumbered by the modes of organization build-ing prevalent at the time of origin.[98] Invoking the assumption that the Japanese economy is becoming more market rational and less adminis-tered and network-y, a reasonable prediction is that older industries such as metals and textiles are more network-embedded in general and keiretsu bound in particular than industries such as chemicals and machinery, which in turn are more so encumbered than autos and electronics.

H4.15: *Relative to younger industries (e.g., autos and electronics), older industries (e.g., chemicals and metals):*
    a. Embed transactions in complex control relations (cross-shareholding, director transfer, reciprocity)[99]
    b. Exhibit big-six homophily and centrality effects.

Global Integration
Another hypothesis suggested by a combination of economic and insti-tutional perspectives is that industries with a strong export orientation – those in which Japan is internationally competitive – differ from industries oriented to the domestic market. The latter are presumably protected to some degree from the harsh competition in the global economy. More-over, they have adapted to a business environment that is highly insti-tutionalized, one that places much store by stable, embedded interfirm relationships. The global players, by contrast, have proven themselves in a competitive environment configured for the most part by a very different and arguably more stringent set of rules.

---

[97] Cusumano (1985); Odaka et al. (1988).
[98] Stinchcombe (1965).
[99] We acknowledge the appearance of some inconsistency here. Earlier we hypothesized (and found) that reciprocity was a functional substitute for formal governance. Now we suggest that both are network forms of organization. The point is that both constitute control structures for the bridging or embedding of exchange.

Table 4.3. *Number of Firms and Shacho-kai Composition by Industry*

Industry	No. Firms	Shacho-kai Proportion
Automobile	20	.199
Electronics and electrical machinery	21	.419
Metals	28	.60
Chemical	31	.524
Nonelectrical machinery	17	.706

Chemicals is an industry in which Japan's comparative advantage has been small. In metals, by contrast, Japan has been a major player but has ceded ground over the years to lower-cost producers. Autos, electronics, and machinery are all sectors in which Japan remains a formidable competitor.

H4.16: *Relative to industries in which Japan is globally competitive (e.g., autos, electronics, and machinery), domestically oriented industries (e.g., chemicals and metals):*

    a. Embed transactions in complex control relations (cross-shareholding, director transfer, reciprocity)

    b. Exhibit big-six homophily and centrality effects.

Methods

We look at five sectors: autos, electronics, machinery, metals, and chemicals. Clearly, with so few and such broad industries, any tests of the hypotheses laid out above are highly exploratory. Our hypotheses thus provide very general conceptual guides to how industries might differ. Table 4.3 gives the number of firms from each industry and the proportion that are shacho-kai members.

The methodological challenge in an industry-specific analysis is how to form the sample of dyads. The obvious choice – restrict it to pairs of firms drawn entirely within industries – is not the way to go. The horizontal keiretsu have by design (the one-set principle) spanned sector boundaries. Firms in any one industry forge exchange and control ties with an array of firms and financial institutions outside that industry. Take again the much-studied case of autos. Japan's auto firms purchase inputs from steel, machinery, textile, and chemical companies; borrow capital from banks; and sell to trading companies and distributors. A totally industry-specific network analysis will perforce miss many auto industry transactions.

Thus, our analytic strategy is to do two sets of industry-specific dyad regressions: (1) firms in industry I send ties (dispatch directors, own shares, lend, and sell) to all 259 (which includes industry I); (2) firms in industry J receive those four ties from the same population. We could in principle estimate four regressions in each industry for each year of data: two for the industry as sender of directors and of equity and two for the industry as receiver of directors and of equity. With data for each of seven time periods, that yields twenty-one regressions. This is too much statistical information to sift through and make sense of. Five time points – 1978, 1982, 1986, 1989, 1993 – give us an evenly spaced (three to four years) series that enables us to gauge shifts across such critical junctures in the evolution of the Japanese economy as the 1986 endaka, the 1989 bubble, and the 1993 recession. We also omit the probit regressions of director dispatch in the industry-to-population data segments. Given the relatively small N's and the low variance of the outcome variable, those results appeared unreliable. We are left, then, with $3 \times 5 = 15$ regressions for each of five industries, still a lot of numbers to be sure but manageable. We shall see, moreover, that, because the results are generally stable over time, the patterns in the data are easily summarized.

As before, we represent the horizontal keiretsu as three dummy variables. First, we formed a dyad-level dummy for whether the pair of firms is in the same group ($= 1$) or not ($= 0$). Second, we coded a dummy for whether the sending firm was a shacho-kai member ($= 0$) versus independent ($= 1$) and another coded the same way for the receiving firm.[100]

Results

The industry-specific results do not deviate greatly from the pooled analysis. Differences appear, but the similarities overshadow them. For example, in every industry we observe the sharp dip in 1989 in the lending effects on control ties, testifying again to the distortions of established economic relations and practices that marked the bubble era. Further, in all industries, strong tendencies exist for lenders to control (via equity stakes and director dispatches) borrowers and much weaker, though still positive, tendencies for borrowers to control lenders. Similarly, the effects of firm size and age are not greatly different across industries. The pattern

---

[100] In the industry-specific analysis, however, we omit two sets of interaction terms, *Equity IJ* * *Equity JI* and *Trade IJ* * *Trade JI* (as reciprocity effects) and the Tokyo–Kansai terms. Included, however, is a dummy variable for joint location in the same prefecture. There are of necessity more receiver firms and fewer sender firms in the *industry from* models than in the *industry to* models. This means that the sender effects will have larger standard errors and receiver effects will have smaller standard errors. The reverse is true of the receiver effects. We interpret the results with this caveat in mind.

(much more consistent for size than for age) is one of larger, older firms extending control to smaller, younger ones.

Where we do find some differences is in the effects of reciprocity, buying and selling transactions, and big-six homophily and centrality. These are at best mildly supportive of our hypotheses and are discussed below.

Autos

Governance and control relations among auto firms are strikingly less symmetric than in other industries (see Table 4.4). Reciprocity, whether in director or equity ties, is zero or less; to wit, the only significant effects are negative. No other industry displays so little reciprocity of control. Further – and again in line with our impressions – the contribution of purchase or supply to the shaping of governance in autos is less symmetric than other industries. Across all fifteen regressions (5 years × 3 outcome variables), only in two instances (models 10 and 14) are buyers less apt to control sellers than vice versa. Finally, the firm size effects in autos bespeak a steeper hierarchy of control from larger to smaller firms than in other industries.[101]

The association of governance and exchange in the auto industry is remarkably stable across the five observation periods with one predictable exception. In 1989, the peak of the bubble, there is a sharp fall-off in the effect of lending to this industry either on the holding of shares or on the sending of directors.

---

[101] In the case of one important industry – automobiles – we have results from a much more fine-grained analysis of exchange and control. Ahmadjian (1996) studied cross-shareholding among Japanese automobile assemblers and suppliers. With extraordinary data compiled by a Japanese consulting firm, IRC, she used a dyad analysis comparable in specification to our own to examine how dependence of each side on the other in a purchase–supply transaction combined with attributes of the part or material purchased (e.g., engineering difficulty, asset specificity) to shape the likelihood of an equity relation between a pair of firms. Our more aggregated data purchase–supply transactions testify only to the *presence* of a customer–supplier tie. Ahmadjian's data spoke to the *volume* of sales from supplier to assembler. She was thus able to measure the dependence of each transaction partner on the other: (1) for customer *I* the percentage of its total procurement of a part sourced from supplier *J*; (2) for supplier *J* the percentage of its total sales of a part to customer *I*. Although both forms of dependence proved to relate significantly to the odds of the customer taking a stake in the supplier, the supplier's dependence had the bigger effect. Ahmadjian's interpretation, consistent with our earlier reasoning, is that cooptation of customer by supplier accounts for most of the process whereby the former is led to take a stake in the latter. This is important, because it is prima facie so at odds with what has been the dominant perspective on control and governance in Japanese supply networks – that customers use equity stakes and director dispatch as a way of imposing their preferences on dependent suppliers. The cooptation view, by contrast, says that customers take stakes in suppliers because of supplier pressure on the customer to make a *credible commitment*, enabling the supplier to manage its dependence on the customer and obligating the customer to support the supplier in difficult times.

Table 4.4. *Probit (Director) and Tobit (Equity) Regressions of Ties From and To Twenty Firms in the Automobile Industry*

Explanatory variable	1978			1982			1986			1989			1993		
	Directors to	Equity from	Equity to	Directors to	Equity from	Equity to	Directors to	Equity from	Equity to	Directors to	Equity from	Equity to	Directors to	Equity from	Equity to
Director IJ	23.119***			.082			1.307			-.514			-.125		
Equity IJ	4.523	-.343	-.907**	52.110***	-.058	-.281	17.196***	-.145	-.513*	50.725***	.119	-.359*	6.700***		-.515**
Equity JI	23.646***		.766***	1.427		.780***	-3.471		.725***	6.627		.299***	-.169	-.062	.568***
Debt IJ				6.260***			5.666***			4.169***			6.018***		
Debt JI		.549			.014			.095			.359			.494	
Trade IJ	-.048	.186***	.104***	.487	.170**	.081+	.052	.190***	.101**	1.412+	.181***	.091***	1.087*	.175***	.096**
Trade JI	3.030***	.197***	.227***	1.544***	.196***	.202***	2.149***	.211***	.226***	-.556	.213***	.203***	1.165***	.239***	.234***
I is financial	-.366	.091**	.103***	-.704	.122**	.026	-.298	.101+	.097***	-1.200	.137***	.061**	-3.408	.142**	.097*
I is trading co.	-1.612*	-.139***	-.113*	-.127	-.128***	-.118+	-.278	-.136***	-.107	.501+	-.761***	-.172**	-.1932	-.635***	-.152*
I is independent	-.191	.047	-.020+	-.248	.067+	.005	-.053	.047	-.022+	-.187	-.020	-.022	-.3826	-.002	-.019
J is independent	.547	.084***	.010	.244	.068*	.015	.484	.060*	.029	-.780	.059*	.036*	.0916	.066*	.029*
I and J in same group	-.233	.108**	.029	-.364	.097***	.082*	1.106*	.092***	.071**	.031	.105***	.076***	.2196	.074**	.046*
I and J in same region	.322	.066*	.041**	-.061	.076**	.047**	.419**	.090***	.033*	-.003	.106***	.042**	.188	.122**	.036**
Assets of I	.167	.052*	.003	.256*	.056*	.026*	.499***	.067*	.008	.013	.060**	.020**	.3900*	.050**	.006
Assets of J	1.019***	-.031**	-.003	.337	-.032***	-.001	.310+	-.020**	.006	.019	-.023***	.000	.3273	-.033*	-.000
Age of I	-.001	.001	-.000	-.011+	.002*	-.000	-.002	.002*	.000	.019	.000	-.000	-.0017	.000	-.000
Age of J	.038***	-.000	-.000	.018***	-.000+	-.000	.010	-.000	-.000		-.001***	-.000	.0121	-.000	-.000
Autoregression	23.550	66.9*	23.377	42.298*	63.648***	14.885+	37.060+	53.545*	11.962+	38.298*	27.840	14.385*	-4.4683	48.509*	18.3*
Constant	-21.369***	-.837*	-.258*	-11.922***	-.935*	-.591**	-15.867***	-1.28**	-.481***		-.958*	-.525***	-14.145**	-.785*	-.345**
Sigma	-11.8***	.098***	.083***	-11.850***	.110***	.092***	70.702***	.116***	.085***	-11.895*	.122***	.070***		.107***	.068***
Pseudo R^2	.806			.760			.7196			.794			.7526		

*** $p < .001$; ** $p < .01$; * $p < .05$; + $p < .10$. Robust standard error estimates (adjusted for clustering by firm).

Note: Columns labeled *to* are the regressions on 5,160 dyads of director and equity ties *to* the 20 firms in the industry *from* the population of 259 firms. Columns labeled *from* are the corresponding regressions *from* the industry to the 259.

With the exception of Honda and Mazda, the major auto assemblers are members of shacho-kai. Their principal vertical keiretsu suppliers often are not, although this is truer of Toyota than Nissan. This plus the relative youth of the industry and its strong global competitiveness suggest weak big-six homophily but strong centrality (i.e., shacho-kai firms control independents). Yet in regard to equity if not director ties, we find a stable pattern of same-group effects. They are stronger in the industry-to-population (*from*) regression than in the population-to-industry (*to*) analysis, however. This may reflect the strong vertical keiretsu organization of the industry: a flow of control from the major auto assemblers to the firms in a variety of industries with which they do business. The evidence for big-six centrality points to the same interpretation. Independents, as expected, are the objects of control (in terms of equity) but only when the issuers are within the industry (i.e., the large assemblers).

Autos also stands out among these industries in terms of the importance of site-homophily, that is, a tendency to forge control links with firms in the same region. This, of course, is consistent with the geographic concentration of the Toyota, Mazda, and other vertical production networks.[102]

Electronics
Like autos, electronics is a highly strategic sector in Japan's export-led post-war economic development. Japanese electronics makers built up a huge competitive advantage on the strength of their products' quality, cost, and fast development cycles. However, compared to autos, electronics is an industry in which the contrasts with U.S. production and supply organization have been less sharply drawn.

These considerations, combined with the high global exposure and low supply chain position of the electronics firms, point to lighter network infrastructure relative to other industries, and the data generally bear that out (see Table 4.5). Reciprocity of director dispatch is strong in every year but 1993 (the last of the series), when it disappears altogether. But like the autos case, equity reciprocity is absent. Unlike autos, however, the control flows between sellers and buyers are consistently symmetric. The size and age effects, here as in other industries, are strongly asymmetric. The big-six role in shaping electronics industry networks is distinctive as well. Consistent with the hypothesis on global competition, it is weaker here. Shacho-kai homophily is evident only in the population-to-industry (*to*) analysis; that is, the control ties electronics firms receive lie within a group,

---

[102] Several factors contributed to the geographic clustering of the automobile supply networks. The just-in-time system put pressure on suppliers to locate in close proximity to assemblers, since frequent small deliveries are required on both ends to keep inventories small. Moreover, many auto suppliers, often being spun-off divisions, grew up in close association with their affiliated automakers (Chapter 2; Odaka et al., 1988).

Table 4.5. Probit (Director) and Tobit (Equity) Regressions of Ties From and To Twenty-One Firms in the Electronics Industry

Explanatory variable	1978			1982			1986			1989			1993		
	Directors to	Equity from	Equity to	Directors to	Equity from	Equity to	Directors to	Equity from	Equity to	Directors to	Equity from	Equity to	Directors to	Equity from	Equity to
Director IJ	3.152***			3.050***			3.269***			2.486***			.096		
Equity IJ	27.488***			36.137***			9.005***			6.286***			4.002**		
Equity JI	-3.568	.152	-.462	-1.892	.742	.071	-2.019	-.428	-.583+	-1.246	.423	-.201	1.966	.636	-.182
Debt IJ	4.334***		.585*	2.136		.659*	9.083***		.752***	2.041		.425*	15.895***		.729**
Debt JI		1.149*			.982			.959*			2.006*			3.102**	
Trade IJ	-.490	.365***	.226**	-.518	.346*	.204	-.278	.392***	.259**	.418	.346**	.152**	1.108**	.220	.175*
Trade JI	.605	.438***	.233**	.456	.424***	.154*	-.066	.382***	.188**	.557	.474***	.144+	.364	.466***	.130*
I is financial	-.442	.214**	.153**	-1.190*	.243*	.024	-.699*	.149*	.117*	-.942*	.148	.057	-.611	.188+	.092**
I is trading co.	-.928+	.030	-.150	-.114	-.070	-.206+	-.597+	-.085	-.191+	-1.183*	-.218	-.117	-.296	-.161	-.073
I is independent	-.118	.164**	.001	.145	.209***	.043	.165	.123+	.003	.169	.248***	.021	.173	.122***	-.008
J is independent	.558	-.009	.005	.628+	.028	.026	.929*	.009	.034+	.856*	.039	.007	.322	-.082	-.009
I and J in same group	1.135*	.164	.162***	1.281**	.340+	.224***	1.598***	.148	.130***	1.460***	.210	.123*	.895*	.149	.086*
I and J in same region	.278	.084*	.027+	.142	.092*	.031	.039	.073**	.001	.165	.155**	.022	.339+	.099***	.017+
Assets of I	.655**	.109***	.010	.677**	.160***	.053+	.406**	.110*	.022*	.539***	.188***	.027	.246+	.211***	.015
Assets of J	.171	-.018	-.029*	.169	-.031	-.030	.107	.000	-.018+	.121	-.009	-.020+	-.030	-.022	-.024*
Age of I	.010+	.004**	-.000	.003	.001	-.000	.002	.001	-.000	.004	.003*	-.000	.001	.001	-.000
Age of J	-.013*	-.001	-.000	-.008	-.002+	-.001+	.000	-.001	-.000	-.002	-.002	-.000	-.005	-.001***	-.000
Autoregression	-21.934	16.457	49.739*	-2.386	48.910	45.523+	16.959	55.919***	36.585*	7.236	64.878***	47.331*	-6.346	-3.198	38.540*
Constant	-14.511***	-2.286***	-.206	-4.985***	-2.903***	-.770+	-1.290**	-2.477***	-.478*	-3.054***	-3.870***	-.477*	-6.169***	-3.536***	-.182
Sigma		.277***	.134***		.334***	.161***		.264***	.118***		.318***	.117**		.229***	.091**
Pseudo R^2	.697			.688			.686			.507			.473		

*** $p < .001$; ** $p < .01$; * $p < .05$; + $p < .10$. Robust standard error estimates (adjusted for clustering by firm).

Note: Columns labeled to are the regressions on 5,418 dyads of director and equity ties to the 21 firms in the industry from the population of 259 firms. Columns labeled from are the corresponding regressions from the industry to the 259.

a pattern that declines with time. But the control ties electronics makers send are not so constrained, indicative of vertical keiretsu organization. This pattern is precisely the opposite of what we saw in the auto industry case. Similar to autos, however, is the absence of big-six centrality. While noncouncil firms in electronics, as in autos, are *slightly* more likely to be targets of control, independents are also significant purveyors of control.

Some regional homophily shapes the electronics industry's control networks but it is less pronounced than in autos.

Metals

Metals, an older and less globally competitive industry than the foregoing two – and one positioned higher in the supply chain – should, by our hypotheses, exhibit strong keiretsu effects of two sorts: more embeddedness of transactions (reciprocity, etc.) and greater propensity to pick exchange partners from the ranks of the group. Big-six homophily in the control networks is indeed quite strong, although, as in electronics, it decays in later periods (see Table 4.6). Big-six centrality, on the other hand, is notably absent. Again, like electronics, independent – not group – firms both issue control and (to a lesser extent) receive it. This declines over time.

Otherwise, there is scant evidence that the metals sector is given to complex governance arrangements. Equity tie reciprocity is positive and generally significant but weaker than in other industries. Most notable here is the marked asymmetry in how buying and selling shape control relations. Sellers – metals producers – control buyers, a pattern found in other industries (autos being the chief exception) but particularly pronounced here. However, buyers in metals (in years 1982, 1986, and 1989 at least) are *un*likely to control sellers. What does this mean? There may be some collinearity induced, in particular, by the dummy for trading company. Metals producers source ore and other raw materials, often through the shosha as intermediary. Note that metals is the only industry in which we observe a significant shosha effect on equity ties.

Chemicals

More than metals, Japanese chemical and pharmaceutical firms are notoriously uncompetitive globally. In line with the hypothesis that the keiretsu have a stronger hold on domestically oriented industries, we find substantial homophily in the control shacho-kai firms direct *to* the industry (see Table 4.7). These effects decay in 1989 and 1993, the bubble and its aftermath. Big-six centrality is nonexistent; on the contrary, independents are more likely to send and receive equity and directors.

Reciprocity of director dispatch is pronounced in all years, but business cycle fluctuations exist: up in 1986 (the endaka recession), down in 1989 (the bubble), and sharply up in the 1993 recession. Equity reciprocity,

Table 4.6. *Probit (Director) and Tobit (Equity) Regressions of Ties From and To Twenty-Eight Firms in the Metals Industry*

Explanatory variable	1978 Directors to	1978 Equity from	1978 Equity to	1982 Directors to	1982 Equity from	1982 Equity to	1986 Directors to	1986 Equity from	1986 Equity to	1989 Directors to	1989 Equity from	1989 Equity to	1993 Directors to	1993 Equity from	1993 Equity to
Director IJ	1.843**														
Equity IJ	30.858***	.473**	.417*	27.485***	.544**	.698*	11.430**	.457*	.368+	12.431**	.481*	.974*	34.167***	.462**	.820*
Equity JI	-12.120		.919***	-17.417		.906**	2.010		.477***	-7.762		.337**	6.834		.592***
Debt IJ	-6.683*	.818*		5.356**	.550*		10.468***	.596*		3.711+	.150		4.967	.429	
Debt JI		.550*													
Trade IJ	1.447**	.102+	.132**	-.232	.13**	.127*	.793	.147*	.079+	1.292**	.087**	.098*	-2.529*	.099*	.112+
Trade JI	-.143	.005	.094*	-1.257+	-.714***	.081	.480	-.793***	.088+	-.205	-.044+	.040	.570+	-.013	.080
I is financial	-1.058+	.042+	.044+	-1.147**	.090***	-.025	-1.692**	.035	.035	-1.476**	.009	.027	-1.901***	.005	.028
I is trading co.		-.000	-.101*		.133**	-.102		.103*	-.063	-1.246*	.018	-.083		-.015	-.081
I is independent	.270	.038**	-.015	.361**	.027	.009	.679**	.029*	-.006	.571**	.040+	-.006	.234	.041**	-.007
J is independent	-.058	.038*	.019	-.130	.064*	.019	.124	.050+	.013	.648+		.011	.211	.036	.013
I and J in same group	1.235***	.145***	.080***	.646***	.170***	.089***	1.127***	.161***	.064***	1.425***	.140***	.061**	.687+	.142**	.050*
I and J in same region	.434**	.051**	.022*	.368+	.057**	.023	.408+	.053**	.028+	.305*	.034*	.017	.345	.024+	.020+
Assets of I	.537*	.040***	.020*	.470**	.051***	.044*	.430**	.053	.023*	.478**	.044**	.017*	.418*	.043**	.011
Assets of J	-.094	-.003	-.007	-.029	-.016	-.007	-.070	-.004	-.002	.025	.007	-.007	-.233	.001	-.005
Age of I	-.004	.000	.000	.000	.000	.000	.000	.000	.000	.004	.001	-.000	.007+	.001+	-.000
Age of J	.010*	-.000	.000	.005	-.000	.000	.004	-.000	-.000	-.006	-.000+	-.000	-.000	-.000	-.000
Autoregression	39.685+	-6.255	2.668	24.561*	16.6+	3.232	15.366	11.363	7.852	33.387	9.056+	29.806***	36.888	14.648*	38.128***
Constant	-10.640**	-.898***	-.450**	-9.857***	-.953***	-.807***	-8.957***	-1.129***	-.518***	-10.842***	-1.115***	-.380**	-6.899	-1.067***	-.330**
Sigma		.114***	.089***		.11***	.100***		.117***	.078***		.090***	.079***		.106***	.128***
Pseudo R^2	.765			.658			.598			.533			.642		

*** $p < .001$; ** $p < .01$; * $p < .05$; + $p < .10$. Robust standard error estimates (adjusted for clustering by firm).

Note: Columns labeled *to* are the regressions on 7,224 dyads of director and equity ties *to* the 28 firms in the industry *from* the population of 259 firms. Columns labeled *from* are the corresponding regressions *from* the industry *to* the 259.

Table 4.7. *Probit (Director) and Tobit (Equity) Regressions of Ties From and To Thirty-One Firms in the Chemicals Industry*

Explanatory variable	1978			1982			1986			1989			1993		
	Directors to	Equity from	Equity to	Directors to	Equity from	Equity to	Directors to	Equity from	Equity to	Directors to	Equity from	Equity to	Directors to	Equity from	Equity to
Director IJ	2.134*			2.053***			2.782***			2.221***			3.560***		
Equity IJ	38.626***			33.34***			57.280***			39.28***			37.405***		
Equity JI	-3.560	1.232*	.161	1.963	1.363+	.297***	-7.162	1.471*	.869**	-4.716	.253	.008	.999	.423	-.062
Debt IJ	2.085			4.404*			1.193			2.183			5.765***		
Debt JI		1.846*	.653***		1.415	.727***		.735	.515**		.871	.288***		.887	.493***
Trade IJ	.431	.163*	.093***	.725+	81.161*	.060***	.802*	70.097*	.049*	1.085**	.292*	.046*	.270	.305*	.063***
Trade JI	-.819+	.098	.064**	.092	.074	.060*	.139	.086+	.079***	.715+	.071	.083***	.169	-.147	.074**
I is financial	-.880**	.045+	.061***	-1.140*	.111+	.024*	-1.271***	-.320***	.057***	-.918*	-.576***	.054***	-.349**	-.600***	.049***
I is trading co.	-.049	-.049	-.045*	-1.133*	-.004	-.041*	-1.615**	-.01	-.028	.123	-.941***	-.038	-.083	-.795***	-.062*
I is independent	.317	-.044	-.006	.213	-.018	-.008	.414+	-.03	-.013+	-.093	-.093	-.013*	-.447*	-.081	-.011*
J is independent	.493*	.020	.021**	.609**	.023	.022***	1.073***	.02	.010+	.384	.024	.015**	.922**	.042	.012*
I and J in same group	.968***	.091**	.062***	1.025***	.128**	.051***	.960***	.093***	.045***	.783**	.141*	.053***	.944***	.151*	.038***
I and J in same region	.166	.034+	.017**	.169	.038+	.018+	.380+	.03*	.015**	.100	.025	.01*	-.187	.057	.013**
Assets of I	.329***	.081*	-.001	.456**	.100*	.009**	.316***	.06+	.000	.168	.046	.004+	.554**	.081	-.000
Assets of J	-.021	-.035**	-.010*	.095	-.046*	-.008+	.239	-.02	-.009*	-.008	-.032	-.012**	.014	.001	-.007*
Age of I	-.001	.000	-.000	-.001	-.000	-.000	-.005	.00	-.000	.003	-.000	-.000	-.001	-.001	-.000
Age of J	-.001	-.001*	-.000	-.002	-.001	-.000+	-.001	-.00	-.000	.001	-.003*	-.000	.004	-.003*	-.000
Autoregression	35.611**	-60.2+	18.234***	24.578+	-81.826	2.099	45.341**	-70.85	13.8**	85.234***	-153.51	18.786***	-17.212	-147.373	19.742***
Constant	-7.659*	-.896*	-.045	-10.873*	-1.004	-.168*	-11.407***	-.71+	-.0342	-6.376*	-.523	-.067	-11.960**	-1.323	-.025
Sigma		.112***	.056***		.127***	.049***		.090***	.048***		.1879***	.051***		.168**	.043***
Pseudo R²	.631			.642			.689			.632			.599		

*** p < .001; ** p < .01; * p < .05; + p < .10. Robust standard error estimates (adjusted for clustering by firm).

Note: Columns labeled to are the regressions on 7,998 dyads of director and equity ties to the 31 firms in the industry from the population of 259. Columns labeled from are the corresponding regressions from the industry to the 259. The N's are slightly reduced in some years due to missing cases.

Table 4.8. Regressions of Director and Equity Ties From and To Seventeen Firms in the Nonelectrical Machinery Industry by Year

Explanatory variable	1978			1982			1986			1989			1993		
	Directors to	Equity from	Equity to	Directors to	Equity from	Equity to	Directors to	Equity from	Equity to	Directors to	Equity from	Equity to	Directors to	Equity from	Equity to
Director IJ	1.922**			2.310***			3.371***			3.720***			2.122***		
Equity IJ	28.980**	.697**	1.296**	27.686**	1.555*	.914**	32.434***	.878	1.273*	42.941***	.539	1.372*	42.431***	.778	1.262*
Equity JI	9.666		.708***	41.087**	.618***		35.614		.432**	69.990+		.049	24.159		.345**
Debt IJ	8.092+	.239		8.129***	-.213+		4.839**	-.358		1.577	-.027		13.017***	-.470	
Debt JI															
Trade IJ	.216	.040+	.053**	-.029	.077***	.062***	1.340**	.043*	.087***	1.092***	.062***	.102***	.160	.074***	.091***
Trade JI	.496	-.010	.045**	.615	.064**	.026*	.706	.023***	.090***	.917	.001	.056*	.513+	.010	.049*
I is financial	-.250	.009	.037***	-1.286***	.019	.071***	-.365	.028*	.060***	-.605	.037*	.070***	-2.109*	.037*	.059***
I is trading co.	-.118	.011	-.002	-.211	-.065*	-.038*	.503	-.031	-.107*	-.021	-.014	-.074*	.720	-.035	-.047
I is independent	-.059	-.193***	-.012	.406	-.012	-.269***	1.185**	-.250*	-.013	.428	-.151	-.016	.112	-.194*	-.020**
J is independent	.882***	-.007	.005	.270	.017+	-.006	.275	.014*	.008	.824**	.019**	.010	.355	.068**	-.000
I and J in same group	.388	.042***	.028***	.183	.028**	.056***	1.348**	.066***	.042***	.721***	.046***	.051***	.465	.092**	.027**
I and J in same region	-.109	.019*	.014*	.072	.019*	.026***	-.112	.038***	.011	.451	.028***	.013*	.261	.056**	2.094
Assets of I	.393**	.015	.002	.603***	.011	.018+	.886*	.009	.002	.234	.003	.003	.322	.010	-.000
Assets of J	.022	-.000	-.005.	-.066	-.011*	-.016**	-.078	-.002	-.003	-.814***	-.002	-.005	-.152+	-.004	-.004
Age of I	.010+	.000	-.000	.004	-.000	.000	.010	.000	-.000	.010	.001**	.001	.021*	.000	-.000
Age of J	.010	-.000	-.000	.000	-.000	-.000	-.020*	-.000	-.000	-.001	-.000	-.000	.009	-.000	-.000*
Autoregression	-19.022	-.356	7.996	-9.647	8.102	18.366**	-21.190	17.728***	11.907+	45.976	6.81***	19.155***	36.73	22.451***	19.30***
Constant	-10.146***	-.379***	-.080	-10.805***	-.145	-.207*	-16.018*	-.323*	-.121*	1.825	-.273**	-.118*	-8.519*	-.343	-.036
Sigma		.045***	.042***		.042***	.034***		.045***	.045***		.030***	.043***		.030***	.039***
Pseudo R²	.591			.592			.727			.683			.727		

*** p < .001; ** p < .01; * p < .05; + p < .10. Robust standard error estimates (adjusted for clustering by firm).

Note: Columns labeled to are the regressions on 4,386 dyads of director and equity ties to the 17 firms in the industry from the population of 259 firms. Columns labeled from are the corresponding regressions from the industry to the 259. The N's are slightly reduced in some years due to missing cases.

on the other hand, is stable through 1986 but is gone in 1989 and 1993. The effect of financial exchange is marked by long-term trend and cyclical fluctuations. Borrowers have some control over (own shares in) lenders in the early years, but this is gone by the end of the series. Similarly the propensity for lenders to own borrowers trends downward, save that 1989 is the trough and 1993 brings a rebound. Unlike autos but similar to steel, sellers consistently have more control over buyers than vice versa.

Machinery
Machinery is a major export industry for Japan. By our reasoning, that portends less big-six structuring and a thinner overlay of control. However, machinery's high location in the supply chain argues for thicker overlay – that is, control ties pegged closely to business transactions and more reciprocity. What do the data say?

In fact, shacho-kai homophily in machinery is only moderate in every year but 1986 and 1989 (see Table 4.8). It surges in the endaka (1986), fades in the bubble (1989), and then returns to pre-endaka levels (1993). The endaka shock, it seems, caused machinery firms to cozy up to big-six kin. This, of course, is a highly cyclical business, prone to sharp contraction in downturns. Second, shacho-kai independents in this industry are less apt to emit interorganizational control and more likely to receive it. Thus, both homophily and centrality tendencies exist: shacho-kai firms forge links to one another via cross-shareholding and director dispatch, and they also extend these control ties to independents. We conclude that the big-six role in structuring the machinery industry network is mostly small.

As for pairwise governance strength, director reciprocity in metals is strong in all years. Equity reciprocity is moderate in the early period and declines thereafter. Lender effects on governance relations are strong in this capital intensive industry in all years but the bubble, when they vanish altogether. As in most of the other industries, sellers have more control over borrowers than the other way around.

Summary and Conclusions

This chapter examined how the control relations of director dispatch and cross-shareholding depend on the exchange relations of lending–borrowing and buying–selling in the largest 259 financial, industrial, and trading companies in the Japanese economy and how that pattern of dependence changed between 1978 and 1993. Our theoretical orientation drew from several paradigms of interorganizational research, all of which address how business exchange between a pair of firms is controlled, managed, governed, embedded, or bridged in various ways by the transacting partners. We also looked into the degree to which control networks are shaped by attributes of the firms involved such as size, age, region, and, most important, horizontal group affiliation. Finally, we considered how patterns of exchange and control varied by industry.

While we proposed and evaluated a number of hypotheses, our chief inspiration was a thoughtful passage from a paper on Japanese business networks by Banri Asanuma of Kyoto University, a colleague and friend until his untimely death in 1996. Asanuma proposed that the keiretsu question reduces to how firms use governance structures to manage exchange. Taking some liberties with his argument, we deduced that, were he right, any evidence of keiretsu effects should disappear with the application of statistical controls for financial and commercial transactions. Our analysis showed this presumption to be wrong. Such controls notwithstanding, we observed substantial effects of groups on cross-shareholding and director transfer networks, although (consistent with the last chapter) such effects appeared to weaken with time. In the language of network analysis, these were of two sorts – homophily and centrality. Homophily means that the odds that a pair of firms might bind to one another through equity and director ties go up if members of the pair are affiliated with the same group. Centrality means that big-six firms are centrally positioned in the sense that control emanates from them to the network as a whole.

More broadly, our interest lay in exploring just how financial and commercial exchange between firms drove the distribution of control ties between them in the fashion proposed by organizational theory. Some results were as we hypothesized; others were not.

1. We expect to find directors being transferred from the owners of equity to the firms owned, not the other way around. This was confirmed in every year until the most recent in our series (1993), when the pattern reversed.
2. As for how resource flows drive control relations, we anticipated and found strong tendencies for lenders to own equity and dispatch directors to borrowers. This was matched by weaker, yet still significant tendencies for borrowers to own stakes in lenders, but no significant evidence in any year that borrowers send directors to lenders.
3. Financial institutions – banks, insurance companies, and so on – are the lenders in systems of financial exchange and industrial firms are borrowers. In like fashion, the general trading companies (sogo shosha) are important brokers of commercial – buying and selling – transactions in Japan. A strict interpretation of transaction cost economics or resource dependence theory – both being

models of how control or governance operates at the dyad level to manage a bilateral exchange – says that the control wielded by banks stems wholly from their role as purveyors or brokers of transactions. Other perspectives – for example, the "bank hegemony" theories of critical political economy or Sheard's network twist on principal–agent theory casting the Japanese main bank as "reciprocal delegated monitor" – see the control exercised by banks as disproportionate to the pairwise management of their transactions with borrowers. The support for this hypothesis is strong: even with the lending–borrowing effect netted out, financial institutions remained significant senders of equity and director ties. A good deal of writing casts the sogo shosha in a similarly monitoring and coordinative role in the Japanese corporate network, but we did not find this to be the case.[103] While the shosha remain central to interfirm trade networks in Japan, any role they play in control networks is entirely explained in bilateral monitoring terms.

4. Another important matter to which we devoted some close attention is the form and strength of reciprocity effects in these networks. Organizational theory (e.g., Williamson), buttressed by some insightful writing by Dore, Sako, and others on the distinctive qualities of Japanese organization, holds that reciprocity in economic exchange serves a governance function, bolstering and signaling commitment and trust while diminishing risks of opportunism and defection. Our hypothesis, then, was that commercial reciprocity (*I* sells to and buys from *J*) lowers the odds of formal control relations (cross-shareholding and director transfer) between *I* and *J*. The evidence in support of this hypothesis was impressively strong.

5. We also considered the roles of firm size, age, and region. The obvious hypotheses on size and age are that larger and older firms are central in the control network – that is, they issue equity and director ties – while small and younger firms are peripheral – that is, the objects of control. The support for this hypothesis was solid. As for region, we again posited a combination of homophily – that is, firms forge control ties to one another within rather than across regions – and centrality effects – that is, control emanates from Kanto (Tokyo)-based firms to the rest of the country. We found significant homophily effects of Kanto and (to a lesser degree) Kansai (Osaka/Kobe) locations, both of which declined over time. As expected, Kanto firms controlled Kansai

[103] Sheard (1989b).

firms – no evidence for the reverse – but the pattern was weaker than expected.

6. Finally, we took up the question of industry differences. For the most part, the picture gleaned from our analysis of how firms in specific industries related *to* and *from* the sample of 259 was not greatly different from the overall analysis, the reporting of which occupied the bulk of our attention. First, we found ample support for the proposition from Asanuma that many of the trappings of keiretsu – cross-shareholding, director dispatch, and reciprocity – are driven by dyad-level financial and commercial exchange. Second, and contrary to the Asanuma thesis, we found strong big-six effects in every industry, although, as in the pooled analysis, these diminished with time. As for the contrasts, some were predictable – in autos, for example, buyers exercised more control over sellers than vice versa, a pattern consistent with most treatments of the hierarchical nature of this industry's supply chains. There was also some support for the idea that Japan's most competitive export industries (autos, electronics, machinery) are less encumbered by keiretsu affiliation, but the differences with less competitive industries (chemicals, metals) were not large. Our suggestions (from institutional theory) that older industries and (from transaction cost theory) industries high in the supply chain have more complex and network-embedded governance arrangements did not find significant support.

Appendix

4.1. Modeling Dyads

The unit of observation in our analysis is a *dyad*, i.e., one of $N(N-1) = 66,822$ ordered pairings of 259 firms. In a matrix representation of the network, e.g., $M(N \times N)$, rows ($i = 1, \ldots N$) represent senders of a relation and columns ($j = 1, \ldots N$) are receivers. We array as a column vector, p, as follows: $p = \{1,2; 1,3; \ldots 1,N; 2,1; 2,3; \ldots 2,N; \ldots N-1, 1; N-1, 2; \ldots N-1, N\}$. A 1,2 pairing and a 2,1 pairing appear as separate observations because an $i \rightarrow j$ tie (e.g., sales) is distinct from a $j \rightarrow i$ tie.

We model the existence of a tie between a pair of firms as a function of attributes of that same pair or of the firms that compose the pair:[104]

$$y_{ij} = \beta y_{ji} + \pi'_{ij} r_{ij} + \gamma'_i x_i + \gamma'_j x_j + \rho W y_{ij} + \varepsilon_{ij}.$$

[104] Lincoln (1984); Holland and Leinhardt (1981); Krackhardt (1988).

Here, y_{ij} measures a relation from firm I to firm J (e.g., share of firm J owned by firm I); y_{ji} measures the same relation from J to I. β is the reciprocity effect; that is, the change in y_{ij} produced in response to a change in y_{ji}. r_{ij} is a vector of variables each defined at the level of the pair. Included are other relational variables (debt and trade relations) plus dyad attributes such as similarity of group affiliation or prefectural location. x_i is a vector of attributes describing firm I (e.g., asset size, age, etc.) and x_j contains the same attributes describing firm J. A positive γ_i means that some x_i, say size, boosts the probability that firm I has a director on J's board. A positive γ_j means that size increases the chance that firm J receives a director.[105]

Dyad Autoregression

A problem in regression analysis where the observations are dyads or *pairs* of actors is that values of the dependent variable are almost certain to be correlated over observations, even with the explanatory variables controlled. Specifically, different pairs with the same units (e.g., I, J and I, K) are more similar than pairs with different units (I, J and K, M). This problem is not unique to dyad data; it is common in analyses of time series, spatially distributed data, multilevel data, and other applications. The consequence is underestimation of the true standard errors of the regression coefficients, inflating statistical significance.[106]

This is a problem for which no consensus solution has evolved.[107] We use a dual approach. First, we construct an autoregression term, $\mathbf{W}y_{ij}$, included in our regressions to absorb the residual similarities in the dependent variable due to overlapping dyads.[108] The $\mathbf{W}y_{ij}$ term also

---

[105] An identical equation can be written for y_{ji}, reversing the i and j subscripts. y_{ij} and y_{ji} are thus simultaneously determined endogenous variables and $\beta_{ij} = \beta_{ji} = \beta$ is the reciprocity effect. Because of low network densities, the relational variables in these data are discontinuous and extremely skewed. We have therefore used the single-equation tobit and probit routines in *Stata*, which preclude simultaneous estimation of the reciprocity effect in the fashion described in Lincoln (1984). Consequently, our estimates of the reciprocity model are biased. However, the correct estimates under the simultaneous model are exactly one-half the single-equation estimates, and t-statistics are unbiased.

[106] Since the usual statistic for assessing the significance of an effect is the t-ratio [computed as $\beta/\text{SE}(\beta)$].

[107] For an alternative methodology, see Krackhardt (1988).

[108] For the ijth dyad, $\mathbf{W}y_{ij} = \Sigma_p w_{pq} y_q$ where $p = q = i, j = 1, 2; \ldots; 1, N; \ldots; 2, 1; \ldots; 2, N \ldots; N-1, 1; \ldots; N-1, N$; and $p \neq q$. $w_{pq} = 1/n_p$ if dyad p and dyad q share a common firm (e.g., 1,2 and 1,4), 0 if not (e.g., 1,2 and 3,4). This methodology is an adaptation of the spatial or network autoregression framework developed by Ord (1975), now widely used to model network interdependencies. It is best understood as a weighted mean of the dependent variable taken over all dyads (excluding ij) that include firm i or firm j. Its inclusion in the regression is analogous to the mean-differencing strategy of controlling the similar biases that arise in panel data when units or time points repeat across observations (Hausman and Taylor, 1981).

gauges how well-specified the model is. If its coefficient estimate, ρ, is not significantly different from zero, we conclude that the explanatory variables in the equation succeed in capturing the firm-level effects. If the autoregressive effect is positive and significant, we conclude that the model is incomplete, and the influence of left-out variables is picked up by $\mathbf{W}y_{ij}$.

The second approach we take to the dyad autoregression problem is to exploit the "correction for clustering" feature in *Stata*.[109] Robust standard error estimation techniques correct for the problems of heteroscedasticity and autocorrelation without strong assumptions about the form of these effects. The correction for clustering option yields standard error estimates that are purged of the effect of clustering on variables such as time, space, or group. In our application, the clustering variable is firm, such that dyad similarities due to same-firm effects are adjusted for.

How do the autoregression term and the clustering correction work together? The latter works on the error or *residual* variation – what is not explained by the included variables. Since the autoregression term is an "included variable" in our framework, it gets first crack, so to speak, at the dependent variable. The autoregression term operates imperfectly and depends on assumptions about the ordering of nodes and so forth. The clustering correction captures residual similarities that the autoregression term fails to absorb.

[109] Stata Corporation (1999).

5

Intervention and Redistribution

How Keiretsu Networks Shape Corporate Performance

The relatively high capacity of the Japanese economy for adjustment to changed market conditions may thus be closely related to the industrial organization in Japan as characterised by group formation.

Nakatani, 1984

Now the keiretsu *system is a nightmare for those desperate for Japan to reinvigorate its economy and help fend off a worldwide slowdown. The* keiretsu *ties that bind can also strangle: The culture of mutual protection makes it hard for strong companies to break free and grow, and forces weak companies to bail out even weaker ones.*

Sugawara, 1998

Introduction

Keiretsu ties showcase the Japanese penchant for meshing market and social relations in a "thick and complex skein," as Caves and Uekusa (1976:59) put it, casting in high relief the Japanese economy's network embeddedness. Companies adjust terms of trade in accordance with their obligations and commitments to one another, factoring into price and contracting decisions nonmarket considerations such as fairness norms or the partner's well-being. Prices, wages, and rates of return are thus set, not so much according to what the market will bear, but rather to what seems just and proper given the identities of the actors and the needs of the community as a whole. Thus, transactions channeled through keiretsu networks distort the operation of market mechanisms, yielding patterns of resource allocation and return that appear deeply suboptimal through a conventional economic lens. Yet, at least until the 1990s, it was not easy to claim that Japanese companies had evolved into world-class competitors despite rather than because of their entanglements in networks. The Japanese economy has been all the more frustrating to mainstream economic thought because the hypotheses most congenial to it – that keiretsu clusterings promote joint profit maximization by dint of monopoly/monopsony rents or greater transactional efficiency – are at odds with the available empirical evidence.

Much research on keiretsu, and this includes our work to this point, deals with problems of structure: the composition of groups in terms of firms represented, the ties such as cross-shareholding and management transfers that bind companies to them, and the transformation of these relations over time.[1] The consequences – for individual firms enmeshed in such networks and for the Japanese economy as a whole – are less studied and firm conclusions are scarce. What difference, if any, have the keiretsu made in the performance of Japanese companies? Are they – particularly the big-six horizontal or intermarket groups on which our inquiry is mostly focused – best cast as dinosaurs, survivals from a prior phase of Japanese industrialization having scant significance today beyond the sharing of some familiar corporate names and logos? In our interviews over the years this was the position often taken by Japanese business and government spokespersons eager to play down the role of keiretsu in Japan's hard-to-penetrate markets and large trade surplus. Now, with Japan struggling year upon year with stagnation, debt, and policy paralysis, a popular view is that the thicket of cozy business and government relations – derisively labeled crony capitalism – does indeed makes a difference: its persistence is why the economy has remained so weak.

From the analyses reported in this chapter, we conclude that keiretsu networks do impact the performance of affiliated firms, but that impact is not one of generally raising or lowering sales and earnings. The keiretsu effect is neither *joint profit maximization*, as an early generation of industrial organization economists believed, nor, as some have argued, is it to induce members to deploy assets and expand sales at the expense of profits.[2] Our evidence, building on that of other recent work, testifies that keiretsu have the consequences associated with collective action of a variety of kinds: they enhance the cohesion and continuity of the group by aligning the membership's resources and prospects. Groups, it appears, work to equalize their members' fortunes, smoothing inequality across firms at any given time and across time as well for any given firm. Such behavior describes both vertical and horizontal keiretsu which, as Sakamoto (1991:59) writes, "are composed of firms that confront

---

[1] See Gerlach (1992a); Lincoln et al. (1992); Okumura (1983); Orru et al. (1997).
[2] Weinstein and Yafeh (1995); Rumelt (1974); Teranishi (1986).

external risks together and facilitate an internal transfer from those firms that are favorably impacted to those that are unfavorably impacted."

This chapter explores the hypothesis of redistributive intervention with a panel data set on the largest in 1980 200 Tokyo Stock Exchange-listed manufacturing firms over the period 1965–95.[3] Our main focus is the horizontal groups, but we give some limited attention to the vertical keiretsu as well. The performance outcomes scrutinized are the profitability (return on assets) and sales growth of the individual corporation in a single year. The goal of the analysis is to evaluate the keiretsu effect on corporate financial performance by studying how it varies across keiretsu ties, industries, and periods.

Research on Keiretsu Effects: From Profit Maximization to Redistribution

A number of arguments advance the hypothesis of joint profit maximization by a Japanese business group. Conventional economic reasoning portrayed the horizontal keiretsu as cartel-like alliances wielding large degrees of market power.[4] A sophisticated version was Caves and Uekusa's (1976:61) model of the big six as reciprocating oligopolists, charging each other efficient prices (i.e., in line with their respective opportunity costs) while collectively extracting monopoly/monopsony rents in their dealings with outsiders.

Later students were less drawn to market domination arguments and more inclined to stress the cost reduction and coordination advantages that groups confer on members.[5] This work drew heavily on organizational economics – transaction cost and agency theory – in arguing that monitoring by groups is superior to that afforded by U.S. market-oriented corporate governance. Yet as a hybrid form, keiretsu were also claimed to avert the pitfalls of bureaucracy (as in the U.S. conglomerate) by keeping contractual arrangements implicit and monitoring and intervention modes flexible and informal. As noted by Nakatani (1984) – the author of an influential paper on the corporate performance implications of keiretsu – the transaction cost and agency theories agree with market power arguments that groups raise profits. The causal mechanism,

---

[3] We selected 1980 as the benchmark year for defining our sample of top 200 firms because it fell near the middle of our 1967–1995 series. This was also a period of relative stability in the Japanese economy in contrast with the Nixon and oil shocks of the early 1970s and the *endaka* (high yen) and bubble economy turbulence of the late 1980s.

[4] Hadley (1970).

[5] See, *inter alia*, Goto (1982); Imai and Itami (1984); Odagiri (1975); Okumura (1983).

however, is presumed to differ: transactional efficiency versus inefficient monopoly/monopsony rents.

While agency/transaction cost accounts of Japanese business groupings have remained relatively fashionable in research on vertical keiretsu (e.g., the Toyota supply network), where the case for an efficiency payoff is prima facie more compelling,[6] the evidence for the horizontal groups has proved sharply at odds with the profit maximizing framework.[7] Econometric analyses of data on large Japanese manufacturing firms conducted first by Caves and Uekusa and later by Nakatani found significant *negative* effects of big-six affiliation on corporate financial performance.[8]

The difficulty with the hypothesis that keiretsu joint profit maximize is that it puts too simplistically the question of how they condition firm performance; that is, that they raise or lower the performance of an average firm. The reality is more complex. What groups do to or for a Japanese company varies with the economic fortunes of the firm and those of other firms to which it has long-term ties, the broader state of the macroeconomy or industry, the strategic concerns of the group, the policies and actions of government ministries, and a host of related constraints.[9] The role of keiretsu, whether vertical or horizontal, is the redistribution of risks, resources, and returns. This ensures the survival and success of members and supports the cohesion and continuity of the group. Murphy (1996:74) writes:

> Companies that stand at the apex of a vertical keiretsu, for example, are generally regarded as being ultimately responsible for the liabilities of their affiliates. Toyota may own only 10.9 percent of Hino, the truck and bus maker, but has an implicit obligation to bail Hino out should the latter ever get into trouble. Companies in the great horizontal keiretsu have what are essentially unlimited obligations to each other. It is inconceivable, for example,

---

[6] See Asanuma (1989); Dyer and Ouchi (1993); Nishiguchi (1994); Sako (1992); Smitka (1991); Womack et al. (1990).

[7] Aoki (1988:225). Also see Blinder (1991). Other research, however, discriminates at least partially between the efficiency and monopoly arguments. Notwithstanding the dearth of evidence that group ties enable Japanese firms to leverage monopoly rents into higher profitability, studies by Lawrence (1991, 1993) and others, showing barriers to import penetration in keiretsu-ridden industries, favor a market domination story. The widespread impression (backed by Weinstein and Yafeh's, 1995, econometric evidence) that groups push client firms to sacrifice profits on the altar of expanded sales growth and market share supports the claim that groups provide strong monitoring.

[8] Roehl (1983a) gives evidence that the effect of big-six membership on corporate financial performance was positive in the early post-war period (the 1950s) but negative thereafter. This reinforces the impression that zaibatsu companies played critical roles in Japan's early industrialization and post-war reconstruction but diminished ones in the post-war period. For another recent keiretsu performance study, see Moerke (1999).

[9] Johnson (1982); Hoshi (2002); Schaede (2000, 2001).

that a Sumitomo group company carrying the Sumitomo name would be allowed by other Sumitomo companies to default on its obligations, but exactly which company is responsible for how much is never defined.

To shepherd a troubled affiliate through bad times, groups reassign employees, adjust prices, roll over loans, raise equity stakes, dispatch executives, extend trade credits, help with asset sales (including cross-held shares), and adjust terms of trade.[10] The notorious opaqueness of Japanese accounting – most concretely the absence of stringent requirements for consolidated reporting of subsidiaries' assets, liabilities, costs, and earnings – encouraged and abetted such maneuverings. The distinctive structure of the Japanese labor market enabled interlinked companies to lend or place employees at all levels within one another with little resistance from unions or the people themselves.[11]

For Nakatani (1984:228), the redistributive activities of business groups are an implicit mutual insurance scheme evolved to absorb business risks in the absence of efficient capital market mechanisms for doing so:

> It is frequently suggested that member firms of groupings help one another in times of serious business hardship. When a financial difficulty arises, for example, the member banks usually render assistance, financial or sometimes managerial, to the firm in trouble, sometimes at a far greater cost and risk than normal business reciprocity requires. Likewise, in a buyer-seller relationship, the buyer will often accept a somewhat higher price if the seller is in the same group and is facing business difficulties. Of course, in the reverse case, when the buyer is in difficulty, the seller is willing to sell at a lower price, or take other measures such as extending usance on buyer's bills. This sort of business reciprocity may be taken to imply an implicit mutual insurance scheme, in which member firms are insurers and insured at the same time. One of the essential functions of the capital market is to allocate risk efficiently among different investors in the economy, but, if the capital market is imperfect some way or other,

---

[10] Similar allocation and adjustment activities operate within multibusiness corporations. Large U.S. companies manage earnings through transfer pricing, the strategic timing of asset sales, and other devices designed to avoid surprises and keep Wall Street expectations in check. General Electric and other large U.S. companies have routinely timed the write-off of losses and charges to coincide with spikes in operating earnings, thus avoiding reported income too high to surpass easily the following year (Smith, Lipin, and Kumar, 1994). A research literature in accounting addresses corporate attempts to smooth and otherwise manage earnings. See, for example, Dechow, Sloan, and Sweeney (1994).

[11] Lincoln and Nakata (1997).

then the grouping of firms can be regarded as an ingenious solution to the problem of the non-existence of contingent markets for "management risks." In other words, the setting up of a mutual insurance scheme among group members, and particularly between the banks and other group members, is an institutional response by the Japanese firm which aims at coping with apparent market failure in contingent claims markets of management risks.

Nakatani's account helped explain the apparent lackluster financial performance of big-six affiliates. Member firms pay a premium for the implicit insurance that insulates each from the ever-present specter of business adversity. In the long run, the rescue and turnaround of a financially distressed business partner might pay for itself (e.g., in loans and contracts otherwise lost to failure), but in the near term the burden on the rescue team may be severe.

Yet to see redistributive intervention merely as an ingenious solution devised by groups of firms to overcome a particular kind of capital market failure is to understate its scope and embeddedness. Such quasi-managerial weighing and alignment of needs and demands pervades the Japanese political economy. It has shaped prices, wages, and rates of return in ways that sometimes augment – more often undermine – market forces. The impact of such processes on the Japanese employment system is well-known. Unions adjust wage demands in times of difficulty for employers, and when business rebounds employers reciprocate with generous opening offers.[12] The reluctance of employers to tolerate large compensation disparities out of concern for employee equity and cohesion is part of the same pattern, as is the *nenko joretsu* compensation system: the pegging of wages to an employee's life course stage and family support needs.

The Role of the State: Crypto-Socialism?

No reasonable analysis of keiretsu risk-sharing and return can ignore the role of government policy and administrative guidance. To quote Murphy (p. 74) again:

> Companies find themselves rescuing their erstwhile "competitors," usually at the behest of the industrial association or governing bureaucracy. At one point or another over the past thirty years, MITI has organized cartels in a number of distressed

---

[12] For example, in the aftermath of the first oil shock; see Dore (1986); Taira and Levine (1985).

industries, such as textiles, rubber, steel, nonferrous metals, ship-building, and petrochemicals. The MOF periodically engineers take-overs of weaker banks by their stronger brethren. The current restructuring of the securities industries has as its explicit purpose the bailing out of weaker firms.

Just how prominent has been the role of government agencies such as MITI and MOF in the execution of bailouts and restructurings? One view, linked most closely to the writings of Chalmers Johnson, sees the state as prime mover and behind-the-scenes manipulator of what appear only to the naïve observer as private sector machinations. When the rescue drama unfolds according to the government's script, the ministries keep a low profile, staying in informal touch with the banks and keiretsu principals but otherwise remaining on the sidelines. However, in the uncommon event that the private sector players fail to follow the script and back away from their assigned obligations, the profile of the state can rise dramatically.

To some, this smacks of socialism:

> Japan has had a more socialist economy than, say, the Eastern Europeans. Our ruling philosophy has been the convoy system, which means that every company must grow together at the same pace, without true winners or losers. As long as Japan was growing fast, we were blinded to the negative side of this system. But it's time to realize that this kind of structure is impossible to maintain (Tadashi Nakamae, President of Nakamae International Economic Research, quoted in French, 2001).

Indeed, the support of weak firms at the expense of healthy ones is a distinctive feature of socialist economies to which scholars have given close attention. The *ratchet effect* is the penchant of state planners to ratchet up demands on strong performers. The complementary *soft-budget constraint* is the well-known tendency in a command economy for the government to prop up or rescue poor-performing firms. Dewatripont and Roland (1997) write:

> Both the ratchet effect and the soft budget constraint syndrome are general incentive problems that apply beyond the socialist system, but were particularly present under socialism given the close relationship between firms and the government.... [B]oth problems are intuitively related: the temptation to extract resources from good firms [the ratchet effect] is particularly high when there is an incentive to refinance bad firms [due to the soft budget constraint]. Moreover, bad firms have few incentives to respect financial discipline if they know they can rely on

> cross-subsidization to be bailed out.... Knowing that they will
> be bailed out, the incentives of enterprises to observe financial
> discipline are weakened.

In a true command economy, of course, how resources are extracted
from good firms and transferred to bad ones is fairly transparent: state
planners impose the reallocation by fiat. The Japanese state is hardly socialist in this sense, however effective it may generally have been in lining
up its private sector ducks in the conduct of bailouts and restructurings.
As Nakamae observed in the quote above, Japanese state-spearheaded
redistribution is most conspicuous in the convoy system, whereby large
and healthy financial institutions are cajoled, if not strong-armed, by the
ministries into rescuing weak ones. This was regulatory policy of the Ministry of Finance, which for years kept troubled institutions afloat at relatively low direct public cost. When one or more banks launched a bailout,
MOF behind-the-scenes guidance and control were usually implicated.[13]
As the government had no equivalent responsibility to shareholders or
employees, its actual regulatory obligation to prop up industrial firms
was small. Yet Japan's history of recession cartels, set up by MITI with
the cooperation of trade associations and major keiretsu companies, testifies differently. The cartels were structured, in part, to phase out declining
industries by shifting investment and labor to growth sectors. In reality,
as Katz (1998:171–2) notes, they often served to maintain those industries. More important for our purposes, to the extent that the cartels did
succeed in reducing industry capacity, they did so in convoy fashion by
maintaining an equitable distribution of cuts, with strong producers taking disproportionate hits in order to make it easier on weak kin.

> In the name of egalitarianism, all firms were obliged to make pro
> rata cuts according to their share of the market or their share of
> capacity. To help out the weakest, the bigger or stronger firms
> were sometimes pressured... under penalty of government fines
> and industry association boycotts... to take an extra-large cut.
> The Japanese call this a "convoy" system in which the whole
> convoy can move no faster than the slowest ship.

---

[13] Schaede (2001:6) describes the role of the MOF in main bank bailouts as follows: "Because guidance was extra-legal and compliance voluntary, effective informal regulation
had to allow for the regulatees' input in the formulation of rules. The system also allowed for pragmatic solutions to problems. For instance, MOF did not design tight and
stringent accounting and disclosure rules for banks. This was helpful when a bank was
asked to bail out a failing company, because it made possible backroom deals between
the bank and the MOF, which could have included full tax deductions of the loss, subsidies from the government for the bank, and other support measures. Yet, whatever the
official support, bailouts were doubtlessly expensive for banks."

Or Network Politics?

Other able observers feel the role of the Japanese state in corporate and industry restructurings is overstated. Sheard writes:

> Most discussion of Japan's industrial adjustment has focused on the role of public policy, and there has been a tendency to equate industrial adjustment in Japan with the policies and programs of the powerful Ministry of International Trade and Industry (MITI).... [T]he private sector plays a much more active and important role in the adjustment process than is suggested by much of the existing literature.[14]

Our own view, in keeping with the structural perspective of this volume, sees the government role less in terms of regulatory command and control and more as behind-the-scenes network politics: an intricate web of company, group, industry, and state interests and relations. (This, indeed, is the view of Sheard as well, who in the paper cited documents the interplay of government policy and keiretsu involvement in the 1970s restructuring of the Japanese aluminum industry.) From the network perspective, MITI and MOF are similarly positioned with respect to the industries they monitor and supervise. Their formal authority to impose solutions is limited and the costs in political capital they incur by doing so are large. The actions available to them are constrained by their dependence on the goodwill and cooperation of private sector actors. Such close connections and mutual trust channel the influence and information that feeds the ministries' policy formulation machinery. Moreover, the bureaucrats as individuals enjoy numerous perks provided by the companies they regulate. Most notable of these is the promise of *amakudari* (descent from heaven) – stepping at an early retirement age into a well-paying executive position in a prominent company under the ministry's tutelage.[15] Bureaucrats thus have a substantial personal stake in remaining on good terms with their corporate clients.

Okimoto (1989:47) notes the critical role played by keiretsu in MITI's stewardship of the Japanese economy.[16] The groups, in his view, facilitated MITI industrial policy by channeling it through "a ready-made network for information gathering, sharing, and policy deliberations; unlike trade associations, that network cuts across industrial sectors, creating the kind

---

[14] Sheard (1991b). Also arguing for the independence of the Japanese private sector and against the Johnson (1982) "developmental state" thesis of ministry-led industrial adjustment is Calder (1993).

[15] Colignon and Usui (1996); Schaede (1995).

[16] Other important institutions are industry associations and "intermediate organizations" in which ministries and companies jointly invest. These serve as network bridges between the public and the private sectors.

of horizontal linkages that Nakane believes are so underdeveloped and hard to establish in Japan." Moreover, the keiretsu safety net relieved the ministry of "the headaches of having to step in directly to rescue firms from the brink of bankruptcy." Historically, the bureaucracy bridged to the groups in three key ways. Japan's main bank system allowed MOF to control flows of capital within Japan's undeveloped financial markets through the large commercial banks, which in turn gave preferred access to funds to client companies. Regulation of international commerce – part of MITI's portfolio – was facilitated by the central role played by the general trading companies (sogo shosha) as the conduit through which imports and exports flowed. Finally, MITI was able to shape industrial resource allocation through major producers' vertical supply and distribution keiretsu.

Government players exploit rich stores of social capital when they orchestrate rescues of companies or restructurings of industries. They activate channels to information networks (e.g., through the *amakudari* officials they have situated at the top of private companies); they pressure member firms, banks especially, to do their part and punish the occasional holdout who balks at going along; they lend their prestige and influence to the orchestration of bailouts; and they absorb a portion of the costs. But they are also constrained by the countervailing forces of private sector power, a power that increased through the post-war period as the economy grew.

They balance these tensions by acting as freelance keiretsu partners, brokering assistance from the central positions they occupied in the network. The facilitator role they played is not fundamentally different from that of main banks acting in aid of troubled client firms or parent manufacturers supporting affiliated suppliers and distributors. In relinquishing direct regulatory control, they kept their financial exposure low, in contrast, say, with the U.S. government bailouts of Chrysler, Lockheed, or the savings and loan industry.

A Case Study in the Government's Role: Toyo Shinkin
A case study in the government's role as network player is the bailout in 1991 of scandal-ridden Osaka credit union, Toyo Shinkin. Setting the context, recall that the story of a top-down, state-administered economy is most convincing in the financial services sector. Absent the direct financing vehicles of the Anglo-American economies, Japanese corporations have been heavily dependent on bank debt.[17] This concentration in financing sources, coupled with the economy's rapid expansion, put great pressure

---

[17] Hoshi and Kashyap (2000); Kobayashi et al. (1993); Suzuki (1987:26); Wallich and Wallich (1976).

on the banks, which despite their large size, chronically loaned out funds in excess of their deposits and capital reserves. The banks' precarious situation rendered them, in turn, highly dependent on borrowing from the Bank of Japan. The Bank of Japan and the Ministry of Finance could then leverage this dependence into top-down control over the financial sector, for example, through window guidance (*madoguchi shido*).

Yet the story this case tells is less one of ministerial fiat than of behind-the-scenes network politics. At the time of the bailout, Toyo Shinkin had debts of $1.9 billion equal to 83 percent of its total deposits. The episode was much discussed in the Japanese press as symptomatic of the breakdown of the traditional main bank/keiretsu system of intervention and rescue. Making the case especially lurid was the arrest of some thirty Toyo Shinkin officials along with Nui Onoue, a notorious Osaka stock speculator, for conspiring to forge Toyo Shinkin deposit certificates, which were then used as collateral to obtain loans from a number of major financial institutions.

Sanwa Bank, Toyo Shinkin's main bank and the core institution in the Sanwa group, declined to take the conventional steps to alleviate the problem: absorb Toyo Shinkin and its huge financial obligations. The massive scale of the debt was a factor in Sanwa's resistance but so was the scandal-tainted nature of the case. Particularly embarrassing to Sanwa was the arrest with Onoue for criminal fraud and conspiracy of Tomomi Maekawa, a branch manager whom Sanwa had earlier dispatched to Toyo Shinkin.

Given Sanwa's resistance, the bailout solution demanded a visible and aggressive intervention on the part of government financial authorities – the Ministry of Finance and the Bank of Japan. To overcome Sanwa's aversion to taking on the whole responsibility, the regulatory agencies put pressure on the Industrial Bank of Japan (IBJ), which was implicated in the scandal by the huge loans it had made to Onoue with few questions asked. While Sanwa ultimately did absorb the thrift and ¥80 billion in debt not written off by IBJ and the other Toyo Shinkin creditors, IBJ reduced the load on Sanwa by providing it with low-interest loans over a ten-year period. The government Deposit Insurance Corporation and the Zenshinren Bank (the central *shinkin* agency) likewise supported Sanwa with cheap credit.

The working out of this arrangement involved multilateral negotiations in which no one side exercised final control. While the bailout took place within the financial industry, where ministerial power has been most persuasive, and despite the government's regulatory obligation to prevent bankruptcies of financial institutions and protect depositors, the ministries were unable to impose a solution over the resistance of the private sector parties. Sanwa's reluctance to take the lead in rescuing the scandal-ridden thrift allowed the bank to emerge from the restructuring deal with a far less onerous burden than it otherwise might have borne.

At the same time, Sanwa *did* shoulder some of the load, as other financial institutions regularly did through the 1990s. The advantages to the government hardly need belaboring. In sharp contrast with the U.S. savings and loan debacle of the late 1980s, the contribution to the bailout by the Deposit Insurance Corporation (Japan's counterpart to the U.S. FDIC) was only about ¥30 billion or 12 percent of Toyo Shinkin's total debt. The lion's share of the cost fell on Toyo Shinkin's main bank, the creditor institutions, and the *shinkin* system. Moreover, as noted, the low exposure by the government in the Toyo Shinkin case is not exceptional. Sheard comments (1991b) that "A rough way to judge the relative magnitudes of internal and external assistance is to note that the level of losses absorbed by parent firms, other shareholder firms and banks in the (aluminum) industry in the 1981–1985 period was almost four times that of government subsidies in the entire 1978–85 period."

Intervention as a *Group* (versus Bank) Phenomenon

On the assumption that the government plays an important but not determinative role in the system of risk-sharing and redistribution – and even then works largely through private-sector channels – our attention henceforth is on the latter. But the question remains of where the agency in keiretsu rescues and restructurings lies. Only in the vertical groups – the pyramidal webs of suppliers or distributors at whose apex stands a Toyota, Toshiba, Matsushita, or Nippon Steel – can there be little doubt about the network's central node or its monitoring and disciplining agent. Among the horizontal groups, however, the issues of centrality and agency are less clear. Even so, few sociologically inclined readers will find terribly novel the idea that a group of firms, like one of individuals, might look after its members' affairs with an eye to sharing risks, maintaining equity, and promoting collective welfare, even at some cost to individuals. It may be less familiar terrain for economists, but they deal with such patterns, too, in collusion and cooperation in cartels, oligopolies, and even trade unions. The enigma of the keiretsu centers less on the *facts* of intervention and redistribution per se than on the mechanisms whereby such processes are organized and executed. Set against the relatively explicit and transparent institutions that govern rescues and restructurings in the Anglo-American economies – government bailouts, merger and acquisition, management buyouts, bankruptcy filings, proxy contests, and outsider-led board revolts – how a keiretsu mobilizes to reshape the fortunes of a distressed or wayward Japanese firm and what rules of membership endow a firm with the rights and obligations of participation are not easily discerned. Such nontransparency explains much of the apprehension that has clouded discussions of the keiretsu issue in U.S. business and policy circles.[18]

The ties that constitute the keiretsu, as previous chapters discuss, are of two main sorts: (a) economic resource or transaction dependencies on a group, and (b) the governance or control relations that overlay those dependencies.[19] The transactions are either financial or commercial: dependence on group banks for borrowed capital and dependence on group manufacturers and trading firms as buyers and sellers of products and services. The assumed governance modes are two: equity and director ties. The shacho-kai is generally thought not to function as a governance device, but we treat that as a testable hypothesis.[20]

A simple perspective on the keiretsu as multiplex networks says that these five ties have equal weight in binding firms to groups and in channeling intervention activity. A more sophisticated view, in line with the Asanuma framework guiding the last chapter's inquiry, is that different forms of linkage have different causal meanings and operate in a causal sequence. Specifically, the equity and director networks represent a control or governance *overlay* on the exchange networks of lending and trade. We thus consider the potential intervention role of each such tie in turn.

Shacho-kai

The presidents' council looks like a keiretsu headquarters or board of directors function and thus might seem an apt candidate for the coordinative body behind the group's redistributive bent. Whereas what transpires in shacho-kai meetings is shrouded in secrecy, most close observers have not seen the councils this way but rather regard them as loose associations that build cohesion and occasionally address group-wide concerns (e.g., brand image) but involve themselves sparingly, if at all, in the business affairs of member firms.[21] As Caves and Uekusa (1976:65) write:

> The clubs, however, are informal groups of ostensibly equal individuals, with neither special staff to coordinate their actions nor enforcement mechanism. They are probably important as channels for collaboration on new ventures and forums for resolving

[18] See Imai (1990); Lawrence (1993); Ozawa (1994); Prestowitz (1989); Sheard (1991a).
[19] Baker (1990); Burt (1983); Lincoln et al. (1992); Pfeffer and Salancik (1978); Williamson, (1985).
[20] The shacho-kai, as elsewhere noted, has no clear counterpart in other countries. A parallel organization in the vertical keiretsu might appear to be the *kyoryoku-kai* or cooperative association of suppliers that most manufacturers maintain (Guillot and Lincoln, 2003; Sako, 1996). However, whereas the horizontal group shacho-kai are, with few exceptions, mutually exclusive, the cooperative associations are not. The same suppliers may participate in the *kyoryoku-kai* of multiple assemblers.
[21] See Gerlach (1992a:106–10); Okumura (1982).

disputes among members, but they do not seem capable of providing the close coordination that was once attained by the top holding companies.

Moreover, Japanese executives we interviewed were quick to note that board-like behavior could well expose the firm to prosecution under Japan's antimonopoly law. From this perspective, the significance of the shacho-kai lies less in what the councils actually do than in their designation of the inner circle of the group. Members are centrally positioned in the keiretsu web of relations and are most likely to use the group name and logo (e.g., the Mitsubishi three diamonds; the Sumitomo *igeta* or well-frame). Outside this inner circle, however, firms connect to councils in varying degrees of intensity through business dealings and the governance processes noted above. Within the shacho-kai, members bind to one another via the same ties, these perhaps figuring more importantly in cohesion and coordination than does the presidents' council itself.

Gerlach's (1992a:111) recounting of the 1982 Mitsukoshi Incident, however, makes clear that at their regular meetings shacho-kai do sometimes take on the problems of group firms and intervene to solve them. Mitsukoshi is one of Japan's leading department stores and a member of the Mitsui *Nimoku-kai*. A series of scandals involving Mitsukoshi's president, Shigeru Okada, was perceived by the group to be tarnishing the name of Mitsui, and the *Nimoku-kai* felt compelled to act. The *Nimoku-kai* reached a consensus that Okada should be dismissed, a decision that Mitsukoshi's board then voted to implement.

Our analysis can discriminate between these models: if the shacho-kai effect is *indirect* – works *through*, not independent of, the network of exchange and control – the inner circle theory finds support; to wit, councils have meaning only in the sense that they delineate a clique of firms at the center of the network. If, however, the council effect is large and direct, support builds for a model of the councils as governance agents *sui generis*.

Financial Exchange

A considerable literature identifies large debt holders as effective corporate monitors. Indeed, one school of thought – prominent in the work of financial economists – finds little mystery in how groups orchestrate bailouts: the active agent is the firm's main bank.[22] In the starkest version of this story, keiretsu is an illusion: apart from the bank–client relationship, it does not exist.[23] Given the high leveraging and low capitalization

---

[22] Aoki and Patrick (1994).
[23] See, for example, Flaherty and Itami (1984); Miwa and Ramseyer (2002).

of the post-war Japanese corporation, the bank's capital is exposed to risk, and it thus seeks to monitor its borrowers. An equity stake and representation on the client's board are rational ways of managing that exposure and thus position the bank for intervention should the client fall on bad times.

The pure main bank model is rather at odds with our perspective on the keiretsu as a layered web of financial, commercial, and governance relations issuing from the shacho-kai to encompass a wide swath of the Japanese corporate economy. As a factual matter, the suggestion that keiretsu interventions devolve to bank monitoring is hard to support. The leading trading companies and manufacturers of a group are known to have spearheaded bailouts and restructurings.[24] The banks, to be sure, are critical players as well, taking the leadership role more often than not. The issue, as we see it, is whether the bank acts as *delegated* monitor, orchestrating an effort to rescue a company to whom the group as a whole is committed, versus acting self-interestedly to prop up a client whose collapse might jeopardize its own financial health.[25]

As with the idea of shacho-kai as governance structure, we can test the hypothesis that group intervention is mostly a matter of bank intervention by evaluating the relative importance of debt ties. If the debt effect is large and direct, while those of shacho-kai and trade are weak and mediated, the bank monitoring model gains support.

Commercial Transactions
Buying and selling transactions do not map the contours of the horizontal groups to the degree that financial dealings, cross-shareholdings, director transfer, and shacho-kai membership do.[26] We might thus expect their role in interventions to be small. Yet case studies and journalistic accounts of keiretsu-orchestrated adjustments regularly identify major manufacturers and trading companies as intervention leaders. Kester's (1991:72–73) comments on the Mitsubishi Bank-led reorganization of Akai Electric, a Mitsubishi Electric affiliate brought close to bankruptcy by the 1986 endaka highlight the group character of the rescue while drawing particular attention to the role of commercial ties:

[24] Morikawa (1993); Murphy (1996); Sheard (1989b, 1991b, 1994b).
[25] The 5 percent legal ceiling on the equity a bank can own in a Japanese corporation ensures that when the bank intervenes it does so on behalf of a broad coalition of investors and business partners (Sheard, 1994b). This is in contrast with the German main bank system where such limits have not existed (e.g., Deutsche Bank's approximate 25 percent share of Daimler-Benz). Deutsche Bank has been criticized for unilaterally imposing restructuring solutions on troubled client firms without the consensus and consultation of other stakeholders (*Financial Times*, 17 January 1994).
[26] Berglof and Perotti (1994) argue, however, that support of bilateral trade is a key function of the horizontal groups.

For a deeply troubled company like Akai, the lion's share of credit must go to the overall effectiveness of the rescue effort mounted by the Mitsubishi group. And it was a group effort in every sense of the word. Although the bank may have been the prime mover at the outset, the actual execution of the rescue plan was customer/vendor led. Consequently, the fundamental thrust of the restructuring was less that of generating cash in the short run to satisfy creditor demands than one of preserving Akai's role in the Mitsubishi group's global network of trading relationships. Rather than restructuring financial claims against the firm, effort was focused on restructuring Akai's function as a purchaser, supplier, and owner of assets used to support transactions occurring in a vertical chain of electronics production and marketing inside the Mitsubishi group.

Our own interviews with Mitsubishi firms relating to the Akai bailout confirm this interpretation. Mitsubishi Bank's assistance, informants said, was limited to restructuring Akai's finances. The rebuilding of Akai's manufacturing organization came from Mitsubishi Electric and other manufacturers of the Mitsubishi group.[27]

Further testifying to the role of trade networks in intervention processes, Sheard (1986b:1–2) documents the centrality of the sogo shosha in restructuring the Japanese aluminum industry and absorbing the risks of their affiliated firms.

The general trading company constituted one of several important institutional mechanisms for diversifying economic risks. Reflecting this risk-diversifying function, general trading companies have played an important role in absorbing structural-change-related losses in post "oil shock" Japan. General trading company loss-bearing and assistance for depressed affiliates has been a major aspect of the operation of internal adjustment mechanisms in the private sector which have operated alongside and

---

[27] Interview conducted 3 June 1994. A more recent case of group effort in the conduct of a bailout is that of Mitsui Construction. The *Nikkei* (Fukuda, 1997) reported that: "Four financial institutions – Sakura Bank, Mitsui Trust, Mitsui Mutual Life Ins., and Mitsui Marine and Fire will offer stop gap loans. Mitsui Fudosan Co., the nation's largest real estate developer and Mitsui & Co., the leading trading house, will support business operations with preferential orders. 'Fortunately our position is not so bad because of the name of Mitsui,' said Susumu Naito, managing director of Mitsui Construction. 'Support from Mitsui group companies will wipe out uneasiness over the company's credibility for at least one year,' Kano [a Yamaichi Securities analyst] said. 'If Mitsui companies approve a capital increase, it will improve financial strength as well. It's far better than if everything were coming from a single main bank.'" See also Murphy's (1996:75) chronicle of the Mitsubishi group bailout of Mitsubishi Oil in 1974.

often in tandem with external government assistance measures and schemes.

Thus, there are ample grounds for a hypothesis that commercial linkage, too, functions as a conduit for keiretsu intervention. We again test that hypothesis by assessing the degree to which the trade effect is large and direct as opposed to weak and mediated.

Equity and Director Ties
Equity and director interlocks are governance or control relations giving council firms and business partners the leverage necessary to monitor and intervene in an affiliate's affairs. Consistent with the perspective of the last chapter, we see such governance ties arising from financial and commercial transactions and mediating the part they play in the keiretsu intervention process. The bank monitoring model, by contrast, says that the bank role is large and direct, well in excess of the relatively meager leverage that the bank's equity stakes and board representation bestow. Similarly, a view of the shacho-kai as governance device *sui generis* says that the adjustments councils make in the behavior and performance of affiliated companies are done directly, not merely indirectly via the cross-shareholdings and director interlocks that council firms maintain.

In addition, equity ties are commonly portrayed as the best single roadmap to the keiretsu network – a sufficient statistic for indexing the alignment of firms with groups. If so, they should prove to be the primary vehicle whereby a group coordinates and channels intervention actions. As a far sparser network, director interlocks only weakly reflect group alignments (see Appendix 3.1), so for that reason they might be thought to play a smaller intervention role. However, a dispatched director can provide close and continuous monitoring of a target firm, and as an operating executive such a director is well-positioned for active intervention. Several studies show that falling performance and other signs of trouble in a firm cause it to take on a director from a bank or trading partner.[28]

Methods

The Sample

We work with the same 200 largest manufacturing firms (as of 1980) studied in previous chapters, but not, in this analysis, with financial institutions or trading companies. These are observed yearly over the period 1965–95. Three manufacturers were lost to merger, reducing the

---

[28] Kaplan and Minton (1994); Kang and Shivdasani (1995).

sample of firms to 197 in 1995.[29] This period covers several significant shocks and transitions in the Japanese economy. The OPEC oil cutoff in 1973 and the subsequent slowdown ended a fifteen-year period of growth rates in excess of 10 percent. The year 1985 marked the onset of the *endaka* shock years when the yen doubled against the dollar, precipitating a decline from which Japan rebounded into the bubble phase of explosive growth and asset inflation (1988–90). This was also a period of significant institutional change for Japanese corporations: rapid deregulation of financial markets, a massive shift from debt to direct (equity and bond) financing, offshore movement of low value-added production, and rising job mobility in labor markets.

Measurement and Descriptive Results

Group Affiliation

The clearest and simplest way to classify firms by horizontal group affiliation is the shacho-kai criterion (see Table 1.1).[30] Of the 197 firms we study, 87 are council members and 110 are not.

Measuring the big-six leanings of noncouncil firms is a long-standing challenge of keiretsu research. Most studies use a few standard classifications; for example, Dodwell, *Keiretsu no kenkyu*, or Nakatani's (1984) taxonomy. Firms are generally coded dichotomously as *group* or *independent*. We, on the other hand, treat keiretsu affiliation as a kind of gravitational field, flowing seamlessly from the shacho-kai core to touch a broad periphery of off-council firms. As in other chapters, we consider four distinct exchange and control ties:(1) buying–selling, (2) lending–borrowing, (3) owning–owned, and (4) sending–receiving directors.

For each such tie, we calculated the proportion of the firm's trading partners, debt, equity, and directors contributed by the shacho-kai with the largest such proportion. For council members, there is no instance in which the group with the largest share does not also have that firm on

---

[29] As previous chapters note, our data come from a variety of archival sources. They include (1) the Nikkei NEEDS financial information on Tokyo Stock Exchange listed firms (Nikkei Databank Bureau, 1989), (2) the Japan Development Bank Corporate Finance Data Bank (2000), and (3) such sources on corporate keiretsu affiliations as *Keiretsu no kenkyu* and *Kigyo keiretsu soran* (Toyo Keizai, various years).

[30] Shacho-kai membership was also the basis for Caves and Uekusa's (1976) classification of groups and independents. Nakatani's (1984) elaboration of the *Keiretsu no kenkyu* classification scheme has been criticized as too encompassing (Hadley, 1984). Given his composite classification, moreover, Nakatani could not ascertain whether different dimensions of group integration (for example, cross-shareholding vs. shacho-kai membership) had contrasting effects on individual firms. Hoshi et al., 1991a, 1991b) used both the dichotomous Nakatani classification and the fractions of debt and equity controlled by the firm's main bank. This procedure equates group involvement with main bank dependence, however, and ignores the network of trading relations among nonfinancial firms.

its council. For shacho-kai firms, then, the measure simply taps a firm's centrality in the big-six network of exchange and control relations. But it also has meaning for noncouncil firms: the degree of dependence on or control by a group.[31] Descriptive statistics on these and all other variables analyzed in this chapter appear in Table 5.1.

Control Variables
Any effort to infer keiretsu effects on the behavior and performance of Japanese firms must take care to rule out confounding variables. Shacho-kai firms are distinctive in several respects: for example, they are larger, older, and in somewhat different industries.[32] They also carry larger debt loads. Japanese companies in general and big-six firms in particular have been heavily dependent on debt financing in the post-war period. We should not confuse the effects of a firm's internal mix of equity and debt financing with those of its financial *ties* to group banks.

Correlations
Table 5.2 gives the correlations among the five indices of big-six affiliation and several attributes of firms: size, age, debt–equity ratio, and a dummy for the automobile industry. (We use autos as an illustrative case, as it is high on some keiretsu measures and low on others.) With two exceptions (shacho-kai and director; debt and trade), the correlations are positive if mostly not large.

Note that firm size (total assets and sales) correlates positively with shacho-kai membership but negatively with the four exchange–control ties. Industry composition differs, too. The auto industry contains a number of off-council firms, for example, assemblers Mazda and Honda and suppliers Aisin, Denso, Kanto, and Nissan Auto Body. However, of the fifteen industries in our data, auto firms (including parts and materials suppliers) have the strongest (by the correlation coefficient) equity and director linkage to the horizontal groups. This highlights the horizontal–vertical keiretsu interface. The archetypal vertical group – Toyota – illustrates. The *shacho* of such leading affiliates as Denso, Aisin Seiki, Hino, Aichi Steel, and Kanto Auto Works are not council members, but their firms align with the horizontal groups (chiefly Mitsui) through the

---

[31] The measure can be written as I_R (where R indexes equity, directors, trading partners and debt). $I_R = (R_{ij}/R_i | R_{ij}/R_i. > R_{ik}/R_i.)$, where $i = 1, 197$ firms; $j = 1, \ldots, 6$ groups; $k = 1, \ldots, 6$ groups; but $j \neq k$; R_i is the sum (of equity, etc.) for firm i. For example, I_E is the proportion of firm I's total equity controlled by group J conditioned on J holding a higher proportion of I's shares than does any other group.

[32] Shacho-kai firms comprise eight of fifteen steel companies; four of seven oil companies; eight of fourteen nonferrous metals companies; five of seven shipbuilders; and seventeen of thirty-two chemicals firms; but only nine of twenty-four electrical and precision machinery firms and four of seventeen auto and auto parts producers.

Table 5.1. *Definitions of Variables, Means, and Standard Deviations*

Label	Definition	Mean	SD
Shacho-kai	Firm is a big-six shacho-kai member (=1; else 0)	.447	.497
Mitsui	Firm is a member of the Mitsui *Nimoku-kai* (= 1; else 0)	.062	.241
Mitsubishi	Firm is a member of the Mitsubishi *Kinyo-kai* (= 1; else 0)	.060	.237
Sumitomo	Firm is a member of the Sumitomo *Hakusui-kai* (= 1; else 0)	.046	.209
Fuyo	Firm is a member of the Fuyo *Fuyo-kai* (= 1; else 0)	.075	.264
Sanwa	Firm is a member of the Sanwa *Sansui-kai* (= 1; else 0)	.102	.302
DKB	Firm is a member of the Dai-Ichi Kangyo *Sankin-kai* (= 1; else 0)	.103	.304
Debt tie	Proportion of firm's debt held by shacho-kai with largest proportion	.222	.133
Trade tie	Proportion of firm's trading partners from shacho-kai with largest proportion	.332	.227
Equity tie	Proportion of firm's equity held by shacho-kai with largest proportion	.152	.128
Director tie	Proportion of firm's directors from shacho-kai with largest proportion	.014	.050
Mitsui debt tie	Proportion of firm's debt held by Mitsui *Nimoku-kai*	.067	.108
Mitsubishi debt tie	Proportion of firm's debt held by Mitsubishi *Kinyo-kai*	.071	.111
Sumitomo debt tie	Proportion of firm's debt held by Sumitomo *Hakusui-kai*	.078	.122
Fuyo debt tie	Proportion of firm's debt held by Fuyo *Fuyo-kai*	.065	.099
Sanwa debt tie	Proportion of firm's debt held by Sanwa *Sansui-kai*	.059	.093
DKB debt tie	Proportion of firm's debt held by DKB *Sankin-kai*	.059	.079
Mitsui trade tie	Proportion of firm's major trading partners from Mitsui *Nimoku-kai*	.1312	.1786
Mitsubishi trade tie	Proportion of firm's major trading partners from Mitsubishi *Kinyo-kai*	.1209	.1759
Sumitomo trade tie	Proportion of firm's major trading partners from Sumitomo *Hakusui-kai*	.0680	.1327
Fuyo trade tie	Proportion of firm's major trading partners from Fuyo *Fuyo-kai*	.1180	.1684
Sanwa trade tie	Proportion of firm's major trading partners from Sanwa *Sansui-kai*	.1029	.1454
DKB trade tie	Proportion of firm's major trading partners from DKB *Sankin-kai*	.1306	.1604

Label	Definition	Mean	SD
Mitsui equity tie	Proportion of firm's equity held by Mitsui *Nimoku-kai*	.0323	.0873
Mitsubishi equity tie	Proportion of firm's equity held by Mitsubishi *Kinyo-kai*	.0253	.0653
Sumitomo equity tie	Proportion of firm's equity held by Sumitomo *Hakusui-kai*	.0245	.0674
Fuyo equity tie	Proportion of firm's equity held by Fuyo *Fuyo-kai*	.0256	.0834
Sanwa equity tie	Proportion of firm's equity held by Sanwa *Sansui-kai*	.0232	.0850
DKB equity tie	Proportion of firm's equity held by DKB *Sankin-kai*	.0205	.0687
Mitsui director tie	Proportion of firm's directors dispatched by Mitsui *Nimoku-kai*	.016	.053
Mitsubishi director tie	Proportion of firm's directors dispatched by Mitsubishi *Kinyo-kai*	.0098	.0308
Sumitomo director tie	Proportion of firm's directors dispatched by Sumitomo *Hakusui-kai*	.0124	.0516
Fuyo director tie	Proportion of firm's directors dispatched by Fuyo *Fuyo-kai*	.0199	.0757
Sanwa director tie	Proportion of firm's directors dispatched by Sanwa *Sansui-kai*	.0084	.0310
DKB director tie	Proportion of firm's directors dispatched by DKB *Sankin-kai*	.0174	.0422
Debt concentration	Herfindahl (Σp_i^2) for debt concentration across top 10 lenders	.1561	.1056
Equity concentration	Herfindahl (Σp_i^2) for equity concentration across top 10 stockholders	.1761	.1276
Return on assets (*ROA*)	(Operating income before taxes)/total assets	.0636	.0615
Sales growth	[Total sales revenue(t)-total sales revenue($t-1$)]/total sales revenue($t-1$)	.0914	.1618
Total assets	Log of total assets in current year	9.693	1.134
Total sales	Log of total sales in current year	9.768	1.059
Debt/equity ratio	Total liabilities /total shareholders' equity	.0044	.0274
Age of firm	Number of years since founding	.0566	.0227
Calendar year	Last two digits of current year	80.45	8.630
Industry dummies	Food, textiles, pulp/paper, chemicals, petroleum, ceramics, iron/ steel, nonferrous metals, nonelectrical machinery, electronics/ electrical machinery, shipbuilding, automotive, rubber and tire, misc. manuf., extractive		

Table 5.2. Zero-Order Correlations of Keiretsu Measures and
Firm Attributes

	Shacho-kai	Debt Tie	Trade Tie	Equity Tie	Director Tie
Shacho-kai					
Debt tie	0.166				
Trade tie	0.079	0.023			
Equity tie	0.190	0.228	0.256		
Director tie	−0.039	0.137	0.268	0.591	
Total assets	0.336	−0.215	−0.049	−0.110	−.213
Total sales	0.216	−0.252	−0.034	−0.100	−.174
Age	0.157	0.099	−0.025	−0.175	−.144
Debt/equity	0.045	0.002	0.048	0.003	.004
Autos	−0.163	−0.147	0.027	0.222	.367

ownership and control of Toyota and its affiliated banks – Sanwa, Tokai
(both merged into UFJ Holdings), and Mitsui (now Sumitomo-Mitsui).

Performance Outcomes: Return on Assets and Sales Growth
A firm's financial performance may be assessed on a variety of criteria:
profitability, sales and asset growth, stock price appreciation, and so forth.
We focus on two: return on assets (ROA; operating income before taxes
divided by total assets) and one-year sales growth (sales in year t minus
sales at year $t − 1$ divided by sales in year $t − 1$). ROA was the measure used in the path-breaking studies by Caves and Uekusa (1976) and
Nakatani (1984) of the economic consequences of keiretsu.

Besides its role as an indicator of corporate health, profit is a performance dimension that is amenable to keiretsu intervention. Stock price
moves with a variety of forces unrelated to corporate financial well-being –
market trends, analyst expectations, and so forth. Sales volume and
growth are responsive to some forms of tinkering but not others. Mazda's
sales got a boost from Sumitomo companies' fleet purchases of Mazda
vehicles. But Mazda's corporate health was also attended to through
channels that left its sales untouched but did adjust its profits; for example, Sumitomo suppliers cut prices and extended trade credits to reduce Mazda's costs, and Sumitomo and other Mazda creditors rolled over
loans and dropped interest rates. Another device commonly employed by
distressed Japanese firms is the selling of assets to offset weak operating income.[33] In particular, the unwinding of cross-shareholdings in bad

---

[33] One variant of this pattern is the *tobashi* practice of core firms selling real estate and other
assets to keiretsu supply-chain partners, paid for with loans supplied by the parent (Dore,
2000:83). This enabled the parent to clean up its books, while keeping the property within
the keiretsu family. "In the case of Asahi Breweries, a distribution subsidiary bought a

times is an agreed-upon means of shoring up balance sheets. Managers we interviewed were forthright in characterizing cross-shareholdings as an insurance policy or nest egg designed to be liquidated in hard times.[34]

Profit might seem a poor measure of performance for a Japanese firm, as until recently at least it was subordinate as a strategic goal to sales growth and market share. This oft-repeated observation gives an incomplete picture, however. To be sure, Japanese corporations have been spared the fixation on quarterly earnings that drives Wall Street's appraisals of U.S. firms. To the patient capital – the large institutional investors (i.e., financial institutions and major trading partners) – that owned them, big profits were not a critical concern. However, moderate and stable profitability *is* critical in keeping firms clear of *akaji* (going in the red).[35] Negative profit sends a strong signal to the business community that a company is in trouble, unable to honor commitments to stakeholders, and in need of assistance.[36]

Analysis

Main Effects

We begin our empirical analysis by revisiting a finding that has long perplexed students of the Japanese economy: horizontal keiretsu companies are both *less* profitable and grow more slowly than independent

trucking site in Yokohama and a cross-held subsidiary bought a plant in Kashiwa, Chiba Prefecture. In both cases, there has been little change in Asahi's operations. Beer delivery trucks continue to go in and out in the Yokohama site. Equipment at the Kashiwa plant is still producing soft drinks" (*Nikkei Weekly*, 7 February 1994). Similar practices of shifting resources in nontransparent fashion ("tunneling") among member companies are typical of business groups in other countries (Bertrand, Mehta, and Mullainathan, 2002).

[34] As Sheard (1991b) documents, the sale of stable shares has also been a mechanism for off-loading the costs of interventions and bailouts from a main bank or parent firm to the wider keiretsu network: "The case of Mitsubishi Chemical illustrates the use of interlocking shareholdings in main banks and group business partners to offset losses. Mitsubishi Chemical registered profits totalling 31.3 billion yen in the 81–83 period from the sale of shares, thus enabling it to absorb the financial impact of the losses it incurred in subsidizing MLM's [Mitsuibishi Light Metal, a distressed aluminium subsidiary] adjustments. ... It is particularly noteworthy ... that the sell-off centered on the sale of shares in Mitsubishi group firms and other business partners, particularly the main banks, Mitsubishi Bank and Mitsubishi Trust and Banking, and key industrial firms, Mitsubishi Mining and Cement and Mitsubishi Rayon."

[35] In recent years Japanese corporations' concern with profitability has grown. More companies are setting *ROA* and *ROE* targets that are ambitious by historical standards. Rather to the consternation of the U.S. auto industry, Toyota, for example, announced in 1998 that it aimed to double profitability from 5 percent to 10 percent. Some firms have sought higher *ROA* or *ROE* by shrinking the denominator, that is, by selling off assets or reducing shareholders' equity through a management buyout (see, e.g., "Kao expects 2.1-point increase in *ROE*," *Nikkei Net Interactive*, 16 January 2001).

[36] Interview with Yasuda Trust managers in January 1991.

counterparts. We think the studies yielding this result had some design deficiencies – their statistical models were misspecified and their estimation techniques were less than state-of-the-art. But for now it is useful to follow these pioneers and address the issue their way.

Thus, because it was the methodology of research we wish to replicate, we use an OLS regression to estimate the main (or additive) effects of big-six membership on profits and growth.[37] Table 5.3 contains the results. Included as controls are the log of total assets: the ratio of total bank debt to shareholders equity, the age of the firm, the calendar year to capture trend, fourteen dummy variables representing industries, and the annual mean of the dependent variable computed across all firms. This last controls for temporal events (e.g., business cycle fluctuations) and regulatory, exchange rate, and other shocks (e.g., the spike in oil prices in 1974–75).

We find consistently weaker performance among firms tied to groups: the shacho-kai and the exchange and control effects are mostly negative and significantly so. It is important to note that the latter are *net* of shacho-kai. Off-council firms tied to council firms via debt, trade, equity, and director relations exhibit lower returns.[38]

This pattern of keiretsu *main* effects – net tendencies for group firms to underperform independents – holds for both performance outcomes, sales growth and profitability. The contrast between group and independent is sharper, however, with *ROA* as dependent variable. This is true even with sales growth on the right-hand (explanatory) side of the *ROA* regression. Clearly, group firms' thinner margins are only in part attributable to lower sales growth. This fits our conjecture that the redistributive efforts of groups are more successfully directed at balance sheet adjustments of

---

[37] Sales growth and to a lesser degree total sales and the debt/equity ratio are arguably endogenous – determined by variables in the model – notwithstanding our modeling of them as exogenous or predetermined. This is a shortcoming of our analysis, but not, we believe, a fatal one. First, the causal model guiding our inquiry is two-stage. The first stage takes sales growth as a function of keiretsu and various controls. The second takes *ROA* as a function of sales growth, keiretsu, and the same controls. In such a recursive system, no special estimation procedure (e.g., that deal with simultaneity) is required. OLS gives unbiased estimates. In the real world of the Japanese economy, *ROA* and sales growth are no doubt simultaneously or reciprocally determined. Through most of the post-war era, Japanese firms traded off profits for growth and market share. In such a framework, sales drive *ROA*, and *ROA*, set in accordance with managerial expectations, constrains growth. Thus, OLS or GLS estimation exaggerates the weights of sales and sales growth. We thus overcontrol sales and sales growth – their true effects on profitability are less than our estimates indicate. That should not bias the estimated keiretsu effects. As Table 5.2 shows, sales and sales growth correlate weakly, even negatively, with group ties. An overestimate of the sales and sales growth effects thus results in underestimation of the group effects, rendering our conclusions conservative.

[38] Substituting *ROE* for *ROA* in these regressions yields the same pattern of results, although the group effects are weaker, and debt-equity, which shares a common denominator with the dependent variable, takes a large positive coefficient.

Table 5.3a. OLS Estimates of Main Effects on ROA of Keiretsu Measures and Controls (197 Manufacturing Firms, 1965–95)

Explanatory Variables	(1)	(2)	(4)	(5)	(6)
Shacho-kai	−0.007***				
Debt tie		−.008			
Trade tie			−.021***		
Equity tie				−.035***	
Director tie					−.025***
Debt/equity (/1000)	−0.082**	−.085***	−.077***	−.081***	−.083***
Year mean ROA	0.493***	.484***	.486***	.474***	.475***
Total sales	0.032***	.033***	.023***	.033***	.033***
Total assets	−0.030***	−.032***	−.031***	−.033***	−.033***
Sales growth	0.084***	.084***	.085***	.084***	.085**
Calendar year	−0.001*	−.000+	−.000+	−.000+	−.000*
Company age (/1000)	−0.283***	−.274***	−.335***	−.303***	−.290***
Constant	0.057	.059*	.068**	.067*	.068**
N	5907	5907	5629	5887	5907
Adjusted R^2	0.28	.268	.278	.272	.272

*** $p < .001$; ** $p < .01$; * $p < .05$; + $p < .10$. Regression includes fifteen industry dummy variables.

Table 5.3b. OLS Estimates of Main Effects on Sales Growth of Keiretsu Measures and Controls (197 Manufacturing Firms, 1965–95)

Explanatory Variables	(1)	(2)	(3)	(4)	(5)
Shacho-kai	−0.433*				
Debt tie		−1.249+			
Equity tie			−1.555*		
Director tie				−2.520**	
Trade tie					−0.403
Year mean ROA	0.598***	0.633***	0.628***	0.620***	0.635***
Debt/equity (/1000)	11.736***	11.558***	11.680***	11.701***	11.713***
Total assets	2.264***	2.145***	2.145***	2.114***	2.220***
Calendar year	−0.131***	−0.125***	−0.123***	−0.124***	−0.125***
Company age (/1000)	−9.070*	−8.129+	−10.118*	−9.692*	−9.719*
Constant	−9.105***	−8.409***	−8.556***	−8.246***	−9.238***
N	5907	5866	5887	5907	5629
Adjusted R^2	0.12	0.12	0.12	0.12	.12

*** $p < .001$; ** $p < .01$; * $p < .05$; + $p < .10$. Regression includes fifteen industry dummy variables.

costs, assets, and liabilities than at the corporate capabilities and demand conditions that drive top-line sales.

While the control variables in our models function chiefly to rule out bias in our estimation of keiretsu effects, it is informative to scan them as well. The negative effect of calendar year taps the secular slowing of growth in the Japanese economy and the corresponding long-term fall in corporate earnings. Older and larger (in assets) firms exhibit lower returns. Both total sales and sales growth, by contrast, drive profits up. Finally, a higher debt/equity ratio, as expected, produces lower *ROA*. Some significant differences among industries also exist, but none is large enough to warrant comment.

Changing the Question: How Groups Affect Weak and Strong Firms

Thus, with a somewhat different set of firms, longer panel, and more nuanced indices of group affiliation we obtain results that parallel prior studies of the economic consequences of keiretsu. This finding, as noted, is hard to reconcile with market power and transaction cost theories of groups as profit-maximizers but it does fit the now-dominant portrait of keiretsu as an obsolete and inefficient economic form. However, this framing of the problem – the group effect on an average member firm – misses the point. More interesting and important is how the keiretsu effect varies with the performance history of the firm.

The idea of a contingent group effect is consistent with the theory of the keiretsu as a risk- and return-sharing community of fate: the support of the group is reserved for its member firms in need – affiliates in dire financial straits or troubled by mismanagement or scandal. Its effect on members whose business is sound is the cost of enlisting in a campaign to bail out or otherwise shore up the ones in difficulty. Healthy companies pay the tax or insurance premium (in time, opportunity costs, submarket prices, the salaries of transferred personnel) required to maintain the safety net. Since at any one time more companies are paying premia than filing claims, as it were, such costs are a drag on the performance of the group.

As noted, an abundance of anecdotal reports testifies that keiretsu interventions often succeed. With the aid of the group, the troubled firm staves off bankruptcy and resumes life as a revitalized concern.[39] Yet systematic evidence was for the most part lacking until an important study by Hoshi et al. (1991a; hereafter HKS). From the population of publicly listed manufacturing firms, these researchers screened for companies that had experienced financial distress (defined as operating income greater than interest payments in one year but less in the following two). This selection criterion yielded a sample of 167 firms entering a spell of distress

---

[39] See Gerlach's (1992a:199) review of the Sumitomo group's rescue of Sumitomo Machinery in 1954; Pascale and Rohlen's (1983) discussion of the Mazda turnaround by the Sumitomo group; Kester's (1991:70) treatment of the Mitsubishi group intervention to save Akai Electric; and Sheard's (1991b) study of the restructuring of the Japanese aluminum industry. Though many such interventions take place with the grateful acquiescence of the turnaround target, instances of resistance on the part of the target firm are not unheard of (Brauchli, 1991; Gerlach, 1992a:200).

within the period of observation, although data problems reduced the final sample to 121. Their regression analyses showed that firms with group ties both invested more than independent firms in the period following the onset of difficulty and subsequently enjoyed stronger sales growth.

The HKS research substantially advanced understanding of the economic role of keiretsu. On top of the anecdotal literature on bank-led bailouts and other interventions geared to reversing the fortunes of troubled firms, it made clear that the Caves and Uekusa and the Nakatani analyses of keiretsu effects, pioneering as they were, missed the mark. The keiretsu effect is firm and sector specific. For troubled firms, keiretsu participation yields real dividends: bankruptcy risk is attenuated, normal operation continues (e.g., via ongoing investment), and recovery is sped up.[40] What neither the anecdotal nor the HKS evidence directly illuminate, however, is the cost to the group – particularly to its stronger members – that intervention activity incurs.

Moreover, group affiliation may be costly for reasons quite apart from the implicit premia that risk and return sharing entail. An affiliate with earnings sharply up in one accounting period may find itself reined in the next as the group reacts to this signal that the firm is extracting rents from transaction partners. In intermediate product markets, high margins for one firm are possible only at the expense of customers and suppliers. When such firms are bound to one another in a keiretsu network, any firm capturing "extraordinary" returns will come under pressure to drop its parts and materials prices. The trading network acting in concert can quickly adjust the profits of a partner dependent on those transactions merely by colluding to fix the prices of their purchases and sales. Discussing T. Boone Pickens' abortive attempt to secure a seat on the board of Toyota supplier, Koito, Zielinsky and Holloway (1992:201) observe:

> Although Pickens was the largest individual shareholder, Toyota and five other stable shareholders controlled 63 percent of the company. The car firm has supplied Koito's president, a vice-president, and one director. But the relationship goes much deeper than that. According to the Pickens camp, Toyota effectively controls the price, the delivery time, and, thus, the profits of Koito. If Koito makes too much profit in one year, it will be asked to reduce it in the next period by discounting its sales.

Alternatively, the manufacturer may discriminate among suppliers as to whom to squeeze the most. The established practice of Japanese auto manufacturers extracting price concessions from suppliers in each model year works to redistribute returns in accordance with member needs and

---

[40] Morck, Nakamura, and Shivdasani (2000).

group norms. Ahmadjian (1997) quotes the purchasing manager of a major Japanese auto firm as follows.

> "We look at the profitability of our suppliers carefully. We don't want them to show a loss. We want our suppliers to have a similar level of profit." He went on to describe a process of price setting in which semi-annual price decisions was based upon a supplier's past performance. Poor performers were "given a break" while excellent performers were hit a little harder.

Ahmadjian sees this redistributive process reflecting the assembler's social capital in the supplier. That capital binds the partners in a community of fate and gives the assembler a stake in the supplier's welfare.

Miyashita and Russell (1994:167) quote the foreman of a small manufacturing subcontractor in Tokyo to similar effect:

> The worst thing in this business is when some other subcontractor finds a way to lower his costs a fraction, and instead of keeping his mouth shut about it and making what profits he can for a few months, reports it to the parent. The big company rep is down there in a flash, demanding that this company lower their costs immediately. Then he comes around to all the other firms in the same general line and say, "X company is doing this for 88 yen. Submit reports about how you will lower your prices to 88 yen."

The hypothesis, then, is that keiretsu interventions are symmetric: weak firms gain while strong ones lose. A complete inquiry must consider both sides of the problem.

What, then, say our data on the question of whether the effects of keiretsu diverge for weak and strong firms? The problem at the outset is how to measure weak and strong. Since we deal with two outcomes – profits and growth – one solution is to use the lag of each dependent variable. It is improbable, however, that when keiretsu monitors spot a downturn in sales they aim to adjust the afflicted firm's sales, but when the shortfall is in profits, they hone in on profits. As we earlier observed, keiretsu interventions – at least in the well-publicized cases of large companies teetering on the brink of insolvency – are broad scope affairs: loans are rolled over, customers offer trade credits and extend discounts, the firm delays payments on debt and to vendors, and so forth.[41]

---

[41] The common Japanese practice of customers extending trade credits to suppliers enables a firm with a cash flow problem to continue buying inputs while deferring payment. Large assemblers such as Toyota or Hitachi routinely bestow such favors on affiliated suppliers and contractors. Viewed from the other end of the supply chain, customers under stress may delay payment to suppliers, a controversial practice as it is typically done without the supplier's consent. Sheard (1989b) describes the role of trade credits

Thus, a better methodology is to pick one measure of prior performance that the group monitors for signs of trouble. HKS used a conventionally accepted technical definition of financial distress: whether a firm's interest payments exceeded its operating income for two straight years. This is a credible tack, but it has some shortcomings. Japanese firms have carried debt loads relative to their assets and earnings that by U.S. standards constitute borderline distress. Another concern is the association between distress and keiretsu affiliation. A company with strong backing from its main bank and other keiretsu allies should tolerate a higher debt- (hence interest payments) to-earnings ratio than a comparable independent firm without such backing. Indeed, a subsequent paper by these researchers shows Japanese companies with big-six ties require less liquidity to finance investment than did independent firms.[42]

A final limitation to the HKS methodology, in our view, is the restriction of their sample to distressed firms. A sample so derived is unrepresentative of the economy and risks selection bias. *Distress,* after all, is just a label given to low values on a corporate performance variable such as *ROA.* We prefer to use a continuous performance measure in order to gauge how interventionism "kicks in" by degrees.

Moreover, we are especially interested in the keiretsu effect on high as well as low performers. If group ties are good for weak firms, it follows from our main effects analysis that at some point on the t_1 performance distribution affiliation becomes a bad thing, for example, an encumbrance impairing rather than enhancing a firm's ability to sell goods and make profits. The appropriate test of this hypothesis, in our view, is the course we chart: draw a sample of firms that is representative on conventional criteria, measure prior performance on a continuous scale, and evaluate group effects on weak and strong performers alike.

Replicating HKS

Still, a useful point of departure is a partial replication of HKS. Thus, we screen for companies that on credible criteria appear troubled. We then look to whether their keiretsu ties make a difference in the rate or extent of their recovery. The hypothesis is that, for distressed or low

as follows: "A feature of interfirm transactions in Japan is the extensive reliance on trade credit. Average amount of trade credit outstanding for manufacturing sector as a whole in 1982 was the equivalent of 13 weeks of annual sales turnover, more than twice that for the U.S., typically provided through trading co. intermediation. Suppliers of intermediate products in Japan typically extend up to several months of trade credit, initially in the form of accounts receivable and then by conversion of accounts receivable to a bill of payment from the purchaser to the supplier." See also Ahmadjian (1997); Aoki (1988:109); and Clark (1979).

[42] Hoshi et al. (1991b).

performing firms, affiliation with a group – hardly a liability as early research proposed – is the *social capital* that enables it to get back on track.

HKS did not use accounting measures of performance such as *ROA* or *ROE* (return on equity). However, as noted, groups may move to adjust an affiliate's bottom line in more and simpler ways than they can rewrite its top line (income from sales). These include intragroup asset transfers, trade credits, sale of land and cross-shareholdings, and an array of creative accounting techniques.

We focus on profitability – return on assets – as the measure of prior (t_1) performance that the group observes and reacts to. *ROA* taps the efficiency or productivity in a company's use of its assets. Low or negative profit *(akaji)* is a clear signal of trouble that firms go to great lengths to avoid. Japanese companies are highly sensitive to reputation, and the adverse reputational effects of *akaji* in Japanese product, capital, and labor markets are nontrivial. Moreover, such effects are not confined to the firm in jeopardy but spill over to tarnish banks and trading partners. Thus the keiretsu network has a strong incentive to rescue a firm in need. The former zaibatsu are most vulnerable to reputational spillovers, since their core members – unlike those of the bank-centered groups – are apt to share the group's name and brand (Mitsui, Mitsubishi, Sumitomo, Yasuda) and thus the benefits and risks associated it.

We report in Table 5.4 the regressions for terciles (thirds) of *ROA* lagged two years.[43] The tercile cutoffs are arbitrary ones, but they facilitate a three-way comparison of low, middling, and high performers.

Consider first Table 5.4a, the *ROA* case. The pattern varies with the tie, but in general the keiretsu effect shifts from positive to negative as we scan from the bottom tercile to the top. Of the bottom tercile firms, those tied to groups by shacho-kai membership, shareholding, bank borrowing, and directors (not significant) outperform independents two years hence. (Trade has no effect.) In the top tercile, by contrast, a big-six equity tie means lower profit performance than the independents achieve. The other

---

[43] We experimented with alternative screens for lower performing firms. We flagged the companies in our sample whose reported profits for the fiscal year were zero or less *(akaji)*. This screen produced 80 firms in 180 firm-year observations. The results were suggestive: none were significant, but the keiretsu effects were positive. However, the "0" *ROA* threshold proved to have no particular significance; that is, other cutoffs in the lower range of t_1 *ROA* (e.g., 0.15, 0.25, 0.33) were as good or better in yielding evidence of intervention. It appeared, however, that the payoff from affiliation was greater on sales growth at lower thresholds (e.g., 0.25) and greater on *ROA* at higher ones. We also considered alternative lags: how long a period from the time a firm is identified as troubled or distressed to the time when its growth or profitability is targeted for adjustment. As a later section notes, we henceforth use ROA_{t-1} to assess trade-based interventions; otherwise ROA_{t-2} is used.

Table 5.4a. *OLS Estimates of Keiretsu Effects on ROA$_t$ by Tercile of the ROA$_{t-2}$ Distribution*

	(1) Shacho-kai Only	(2) Shacho-kai and Debt Tie	(4) Shacho-kai and Equity Tie	(5) Shacho-kai and Director Tie	(6) Shacho-kai and Trade Tie
			Top tercile		
Shacho-kai	−0.002	−0.001	−0.002	−0.002	−0.001
	(0.71)	(0.40)	(0.42)	(0.71)	(0.18)
Tie measure		0.001	−0.035	0.001	−0.004
		(0.05)	(2.91)**	(0.08)	(0.61)
			Middle tercile		
Shacho-kai	0.001	0.001	0.001	0.001	0.001
	(0.72)	(0.60)	(0.91)	(0.99)	(0.63)
Tie measure		0.004	−0.001	−0.014	−0.002
		(0.90)	(0.29)	(2.25)*	(0.77)
			Bottom tercile		
Shacho-kai	0.002	0.002	0.002	0.003	0.002
	(1.89)+	(1.19)	(1.41)	(1.97)*	(1.47)
Tie measure		0.015	0.011	0.008	0.000
		(3.25)*	(2.22)*	(1.31)	(0.04)

*** $p < .001$; ** $p < .01$; * $p < .05$; + $p < .10$. Control variables not shown.

Table 5.4b. *OLS Estimates of Keiretsu Effects on Sales Growth by Tercile of the ROA$_{t-2}$ Distribution*

	(1) Shacho-kai Only	(2) Shacho-kai and Debt Tie	(4) Shacho-kai and Equity Tie	(5) Shacho-kai and Director Tie	(6) Shacho-kai and Trade Tie
			Top tercile		
Shacho-kai	−0.018	−0.019	−0.016	−0.019	−0.024
	(2.06)*	(2.11)*	(1.74)	(2.09)*	(2.49)*
Tie measure		0.011	−0.014	0.017	0.025
		(0.38)	(0.46)	(0.41)	(1.33)
			Middle tercile		
Shacho-kai	0.000	0.001	0.000	0.000	0.001
	(0.04)	(0.14)	(0.04)	(0.05)	(0.14)
Tie measure		0.002	0.011	−0.004	−0.005
		(0.07)	(0.46)	(0.13)	(0.45)
			Bottom tercile		
Shacho-kai	0.006	0.003	0.005	0.006	0.006
	(1.01)	(0.53)	(0.86)	(0.91)	(1.00)
Tie measure		0.049	0.015	0.046	−0.008
		(2.11)*	(0.60)	(1.61)	(0.66)

*** $p < .001$; ** $p < .01$; * $p < .05$; + $p < .10$. Control variables not shown.

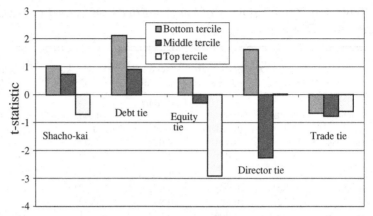

Figure 5.1. Keiretsu effects on ROA_t by tercile of ROA_{t-2}.

keiretsu effects are also negatively signed in the top tercile, but not significantly so. Finally, save on one dimension (directors), big-six linkage has no bearing on the t_2 ROA of middle-tercile firms.

The intervention pattern also holds for sales growth, controlled in the ROA regression. The main differences are that the equity effects are nonsignificant, while the negative shacho-kai effect in the top tercile is. Consistent with our knowledge that commercial ties only weakly index big-six commitments, trade again plays no role.

Figures 5.1 and 5.2 tell the story graphically. Each vertical bar represents the t-statistic indexing the keiretsu effect on ROA or sales growth for firms at each tercile of ROA_{t-2}. Aside from trade, the pattern overall is clear: groups help weak firms, hurt strong firms, and mostly leave the mediocre ones alone.

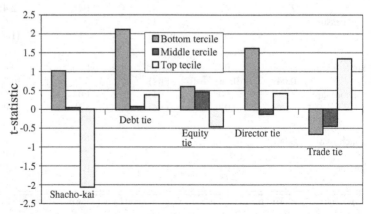

Figure 5.2. Keiretsu effects on sales growth by tercile of ROA_{t-2}.

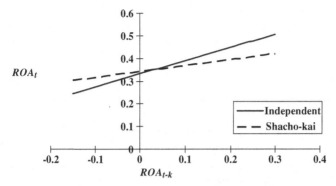

Figure 5.3. ROA_t regression on ROA_{t-k} for shacho-kai and independent firms.

Modeling Intervention

Now we shift strategy and study group effects on the performance of firms in a more general and rigorous way. The core of our analysis is an empirical model of intervention. Atop an abundance of anecdotal evidence, HKS showed that linkage to a group reverses the fortunes of a distressed Japanese firm. For this segment of the economy, the Caves and Uekusa and Nakatani studies miss the mark: keiretsu ties enhance, not impair, performance. However, intervention on behalf of a weakened partner is not costless. Banks tolerate lower returns on their capital; purchasers accept higher prices while suppliers accept lower; know-how, capital, and labor time are diverted from the aid-givers to the target firm. Thus:

H5.1: *The impact of big-six affiliation on a Japanese firm's performance is conditioned on the prior performance of that firm: weaker firms do better but stronger firms do worse.*

This implies for our analysis of keiretsu effects on corporate profitability a negative statistical interaction between group affiliation and prior performance, the latter lagged a sufficient length of time for an intervention to occur and the results to become apparent. Figure 5.3 shows how such a negative interaction connotes redistributive intervention. The regression of ROA_t on ROA_{t-k} is flatter for group firms compared to independents, and, at a point just right of the intercept, the lines cross. Thus, for firms with low ROA at time $t - k$ (e.g., near-zero or negative profitability), big-six affiliation is a net plus. Above that threshold, on the other hand, group firms underperform independents. Another way to read the figure is that group firms undergo more change, that is, regress faster to the mean. The independents show more inertia. Modeled as a linear equation,

$$ROA_{it} = \alpha + \beta' \mathbf{x}_{it} + \delta ROA_{it-k} + \gamma TIE_{it} + \lambda TIE^* ROA_{it-k} + \varepsilon_{it}$$
$$(5.1)$$

where α is the constant term, β is a vector of regression slopes, $\mathbf{x}_{it}$ is a vector of control variables (asset size, etc.), ROA_{it-k} is ROA lagged k years, TIE measures the strength of a firm's tie to a big-six group, $TIE^* ROA_{it-k}$ is the product of ROA_{it-k} and TIE, and ε_{it} is the stochastic error term. The difference between group and nongroup firms in the ROA_{it} on ROA_{it-k} slopes is measured by λ, and the difference in the intercepts is measured by γ. Our specific predictions are:

$$\gamma > 0 \qquad\qquad\qquad\qquad\qquad\qquad\qquad\qquad\qquad (5.2)$$
$$\lambda < 0 \qquad\qquad\qquad\qquad\qquad\qquad\qquad\qquad\qquad (5.3)$$

Thus, the slope of current on prior profitability is flatter for group firms than for independents and the intercept is larger. At values of ROA_{it-k} exceeding 0, independents outperform their keiretsu counterparts.[44]

For a set of large Japanese firms over the period 1965–95, a thirty-year period, we search for evidence that keiretsu orchestrate adjustments of the sort this model describes. Having found such evidence for the sample as a whole, we then explore the conditions that shape the strength and form of intervention: whether some groups are more interventionist than others (the former zaibatsu versus the post-war bank-centered groups), whether alternative forms of linkage to a group trigger distinct intervention patterns, and whether intervention activity is concentrated in certain industries. These analyses revolve around a core theme: the big-six groups are multiplex interfirm networks, and intervention is a collective undertaking.

So we specify a regression equation for ROA and another for sales growth. Both use ROA_{it-k} as a right-hand side (explanatory) variable (see Equation 5.1). It appears in two guises: alone (i.e., as a "main" effect) and as a component of an interaction with each of the five ties.

Setting the Lag

Setting the lag in our intervention model is an important matter. The time it takes a group to detect distress and intervene to effect a change is not fixed. But our performance data are available only at yearly intervals.

---

[44] Obviously, the threshold of "0" profitability is arbitrary, although it is close to the empirical reality (see Figures 5.1 and 5.2). The "0" ROA_{t-k} threshold merely signifies that there is some level of prior profitability below which keiretsu firms subsequently outperform independents.

There is reason to suppose that different keiretsu forms are associated with interventions on different timetables. Bearing in mind that, with the exception of shacho-kai, our keiretsu dimensions correlate positively (if not strongly), we argue as follows. Trade- and debt-based interventions should induce the quickest returns, for example, in terms of improved *or* diminished performance by the target firm. Those brought about by governance ties demand a longer lag, as they operate not directly on supply costs, earnings from sales, or the cost and availability of financing, but via an overhaul of the structure, strategy, and leadership of the firm. Yet this reasoning speaks less to the *speed* than to the *magnitude* of response. A firm dependent on group trade or debt but unattached in terms of directors, equity, or shacho-kai, may see its sales and profits swiftly adjusted if trading and lending partners collude to rewrite the terms of the exchange. Doing so, however, will cost the partners. Thus, these will be short-term, stop-gap interventions, whereas deep restructuring is only feasible when the group inserts itself into the company's governance machinery.

We experimented with one-, two-, and three-year lags, and, while the *pattern* of effects held up, some variations in their size and significance appeared. These make substantive sense. Moves by trading partners to reverse the fortunes of a member firm by adjusting volumes and prices of purchases and sales will immediately impact the target's financial health. Interventions by lenders (e.g., a restructuring of debt) may take longer to work through to profitability and growth. The returns to raising equity stakes or seconding executives take even longer. These conjectures are born out by our analysis. The intervention effect of big-six trade is largest with the one-year lag – in fact, it is nonsignificant with longer lags. For the other four affiliation measures, the two-year lag gives stronger results. Thus, we report the one-year lag results in the trade case but otherwise use the two-year lag.

Estimating the Model

Table 5.5 gives the estimates of the intervention model (Equation 5.1). We present them in a somewhat unconventional way. For each performance outcome – ROA and sales growth – five regressions were run. They differ in the keiretsu indicator: that is, the first includes the shacho-kai dummy and its interaction with ROA_{t-k}, the second includes equity tie and its interaction with ROA_{t-k}, and so on. The same sequence applies to sales growth.

Consider first shacho-kai, the cleanest and simplest indicator of group (column 1 of Table 5.5). The pattern of results supports the intervention theory: the shacho-kai effect on the performance of a firm – whether indexed by *ROA* or sales growth – is conditioned on prior profits; that

Table 5.5. *Regressions of ROA and Sales Growth on Keiretsu Measures and Controls (197 Japanese Manufacturing Firms, 1966–95)*

	(1)	(2)	(3)	(4)	(5)	(6)	(7)	(8)	(9)	(10)	(11)	(12)	(13)	(14)
	ROA_t	Sales Growth	ROA_t	Sales Growth	ROA_t	Sales Growth	ROA_t	Sales Growth	ROA_t	Sales Growth	ROA_t	ROA_t	ROA_t	ROA_t
Shacho-kai	.014***	.024***	.008**	.021**	.008**	.011+	.010**	.020**	.014***	.023***	.006**	.008***	.005*	.008***
Shacho-kai*ROA_{t-k}	−.208**	−.431***	−.129**	−.400***	−.118**	−.278**	−.137**	−.383***	−.207***	−.428***	−.091*	−.136**	−.068+	−.118**
Debt tie			.047***	.025							.037***	.044***		
Debt tie*ROA_{t-k}			−.594***	−.193							−.460***	−.546***		
Trade tie					.005	−.009							−.041	.002
Trade tie*ROA_{t-k}					−.133**	.062							−.002	−.079
Equity tie							.042***	.036			.027**		.032**	
Equity tie*ROA_{t-k}							−.729***	−.462			−.557**		−.536**	
Director tie									.028+	.018		.015		.030+
Director tie*ROA_{t-k}									−.517**	−.033		−.354*		−.485*
ROA_{t-k}	.741***	.064*	.807***	.090*	.872***	−.031	.791***	.096*	.772***	.067+	.828***	.106**	.882***	−.036
Constant	−.146***	.004	−.149***	−.001	−.078**	−.015	−.141***	.002	−.143***	−.001	−.142***	.000	−.078	−.013
N	5882	5882	5841	5841	5605	5605	5862	5862	5882	5882	5882	5882	5882	5882
Adjusted R^2	.687	.337	.696	.337	.807	.331	.695	.335	.689	.334	.700	.340	.813	.336

*** $p < .001$; ** $p < .01$; * $p < .05$; + $p < .10$, based on robust standard error estimates. Control variables not shown. $k = 1$ when trade is the tie; otherwise $k = 2$.

is, as Equations 5.2 and 5.3 predict, γ, the main effect (the adjustment to the intercept) is positive, while λ, the interaction effect (the adjustment to the slope) of ROA_{t-k}, is negative. Thus, groups favor weaklings at the expense of stronger firms.

The negative $\{\lambda\}$ have two interpretations: (1) that the group effect varies from high to low (including high positive, zero, and high negative) as t_1 performance ranges from low to high, or (2) that the inertia in performance – the effect of past on present performance – is greater for independent firms than for group firms. Put another way, keiretsu firms regress to the mean faster than do independent firms.[45] Those whose profits are high or low at t_1 find themselves closer to the mean by t_2.[46]

The autoregressive effect of ROA_{t-k} on current ROA_t is strong: 0.741 in the baseline shacho-kai regression.[47] For council firms, however, it is less (0.741 − 0.208 = 0.553). In other words, among weak (low profit) firms at t_1, the stronger the keiretsu tie, the greater the shift to average performance at t_2, signifying intervention by the group.[48] The positive main effect of council ($\gamma = .014$) says that, for firms with 0 to negative profitability at t_1, members are subsequently (t_2) more profitable than nonmembers. It also says that council firms that are strong at t_1 are weaker – closer to the mean – at t_2. Due to the linear model's symmetry, we cannot tell the difference, but we know from the tercile analysis that both are true.

Next consider the exchange and control ties, which tap a firm's involvement in a group via debt, equity, trade, and directors relations. With ROA as outcome, the intervention pattern holds in every case. The trade and director effects are weaker than the debt and equity coefficients (as the tercile analysis in Table 5.4 indicated) but all are significant.

The intervention model fares less well with sales growth as performance outcome. Only shacho-kai displays a strong intervention effect.[49] Except

---

[45] For a similar methodology applied to a related problem, see Greve and Taylor (2000).

[46] *Regression to the mean* is the tendency for observations at the extremes of a distribution at t_1 to move closer to the mean at t_2. This happens whenever the correlation between the t_1 and t_2 values is less than one. The mean of a distribution is typically the value with the highest probability. If improbable values at the extremes are selected, the likelihood is high that, upon remeasurement, they will have converged toward the average.

[47] If it were 1.0 with an intercept of 0, the angle of the slope of the regression plane would be forty-five degrees, signifying that t_1 performance maps perfectly to t_2 performance.

[48] Evaluation studies of the effectiveness of an intervention, whether a drug to cure illness or a treatment program for troubled children, often use a similar research design. Because of regression to the mean, many physical or social problems cure themselves with time. To evaluate the effectiveness of treatment, the researcher monitors change in both the treatment and the control groups. Faster regression to the mean ("normalcy") on the part of the treatment group implies treatment effectiveness (see, e.g., Judd and Kenny, 1981).

[49] The main effect of ROA_{t-k} on sales growth is weak and, depending on the mix of explanatory variables, fluctuates between positive and negative. In terms of the intervention

for trade, the exchange (debt and trade) and control (equity and directors) effects have the right signs ($\gamma > 0; \lambda < 0$) but none is significant. This pattern conforms to the tercile analysis except for the debt effect, which was significant there.[50]

Now we address the causal sequencing of ties in shaping interventions. Specifically, do cross-shareholding and director interlocks work as governance structures to mediate the effects of shacho-kai and financial/commercial exchange? (As only shacho-kai plays a significant intervention role in sales growth, we deal here just with ROA.) The answer is yes for trade but largely no for debt ties and shacho-kai. With the equity and director variables included in the ROA regressions (see the last four columns of Table 5.5), the trade effects vanish (suggesting mediation), but the shacho-kai and debt effects, while attenuating some, hang on. Thus, lenders *and* councils appear to be active monitors whose adjustments to their member and client firms' performance are made directly (i.e., through such unobserved processes as face-to-face relations), not merely indirectly via cross-shareholding and director dispatch.

model, it matters little whether the slope of the regression of t_2 sales growth on t_1 ROA is positive, flat, or negative, so long as the group slope tilts below the independents' slope. If so, the intervention interpretation applies. A stream of business strategy research argues that a negative correlation between profitability and sales growth is normal – that a firm committed to high profits thereby restricts its capacity for growth (Rumelt, 1974). Again, this describes the post-war competitive strategy of the Japanese firm: pursuit of growth to the relative neglect of profit and share price.

50 With the exceptions of Hitachi and Kobe Steel, every shacho-kai firm is uniquely assigned to one council. Thus, we can straightforwardly examine the effects of shacho-kai dummies where the baseline (excluded) category is *independent*. The interpretation of exchange and control measures is trickier. As in the blockmodel analysis, it makes sense to identify firm I as a member of group J to the degree that I is (a) involved in J *and* (b) uninvolved in groups $K - J$. We view the group with the greatest share of a firm's debt, equity, and so on as the group to which the firm belongs. The problem is that some firms link to several groups, while others align strongly with one and only weakly with others. The two companies may have comparable keiretsu involvement in the sense of dependence on shacho-kai firms, but the first firm is much more a member of a group than is the second. This is important. Our story is that keiretsu look after their own, tending to member needs by, for example, sharing risks and redistributing resources, thus reducing performance gaps and smoothing performance trajectories. But we cannot rule out the possibility that a company's ties to one group matter not – what counts is its involvement with the community of keiretsu firms as a whole. If so, a different story is called for, one framed in terms of strata or sectors (big-six vs. independent) versus groups or networks. The shacho-kai firms at the core of the economy, for example, might as a set conduct better monitoring of partners than independents can. They may, for example, draw closer scrutiny from government agencies or major banks. Yet our evidence shows generally, if imperfectly, that it is alignment with *one* group that matters. With ROA as outcome, the *other* group effects are either nonsignificant or (in the case of directors) have the wrong signs. The sales growth case is unclear, in part because shacho-kai, as noted, is the only tie that affects it significantly, but also because the *other* group pattern (again excepting directors) is closer to the hypothesized one. Still, in these instances, the one group tie has the stronger intervention effect.

So, we have general support for the theme of this chapter – that redistributive intervention is a *multiplex network* process operating similarly along the diverse relational dimensions whereby firms bind to groups. However, we also acknowledge that the strong and direct effects of lending relations and shacho-kai are consistent with models of (a) bank monitoring as a key, if not the dominant, mechanism of keiretsu intervention; and (b) shacho-kai as governance structure *sui generis*.

Is the Intervention Process Linear?

Our analysis assumes that that the function relating present to past performance is linear. This is a simplifying assumption that distorts reality. Ceiling and floor effects are apt to exist: because of limits on how low and how high profitability and sales growth can go, a decrement at the bottom of the distribution or an increment at the top induces less change than in the middle. The conventional way of capturing such nonlinearity is to add higher-order polynomials to the regression:

$$ROA_{it} = \alpha + \delta_1 ROA_{it-k} + \delta_2 ROA_{it-k}^2 + \delta_3 ROA_{it-k}^3 + \varepsilon_{it} \quad (5.4)$$

δ_2 is the second derivative, and it tells whether the function relating Y (outcome variable) to X (explanatory variable) accelerates ($\delta_2 > 0$) or decelerates ($\delta_2 < 0$) across the range of X. The third derivative, δ_3, tells whether that acceleration or deceleration shifts across the range of X. A negative δ_3 says that at some point the curve tops or bottoms out and moves in the opposite direction. An S-shaped curve implies that $\delta_1 > 0$, $\delta_2 > 0$, and $\delta_3 < 0$.

The autoregressive ROA function does take this curvilinear form. Moreover, the S-shape is sharper (flatter at the tails than in the middle) for group-aligned firms. We regressed ROA and sales growth on ROA_{t-k}, ROA_{it-k}^2, and ROA_{it-k}^3 and the corresponding interaction terms. We also varied the lag between one, two, and three years. The general pattern was mostly the same. (We depict it for trade in Figure 5.4.) The stronger the keiretsu tie, the more S-shaped is the function. Compared to independents, group firms located at the extremes of the t_1 performance distribution regress more rapidly to the mean.[51]

Relaxing the linearity constraint thus gives a clearer picture of the intervention process: groups apply the greatest pressure to the weakest and

---

[51] Using the estimates from a regression containing both nonlinear and interaction terms, we plotted in Figure 5.4 the function of ROA_t on ROA_{t-k} at two hypothetical levels of big-six tie: 0 percent and 50 percent, that is, no trading partners from the dominant big-six group and half of all trading partners from that group. The corresponding plots for debt, equity, and director ties are similarly S-shaped but less well-defined.

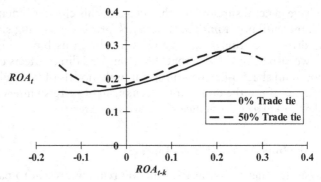

Figure 5.4. ROA_t regression on ROA_{t-k} at 0 percent and 50 percent trading partner ties to a big-six group.

the strongest firms. This fits our understanding of the intervention process. The network's aim is not merely to keep troubled affiliates alive or to punish, for example, rent-seekers. It is an equitable – even decorous – distribution of assets and returns across the membership and a smooth performance trajectory over time. Firms whose behavior and performance approximate the average for the group require little monitoring or adjustment.

Still, for the bulk of our analysis, the linear model is an acceptable simplification. The nonlinear specification adds little to the explained variance in performance (1–4%). Also noteworthy is that the shacho-kai effect is linear. In a previous paper, we speculated that interventions within the shacho-kai elite were "more incremental" whereas those targeting council firms were "episodic."[52] Thus, we stick with the linear models, even while we recognize that, as in all modeling, they oversimplify.

Cohesion and Intervention

To this point we have ignored differences among the big six in monitoring and intervention roles. We know from both prior work and our own inquiries (Chapters 3 and 4) that the horizontal keiretsu vary in cohesion. The former zaibatsu – Mitsui, Mitsubishi, and Sumitomo – and (due to its inclusion of the prewar Yasuda zaibatsu) Fuyo have been more tight-knit than the bank-centered groups (DKB and Sanwa). Moreover, of the zaibatsu, Mitsubishi and Sumitomo are best defined and most cohesive.

A straightforward hypothesis is *the more cohesive the keiretsu, the more interventionist it is*. The tighter-knit the group, the greater, presumably,

---

[52] Lincoln et al. (1996).

is its commitment to the welfare of the membership and the stronger are its norms of internal equity.[53] Sakamoto (1991:59) agrees: "In general, when the tie within the group intensifies, frequently the group takes on the role of mutual relief in times of adversity."

We studied the variation in the interventionist propensities of groups as follows: each shacho-kai was represented by a single dummy variable, the baseline again being noncouncil firms. We further calculated group-specific exchange and control ties, that is, the shares of each firm's equity, debt, suppliers or buyers, and directors supplied by each shacho-kai.[54] The correlations are in Table 5.6. They vary by group in the predictable way: stronger in the zaibatsu and weaker in the bank-centered groups.

Table 5.7 gives the group-specific results. Consider first the simplest case: shacho-kai as the only tie (column 1).[55] The pattern is strong. By either performance criterion, the most cohesive of the big six – Sumitomo – is the most interventionist. The least coherent – DKB and Sanwa – are the least so. The Fuyo, Mitsui, and Mitsubishi cases are less neat. With ROA as outcome, Mitsubishi is second-most interventionist, and Fuyo is third, but Mitsui – one of the big three former zaibatsu – is tied for last with DKB and Sanwa. With sales growth as outcome, Fuyo and Mitsui tie for second place in the intervention sweepstakes, while Mitsubishi is a distant fourth.[56]

The group-specific intervention pattern may be rendered graphically. Figure 5.5 shows the dependence of ROA and sales growth on ROA_{t-k} for shacho-kai and independent firms. (The corresponding regression is labeled shacho-kai in Table 5.7.) Whether the bar represents the effect on ROA (all in positive territory) or sales growth (all in negative territory except for the independents), the interpretation is the same: lower bars

---

[53] Moreover, as noted, the bank-centered groups are larger and contain more cases (e.g., Hitachi, Kobe Steel) of firms spanning big-six boundaries by occupying seats on multiple shacho-kai. These patterns figure in their lower cohesion.

[54] We thus ran five ROA and five sales growth regressions for each group: (1) including the shacho-kai dummy for that group and (2) including that dummy plus each group-specific exchange and control measure. As before, in an ROA or sales growth regression shacho-kai and exchange and control play complementary roles. The shacho-kai dummy captures the council effect, while the continuous measures tap the effects of big-six business–governance relations with council status controlled. Shacho-kai members may have debt, trade, director, and equity links to one another. Thus, our two dimensions of group alignment overlap. Entering them in a two-step sequence assesses whether gross shacho-kai effects apparent in the first-step are direct or net effects, operating through exchange and control.

[55] Note that, unlike previous tables, each column is one regression; that is, all terms are included.

[56] The coefficient on the interaction term in the Mitsui case, however, has a large standard error, indicating some instability. Indeed, if we switch the criterion for ranking groups on intervention intensity from raw slope to t-statistic (slope divided by standard error), Mitsui's interventionism lags Mitsubishi's.

Table 5.6. *Zero-Order Correlations among Group-Specific Measures*

		Mitsubishi				
		Shacho-kai	Debt Tie	Trade Tie	Equity Tie	Director Tie
Sumitomo	Shacho-kai	1.000	.586	.406	.718	.657
	Debt tie	.468	1.000	.339	.691	.595
	Trade tie	.388	.343	1.000	.478	.438
	Equity tie	.738	.656	.474	1.000	.702
	Director tie	.441	.481	.381	.615	1.000

		Fuyo				
		Shacho-kai	Debt Tie	Trade Tie	Equity Tie	Director Tie
Mitsui	Shacho-kai	1.000	.425	.077	.154	.018
	Debt tie	.480	1.000	.285	.560	.350
	Trade tie	.278	.334	1.000	.499	.502
	Equity tie	.435	.631	.489	1.000	.732
	Director tie	.082	.385	.307	.711	1.000

		DKB				
		Shacho-kai	Debt Tie	Trade Tie	Equity Tie	Director Tie
Sanwa	Shacho-kai	1.000	.505	.256	.306	.425
	Debt tie	.683	1.000	.151	.445	.444
	Trade tie	.172	.087	1.000	.203	.349
	Equity tie	.576	.559	.002	1.000	.730
	Director tie	.557	.514	.088	.607	1.000

Note: Correlations in the upper off-diagonal refer to the horizontally labeled group. Correlations in the lower off-diagonal refer to the vertically labeled group.

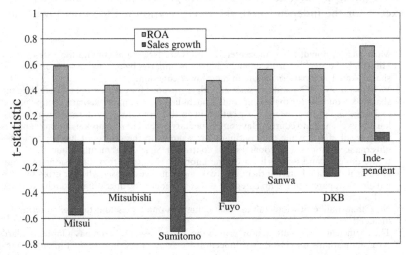

Figure 5.5. ROA_{t-k} effects on ROA_t and sales growth by shacho-kai.

Table 5.7. Regressions of ROA and Sales Growth on Group-Specific Ties and Interactions

	Shacho-kai		Shacho-kai and Shacho-kai Debt Tie		Shacho-kai and Shacho-kai Trade Tie		Shacho-kai and Shacho-kai Equity Tie		Shacho-kai and Shacho-kai Director Tie	
	ROA_t	Sales Growth	ROA_t	Sales Growth	ROA_t	Sales Growth	ROA_t	Sales Growth	ROA_t	Sales Growth
Mitsui shacho-kai	.010+	.027*	.007	1.041**	.004	.025*	.012*	.038**	.006	.027*
Above*ROA_{t-k}	-.151*	-.637**	-.101	-.770***	-.062	-.591**	-.176*	-.743**	-.054	-.583*
Mitsubishi shacho-kai	.019***	.020*	.017***	.027	.010+	.029*	.015*	.041*	.019***	.048***
Above*ROA_{t-k}	-.303*	-.396**	-.306**	-.569+	-.129+	-.454*	-.243**	-.867***	-.395**	-.972***
Sumitomo shacho-kai	.021***	.045***	.016***	.055***	.013*	.044***	-.010	.044+	.011+	.046***
Above*ROA_{t-k}	-.402***	-.767***	-.370***	-.915***	-.323***	-.869***	.076	-.785*	-.265**	-.825***
Fuyo shacho-kai	.021***	.033**	.020**	.018	.017***	.029*	.017***	.028*	.015***	.029*
Above*ROA_{t-k}	-.268***	-.533**	-.248*	-.379*	-.212**	-.489*	-.199**	-.446*	-.159**	-.433*
Sanwa shacho-kai	.012*	.022**	.014+	.002	.006	.023*	.019***	.014	.011*	.010
Above*ROA_{t-k}	-.181+	-.321*	-.246	.035	-.108	-.348*	-.395**	-.220	-.250**	-.191
DKB shacho-kai	.010*	.014*	.013**	.004	.005	.013	.008+	.017*	-.002	.006
Above*ROA_{t-k}	-.175*	-.339***	-.192*	.023	-.064	-.377**	-.097	-.309*	.084	-.168
Mitsui tie			.033*	-.015	.016+	.026	.026	-.037	-.005	-.038
Above*ROA_{t-k}			-.421+	.182	-.415*	-.499*	-.616**	.601	-.179	.534
Mitsubishi tie			.023	.012	.018+	-.019	.038	-.093	-.044	-.306**
Above*ROA_{t-k}			-.143	.301	-.408+	.001	-.708+	2.565*	1.821*	6.597***
Sumitomo tie			.039***	.012	.019	.007	.138+	.026	.040	-.033
Above*ROA_{t-k}			-.353*	-.015	-.138	.435	-2.284*	.112	-.468	1.285
Fuyo tie			.025	.084+	-.035+	.032	.047***	.067*	.013	.051
Above*ROA_{t-k}			-.291	-.567	.601+	-.408	-.922***	-.910*	-.373*	-.663*
Sanwa tie			.007	.098+	.016	.000	-.055*	.091	-.095	.132
Above*ROA_{t-k}			.129	-1.34*	-.136	.106	1.631***	-.617	3.642***	.016
DKB tie			.004	.089+	.005	.031	.028	.011	.081+	.067
Above*ROA_{t-k}			-.093	-2.152**	-.204	-.256	-.840+	-.293	-2.518***	-1.204
ROA_{t-k}	.740***	.065*	.807***	.209***	.731***	.162	.791***	.071	.614***	-.025
Constant	-.144***	.006	-.154***	-.021	-.142***	-.026	-.124***	.003	-.114***	.005
N	5882	5882	5434	5434	5604	5604	5862	5862	5882	5882
Adjusted R^2	.688	.334	.696	.340	.701	.335	.704	.336	.705	.339

*** $p < .001$; ** $p < .01$; * $p < .05$; + $p < .10$, based on robust standard error estimates. Control variables not shown.

Note: Tie in this table refers to the group-specific debt, etc., tie; e.g., Mitsui debt tie (see Table 5.1). $k = 1$ when trade is the tie; otherwise $k = 2$.

247

signify greater intervention. Again, save for Mitsui (*ROA*) and Mitsubishi (sales growth), the ordering by interventionist proclivity is clear: independents anchor the comparison at none; the bank-centered groups (DKB and Sanwa) *sans* zaibatsu history follow; next is Fuyo, a bank-centered group with a zaibatsu history; and finally the former zaibatsu led by Sumitomo.

We further expect that the greater each group's share of a firm's debt, trade, equity, and directors, the greater is its inclination to adjust that firm's performance. Two questions are key: (a) do the intervention effects of these exchange and control ties differ by group, perhaps in proportion to the role of the tie in the cohesion of the group; and (b) do they mediate the shacho-kai effects?

Table 5.7 shows ROA adjustments stemming from debt ties to Mitsui and Sumitomo; trade ties to Mitsui and Mitsubishi; equity ties to Mitsui, Mitsubishi, Sumitomo, Fuyo, and SKB; and director ties to DKB.[57] Sales growth interventions flow from debt ties to DKB and Sanwa, trade ties to Mitsui, and equity and director ties to Fuyo.

Although the shacho-kai effects are approximately the same on growth as on profits, the exchange and control effects are weaker. Our conjecture again is that adjustments to the bottom line are easier to engineer.[58] The strong shacho-kai role in sales growth intervention may testify to better monitoring within the councils than between them and the noncouncil firms whose big-six links are exclusively those of pairwise exchange and control.[59]

[57] Table 5.7 shows a few exchange and control effects with the wrong signs: for *ROA*, Mitsubishi and Sanwa directors and Sanwa equity; for sales growth, Mitsubishi and Sumitomo equity. These are symptomatic of multicollinearity, not unexpected with so many overlapping terms in the same regression. Still, flipped signs, inflated coefficients, and other signs of collinearity are rare in these analyses.

[58] As the Enron debacle so dramatically shows (see Chapter 6), this is not unique to Japan. Many U.S. firms have come under intense scrutiny and criticism for their use of questionable techniques to demonstrate steady earnings growth. Some of these – the shifting of costs and earnings between parent firm and off-balance sheet subsidiary or partner – are reminiscent of the *tobashi* practices of the keiretsu.

[59] There is again the question of attachment to multiple groups. A group's propensity to intervene should be greatest in those firms who belong to it alone. Until the 1990s, the largest cases of post-war bankruptcy (e.g., Sanko Steamship) were companies that sought to diversify their portfolio of keiretsu commitments by, for example, having several main banks. When they ran into trouble, no one bank or group was willing to throw them a lifeline (Gerlach, 1992a:200; Murphy, 1996:47). Although shacho-kai memberships are mostly mutually exclusive, large firms routinely select lenders, shareholders, suppliers, and even directors from multiple groups. A major bank such as Mitsubishi or DKB might be a substantial holder of firm A's debt and equity but still rank third or fourth among A's creditors and stockholders. For example, in 1982 Mitsui Bank was Toyota's largest shareholder, owning 5 percent of its stock, while Sanwa Bank owned 4.8 percent. While the difference in the two banks' Toyota stakes is small, it symbolizes Toyota's longer and closer association with Mitsui. Thus, we should consider not merely the magnitude of a council's business with or control of a firm, but also whether it is the firm's *lead* group. We coded dummies for whether (= 1) or not (= 0) each shacho-kai was the firm's lead group

Several of the shacho-kai effects are, in fact, mediated. Debt ties take out the *Sankin-kai* (DKB) and *Sansui-kai* (Sanwa) adjustments to sales growth. Director ties explain DKB's contribution to both performance outcomes and Mitsui's role in *ROA*. Trade relations mediate much of the Mitsui *Nimoku-kai* and Mitsubishi *Kinyo-kai* effects on *ROA*. Finally, equity accounts for the Sumitomo *Hakusui-kai* effect on *ROA*. There is some correspondence here between the tie's role in the definition of a group and its role in the group's intervention pattern. Lending networks are clearly key to the definition of the bank-centered groups; and we know from Appendix 3.1 that commercial relations figure in the structuring of Mitsui and Mitsubishi, as do director ties in that of DKB.

Still, the bulk of the group-specific shacho-kai effects are direct, so our earlier conclusion stands: the shacho-kai looks to be a real governance structure, not merely an inner circle of closely linked and centrally positioned companies.

Size and Stakeholder Concentration: *Too big to fail?*

Does the magnitude of intervention vary with the target company's size? Groups should be more committed to their large affiliates than their small ones. At the time of its bailout in the mid-1970s by the Sumitomo group, Mazda was the largest employer in the Hiroshima region. The salvation of a smaller automaker might have had less priority. The pressure to intervene from government agencies such as MITI would likely have been less as well. The U.S. government bailouts of Chrysler, Lockheed, and Penn Central all were justified on the ground that these were huge employers and therefore vital to the country's economic health.

In early 1996, when slack demand for capital was driving the major commercial banks to expand their business with small and medium-sized corporations, we asked executives in an interview at Sumitomo Bank headquarters if the bank would as soon come to the aid of a small client as a large one.[60] They said they would not allow a client firm to fail just because it was small. They acknowledged that Sumitomo might have less

by the criteria of debt, trade, equity, and directors. We then formed three-way interactions of the following sort: shacho-kai dummy*exchange/control tie*ROA_{t-k}. The pattern was intriguing. For the bank-centered groups, but not the zaibatsu, the ROA adjustments associated with debt and trade were enhanced by lead-group status. They were weaker (debt) or nonexistent (trade) in the case of the zaibatsu groups. The lesson may be this: the former zaibatsu – Mitsubishi and Sumitomo in particular – have been aggressively – even indiscriminately – interventionist. The bank-centered groups, by contrast, target their interventions more. They are less apt to bail out any council member with a problem and are disinclined to assist a noncouncil firm without a clear claim to affiliate status.

[60] Interview conducted on 5 July 1996 at Sumitomo Bank's Osaka headquarters.

direct and short-term incentive to help, but the long-term *reputational* cost of inaction required that they intervene as readily as with a large firm.[61]

While reputational constraints in Japanese corporate networks are by all accounts important, our data do not bear this comment out. The evidence for performance-adjusting interventions is greater for large firms (except in the case of director ties). We tap this tendency with two interaction terms: TIE*SIZE and TIE*ROA*SIZE. The results for ROA_t take the familiar form: the first coefficient is positive and the second is negative (see rows 3 and 5 of Table 5.8a). Thus, as the size of the target firm increases, the keiretsu main effect (γ) goes up and the interaction effect (λ) goes down; that is, the intervention pattern strengthens.[62]

As usual, the results are weaker with sales growth as outcome: the intensification of the intervention pattern as a function of firm size materializes only with respect to debt.

The one strongly disconfirmatory result in this analysis is the director effect. Interventions channeled through director networks are stronger in *smaller* firms. Since this pattern holds for both performance outcomes, we cannot discount it, but neither can we explain it.

Debt and Equity Concentration

Could the intervention effects of big-six debt and equity ties reflect a more general corporate governance phenomenon: monitoring by large debt- and shareholders?[63] The question should be addressed for two reason: first, because stakeholder concentration constitutes a competing interpretation of our results – one that may not require the concept of keiretsu – and, second, because the issues are interesting and important in their own right.

The effects of equity and debt concentration on the behavior of managers and the performance of firms are widely studied. Berle and Means' (1932) pioneering treatise on the modern public corporation saw

---

[61] Aoki (1988:148), too, noted the role played by reputational concerns in main bank interventions: "it is vital for the main bank to maintain its reputation as a competent and responsible monitor. This may explain ... the rescue operation put forth by a main bank when it discovers serious financial difficulties in a customer company, yet judges that the ailing company has a chance to recuperate. ... [W]hat is at stake when a customer company fails is the main bank's reputation as a responsible monitor, and the cost [of the bailout to the bank] – bearing may be understood as a price for the misjudgment that led to the financial trouble of the customer company."

[62] Splitting the sample at the median, we find the intervention effect of shacho-kai to be half in the small firm segment what it is in the large firm segment. The director effect is entirely confined to small firms.

[63] Schleifer and Vishy (1986); Morck and Nakamura (1999).

Table 5.8a. Firm Size Conditions the Intervention Effects of Keiretsu Ties on ROA

Explanatory Variables	(1)	(2)	(3)	(4)	(5)	(6)	(7)	(8)	(9)	(10)	(11)	(12)
	Shacho-kai				Debt Tie		Trade Tie		Equity Tie		Director Tie	
Tie	.016***	.014***	−.086**	−.133**	−.152	−.414*	.797	1.871	3.502+	5.601+	−.905	−.792
Tie*ROA_{t-k}	−.238**	−.216**	1.427***	1.852**	3.808+	6.598**	−.021	−.086	−.068	−.250	.318**	.220
Tie*Assets			.010**		.022		.004		.014		−.031**	
Tie*Assets*ROA_{t-k}			−.173***		−.495*		−.125		−.496*		.029	
Tie*Sales				.015***		.047*		.010		.031		−.022
Tie*Sales*ROA_{t-k}				−.211***		−.750**		−.229		−.691*		.054
Assets*ROA_{t-k}	.066*		.107***		.107+		.076*		.080*		.036	
Sales*ROA_{t-k}		.128**		.173***		.210**		.186*		.162**		.117*
ROA_{t-k}	.124	−.512	−.263	−.962*	−.197	−1.289+	.106	−1.018	.047	−.805	.413	−.421
Total assets	.016***	.006	.016***	.002	.017***	.002	.013***	.001	.015***	.006	.014***	.007
Total sales	−.021***	−.016***	−.023***	−.016***	−.022***	−.016***	−.017***	−.013***	−.019***	−.016***	−.015***	−.015***
Constant	−.110***	−.056	−.078***	−.011	−.106*	−.009	−.135***	−.049	−.122***	−.049	−.158***	−.085*
N	5882	5882	5882	5882	5841	5841	5604	5604	5862	5862	5882	5882
Adjusted R^2	.690	.702	.695	.709	.699	.711	.687	.701	.698	.708	.686	.697

*** $p < .001$; ** $p < .01$; * $p < .05$; + $p < .10$, based on robust standard error estimates. Control variables not shown.

Note: Tie refers to shacho-kai, debt tie, etc., depending on the column label. $k = 1$ when trade is the tie; otherwise $k = 2$.

Table 5.8b. *Firm Size Conditions the Intervention Effects of Keiretsu Ties on Sales Growth*

Explanatory Variables	Shacho-kai				Debt		Equity		Trade		Director	
	(1)	(2)	(3)	(4)	(7)	(8)	(5)	(6)	(11)	(12)	(9)	(10)
Tie	.022***	.023***	-.036	-.102	-.588	-.673*	-.009		-.148	-.038	.935**	1.027**
Tie*ROA_{t-k}	-.452***	-.471***	-.179	.194	1.045	9.526*	-.164		.725	-.024	-1.348	-2.611
Tie*Assets			.006		.068		.223	-.869	.014		-.094**	
Tie*Assets*ROA_{t-k}			-.025		-1.177+		.184	.307	-.054		.065	
Tie*Sales				.012+		.075*		-.022		.002		-.104**
Tie*Sales*ROA_{t-k}				-.063		-1.089*		-.044		.028		.244
Assets*ROA_{t-k}	-.045	-.017	-.033		.089		-.084		-.041		-.088	
Sales*ROA_{t-k}				.007		.083		-.055		-.017		-.043
ROA_{t-k}	.469	.217	.358	-.026	-.742	-.723	.891	.626	.314	.084	.860	.427
Total assets	-.028**	-.030***	-.030**	-.031***	-.035*	-.029***	-.022*	-.031***	-.031***	-.029***	-.016+	-.031***
Total sales	.031***	.032***	.031***	.026***	.029***	.021+	.030***	.037***	.030***	.028*	.027***	.038***
Constant	-.421***	-.404***	-.398***	-.351***	-.359*	-.341**	-.491***	-.486***	-.441***	-.446***	-.535***	-.513***
N	5882	5882	5882	5882	5841	5841	5862	5862	5604	5604	5882	5882
Adjusted R^2	.251	.251	.251	.251	.254	.253	.250	.249	.244	.244	.250	.249

*** $p < .001$; ** $p < .01$; * $p < .05$; + $p < .10$, based on robust standard error estimates. Control variables not shown.

Note: Tie refers to shacho-kai, debt tie, etc., depending on the column label. $k = 1$ when trade is the tie; otherwise $k = 2$.

dispersion of ownership divorcing the interests of managers from those of owners and reducing the ability of owners (principals) to monitor managers (their agents). When ownership is in few hands – when one or more stockholders hold large blocks of shares – they have the incentive and the means to monitor and discipline management for deviations from profit and share-price maximizing behavior. The same reasoning applies to debt holding, particularly outside the Anglo-American economies. In the absence of efficient markets for corporate control (i.e., ease of merger and acquisition), the German and Japanese economies evolved main bank systems, which put one large debt (also typically an equity) holder in a position to scrutinize and redirect, if need be, the workings of a client firm.[64] When equity and debt holders are large in number and small in size, no one has the scale and stature to oversee the company and keep it on course.[65]

A key prediction of large stakeholder theory is that profit and stock performance benefit because incumbent management has less leeway to pursue suboptimizing goals (e.g., expansion of assets for the sake of personal aggrandizement). But it applies as well to performance interventions of the sort we study here: a capacity to force the firm to react quickly to performance deviations from a baseline norm. Usually the adjustment is recovery from a downturn, but we have cited reasons why monitors might also seek to temper "excessive" success.

Equity and debt concentrations were measured with Herfindahl indices of concentration in the proportions of equity or debt held by the ten largest equity or debtholders. Table 5.9 shows no more than a trivial correlation (−0.047) between the two, possibly because of the low cap (5 percent) on the equity a bank was allowed to hold in a firm until the cap was raised to 10 percent in 1997. Not surprisingly, the Herfindahls correlate positively with the corresponding keiretsu ties (for equity: 0.366; for debt: 0.280). When a large share of a firm's debt or equity is held by the members of a shacho-kai, ownership is obviously concentrated. The Herfindahl for equity, but not debt, also correlates positively with director tie (0.323). The correlation between equity concentration and shacho-kai, however, is negative (−0.113). The firm size correlations suggest why. Companies with few stockholders tend to be small, whereas shacho-kai firms are large.

---

[64] Cable (1983); Cable and Yasuki (1985).

[65] Roehl (1983a) suggests that concentrated shareholding in the context of keiretsu cross-shareholding may in fact give firms *more*, rather than less, leeway to pursue goals other than profit and share price maximization. This calls to mind the finding of Schleifer and Vishy (1986) that the effect of shareholder concentration on corporate performance is curvilinear – when a very small number of extremely large stockholders control a corporation they, too, may opt for goals other than earnings or share price maximization.

Table 5.9. *Correlations of Debt and Equity Concentration with Keiretsu Ties, Size, and Industry Measures*

	Debt Concentration	Equity Concentration
Debt concentration	.0473	1.0000
Equity concentration	1.0000	.0473
Total assets	−.0783	−.2018
Total sales	−.0613	−.1188
Shacho-kai	−.0586	−.1128
Debt tie	.2798	.0343
Trade tie	.0657	.0531
Equity tie	.0387	.3655
Director tie	.0732	.3223
Textiles (= 1)	.0079	−.1036
Chemicals (= 1)	−.0870	−.1622
Electronics (= 1)	−.0282	.1561
Shipbuilding (= 1)	.0391	−.0404
Autos (= 1)	.0256	.2241

The question before us is whether the phenomenon of intervention by a big-six horizontal group reduces to the more general one of monitoring by large debt or stockholders, whether keiretsu-affiliated or not. Such a finding would undercut our perspective on the keiretsu network as a risk-sharing community of fate.

Table 5.10 shows equity concentration following the script: we observe the familiar intervention pattern ($\gamma > 0$; $\lambda < 0$) for both performance outcomes. These persist, and even increase in the case of sales growth, with equity tie in the regression. Debt concentration, however, behaves differently. Its effects ($\gamma < 0$; $\lambda > 0$) take the wrong signs under the intervention hypothesis. Further, when debt ties enter the regression, those effects lose all significance.

What do we conclude? First, in the debt case, it is the *tie* that matters, not concentrated debt-holding per se. Equity concentration, by contrast, behaves so much like equity tie that it seems a single process is at work. One possibility is this: keiretsu intervention of the sort we study is not exclusively a horizontal group activity; it is practiced by the vertical groups as well. The keiretsu ties we consider (membership in and dependence for debt, etc., on a shacho-kai) are specific to the horizontal groups. Thus, we ignore variation in the nonfinancial (chiefly equity) ties that make up the vertical nets, for example, Nissan, Toyota, Matsushita, Hitachi, and so on. The net effects of equity concentration may thus represent unmeasured vertical group activity.

Table 5.10. *Intervention Effects of Shacho-kai, Debt and Equity Ties, and Debt and Equity Concentration*

	(1) ROA$_t$	(2) Sales Growth	(3) ROA$_t$	(4) Sales Growth	(5) ROA$_t$	(6) Sales Growth	(7) ROA$_t$	(8) Sales Growth
Shacho-kai	.011*	.018*	.007*	.018*	.014***	.024***	.011***	.022***
Shacho-kai*ROA$_{t-2}$	−.166*	−.349***	−.112+	−.347**	−.218***	−.440***	−.163***	−.411***
Debt tie			.040***	.008				
Debt tie*ROA$_{t-2}$			−.545***	−.038				
Equity tie							.031**	.032
Equity tie*ROA$_{t-2}$							−.542**	−.285
Debt concentration	−.012	−.020	.000	−.021				
Debt concentration*ROA$_{t-2}$	.323	.618+	.169	.557				
Equity concentration					.032*	.009	.028*	.000
Equity concentration*ROA$_{t-2}$					−.536***	−.423	−.434***	−.369
ROA$_{t-2}$	.640***	−.130	.747	−.103	.834***	.138*	.855***	.150*
Constant	−.130***	.029	−.140***	.024	−.148***	.007	−.246***	.007
N	5882	5882	5882	5882	5882	5882	5882	5882
Adjusted R^2	.691	.338	.699	.340	.693	.337	.699	.338

*** $p < .001$; ** $p < .01$; * $p < .05$; +$p < .10$, based on robust standard error estimates. Control variables not shown.

255

In any case, the bottom line is clear: neither debt nor equity concentration behaves in such a way as to require revision of our general theory of big-six debt- and equity-based intervention. Debt concentration bears no resemblance to debt tie, and equity concentration seems to proxy equity tie, not the other way around. Much research on corporate governance in Japan conveys a different sense. It downplays the interventionism of groups while highlighting that of banks. Our evidence suggests that bank monitoring is part and parcel of the broader keiretsu intervention process.

Industry Patterns

At an interview we conducted with Toyota in the mid-1990s, an executive asserted that the critical cleavage in the Japanese economy was no longer that of management and labor; it was now between the keiretsu-ridden, protected, and uncompetitive industries and the unregulated, flexibly organized, and globally powerful industries such as autos. We were intrigued at his suggestion that the Japanese automotive industry in general and Toyota in particular might be thought free of the encumbrances of keiretsu.

Still, there is good reason to suppose redistributive interventionism to be spread unevenly across sectors of the Japanese economy. For one thing, the density of keiretsu connections varies by industry. Table 5.11 measures the prevalence of group affiliation in the fifteen industries in our sample. The proportion of each industry's firms on shacho-kai varies from roughly 17 percent to 71 percent with eleven of the fifteen in the 40–60 percent range. In addition, 20–30 percent of each industry's debt and trading partnerships is big-six based, as is 10–20 percent of its shareholders' equity, and 5–10 percent of its directors.

Whether an industry has a larger or smaller big-six presence, however, varies with the tie. Of these industries, autos has the lowest rate of shacho-kai representation. This, perhaps, was what our Toyota informant had in mind. Debt ties to big-six financials are also low, yet the car industry's big-six trade ties are average and its equity and director linkage is above average. Some consideration of the Toyota case helps to clarify. Of its core members (Aisin Seiki, Daihatsu, Denso, Hino, Kanto Auto, Toyota Automatic Loom), only Toyota and Daihatsu hold shacho-kai seats (Mitsui and Sanwa, respectively). But the remaining firms – all high in the Toyota supply chain – link indirectly to Mitsui and (to a lesser degree) Sanwa through their equity and director involvement with Toyota.

A second globally competitive industry – electronics and electrical machinery – is much more consistently low (negative correlation) on all

Table 5.11. Means and Correlations of Keiretsu Variables by Industry

Industry	No. Firms (1980)	Shacho-kai		Debt Tie		Trade Tie		Equity Tie		Director Tie	
		Mean	Correlation	Mean	Correlation	Mean	Correlation	Mean	Correlation	Mean	Correlation
Food	26	.233	−.194	.237	.046	.323	−.013	.114	−.113	.059	−.052
Textile	12	.416	−.016	.214	−.013	.283	−.055	.099	−.111	.030	−.105
Pulp and paper	8	.489	.018	.236	.027	.377	.043	.146	−.005	.050	−.035
Chemicals	33	.524	.071	.200	−.084	.344	.031	.143	−.034	.045	−.116
Petroleum	7	.571	.044	.202	−.025	.316	−.013	.086	−.103	.040	−.057
Ceramics	9	.659	.074	.303	.125	.398	.061	.191	.071	.097	.073
Iron and steel	15	.475	.022	.264	.094	.300	−.053	.165	.023	.067	−.011
Nonferrous	13	.615	.092	.305	.174	.350	.022	.232	.166	.086	.042
Machinery	17	.706	.190	.229	.025	.353	.029	.135	−.028	.069	.006
Electrical	22	.419	−.033	.184	−.102	.252	−.123	.121	−.089	.047	−.080
Shipbuilding	2	.500	.011	.242	.016	.313	−.008	.166	.009	.136	.067
Automobile	20	.199	−.163	.165	−.147	.350	.027	.231	.222	.173	.367
Rubber and tire	3	.666	.056	.243	.021	.262	−.039	.157	.002	.059	−.014
Misc. manufacturing	7	.416	.098	.271	.074	.456	−.025	.233	.226	.072	.236
Extractive	6	.165	−.091	.149	−.092	.432	.081	.101	−.069	.028	−.071

Note: Table entries are industry-specific means of keiretsu ties and correlations of keiretsu ties with industry dummy variables.

Table 5.12. *Industry Conditions the Intervention Effects of Keiretsu Ties on ROA and Sales Growth*

Keiretsu Tie Measures	(1) Shacho-kai ROA_t	(2) Sales Growth	(3) Debt Tie ROA_t	(4) Sales Growth	(5) Trade Tie ROA_t	(6) Sales Growth	(7) Equity Tie ROA_t	(8) Sales Growth	(9) Director Tie ROA_t	(10) Sales Growth
Baseline ROA_{t-k}	.850***	.052	.873***	.069*	.980***	−.051	.901***	.075*	.864***	.061
Baseline tie	.017*	.046***	.028	.065	.017*	.130	.098***	.105*	.045+	.074
Baseline tie*ROA_{t-k}	−.302***	−.642***	−.553***	−.700**	−.298***	−.169	−1.593***	−1.265*	−.533	−.791
Food*ROA_{t-k}	−.252***	.047	−.275**	.006	−.201***	−.268	−.346***	−.156	−.372***	−.538*
Food*tie	−.012	−.018	−.066	.082	−.019*	−.057	−.127**	−.174	−.112*	−.314*
Food*tie*ROA_{t-k}	.259**	.170	.499**	.518	.273*	1.169	1.949***	2.439	1.663***	6.099***
Textiles*ROA_{t-k}	−.608***	.185	−.916***	.656+	−.541*	−.549	−.556*	.259	−.647***	−.060
Textiles*tie	−.010	−.041*	.000	.000	−.041	.080	−.010	−.098	−.035	−.368+
Textiles*tie*ROA_{t-k}	.275*	.368	1.813+	−1.918	.215	−.206	.480	−.611	1.135	5.204
Chemicals*ROA_{t-k}	−.271***	−.059	−.415***	.102	−.186**	−.097	−.224***	−.046	−.217*	−.069
Chemicals*tie	−.019**	−.051*	−.063	−.019	−.008	.001	−.063*	−.055	.030	.103
Chemicals*tie*ROA_{t-k}	.316**	.405	1.166*	−.196	.278	.119	1.029+	.440	−.733	−1.498
Iron and steel*ROA_{t-k}	−.625***	−.339**	−.731***	−.432***	−.421***	.163	−.822***	−.411*	−.685***	−.417*
Iron and steel*tie	−.009	.001	−.038	−.083	.032	.193	−.131***	−.037	−.042	.016
Iron and steel*tie*ROA_{t-k}	.196*	.112	.717**	.347	.048	−1.079	2.043**	.708	.649	.371
Nonferrous*ROA_{t-k}	−.376*	−.422*	−.331	−.590	−.176+	−.745	−.449*	−.371	−.341*	−.517
Nonferrous*tie	−.015+	−.052**	−.024	−.151	−.005	−.025	−.094*	−.080	−.021	−.120
Nonferrous*ROA_{t-k}	.216	.322	.234	1.042	−.296	.311	1.569***	.651	−.470	.916
Machinery*ROA_{t-k}	−.237***	−.259	−.235***	−.407+	−.306***	.042	−.276***	−.380+	−.264***	−.447*
Machinery*tie	−.012	−.037*	−.007	−.022	−.025***	−.039	−.070*	−.092	−.023	−.133
Machinery*tie*ROA_{t-k}	.198*	.446	.185	1.065	.368*	.504	1.046*	1.481	.064	2.088
Electronics*ROA_{t-k}	−.201***	.159	−.198***	−.164	−.183***	−.004	−.290***	.110	−.229***	.049
Electronics*tie	−.005	−.010	.014	−.062	−.013+	−.036	−.107*	−.018	−.029	.003
Electronics*tie*ROA_{t-k}	.129	.436	.224	1.881	.214+	1.324	1.689***	.913	.236	1.414
Automotive*ROA_{t-k}	−.335***	.069	−.205***	.206	−.213***	.075	−.361***	−.085	−.321***	.034
Automotive*tie	−.024	−.042	.017	.044	−.016+	−.072	−.105	−.167	−.068	−.106
Automotive*tie*ROA_{t-k}	.400***	.391	−.231	−.632	.267	.075	1.656***	1.715*	.596	.602
Constant	−.123***	.002	−.127***	−.007	−.090***	−.037	−.126***	−.011	−.130***	−.011
N	5686	5686	5653	5653	5423	5423	5668	5668	5686	5686
Adjusted R^2	.713	.335	.714	.336	.824	.340	.715	.333	.711	.334

*** $p < .001$; ** $p < .01$; * $p < .05$; +$p < .10$, based on robust standard error estimates. Control variables not shown.

Note: Tie refers to each of the five keiretsu tie measures, depending on the column. *Baseline tie* refers to the keiretsu tie measure computed over all industries not coded as dummy variables and included in the regression (see Table 5.11). $k = 1$ when trade is the tie; otherwise $k = 2$.

dimensions of affiliation. Food, extractive industry (mining, fishing, and forestry), and, to a lesser extent, textiles are also largely uninvolved on four of the five criteria (exceptions being debt in the food case and trade in extractive). The industries with strong and multidimensional big-six ties are ceramics, nonferrous metals, nonelectrical machinery, and miscellaneous manufacturing. Iron and steel exhibit average involvement as do paper and rubber. Chemicals and petroleum are high in shacho-kai representation but low in exchange and control.

The key question, however, is whether industry differences exist in the form and strength of intervention. Beyond the commonsense prediction that the more keiretsu-ridden the sector, the greater the interventionism, industries differ in need for adjustment. Declining sectors such as metals or shipbuilding have more firms in need of bailout.[66] Less cyclical industries such as food and textiles should draw fewer interventions. Finally, in line with our Toyota interview, we expect more intervention activity in old-line, uncompetitive industries, regardless of how keiretsu-penetrated they are, simply because such forms of protection and guidance are more institutionalized than in autos and electronics where the rules of play are those of hard-ball global competition. On the other hand, firms in mature and declining industries might seem poor bets for intervention, for their difficulties are structural and systemic – rooted in the weakening competitive position of the sector rather than in the remediable problems of firm-specific bad management, bad strategy, and bad luck.

We evaluate the industry-specific results with caution, as they are based on fewer firms and so are more susceptive to sampling and measurement errors. Table 5.12 gives the evidence on intervention effects on *ROA* and sales growth by industry. The analysis is structured as follows. Because some of the industries in our sample (miscellaneous manufacturing, ceramics, rubber, shipbuilding, petroleum) lack sufficient firms to enable a reliable look at within-industry patterns, we pool these firms, making them the baseline against which to assess intervention activity in larger industries. Thus, the intervention evidence within the industries to which we do give consideration is interpretable only with reference to this baseline.[67] Fortunately, the intervention effect is strong in this residual group,

---

[66] Sheard (1991b).
[67] The model is a straightforward extension of Equation (5.1). *IND* is a dummy for the jth industry, and the other terms were earlier described.

$$ROA_{it} = \alpha + \beta' x_{it} + \pi_j IND_j + \delta_1 ROA_{it-k} + \delta_2 ROA_{it-k}{}^*IND_j$$
$$+ \gamma_1 TIE_{it} + \gamma_2 TIE_{it}{}^*IND_j + \lambda_1 TIE_{it}{}^*ROA_{it-k} \qquad (5.5)$$
$$+ \lambda_2 TIE_{it}{}^*ROA_{it-k*}IND_j + \varepsilon_{it}.$$

Thus, for the baseline industries, $IND_j = 0$, so the model reduces to Equation (5.1):

$$ROA_{it} = \alpha + \beta' x_{it} + \delta_1 ROA_{it-k} + \gamma_1 TIE_{it} + \lambda_1 TIE_{it}{}^*ROA_{it-k} + \varepsilon_{it}.$$

rendering it a useful benchmark. The expected configuration of positive main (γ) and negative interaction effects (λ) materializes in the baseline sector for every pairing of tie and outcome save one: trade and sales growth. Of the effects whose signs do fit the intervention model all are significant but that of directors.

The table gives three terms for each tie–outcome–industry combination: an industry–ROA_{t-k} interaction, an industry–tie interaction, and a three-way industry–tie–ROA_{t-k} interaction. (Excluded from the table are industry main effects, which add little useful information.) The coefficients on these terms contain all the information needed to assess how intervention varies by industry.

Table 5.12 reveals considerable variation across industries and, within them, across ties. Shacho-kai is the clearest form of keiretsu linkage, but on an industry-specific basis, it is often less important than other ties. This may be true because, within industries, vertical keiretsu ties are key. A shacho-kai firm (e.g., Toyota, Nissan, or Hitachi) links to up- and downstream affiliates through trade, equity, and director ties and through the group's primary banks (Mitsui, Sanwa, and Tokai in the Toyota case).

Considering ROA as outcome and shacho-kai as tie, the baseline model fits the nonferrous metals and electronics industries; that is, λ_2, the coefficient on $TIE^*ROA_{t-k}^*IND$, is not significant. In other industries, λ_2 is significant and *positive*; thus, the intervention effect of shacho-kai in those industries is attenuated relative to the baseline effect. Shacho-kai intervention is altogether absent in autos ($\lambda_1 + \lambda_2 = -0.302 + 0.400 = 0.098$) and chemicals ($\lambda_1 + \lambda_2 = -0.302 + 0.361 = 0.059$), and nearly so in food ($\lambda_1 + \lambda_2 = -0.302 + 0.259 = -0.043$) and textiles ($\lambda_1 + \lambda_2 = -0.302 + 0.275 = -0.027$). It is weaker but still present in iron and steel ($\lambda_1 + \lambda_2 = -0.302 + 0.196 = -0.106$) and machinery ($\lambda_1 + \lambda_2 = -0.302 + 0.198 = -0.204$).

With sales growth as outcome, the pattern at first glance is similar: all the $\{\lambda_2\}$ are positive; that is, shacho-kai interventionism in the included industries is weaker than in the baseline group. However, none is significant, so the baseline model applies.

As for the exchange and control ties, the evidence for intervention is weaker – that is, more positive and significant $\{\lambda_2\}$ – in foods, iron and

For each included industry, j, then, the intervention model becomes:

$$ROA_{it} = (\alpha + \pi) + \beta' x_{it} + (\delta_1 + \delta_2)ROA_{it-k} + (\gamma_1 + \gamma_2)\,TIE_{it}$$
$$+ (\lambda_1 + \lambda_2)TIE_{it}^*ROA_{it-k} + \varepsilon_{it}.$$

While this model assumes constant industry-specific slopes of the $\{x_{it}\}$, δ_2 allows the main effect of ROA_{t-k}, to vary (as, of course, do the *TIE* terms). In two industries – textiles and iron and steel – it is well below the baseline. This says that these are industries in decline: their performance in each year falls short of a projection from two years before.

steel, and machinery. It is stronger – fewer positive and significant $\{\lambda_2\}$ – in chemicals, textiles, and nonferrous metals.

The key sectors of autos and electronics deserve close attention. In electronics, judging again by the lack of significant $\{\lambda_2\}$, the baseline model fits. The main exception is the absence of an equity effect on *ROA* (i.e., $\lambda_2 = 1.689$ cancels the baseline $\lambda_1 = -1.593$).

Although the debt, trade, and shacho-kai (sales growth only) intervention models (weakly) fit the autos case, equity and director effects are absent, both on profit and on growth. This is a puzzle, for as earlier noted the industry's big-six equity and director links are strong.[68] The very prevalence of these ties in autos – much of it vertical between the assemblers (most of whom are shacho-kai members) and their major suppliers – could be the explanation. Both Nissan and Toyota, for example, have been densely tied by equity to their suppliers, but, as the next section shows, the intervention effect is strong in the first case and weak in the second.

Thus, keiretsu intervention is not a simple function of the sector's keiretsu strength. Food and electronics, for example, have low to average big-six exposure, yet the intervention pattern is weak in the former and relatively strong in the latter. The auto industry's big-six exposure is low in terms of shacho-kai membership but high by equity and director linkage, yet none of the three provides an intervention vehicle.

Nor do fading industries, whose need for intervention is presumably high, seem to be particularly targeted for intervention. Japanese textiles and iron and steel have long been in decline – confirmed in our analysis by their low level of profit persistence (i.e., the weak autoregressive effect of ROA_{t-k}). It is noteworthy, on the other hand, that the food sector – the least cyclical of these industries – displays the lowest interventionism.

Following up on our Toyota informant's comment, are there indications here that Japan's most competitive export sectors – autos, electronics, and machinery – are propped up or pulled down by keiretsu any less than in

---

[68] As a check on the validity of the pooled analysis reported in Table 5.12, we ran separate regressions on each industry subsample. As this method allows all coefficients (including controls) to vary freely over industries, the results need not be identical to those based on the footnote 67 equation and reported in Table 5.12, but, in fact, for both performance outcomes, they essentially were identical. For the twenty automotive industry firms, for example, the subsample regression yielded no intervention effects of shacho-kai, equity, or directors but did give correctly signed and significant (by a minimum criterion of 10 percent) intervention effects of debt and trade. The one discrepancy between the two methods is the intervention effect of shacho-kai on sales growth indicated in Table 5.12 (i.e., no significant deviation from the baseline). The subsample regression disagreed. The λ estimate had the right sign ($-.058$) but no significance. This is a standard application of the rule of parsimony: the less complex model (assuming *additive* industry effects) is preferred to a more complex model (assuming *interactive* industry effects) unless the latter better fits the data by a large margin of confidence.

such domestically oriented counterparts as chemicals or textiles? Fewer exceptions to the baseline model do materialize in the domestic sectors, thus favoring the hypothesis. But intervention effects on some keiretsu dimensions (shacho-kai, debt, trade) are evident in the competitive sectors as well.

Our broadest conclusion is that, for a variety of idiosyncratic reasons, industries differ in how keiretsu redistributive intervention plays out, but it appears in some form and to some degree in all of them.

Vertical Group Interventions

We have the data for a limited study of vertical keiretsu interventionism. The measurement is crude: we use the Dodwell typology of vertical groups in 1980 to classify firms as members or independents.[69] The Dodwell classification is based on the same criteria of group assignment used thus far – cross-shareholding, director transfers, and trading relationships – but it combines them with subjective assessment to identify individual firms as simply in or out of a vertical network. Further, since we deal only with the 200 largest industrials as of 1980, we overlook a number of firms identified by Dodwell as affiliates. The vertical groups we examine are in three industries: Nippon Steel in metals, Toyota and Nissan in automobiles, and Hitachi and Matsushita in electronics. All comprise major manufacturers and their subsidiaries and affiliates. Published classifications of Japanese business groups routinely cite them as key vertical groups.[70] All were shown by the blockmodel analysis of Chapter 3 to exert considerable pull on the corporate network. The Toyota group spans Mitsui and Sanwa, while Hitachi spans Fuyo and Sanwa. Matsushita is an off-council firm, but, due in part to its Osaka location, it has leaned toward Sumitomo. As Chapter 3's analysis showed, all such vertical clusters have evolved over the period we observe. Toyota has drifted away from Mitsui as has Matsushita from Sumitomo. However, except for Nippon Steel, these groups have stayed cohesive. Indeed, as we have written elsewhere, both Toyota and Matsushita have moved in recent years to revitalize their core alliances for the sake of competitive advantage.[71] On the other hand, Chapter 3's blockmodel analysis revealed clear signs of decay, first in the Nippon Steel cluster and later in the Nissan group.

The question now is whether firms involved in these clusters exhibit the intervention pattern modeled by Equation 5.1. We might expect them to vary in the manner of the horizontal groups: the more tight-knit the group,

---

[69] Dodwell Marketing Consultants (various years).
[70] Career Development Center (2002).
[71] Ahmadjian and Lincoln (2001); Lincoln, Ahmadjian, and Mason (1998); Guillot and Lincoln (2003).

the greater the monitoring of members and adjustment of performance up or down. By this logic, Nippon Steel's post-1980 disappearance as a network position (Chapter 3) points to weak interventionism there. By the same logic, Toyota should prove more interventionist than Nissan. Yet Toyota, if not exactly "dry" (cold and arm's length) in its dealings with its affiliates, is reputed to be *kibishi* – rigorous and demanding. Nissan has been less so. Nissan's new CEO, Renault executive Carlos Ghosn, set about first to discipline, later in large measure to dispose of, a supplier network that by all accounts fell far short of Toyota's standards for supply chain discipline and control.[72]

Both the Hitachi and the Matsushita nets are rather tight-knit, a bit of testimony for which is the number of members that bear the parent company name. Our sense for the two firms' corporate and keiretsu cultures inclines us to view Hitachi as the more interventionist. We have done interviews at both. Matsushita prides itself and is reputed to be *dorai* (dry vs. wet or sentimental) in its dealings with suppliers and other affiliates. Hitachi, on the other hand, is an old-line, traditional Japanese company, holding equity stakes in an array of ancillary firms and routinely *shukko*-ing (transferring) employees to them.[73]

The data shortcomings notwithstanding, the Dodwell classification yields clear evidence of interventionism in two of the five vertical groups. The results appear in Table 5.13. As in the broad industry analysis, we use as t_1 performance criterion the industry-specific ROA_{t-2}. We find strong interventionism in Nissan and Hitachi and none in Matsushita, Toyota, or Nippon Steel.

This analysis does raise an issue in the conceptualization and measurement of the intervention effect. We do not suggest that Toyota refrains from assistance or adjustment of its satellite firms. The record says otherwise. However, if the Toyota group's redistributive adjustments occur in high-frequency real time, our modeling strategy (Equation 5.1) cannot detect them. For it to do so, a firm must veer off – either higher or lower – from a prior norm, then be jerked back, as it were, into line. If monitoring by the group is so fine-grained that member firms do not

---

[72] Shirouzu (1999c). At the time of its brush with bankruptcy in the mid-1970s, Mazda's relations with its suppliers were similar. As Pascale and Rohlen (1983:226) describe it, "suppliers were dealt with in a patronizing manner that simultaneously protected them, made them subservient, and prevented them from progressing rapidly in terms of productivity.... 'It was an old style ('wet') kind of relationship,' states one supplier, with each side asking favors at times and neither side introducing the kind of scientific managerial thinking that would have forced rapid progress. Top officials spent time entertaining suppliers, but not time working with them to strengthen their common business." As Whittaker (1997:96) notes, the language of wet, parent–child relations has been disappearing from Japanese customer–supplier relations and with it the assumption that the parent (customer) firm will look after the child (supplier) company in difficult times.

[73] Lincoln et al. (2000); Guillot and Lincoln (2003).

Table 5.13. *Intervention Effects of Vertical Keiretsu on ROA and Sales Growth*

Explanatory Variables	(1) ROA$_t$	(2) Sales Growth	(3) ROA$_t$	(4) Sales Growth	(5) ROA$_t$	(6) Sales Growth	(7) ROA$_t$	(8) Sales Growth	(9) ROA$_t$	(10) Sales Growth	(11) ROA$_t$	(12) Sales Growth	(13) ROA$_t$	(14) Sales Growth
Toyota (10 firms)	.002	.003			.002	.005								
Toyota*ROA$_{t-2}$	.011	-.037			-.007	-.085								
Nissan (4 firms)			.002	.009	.003	.012								
Nissan*ROA$_{t-2}$			-.114+	-.225	-.114+	-.270+								
Autos*ROA$_{t-2}$	-.150*	.111	-.126	.131	-.126+	.175								
Nippon Steel (4 firms)							-.006	.000						
Nippon Steel*ROA$_{t-2}$							.007	-.167						
Steel*ROA$_{t-2}$							-.529***	-.400**						
Hitachi (4 firms)									.012***	.059*			.012***	.058*
Hitachi*ROA$_{t-2}$									-.148***	-.717***			-.148*	-.795***
Matsushita (5 firms)											-.003	-.006	-.003	-.006
Matsushita*ROA$_{t-2}$											.029	-.073	.024	-.083
Electronics*ROA$_{t-2}$									-.073	.181*	-.083	.212*	-.079	.218*a
ROA$_{t-2}$	.733***	-.011	.733***	-.012	.733***	-.011	.753***	.011	.735***	-.021	.735***	-.024	.735***	-.021
Constant	-.168***	-.012	-.167***	-.011	-.168***	-.012	-.162***	-.009	-.165***	-.012	-.166***	-.017	-.164***	-.014
N	5686	5685	5686	5686	5686	5686	5686	5686	5686	5686	5686	5686	5686	5686
Adjusted R^2	.682	.332	.682	.333	.682	.333	.695	.334	.682	.333	.682	.333	.682	.333

*** $p < .001$; ** $p < .01$; * $p < .05$; + $p < .10$, based on robust standard error estimates. Control variables not shown.

deviate from the norm, then intervention, modeled as fast regression to the mean, cannot be discerned.[74]

The Intervention Pattern over Time

Our inquiry to this point permits a number of observations on the keiretsu intervention process: it is evident over a variety of ways of operational-izing group affiliation: as membership on a shacho-kai, as exchange and control relations with a horizontal keiretsu, and as the Dodwell classifi-cation of vertical manufacturing groups. The intervention effect appears in regard to both profits (ROA) and sales growth, although – in line with reasoning that profit margins are easier to adjust than sales volumes – the ROA evidence is stronger. It is most pronounced for large firms and in the more cohesive groups (e.g., Mitsubishi and Sumitomo). Although the magnitude of the effect and the delivery channel varies, it appears in all industries. It varies markedly across major vertical keiretsu – Nippon Steel, Nissan, Toyota, Hitachi, and Matsushita – in ways consistent with our sense for the cohesion of these groups and the parent firm's corporate culture.

We have yet, however, to consider that factor bearing on the form and strength of redistributive intervention that is perhaps of greatest interest in a turbulent spell in the evolution of the Japanese economy: time. There are strong reasons to suppose that the interventionist bent of Japan's keiretsu groupings has not been stable over the thirty-year period we study.

Two Models of Change

The Hypothesis of Steady Decline
We entertain two main hypotheses, based on considerations similar to those underlying Chapter 3's analysis of corporate network change. The first is this: owing to the liberalization of financial markets ushered in by

---

[74] A *Wall Street Journal* account of Nissan's intervention in keiretsu affiliate, Ichikoh Indus-tries, questions the smoothness of Nissan's handling of interventions (Brauchli, 1991): "In a rare outburst of dissent from corporate Japan, the former chairman of a big automotive-parts company accused Nissan Motor Co. of meddling in the supplier's business. Tetsuyo Tsukatani, 71 years old, who was ousted in a board revolt in February as chairman of Ichikoh Industries Ltd., said Nissan used threats and intimidation to remove him from the leadership of the automotive-lighting company.... Mr. Tsukatani accused Nissan of waging a four year campaign to take over Ichikoh's business, even though the auto maker owns only 20.9 percent of the lighting supplier's stock. He said Nissan executives told him that if he didn't resign, they would slash orders from Ichikoh. Nissan accounts for half of Ichikoh's business.... Mr. Tsukatani and his attorney also alleged that Nissan ex-ecutives insisted on being consulted in advance of any personnel moves at Ichikoh, and demanded frequently that the company lower its parts prices for Nissan, even though it serves 50 other customers, including Detroit's auto industry."

deregulation, the Plaza accord, globalization, the rule-destroying turbulence of the bubble, and other forces elsewhere reviewed, the pattern of keiretsu intervention was largely broken, first by the upside turbulence of the mid-to-late 1980s' market deregulation, *endaka*, and asset bubble, and then by the downside macroeconomic weakness, recurrent financial crisis, and regulatory and corporate governance changes that marked the 1990s.[75]

With the late 1980s escalation of asset prices, Japanese firms ratcheted down their dependence on bank borrowing even as total investment in this period doubled over the previous interval.[76] Hoshi and Kashyap (2000) show the ratio of bank debt to assets for publicly listed manufacturing firms falling every year from a peak of 38.1 percent in 1976 to a trough of 12.7 percent in 1990. It then rose steadily to a high of 15 percent in 1994 when the trend reversed, dropping to 12.6 percent in 1997, the last year of their series.

In an interview we conducted at Mitsubishi Bank headquarters in 1989, a manager gave us the bank's view of the bubble-era abandonment of bank debt for retained earnings, bond issues, and equity. "They are independent companies and free to make their own decisions," he said. "But if they get in trouble we would have to think twice before coming to their aid."

The recent history of Sakura (Mitsui) Bank, the lead commercial bank of the Mitsui group, is an interesting case study in the newfound reluctance of keiretsu partners to shepherd one another through hard times. Sakura (now Sumitomo-Mitsui), which, as leader of the Mitsui Group had often led the charge to rescue troubled member firms, was brought low by the fall in asset prices that marked the bubble's collapse. Hat in hand, Sakura made the rounds of Mitsui companies, but could not garner the support to stay in business on its own. Sakura succumbed on 1 April 2001 to a de facto takeover by Sumitomo Bank. The Mitsui group firm best positioned to rescue Sakura was Toyota. Despite Mitsui's bailout of Toyota in the auto firm's own financial distress in the early 1950s, Toyota said no. The reasons were several. One was simply the times – the economy as a whole was so troubled and the demands for industrial adjustment so great that groups were turning deaf ears to the pleas of desperate partners. The government was assembling a massive bailout package but it came with many strings attached. Few observers expected the convoy system of keiretsu-orchestrated bailouts to kick in as it had in the past. Another consideration specific to Mitsui's circumstances is the

---

[75] Hoshi and Kashyap (2001); Zielinski and Holloway (1992).
[76] Kobayashi et al. (1993) find that bank borrowing, which had averaged 56.2 percent of total corporate external finance between 1965 and 1985, fell from 22.6 percent in 1980–1985 to −8.5 percent in 1986–1989 (the negative sign indicating that companies were paying off loans in excess of their borrowing).

relatively low cohesion of the Mitsui group. Despite its reliance on Mitsui-Sakura as its main bank, Toyota, for example, always portrayed itself as something less than a full-blown Mitsui group member. Most shacho-kai membership lists footnote Toyota as an observer on the Mitsui *Nimoku-kai*.[77]

But perhaps the key factor in Toyota's reluctance to bail out Sakura was the inclination of its president (*shacho*) at the time, Hiroshi Okuda. Okuda was the first Toyota chief executive outside the Toyoda family, and his aggressive and individualistic management style was a marked departure from the conservative traditions of Japan's preeminent manufacturing corporation. It was also the cause of some rancor within the company. Okuda embarked on a diversification and acquisition spree, got tough with Toyota suppliers, and effectively took over Toyota keiretsu companies such as Daihatsu and Hino.[78] He was eventually pushed upstairs to the largely ceremonial post of chairman (*kaicho*), his successor as *shacho* being Fujio Cho, a lower-key manager close to the Toyoda family. Media reports indicated that the Toyodas favored the bailout of Sakura but were overridden by Okuda.[79] Even in the twenty-first-century Japanese economy when keiretsu obligations lack the force they once had, Okuda was an unusual CEO. Few Japanese corporate leaders have pushed so forcefully onto new terrain.[80]

Such reports also suggest that industrial firms, as with keiretsu financials, have been content to sit on the sidelines more than in the past. The failure of Nissan Mutual Life, the only insurance company to go bankrupt since the war, is a conspicuous case of powerful keiretsu partners (the Nissan group) refusing, despite pressure from the insurance industry and

---

[77] Miyashita and Russell (1994); Fair Trade Commission (1992).
[78] Treece (1998).
[79] See Shirouzu (1999a, 1999b, 1999c); Thornton (1999).
[80] Mazda's recent leadership history offers an interesting counterpoint. Mazda is controlled by Ford, which since 1996 held a 33.4 percent stake in the automaker. However, despite the American control and Mazda's shaky financial condition, restructuring at Mazda proceeded cautiously. Fears in Hiroshima, Mazda's headquarter city, that Ford would get tough with employees and suppliers proved largely unfounded. Mazda's first Ford-dispatched president – Henry Wallace – made an effort to reassure Mazda stakeholders that the partnership with Ford did not spell the end of the traditional Mazda organization. Part of the reason, it seems clear, was that Sumitomo Bank was still playing *nakodo* – matchmaker – in brokering the Mazda–Ford marriage. Wallace, who returned to Detroit in 1997, was replaced by a much more aggressive Ford executive, James Miller, who in short order strained relations with Mazda's union, parts suppliers, and longtime patron, Sumitomo Bank. Miller was replaced in 1999 by thirty-eight-year-old Mark Fields, a protégée of Wallace, who in turn became chief financial officer at Ford. A president so young is a sharp break with Japanese tradition, something that concerned a number of Mazda managers. A senior Ford official commented, however, that Fields is "certainly young, but there will be no problem because Wallace will hold full power" (Yokei and Kanno, 1999).

government officials, to come to the aid of an unhealthy affiliate. Both Nissan Motors and Hitachi had directors on Nissan Life's board, but a spokesman for the car company characterized these ties as merely *tsukiai* ("socializing"), not a keiretsu commitment to Nissan Life that would justify assistance. The comment squares with our view that, while network leaders have not altogether sworn off risk-sharing interventions, they are picking them more judiciously and strategically than in the past.[81] Nissan Mutual was later bailed out by a French insurer, Artemis. Indeed, of six small failed Japanese life insurers since 1997, only one, Taisho Life, was able to find a Japanese buyer.[82]

A survey conducted of Tokyo Stock Exchange-listed companies by the Economic Planning Agency, finds that for 50 percent of those experiencing financial distress in the mid-1990s, main banks *reduced* loans, rather than increased them as would be expected in a bailout.[83] Thirty-seven percent reported no such reductions. Gao comments that "This indicates that the main banks took the passive position of reducing their loans to troubled companies rather than providing them with active rescues."

None of this says that bailouts and other risk-sharing interventions have vanished from the Japanese economy. They continue but with less frequency and legitimacy than in the past.[84] Banks' efforts to keep troubled borrowers' afloat are seen as a primary cause of Japan's bad loan crisis. In contrast with just a few years ago when foreign-controlled firms such as Shinsei Bank or Nissan were receiving harsh criticism from the press and politicians for their aggressiveness in cutting jobs and suppliers, their relative success has now won them a certain grudging respect.[85]

> For conservatives, Shinsei Bank's success is worrisome, possibly heralding more takeovers.... The bank has become synonymous with "hagetaka" or "vultures" – the way Japanese are referring to foreign investors these days.... Although reprimanded by the government for holding back on lending, Shinsei Bank is gradually winning over Japanese who see its approach as simply smart

---

[81] Another noteworthy case is Fuji Bank's refusal to rescue Yamaichi Securities (not a *Fuyokai* member). Fuji had bailed out Yamaichi in a brush with bankruptcy in the 1960s. Yoshiro Yamamoto, president of Fuji Bank, was quoted by *Financial Times* reporter Gillian Tett (1997) as saying, "The degree of dependency of companies on banks has fallen, and so the sense of identity as members of a (keiretsu) group has fallen." Mr. Yamamoto says, "I really do not think that all the liabilities of the Fuyo group are the liabilities of Fuji."
[82] Suzuki (2001).
[83] Keizai Kikakucho (1997), cited in Gao (2001:251).
[84] The Sumitomo group, for example, has pumped capital into Sumitomo Metal Industries Ltd. in order to bolster the troubled affiliate's creditworthiness and stock price (*Nikkei Net Interactive*, 19 October 2002).
[85] See, e.g., Kageyama (2003).

policy.... Many Japanese have long suspected banks of lending to money-losing "zombie" companies with connections, while scrimping on lending to innovative but powerless ventures.

There are also signs that government authorities are becoming less tolerant of nontransparent and legally dubious, if time-honored, keiretsu risk-sharing practices. In November 2002, the Nagoya Regional Taxation Bureau found that Toyota had failed to declare ¥2 billion in income and fined the automaker ¥400 million in penalties and additional taxes. At issue was Toyota's extraordinarily high payments for automotive filters to a parts-making affiliate, Toyota Boshoku Corp. The tax agency ruled that Toyota's overpayments for the procured parts were transfers designed to assist the struggling supplier and thus should be reported as income rather than ordinary operating expenses.[86] Redistributive activity of this sort had been routine keiretsu practice, and the government's willingness to let it pass with a wink and a nod amounted to an indirect subsidy of private sector efforts to keep weak firms afloat.

Another significant indicator of change is that the Tokyo stock market has in recent years responded positively to news that troubled Japanese firms were going bankrupt as opposed to being bailed out by banks and keiretsu partners as in the past. The Nikkei index rose 6 percent – bank stocks in particular – on 3 March 2002 amid reports that large construction firm Sato Kogyo had been forced into bankruptcy by its main bank, Dai-Ichi Kangyo. "It's positive as the bank cut off support to a troubled company instead of providing a simple bailout, which can delay much needed corporate realignments," Shinko Securities analyst Tsuyoshi Segawa was quoted as saying.[87] Others, however, suggested that the Koizumi government had allowed Sato Kogyo to fail in order to give it the cover it needed to use the convoy system to bail out other ailing firms. Sato Kogyo was winning few new contracts, and its prospects for rehabilitation appeared poor.

However, amid the fast-pitched drama of change in Japan's industrial adjustment regime, the old ways still resurface. A high-profile example commanding attention as we write is Toyota Motor Corporation's change of heart on the wisdom of bailing out its partners. Toyota's current CEO, Fujio Cho, seems much more inclined than was his predecessor, Okuda, to use the automaker's vast cash reserves to help distressed partners. Much in the news is Toyota's rescue of troubled mid-sized sogo shosha, Tomen. Tomen's president does not sit on a big-six shacho-kai, but the company is tied to the Mitsui and Sanwa groups and, within them, the Toyota keiretsu.

---

[86] *Nikkei Net Interactive*, 12 November 2003.
[87] *Wall Street Journal*, 4 March 2002.

Chapter 3's blockmodels show Tomen's proximity to Toyota rising over the years. In 1978 and 1986 the trader was firmly with the Sumitomo Group (Tables 3.2 and 3.3). In 1989, however, Tomen appears in the Toyota block, and in 1993, 1995, and 1997 it is in the company of Mitsui and Sanwa, Toyota's primary big-six affiliations. The Toyota group is plowing ¥10 billion into Tomen in the form of increased stock ownership, primarily by Toyota trading firm, Toyota Tsusho, now Tomen's largest shareholder with an 11.5 percent stake. Toyota Tsusho and UFJ Bank (the merger, with Toyo Trust, of Toyota-affiliated Tokai and Sanwa) have dispatched executives to fill the roles, respectively, of Tomen chairman and president and a merger of Tomen and Toyota Tsusho is in the works. Toyota is also infusing cash into UFJ itself, teetering on the brink in part from its exposure to Tomen.

Toyota's bailout of Tomen has drawn loud condemnation from the Western business press. An op-ed piece in the *International Herald Tribune* bears reproducing for its blunt summation of the case against keiretsu intervention:[88]

> [Toyota] seems to be doing its share to perpetuate Japan's malaise. On Dec. 27, a Toyota group agreed to inject ¥10 billion ($84 million) into one of Japan's money-losing, debt-ridden trading houses. It was a drop in the proverbial bucket for Japan's most profitable automaker, but the move's symbolism eclipsed its cost. The trading house, Tomen, is part of Toyota's extended business family, or keiretsu. And so Toyota . . . felt obliged to help its less fortunate brethren. Trouble is, the rest of Japan may be encouraged to hit up Toyota and others for handouts. Corporate beggars of Japan, unite! Tomen should be allowed to fail. So should myriad other companies in an economy wracked by deflation, overcapacity and questionable competitiveness. Yet the strongest companies continue to bail out the weakest, regardless of how feeble. It's only a matter of time before the weakest links undermine the strongest ones. Keeping zombie companies afloat is why Japan is grappling with deflation. Banks are loaded down with at least $430 billion of bad loans because they have refused to cut off loser businesses. And that's why Toyota's decision to throw Tomen a lifeline is so worrisome. It shows that even as Japan Inc. talks about change, it's running way from it. . . . [T]his bail-out-the-vanquished mindset is behind Japan's 12-year malaise. Saving weak companies won't help the economy but merely punt

---

[88] Pesek (2003). See also "Stop feeding the losers, Toyota," *Business Week Online*, 13 January 2003; and Ibison (2003b).

its problems a couple years further into the future. Toyota's willingness to keep dying companies alive ... [is] only helping to perpetuate a bankrupt economic model in which the bad businesses are supported by good ones. The losers aren't only shareholders but the entire economy.

The view from the Japanese business press could not be more different. The Yomiuri Shimbun applauded Toyota's rescue of a weak affiliate and called on other strong firms to do the same[89]:

Toyota's preeminence in the nation's business world also is signified by its willingness to extend financial help to or acquire other companies in trouble. In the United States and Europe, it is seen as a matter of course for a company to expand its business by taking advantage of its rivals' misfortune, and mergers and acquisitions are routine. To materialize a business resuscitation of this country, not only Toyota, but also many other companies must come up with aggressive plans to provide financially struggling firms with various forms of assistance. It is strongly hoped that even companies that do not have so much financial clout as Toyota will become ready to take risks in extending assistance to those on the wane. Should such assistance providers be limited to Toyota and foreign investment funds, which are often referred to as nothing better than corporate vultures, the Japanese economy cannot expect to see a ray of hope for its rebirth.

The Yomiuri, Japan's largest circulation daily, leans right on most issues, but other domestic press commentary on the Tomen bailout has also been favorable or neutral. Deflation is now seen as the country's greatest economic problem, and fears run deep that tough measures to dispose of bad loans (and with them a legion of struggling companies) will exacerbate it. Also, too, as the next chapter discusses, the still-reverberating corporate scandals and flagging economic recovery in the United States have tarnished the allure of American ways while restoring that of old-line Japanese practice. Moreover, as the Koizumi government sets up a new government–sponsored entity – the Industrial Revitalization Corporation – to take on the task of rehabilitating problem firms, opposition parties have been mobilizing resistance to what they view as a massive bailout with taxpayer funds. The convoy system of old – like the corporate rescues Toyota is now embarked upon – were largely, if by no means entirely, private sector affairs, thus seeming to spare the taxpaying public.

---

[89] Sugiyama (2003).

272   *Japan's Network Economy*

There are still those in Japan (as indeed in the West until recently) who believe that the keiretsu system of industrial adjustment once worked well and might be made to do so again. Still, a return to keiretsu interventionism of more than a sporadic sort seems unlikely if only because the network infrastructure necessary to support it has so withered away.

The Bubble as Anomaly

Consider the following take on Japan's recent past: one that adds credence to Western critics' claims that Japan has not changed nearly enough; that deep-seated reluctance to let failing partner firms die and be done with it is still endemic to the Japanese network economy. The hypothesis here is that the *endaka*-bubble (1986–90) was an aberration: a time when business actors were swept up in a tsunami of irrational exuberance, and while it lasted, the core norms and practices of the Japanese way of business were shunted aside. Speculation in asset values was the order of the day, driven by a seemingly un-Japanese "Wild West" mentality that had little grounding in business fundamentals – investing for the long term, developing strategic capabilities, and cultivating manufacturing expertise. The neglect of fundamentals and the speculative frenzy that distinguished the late 1980s bubble are practices for which U.S. business is regularly chastised and to which it again succumbed in the dot-com fever of the late 1990s.

This bubble-as-anomaly model implies that, with its passing, Japan Inc. would revert to business as usual. On the face of things, the 1990s were hardly a time of retrenchment around the values, commitments, and strategies of the pre-bubble network economy. It was rather one of weak and unstable growth, offshore migration of production, intensified foreign competition, fraying ties to business partners, recurrent financial crisis, significant regulatory change, and, if not the wholesale abandonment, certainly the scaling down of entrenched labor practices such as lifetime employment and seniority-based pay.

Still, unlike the bubble, the 1990s were also a time when many corporations and financial institutions were in financial trouble and in chronic need of assistance. As this chapter's lead quote from Nakatani suggests, it has been precisely in such periods of stress that keiretsu networks mobilized for structural adjustment, a major component of which was the easing of weak firms through hard times.

Moreover, our analysis in Chapter 3, plus a good deal of other evidence, suggests that some tightening of these networks – the zaibatsu-based groups in particular – occurred in the wake of the bubble. The densities and connectivities of the debt, equity, and director networks moved up in the subsequent period, but then (most notably in the debt case) declined in the decade's second half.

The hypothesis, then, is that keiretsu intervention activity scaled down sharply in the bubble years but ticked up again when the bubble ended in 1991.

The third, and perhaps most realistic, possibility – this also being Chapter 3's conclusion – is that the truth lies in between. With the tightening of networks and the deterioration of the economy, some postbubble resurgence of keiretsu interventionism may have taken place, but the longer term trend, accelerated at the turn of the century, is decline.

Our empirical results appear in Table 5.14a. Ending our panel in 1985 as opposed to 1995 puts the evidence for keiretsu interventions in much higher relief. The intervention pattern ($\gamma > 0, \lambda < 0$) is stronger in 1966–85 than in 1966–95 (Table 5.5). Despite the reduction in sample size, more of the keiretsu effects reach significance in the shorter period.

The temporal shifts in intervention activity follow the structural trends mapped by Chapter 3: cyclical and secular change combined with a degree of pattern persistence. On the cyclical side, we find the drop in interventionism after 1985 to be largely limited to 1986–90. The estimates for this interval are sharply at odds with the intervention model and our findings heretofore: the relevant effects are either not significant or if significant have the wrong signs. In the last five years of the panel, interventionism, by several indicators, resumed. This describes the equity and director effects in the *ROA* and sales growth regressions and (less clearly given the lack of significance) the debt and trade effects in the sales growth case. The secular changes are the roles of shacho-kai and debt ties in *ROA* adjustments: both fell sharply after 1985 and show no post-1991 resurrection. The stability is in the part played by shacho-kai in sales growth – it is strong in each period. Stability is secondarily evident in the trade effect on *ROA*, which loses significance in the five-year intervals (due perhaps to smaller N's), but is otherwise stable.

Thus, the powerful intervention effect of bank ties earlier observed holds only up to 1986, the watershed *endaka* year that set the stage for the bubble. Thereafter, big-six debt relations played no discernible role in profit adjustments. A trace of debt-related intervention in sales growth is evident before and after the bubble period, not during it. As before, however, statistical significance is lacking.

What should we make of the strong and consistent evidence that keiretsu intervention activity evaporated in the *endaka*/bubble era only to resurface in the following years? Perhaps it testifies to the ongoing viability of the vertical groups amid scaled-down bank monitoring and general fraying of big-six keiretsu ties. We do know that in the 1990s some vertical groups – most prominently Toyota – stepped up cross-shareholding and director dispatch, in part due to the banks' shedding of shares in Toyota group companies. In a time of increased foreign participation in

Table 5.14a. *Regressions of ROA on Shacho-kai and Exchange and Control Ties by Period*

	(1) 1966–85	(2) 1986–90	(3) 1991–95	(4) 1966–85	(5) 1986–90	(6) 1991–95	(7) 1966–85	(8) 1986–90	(9) 1991–95	(10) 1966–85	(11) 1986–90	(12) 1991–95	(13) 1966–85	(14) 1986–90	(15) 1991–95
Shacho-kai	.026**	.002	.004	.011*	.007*	.005	.015**	.001	.002	.017**	.010**	.003	.026**	.009**	.004
Shacho-kai*ROA_{t-k}	-.331***	-.053	-.126	-.166*	-.151**	-.137	-.193**	.049	-.076	-.213**	-.188***	-.065	-.331***	-.181***	-.103
Debt tie				.113***	.020+	.002									
Debt tie*ROA_{t-k}				-1.263***	-.178	.060									
Trade tie							.011	.009	.002						
Trade tie*ROA_{t-k}							-.190*	-.257	-.134						
Equity tie										.086***	-.014	.023*			
Equity tie*ROA_{t-k}										-1.162***	.111	-.856**			
Director tie													.072**	-.006	.032*
Director tie*ROA_{t-k}													-.945***	-.221	-1.589***
ROA_{t-k}	.856***	.455***	.699***	1.012***	.606***	.695***	.952***	.683***	.729***	.943***	.591***	.751***	.921***	.606***	.729***
Constant	-.146	.068	-.332	-.162***	-.118*	-.339***	-.090	-.132*	-.329***	-.143***	-.112	-.303***	-.145***	-.108	-.308***
N	3931	985	966	3895	1178	965	3742	1130	922	3911	1182	966	3931	1182	966
Adjusted R^2	.703	.642	.678	.727	.670	.669	.829	.674	.681	.718	.669	.674	.706	.670	.677

*** $p < .001$; ** $p < .01$; * $p < .05$; + $p < .10$, based on robust standard error estimates. Control variables not shown. $k = 1$ when trade is the tie; otherwise $k = 2$.

Table 5.14b. *Regressions of Sales Growth on Shacho-kai and Exchange and Control Ties by Period*

Explanatory Variables	(1) 1966–85	(2) 1986–90	(3) 1991–95	(4) 1966–85	(5) 1986–90	(6) 1991–95	(7) 1966–85	(8) 1986–90	(9) 1991–95	(10) 1966–85	(11) 1985–90	(12) 1991–95	(13) 1966–85	(14) 1985–90	(15) 1991–95
Shacho-kai	.032***	.011	.018	.026**	.021	.015+	.023**	−.025+	.000	.025**	.012	.012	.031***	.009	.018*
Shacho-kai*ROA_{t-k}	−.472***	−.424*	−.478*	−.409***	−.544*	−.401*	−.395***	.063	−.021	−.379***	−.400*	−.327	−.465***	−.320	−.457*
Debt tie				.050	−.054	.023									
Debt tie*ROA_{t-k}				−.437	1.293+	−.501									
Trade tie							.001	−.053+	−.001						
Trade tie*ROA_{t-k}							−.037	.701*	.046						
Equity tie										.069	−.023	.083*			
Equity tie*ROA_{t-k}										−.847*	.812	−2.146*			
Director tie													.078	.011	.040
Director tie*ROA_{t-k}													−.652	.261	−1.406
ROA_{t-k}	.063	−.018	.103	.124*	−.129**	.147	.015	.479*	−.153	.125**	−.094+	.236*	.108*	−.074	1.131
Constant	.134	−.325	.170	.125*	−.329	−.168	.106+	−.188	−.167	.134*	−.357	−.108	.127*	−.368	−.154
N	3931	985	966	3895	1178	965	3742	941	922	3911	1182	966	3931	1182	966
Adjusted R^2	.271	.275	.154	.270	.250	.235	.271	.295	.252	.269	.246	.241	.268	.246	1.236

*** $p < .001$; ** $p < .05$; * $p < .05$; +$p < .10$, based on robust standard error estimates. Control variables not shown. $k = 1$ when trade is the tie; otherwise $k = 2$.

the Japanese economy, the auto firms had reason to worry about takeover risk.

Thus, the bubble era was seemingly anomalous in abruptly lowering the profile of the horizontal groups as agents of risk and return sharing. As discussed below, this fits the view that the salient institutional changes in the Japanese economic environment were accelerated financial deregulation and the abandonment by groups of bank-mediated debt for direct forms of financing.

How Groups Smooth Performance Trajectories: A Year-by-Year Analysis

Were other periods of our thirty-year panel marked by fluctuations in the intensity of keiretsu interventionism? It was less prevalent in the early post-war years, when the joint pursuit of technological and market opportunities, plus the implementation of state economic policy mandates, were critical imperatives. Spells of high uncertainty, such as the Nixon shock of 1971 and the oil shock of 1974, were temporary jolts to the system.[90] Such shocks aside, the 1980s were a time of financial market deregulation and disintermediation, reduced reliance by manufacturers on trading companies for procurement and distribution, and like processes of keiretsu disengagement. We explored the possibility that the early 1980s and early 1990s were exceptional by dividing our panel into five-year intervals and reestimating the intervention model. Yet only 1986–90 proved to be so: otherwise, the intervention pattern held.

For a finer-grained study of how the intervention pattern has fluctuated over time, we calculated year-to-year shifts in the effects of ROA_{t-k} on ROA_t and sales growth by degree of keiretsu attachment. The model is

$$ROA_{it} = \alpha + \beta' x_{it} + \sum_t \pi_t YR_t + \sum_t \delta_t ROA_{t-k}{}^* YR_t$$
$$+ \sum_t \gamma_t TIE^* YR_t + \sum_t \lambda_t TIE^* ROA_{t-k}{}^* YR_t + \varepsilon_{it}$$
$$(5.6)$$

where ROA_{it} = current ROA, YR_t = a dummy variable for each year from 1969 to 1995, TIE = a keiretsu tie, ROA_{t-k} = lagged ROA, and x_{it} is the usual vector of covariates. The $\{\delta_t\}$ gauge the dependence of present on past performance in each year for nonaffiliates, and the $\{\delta_t + \lambda_t\}$ do the same for keiretsu firms. Since shacho-kai is the only natural dichotomy, we set each of the four exchange and control measures to zero and to its

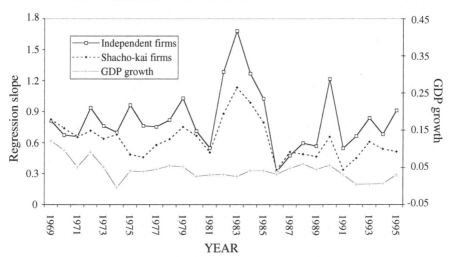

Figure 5.6. ROA_{t-2} effect on ROA_t by year for firms with and without a big-six shacho-kai membership.

mean to produce, respectively, the independent and keiretsu conditions required for the graphs.

ROA as Outcome

As before, consider first the simplest indicator of group affiliation: shacho-kai membership. Figure 5.6 plots the regression of ROA_{it} on ROA_{it-k} for member and nonmember firms from 1969 to 1995. The intervention effect appears in each year that the independents plot exceeds the shacho-kai plot. It exists in most years. A first conclusion, then, is that profit adjustments within the shacho-kai have been a stable feature of the large-firm economy since the 1960s.

When does the intervention pattern disappear? The figure points to business cycle downturns: 1971 (the Nixon shock), 1973–74 (the first oil shock), 1980–81 (the second oil shock recession), and 1986–87 (the *endaka* shock). In these spells, the performance inertia of independents firms slips below that of council firms, causing the gap to disappear. This happens in two sustained periods: (1) at the onset of the series – from 1969 to 1971 (the end of the high-growth era), and (2) from 1986 through 1987 (the endaka and early bubble). From 1988 to 1995, the intervention effect is clearly evident.

Our attention now shifts to exchange and control. Of these ties, equity (Figure 5.9) best resembles the shacho-kai case just considered: the intervention effect materializes in most years, the exception being the anomalous *endaka*-bubble (1986–90) era. Also striking is the smoothness of the

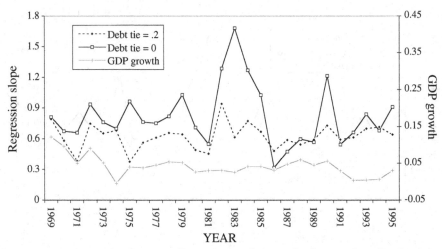

Figure 5.7. ROA_{t-k} effect on ROA_t by year for firms with and without a big-six debt tie.

inertia curve. When the independents' curve spikes up (1982, 1983, and 1990), the keiretsu curve either does so in lesser degree or not at all. When the independents' curve troughs – most notably in the recession years of 1973, 1981, and 1986 – keiretsu inertia falls less or not at all. At these junctures, the inertia gap closes; that is, the intervention effect disappears.

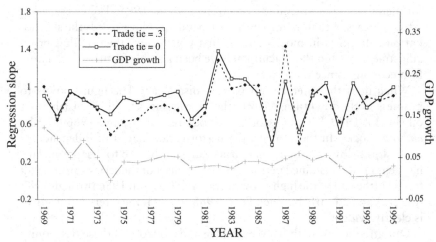

Figure 5.8. ROA_{t-1} effect on ROA_t by year for firms with and without a big-six trade tie.

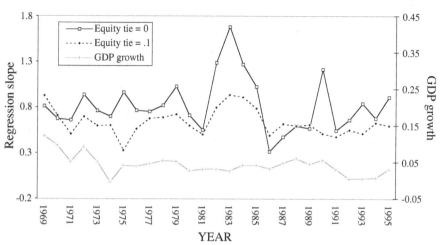

Figure 5.9. ROA_{t-2} effect on ROA_t by year for firms with and without a big-six equity tie.

These patterns provide additional insight into the nature of the intervention phenomenon. Our keiretsu intervention model (Equation 5.1) is a crude gauge of a complex process. It makes sense when the main effect of ROA_{t-k} (δ) is strong, as in most years of our series. But when that dives – due typically to a patch of macroeconomic turbulence that lifts or sinks all ships – the closing of the gap also testifies to intervention activity.

We noted some of the changes occurring in Japanese financial markets from the mid-1980s on. Their principal thrust was to give Japanese corporations a larger set of financing options, reducing dependence on bank debt and therefore main bank ties. A reasonable hypothesis, then, is that interventions based on banking ties fell off earlier than was true of those channeled through other forms of big-six linkage. That proves not to be the case (Figure 5.7). The ROA inertia curves for independent (0 percent debt tie) and keiretsu (a 20 percent debt tie) reveal 1986 – the *endaka* downturn – as the start of the period of diminished debt-based interventionism. As Table 5.14 showed, these effects, unlike those of shacho-kai and equity ties, do not reappear postbubble. However, the figure does suggest that big-six debt dependence worked to smooth firms' performance trajectories in the 1990s.

The picture in Figure 5.10, the directors case, is fuzzy, as is true of all the evidence on this particular tie. First, the inertia gap in the pre-endaka era is narrower, particularly after 1981. Consistent with Table 5.14a, it is

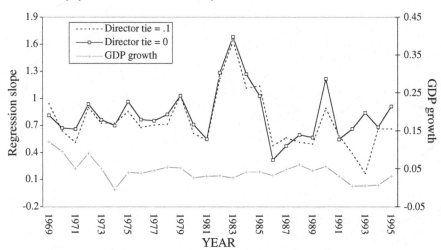

Figure 5.10. ROA_{t-2} effect on ROA_t for firms with and without a big-six director tie.

pronounced from 1988 on. However, the director plot appears less stable than are the shacho-kai, equity, and debt plots.[91]

Figure 5.8 reveals evidence of trade-based intervention activity only between 1974 and 1984, not before or after that period. Also, trade ties to a big-six group seem not to smooth the inertia curve the way the other ties do.

Sales Growth as Outcome

The graphic evidence on keiretsu adjustments to sales growth is, as in our previous analyses, less sharp than in the *ROA* case, but some noteworthy patterns nonetheless materialize. Until 1984, Figure 5.11 documents shacho-kai intervention activity in all but three widely separated years – 1970, 1977, and 1982. It then vanished in 1984–88, just before the 1986–90 *endaka*-bubble period. After 1989, it reappeared intermittently, lacking the consistency of pre-1985. But what is striking here is the smoothness of the shacho-kai inertia curve compared to the independents' curve, which, as in the other graphs, exhibits high volatility. Thus, indexed by growth as well as profitability, shacho-kai firms managed to chart a remarkably stable course through very choppy seas.

---

[91] These are plots of unadjusted slopes. Due in part to the sparseness of the director network and measurement error in determining any given director tie, there is considerably more variability in the regression estimates in the director case (implying large standard errors, small R^2's, and less statistical significance). The graphs do not adjust for this, so what look to be large movements in the director data may simply be sampling and measurement fluctuations.

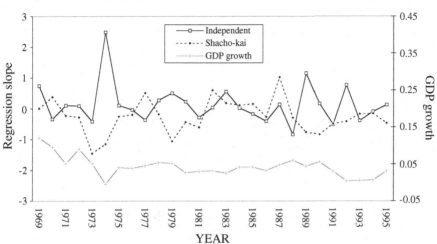

Figure 5.11. ROA_{t-2} effect on sales growth by year for firms with and without a big-six shacho-kai membership.

The evidence on big-six debt-tie adjustments to sales growth has been weak throughout, although in the bank-centered groups and in some industries (the baseline set and autos) it is stronger. Recall Table 5.14b's revelation of no debt tie effect on growth before, during, or after the endaka-bubble. Figure 5.12, by contrast, shows it to be strong and consistent

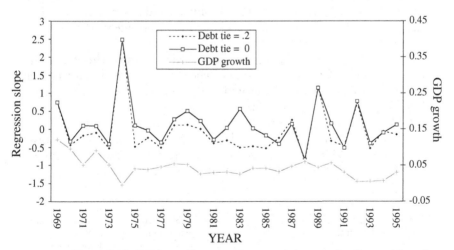

Figure 5.12. ROA_{t-2} effect on sales growth by year for firms with and without a big-six debt tie.

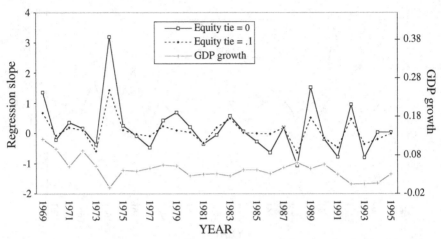

Figure 5.13. ROA_{t-2} effect on sales growth by year for firms with and without a big-six equity tie.

up to 1986, the endaka year.[92] Between 1986 and 1989 it is gone. The signs that it resurfaced in the 1990s are slight (i.e., in 1990, 1993, and 1995).

Table 5.14b revealed strong equity tie intervention before and after the endaka-bubble (1986–1990) but not during it. Figure 5.14, again, paints a different picture. It shows an inertia gap in most years up to 1981 and no consistent pattern thereafter. Most notable, once again, is that groups smoothed the performance trajectories of equity-tied firms. The inertia curves of both sets of firms fluctuate sharply up and down after 1985, but each such peak and trough is steeper for the independents than for the affiliated firms.

Figure 5.13 gives the inertia plots for trade-linked firms. The figure confirms the thrust of Table 5.14b: the evidence for a consistent intervention effect of big-six trade on sales growth is nil. But evidence that the groups damped down volatility is strong.

Table 5.14b showed director-based intervention in sales growth lacking significance but taking the expected form: negative before 1986, positive from 1986 to 1990, and negative from 1991 to 1995. Figure 5.15 shows essentially the same thing and thus adds no new information.

---

[92] A reason for the difference may be that, unlike the tabulated regressions, shacho-kai is uncontrolled in the graphical depiction of debt intervention. Arguing against this interpretation, however, is that the debt graph paints a sharper picture of interventionism than does the shacho-kai graph.

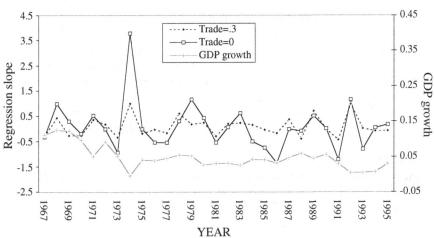

Figure 5.14. ROA_{t-1} effect on sales growth by year for firms with and without a big-six trade tie.

Year-by-Year Analysis: Discussion

In general, the performance inertia graphs both reinforce and extend the period-specific analysis of Table 5.14. Intervention activity by the horizontal groups to adjust the profit and sales growth of affiliated firms relative to a baseline of prior profitability persists until the mid-eighties – the *endaka*-bubble (1986–90) in particular – at which time it disappeared.

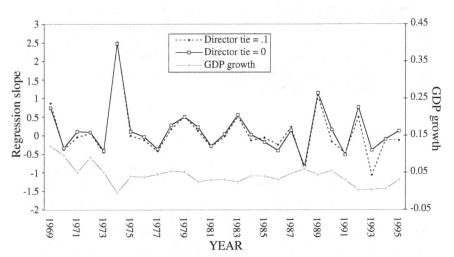

Figure 5.15. ROA_{t-2} effect on sales growth by year for firms with and without a big-six director tie.

In the 1990s, the intervention pattern resurfaced to some degree, conditional on the performance outcome and the tie: stronger for *ROA* than sales growth and stronger for shacho-kai, equity, and directors than debt and trade. What the graphical evidence reveals that the regression analysis could not is that the performance trajectories of keiretsu firms are smoother, less volatile. The pattern of fluctuations is similar – spells of stable GDP growth boost the performance stability of all firms. Times of rapid macroeconomic change – mostly downturns but, in the bubble at least, upturn as well – reduce it. When economic conditions are stable, such that most firms' performance inertia is moderate to high, we observe the intervention pattern on which this chapter dwells, that is, less inertia on the part of big-six affiliated firms. Specifically, low *ROA* firms at t_1 show greater t_2 profits and growth the stronger their ties to groups. Conversely, for profitable firms, such ties portend diminished performance down the road.

In times of change, however, interventions take a different form. When a turbulent environment puts *all* firms in free fall, so to speak, groups strive to keep performance in line with historical norms. In a recession, this means placing a safety net under the membership – affiliated firms do not fall as fast or as far from "normal" performance ranges as independents are wont to do.

Recalling the industry-specific analysis (Table 5.12), our reasoning here is similar to that we applied to the seeming absence of keiretsu interventionism in the textile and steel industries. Both sectors have long been declining in Japan, as in other mature economies. Inertia or persistence in profit and sales performance is thus low. The significance of keiretsu alignment in these industries differs from those in which historical performance levels have been more or less maintained: the group keeps its members afloat, staving off the drift to insolvency that is the fate of firms that lack keiretsu life supports.

Summary and Conclusions

Building on a diverse body of evidence that corporations with keiretsu ties are, on the one hand, less profitable than unaffiliated firms, and, on the other, more apt to recover from financial distress, we have produced some rich empirical results on the strength and form of keiretsu interventions and their significance for the structure and functioning of Japan's business groups. The indications that groups are weak financial performers have been offered as testimony for their dinosaur status – that keiretsu is an obsolete form with few attractions for the more nimble and aggressive companies on the Japanese economy's frontiers. There is some truth to that view. But any suggestion that the groups are a cultural–historical residue of no economic consequence is either wrong or if true at all only since the late 1980s when deregulation, the bubble, recession, and a tsunami of regulatory changes transformed the Japanese economy in fundamental ways.

The fact is that some Japanese firms have derived real benefit from their keiretsu attachments while others paid a price. Groups allocate resources among the members in line with a vision of collective welfare. They provide safety nets for their weak, they police profiteering by penalizing affiliates that do too well, and they insulate members from the harsh scrutiny of tax authorities and investment analysts by managing the reporting of earnings and losses to yield steady growth.

Establishing that Japan's keiretsu networks bail out weaklings, rein in high flyers, and otherwise adjust and align the performance trajectories of their members was the starting point for our analysis. From there we sought to answer several questions regarding the structure and behavior of the horizontal groups: (1) are they bona fide networks, bundling financials and industrials in a web of indirect as well as direct, commercial as well as financial, control as well as exchange relations? Or (2) are they hub-and-spoke pairings of firms with leading banks who help clients through rough patches chiefly to safeguard the bank's investment? The evidence favors the first view. Lending–borrowing is one keiretsu tie; others work similarly as intervention channels. Combined with the evidence that more cohesive groups are more interventionist, we have a reasonable case against a reductionist model of big-six interventionism as simple bank control.

To be sure, the intervention effect of banking ties up to 1985 is strong, if only on profits, not sales. Moreover, it is mostly unmediated by control or governance (equity and director) relations. Whether control ties convey the effects of commercial and financial exchange on performance is a core issue for our inquiry and point of continuity with the last chapter. The direct effects we find of keiretsu debt relations are presumptive evidence that bank control is both more extensive and more nuanced than our hard governance measures can detect.

The intervention effects of trade relations are weaker than those of debt and mediated more by equity and directors. Yet in certain industries (metals, textiles) and groups (Mitsubishi and Mitsui), trade proved an important intervention channel. Trade ties also figure importantly in the definition of the Mitsubishi and Mitsui groups (Appendix 3.1). In like fashion, director interlocks are key to the structuring of the DKB group *and* to the channeling of its redistributive interventions.

Our analysis suggests that the shacho-kai is itself a governance structure, not merely an inner circle of closely linked and centrally positioned companies. The council effects are proportionate to the cohesion of the group: weaker in the bank-centered clusters (DKB and Sanwa) and stronger in the former zaibatsu. In general, the councils' role relative to that of exchange and control ties is greater in sales than in profit adjustments. The probable reason is that sales adjustments require more intrusive action than profit adjustments do. Moving costs and assets around the network (e.g., via *tobashi*) to make a bottom line look good takes less coordinated effort.

The evidence is clear that the larger the firm, the more likely it is to be an intervention target. This stands to reason, despite the reticence of group spokespersons (e.g., our Sumitomo informants) to acknowledge it. The probable failure of a bigger firm not only has more adverse significance in terms of business lost and reputations damaged; government pressure is apt to be greater as well.

The analysis of debt and equity concentration established that keiretsu intervention is distinct from the monitoring that corporate governance theory in a principal–agent vein attributes to large equity and debt holders of any sort. Debt concentration bore no resemblance in our regressions to keiretsu debt relations, taking a form inconsistent with the intervention model. But the equity concentration effect so resembled (while not diminishing) the equity tie effect that it seems the causal processes are the same. Our conjecture is that the equity concentration variable picks up vertical keiretsu effects that the horizontal keiretsu measures do not tap.

We found some industry variability in the strength and form of intervention, but, with the possible exception of food, it appeared in all industries. It did not vary systematically with the industry's keiretsu composition, but the industry differences in that respect are not large. Nor do industries known to be declining – hence in need of structural adjustment – exhibit more interventionism. The evidence better fits the hypothesis of less keiretsu activity in globally competitive sectors as autos, electronics, and machinery than in domestically oriented ones such as chemicals and textiles. Indeed, a probable reason the intervention model fits our baseline industries (e.g., ceramics, paper, extractive, shipbuilding) so well is their distinct tilt toward the domestic economy.

Our treatment of vertical groups using the Dodwell typology was limited but still suggestive. No trace of the intervention pattern materialized in the two groups most reputed to be stringent (*kibishi*) with their affiliates – Matsushita and Toyota. By contrast, two others (Hitachi and Nissan) in the same manufacturing industries, both with some reputation for "wet" (*amae* or coddling) treatment of suppliers, did show such effects. Nor was intervention detectable in the once-prominent Nippon Steel group, whose position in the network had disintegrated by 1980.

Finally, we addressed the question of change. The hypothesis that interventionism waxes and wanes with temporal fluctuations in keiretsu cohesion finds considerable support. In particular, in 1986–90 – the *endaka*-bubble era – cohesion *and* interventionism fell. With the bubble's collapse, not only did some groups – the former zaibatsu – close ranks, but intervention activity picked up, too. This varied with the tie. The role of keiretsu debt relations – so strong up to 1985 – is absent afterward. This conforms to the oft-rendered portrait of an injured and enfeebled banking sector in the 1990s. The shacho-kai effect also dissipated in the latter 1980s, reappearing only weakly in the 1990s. The postbubble resumption of the intervention pattern is mainly equity and director based. Both vanished in the *endaka*-bubble, resurfacing in the 1990s.

The picture of change is further fleshed out by our charts of year-by-year fluctuations in the intervention effect. Varying the tie and the outcome variable, they reinforce the picture of a stable system of keiretsu interventionism torn asunder by the bubble and only partly restored in the 1990s.

The chapter's findings on the whole support our view of keiretsu as multiplex networks that take collective action to restrain both the bearing of risks and appropriation of returns by member firms. The benefits to weak affiliates go without saying. Why the best performers of a group maintain their membership is one of the mysteries of the keiretsu. That today's strong firms keep their ties as a hedge against tomorrow's failure is an answer consistent with the view that Japanese business is often risk-averse.[93] But this reasoning assumes a degree of individual self-interest seeking unconstrained by social commitments and normative rules that is scarce in Japan.[94] The networks within which Japanese economic action is embedded give corporations limited freedom to chart their own course, to pick and choose alliances (or whether to align at all) on the basis of unilateral calculations of advantage. There is a collective – embedded network – logic to the keiretsu phenomenon that is not reducible to rational optimizing on the part of individual firms.

Of course, the looming question that our analysis cannot directly address is the impact of keiretsu intervention activity on the economy's general well-being. Many now see it as disastrous – that Japan's penchant for propping up weakling firms figures prominently in the financial crises of the 1990s, the declining competitiveness of Japan's industry base, and the country's dismal rates of economic growth. Keiretsu bailouts and other

---

[93] Aoki (1988:280); Morikawa (1993).
[94] Dore (1983, 1986).

adjustments, critics say, simply stave off the creative destruction that Japan now desperately needs to sweep out its corporate deadwood and put the economy on new and firmer footing.

While there is little hard proof that the redistributive bent of Japanese network capitalism explains the country's current malaise, some of the circumstantial evidence is persuasive. One recent study concludes that keiretsu adjustments have exacerbated the stock market's decline. Hamao, Mei, and Xu (2002) find that in the 1990s the Japanese market deviated from the normal recessionary pattern of heightened price variability. When markets are weak, investors are more discriminating: capital leaves weak firms in search of safe havens in strong ones. Japan, however, is different:

> When the rate of economic growth is low (i.e., post-bubble), there tends to be greater disparity of stock performance among non-keiretsu firms and firms without main banks, compared to their counterparts. This suggests that keiretsu firms and firms with main banks are less sensitive to negative economic conditions compared to independent firms, indicating the presence of protection of weak firms by keiretsu groups or main banks.... [T]his... misallocation of capital by Japanese keiretsu or main bank groups in the form of lack of corporate bankruptcy and the presence of group protection may have contributed to a reduction in Japanese equity market efficiency.

In the three recessions since the bubble burst, individual stocks closely followed market indices. The authors suggest that keiretsu supports block the market cleansing function of a downturn whereby unfit companies are starved of capital and cleared away. Like the profit and sales measures we study, Japanese stock prices are made more uniform and equal by the economy's network interdependencies. Were weak stocks decoupled from strong ones, these authors suggest, the latter would rise and the market recover.

Notwithstanding Toyota's rescue of Tomen and other recent cases of bailout, the evidence is clear that keiretsu risk-sharing has fallen since the late eighties, the steep rise in bankruptcies through the 1990s being a probable consequence.[95] Whatever its role in the past, intervention thus seems an unlikely near-term cause of the economy's problems today. Moreover, to return to an early theme, Japan's network structures are always easy targets when the country hits the skids. In spells of growth, by

---

[95] Corporate bankrupties of companies with debt of ¥10 million or more peaked at 20,052 in FY 2001, declining 5.6 percent to 18,928 in FY 2002. Bankruptcy cases in FY 1989 numbered 6,653 (Teikoku Databank America, 2003).

contrast, they elicit praise. Japanese-style private sector–based keiretsu-managed restructurings once seemed to generate minimal dislocation (in layoffs and closures) at relatively low transaction cost (in accountant, bank, and lawyer fees). By contrast, critics found little to admire in the U.S. pattern of large corporations (Chrysler, Lockheed, Long-Term Capital Management, Enron, WorldCom), if not whole sectors (the savings and loan industry), running headlong, largely unmonitored (as the Enron record shows), off cliffs, leaving the government to pick up the pieces and the tab. Public expense aside, Chapter 11 filings decimate shareholder value, jobs, and reputations, all the while piling up the professional and legal costs. With all that, they do not seem to unleash much creative destruction.[96] In giving distressed companies an easy escape hatch, U.S. court-ordered restructurings and government bailouts arguably breed as much if not more moral hazard than does the Japanese tradition of falling back on business partners.

Moreover, the mobilization of networks to share risks and give assistance is by no means foreign to U.S. business. Uzzi's (1996) study of subcontracting in the Manhattan garment industry shows manufacturers regularly supporting subcontractors with whom they have *embedded* (reciprocal, high trust) ties, even when the former stands to realize no direct economic gain. Saxenian (1991:147) found the same in Silicon Valley:

> Reciprocity guides relations between Silicon Valley's systems firms and their suppliers. Most of these relationships have moved beyond the inventory control objectives of JIT [just-in-time] to encompass a mutual commitment to sustaining a long term relationship. This requires a commitment not to take advantage of one another when market conditions change, and can entail supporting suppliers through tough times – by extending credit, providing technical assistance or manpower, or helping them find new customers.

As these examples attest, reciprocated risk-sharing among closely networked transaction partners is still looked upon in many global business settings as economic virtue, not vice, offsetting the failings (e.g., opportunism and information blockage) to which atomistic markets are

---

[96] Indeed, U.S. Chapter 11 filing is now criticized because it does precisely what keiretsu intervention in Japan is thought to do: "create zombie companies that live on, only to drag other firms into their graves. Nor is the reputation of Chapter 11 helped by the sight of lawyers, accountants and other restructuring experts feeding off the carcass. The headline figures for professional fees for the latest batch of bankruptcies are likely to break all records. One creditor committee at Enron, for instance, guesses that fees may hit $700m for the two years or more that the firm thinks its bankruptcy will take. On recent trends, fees related to WorldCom could easily top $1 billion" (*The Economist*, 12 December 2002).

inclined. Even now in Japan, some make the case that the shoring up of weak companies strengthens the economy's longer-term prospects. Japan's persistent problems – price deflation, depressed demand, and capital shortages – have produced an environment in which many firms struggle to survive. Such companies are of two types: (a) those whose fundamentals render them unfit for any competitive market, (b) and otherwise sound enterprises whose balance sheets are laden with debt and unproductive assets, much of it a hangover from the bubble. In a reasonably healthy economy, the latter would be viable competitors, belying the lazy journalistic labeling of the lot as "deadbeat" or "zombie." Letting the first succumb while keeping the second on temporary life support might be sound policy. In any case, as Chapter 6 discusses, it is the course Japan for now has chosen to follow. The Industrial Revitalization Corporation, which came on line in the spring of 2003, will sift and sort through the ranks of troubled firms. Working in concert with banks and investments funds, its charge is to separate the terminally unfit from the potentially salvageable and then recapitalize and restructure the latter. How effectively this new convoy system will perform long term remains to be seen, but in its mandate to target and aid only the most promising cases of corporate distress, it looks to be an advance over the keiretsu convoys of the past.

However, in propping up weak firms to preserve jobs for employees, customers for suppliers, clients for banks, and so on, the Japanese economy is seemingly made a less fertile environment for new enterprise and new jobs. In a setting where it is difficult to found and grow a firm, contract with suppliers and distributors, and change careers, the perceived cost of bankruptcy and layoff is huge. Some of Americans' much marveled-at propensity to spend and borrow through bad times may be a culturally ingrained optimism or risk tolerance that contrasts with the pessimism and risk-sensitivity of the Japanese. But a portion of it surely springs from the conviction that, while well-oiled markets do cause firms to go under and people to be out of work, they are also reliably conducive to the founding of new firms and the generation of new jobs. Much of the pressure in Japan to keep old firms, old jobs, and old ties intact is that the price of failure in terms of picking up and starting over remains higher than in the United States.

Appendix

5.1. Modeling Panel Data

The analysis of panel data such as ours poses a number of statistical issues in model specification and estimation. There is considerable certainty on the point that OLS estimation or the sort performed earlier in this chapter is an inferior technique, particularly in giving correct estimates of standard errors and therefore significance tests. The problem is fundamentally that OLS assumes each observation to be independently sampled. In panel data, in which observations vary both over time periods and across units (here, firms), that assumption is not tenable: observations made at different times on the same firms will be similar owing to unmeasured and uncontrolled firm effects. Likewise, observations made on different firms at the same time may be similar because of unmeasured time effects: that is, arising from events in the broader economy during that period in time.

The usual choice of statistical techniques for analyzing panel data is between the fixed-effects (or least-squares dummy variable) model and the random-effects or random coefficient model. Both contain explicit built-in parameters for the unit and temporal effects referred to above. Both have disadvantages, however, and it is in the nature of our data that neither wholly suffices. The fixed-effects model estimates a within-groups regression, where the "groups" are not keiretsu, but, in our case, the firms and years on which observations are made. That is, it nets out all the between-unit and even between-period variation in the dependent variable. The problem is that in discarding so much of the variation in the variables of interest, the coefficient estimates under the fixed-effects model are inefficient – prone to high sampling fluctuation. A greater problem for our purposes is that variables exhibiting little or no variation either across units or over time (in the two-way fixed-effects framework) cannot be accommodated. Several of the characteristics of firms that interest us are temporally invariant (e.g., industry) or nearly so (e.g., shacho-kai).

The random-effects or error components model, like the fixed-effects model contains explicit parameters for unmeasured firm (and/or time) effects, but it treats these as stochastic (not fixed) components of the error term. While this is a more realistic assumption than that of fixed effects in repeated samples, it comes at some cost: the random-effects model requires an assumption that the stochastic error components are uncorrelated with the firm- and time-level explanatory variables. The fixed-effects framework requires no such assumption because it sweeps all the between-firm or period variation into the fixed effects. As noted, this in essence overcontrols for unmeasured cross-sectional and temporal effects, as it parcels out much of the variation in the explanatory variables. But that is a problem of statistical efficiency, whereas the random-effects model arguably risks the more serious problem of error correlated with regressor, hence bias and inconsistency in the coefficient estimates. Hausman (1978) has devised a test for specification bias in the random-effects estimator. It assumes that the fixed-effects estimates are unbiased and consistent albeit inefficient. If the random-effects estimates deviate substantially from their fixed-effects counterpart (as measured by a chi-square statistic), the investigator concludes that the random-effects estimates are biased.

The dilemma is that our use of (nearly) time-invariant regressors rules out the fixed-effects model. However, when we estimate a simple random-effects model of ROA_t that includes the lagged dependent variable, ROA_{t-k}, (excluding the unit- and time-invariant regressors), the Hausman statistic is significant at a high probability. An inspection of how the random-effects estimates differ from their fixed-effects counterparts reveals that the former technique produces a much larger coefficient estimate for the ROA_{t-k}. Since much of our analysis and discussion hangs on the effects of the interaction between ROA_{t-k} and the measures of keiretsu tie, this bias has implications for our research.

Another approach to estimation of panel and time-series models has rapidly gained acceptance among econometricians.[97] This is to use the simple tried-and-true procedure of OLS but augment it with estimates of standard errors that are robust to violations of the usual assumptions of homoscedasticity (constant variances) and autocorrelation (independent disturbances). Our solution is thus to use OLS with robust standard error estimation. In fact, in our data, this gives more conservative estimates of standard errors (larger) and test-statistics (smaller) than the random-effects estimation provides.

A critic might concede that the method of OLS with robust standard errors is adequate to handle the sort of panel data problems to which the fixed- and random-effects estimators offer solutions: adjusting estimates of standard errors to account for clustering of observations within units or periods. However, it is not a satisfactory method for dealing with the common time-series problem of temporally autocorrelated errors, particular in the case of models with lagged dependent variables. In a panel model without temporal autocorrelation, the OLS estimate for a lagged dependent variable is biased but consistent, meaning that the bias is negligible in large samples. Our sample of observations on thirty periods for each of 197 Japanese firms is fairly large by the usual standards of time-series analysis, so we may reasonably assume that the bias in our estimates is small. Indeed, strictly speaking, in such a model we may still tenably assume that that the lagged dependent variable regressor is uncorrelated with the *contemporaneous* error term. But it will certainly be correlated with the errors at prior observation periods.

However, in the presence of first- or higher-order temporal autocorrelation, a lagged dependent variable regressor poses a much more serious problem of bias and inconsistency. The only available solution is

[97] Greene (1997).

instrumental variables estimation of the lagged dependent variable model combined with an adjustment for autocorrelation. The Durbin-Watson test for first-order autocorrelation requires some modification to adapt it to our data. First, the Durbin-Watson d is inappropriate for models containing lagged dependent variables, but the alternative Durbin-Watson h and t statistics designed for this purpose are easily obtained. The second issue is that the Durbin-Watson test must be performed separately on each of the 197 firm-specific time series and averaged to form a single overall statistic. The test statistic so constructed fell far short of significance by the usual criterion of .05. A few of the individual tests performed on particular firms reached significance but these were a small minority.

Notwithstanding the absence of evidence from the Durbin-Watson test for temporal autocorrelation, we estimated several models incorporating adjustments for autocorrelation, for example, OLS with standard errors made robust to heteroscedasticity and within-firm clustering (our primary method) and generalized least squares with first-order autoregression and heteroscedasticity-robust standard errors. The differences between the slope and standard errors estimates obtained under the two techniques were miniscule. A more elaborate methodology is a random-effects model with parameters for firm and time effects plus a two-year moving average error structure. We estimated such a model via the De Silva generalized least-squares procedure available in the TSCSREG panel analysis package within SAS.[98] Again, the results were similar to those given by our chosen OLS-robust methodology.

The evidence, then, is that autocorrelated error is not a significant problem in our data, and models that are explicitly structured to represent such processes offer no visible improvement over our OLS-robust estimator. Most important, in the absence of autoregression and given our reasonably long series, we would appear to be on fairly safe ground in supposing our lagged dependent variable (ROA_{t-k}) effects to be asymptotically unbiased. Even so, to address the issue, we experimented with a two-stage least-squares estimator (2SLS). Predicted values for the lagged dependent variable were generated by regressing it on prior lags plus our explanatory variables. Comparing the OLS and 2SLS estimates of a typical model, the estimates for the ROA_{t-k} coefficient in a regression of ROA_t were trivially different. However, the standard errors from the two methods were substantially different: the 2SLS estimate was much larger. This is symptomatic of the inefficiency and instability of 2SLS estimators generally. Given that the 2SLS slope estimate was virtually identical to the OLS estimate, it seemed once again that OLS-robust was the procedure to use.

[98] SAS Institute (1990).

We have thus applied a number of estimation techniques to these data and models. OLS-robust gives us estimates as precise and conservative as any and with greater stability and efficiency than most. The bottom line is that we have taken some care to ensure that the results we report are not inflated by any unadjusted features of the data or inappropriate choice of estimator.

6

Japan's Next-Generation Industrial Architecture

Japan is going through its biggest social upheaval since the Meiji Restoration.

Masayoshi Son, founder and CEO, Softbank Corporation.[1]

Introduction

As to what degree the network structure of the Japanese economy has withered away, our analysis from the 1960s to the 1990s yields a mixed picture. Signs of disintegration abound – in the fabric of the corporate network as a whole, in the boundedness and coherence of individual keiretsu groupings, and in the general decline of redistributive intervention to align and smooth the growth and profitability trajectories of affiliated firms. Yet the indications are also substantial that, at odds with the recent conventional wisdom, the recessionary 1990s were to some degree a time of retrenchment, not abandonment, of dense networks, keiretsu forms, and performance alignment. This pattern, we think, comports with the core function that keiretsu serve: as mutual support networks that sustain member firms through difficult times. Critics, however, argue that the system of risk-sharing and reciprocal obligation is the reason that the Japanese economy got in trouble in the first place and is having such difficulty extricating itself from bad times. *The Economist* (2002), ever critical of Japan's network economy, noted:

> According to Goldman Sachs, as of November 5th, the share price of only 60 of the more than 1,400 companies currently listed on the first section of the Tokyo Stock Exchange had risen at all since

---

[1] *Business Week Online*, 13 March 2000.

295

the start of 1990.... What sets such companies apart?... Most
of them...have high levels of foreign ownership.... Many are
also considered to have above-average standards of corporate
governance.... Most striking of all, almost none of the best performers belong to keiretsu, the corporate families bound together
by cross-shareholdings that traditionally dominated most industries. Because the outperformers were less protected by strategic
owners, argues Kathy Matsui, a strategist at Goldman Sachs, they
were more exposed to market forces, and so forced to sharpen
up their performance.

This bleak view of the part played by keiretsu, ministry guidance, traditional corporate governance (e.g., insider boards, opaque accounting
practices), and even, it would seem, Japanese business culture in the
economy's persistent malaise is now widely held, certainly outside but
also inside Japan. In consequence, the last few years have seen a wave
of restructuring and innovation in corporate governance and regulation
with no precedent since the early post-war period. Whatever serious flaws
Japan's economic organization may have, and notwithstanding the well-
documented virtues that offset them, reform and restructuring are now
clearly on the policy agenda. They are likely to remain so in the future,
whether or not the economy regains anything like its pre-1990s luster.
Japan would seem to have little alternative, given the forces of technological change and the market integration that are reshaping business systems
worldwide.

The restructuring of the Japanese economy – from spurring entrepreneurial innovation to breaking up insulated markets – demands
transformation of its network infrastructure. This we refer to as Japan's industrial architecture: the fabric of relations among the large Japanese companies that constitutes the economy's strategic core, small and medium-
sized enterprises that are its backbone, and the state agencies that provide
the political backdrop and regulatory rules of the game. How are the network structures underpinning the Japanese economy responding to the
forces that buffet the country today? How has the pace of change been
conditioned by historical legacies, institutional interconnections, and political realities? What efforts are currently under way to reform Japan's
network forms of organization, and where will reform have the biggest
impact?

The chief contours of change are the following. Beginning in 1997,
Japan's moribund financial sector was exposed over three years to a major deregulatory shock ("Big Bang"), intended, like the 1999 repeal of
the Glass-Steagall Act in the United States, to bring down the regulatory
firewalls between commercial and investment banking, eliminate fixed
commissions and rates, give financial services consumers new investment

vehicles (e.g., mutual funds), and thus spur greater competition and innovation. An array of new corporate governance rules were proposed, the most substantial of which was the lifting of the ban on holding companies imposed by the U.S. Occupation in 1947. A surge in foreign direct investment – taking quick advantage of Japanese disarray – brought a spate of high-profile takeovers of financial institutions. Even the country's still leading-edge manufacturers were constrained to adapt to the new global economic reality in weeding out inefficient and dependent suppliers, shifting production overseas, and selling stakes – sometimes controlling ones – to foreign interests. Finally, the Internet tsunami promised to sweep away the vestiges of the old business regime and in the process revolutionize time-honored industry practices (including keiretsu-based procurement relations) and the economy as a whole.

Some observers herald these changes as a straight-line march from old to new economy – from the traditional hidebound model of Japanese network capitalism to the modern, streamlined, market-oriented Western model. The business press recounted with predictable simplism the (new) conventional wisdom: "The tenets of the 'Japanese model,' so lauded in the 1980s, are now widely discredited."[2] However, the reality has been more complex and interesting, particularly given the 2001–2002 explosion of corporate accounting scandals in the United States, which have undercut U.S. claims to economic superiority. The driving forces of the new economy, globalization and innovation, have sped the pace of reform in Japan, as elsewhere. But the process of restructuring has proceeded down pathways well-carved by Japan's distinctive historical and institutional legacies.

We begin with a review of these legacies as they emerged from Japan's pre-war and post-war periods – the first two critical generations in Japan's modern industrial architecture. Following this is an assessment of the forces driving change in contemporary Japan, focusing on the two broad categories of relationship that have been the analytic focus of this study: the strategic ties of finance and corporate governance and the operational ties of production and technology. For each relationship, we evaluate the patterns of reform and restructuring and then offer some assessment of prospects for the future.

Japan's next-generation industrial architecture is still very much in the making, so it is hard to say with any certainty what its ultimate shape will be. Still, the evidence accumulated to date provides some road maps to the pace and trajectory of change. These demonstrate accelerated restructuring in several important *patterns* of strategic and operational relations. What they do not indicate is the wholesale disappearance of networks as the connective tissue of Japanese industrial architecture. Many of the core

---

[2] From an editorial in the *Wall Street Journal*, 1 November 1999.

patterns of Japanese alliance formation remain largely intact, even after the 1990s reforms: companies still make strategic investments in each other, forming extended families of affiliated enterprises, and emphasizing long-term relationships over short-term transactions, at least where they serve the needs of the business.

These patterns continue not because corporate managers and national policy makers are exceptionally stubborn, unwilling to recognize the manifest superiority of a market economy. Nor is it even because vested interests have become so entrenched or inherited business practices so institutionalized that true reform is out of reach. The reason is more fundamental: network structures and processes persist because the reciprocity and reliability that comes from knowing and caring about the identities of business partners, taking a trusting if not benevolent posture toward them, and otherwise crafting mechanisms for ensuring good working relations is a universal logic of organization – one that explains not only the rise of keiretsu affiliations but also of firms themselves.

The new economy has not repudiated this logic of interfirm ties any more than it has for intrafirm relations. Even in the globalized, information technology-dominated business world of today, firms still buffer themselves from the vicissitudes of markets by building formal and informal mechanisms of trust and reliability: vertically integrating, forming joint ventures with rivals, or building elaborate networks that allow for fast leveraging of capital and technology in turbulent market environments. The network logic explains why a new economy revolutionary like Masayoshi Son of Softbank could label his emerging empire a zaibatsu, invoking Japan's pre-war era of buccaneering capitalism. It also explains why Silicon Valley firms will refer to their "keiretsu of" partner companies – or the popular hybrid neologism *netbatsu* – without seeming to embrace stale Asian crony capitalism.[3]

The logic of networks is dynamic, however, as organizational patterns adapt to changing circumstances. The most fundamental change in Japan's industrial architecture is the gradual but probably irreversible shift away from the keiretsu-based macro-network webs and clusterings to a system of less stable and more market-oriented micro-networks, born of strategic alliances that are unconstrained by the old loyalties and enmities and designed to advance the near-term business agendas of the firms involved. This transformation is reflected most clearly in the breakdown of horizontal keiretsu groupings that, as Chapter 3 demonstrated, configured

---

[3] Perhaps the most conspicuous use of the keiretsu terminology is by Kleiner Perkins Caufield & Byers (KPCB), the largest and most influential venture capital firm in Silicon Valley. John Doerr, its highest profile partner, has been preaching the virtues of a tight network of KPCB-funded firms for years.

Japanese business networks from the 1960s into the 1990s. Accelerating this shift in recent years is the consolidation of the Japanese banking industry, plus the rapid interpenetration of foreign investment in a number of crucial industries, including finance and motor vehicles.

How far and how fast this change is occurring varies by sector and type of relationship. Some of the most dramatic changes took place in Japan's most competitive and internationalized industries: the auto industry now has a number of major foreign producers that own large stakes in erstwhile rivals, while its computer industry is more dependent on foreign technology than at any point in thirty years. But important changes are evident as well in some of Japan's least competitive and internationalized industries. In the financial sector, for example, the ties between city banks and their largest clients have been weakening as a result both of financial liberalization (which has opened up new channels of capital) and of industrial success (which has reduced the need of many companies to borrow). E-commerce threatens to do the same to the convoluted networks of the Japanese distribution system.

Even at the extreme frontiers of Japan's new economy, the trajectory of change is shaped by legacies of the past: idealized images of how business should be conducted, the slow and haphazard process of deregulation, and the residue of historical affiliations. Japan's next-generation industrial architecture, therefore, is being built atop or perhaps alongside its earlier architectures. Evidence of this comes from METI, the renamed and, presumably, revamped MITI. Even at the end of the 1990s, the ministry's surveys indicated that over 90 percent of all companies, large and small, still relied on a main bank as their lead financial patron, with more than three-quarters reporting that they had *never* changed main banks. These same surveys indicated that the primary subcontracting relations among over two-thirds of all industrial enterprises had remained stable in recent years; among those where relationships had changed, the vast majority (over three-quarters) reported a *strengthening* rather than weakening of business ties.[4]

A Synopsis of Japan's Industrial Architectures

Since the "software" of industrial architecture evolves from prior generations in much the same way that computer architectures do, it is worth reviewing the contours of these legacies. Japan's first-generation modern industrial architecture originated in the post-Meiji era, a period marked by the tremendous transformations that took place following Japan's

---

[4] MITI (1999).

opening to the outside world and the rapid modernization that resulted. The period from the late 1800s to the 1930s witnessed considerable entrepreneurial initiative, as thousands of new companies were founded and whole new industries forged. (The bulk of our own core sample of 259 firms got their start during this period.) It was also marked by significant technical and organization learning from foreign enterprises, some of which took substantial positions in Japanese companies.

As a result of these dynamic technological and geopolitical conditions, the structure of relations among companies, as our earlier analysis showed, was considerably more open and flexible than in the architecture that emerged out of the wartime and post-war period. That this more open structure did not get in the way of Japan's economic development is evident in the high rates of growth achieved during this period.

Within this overall industrial architecture, two general patterns emerged. One was the zaibatsu – the leaders of most of Japan's modern industries: international commerce, finance, and science- and technology-based fields (e.g., chemicals and electrical machinery). Here finance arose from commercial and industrial enterprise, and strategic control was centered at the top of a holding company. These holding companies also provided critical channels of access to the Japanese state, as zaibatsu leaders such as Iwasaki (Mitsubishi) and Minomura (Mitsui) cultivated ties to political and ministerial leaders in order to gain favored treatment in the dispensing of licenses and subsidies. Following a second pattern was much of the remainder of Japanese industry, including an important leader in the early modernization process, cotton spinning. Companies in these industries generally operated independent of both banks and the state. Funding came chiefly through direct finance, especially from affluent individuals who, unlike the zaibatsu holding companies, were more interested in profitability than in growth and preferred high dividends over capital reinvestment.[5] Management and control was often integrated in these enterprises (as it still is in the family-centered enterprises that dominate Japan's medium- and small-firm sectors).

The requirements of wartime (a period beginning in the early 1930s) wrought significant changes. The state increased its control over the economy by organizing firms and industries into carefully structured webs of associations and councils assigned the job of supporting wartime activities. The construction of these webs eliminated the second pattern outlined above, forcing all enterprises to follow paths laid down by the zaibatsu. Even more important were wartime changes affecting the corporate governance and structure of the Japanese firm. Because the capitalist conception of the firm, with its emphasis on shareholder control and investment

[5] Okazaki (1993).

returns, was at odds with the imperatives of the wartime economy, the government sought to enact policies to remold the corporation itself. Ownership was separated from management and the strategic goal of the enterprise became faithful execution of the apportioned production plan as opposed to profit or growth maximization.

Wartime demands also forced dramatic shifts in the ordering of relations within and between industries. From the late 1930s to early 1940s, the Japanese economy was reorganized into a hierarchical structure of enterprises, the function of which was to carry out wartime resource production and allocation plans. International sources of supply were cut off, foreign technology licensing was severely restricted, and external capital flows were rechanneled into domestic uses. Government agencies exercised increasing control over major business decisions, such as whether and where to invest in plant and equipment.

These wartime changes in the mission and structure of the corporation became a significant legacy on which Japan's second-generation industrial architecture, introduced after the war as part of the U.S. Occupation reforms, would build. The immediate post-war period saw the rationalization of finance and corporate governance relations but not the elimination of the densely connected intercorporate hierarchy that had developed during the war years. Indeed, one of the great ironies of post-war Japanese history is that, despite the fact that the Occupation set out to purge the Japanese economy of zaibatsu influences, economic reforms initiated by the Occupation actually helped to institutionalize tightly organized network structures *throughout* Japan's industrial architecture.[6]

The post-war reforms also put an end to the most rigid trappings of the state economic planning apparatus, while fostering a continuation of – even reinforcing – the hierarchical private-sector structures already in place. The demands of Japan's high-growth economy of the 1950s and 1960s forced large producers to rely heavily on subcontractors to increase production capacity. The core firms provided these satellite suppliers with capital, equipment, and raw materials, organizing them into *cooperative factories* (*kyoryoku kojo*) and consigning them to specialized and dependent roles. Under the pressure of rapid growth, primary subcontractors turned to secondary subcontractors and so on down the line. The result was the elaborate, multitier structure supplier and subcontracting relationships for which such Japanese industries such as motor vehicles and machinery are famous today. The keiretsu terminology itself came into being during this period, beginning sometime in the early 1950s.[7]

[6] Johnson (1982).
[7] Nakamura (1983) attributes the first use of the term to a textile producer, Toyoran, circa 1952.

The process of keiretsu-ization during Japan's high-growth era altered not only supply and distribution relations but those of technological development as well. With the institutionalization of permanent employment in large firms came an increasingly clear interfirm division of labor, with research and development functions in science and technology fields centralized in core firms. These companies combined their greater technical expertise with financing from affiliated banks to take the lead in new industries and technologies. This continued a pattern started by the zaibatsu, only with an important difference: unlike the earlier years of business group development, new companies emerged within an increasingly institutionalized system of preexisting relationships that greatly limited access to critical resources and markets.

Japan's New Economy, Part 1: Finance and Corporate Governance

Japan's systemic shift to a new industrial architecture in the late 1990s may prove as significant a historical juncture as 1868 (the Meiji Restoration) or 1945–52, the U.S. Occupation. During this decade, the bursting of the asset-price bubble in 1991 severely challenged policy makers' long-held legitimacy, spurring active debate on major reform, just as Japan's growing exposure to the forces of globalization and technological change was sharply increasing. In considering the specifics of the reform and restructuring program, we begin by looking at the institutional glue that held the network economy together – its financial and corporate governance systems. Reforms here are as significant as anywhere in changing the face of Japan's industrial architecture, but this also makes them contested terrain.

The roots of financial system change, as we suggested in earlier chapters, go back decades earlier, as the 1970s and 1980s witnessed initial efforts to deregulate and internationalize Japanese financial services. Beginning in the late 1970s, financial authorities liberalized interest rates, relaxed international capital controls, permitted firms to offer a broader range of products and services, and eliminated some of the functional divisions within the financial services sector.[8] Japanese financial institutions also began opening up foreign branch offices to learn about and tap into the Euromarkets, where financial deregulation was already far along and a wide variety of innovative financial instruments were being created.

The reforms also affected Japan's industrial corporations, as the emergence of a corporate bond exchange and liberalization of stock market

---

[8] Rosenbluth (1989); Schaede (2001).

listing requirements greatly increased the availability of direct, nonbank financing. More important, Japan's manufacturing competitiveness enabled some firms to finance investments wholly from internal cash flows and thus escape bank dependence altogether. As the Nikkei index soared in the late 1980s bubble, Toyota, for example, ceased all borrowing and became a de facto bank for its affiliated firms.[9] The chronic capital shortages of the early post-war period – which had been the foundation for the main bank relations and the emergence of the bank-centered groups – evaporated for many of Japan's largest companies.[10]

While financial services were thus restructuring, no comparable transformation of corporate governance was taking place. Indeed, this was a time when the seeming virtues of Japanese capitalism – a dedicated and well-trained workforce, stable growth, smooth adaptation to the macroeconomic shocks of oil and exchange rate shifts, technological and manufacturing leadership – were conspicuously on display. Financial sector reform was spurred by concerns over the relative global backwardness and uncompetitiveness of Japan's financial services, but there was widespread faith both within and outside the country that the traditional systems of employment, managerial decision making, and organization (where the survival of every company was more or less guaranteed as long as it did right by its employees, business partners, and the state) were integral to Japan's post-war economic miracle and thus beyond reproach. Less apparent at the time was that, while large companies were reducing their dependence on main banks and other external monitors, no well-defined system of checks and balances was being put in place.

The Financial System in the 1990s

The 1990s ushered in dramatic change in how Japan assessed itself, as the debate over financial system and corporate governance reform, previously at low ebb, took on new urgency. Banks were crippled with nonperforming loans stemming from failed bubble-era investments, downgrades in credit ratings, and (due to falling markets) insufficient capital reserves to meet the Bank for International Settlements' standards. In this section, we address four broad forces driving the financial reforms of the decade: changes in the regulatory environment, the declining role of banks as financial intermediaries, financial consolidation, and the sale of financial institutions to foreign investors.

---

[9] As we note below, banks themselves often shifted loans from parent companies to the growing family of vertical affiliates.
[10] Hoshi and Kashyap (2000).

1. Regulatory Politics in the 1990s: The Death of the Convoy System?

The decade's reforms began with a revision of securities and banking regulation, allowing banks for the first time to establish securities subsidiaries. The Big Bang package of regulatory changes initiated in 1997 was designed to bring down the firewalls between segments of the financial services industry. Scheduled for completion in 2001, the program was to revitalize the banking, insurance, and securities sectors. It comprised market-opening liberalization of several kinds, among them revision of the Foreign Exchange and Foreign Trade Control Law to remove the licensing requirement for foreign activities (although extensive reporting requirements remained); elimination of barriers to entry to different markets, enabling commercial banks, securities brokers, and insurance companies to compete directly; and deregulation of the system of fixed commissions that had slowed development of Japan's securities industries.[11]

In the interim other reforms tightened regulatory control, subjecting financial services to stricter prudential rules. Banks had long been exempted from many of the annual reporting requirements imposed on other companies. But as the financial crisis spread and more banks were charged a "Japan premium," the Federation of Bankers Associations (*Zenginkyo*) worked with the MOF to close the regulatory loopholes that were damaging the reputation of Japanese financial institutions and their ability to lend and raise capital in international financial markets.[12] A profoundly important shift during the end of the decade was the slow demise of the convoy system, whereby financial regulators, through a process of prodding and cajoling main banks and other partners to join together in a bailout and turnaround attempt, allowed no firm to fail.[13]

> The convoy system has been credited for a large part of Japan's impressive postwar economic development, and certainly imbued banks with godlike powers as dictators to the corporate sector.

[11] The elimination of fixed commissions in October 1999 occurred in tandem with the appearance of online trading. Together, these changes opened the door for the first time to cost-effective trading by individual investors in Japanese corporate shares. Even into the late 1990s, individuals still accounted for only one-quarter of total shareholding on the Tokyo Stock Exchange, about half the number in the United States and one that has changed little over decades. If the high costs of trading for individual investors could be brought down, the hope was that more individual investors might enter the market and increase their voice relative to stable corporate investors.

[12] Schaede (2001).

[13] Hoshi (2002) argues that the convoy system, which worked well before the 1980s, began to decay in that decade as deregulation limited the ability of the Ministry of Finance to induce financial institutions to join the convoys. On the fate of companies that failed to honor their main bank obligations, see the discussion by Gerlach (1992a) of the Mitsukoshi and Sanko Steamship cases.

The banks told their corporate clients when to borrow and when to go into new businesses. When troubles arose, the banks made their divination: restructuring or liquidation. But the convoy system has been crumbling since 1997, when banks virtually stopped lending and rather than protecting their corporate flock, turned inward to focus on their own survival. Banks grasped at the public-funding lifeline and launched successive rounds of mergers and tie-ups that weakened traditional keiretsu links.[14]

One of the first departures from the MOF's long-standing "no failure" policy was the ministry's decision to allow several distressed institutions to close in 1997. Prominent among these were Hokkaido Takushoku Bank (Japan's sixteenth largest) and Yamaichi Securities (fourth largest). However, the closures only came about after two years of unsuccessful efforts to restructure Hokkaido Takushoku within the old convoy framework. As the *Wall Street Journal* noted:

> Japan finally may be abandoning some of its time-worn practices of forcing strong financial institutions to bail out the weak.... The fate of Hokkaido Takushoku ... shows Japan's normal solutions are no longer sufficient.... Yet, Japan got radical only after exhausting all other options. Regulators tried to corner other banks into merging with Hokkaido Takushoku. But ... potential partners, nursing their own problems in a time of growing competition, showed unprecedented pluck in saying no to the bureaucrats.[15]

Thus, the MOF gave up on the convoy system only after it had ceased to be a useful tool. As Ulrike Schaede (1995) has shown, the *jusen* crisis – the failure of seven mortgage-lending institutions in 1996 – became a ¥700 billion government bailout after the city banks, which in several cases were using the *jusen* to front their mortgage business, refused to honor the usual keiretsu obligations to rescue distressed affiliates and absorb their losses.[16]

---

[14] *Nikkei Weekly*, 10 July 2000.
[15] *Wall Street Journal*, 18 November 1997.
[16] A suit brought by the Housing Loan Administration Corporation in 1998 alleged that Sumitomo Bank had induced its affiliated *jusen* to loan to highly unsuitable clients. Nakabo Kohei, president of Housing Loan Administration Corporation, accused Sumitomo Bank of a "serious lack of morals" in its involvement in the *jusen* affair (*Financial Times*, 1 July 1998). In the end, after a good deal of government arm-twisting, the large commercial banks did contribute some ¥500 billion to an investment fund set up to pay for the *jusen* debacle. Investment banks contributed somewhat less than this. However, only the income earned from managing the fund could be used to offset *jusen* losses.

The regulatory agencies themselves were by no means off limits to the reform process, the MOF most of all. The ministry was widely accused of having helped foster and subsequently mismanaged the country's succession of financial crises in the 1990s – the crash in equity markets, the *jusen* scandal, and the persistent bad loan and asset adequacy problems of the banks. The agency was further tarnished by accusations of corruption that highlighted its incestuous relationship with the industry. In exchange for bribes, MOF officials were reportedly alerting banks to impending inspections. One official committed suicide when the scandal broke, and the minister along with two other officials resigned.

As an early step in breaking up the MOF's "excessive concentration of power," the Securities Exchange Surveillance Committee (SESC) was established in 1992 as a separate agency, charged with monitoring the securities industry.[17] More important was the creation in mid-1998 of the Financial Supervisory (later Services) Agency (FSA) to license, supervise, and inspect financial institutions. The FSA's preemption of MOF's traditional functions was the ultimate affront in a string of humiliations heaped on the once-proud and powerful ministry. Rubbing salt in the wound was the change in the MOF's Japanese name in 2001 from *okurasho* (storehouse), in use since the fifth century, to *zaimusho* (treasury).

The performance of the FSA, working through its Financial Reconstruction Commission, has itself been uneven. A spin-off of the MOF (from which it took its staff), it proved a surprisingly tough watchdog in its first year, overseeing the closure of two banks (Long Term Credit and Nippon Credit) and restructuring others under the pressure of a major loan program to assist in disposing of bad debt. The FSA also played a significant role in arranging the banking mergers discussed below.

With FSA head Hakuo Yanagisawa's late 1999 departure (on the presumption that the large banks were back on stable ground), the FSA fared less well. Under new chief Michio Ochi, the agency turned its attention to the bad loan problems of local credit unions and regional banks. In a public speech, Ochi reassured the industry that he would go easy on it, provoking an outcry from bureaucrats and politicians that forced his resignation in February 2000. In fact, the FSA did go easy. It slowed plans to allow: the entry of nonbanks (such as 7–11 chain owner Ito Yokado) into banking, banks to offer insurance policies, and nonlife insurers to write certain health-related policies.[18] Moreover, while Yanagisawa was open to foreign capital takeovers of failed banks, his successors were less so. When another large bank, Nippon Credit, was declared insolvent and nationalized, the FSA turned aside the foreign "vulture" funds,

17 Norville (1998).
18 Schaede (2001).

placing Nippon Credit in the hands of a domestic investment group led by Softbank.

The reform agenda seemed back on track with the election in 2001 to prime minister of Junichiro Koizumi, a career Liberal Democratic Party (LDP) politician and former minister of Health, Labor, and Welfare.[19] Posing as a radical reformer, Koizumi pledged to clean up the bad loan mess within three years. Once in office, his follow-through was uneven. Proclaiming that markets should decide the fate of ailing firms, he allowed the collapse in September 2001 of retailer Mycal, the second largest nonfinancial post-war bankruptcy, on the heels of the failure of retailer Sogo, the largest, one year before. Both firms were encumbered by soured bubble-era real estate investments, and their main banks, IBJ and DKB, respectively, were unwilling to go the extra mile to keep them alive. At a press conference with foreign reporters shortly after the Mycal bankruptcy, bound to eliminate tens of thousands of jobs, Koizumi said, "I have no intention to stop reform because unemployment has reached a certain level."[20]

But six months later, with unemployment rising, the prime minister changed course and endorsed a government-led rescue of Daiei Inc., a major supermarket chain operator. Further, despite the campaign rhetoric, his administration was slow to tackle the bad loan crisis, delegating the matter to Financial Services Agency head Yanagisawa, who returned to the post in January 2000. Yanagisawa was effective in his first term, but he then had the leverage of ¥7.5 trillion in government loans to distribute to the banks. Now he steadfastly opposed new public funds for troubled banks. As criticism of his reform program mounted, Koizumi replaced Yanagisawa as FSA chief with Heizo Takenaka, a Keio University economist unbeholden to the business and political establishment and thus with little to lose from an aggressive reform campaign.

Takenaka's tough first plan as FSA head, revealed in October 2002, was strong medicine. First, it would have forced banks to recalculate assets so that most would fail to meet Bank for International Settlements (BIS) capital adequacy standards. Second, it required banks to convert

---

[19] Okuno-Fujiwara (1991).

[20] In opting for court protection, both Sogo and Mycal took advantage of a Big Bang adjustment to Japan's bankruptcy laws, effective 1 April 2000, allowing firms to file for protection before they reached full insolvency. The new rules, closer to U.S. Chapter 11, had the courts working out an arrangement with creditors, enabling the firm to be back in business sooner. The change struck a blow at the main bank system, as the courts preempted some of the main bank's historical role as a broker of bailouts and restructurings. By the same token, the stringency of the old bankruptcy rules had been a factor in the keiretsu/convoy system of private sector bailouts, as a firm declared legally bankrupt was essentially guaranteed destruction as a functional business entity (Landers, 2001a, 2001b, 2001c).

preferred shares (received by the government in exchange for the loans of 1998) to common stock, thus giving the state majority voting rights in some banks, effectively nationalizing them. Crashing bank stocks and a firestorm of criticism from bankers, bureaucrats, and LDP politicians (who moved to censure Takenaka in the Diet) forced rapid back-pedaling. Hardcore reformers saw a cave-in to the usual powerful interests, but even some Western observers, unlikely to be called apologists for Japan, Inc., saw the plan as draconian. Glenn Hubbard, head of the Bush administration's Council of Economic Advisors, commented that "Takenaka's original plan would have been a very constructive step to solve the non-performing asset problem, but in itself it would be quite deflationary."[21]

The revised Takenaka–Koizumi proposal, modified to offset the deflationary effects of bad loan clean-up, called for the creation of a new government entity to oversee the rehabilitation of failing firms, the Industrial Revitalization Corporation (IRC), which began operations in the spring of 2003.[22] The charge to the IRC is to "pick winners and losers" – target some firms for rehabilitation and leave others to die. It will not act alone but in concert with the private sector, including the growing number of equity funds specialized in salvaging distressed assets. METI officials voiced opposition to the government thrusting itself so explicitly (unlike the covert practices of the past) into the targeting and turnaround of troubled firms, but they were overruled.

The IRC, in league with its private sector partners, has some of the earmarks of the old convoy system, albeit with important differences. It is a more transparent instrument of industrial adjustment policy. Its charge is not to save every troubled firm, but only those whose shot at revival is strong. Finally, the private sector parties to the IRC include investment funds and banks, both foreign (e.g., Ripplewood) and domestic, whose own earnings and market value hinge on the success of their turnarounds in a fashion quite different from the keiretsu convoys of old. The view from the Bank of Japan and the United States is that deflationary policy should mean monetary easing, nothing more. Picking winners and losers and otherwise trying to preserve jobs and protect stakeholders is just a replay of a tired old network economy refrain and is destined to failure.

2. Declining Role of Banks as Financial Intermediaries
Even as Japan's policy machinery lurched from one reform campaign to another, market forces were relieving banks of the powerful intermediation role they had played in the high-growth era. Financial market deregulation since the late 1970s, coupled with the shift to slower economic

[21] Sevastopulo (2002).
[22] Pilling (2001).

growth after 1974, had reduced corporations' dependence on bank borrowing, as firms with large cash flows and strong balance sheets funded investment from their own reserves or through the issuance of corporate bonds. This pattern intensified in the 1990s, as the banks, beset by mounting financial problems, found themselves no longer able to fund large-scale industrial projects.

However, while the *ginko banare* (bank separation) process was quite real for some companies, it was not the end of financial intermediation and the hegemonic role of banks. Dependence on bank borrowing remained high in heavy industry and other mature and declining sectors where profit margins were low and unattractive to the corporate bond and equity markets. Banks increased their lending to small and medium-size enterprises as these heretofore neglected clients expanded overseas and upgraded technologically. In many cases, parent companies helped make the introduction and provided the guarantees for their own, more needy, affiliates, thereby extending bank ties to the broader corporate family.

Japanese firms with large cash flows and balance sheets maintained strong main bank ties for other reasons: as the banks served as underwriters of bond issues, providers of guarantees in overseas bond issues, holders of companies' deposits, handlers of employee accounts for salary receipts, and so on.[23] Similarly, the banks themselves took advantage of deregulation to increase their portfolio of services, adding bond issuance, consulting, and assistance with overseas operations. In expanding relation-based management to include companies' affiliates and foreign subsidiaries, a team in the bank's wholesale division would serve as a unified window for all the transactions of a group.

Representative of this expanded role were the lead banks of Toyota Motor Corporation. Toyota boasted an enormous war chest of cash, a pristine balance sheet, easy access to world capital markets, and the apt moniker "Toyota Bank." It had not borrowed money from its three primary lender banks (Sanwa, Sakura [Mitsui], and Tokai) for many years. Yet when asked why his company maintained its long-standing relationships with these three, Toyota's executive vice president in charge of financial affairs stated: "It might be true that Toyota Motor Corporation enjoys strong

---

[23] According to one study, 77 percent of all warrant bonds issued between 1984 and 1987 were guaranteed by banks, and these were normally the company's main bank. As Miyajima (1998) writes: "The corporate bonds issued in the 1980s were thus a form of public debt as well as a private debt supported by the main bank relationship. Secured bonds and warrant bonds backed by bank guarantees can be understood to be another form of bank borrowing in the sense that the main bank would still be in charge of managing the debt if the company issuing the bonds faced financial distress." The bank's role as trustee was simplified in 1993 and finally eliminated in 1996.

surplus capital. . . . But when you think about the whole Toyota group, in auto financing, suppliers, imports and dealers, on a consolidated basis, we need access to a bank."[24]

In short, the changes begun in the 1980s and continued into the 1990s were less a sharp break with the system of bank dependence and control than a gradual diversification into external financing sources, one focused chiefly on the most successful export industries. Banks still supplied over half the external capital used by the corporate sector well into the 1990s, a very high proportion compared to other advanced economies.[25] A survey conducted by the Japanese government at the end of the decade found that over 90 percent of all Japanese companies, large and small, still used one main bank. Furthermore, more than three-quarters reported that they had never changed main banks since the company's founding.[26] Even at the end of the 1990s, Western critics such as Alan Greenspan were calling upon Japan to abandon its "archetype of virtually bank-only financial intermediation."[27]

3. Sale of Financial Institutions to Foreign Investors
The second half of the 1990s saw the introduction of another private-sector-initiated force for reform, as several major financial institutions were sold to foreign investors. Financial services had been one of Japan's most protected sectors, but a mountain of bad debt and a host of other problems had sufficiently enfeebled a number of institutions so that an infusion of capital from abroad seemed their only hope. In 1999 alone, GE Capital purchased Japan Lease (for $6.6 billion), while a French company, AXA, acquired 70 percent of the shares of Japan Group Life (for $1.9 billion).[28] These were the two largest foreign direct investments of the year.

Setting the stage for the foreign acquisitions was Travelers Insurance, which bought a 9.5 percent stake in Nikko Securities in May 1998, assuming Nikko's investment banking and international operations. Nikko was a core Mitsubishi group member whose largest shareholder was Bank of Tokyo–Mitsubishi. Complaining that they had no advance warning of the Travelers' deal, executives at the bank were outraged at Nikko's breach of keiretsu etiquette, reportedly refusing to speak to Nikko managers for months. Despite having listed Nikko first among its underwriters

[24] Iwao Okijima, quoted in the *New York Times*, 20 November 1998.
[25] Miyajima (1998).
[26] MITI (1999).
[27] Greenspan made this comment at the annual meeting of the World Bank and the International Monetary Fund on 27 September 1999. *New York Times*, 28 September 1999.
[28] *Business Week*, 10 April 2000.

for years, the bank made it known that henceforth it would divvy up its business purely on a case-by-case basis.[29]

Of major significance was the sale in September 1999 of bankrupt Long-Term Credit Bank (LTCB), renamed Shinsei Bank, to a foreign investment consortium, Ripplewood Holdings. LTCB had been the linchpin institution in Japan's post-war reconstruction, in the words of one report, "at the very heart of the bureaucratic-corporate alliance which built up the nation's economy in the decades after World War II."[30] The deal included a quid pro quo designed to soften the blow to LTCB's corporate clients. To make LTCB more attractive to Ripplewood's investors, it guaranteed protection against large losses. If LTCB loans proved bad, the government would buy them back at original face value. In return, Ripplewood's investors had to agree that they would not cut off any LTCB borrowers for at least three years from the time of purchase, thus granting a breathing spell to client firms in such recession-battered industries as construction and retail.[31]

By decade's end, questions persisted about the solvency of Japanese financial institutions and the role foreign banks might play in their restructuring. The predictions of collapse (especially in the 1997–98 period) had not yet come to pass. Nor, despite a few high-profile successes, had foreign investment yet made large inroads. Moreover, unlike say, the auto industry, the restructuring to that point had produced neither large-scale workforce reductions nor the abandonment of major clients. The industry was changing, to be sure, but the change was less cataclysmic than many had expected.

4. Bank Consolidation

Under pressure from the FSA, and with the memory of the LTCB and Nippon Credit closures fresh in managers' minds, other banks rushed into alliances. The wave of major bank consolidations at the end of the 1990s was a dramatic and sweeping change in the Japanese financial landscape. Bank mergers have a lengthy history in Japan, one key to the formation of the country's modern industrial architecture.[32] What made the 1990s merger wave distinctive was the scale of the institutions involved and of their problems. The early years of the decade had seen two important

---

[29] *Wall Street Journal*, 19 May 1999.

[30] *Wall Street Journal*, 23 September 1999.

[31] *Wall Street Journal*, 29 September 1999. These guarantees were later criticized by politicians (see *New York Times*, 7 June 2000).

[32] As the corporate history trees (Figures 2.5 and 2.6) demonstrate, Sumitomo Bank and Dai-Ichi Kangyo Bank grew primarily through a process of merger and acquisition, especially during the pre-war period. This pattern was followed by other large banks as well.

bank mergers, Mitsui Bank and Taiyo-Kobe Bank in 1990 to form Sakura, and the Mitsubishi–Bank of Tokyo merger in 1996. Another series of mergers linked the trust banks of the big-six groups to their counterpart city banks.[33] All these were dwarfed, however, by a series of mega-mergers that fundamentally changed the complexion of Japanese banking and its interface with the big-six keiretsu groups.

The first such major announcement came in August 1998, when three of Japan's largest banks – Fuji, Dai-Ichi Kangyo, and Industrial Bank of Japan – announced their plans to merge into a gargantuan entity, later named Mizuho Bank, with ¥140 trillion in assets. The resulting behemoth was to be half again the size of the world's next-largest institution, Deutsche Bank. There followed in October 1999 the news that Sumitomo Bank and Sakura (Mitsui) would merge. Together, these two combinations meant that the six large city banks that had provided the core leadership of the horizontal keiretsu would soon reduce to four.

However, the creation of Mizuho, while certainly a dramatic turn of events, is in retrospect unsurprising in view of the overlapping network positions of the participating banks and their corresponding keiretsu groups.[34] This meant fewer competitive rivalries among the corporate clients of the banks. Such rivalries had brought down similar mergers in the past (notably that between Dai-Ichi Bank and Mitsubishi Bank in the late 1960s). Indeed, the president of IBJ was explicit on the point, telling the Japanese press that, "I chose DKB and Fuji Bank (as merger partners) because neither belongs to a tight corporate group."[35]

One reason for the overlap of the Fuyo, IBJ, and DKB networks was the cross-cutting Nissan and Hitachi vertical keiretsu. The two manufacturers were the lead companies of the Nissan zaibatsu before the war, and they retained a close keiretsu connection to the present. Nissan's main banks were Fuji and IBJ, while Hitachi – uniquely among large industrial firms – had balanced its ties with four principal banks: Fuji, DKB, IBJ, and Sanwa.[36] Moreover, Hitachi and Nissan's vertical groups of affiliated industrial firms relied on the same handful of banks, effectively extending the networks of the Mizuho partners to dozens of other companies.[37]

[33] Among these, Sumitomo Trust and Banking merged with Sumitomo Bank in October 1998 and Yasuda Trust and Banking merged with Fuji Bank in January 1999. In April 2000, Bank of Tokyo-Mitsubishi announced that it would merge with Mitsubishi Trust and Banking.

[34] Gerlach (1992a).

[35] *Daily Yomiuri*, 7 September 1999. The IBJ president also emphasized geographical considerations, saying, "What helped us in the negotiating process was that I had many chances to talk with the two banks since we are all based in the Kanto region."

[36] As earlier noted, Hitachi is the only Japanese company seated on three different presidents' councils – Fuji, DKB, and Sanwa.

[37] Table 3.5 shows several hybrid blocks in which these and other connections were played out. Block *2A1a* has Nissan and its affiliates clustered with Yasuda Fire and Marine from

A glance at Table 3.4, our CONCOR blocking of the large-firm network in 1993, makes clear how little violence to the extant patterns of keiretsu alignment was done by the Mizuho consolidation. By the early 1990s, neither the Fuyo nor the DKB groups had distinct identities, owing to the intermingling in the network of their and Sanwa's affiliated firms. The 1993 blockmodel image shows all three banks in the *1A1a* block, with DKB and Fuji adjacent in the CONCOR tree.[38]

Also significant is that DKB was already a model for a large-scale financial combination. Formed from a merger in 1971 of Dai-Ichi and Nippon Kangyo banks, it embraced several preexisting clusterings, such as the formerly independent Kawasaki and Furukawa groups. In cobbling these disparate pieces together, the merged firm struggled to forge a common identity. DKB's personnel department was segmented into three divisions serving DKB employees, Nippon Kangyo employees, and postmerger employees. Moreover, the presidency was held by an employee of one of the merging firms and the board chair was held by another. Because the DKB group included so many companies, with such different histories, it never conformed to the one-set principle of a single large affiliate in each industry. Furthermore, its presidents' council met only once every three months, rather than monthly. It is hardly surprising that the group's cohesion was the lowest of the big six.[39]

The formation of the Mizuho Group is thus comprehensible within the framework of Japan's prevailing industrial architecture as it had evolved over the previous several decades.[40] The same could be said of the merger in October 1999 of Sanwa Bank with Tokai Bank and Toyo Trust. Sanwa in effect intruded on what began as an Asahi–Tokai alliance with anticipated participation by Daiwa and Yokohama Banks. The strategy was to create a super-regional banking institution of the sort that was emerging in the United States. After Sanwa's entry, Asahi pulled out of the merger. Replacing Asahi was Toyo Trust, a Sanwa *Sansui-kai* member. Sanwa is a major shareholder in Tokai, and both banks had long-standing ties to the Toyota group (Toyota affiliate Daihatsu being a *Sansui-kai* member).

---

the Fuyo group, along with some council independents that include a number of Nissan affiliates that have IBJ ties as well. Block *2A2a(1)* shows Hitachi and its own affiliates also clustered with some independents affiliated with IBJ. A third block, *2B2a*, has an equal number of Fuyo and DKB members, as well as several more Nissan affiliates.

[38] Other alliances appearing to cross conventional keiretsu lines are similarly between groups whose positions in the network have either been adjacent or overlapped for years. An example is the merger in 2000 of Chuo Trust and Mitsui Trust, which appear together in the *1A1a* block in 1993.

[39] Gerlach (1992a).

[40] We are particularly indebted here to Kyoto University professor Masahiro Shimotani for his observations on the implications for keiretsu of Japan's recent financial consolidations.

Thus, the new UFJ (United Financial of Japan) Bank group was shaping up to be very Sanwa-centered.

Due in part to their common alignment with the Toyota keiretsu, Chapter 3's blockmodel analysis shows Sanwa close in network space to Mitsui (see Table 3.5), and, indeed, speculation at the time had it that this would be the next large consolidation.[41] To general surprise, Sakura–Mitsui fell into the arms of Sumitomo, a marriage announced in October 1999. In a period of almost daily press reporting of huge new business combinations, this more than any other merger cut across the traditional fault lines of the network economy. With some 800 years of history between them, the Mitsui and Sumitomo names represented Japan's oldest business houses. Unlike the Mizuho merger, these banks were the lead institutions of two of the big-three pre-war zaibatsu and were major competitive rivals. The Sumitomo group, of course, is well known for its cohesiveness and insularity.

Thus, the Sumitomo–Sakura merger "blurred old zaibatsu lines," as a *Nikkei Weekly* headline put it (Sato, 1999b). Its implications for the imminent demise of the zaibatsu-based groups, however, were less clear. Notwithstanding the two banks' protestations to the world that theirs would be a marriage of equals, the merger was a transparent bailout and takeover of Sakura, at the time the weakest of the city banks, by Sumitomo, one of the strongest. Sakura, as noted, was beset by bad debts and a huge portfolio of declining stocks.[42] By early 1999, just before the Sumitomo merger was announced, its stock came under heavy selling pressure from investors concerned with its shaky standing and bleak prospects for recovery. The bank announced plans to shrink employment and branches by 25 percent and was in line for a large infusion of public funds. Some months before, Sakura had sought assistance from major Mitsui group companies, including Toyota, but its pleas for aid were rebuffed.[43] Thus, the Sumitomo–Sakura partnership is best seen as a strong bank in a tight group devouring a weak bank in a loose group. The executive ranks of the new entity are mostly Sumitomo with relatively little high-level Mitsui participation. The Mitsui keiretsu – never as crystallized as Mitsubishi and Sumitomo – may have been weaker than Chapter 3's analysis suggests. The group's reluctance to bail out its lead bank – setting up Sakura to be absorbed by a stronger institution and key competitor – did not bode

---

[41] Sato (1999a).

[42] Spindle (1998).

[43] As earlier chapters note, the Toyoda family reportedly favored a bailout of Mitsui, which they saw as reciprocity for Mitsui's rescue of Toyota when the automaker veered close to bankruptcy in the early 1950s. They were overruled, however, by then-*shacho* Hiroshi Okuda, a Western-style executive with little regard for keiretsu obligations (Shirouzu, 1999a).

well for the Mitsui group's survival. On the other hand, there is little basis here for a conclusion that the Sumitomo–Mitsui merger diminished the Sumitomo group or Sumitomo bank's historic role as its leader.

Thus, the Mizuho consortium is the one financial consolidation that seems truly a marriage of equals in bringing together Fuji – the lead firm of the Fuyo group and chair of the *Fuyo-kai* – and DKB, kingpin of the DKB group. The Mitsui–Sumitomo and Sanwa–Tokai–Toyo mergers are best viewed as developments that strengthened Sumitomo and Sanwa at the expense of one ailing city bank and two midsize institutions.

To what extent is the turbulence in the banking industry the leading edge of a broader restructuring of Japan's business industrial architecture? First, the bank mergers appear to be toppling a major barrier to large-scale industrial restructuring. According to Takashi Imai, chairman of Nippon Steel and former chief of Keidanren, a reason the nation's steel industry had yet to consolidate was the diversity of the steelmakers' primary banking relationships.[44] The consolidation of the banks presented a solution. The merged banks continued to hold large equity stakes in their industrial clients. With the Mizuho merger, for example, the three participating banks controlled 12.4 percent of NSK, a huge ball-bearing and machine-parts maker, and 10.5 percent of Nissan. While the law permitted them to own no more than a 5 percent share of any given company, their affiliated enterprises could purchase more shares and thus get around the restriction.[45] The aggregate ownership was enough to force consolidation among the industrial firms.

Indeed, some restructuring of manufacturing and trade has been proceeding within the footprints of the new bank groups. Kawasaki Steel of the DKB group and Nippon Kokan (NKK) of Fuyo announced in 2000 that they would ally in distribution, maintenance, and materials purchasing. A month later, Fuyo sogo shosha Marubeni and DKB trader Itochu announced a consolidation of steel operations in China, prompting rumors that merger plans would follow. Tie-ups between Mitsui and Sumitomo industrial companies are also proceeding apace. Mitsui Chemical and Sumitomo Chemical announced a merger in the fall of 2001, labeled by the business press "the first alliance on such a scale beyond the boundaries of zaibatsu business groups in the manufacturing industry."[46] Mitsui Construction and Sumitomo Construction made plans to merge in April 2003.[47] Sanwa group trading companies Nissho Iwai and Nichimen are

---

[44] *New York Times*, 15 October 1999.
[45] Executives in Sakura and Sumitomo, for example, made clear that while they expected to reduce some of their cross-shareholdings with client firms, they would first seek the clients' approval.
[46] *Nikkei Weekly*, 27 November 2000.
[47] *Kyodo News*, 14 November 2002.

also folding their operations into a holding company effective April 2003. The Mitsui and Sumitomo shosha, while not planning to merge, are pursuing a series of alliances in construction materials, sheet steel, and other activities.[48]

What should we make of this chain reaction of consolidations cascading from financials to industrials down horizontal keiretsu lines? Many heralded it as a toppling of the pillars of the network economy – the end of keiretsu, main bank ties, and convoy system bailouts. Yet the observable tendency for new industrial mergers and alliances to follow the paths of the financial mergers may also be read as testimony to the persistent power of keiretsu alignments. If keiretsu loyalties had little current salience, manufacturing and commercial enterprises should not be joining hands in ways that complement the keiretsu contours of the bank tie-ups. The processes of corporate merger appear to embrace, not merely banks, but whole groups. The former six horizontal groups are indeed compressing into four, but to label this transformation a breakdown of the keiretsu is off the mark.[49]

Moreover, both the Mizuho and Sumitomo–Sakura mergers arrived on the heels of an important regulatory change: the legalization of holding companies in 1997. The holding company had been outlawed since the U.S. Occupation, but in the 1990s sentiment in the business community shifted strongly in favor of lifting the ban. By most accounts, the ban figured in the post-war creation and spread of the keiretsu form, since mutual cross-shareholdings and interlocking directorates permitted a degree of coordination that would otherwise (as in the pre-war zaibatsu or the Korean *chaebol*) be administratively formal, direct, and centralized.

In the new climate of merger and restructuring, holding company organization enables firms to bring discrete businesses under a single legal-administrative umbrella without erasing corporate identities or even fully integrating day-to-day operations. Distinct personnel and other systems can be maintained at most levels. And if the merger fails – or the component operations' financial condition improves to the point of self-sufficiency – the companies can separate with little trauma. Some observers saw the financial mega-mergers as temporary expedients, which the players might undo at some future point in time. All followed the same series of steps: first the creation of an alliance, second the adoption

---

[48] *Nikkei Net Interactive*, 29 May 2001.
[49] Contrary to the view that the bank mergers have reduced the horizontal groups from six to four are reports that the Fuyo and Mitsui groups have reaffirmed their group identities and have committed to carrying on, despite the loss of their lead banks. The Japanese press reported that the member companies of the *Fuyo-kai* and *Nimoku-kai* requested that the banks relinquish their council chairmanships. We are again indebted to Masahiro Shimotani for his observations here.

of a holding company, and only later the integration of system operations. This sequential strategy allowed for relatively easy decoupling should major roadblocks arise or if the banks' financial circumstances improved to the point that a merger was unnecessary.[50] As of early 2003, there is little sign of that. As we write, Mizuho is in danger of failing to meet BIS capital asset requirements and, in one rendition of the keiretsu bailout scenario, is peddling preferred shares to its partner firms in hopes of securing new capital.[51]

There was clearly an element of contagion in the 1990s consolidation wave. Executives of the later merging banks acknowledged the pressure they were under to respond to rivals' earlier announcements. No one at this dance wanted to be the last without a partner. The merger mania, moreover, was not confined to Japan, as U.S. and European firms were aggressively building vast financial empires, against which, Japanese business leaders feared, their financial players could not successfully compete.

Thus, the six horizontal groups that dominated Japan's industrial architecture since the early 1970s were evolving into something new. The groups had key features in common: the one-set principle of membership, presidents' and other executive councils, and group-wide undertakings aimed at building cohesion. Their consolidation into four may not spell the end of main bank relations, stable shareholding, risk-sharing interventions, or other trappings of the keiretsu system. The big six was an arbitrarily contrived network configuration emerging from a particular mix of historical events some decades before (among them, the merger of Dai-Ichi and Nippon Kangyo banks in 1971). Japan's corporate and financial networks predated the seventies and they may in some form survive the current restructuring wave as well.

Changing Corporate Governance Relationships in the 1990s

The 1990s witnessed the first move to change the fundamentals of Japanese corporate governance since the early post-war period. With the collapse of the bubble and the long decline in stock values, investors had lost sizable fortunes and were demanding more accountability from corporations. *Gaiatsu*, the foreign pressure that domestic reformers had often seized upon in pushing a reform agenda, played a role as well. The OECD and G7 industrial nations pressed Japan for greater disclosure and

---

[50] Indeed, many observers were critical of the slow progress being made in attaining the efficiencies that were the rationale for the earlier mergers (e.g., ending duplication of operations and administrative structures) and pointed instead to bank managers' continuing concern with protecting market share. Banks were even maintaining separate administrative structures and promotional lines years after their supposed integration.
[51] *Japan Times*, 6 February 2003.

transparency in corporate governance and accounting practice. Regulators and executives responded with an array of reform initiatives. Among them are the reintroduction of the holding company, adjustments to financial reporting requirements, new rules for boards of directors, and steps to discourage cross-shareholding.

1. Reintroduction of the Holding Company Structure

Holding companies had been banned in Japan since the U.S. Occupation sought to quash the economic and political power of the zaibatsu.[52] After years of lobbying by the business community, the Commercial Code was amended in 1997 to drop the ban, and in short order numerous companies announced plans to reorganize under holding companies. Already in wide use in U.S. financial services industries, the form was rapidly embraced by Japanese banks. Daiwa Securities became the first such firm to take advantage of the new law, and, as noted above, holding companies provided the umbrella structure for such new financial consolidations as Mizuho. Beyond financial services, fewer firms have thus far implemented the form, although for many the change is in the works. An example is Sanyo Electric, now converting to a legal holding company from the ersatz holding company or company system form it maintained for several years.[53] Each of the five Sanyo in-house companies is to become a wholly owned subsidiary, tailoring its employment and accounting systems to its particular line of business. In addition to corporate strategy, the parent company's responsibility will be group-wide administrative and financial activities.[54]

Thus, one use of the holding company is to enable the highly unitary Japanese corporation to shift decision making to the line-of-business level, encouraging product divisions to act as though they were independent firms. Why Japanese executives seem to feel that business unit decentralization demands a new structural and legal device is not

[52] According to Article 9 of Japan's Antimonopoly Law, holding companies are defined as "pure stockholding companies" in which the principal business consisted of controlling business activities of a company or companies in Japan.

[53] Perhaps in anticipation of the eventual removal of the holding company ban, a number of large corporations in the 1990s adopted a fictive or ersatz holding company form, the "within-company system" (*sha-nai bunsha seido*), devised by Sony in 1994. The structure is claimed to allow greater decentralization to the business unit level, more sensitivity to profit and loss, and faster response to market conditions. Sony president Nobuyuki Idei explained: "I want to see Sony grow by means of business units that are increasingly managed independently while interacting in a complementary fashion, influencing and helping one another." Hitachi announced in April 1999 it would set up ten independent in-house companies, each with its own management hierarchy and bottom line. Toshiba did the same with eight internal divisions (Ogawa, 1995; Shimotani, 1996).

[54] The new rules on consolidated earnings reporting have also been a factor in the adoption of holding companies (*Nikkei Net Interactive*, 23 August 1999).

altogether clear. Large U.S. firms such as General Electric or Johnson & Johnson endow operating divisions with broad autonomy without recourse to the holding company mechanism. The Japanese firms adopting the form, such as Sanyo, see the holding company as the strategic center of the corporation. Thus, they do not appear as true holding companies in the American sense of a legal and financial shell that merely owns the stock and aggregates the finances of a set of operating businesses.[55] Japanese executives' adoption of the holding company in their quest for decentralization may speak to the organic character of the Japanese corporation. Unless a division is organized as a bounded entity with its own president and board, employees identify less with *it* than with the broader corporation of which it is a part. Japanese firms have seized on the holding company structure as a template on which to forge a truly decentralized corporation – a network of semiautonomous product divisions monitored and coordinated through accounting controls. While divisionalized Japanese firms have been around for some time – most notably the large electronic and electrical machinery makers such as Hitachi and Matsushita – they are much more culturally and structurally unitary than has been the U.S. pattern.[56] Figuring in this is Japan's highly institutionalized internal labor market arrangements. Rewarding one division manager for strong financial performance while punishing another for poor results was simply not feasible under the prevailing rules of lifetime employment (*shushin koyo*) and seniority pay (*nenko joretsu*).[57]

A second use of the holding company form has more significance for the keiretsu question. Besides the big bank mergers, the consolidation under holding companies of Sogo and Seibu Department Stores, trading companies Nissho Iwai and Nichimen, Kawasaki Steel and NKK, and Konica and Minolta are pairings of this sort. The holding company is in effect a compromise solution that permits firms to retain their distinct identities while joining hands within a unified strategic and administrative framework.

Thus far, the new holding companies in Japan are serving either to consolidate independent firms of comparable stature or decentralize as wholly owned subsidiaries, the international product divisions of an existing corporation. They have yet to become the vehicle for converting a vertical keiretsu into a centrally owned and managed entity. The keiretsu form in which the parent company holds minority equity positions and participates in but does not dominate the management of affiliates still

---

[55] Williamson (1975), for example, contrasts the holding company structure ("H-form") with the multidivisional structure ("M-form") on this point. The M-form, in his view, is a strategically unified entity. The H-form is merely a shell.

[56] Fligstein (1990); Freeland (2001).

[57] Beer and Spector (1981); Sako (2004); Shimotani (1998).

has its uses and its supporters. Matsushita and Toyota have given active consideration to the holding company form as a means of bolstering the strategic unity of the group and, in Toyota's case, resisting foreign ownership. For the present, however, both have chosen instead simply to increase ownership of and impose more control over (e.g., through executive dispatches to) their affiliated firms.

Japanese companies have resisted merger for fear of losing corporate autonomy and commanding less business in combination than they could secure on their own. Construction firms, for example, have objected to government efforts to shrink the sector on the grounds that a large merged firm might win fewer government contracts than the merger partners could obtain independently. The Ministry of Land, Infrastructure, and Transport has reassured them that, if they convert to subsidiaries managed by a holding company, each such subsidiary may bid for contracts.[58]

A third use is to facilitate the closing or selling of a failing business. A holding company, reasoning went, makes it easier for a corporation to identify money-losing subsidiaries and declare them nonviable. Japanese courts require that firms act "reasonably" in their restructuring plans, generally interpreted to mean that marginally profitable enterprises may not eliminate jobs. Managers hope that a holding company might enable them to circumvent this rule by delegating more responsibility to business units and highlighting the performance differences. Also claimed is that the spin-off of failing businesses would help develop the merger and acquisitions market in Japan.

In 1995, for example, Reiichi Yumikura, the chairman of Keidanren's Committee on Competition Policy, argued that a holding company would enable the "quick decision-making, drastic actions, and continual searches for a new corporate structure . . . key . . . to survival in a borderless global economy." The holding company, in his view, would allow a parent firm to "attain flexible and efficient management for its group firms . . . by ensuring a constant flow of personnel and other business resources within the group." Holding company organization would encourage venture capital and enable firms to achieve the scale and scope essential to competitive success in the global economy.

What, then, is likely to be the impact on Japan's industrial architecture of the lifting of the holding company ban? Although it has its merits as a restructuring tool, skeptics see them fitting within the framework of the existing industrial architecture. The holding company facilitates merger and decentralization in the absence of a merger and acquisition market and in the presence of strong internal labor markets, without challenging these institutional arrangements head-on. Critics also see irony and

---

[58] *Nikkei Net Interactive,* 30 January 2002.

danger in the resurrection of the organizational form on which the pre-war zaibatsu were constructed.[59] Kazuo Inamori, chairman of Kyocera, a post-war corporation that, as a startup, struggled to overcome keiretsu barriers in supply and distribution, told the press: "The liberalization of holding companies would create monopolistic power in the economy, which would lead to the rebirth of the zaibatsu."[60] Champions of the form counter that the far more open economic and political environment of contemporary Japan renders that scenario unlikely. However, their vision of the holding company as a complete structural solution to the problems of organizational rigidity and centralization that beset the Japanese firm is hardly less fantastic.

2. Modifying Financial Reporting

Revision of financial reporting requirements is another key reform initiative aimed at increasing transparency and forcing responsiveness to shareholder interests. Among the Big Bang reforms were several provisions to bring Japanese accounting practice, infamous for its opaqueness, into line with International Accounting Standards. In their financial reports for the FY 1999 (ending 31 March 2000), public firms were required for the first time to generate consolidated accounts that subsume results from affiliates over which they have de facto control, even if the equity stake is small.[61] One of the ways keiretsu are thought to play a role in Japan's current economic crisis is that under the old accounting rules companies could hide both liabilities (e.g., from banks and investors) and assets (e.g., from tax authorities) in partner firms.[62] The accounting change may also curtail such keiretsu practices as moving personnel (*shukko*) to affiliates or the bailouts and restructurings that depend on clandestine resource transfers.[63] The accounting change led to a wave of liquidations as firms rushed to dispose of ailing subsidiaries in advance of the law's implementation.[64]

Another required change is the shift to mark-to-market accounting. Japanese banks and corporations have reported assets such as stocks and real estate at book rather than market value. In the bubble years, this practice enabled them to accumulate huge unrealized capital gains, which they leveraged into a worldwide buying spree. With the plummeting of

---

[59] Miyajima (1998).

[60] Interview at Kyocera headquarters, Kyoto, 2 June 1996.

[61] Beginning with FY 2000, companies were required to report their stockholdings at market rather than book value. For FY 2001, other assets must be reported at market value.

[62] At the end of the 1999 fiscal year, Nissan Motor's unconsolidated debts stood at ¥2.91 trillion. On a consolidated basis, they summed to ¥3.53 billion (Strom, 1999).

[63] *Nikkei Net Interactive*, 23 August 1999.

[64] *Nikkei Net Interactive*, 2 January 2000.

asset prices, the same accounting rules enabled firms to conceal large losses, which, if revealed, would threaten their capital reserves and ability to lend. In anticipation of the new rules, which came into effect on 1 April 2001, financial institutions began selling cross-held shares in client companies in order to erase from their books capital losses that might expose them as weaker than they had appeared.

Critics of Japan's network economy, whether domestic or foreign, see the new accounting rules as essential and overdue. How deep is their impact likely to be? Much of the pressure for accounting change was to harmonize Japanese standards with those of the world, thus removing a barrier to foreign capital flows into Japan. The new rules on the reporting of consolidated results and the current market value of assets (including cross-shareholdings) do go directly to the institutional basis for keiretsu structures and practices. Yet as the Enron, WorldCom, and the other recent U.S. accounting scandals show, given enough talented and creative accountants and lawyers, even the most transparent accounting systems can be effectively circumvented if the will to do so is there. It may have been easier to mask a company's true financial picture and its dealings with a network of partners under the old Japanese accounting regime, but it would be naïve to suppose that such practices cannot survive the new one.

3. Board Reform

Also geared to improving managerial accountability were proposals to change the structure and composition of boards of directors. An amendment to the Commercial Code in 1994 required the addition of an outside auditor to the board to ensure independent oversight of corporate finances. Another amendment in 1997 removed legal strictures on stock options, thereby making available an incentive mechanism popular in the United States and thought to be effective in aligning the interests of management with those of shareholders.

Beyond these regulatory changes, a number of large companies announced plans to reduce the size of their boards in order to speed decision making and end the practice of routinely granting director status to high-ranking executives. In the lead was historical pace-setter, Sony, the first Japanese company to list on an overseas stock exchange (New York), which had taken on independent (including foreign) board members at a time when few Japanese firms were doing so. Many such firms also announced changes in the duties performed by directors to improve their oversight capabilities. Under the new rules implemented in the commercial code in April 2003, firms have the option of keeping the traditional system of internal auditors or adapting the U.S. model of outside directors and an audit committee. In 2003, Sony, having trimmed its board from thirty-eight to ten in 1997, switched to the U.S. system and increased its outside directors from three to five.

Such moves, portrayed by the business press as major reform, are again of uncertain impact. In keeping with established practice, the outside auditor generally hailed from a partner company in the same keiretsu group.[65] Moreover, the firms adopting voluntary changes to their boards were typically mavericks like Sony: Westernized, sophisticated, and adroit at playing by global rules.[66] They were not, in other words, the firms most in need of the discipline that modern corporate governance might afford. According to a survey conducted by the Tokyo Stock Exchange, fewer than 40 percent of Japan's listed companies in the late 1990s planned or had already downsized their boards or appointed independent directors.[67] And even in the reform-minded companies, boards were dominated by insiders, the only outsiders being dispatched by a main bank or other keiretsu partner. In the wake of the U.S. corporate scandal wave of 2001–02, Japanese executives have became more resistant to corporate governance reforms designed to move Japan closer to U.S. practice. As we discuss at greater length below, Canon CEO Fujio Mitarai defended his firm's large board (twenty-one) of inside directors, saying that it breeds loyalty to the corporation.[68]

4. The Unwinding of Cross-Shareholding

Perhaps the most important change in the Japanese corporate governance system was the opening up of ownership to new investment groups and the associated decline in stable cross-shareholding by interlinked Japanese firms. Especially ominous for entrenched management teams was the rising share of stock controlled by overseas investors. At the end of FY 2001, foreigners controlled 19 percent of total market capitalization of domestically listed Japanese companies, up from 5 percent a decade earlier.[69] Foreign investors turned their shares over more frequently than domestic institutional investors did, thus ratcheting up the pressure on companies to improve earnings and share price. Moreover, the Commercial Code as amended in 1993 lowered the barriers to shareholder litigation in response to management misconduct. For example, the huge pension fund CalPers, with more than ¥4 billion in Japanese equities, proposed in March 1998 a series of steps Japanese corporations should take to bolster their governance practices.[70]

---

[65] Miyajima (1998).
[66] Ahmadjian (2003).
[67] Reported in Yasui (1999).
[68] *Business Week Online*, 13 September 2002.
[69] Tokyo Stock Exchange (2002).
[70] Yasui (1999).

Table 6.1. *Stability in the Ownership of Japan's Big-Five Steel Firms, 1979–99*

Company	1979 %	1989 %	1999 %
Nippon Steel			
1. IBJ	3.0	3.4	3.1
2. Nippon Life	2.9	3.0	4.1
3. Daiichi Life	2.0	1.8	2.7
4. Fuji Bank	1.8	1.8	
5. Asahi Life	1.8	2.0	
Sumitomo Metal Industries			
1. Sumitomo Trust Bank	6.0	5.5	7.5
2. Sumitomo Life	4.8	4.2	4.1
3. Nippon Life	4.6	3.9	4.0
4. Sumitomo Bank	4.1	3.7	3.5
5. IBJ	2.9	2.5	
NKK			
1. Fuji Bank	4.3	4.0	3.4
2. Daiichi Life	3.7	3.6	4.3
3. Nippon Life	3.3	3.0	3.2
4. Yasuda Life	2.8	3.1	2.6
5. Toa Life	2.5	3.0	2.1
Kobe Steel			
1. Sanwa Bank	4.5	3.6	3.4
2. DKB	4.5	3.6	3.7
3. Nippon Life	4.3	3.3	6.3
4. Taiyo-Kobe Bank	3.1	2.6	3.0*
5. IBJ	2.9	2.5	2.4
Kawasaki Heavy Industries			
1. DKB	4.7	4.5	4.5
2. LTCB	4.6	3.8	3.6
3. Nippon Life	4.5	3.5	5.5
4. Daiwa Bank	3.3	3.5	3.8
5. Taiyo-Kobe Bank	2.9	2.6	2.8*

* = Sakura Bank (formed out of merger of Taiyo-Kobe and Mitsui Banks).
Source: *Kigyo keiretsu soran*, various years. Tokyo: Toyo Keizai Shinposha.

The figures highlight a sea change in Japanese equities markets, with domestic banks and corporate clients moving to unwind long-standing interlocking shareholding relationships and foreign investors actively buying Japanese stock with the simple intent of reaping future capital gains. The shift spells changes in the way Japanese companies are managed. As major new shareholders, foreign investors have clamored for a bigger voice in Japanese corporate governance.

Despite these changes and press announcements to the contrary, stable and patient institutional shareholding remained the norm for most large

Table 6.2. *Stability in the Ownership of Japan's Big-Five Electronics Firms, 1979–99*

Company	1979 %	1989 %	1999 %
Hitachi			
1. Nippon Life	4.2	4.1	3.9
2. Dai-Ichi Life	2.7	2.7	2.7
3. Asahi Life	2.6	1.0	
4. IBJ	2.4	2.4	2.0
5. Hitachi group employees	2.3	2.1	3.2
Toshiba			
1. General Electric	10.2		
2. Dai-Ichi Life	4.8	4.3	3.8
3. Nippon Life	3.7	3.6	3.4
4. Mitsui Trust Bank	2.4	3.1	1.3
5. Mitsui Bank	2.3	3.1	3.7*
Mitsubishi Electric			
1. Meiji Life	5.2	3.9	4.2
2. Nippon Life	4.6	3.6	3.6
3. Mitsubishi Bank	3.3	3.1	4.1**
4. Mitsubishi Trust Bank	3.2	5.0	1.7
5. Mitsui Trust Bank	2.5	4.1	1.6
NEC			
1. Sumitomo Life	9.4	7.0	4.7
2. Sumitomo Bank	6.8	4.7	4.7
3. Nippon Life	3.9	3.6	3.2
4. Sumitomo Marine & Fire	3.8	2.7	2.5
5. Dai-Ichi Life	3.6	3.1	2.2
Fujitsu			
1. Fuji Electric	21.7	13.9	12.6
2. Asahi Life	9.5	6.7	6.2
3. DKB	9.1	4.7	4.1
4. IBJ	3.4	2.4	2.2
5. Mitsui Trust Bank	2.9	1.6	

* = Sakura Bank (formed from the merger of Taiyo-Kobe and Mitsui Banks).
** = Tokyo-Mitsubishi Bank (formed out merger of Bank of Tokyo and Mitsubishi Bank).
Source: Kigyo keiretsu soran, various years. Tokyo: Toyo Keizai Shinposha.

companies through the nineties, as Tables 6.1–6.3 make clear.[71] Tables 6.1 and 6.2 provide a list of the five largest shareholders in 1979 in Japan's big-five steelmakers and big-five electronics producers, as well as their shareholding percentage that year. To map ownership over time, the table also shows these investors' percentages at two later points: ten years later (1989), at the peak of the bubble economy, and twenty years later (1999),

[71] Gerlach (1991).

Table 6.3. *Overall Patterns of Stability and Change among Major Steel and Electronics Firms, 1979–99*

	1979–89	1989–99	Subtotal
Stable[a]			
Steel	25	18	43
Electronics	13	16	29
SUBTOTAL	38	34	72
Increases[b]			
Steel	0	4	4
Electronics	2	1	3
SUBTOTAL	2	5	7
Decreases			
Steel	0	0	0
Electronics	9	5	14
SUBTOTAL	9	5	14
Eliminations[c]			
Steel	0	3	3
Electronics	1	2	3
SUBTOTAL	1	5	6

[a] "Stable" shareholding is defined as proportional increases or decreases in ownership (out of 100%) of 1.0% or less during the decade.
[b] Increases and decreases are defined as changes in ownership over the decade of greater than 1.0%.
[c] Eliminations are those investors that no longer appear in top-shareholder lists in the following decade.
Source: Calculated from Tables 1 and 2.

at the end of the lost decade. A casual eyeballing of the tables suggests that most owners of stock appear as major shareholders in all ten companies in the later two periods and in most cases their ownership stakes are fairly similar to the initial period.

Table 6.3 provides some summary statistics from the tables that make this stability clearer. Taking as our basis the assumption that a proportional change in total ownership of plus or minus 1 percent or less over a decade represents stable shareholding, we can demonstrate several patterns. First, the vast majority of shareholders in 1979 remain stable using this definition throughout each of the two following decades (thirty-eight out of fifty in the 1980s and thirty-four out of fifty in the 1990s). Not surprisingly, given the turbulent nature of the industry, ownership of electronics firms is somewhat more dynamic than in steel, but even here, the majority of investors appear as leading shareholders throughout the twenty-year period. When comparing the two decades, we find a slight decline in investors classified as stable during the later decade (thirty-four vs. thirty-eight), but this is countered by the fact that the number of investors increasing their positions is larger (five vs. two) and the number of investors decreasing their positions is smaller (five vs. nine). Taken together, these data show no evidence for increasing shareholding instability for these ten companies in the 1990s. Instead, we find a remarkable degree of stability across both decades and across both sectors.

How do we square these patterns with all the recent talk of declining stable shareholding in Japan? Consider the *process* involved when a hard-pressed bank or corporation is forced to sell its holdings in affiliated firms. In fact, the seller typically has the acknowledgment and acquiescence of the partner firms and the transfer of the shares is handled so that they are sure to remain in friendly hands. Sometimes the selling firm immediately bought back the shares at market prices, enabling it to report profit from the sale while honoring its obligations as stable shareholders. In others cases, the firms arranged inside deals with affiliated third parties to buy back those stocks in order to maintain both the price and solidarity of the group.

Still, if the pattern of stable shareholding remained largely unaltered through the end of the 1990s, the picture changed as the century turned. A major spur was the 1 April 2001 accounting rule change, requiring corporations to report assets at market, rather than book, value.[72] Given the depressed stock market, the new rules exposed many banks as much worse off than under the old reporting regime and with inadequate capital to support their lending. Consequently, in anticipation of the change, the banks rapidly unloaded cross-held shares. The *Wall Street Journal* commented:

> For more than a century, interlocking shareholdings have defined corporate Japan. Banks have owned chunks of their borrowers, and borrowers their banks; many of these companies have banded into vast corporate groups with names like Mitsubishi, Mitsui and Sumitomo. Such ties have bound their fortunes together and protected them from takeovers. . . . Japan is lurching through one of the biggest transfers of corporate ownership in the past 50 years. The relentless selling of once-stable shareholdings is a prime force behind both the recent plunge in the benchmark Nikkei stock average and the nation's broader decade-old bear market. . . . According to a study by NLI Research Institute, "stable" shareholdings accounted for 38% of all Japanese stocks, by value, in 1999, the most recent year for which data are available, down from 48% in 1992. In 1999 alone, one out of 12 stable

---

[72] Another deadline looming is September 2004, at which time Japanese banks must lower their shareholdings to equal or less than their core capital. As noted previously, Sumitomo Mitsui Banking Corporation reduced its holdings in Toyota Motor by 65 million shares or a decrease from 5 percent to 3.2 percent. See *Nikkei Net Interactive*, 16 November 2002.

shares – defined as those held long term by financial institutions and other corporations for relationship reasons – changed hands. And Shuhei Abe, president of Sparx Asset Management here, predicts that Japanese banks, which have already been prime sellers, will unload the equivalent of an additional 3% to 5% of the market's capitalization this year.[73]

It is useful to take a closer look at the NLI (Nippon Life Insurance) Research Institute analysis of recent cross-shareholding trends from 1987 to 2000 referred to in the *Journal* piece.[74] Figure 6.1 reproduces a graph from the NLI report. We have used the term *cross-shareholding* to refer to one firm's stake in another. NLI calls this "long-term shareholding" and restricts the term *cross-shareholding* to *reciprocated* cross-ownership. It gives the ratio of the value of cross-held shares to total market capitalization of Tokyo Stock Exchange-listed firms, as well as ratio of the *number* of shares to the volume of shares held.[75] In fact, all four measures trend

[73] Dvorak, Guth, Singer, and Zaun (2001).
[74] Kuroki (2001).
[75] Due to a number of significant institutional alterations in Japan's economic environment in fiscal year 2000 (1 April 2000–31 March 2001), NLI adjusted its data for this year. For the first time in the survey's history, firms were included that had been delisted at the fiscal year's close due to merger or acquisition. The biggest mergers were the large financial consolidations (the consolidation of the Fuji, DKB, and IBJ banks into the Mizuho Group; Mitsui and Sumitomo Banks into Sumitomo-Mitsui; Mitsubishi Trust and Tokyo-Mitsubishi Bank into Mitsubishi Tokyo Financial Group; Sanwa, Tokai, and Toyo Trust Banks into UFJ). Thus, their survey covered 2,587 Tokyo Stock Exchange-listed companies and 14 delisted companies for a total of 2,601 whose total market capitalization was ¥368 trillion. Another regulatory change in the financial reporting of retirement benefits caused many firms to place cross-shareholdings in pension trusts at the close of FY 2000. NLI assumes that this does not constitute the unwinding of cross-shareholdings, since the company contributing the shares kept its voting rights over them. Similarly, NLI assumes that cross-shareholdings between the member banks of the Mizuho group and their corporate partners were not materially changed by their folding into a holding company in FY 2000. Thus, DKB and Hitachi Ltd. are presumed to have an equity-holding relationship, but Hitachi's stock is now in Mizuho, not in DKB. Finally, a change in Ministry of Finance disclosure rules affected reporting in one of the survey's key sources, the *Yuka shoken meisaihyo*. Beginning in FY 2001, publicly listed Japanese companies were required to use fair value accounting standards to price their stockholdings and other assets at current market values. Some companies, however, had already made the conversion and reported their holdings under the new FY 2000 rules. While we take no particular issue with any one of NLI's adjustments to deal with the accounting and governance changes clumped at the millennium's end, they do highlight the problems of taking a long panel such as ours up to the present. After 1997, the last year of data we collected and analyzed, the systemic discontinuities in Japanese economic organization reached a point that the assumptions framing our research no longer hold. We deal with a regime that remained largely in place, albeit with various piecemeal institutional changes along the way, from the late 1960s to 1997. Thereafter, restructuring consisted of fundamental shifts in the legal and other institutions governing economic play. The questions of further evolving network form must be addressed within a different framework from that in which our research has been set.

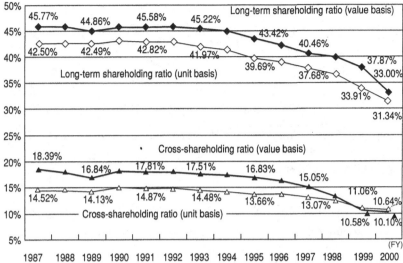

Figure 6.1. Trends in cross-shareholding for publicly listed corporations. *Source:* NLI Research Institute.

about the same. The bubble is shown to be a trough in the incidence of stable and reciprocal shareholding, the next two years bringing a rise. Apart from the fall-off in 1989, both indicators held steady until 1994. The subsequent decline, steeper in stable shareholding than in cross-shareholding, was mild until 1997, the year of the Asian financial crisis, when it picked up speed. Interestingly, from the 1999 to 2000 fiscal year, stable shareholding fell sharply, but cross-(reciprocated) shareholding leveled off. It appears that banks and corporations exercised some selectivity in their elimination of stable holdings: They retained the reciprocated ones – those most symbolic of keiretsu commitments – while quickly disposing of others.

NLI also compiled data on cross-shareholding trends within the big-six horizontal groups (Figure 6.2). They, too, reveal relative stability up to 1999, followed by marked declines from 1999 to 2000. The descent is particularly steep in the case of Mitsubishi group, where cross-shareholding declined by 2.5 percent, as compared with the other groups' 1 percent drops. Mitsubishi firms had been increasing their cross-shareholding through the decade, so that by 1999 it was roughly twice that of every group save Sumitomo. Mitsubishi's decline put its intragroup holdings where they were in 1988 and on a par with Sumitomo (at ~9 percent).

How can we reconcile the seemingly contradictory trends revealed in Figures 6.1 and 6.2: stabilization of cross-shareholding in 1999–2000 for the population of Tokyo Stock Exchange public firms combined with

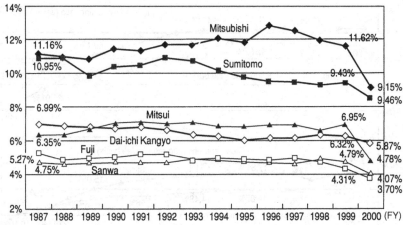

Figure 6.2. Trends in cross-shareholding within the big-six horizontal groups.
Source: NLI Research Institute.

sharp declines for the same period within the horizontal groups? Clearly, the lead financials of the groups were dumping cross-held shares in anticipation of the 2001 accounting rule change. Otherwise, the densities of intragroup equity ties held stable.

The Shoei Case: Cross-Shareholdings Block a Takeover

The attempted takeover of trading company Shoei at the end of the decade, reported as emblematic of the breakdown of stable shareholding, is in fact a case study in the opposite. Shoei was a little-known real estate and electronics parts company that had long been a member of the Fuyo group. Its leading shareholder was Canon, a Fuyo member, which together with Fuji Bank owned 16.25 percent of Shoei's shares. Dispatched Fuji managers had held the president's spot at Shoei for the past fifty years and, at the time of the takeover move, two of the six board seats and one of the two corporate auditor positions. Excluding board members, the company had only forty-four employees.[76] According to one account, "Shoei served as a place to give former directors of Fuji and its sister financial companies, Yasuda Trust and Banking Company, Yasuda Fire and Marine Insurance Company, and Yasuda Mutual Life Insurance Company, a second job and a means of maintaining their golf club memberships and chauffeured car service after retirement."[77]

[76] Landers (2000a).
[77] Landers (2000c).

In January 2000, Yoshiaki Murakami, a former MITI bureaucrat, started an acquisition fund and made Shoei his first target. While Fuji Bank's president had publicly signaled intentions to sever equity ties with Fuyo group firms, the bank and its sister insurers and trust banks chose to stand by Shoei and refused Murakami's tender offer. "Things are OK as they are," a Canon spokesman said. "We take a long-term view. We're not seeking a short-term profit."[78] As a result, Murakami upped his stake in Shoei only slightly – from 2.78 percent to 6.52 percent – and gave up the battle. In the end, therefore, the significance of the Shoei episode is not the takeover attempt per se. Such actions, generally aimed at greenmail (getting management to buy the raider's shares at a steep premium), are not uncommon in Japan (most notably the T. Boone Pickens move on Toyota supplier, Koito). The real significance of the case is in the continued reluctance of stable shareholders, including hard-pressed financial institutions, to sell their shares to unfriendly investors, even in a weak economy and at the end of a decade of falling share values.

Another regulatory change actually strengthened incumbent management teams' ability to fend off takeover threats: an amendment to the Commercial Code in 1995 lifted a post-war ban on stock buybacks. A management buyout, in which a company takes shares off the market, is a common U.S. corporate tactic to lower takeover risk and bolster sagging stock prices. The regulatory change was strongly supported by Japanese business leaders, alarmed at the steep descent of asset values through the 1990s. By the middle of 1998, nearly half of all publicly traded Japanese firms had announced plans for buybacks.[79]

Japan's New Economy, Part 2: Production and Technology Systems

Japan's manufacturing industries were powerful drivers of the country's pre- and post-war economic growth, but in the 1990s they, too, faced a combination of threats unparalleled since the early post-war years. New technologies and business models, most notably those based on information technology and the Internet, exposed firms in all major industries to wrenching shifts in core markets. Global integration (including trade tensions) and competition were altering cost structures and driving manufacturers to move production and procurement offshore. Similar forces challenge intensified and economic planners everywhere, of course, but

[78] Landers (2000b).
[79] Yasui (1999).

they were exacerbated in Japan's case by the problems of high factor costs, overcapacity, and persistent economic stagnation.

As with the financial system, the changes in Japanese manufacturing are rooted in the appreciation of the yen and the heightened trade frictions of the 1980s. Along with intensified competition from other Asian economies,[80] such pressures accelerated worldwide dispersion of Japanese production, as transplants in automobiles, electronics, and machinery negotiated favorable arrangements with local authorities, hired local labor, and launched operations abroad. However, the shift to offshore operations had limited impact on management and governance practice, for iron-clad control from Tokyo or Osaka generally preserved the carefully orchestrated employment and technical relationships at the core of the Japanese firm.

Instead of substituting genuinely foreign goods for domestic ones, Japanese companies often sourced from their own foreign-based subsidiaries. Thus, in contrast to the pattern of international vertical integration set by U.S. and European multinationals – moving forward from production to market – Japanese firms reversed the sequence by integrating backward from control of markets to sources of supply.[81] As pressures on Japan to increase imports grew, Japanese companies often chose to buy the foreign producers rather than the foreign products. Thus, production, distribution, and even some design and development shifted overseas while ownership and control stayed in Japanese hands.[82] What restructuring took place did little violence to the complex hierarchical system of network positions and roles.

The Evolution of Production Networks in the 1990s

The downwardly spiraling economy of the 1990s and the escalating demands of the emergent new economy sped the process of restructuring already under way, but it also triggered a more fundamental reevaluation of production systems by Japanese manufacturers. Managers and policy makers debated which activities should be performed in-house and which should be spun-off and outsourced. They reconceptualized supply chain organization and took steps to rationalize it, for example, by cutting off long-term keiretsu suppliers and taking procurement online. In some industries, foreign firms acquired large equity positions in Japanese

---

[80] See Abegglen and Stalk (1985).

[81] Some have suggested that this distinctive pattern explains Japan's lack of intraindustry trade. See Lawrence (1991).

[82] Katz (1998) reports, for example, that by the mid-1990s, 80 percent of Japan's lost domestic output in the aluminum industry was supplied by imports from Japanese-owned plants overseas.

producers and globalized strategic functions that had long been controlled from Japan.

While the business press portrayed these changes as a series of linear moves toward an open market economy, the restructuring in fact consisted of a good deal of zigzagging. Centrifugal and centripetal forces clashed in drawing the boundaries between core firms and satellite affiliates, so that, instead of disappearing, keiretsu supply relations were in many cases reshaped and extended in altered form. How the restructuring process played out varied from one sector to the next, as domestically oriented industries such as construction or chemicals were much slower to change than industries facing strong international competition, such as automobiles and electronics.

In this section, we consider the following forces for change: the shifting boundaries of large firms as they shrank core workforces while increasing reliance on strategic partnerships, the global keiretsu-ization of Japan's automobile industry, Renault's takeover of Nissan, and Toyota's moves to protect and control its supply chain. Our focus is the automobile industry, which found itself again at the forefront of industrial change. While Japan's automakers' mastery of the lean manufacturing paradigm had given it a significant advantage in production efficiency and quality, they now found global competitors catching up in many areas and were thus in need of new strategies. What adjustments was the industry making and with what impact? Would they lead Japan to a new era of genuine globalization – one in which investment and business models flowed not only out of Japan but in as well?

1. Shifting Boundaries of the Firm

Even as the Japanese economy stagnated in the 1990s, the yen stayed strong and the domestic costs of doing business remained high. For large manufacturers a solution was to make less and purchase more from lower-cost suppliers. The decade thus witnessed heightened attention to *boundary management* – the strategic sorting of business activities into what stayed in and what was shifted outside the boundaries of the firm. Large manufacturers sought to assess their capabilities at each stage of the supply chain; they then rearranged production activities to make the best use of core competencies.[83]

Thus, manufacturers increased both domestic and offshore outsourcing, both overseas and domestically, while retaining control over core

---

[83] This process was not limited to Japanese manufacturers, of course. But what distinguished Japanese companies was the extent to which outside suppliers – most importantly, keiretsu affiliates – were included in the strategic reorganizing process. See Ahmadjian and Lincoln (2001) on the implications of Toyota's vertical integration into electronics for its relations with Toyota group suppliers of electronic components.

strengths in design, systems coordination, and marketing. Offshore procurement had also accelerated in the 1980s owing to trade pressures and domestic-content rules, but in the 1990s the focus shifted from North American and European sites to Asian venues, as concerns with cost reduction prevailed over those of accommodating trading partners. Coupled with the growth in offshore procurement, the offshore workforce of many large firms grew at the expense of domestic employees. Matsushita doubled its overseas workforce from the early to late 1990s (to 134,000 employees) but took on only 6,000 new workers in Japan (to a total of 148,000). Hitachi also nearly doubled its overseas workforce, but reduced its domestic employment by 3 percent.[84]

Has the geographic dispersion of Japanese manufacturing supply chains marked the end of keiretsu (long-term, high trust) supply relations? Evidence from a MITI survey of small and medium-sized enterprises (SMEs) at the end of the 1990s suggests not. As of 1998, 55 percent of the manufacturing SMEs in the survey remained primarily involved in subcontracting work for large parent companies. Although this figure was down from a peak of 66 percent in 1981, it remained enormous by international standards and was a 52 percent increase over two years before.[85] Among SMEs that were primarily subcontractors, more than four-fifths (81.6 percent) reported that their largest trading partner had remained unchanged over *the entire lifetime* of the company, while an additional 11.2 percent reported that they had changed principal customers only once. Less than 8 percent in other words, or one in twelve, had changed parent companies more than once. Moreover, the reasons these firms gave for working as subcontractors were familiar from the past: to stabilize demand and reduce sales risks. Despite the increased attention to Japanese manufacturers devoted to boundary management, the structure of domestic supply networks displayed considerable stability.[86]

There are several reasons for the stability. First, the shift to Asian sourcing was limited to two main sectors, electrical and transportation machinery, whose well-established keiretsu networks were transferable overseas.[87] Second, the offshore movement of production in these industries was carried out through the same process of *uchi-soto* (inward-out) internationalization that had characterized Japan's Western transplants in

---

[84] *Economist*, 27 November 1999.

[85] Reported in the *Chusho kigyo hakusho* (MITI, 1999).

[86] Reviewing the same MITI study, Dore (2000:140) likewise comments that "there is no evidence of substantial change in subcontracting patterns." He cites the Toyota supply network's smooth response to the Aisin Seiki plant fire in 1997 as testimony to the continuing efficiency advantages of keiretsu-style subcontracting. See Nishiguchi and Beaudet (1998).

[87] Lawrence (1991) cites evidence of vertical keiretsu participation of 43 percent in electrical machinery and 63.9 percent in motor vehicles.

the 1980s. That is, manufacturers outsourced the more peripheral, lower value parts of the supply chain while keeping the high value parts and all the strategic control in Japan.[88]

Third, and most important, balanced against the centrifugal force of offshore procurement was an equally powerful centripetal force: Japanese manufacturers were reducing domestic workforce size by increasing reliance on *domestic* suppliers. This helps to explain the MITI survey result that, of those supplier relations changing in recent years, most were *strengthening* rather than weakening ties. The domestic suppliers remained the preferred providers of those critical components, the disruption of which could shut down the entire supply chain. These suppliers had long histories as trustworthy and reliable partners; the relationships were reinforced by ownership stakes taken and executives dispatched by customer firms.

Moreover, subcontract relations were carrying into the postindustrial, service-oriented economy emerging over the decade. According to the MITI survey, more SMEs were involved in subcontracting work in information services than in any other sector (at 72.2 percent). This was probably because many of the firms providing those services began life as spin-offs of larger companies. But whatever the reasons, it appears again that new economy networks were being recast in an old economy mold.

Still, amid the continuing pressures of a weak economy, the most recent signs are that large manufacturers are paring their domestic supplier base. In 2002, the major electronics firms all announced plans to lower their procurement costs by standardizing parts and reducing the number of suppliers they buy from. Many customers have also been switching to online procurement systems, which give them fast access to a worldwide vendor network.[89]

2. The Global Keiretsu-ization of Japan's Automobile Industry
While the Asia shift of the first half of the 1990s represented a continuation of the inward-out internationalization patterns pursued by Japanese manufacturers in the 1980s, a new shift appeared in the second half of the decade: sharply rising foreign direct investment, most notably in motor vehicles. Foreign companies had complained for years about Japan's structural trade barriers, with automobiles and auto parts routinely topping

---

[88] See Lawrence's chapter in Okuno-Fujiwara (1991) and comments by Nolan.
[89] *Nikkei Weekly*, 3 June 2002. We have interviewed several firms switching to online procurement systems about the meaning of this shift for Japan's vaunted high-trust, long-term supplier relations. Their response is generally that electronic sourcing augments rather than substitutes for close, face-to-face transactions. A trusting relationship with a supplier cannot be created online, but the online system is useful in identifying potential suppliers and, once the relation is established, expediting transactions.

the trade negotiations list. Ironically, it was not government mandates but private sector choices that provided the impetus for change. By the end of the decade, it could reasonably be said that the automobile industry was Japan's (and probably the world's) most global industry.

The introduction of foreign capital into the Japanese auto industry, although hardly representative of the low foreign direct investment (FDI) flowing into the economy as a whole, posed for the first time since the pre-war period the possibility of the kind of *soto-uchi* internationalization of a key sector that might fundamentally challenge how Japanese business was done. How were these investments transforming the Japanese automobile industry? Were foreign stakeholders demanding radical restructurings from the Japanese firms they bought into – such as layoffs or the streamlining of supplier relations? Renault's acquisition of a controlling stake in Nissan in 1999 and the French company's restructuring plan for the troubled Japanese automaker offer one sharply defined answer (discussed below), but it was arguably an atypical one.

The evidence available as of this writing suggests a different interpretation. Foreign producers were forming alliances with their Japanese rivals less to garner the rents from restructuring inefficient operations than to circumvent the still formidable structural barriers to Japanese market access, acquiring important capabilities in supply chain management and manufacturing, and establishing beachheads in other Asian markets. Further, they took partial equity positions because full vertical integration remained difficult in Japan due to regulatory barriers, keiretsu obligations, and internal labor markets conditions. These foreign companies, in other words, were not so much sweeping aside the extant industrial architecture as they were redirecting and realigning that architecture. The global keiretsu-ization of Japanese auto production is an apt characterization of what went on.

The phenomenon was not confined to motor vehicles. An official of Texas Instruments, for example, explained to the *Wall Street Journal* (7 June 1993) that the expanding success of foreign semiconductor chip makers in Japan was chiefly because "foreign partners are becoming part of the Japanese keiretsu." Similarly, *Business Week* (22 July 1996) described the "keiretsu connections" that were introducing foreign computer, power generating equipment, and industrial machinery companies into the Japanese market. Still, it was among Japan's motor vehicle producers that the process by the end of the 1990s had progressed the most.

The groundbreakers were Ford and Mazda. Ford began buying Mazda trucks for sale in Asia in 1971 and approached Mazda soon after about buying a share in the company. Ford's overtures were rebuffed by Mazda management until the late 1970s, when Mazda's main bank, Sumitomo, arranged for Ford to help Mazda recover from the devastation of the oil shocks.[90] By the early 1990s, Ford held 25 percent of Mazda's stock and had placed three outside directors and one full-time dispatched director on its board. It had also managed to cut costs at Mazda in the Japanese manner: by freezing wages and paying down debt rather than imposing layoffs or cutting off suppliers.

These foreign partners involved themselves in a wide range of operational activities, reinforced by periodic senior management strategy group meetings. Know-how sharing included Ford providing expertise in styling, international marketing, and finance to Mazda and Mazda providing know-how in supplier management to Ford. (Ford was especially interested in learning from Mazda how to improve the quality and delivery performance of its suppliers.) By one estimate, one-quarter of all Ford cars by this time and two-fifths of all Mazda cars were produced with some tangible input from the other company.[91] Mazda also used its distribution channels to sell Ford vehicles, and Ford became the best-selling American nameplate in Japan. This relationship continued deepening through the decade, and by the late 1990s, Ford controlled 33.4 percent of Mazda and so gained veto power over important company decisions. It had also installed more of its own executives, including Mazda's president.

Following Ford's example was General Motors (GM), which for years had tried to sell into Japan with little success. GM instead made a different kind of headway by taking advantage of the fall in Japanese share prices to piece together a number of equity alliances with Japanese automobile makers. For GM's partners, here was an opportunity to consolidate operations – ironically, something MITI industrial policy makers had repeatedly attempted and failed to do. This network included a new 20 percent stake in Fuji Heavy Industries (Subaru), announced in December 1999, and gradual steps to boost its existing stakes in Isuzu (now 49 percent) and Suzuki Motor (10 percent). The combined share of this network in Japan, the world's number two market, was 18 percent in 1999, second only to Toyota and its affiliates (with 38 percent). By the end of the decade, Japanese executives were starting to refer with both respect and fear to the "GM keiretsu."[92]

European auto firms were slower to become involved in direct investment networks, but they maintained a number of significant sales and production outsourcing arrangements among various manufacturers. Mitsubishi Motors and Volvo formed the first significant direct investment relationship when, in October 1999, Mitsubishi Motors announced that it would spin off its bus and truck divisions by the end of 2001 and sell

[90] Pascale and Rohlen (1983).
[91] *Business Week*, 10 February 1992.
[92] *Wall Street Journal*, 26 January 2000.

a 20 percent stake in the unit to Volvo. In another example of global keiretsu-ization, Mitsubishi and Volvo agreed to a cross-shareholding arrangement whereby each took a 5 percent stake in the other.[93]

3. The Nissan Shock

The above deals all involved second-tier Japanese automakers. That changed when Nissan stunned the Japanese business community with its announcement in March 1999 that it would sell a substantial stake to the French automaker Renault and form a far-ranging alliance. From its pre-war role in the Nissan–Hitachi zaibatsu to its head-to-head rivalry with Toyota for dominance in the 1980s Japanese auto market, Nissan had been a symbol of Japanese manufacturing might, and its steep descent into insolvency and humbling takeover by Renault was poignant testimony to how weak Japan had become.

Nissan had struggled for years with shrinking market share and falling revenues. It had a $4.1 billion line of credit with a group of ten banks, but this consortium (led by Nissan's main banks, IBJ and Fuji, whose ties to Nissan went back before the war) lacked the strength to nurse Nissan back to health. Nissan hung on with large infusions of government assistance: it issued large sums of short-term commercial paper that were bought by the Bank of Japan, and it received $7 billion in credit from the government through the Japan Development Bank. Nissan's restructuring efforts preceded the Renault alliance, as it had sold assets, including its Ginza headquarters, a piece of its textile machinery business, and stakes in an advertising agency and a printing company.[94]

While Renault was a smaller company and lacked the global cachet Nissan once enjoyed as a heavyweight industrial player, it had successfully turned its own troubled operations around and sought an encore performance in Japan. Renault bought 36.8 percent – a controlling share – of Nissan's stock, with warrants that could eventually raise its stake to 44 percent. In addition, Renault bought 22.5 percent of Nissan's deeply troubled subsidiary, Nissan Diesel Motor Company. In return, Nissan got the option to buy some of the French government's 44 percent stake in Renault and a promise that Nissan's CEO would eventually get a board seat.[95]

The leader of Renault's earlier turnaround, Carlos Ghosn, known at Renault as "Le Cost Killer," took on the post of president and chief operating officer at Nissan, bringing with him to the 40,000-employee firm forty French executives.[96] After half a year of study, the Ghosn team and

[93] *Wall Street Journal*, 11 October 1999.
[94] *New York Times*, 11 March 1999.
[95] *New York Times*, 28 February 2000.
[96] *New York Times*, 27 March 1999.

Nissan sent additional shockwaves by announcing the Nissan Revival Plan in October 1999. This draconian cost reduction plan included five plant closings in Japan, a 14 percent headcount reduction of 21,000 jobs, and a ¥1 trillion ($9.48 billion) cut in annual costs over three years.[97] The news of the employment cutbacks was softened, however, by Ghosn's announced intention to achieve them through attrition, use of part-time employees, spin-offs, and early retirement.

One of the most interesting features of Renault's restructuring plan for Nissan was its provisions for Nissan's network of parts suppliers. The Ghosn team announced plans to halve the number of suppliers Nissan buys from, from 1,145 to some 600, over a three-year period, as well as to reduce its cross-shareholdings in these firms. Renault also announced plans to winnow equipment and service suppliers from 6,900 to no more than 3,400 and close 10 percent of its dealerships.[98] Ghosn expressed concern that multiple sourcing, intended to encourage competition among suppliers and build a stable supply base, had in fact pushed costs up by reducing scale economies. It thus appeared that the pain of restructuring would fall most heavily upon Nissan's smallest and most specialized suppliers, many of which had done business only with Nissan and whose margins were too thin to absorb a 20 percent cost cut.

The business press was quick to cast this aggressive cost-cutting plan as the death-knell of the Nissan vertical keiretsu. The *Wall Street Journal* wrote,

> The tough restructuring plan unveiled Monday by Nissan Motor Co. deals another blow to a time-honored but tottering pillar of Japan Inc.: the keiretsu system of suppliers.... Nissan's plan marks only the latest move to unwind keiretsu ties here, but it is the most dramatic yet. It could put into play dozens of components makers, and thus spark more purchases of Japanese suppliers by big foreign parts makers.[99]

While Western journalists applauded Ghosn's assault on the Nissan supply keiretsu, Japan's political establishment saw it differently. Less than twenty-four hours after Ghosn's announcement, Prime Minister Keizo Obuchi and other cabinet-level officials issued statements criticizing Renault and offered assurances that the government would mitigate the impact of the Nissan cutbacks on suppliers and local communities. Said Obuchi, "We are not in a position to interfere in individual management decisions, but we believe it is necessary for them [the Ghosn team] to cope

---

[97] *Wall Street Journal*, 18 October 1999.
[98] Ibid.
[99] *Wall Street Journal*, 20 October 1999.

as much as they can with the plan's effect on the company's employment situation and subcontractors." He then ordered the Labor Ministry to prepare a report on Nissan's restructuring plan.[100] Chief Cabinet Secretary and top government spokesman Mikio Aoki suggested that Nissan was forfeiting its obligations to society: "Restructuring is necessary, but we believe that companies should also shoulder big responsibilities that are brought about by such a step, such as unemployment problems." Similarly, Japan's trade minister, Takashi Fukuya, told reporters, "I'm very worried about the affiliated subcontractors.... These companies have to study ways to survive on their own, but the government would like to extend as much help as possible."

4. Toyota's Countervailing Moves to Protect Its Own Supply Chain

While Japan's weakest motor vehicle producers were being drawn into the vortex of a global ownership network, the industry's strongest player was taking steps to protect its affiliated suppliers and subcontactors from the overtures of foreign suitors. Toyota Motor was not only far and away Japan's largest and most powerful automobile company. Its enormous international prestige, leadership role in Keidanren (Japan's foremost trade association), and competitive track record had positioned it over the past several decades as Japan's most influential company in any industry.

One of Toyota's concerns was that foreign auto parts producers were to follow the lead of the major foreign car companies in scoping opportunities in the Japanese market. Germany's Robert Bosch took stakes in several Japanese parts suppliers, including 5.2 percent of Denso – perhaps the most prominent member of the Toyota vertical keiretsu. Delphi Automotive Systems, a divested (in 1999) parts division of General Motors, had purchased a 6 percent stake in Akebono Brake Industry Company, 14 percent owned by Toyota, and was eyeing other prospects in Japan. French auto parts producer Valeo was also shopping for Japanese parts suppliers.[101]

These encroachments by foreigners did not sit well with Toyota. Said Toyota's chairman, Hiroshi Okuda: "We still have the sales and marketing abilities and vitality to remain pure-blooded.... Why mix different nationalities and cultures at this stage of our development when we don't have to?" The reference to pure-bloodedness recalls the 1960s, when Japanese auto assemblers moved aggressively to raise their stakes in core parts producers in anticipation of capital market liberalization.[102] In his nativist wording, Okuda was taking aim, not merely at outsider control

[100] *New York Times*, 20 October 1999.
[101] *Wall Street Journal*, 3 August 1999.
[102] Mason (1992).

of Toyota's supply network, but specifically *foreign* influence. For their part, Toyota's parts suppliers said that they too were concerned about foreign encroachment and would welcome closer ties to Toyota. A Denso spokesman was quoted as saying "we wouldn't sleep well" if a foreign company took a "large" stake.[103]

Thus, while Nissan under Renault's stewardship was severing keiretsu supply ties, Toyota was busy tightening them.[104] The company raised its ownership of affiliates Daihatsu and Hino from 33.4 percent and 20 percent, respectively, to majority stakes in each. Toyota also sent executives to occupy the post of chairman (*kaicho*) or its equivalent at Denso, Toyoda Automatic Loom Works Ltd., and Aisin Seiki. As noted, Toyota also gave active consideration to a holding company structure that would administer all Toyota group operations, but as of now this is on hold, in part, it appears, because of resistance from the Toyoda family.

As in the past, core suppliers were Toyota's primary concern.[105] While Toyota could accept foreign purchases of stakes in fringe suppliers such as Akebono Brake (nominally a Nissan keiretsu firm), it could not countenance foreign control spreading to strategic partners such as Denso or Aisin. Denso was Japan's largest automotive parts producer and a spinoff of Toyota itself. Denso was a producer of a wide range of high-value electrical and electronic components, such as fuel-injection systems and car navigation systems. Aisin was also a core member of the Toyota group on which Toyota had been heavily dependent for key components.[106]

The Transformation of Technology Relations in the 1990s

Another set of challenges faced Japan in the 1990s: a wave of technology-based creative destruction swept across industry after industry. Leading the charge were the information industries: businesses based on the new technologies of microelectronics, computers, software, information processing, telecommunications, and the Internet. Such industries are distinguished by fast growth levels, rapid technical change, steep learning curves, short product life cycles, and high R&D investment. Given their potential to transform production processes, product components, and business models, they are also strategically important to the economy as a whole.

Between the middle and the end of the 1990s, production in Japan's information and technology sectors exceeded output in other industries by a factor of three to one. Information services employment expanded by

---

[103] *Wall Street Journal*, 3 August 1999.
[104] *Nikkei Net Interactive*, 9 October 2000.
[105] *Nikkei Net Interactive*, 13 June 2000.
[106] Ahmadjian and Lincoln (2001); Nishiguchi and Beaudet (1998).

3 percent annually while declining in the economy as a whole.[107] However, while Japan continued to plow investment into new technologies, the country was falling farther behind the global competitive curve. At the beginning of the decade, Japan cast the specter of technological Armageddon over the West, its corporations posed to overtake U.S. and European firms in an array of leading industries. By the late 1990s, the situation was reversed. It seemed that Japan was being left behind in the race to build a global new economy. Japan's talent at technological catch-up was unparalleled once, but the suitability of its entrenched industrial architecture for competition at the technological frontier was more and more in doubt.

What forces were driving the information technology (IT) industries worldwide, and how were they shaping developments in Japan? What were the limitations on the competitive capabilities of Japanese IT firms, and what changes were taking place? We consider five key forces for change: the shift from proprietary to universal IT standards, the accelerating pace and unpredictability of change in the IT industry, the creation of the Softbank zaibatsu, the emergence of other homegrown start-ups, and the development of the Mothers and NASDAQ Japan stock exchanges for the promotion of high-risk and entrepreneurial ventures.

1. The Shift from Proprietary to Universal IT Standards
Japan's earlier prowess in information technology was in mainframe computer hardware and software. Operating systems were proprietary, and efficiency and reliability were achieved and efficiencies created by routinizing software production in a fashion similar to the routinization and rationalization of autos or machinery production at which Japan had long excelled.[108] In the 1980s, however, the mainframe gave way to personal computers (PCs) and client–server networks, yet Japanese IT stayed focused on proprietary in-house systems. As the "Wintel" (Microsoft-Intel) standard diffused worldwide, Japanese industry found itself mired in a legacy of balkanized and incompatible products and standards.

This changed with the product announcement by IBM Japan in 1990 of DOS/V, the Japanese version of the DOS operating system that ran on IBM-compatible personal computers. Another watershed event was the formation of the Open Architecture Development Group by major computer and electronic firms in the following year. At the time, the dominant personal computer operating system in Japan was NEC's proprietary PC9800 series. NEC and the computer manufacturers that followed it each produced a distinct system of *kanji* (Chinese character) input, output,

---

[107] *Business Week*, 25 October 1999.
[108] Cusumano (1991).

and conversion as firmware, typically derived from the firm's own mainframe *kanji* processing system. The DOS/V operating system design freed Japanese personal computers from kanji firmware for the first time, making it possible to process *kanji* entirely within a software environment compatible with global IT standards.

The first successful challenge to NEC's dominance came from Fujitsu, which introduced a low-cost product line of PCs at the beginning of the decade. Fujitsu saw its market share rise from under 10 percent in the early 1990s to 22 percent in 1996.[109] Fujitsu also kept costs down by adopting the strategy of U.S. computer makers: concentrate on design and marketing and shift most production overseas (primarily to Taiwan). For Japan, this was a significant departure from the traditional manufacturing–supply chain paradigm, one soon followed by other Japanese makers.

The next challenge to NEC came from an American company, Compaq, which in 1992 began offering an IBM-compatible base machine for what was then a remarkably low price in Japan: ¥120,000 (~$1,000), just half of NEC's price. Believing that its market position could withstand the challenge, NEC was slow to respond. The door was thus opened to other foreign producers, whose collective share of the Japanese market went from 8 percent in 1988 (vs. 51 percent for NEC) to 30 percent in 1994 (vs. NEC's 43 percent). More Japanese manufacturers were thus spurred to adopt the DOS/V standard, including holdout NEC in 1998.

As Japanese manufacturers learned to work within the new, standardized and globalized computer production system they regained some of the market share lost to foreign companies by the late 1990s. However, by this point they had fallen far behind their American rivals in important underlying technologies. Unlike the VCR and other major consumer electronics products, Japanese firms found themselves unable to control any of the global standards for hardware and software. Most Japanese personal computers carried the "Intel inside" logo on their box, a sign of their foreign dependence around the brains of the computer, microprocessors. Their operating system was Microsoft Windows. And Japan found itself shut out of the market for packaged software, a business dominated by foreign producers not only globally but in Japan as well.

2. The Increasing Pace and Unpredictability of Change

Despite the challenges posed by the shift to universal IT standards, this was not the main problem facing Japanese computer firms. The closely connected, hierarchical network structure that dominated the sectors existed in other industries where universal standards were present and where Japanese manufacturers had nonetheless performed admirably: cars,

---

[109] Dedrick and Kraemer (1998).

machinery, consumer electronics. Indeed, efficient mass production for global markets was the essence of Japanese strategy in most industries in which Japanese firms were competitive. Japan's industrial architecture, in other words, could be adapted either to proprietary or to universal standards.

The problem, instead, was the high uncertainty and fast pace of change in the IT industry in the 1990s. Its evolution was punctuated by systemic shifts arising from successive waves of innovation: mainframe computers gave way to personal computers, which gave way to networked computing and the Internet. With each shift in technological regime came transformations of the whole industrial architecture of the industries themselves – in the basic capabilities of individual firms, in procurement patterns, in supplier relations, and in target product markets.

The industry was awash in Schumpeterian creative destruction, yet Japanese IT firms strove to adapt to this evolutionary environment without much creation *or* destruction. IT remained the domain of large, diversified, and vertically integrated firms whose roots lay with the electrical machinery and consumer electronics industries. Of Japan's five leading PC makers in the 1990s, all but one (Seiko Epson) was a large electronics conglomerate that had existed since before the war. The companies that had built Japan's computer industry in the 1960s were still the dominant players in the 1990s.

To be sure, these evolutionary patterns were not limited to information technology. According to a MITI study in the late 1990s, Japan had the lowest rates of company foundings and failures across all industries in the developed world during the period covered (1988–94).[110] While annual founding and failure rates of U.S. firms were in the range of 11–14 percent – at the upper end of the distribution worldwide – the range in Japan was 3–5 percent. Moreover, founding rates in manufacturing had declined substantially over time, especially in the early 1990s just as the industry's transformation was accelerating. By the end of the decade, Japan was generating about 100,000 new businesses every year versus 750,000 foundings in the United States.[111] Moreover, far fewer of the Japanese start-ups were in technology fields.

Where were the entrepreneurial companies able to achieve the necessary breaks with the past? Due in substantial part to keiretsu barriers, they faced severe discrimination in capital, labor, product, and technology markets. Large firms dominated R&D spending and access to the best-trained researchers. Their dominance had begun in the mid-1970s

[110] MITI (1999).
[111] *Daily Yomiuri*, 8 September 1999.

and continued growing throughout most of the 1990s.[112] Even at the end of the decade, few medium- and small-sized Japanese enterprises used computers in their businesses. Most reported no plans to sell or purchase online or set up local area networks, a primary reason being insufficient staff with the requisite technical skills. These firms also lacked venture capital from risk-tolerant investors (which the mainstream banks were clearly not). Nor were there many early technology adopters willing to bet that existing systems and standards would soon be obsolete.

Compounding the absence of entrepreneurial foundings was the slowness of incumbent firms in adapting to the new regime of rapid and discontinuous innovation. Companies like NEC, Fujitsu, and Hitachi had modeled themselves on IBM's vertical integration and product diversification from the 1960s to 1980s in everything from semiconductors to computer hardware to software to services.[113] Not surprisingly, they experienced many of the same problems that had beset IBM: weddedness to proprietary technologies in an era of open systems, a corporate culture that resisted radical innovation, and ponderous inability to change course when market and technology conditions demanded it – notably mainframes while the global industry transitioned to PCs and networks.

High-level decision making remained the province of older executives, most of whom lacked day-to-day working familiarity with the technologies (e.g, personal computers and the Internet) that were increasingly the industry's lifeblood. Ironically, the old Japanese criticism of U.S. industries such as automobiles and steel in the 1980s – that they were mostly run by financial and legal types with little understanding of manufacturing or technology – came to apply to Japan's leading IT firms. Moreover, unlike IBM, which underwent a painful but largely successful restructuring in the 1990s, Japan's dominant computer companies were hamstrung by employment practices and organizational cultures that made wholesale replacements of top management teams out of the question.

3. Creation of the Softbank Zaibatsu

By the late 1990s, the dominance of IT by the established electronics makers was being challenged for the first time. Interest in the Internet, which had been high in the United States for a number of years, was spreading rapidly in Japan, and along with it came a new generation of dot-com start-ups that followed few of the conventions of the industry's established corporations. By far the most important of the new companies was Softbank Corporation.

---

[112] MITI (1999).
[113] Anchordoguy (1989).

Sometimes heralded as the Microsoft of Japan, Softbank was a software start-up that moved into communication and Internet business, achieving, at least for a period, phenomenal success. To characterize Softbank as a software player, however, both over- and understates its importance. On a global plane, Softbank had none of Microsoft's significance. By most criteria other than sheer market capitalization it was a middle-tier company, whose revenues, profits, assets, and workforce were far smaller than Japan's blue chip companies. On the other hand, Softbank was in many ways more revolutionary than Microsoft (widely regarded as a marketing powerhouse but a technology follower rather than leader). Indeed, by the end of the decade, Softbank could plausibly be cast as the single most important start-up in Japan since Sony, which, founded in 1946, was no longer a new face on the world IT stage.[114] Softbank's importance was not so much its size but how it leveraged its resources to recraft corporate structure and industrial organization in Japan.

Softbank was founded in 1981 in Tokyo by Masayoshi Son, an ethnic Korean raised in Japan and educated at UC Berkeley. Son got a foothold in the IT business by selling Sharp a design for an electronic translator. He used the profits to found Softbank, initially a distributor of Microsoft products. Taking advantage of the mushrooming growth of packaged commodity software and the hidebound parochialism of marked Japan's proprietary-systems makers, Softbank soon became Japan's leading software distributor.

Son's company expanded into the mid-1990s by leveraging the returns from the distribution business and a stratospheric market valuation to move into related industries, both in Japan and abroad. His ambition, as he described it, was to create a dynasty that would dominate digital infrastructure.[115] He thus added to Softbank's portfolio a wide array of technology and media companies. In the media field, Softbank acquired Ziff-Davis, the publisher of leading technology magazines. In multimedia programming, Softbank formed a joint venture with NTT to distribute by phone line digital movies and software to Japanese homes and took a 21.4 percent stake in TV network Asahi. And in networking technology, Softbank acquired 20.4 percent of Novell Japan, a subsidiary of the leading network software supplier, and in 1993 formed an alliance with Cisco Systems to promote a Japanese standard for network equipment.

What contributed most to Softbank's establishment as a force in Japan's IT industry, however, was its savvy (and lucky) investments in a number of Internet start-ups in the United States. Between 1995 and 1999, Softbank

---

[114] Granted, there is not much competition for the title of "new Sony." The post-war period was remarkably devoid of successful entrepreneurial start-ups with a claim to having revolutionized Japanese industry.

[115] *Red Herring*, August 1997.

parlayed an initial investment of $200 million, spread over some thirty Internet companies, into an Internet empire valued at over $9 billion by early 1999.[116] The biggest and most successful stake was the $100 million Softbank invested in Yahoo! Japan, reportedly on the basis of a two-hour pizza dinner and little background research. Other highly successful investments included E*Trade, GeoCities, USWeb, and CyberCash.

By the end of the decade, one could scarcely pick up a business weekly without reading about a new venture in which Softbank was involved. Softbank had established a distinctive business model, one that would be adopted by other IT start-ups in Japan. Son liked to evoke images of earlier Japanese capitalism by calling his emerging empire a zaibatsu, claiming at one point that "the new zaibatsu will transform Japan from an industrial to an information society."[117] In a variation on this theme, his U.S. affiliate, Softbank Venture Capital, termed its interconnected interests a netbatsu. Strictly speaking, the model Son sought to emulate was not zaibatsu – the centrally controlled pre-war conglomerates – but keiretsu – the looser-knit network organizations of the post-war era. Softbank did not try to own companies outright or even run them. Rather, it sought monitoring capability and network control through minority stakes and synergies across a web of investments in sales and technology. As Son put it in an interview: "I envision us as a group of companies. We already have 100 companies, and in ten years we will have 1,000."[118]

Another perspective on Son's network-building strategy was the Silicon Valley venture capital model, applied, with some twists, to Japan. The difference, according to Son, was

> They look only at returns on their investments. We look at synergies with the operating company that we own. We don't do pure financial investment. We expect our investments to gain from synergies.... We helped Yahoo in many different ways. Through Ziff-Davis we helped Yahoo launch Yahoo Internet Life magazine. We provided them with introductions to our portfolios companies. We own 60 percent of Yahoo Japan and made it profitable from the first month of service.[119]

Softbank's strategy of building durable networks through cross-cutting investments in a broad range of industries does have its obvious parallels with the pre-war zaibatsu and post-war keiretsu. Was Japan's business culture thus reverting to the buccaneering spirit of Japan's Meiji era

---

[116] *Wall Street Journal*, 3 February 1999.
[117] *Business Week*, 6 March 2000.
[118] Interviewed in *Red Herring*, August 1997.
[119] Ibid.

entrepreneurs – where whole empires could be created by the bright, the visionary, and the well-connected?

4. The Emergence of Other Successful Start-Ups

While Softbank was the acknowledged leader of Japan's emerging Internet business world, on its heels came a number of similarly innovative Japanese companies founded by a new breed of young, dynamic, and aggressive entrepreneurs. Most visible of these was Hikari Tsushin, a mobile-phone retailer turned Internet investor. Founder Yasumitsu Shigeta converted money made in the booming retail market for cell phones in more than seventy Internet ventures in Japan, the United States, and elsewhere.[120] In September 1999, his firm was listed on the first section of the Tokyo Stock Exchange – the fastest founding-to-listing time (twelve years) in the history of the exchange. Despite its membership in this elite club of established Japanese companies, Hikari hardly fit the profile. The average age in Hikari's headquarters office in 1999 was twenty-six and that of its board, at thirty-five, was not much older (one year more than Shigeta himself). The directors included foreign nationals from China and elsewhere, whose work visas Hikari sponsored. No office ladies served tea, and Hikari had no main bank. As a poster in Hikari's lobby proclaimed, "Companies that are growing quickly and those that are not are different in every imaginable way."[121]

A third example was Trans Cosmos, founded in 1966 as a data-processing venture by Osaka entrepreneur Koki Okuda, which eventually grew into a leading network services firm. Early on, Trans Cosmos set up an office in San Francisco to position itself for investments in technology ventures it wished to bring to Japan. It eventually took equity stakes in more than fifty U.S. Internet start-ups, including Amazon.com, Autobytel.com, DoubleClick, and Liquid Audio. As these grew, Trans Cosmos took to forming Japan-based joint ventures with several such firms.[122]

Completing our list of high-profile homegrown start-ups at the end of the decade is Rakuten Ichiba. This was the youngest of the four and the only one to have embraced from the start the Internet as its core business model. Rakuten was founded in 1997 by Hiroshi Mikitani, who left the Industrial Bank of Japan in 1995 at age thirty to work briefly as a consultant before moving into e-commerce. As he later put it, "I just got tired of working for a large organization."[123] Having earned an MBA at Harvard, Mikitani raised seed money from classmates to found a Japanese hybrid of Amazon.com and eBay: an e-commerce Web site

---

[120] *Business Week Online*, 6 March 2000.
[121] *Forbes*, 13 December 1999.
[122] *Business Week*, 6 March 2000.
[123] *Far Eastern Economic Review*, 29 July 1999.

with virtual stores, auction platforms, customer bulletin boards, selling everything from fish to kimonos. Rakuten built its own distribution system by offering itself as an online platform for thousands of small brick-and-mortar stores, each of which paid ¥50,000 per month (~$400) to link their Web sites to Rakuten's. By mid-1999, less than three years from its founding, Rakuten was generating revenues of $2 million per month and attracting 80,000 shoppers per day.[124] It had in one breathtaking swoop fashioned Japan's first online shopping mall.

What can be learned from this new generation of start-ups – perhaps the most successful cohort of entrepreneurial firms since the early days of post-war Japan? As a set they provide some broad lessons in Japan's evolving industrial architecture – lessons both promising and cautionary. One feature common to all is the leveraging of the exploding Internet as a base for business expansion. Although the Internet was only just coming into its own as a significant economic force in Japan by the late 1990s, the new companies had accurately gauged its potential and were shifting revenues into strategic investments in the new medium. The risks were also plain: the remarkable run-up in Internet stock prices that had funded these companies' expansion (either through investments in others or by opening doors to venture capital) also made them highly vulnerable to market crashes. The sustainability of a gold rush depends on the price of gold remaining high.

The four firms also shared a strong global outlook. Three (Softbank, Hikari Tsushin, and Trans Cosmos) aggressively built alliances with foreign companies, primarily in the United States, which paid off handsomely and supplied the financial means to grow Japan-side businesses. These also teamed up with those foreign partners to exploit the Japanese market, thus enabling two-way flows of expertise and innovation. Rakuten, while oriented primarily to the Japanese market and shunning partnerships, was nonetheless a true Internet pioneer whose business was bounded more by cyberspace than geography. Referring to Rakuten's relative immunity to government regulation, founder Mikitani said, "What can they do? Shut down a server? ... All you have to do is move the server to the U.S., and you're back in business."[125]

But this also pointed up the large disparity in the IT industry in Japan and high-tech bastions such as Silicon Valley, for the Japanese companies made much of their money in U.S.-based activities. Japan had nothing remotely comparable to Silicon Valley levels of new-firm generation and early technology adoption. Was it just a matter of time before Japanese commitment to and capabilities in the Internet and e-commerce caught up, or were there more fundamental institutional and structural constraints

---

[124] *New York Times*, 30 August 1999.
[125] *New York Times*, 7 June 2000.

that would put Japan ever farther behind in the race to embrace the new economy? Japan's new institutional infrastructure and regulatory reform were promising, but it remained to be seen how far these would go and how successful they would ultimately be.

Especially problematic for the cultivation of a rich entrepreneurial culture in Japan was that the barriers to enterprise creation were greatest upstream in Japan's production and technology value chain. All four start-ups began life as downstream intermediaries in the marketing and distribution of other multilayered products. They found ways to exploit the weaknesses in Japan's notoriously complex and inefficient distribution network, using the Internet to get goods and services into consumers' hands much more quickly and at considerably lower cost. The traditional distribution channels were already being bypassed by mass discounters and direct marketers. Distribution was thus proving to be the most adaptive and responsive segment of Japan's industrial architecture – at least insofar as new economy products and services were involved. On the other hand, the upstream functions of design and engineering remained dominated by the large, established corporations and their satellite spin-offs. The rate at which new firms were generated began slowing, and they were less likely to be directly involved in technology-intensive activities.

5. Creation of New Stock Exchanges

Beyond the impact of the Internet in loosening up Japan's network economy, there was an institutional change designed to make Japan a more fertile environment for the creation and growth of new firms. Among the Big Bang financial system reforms was a plan to create new stock exchanges oriented to the needs of entrepreneurial and high technology firms and investors. According to MITI, venture capital invested in Japan in the 1990s was less than one-fifth of that available in the United States, a probable overestimate as most venture capital went to well-developed firms and spin-offs of established corporations, rather than true start-ups.[126] A key reason for the paucity of real venture capital was the absence of a market for initial public offerings (IPOs), enabling venture capitalists to cash out with large realized capital gains. Japan's eight exchanges had some 2,500 listed companies, compared with 8,850 on the three largest U.S. exchanges: 5,100 on the NASDAQ, 3,100 on the NYSE, and 650 on the American Stock Exchange. Moreover, Tokyo Stock Exchange companies waited an average of thirty-four years before going public, compared with ten years in the United States.[127]

---

[126] *Wall Street Journal*, 29 November 1999.
[127] Ibid.

In December 1999, the Tokyo Stock Exchange launched a new stock market section, fancifully called the Mothers market (from Market for the High-Growth and Emerging Stocks). It targeted technology and Internet start-ups, in-house venture companies, and the like. Unlike the Tokyo Stock Exchange's first and second sections, there were no minimum financial performance, time since founding, or capitalization requirements. The Mothers section also shifted emphasis for prudential oversight from the exchange itself to "investor self-responsibility," but at the same time toughened public disclosure requirements, for example, of quarterly earnings reports versus Japan's standard semiannual reports.

The second new exchange was NASDAQ Japan, which opened in June 2000 as a joint venture of NASDAQ U.S. and Softbank Corporation. Unlike the Mothers section of the Tokyo Stock Exchange, NASDAQ Japan traded in U.S. stocks as well as Japanese listings. Indeed, Softbank's president, Masayoshi Son, made clear that he expected much of the interest in Japan to come from Japanese investors wishing to explore IPOs launched in the United States.[128] Taken together, the Mothers market and NASDAQ Japan were intended to foster vitality in Japanese corporate financial markets and an environment in which an entrepreneurial culture could take hold.[129] In 2002, however, NASDAQ U.S., suffering from the steep decline in technology stock values, caused shock waves by abruptly pulling out of the partnership. The Osaka Securities Exchange is now operating NASDAQ Japan under the name Nippon New Market – Hercules. Mothers, if not exactly thriving, is nonetheless doing relatively well. The banks' unwillingness to lend has driven more firms to equity financing, and fears that the Koizumi government's get-tough policies will lead to further stock market declines are motivating start-ups to go public early.

6. The Influx of Foreign Investment
Bank consolidation and the reshaping of the horizontal keiretsu were processes driven chiefly by domestic forces, mainly deregulation, the financial system crisis, and the twelve-year downward spiral of the economy as a whole. A second force for widespread corporate organization and governance change was of external origin: rising foreign direct investment. The number of foreign takeovers of Japanese companies rose dramatically at the end of the 1990s, branching from financial services to other industries. In dollar value, inward FDI doubled between 1997 and 1998, more than doubling again in 1999. To be sure, the base of FDI in Japan was so small that any increase appeared significant in percentage terms. Even after the late 1990s surge, Japan's inward FDI still ranked at the bottom of the

---

[128] *San Francisco Chronicle*, 16 June 1999.
[129] *Nikkei Net Interactive*, 31 October 2002.

list of industrialized nations. Even so, foreigners acquired nearly $16 billion of Japanese corporate assets in 1999, far more than in any previous year.

Thus, if the 1980s were Japan's era of outward integration – a time of massive overseas investment overseas in the United States, East Asia, and elsewhere – then the 1990s marked the onset of a complementary process that was equally if not more important to Japan's economic maturation: the inward integration into the global economy through increasing foreign investments in Japan itself. Widespread availability of foreign products sharpens price competition, while the presence of foreign firms serves to break up entrenched business practices.[130] Moreover, even sacred cows, such as Japan's financial institutions, were clearly no longer exempt from takeover or dissolution. The branches of failed Yamaichi Securities, a former big-four broker, were snapped up by Merrill Lynch, and Long-Term Credit Bank was sold to Ripplewood Holdings, an American investment consortium. Even Japan's most competitive sectors were not immune, Renault's acquisition of a controlling stake in Nissan being the most visible example.

However, once again the change in the *pattern* of outcomes within Japan's industrial architecture were greater than any change in the *processes* creating them. Like the large-scale foreign takeovers that occurred in earlier decades, nearly all such deals involved the purchase of distressed assets. Japan's decade-long economic malaise had made these available in abundance, but it remained the case that even moderately successful firms were rarely sold to foreign *or* domestic acquirers. At the end of the 1990s, in other words, Japan had nothing remotely comparable to the active market for corporate control found in the Anglo-American economies, where public firms could generally be had for a price. Hostile takeovers, moreover, were a practical impossibility given the cross-shareholding and other barriers still largely in place.

The managers involved in these deals had to contend with powerful structural and institutional constraints. Typically, foreign investors guaranteed continued employment to the workforce and continued business for close vendors and clients. In most deals, the acquirer took a partial equity position in the Japanese firm or participated in a new entity designed to shield the Japanese parent from foreign control. As Sanford Weill, CEO of Travelers Group put it in explaining why his firm had not purchased Nikko Securities outright, "You can do a lot of deals. . . . But in Japan, the culture is so different you just have to do things differently."[131]

---

[130] For a general discussion of this point, see Olson (1982). For an application to Japan, see Katz (1998).
[131] *Wall Street Journal*, 19 May 1999.

An example of the difference is the case of "vulture capital" firm, Rothschild Inc., which worked with Japan Recovery Capital (jointly owned by Daiwa Securities and Sumitomo Bank) to buy Nikko Electric Industry. Nikko Electric was an auto parts supplier that gained local fame as the first company to be sent into bankruptcy by its own employees. In restructuring the company, the investors departed from the standard U.S. blueprint by inviting some of Nikko Electric's biggest suppliers, including Mitsubishi Heavy Industries, Isuzu Motors, and Komatsu, to join the investment consortium. The goal was to ensure their goodwill and continued patronage. Said a senior manager at Rothschild: "That would make it more like the Japanese system, where customers and vendors traditionally have counter-invested in each other.... We're trying to blend American techniques with the historical way things are done in Japan."[132]

Thus, even those with the most to gain from a freewheeling market for corporate control – foreign investors – must adapt to the local rules of the game. In the words of the Japanese chairman of Goldman Sachs (Japan), a foreign-owned investment bank with similar interests in shaking up the status quo:

> To sum up, our problem is that the Japanese market is an extremely difficult one for newcomers to enter, be it Japanese or foreigner. Our task is to transform it into a more open and more accessible market. Having said that, I am not advocating outright change to an American practice of corporate raids and hiring and firing. We still attach great value to the traditional Japanese management style of long-term perspective and stable employment. We believe that only with stable employment were Japanese companies able to accumulate technology and skill, and attain the highest level of quality control, thereby achieving their present global positions.[133]

Keiretsu and Strategic Alliance Formation in the Japanese Electronics Industry[134]

In keeping with the last section's focus on innovative ventures in Japan's changing network economy, we summarize a recent study from our research program on the formation of new strategic alliances in the

---

[132] *New York Times*, 29 October 1999.
[133] From a speech by Ishihara Hideo to the 1995 Japan Canada Business Conference, as quoted in Schaede (2001).
[134] This section was authored by James Lincoln and Didier Guillot.

electronics industry. This section follows the discussion in Guillot and Lincoln (2001) and presents some abbreviated tables from that research.

We argued in the section above that some alliance forms that materialized in the Japanese economy at the turn of the century have distinct continuities and commonalities with the old. With the exception of Sumitomo–Mitsui, for example, the large banking combinations created in the late 1990s are predictable (e.g., by a blockmodel analysis) from the established horizontal keiretsu configurations. We now give more explicit consideration to the question of whether new strategic alliances among Japanese firms in a key manufacturing industry – electronics – derive from the established keiretsu networks. In recent decades, Japanese manufacturing companies have greatly expanded their participation in an array of international as well as domestic partnerships. To what degree are these rooted in the networks of the past, specifically the vertical and horizontal keiretsu?

A theme of Chapter 3's network analysis was that the odd pattern of change in the large-firm equity network – rising density combined with falling connectivity – meant that capital tie-ups were becoming more strategic and firm- or dyad-specific. Japanese capitalism remains network capitalism, we argued, but its fundamentals are changing. In a way uncommon in the past, firms are leveraging relationships to advance their business agendas – seeking partnerships that endow the individual firm or transacting pair with competitive advantage but are less embedded in – that is, integrated with and consequential for – the keiretsu group and corporate network as a whole. The research reviewed in this section is in line with this theme. It appears that new electronics alliances that have a manufacturing (e.g., capacity reduction or expansion; supply chain) rationale are more likely to involve members of the same vertical keiretsu. If the rationale is research and development, however, the keiretsu effect disappears. We also find members of the big-six horizontal groups to be more active than are unaffiliated firms in alliance formation, but no evidence that they favor partners within their own groups.

Firms seek strategic alliances in order to acquire assets they cannot generate internally or obtain through merger and acquisition.[135] They also seek economies of synergy or complementarity that are realizable through a partnership in which the members retain distinct identities.[136] But how do firms select suitable partners in possession of resources and capabilities that complement their own and with whom the potential for productive synergy exists? Strategic alliances regularly fail because the process of choosing partners and assessing "fit" is mismanaged. Scanning the

[135] Pfeffer and Salancik (1978).
[136] Williamson (1985).

environment for alliance opportunities, committing to a qualified partner, and then aligning structures and processes are skills in the fashioning of alliances that organizations can acquire. A history of tie-ups provides firms with information about partners' capabilities. A study of strategic alliances by Gulati and Gargiulo (1999) finds that the likelihood that two firms will form a strategic tie is considerably higher if they have collaborated in the past.

Thus, organizations learn about and try out potential alliance partners through their experiences in interorganizational networks. Stable customer–supplier transactions, common third-party relations – for example, to the same bank, trading company, or consulting firm – joint membership in an industry association or government-sponsored consortium, and interlocking director and equity ties are among the ways Japanese firms discover and bridge to one another and thus sift and sort among strategic partner candidates.

From a transaction costs perspective, alliances are hybrid governance forms – more structured and permanent than a licensing agreement or other long-term contract – yet absent the monitoring and control mechanisms for freeing information and averting opportunism that full internal organization (e.g., vertical or horizontal integration) might provide. The attractions of the alliance form also depend, of course, on what alternatives are available. In the Japanese context, where neither formal contracts nor full-blown mergers and acquisitions have been easily preferred options, a flexible alliance reinforced by reciprocated equity holdings and other credible commitments may be an attractive governance choice.

Thus, firms enter alliances because they perceive that pooling resources in a joint enterprise will generate more value at less cost than if each pursues it alone and, further, that other means of resource and know-how pooling are unattractive or unavailable. Sometimes the venture per se is secondary and the tie-up's real aim is to give each partner access to the other's knowledge stock. The knowledge or skills that one brings to the table and the other covets are generally intangible – hard to observe and copy – and inseparable – their value dependent on a unique combination of assets or supportive environments.[137] Copying, buying, or contracting for a narrow set of capabilities while failing to acquire or recreate the context in which they can flourish is an error organizations all too often commit. An oft-cited example is the firm that hires away or buys *en masse* some talented engineers, only to fail (for reasons of culture or structure) to integrate them in its organization, such that the value gleaned by the former employer cannot be realized again.[138]

---

[137] Itami and Roehl (1987).
[138] Branstetter (2000).

A reasonable supposition is that keiretsu facilitate the joining of corporate hands in new endeavors. Common membership in an established corporate network, as our Mitsui group informants indicated (see Chapter 3), infuses business dealings with trust and goodwill, thus reducing the frictions in, and hence costs of, transactions.[139] Such cultural qualities, Ronald Dore (1983) and others suggest, figured prominently in the institutionalization of keiretsu as a unique organization/governance form. The keiretsu evolved distinctive organizational cultures in terms of shared values and traditions, the work styles of people (homogenized in part by the circulation of employees among the member firms), and competitive strategies. Some such commonalities were born of long history (e.g., the Edo era origins of Mitsui and Sumitomo), others stem from regional insularity (e.g., the concentration of the Toyota keiretsu in Aichi Prefecture or Sumitomo's roots in Osaka), and still others from the enterprise culture of a lead firm. Matsushita Electric claims not to have a keiretsu supply network of the Toyota or Nissan sort, but our interviews with Matsushita suppliers turned up numerous indications that the charismatic vision and teachings of founder Konosuke Matsushita figured powerfully in their commitment to the parent firm.[140] Given the significant costs and uncertainties involved in two firms scoping out each other's resource profiles, synergy, and alignment, the attractions of a tried and true keiretsu partner are easy to discern.

Further, the embedding of an alliance in a far-flung, multiplex keiretsu network implies a profusion of third-party ties. Such indirect connections have important monitoring and governance properties. In a much-cited study of supply relations in the New York garment industry, Uzzi wrote[141]:

> In the firms I studied, third–party referral networks were often cited as sources of embeddedness. Such networks operate by fusion: one actor with an embedded tie to each of two unconnected actors acts as their go-between by using her common link to establish trustworthiness between them. The go-between performs two functions: he or she (1) transfers expectations of behavior from the existing embedded relationship to the newly matched firms, and (2) "calls on" the reciprocity "owed" him or her by one exchange partner and transfers it to the other.

Alliances reinforced by indirect ties are thus superior to unembedded, strictly dyadic alliances in limiting opportunism, as they imply a

---

[139] Lincoln (1990); Sako (1992); Smitka (1991).
[140] Guillot and Lincoln (2003); Lincoln et al. (1998).
[141] Uzzi (1996).

cross-cutting web of trust and obligation operating to spread information, share risks, and allocate resources.

The two primary keiretsu forms – the big-six horizontal *kigyo shudan* and the vertical manufacturing keiretsu – have different organizational structures and functions and thus constitute different platforms for the construction of new alliances. The vertical keiretsu are generally nested within industries and centered on large end-user manufacturers. They arose as solutions to problems of procurement after the war and to regulatory and capital market constraints on the scale and scope of corporations.[142] Such networks enabled large firms to launch new businesses and diversify product lines industries by, for example, spinning-off divisions as affiliated firms.[143] They have also endowed competitive industries such as autos and electronics with the scale and support networks necessary to compete aggressively in global markets.[144]

While tight collaboration along the supply chain between parent manufacturers and affiliated suppliers is less characteristic of the electronics industry than of automakers, vertical keiretsu networks enable the integrated electronics makers to acquire competitive advantage through access to stable supply and distribution networks and ease of technical cooperation.[145] Strong communication channels exist, both vertically between core firm and supplier and horizontally among the suppliers themselves, particularly when the suppliers are organized in supplier associations or *kyoryoku-kai*.[146]

The horizontal keiretsu are configured differently. Because member firms are large, each representing a broad industry sector (the one-set principle), their raison d'etre has been less the exchange of products or technologies than the maintenance of stable, mutually supportive capital and governance ties. Members are not as complementary in a purchase–supply sense as in the vertical keiretsu. Strategic alliances often serve as extensions to or consolidations of supply and distribution channels. We might thus expect them to be grounded more in vertical keiretsu ties and less in horizontal group relations. On the other hand, the large engineering and R&D staffs of the big-six-affiliates facilitate the formation of intragroup partnerships targeted at the development and application of new technologies. Moreover, shared business culture, experience-tested relationships, and the monitoring afforded by third-party ties typify the horizontal as well as the vertical groups, potentially making them, too, fertile soil for new alliances.

---

[142] Odaka et al. (1988).
[143] Gerlach and Lincoln (2000).
[144] Nishiguchi (1994).
[145] Asanuma (1989); Lincoln and Ahmadjian (2001).
[146] Guillot and Lincoln (2003); Nishiguchi (1994); Sako (1996).

H6.1: *Two Japanese firms are most likely to form a strategic alliance if they are members of the same keiretsu group.*

Our reasoning to this point stresses the value of interorganizational familiarity in inclining two firms toward a strategic alliance. Through the communication channels of a keiretsu network, information circulates on the assets and skills that might productively be combined. For example, a supplier and an assembler who have done business for years and, supported by keiretsu ties, share proprietary knowledge of one another's structures and processes may see few perils in a new joint venture. Their partnership has a track record, and they expect it to yield good results again, particularly if the enterprise contemplated is an extension of, not a radical departure from, the projects of the past. Over the years, they have evolved a rich set of routines for working together that must otherwise be built from scratch if either opted for a new and unfamiliar partner.

There are, on the other hand, alliances that firms pursue in order to acquire or create knowledge assets that depart substantially, not only from their own resource base and skill set, but from those available from their keiretsu networks as well. Because of the generally tight coordination of a manufacturing keiretsu division of labor, each vertical group firm is apt to have good information on the capabilities of others; for example, as to who can improve process or product technology within given cost and time frames. Such information, which may only incrementally exceed every other affiliate's knowledge base, can be quickly digested and acted upon. Thus, the selection of a partner from the ranks of the same vertical keiretsu may speed the process of search for productive routines and agreement upon a division of responsibility.

But the downsides to picking new alliance partners from the ranks of the same keiretsu are transparent as well. While mutual trust, familiarity, and thus smooth coalignment of processes and strategies may prompt firms to look for candidates within the group, they risk the opposite problem that the allying firms will be insufficiently distinct to endow the new enterprise with real synergy. In an industry (electronics) and era marked by sharp product and technology cycle discontinuities, such companies might be better advised to seek out new and untested partner prospects.[147] In such an environment, the alliance must achieve not merely an incremental improvement on the extant knowledge base but altogether new knowledge. These trade-offs are to some degree endemic in any partnership, keiretsu based or not: tough going at the outset in melding the styles and capabilities of the participants may, if weathered successfully, pay dividends

---

[147] Tushman and Anderson (1986).

down the road in new and lasting capabilities that neither partner could master on its own.

Indeed, while keiretsu networks clearly facilitate innovation diffusion *within* the group, they also erect tall barriers to the transmission of knowledge *between* groups.[148] Research on R&D consortia, for example, documents case after case in which Japanese firms have been reluctant to cooperate across keiretsu lines. MITI, for example, was forced to create two distinct research laboratories in the 1970s in order to encourage firms to join the VLSI (Very Large Scale Integration) project.[149] MITI also had difficulty persuading Japanese electronics firms to collaborate in the Fifth Generation Computer Projects in the 1980s.[150]

Rtishchev and Cole (2003: 143–44) highlight the trade-off between the gains in compatibility and trust that keiretsu-based strategic alliances afford and the potential costs in innovativeness foregone. Japan, they argue, must embrace the "organizational discontinuities" that in Silicon Valley, for example, have enabled breakthrough innovation and commercialization to proceed. Reliance on keiretsu partners in mounting new R&D ventures exemplifies the kind of incremental adjustment that arguably served Japanese companies well in the past, but in the turbulent global economy of the twenty-first century may not do so.

> We do not argue, however, that alliances [by which they mean keiretsu] in the Japanese economy always hinder innovation. In some cases, intra-alliance R&D projects benefit from effective combination of technological capabilities and low transaction costs. For example, Kodana's (1995: Ch. 5) analysis of technology fusion across industry borders as a basis for innovation in Japan attributes success in fiber-optics to collaboration among three firms within the Sumitomo group. Nevertheless, Kodama concludes that intra-keiretsu R&D is neither a necessary nor even a primary factor for successful technology fusion (p. 203). We go further to claim that sometimes the predilection toward intra-keiretsu R&D in Japan precludes potentially more beneficial fusion across alliance boundaries.

Thus, when the aim of the alliance is research and development – the creation of new technology – a rational Japanese firm in pursuit of an alliance partner will not confine itself to established keiretsu ties.

H6.2: *In forming a strategic alliance with an R&D focus, Japanese firms will select partners from outside their keiretsu groups.*

---

[148] Nishiguchi (1994).
[149] Fransman (1990); Sakakibara (1993).
[150] Guillot et al. (2000).

Does Hypothesis 6.2 apply to both keiretsu forms? Guillot and Lincoln reasoned that R&D tie-ups within the same horizontal group risk less creativity loss than those launched within a vertical keiretsu. Two members of the same horizontal group in the same industry will be competitors. As both are large end-user manufacturers, their businesses are apt to be less intertwined than is generally true of partnerships within a vertical keiretsu. However, by virtue of their keiretsu bond, the two firms share membership in a risk- and resource-sharing community and hence can access information about each other through the community's web of direct and indirect ties. Thus, compared to alliances forged within a vertical keiretsu, alliances within a horizontal group might be a workable solution to the familiarity–creativity trade-off: such firms are sufficiently different that real synergies are possible but sufficiently familiar to allay concerns about fit.

Guillot and Lincoln tested these hypotheses with longitudinal data on new strategic alliances among Japanese electronics firms between 1992 and 1997. Their focus was the electrical machinery industry, after autos Japan's most competitive sector, and its own travails notwithstanding, one that survived the lean 1990s with less radical restructuring than the automobile industry has undergone.[151] This plus a high rate of technological change and short product cycles makes the electronics industry a better candidate for a study of strategic alliance formation, since in the autos case a foreign partner might be calling the shots. Under the foreign management, respectively, of Renault and Ripplewood Holdings, Nissan Motors and Shinsei Bank (the former Long-Term Credit Bank) have moved more aggressively to dispose of keiretsu ties – including cutting off struggling client firms – than has been the pattern for Japanese corporations under domestic control.[152]

The information on alliances was coded from press accounts published in the five largest economic and industrial Japanese newspapers over an eleven-year period from 1987 to 1997 (*Japan Economic Newspaper, Japan Industrial Newspaper, Daily Industrial Newspaper, Japan Economy and Industry Newspaper, and Japan Distribution Newspaper*). The reported alliances were generally of three kinds: (1) R&D-related tie-ups done for the purpose of developing a new product or process technology[153]; (2) supply-chain-related tie-ups: new supply and distribution

---

[151] Today only Honda and Toyota remain totally independent auto firms – Isuzu, Mazda, Nissan, Subaru, and Mitsubishi all have acquired major if not dominant participation by foreign partners. The large electronics firms – Hitachi, Matsushita, Sony, NEC, and Toshiba – have remained entirely under Japanese control, despite some significant internal reorganizations.

[152] *Wall Street Journal*, 28 June 2002.

[153] "Oki Electric and Sony announced on Dec. 7 that they have agreed to collaborate on the development of new technologies for the production of 256 Megabit DRAM's. The two firms will invest about ¥100 billion" (*Nihon Kogyo Shinbun*, 8 December 1995).

arrangements with partner firms (e.g., because a corporation has decided to end production of a component and begun to outsource it)[154]; and (3) joint-venture tie-ups, where a new corporate entity is created in which the participating firms become equity partners.[155]

The data pertain to 128 large publicly held companies. This is the full set of Tokyo, Nagoya, and Osaka stock-exchange-listed companies in the electronics industry. In 1992, there were 164 such firms. In 1997, owing to new listings, there were 178. The sample of 128 firms includes every such company that was in at least one alliance, be it domestic or international, over the eleven-year period.

The analysis examined the factors that affect the likelihood that a pair of firms – a dyad – will enter an alliance in a given year.[156] The unit of observation is therefore the dyad-year.[157]

The statistical methodology is an elaboration of the dyad models of Chapter 4. There, in order to gauge period effects and because of the sizable intervals between measurements, a series of cross-sectional regressions on dyad observations (firm pairs) was run. Here, the yearly data allow us to use a dynamic event history/hazard rate modeling approach. Specifically, the data have the form of a cross-sectional time series in which the units of observation are unique dyads. For each year, the dyad data are configured as follows: $I_1, J_2; I_1, J_3; \ldots;$ $I_1, J_N; I_2, J_3; I_2, I_4; \ldots I_2, J_N; \ldots; I_{N-1}, J_N$, where $I_i = \text{firm } I; J_j = \text{firm } J$; and $i = 1, \ldots, N-1$; $j = 1, \ldots, N$, and $i \neq j$. Thus, for every year there are $N(N-1)/2 = 8,192$ dyads or 48,768 year-dyads across all

---

[154] "Sharp announced on April 15 that its new cellular phone to be commercialized will be manufactured by Nihon Musen Co." (*Nihon Kogyo Shinbun*, 16 April 1995).

[155] "Matsushita Denshi and Matsushita Electric Industrial announced on Nov. 30 that they will establish this month a Joint-Venture to produce nickel and nickel-cadmium batteries. The total investment will be $2 billion, 60% from Matsushita Denshi, 40% from Matsushita Electric Industrial." (*Nihon Kogyo Shinbun*, 1 December 1994).

[156] The financial data used in this analysis are derived from the Japan Development Bank Corporate Finance Data Bank, which records both the unconsolidated and the consolidated accounting data of companies (excluding finance and insurance companies) currently listed on the first and second sections of the Tokyo, Osaka, and Nagoya Stock Exchanges. The Japan Development Bank data come from the annual securities reports (*Yuka shoken hokokusho*) that listed firms submit to the Ministry of Finance.

[157] Chapter 4 discussed the problem of statistical nonindependence of observations arising from the repetition of nodes (firms) across dyads (Lincoln, 1984). Again, there is an analogy with the panel data case in which repetition of units over time periods over units produces unmeasured similarity in the data. The consequence is the same: underestimated standard errors and overestimated significance tests. As these data were on dyads, Guillot and Lincoln encountered all three kinds of nonindependence. They dealt with the problem as follows. They used a random effects probit model specifying and measuring error components for unit and for time, thus adjusting standard error estimates upward. In addition, they used the robust standard error option available in *Stata* 6 (Stata Corporation, 1999) to adjust dyads for clustering on firm. *Stata*, unfortunately, has no routine allowing for simultaneous adjustment for the time and unit effects in the panel data *and* dyad overlap. Thus, these analyses were done sequentially. The results were similar, however, indicating that the reported significance levels are not biased.

years $(NT = 48,768$, i.e., $([128*127]/2)*6)$. Guillot and Lincoln used random effects probit to model the probability that an alliance was reported for each pair of firms in each year. Every firm (or dyad in our case) at risk of entering an alliance is included.

The dependent variable is a dichotomy: coded 1 if a pair of firms entered an alliance in a given year, 0 otherwise. Each dyad-year record included attributes of both members of the dyad, plus a number of relational measures tapping prior and third-party alliance activity and affiliation with keiretsu groups.

The alliances were also coded for content or purpose. Those involving the joint development of a new product or a new technology were classed as R&D alliances. The remainder was generally collaborations in production, distribution, or marketing.

Keiretsu membership was ascertained using the classification in *Kigyo keiretsu soran* (various years). Firms seated on the big-six shacho-kai were coded as horizontal keiretsu. Because the unit of analysis is the dyad or pair, four dummy variables are needed. "Same horizontal keiretsu" = 1 when both firms in the dyad are in the same shacho-kai. "Different horizontal keiretsu" = 1 when the firms are in different shacho-kai. "Both nonhorizontal keiretsu" = 1 when the two firms in the pair are independent (noncouncil) firms; and "horizontal keiretsu and nonhorizontal keiretsu" = 1 when one firm is a council member but the other is not.

Similarly, four measures tapped each firm's vertical keiretsu affiliation.[158] "Same vertical keiretsu" = 1 when both firms are in the same group. "Different vertical keiretsu" = 1 when the firms are in different groups. "Both nonvertical keiretsu" = 1 when the two firms were in none of the eleven vertical groups, and "vertical keiretsu and nonvertical keiretsu" = 1 if one firm is in a group but the other is not.

Results

Tables 6.4 and 6.5 present the relevant the descriptive statistics and regression results.

As hypothesized, firms in the same vertical keiretsu are more likely to form an alliance than are firms in different keiretsu or where one or both companies have no keiretsu affiliation. The dummy variables for the three alternatives to the baseline condition of "same vertical keiretsu" have highly significant negative coefficients.

---

[158] Guillot and Lincoln considered the following eleven vertical networks, because at least one of the 128 sampled firms was a member: Hitachi, Toshiba, NEC, Fujitsu, Sony, Matsushita, Oki Electric, Mitsubishi Electric, Kobe Heavy Industry, Sumitomo Electric, Yasukawa Electric.

Table 6.4. *Descriptive Statistics*

Variable	Mean	Std Dev.
1. Any alliance	.0051	.071
2. R&D alliance	.0029	.037
3. Non-R&D alliance	.0031	.023
4. Same vertical keiretsu	.018	.133
5. Different vertical keiretsu	.145	.352
6. Vertical keiretsu and nonvertical keiretsu	.486	.500
7. Both nonvertical keiretsu	.351	.477
8. Horizontal keiretsu	.003	.053
9. Different horizontal keiretsu	.008	.091
10. Horizontal keiretsu and nonvertical keiretsu	.196	.397
11. Both nonhorizontal keiretsu	.792	.406
12. Prior tie	.031	.347
13. Third-party tie	.044	.204

Moreover, the horizontal keiretsu dummies have negatively signed coefficients that reach significance in two out of three cases, yet the pattern differs notably from the vertical keiretsu case. A pair of firms in the *same* vertical keiretsu is more likely to form an alliance than are *all three* alternative configurations: (1) the pair spans different keiretsu; (2) one firm is keiretsu, the other is not; (3) both are not. This, again, is a *homophily* effect: ties are strongest when the actors have something in common; here, same keiretsu membership (configuration 1).[159] But the horizontal keiretsu evidence reveals no difference between the baseline (same group) and the first dummy (different groups). A keiretsu–independent pairing (configuration 2) is less likely to start an alliance and a pairing of two independents (configuration 3) is least so. This, again in network theory terms, is a *centrality*, not a homophily, effect. Big-six companies start alliances at higher rates, usually with other horizontal keiretsu firms, but whether the group is the same or not makes no difference. Independents join fewer alliances, so a partnership between a big-six firm and an independent is less likely – and between two independents least likely.

Apart from the keiretsu effects, prior strategic alliances and third-party ties raise the odds that a pair of firms will forge a new alliance. The first is analogous to the vertical keiretsu effect; a history of joint endeavors makes it likely that the partners will come together again. This supports Uzzi's observations on the role of third-party ties: firms with the same partners are themselves likely to become partners.

[159] Lincoln and McBride (1985).

Table 6.5. *Random-Effects Panel Probit Estimates of the Likelihood of Strategic Alliance Formation for Each Dyad of Japanese Electronics Firms for Each Year of the Period 1992–97*

Variables	(1) Any Alliance	(2) R&D Alliance	(3) Other Alliance
Compared to same vertical keiretsu			
Different vertical keiretsu	−1.16***	−.04	−1.29***
	(.14)	(.54)	(.14)
Vertical keiretsu & nonvertical	−1.19***	.19	−1.25***
keiretsu	(.12)	(.51)	(.13)
Both nonvertical keiretsu	−1.38***	.45	−1.33***
	(.14)	(.51)	(.15)
Compared to same horizontal keiretsu			
Different horizontal keiretsu	−.18	−.34	−.07
	(.22)	(.47)	(.29)
Horizontal keiretsu and	−.62**	−.81*	−.33
nonhorizontal keiretsu	(.20)	(.46)	(.25)
Both nonhorizontal keiretsu	−1.08***	−.59	−.68*
	(.22)	(.47)	(.28)
Other ties			
Prior tie	.18***	−.03	.09
	(.04)	(.06)	(.05)
Third party tie	.29**	−.14	−.18*
	(.09)	(.24)	(.09)
N	48,678	48,678	48,678
Constant	−15.43***	−12.39**	−11.33**
	(3.93)	(4.25)	(4.01)
Chi square	765.05	154.02	523.06

Notes: Standard errors in parentheses, $*p < .05$, $**p < .01$, $***p < .001$ (two-tailed test). The dependent variable in Model 1 is the occurrence of any new alliance in year t; in Model 2, the occurrence of an R&D alliance in year t: and in Model 3, the occurrence of a non-R&D alliance. Also included in the models are measures of the centrality of each firm in the network of prior alliances; a measure of the interdependence of the industries; the sales volume, profitability, solvency, and liquidity of each firm in the dyad and the interactions of the two; year dummies (1992 omitted), the total number of alliances of each partner, and the density of past alliances.

R&D Alliances Are Different

With the data on alliances broken into R&D and non-R&D types, interesting and important differences emerge. First, for R&D alliances, the strong vertical keiretsu homophily effects vanish as do those of prior and third-party ties. For non-R&D alliances, they persist. (They are weaker in the non-R&D regression than in the pooled regression, but this is likely due to the reduced variance of the dependent variable.)

The horizontal group centrality effects, on the other hand, hold up regardless of the purpose of the alliance. Alliances are more likely when the participating firms are affiliated with the big-six groups, but whether the affiliated firms are in the same or different groups is immaterial.

Keiretsu Ties and Strategic Alliances: Discussion

What, then, does this analysis say about the interface between the Japanese economy's old and new network forms? The most general conclusion is that keiretsu, whether vertical or horizontal, is a significant force in the structuring of new strategic alliances in a fast-paced, globally competitive industry. The pattern of vertical keiretsu effects on non-R&D alliances accords with various theories that portray networks as the circuitry through which flows the information and other resources essential to the creation of enterprise.[160] Access to and skill in navigating networks endows a firm with the social capital needed to pursue cooperative ventures and make them succeed. Finally, it is in the nature of networks that members are to some degree bound to one another by trust, commitment, and reciprocity, qualities that smooth the workings of a strategic alliance.

However, when the alliance aims at creating new knowledge – as opposed to leveraging old knowledge into new venues – the picture shifts. Quick access to information on others and ease of combining forces and meshing routines is less a priority than finding a partner whose capabilities add new and distinct value. This recalls the familiar strong tie–weak tie conundrum of classical network theory.[161] The strong ties, of which the vertical keiretsu are arguably composed, are easily accessed and mobilized, but they suffer from redundancy and thus have low creativity–synergy potential. Weak ties are harder to access and exploit, as they are sparser and connect a more diverse set of actors. When the contemplated venture demands tight top-to-bottom coupling of two firms' structures and processes, a rational company will leverage strong ties. But when the goal is innovation, ease of integration takes a backseat to uniqueness and complementarity. The risk that the marriage might prove rocky pales against the risk that nothing new or interesting will come of it.

It would thus seem that Japanese firms exploit their keiretsu networks in forging tie-ups that have a logic that is more micro-strategic than that of the keiretsu form itself. This analysis also shows, however, that electronics firms are not averse to abandoning old partners and searching for new ones, even if it means that keiretsu boundaries are crossed. In recent years, Japanese companies have acquired much experience in partnerships with foreign firms, where no keiretsu barriers or platforms exist. Clearly, a firm can learn the ability to ally or network effectively with unfamiliar others whose style of business is different from one's own.[162] If Japanese companies can in fact discriminate between alliances that take advantage of old ties and alliances better enacted with new ones, it is to their credit

---

[160] Burt (1992).
[161] Granovetter (1973).
[162] Ahmadjian and Lincoln (2001).

and bodes well for the Japanese economy's capacity to absorb organizational and technological discontinuities and thus bridge to a future that
in more and more ways is different from the past.

Japanese Restructuring and the American Corporate Scandal Wave

Coupled with persistent macroeconomic weakness, a powerful spur to
the restructuring of Japan's industrial architecture in the 1990s was the
strong performance of the U.S. economy through much of the same period. From 1995 until 2000, when the bursting of the dot-com bubble
brought recession and stock market decline, the U.S. economy, whether
indexed by stock returns, entrepreneurial innovation, or unemployment
rates, was without peer. In 1997, with the United States in steep ascent and
Asia in the depths of financial crisis, the *Wall Street Journal* trumpeted
the victory of the American strain of capitalism over once-celebrated,
now disgraced East Asian and continental European forms.[163] Harvard
Business School professor and corporate strategy theorist Michael Porter
was quoted thus: "The strength of the American system is its very tight
corporate-governance system, [which] provides enormous scrutiny of corporate behavior and corporate investments." A similarly triumphal piece
on the global supremacy of U.S. economic practice appeared a year later
in the *New York Times*.[164] Reporter Nicholas Kristof wrote:

> To be sure, virtually everyone believes that the American boom is
> genuine and unlikely to run off a cliff the way Japan's did in 1990
> or Southeast Asia's did last year.... "Market capitalism certainly
> had its defects, but a number of them were addressed during
> the '70s and '80s," said Robert Alan Feldman, chief economist
> of Morgan Stanley in Tokyo.... "Now almost everyone believes
> that the great American advantage is the flexibility of its busi-
> nesses and the lack of government intervention in the economy."

However, in the summer of 2002 each day seemed to bring a report of
another U.S. company accused of accounting fraud, insider self-dealing,
negligent board and auditor oversight, and worse. Porter's eulogy to the
"tight" U.S. corporate governance system and the close "scrutiny of corporate behavior and investments" is today grimly ironic, as, it would seem,
is Feldman's paean to the flexibility that deregulation has wrought. Enron,
Global Crossing, Adelphia, Tyco, Merrill Lynch, Sunbeam, WorldCom,

---

[163] Murray (1997).
[164] Kristof (1998).

Xerox, Bristol-Meyers, Arthur Andersen, and Merrill Lynch were indeed flexible to an extreme, but perhaps not in ways that the rest of the world would care to emulate. These and other companies stand accused of deceptive and unethical, in some cases criminally fraudulent, maneuvers contrived to hide debt in phony partnerships, inflate and smooth earnings, and manipulate analysts' and auditors' assessments (and thereby stock prices and capital costs), all the while diverting vast sums into the pockets of high-ranking insiders. Proud accountancy Arthur Andersen – a onetime industry standard-bearer for untouchable auditing – is convicted of felony obstruction of justice and driven out of business for its overt complicity in Enron's shady schemes to hide liabilities and pad earnings. The ensuing crisis of confidence and legitimacy has weighed heavily on investor and consumer confidence, driving stock prices down to 1997 levels (thus obliterating most of the bubble era gains), weakening the dollar against foreign currencies, and, as of this writing, pushing the shaky economy to the brink of double-dip recession.

Against this backdrop, the rules of play in U.S. competitive capitalism appear much changed. Widely admired blue chip General Electric (GE)is a case in point. Year upon year GE enjoyed rave reviews from business pundits and an ever-rising stock price for its remarkable talent at generating earnings that bested Wall Street forecasts by a hair. But in the second quarter of 2002 with anger over corporate accounting scandals running high, GE's deftly executed earnings management fell flat. In the new climate of cynicism as to financial performance claims, the conglomerate's perfect numbers smacked of yet another case of deceptive accounting and investors dumped GE's stock.[165]

The corporate governance failures brought to light in late 2001 to mid-2002 tell a tale of crony capitalism writ large.[166] Oversight failed, it would seem, because the erstwhile monitors were snug in bed with the monitored. Even when a company's bankers, auditors, lawyers, board members, analysts, and suppliers were not directly complicit in its exercises in deceit, they had ample incentive to look the other way. Combined with the irrational exuberance of the turn-of-the-century bubble, the seeds of the new American cronyism were sewn by deregulation, perhaps most conspicuously the 1999 repeal of the depression-era Glass-Steagall Act, formerly a bulwark against financial conflicts of interest. As Joseph Stiglitz, Nobel Prize winning economist, former senior vice president of the World Bank,

---

[165] As noted in Chapter 5, a front-page *Wall Street Journal* article in 1996 provided extensive documentation of how General Electric moved costs and revenue around its divisions while timing charges and the booking of sales to give investors exactly what they wanted (Smith et al., 1994).

[166] Sanger (2003).

and member of the Clinton Council of Economic Advisors observed in the *Atlantic Monthly* in 2002[167]:

> If there was ever a time not to push deregulation further, the nineties was it. Even legitimate new financial-engineering techniques meant that investors and regulators alike were having an increasingly difficult time assessing companies' balance sheets. Such innovations had created new opportunities for those who wished to provide misleading information; deregulation would simply expand those opportunities. But the forces for deregulation were never greater than in the Roaring Nineties: the profits to be made were enormous, and with the abiding faith in the market economy seemingly confirmed by that economy's stupendous performance, banking interests saw an unprecedented opening. For more than half a century commercial banking had been separated from investment banking, with good reason. Investment banks push stocks, so if a company whose stock they have pushed needs cash, it becomes very tempting to make that company a loan.

Accounting rules – chiefly the absence of a requirement that stock options be expensed on balance sheets – were important as well. On the presumption that it would solve the agency problem of incentive misalignment between shareholders and managers, economists such as Michael Jensen devised elaborate theoretical arguments for coupling executive pay to shareholder value. The shift of stock options to center stage of U.S. compensation practice did change the incentives of managers: it drove many to measures that compromised the assets and mortgaged the future of the firm in order to achieve near-term run-ups in the stock. Few stakeholders of any sort saw fit to complain with the stock market barreling along, but when the train ran off the tracks, due in part to general macroeconomic weakness but mostly to the revelations of balance sheet fraud, the outrage was intense. It compounded as the news broke that top-flight executives of the implicated companies, acting on inside information, were cashing in and bailing out just before the company's deteriorating fortunes became public knowledge and the stock price and credit rating collapsed.

Incentive compensation also motivated executives to sacrifice long-term values on the altar of short-term gains. A reason Arthur Andersen so tilted its audits to make customers look good was that the firm had moved its pay practice away from fixed commissions toward bonuses tied to revenue brought in, thus ratcheting up the pressure on auditors to please clients and win their business. An auditor gutsy enough to blow the whistle on a

---

[167] Stiglitz (2002).

dubious case soon found him or herself off the account, if not out of a job, when the client complained. Similar conflicts of interest were prevalent among the bankers and brokerage firms servicing large corporations. Analysts' incentives were skewed toward extracting more and more of the client's money – achieved through aggressive promotions of its stock – and away from objective reporting on its fundamentals and long-term prospects.

Thus, the American model of capitalism in 2002 appeared much less the beacon light of economic rationality on which such a global consensus had existed just a few years before. This was not just a "few bad apples" as Paul O'Neal, Treasury Secretary (and former Alcoa CEO), ventured to claim. U.S. capitalism of late 1990s vintage looked rotten to the core. The roots of the market manipulations, cooked books, and self-dealing cronyism ran deep. As the *Wall Street Journal*, the foremost voice of 1990s American triumphalism, put it in what might fairly be called a crow-eating piece:

> "The investing public is infuriated with the financial information that they've been receiving – this is the U.S. in 2002 and we have a financial reporting system that resembles some sort of banana republic," said Brian McQuade, managing partner at Columbia Financial Advisors, an asset-management firm in Washington, D.C. "We have always been the leader in dictating corporate reporting standards to the rest of the world, and our own backyard is a mess."[168]

Among the many criticisms of East Asian and continental European capitalism floated by U.S. economists and consultants in the 1990s was that those managers lacked the high-powered incentives that so inspired U.S. executives' single-minded pursuit of shareholder value. Today, with stock options, bonuses, and other performance rewards exposed as drivers of the self-dealing and deception that brought to ruin the likes of Enron and WorldCom, the low-powered executive incentives typical of the Japanese corporation deserve another look.[169] As Dore (2000) notes, Japanese executives generally do not stand to profit personally by pushing their firms to overreach to the point of ruining stakeholders, destroying reputation, and decimating corporate assets. Within the framework of the permanent employment system, management incentives have been geared

---

[168] *Wall Street Journal*, 9 July 2002.
[169] The U.S. accounting scandals have bolstered European and Asian resistance to the U.S.- based Generally Accepted Accounting Principle (GAAP) in favor of International Accounting Standards, or IAS, as the global standard. Critics of GAAP complain of its complexity and its ease of manipulation: it allows a company bent on deception to adhere to the letter of the rules while violating the spirit.

to building a durable institution designed to do right by a diverse portfolio of constituents – customers, suppliers, employees, creditors, local
communities, *and* stockholders.

Some of the misdeeds catapulting major U.S. firms into bankruptcy
and disgrace were garden-variety fraud – crude violations of elementary
accounting rules – such as WorldCom's misrepresentation of operating
expenses as capital investment. They are noteworthy less for the size and
prestige of the corporate perpetrators than for the failure of auditors,
directors, banks, lawyers, and other erstwhile "monitors" to catch and
expose what was going on. Other corporate sins were more subtle and,
for our purposes, interesting for their parallel with keiretsu practice in
Japan.[170] Particularly instructive is Enron's leveraging of phony partnerships to shift debt and costs off the balance sheet and to engineer ersatz
trades that gave the appearance of high-volume transactions without any
value being added or real money being made. As earlier chapters note,
one of numerous ways keiretsu networks redistribute costs and assets
is the practice of *tobashi*, whereby one firm sells a property to another
with an under-the-table agreement to buy it back at a premium at a later
point in time and perhaps a loan to facilitate the purchase.[171] In either
case, pulling the wool over the eyes of stockholders, tax authorities, and
other monitors is part of the game. Yet Enron's practices are prima facie more manipulative and reprehensible if only because the "partners"
with whom the energy trader was exchanging liabilities and earnings were
paper entities set up expressly to obfuscate and deceive. In *tobashi*, the
partners may be cozily tied and the "sale" a contrivance with undisclosed
strings attached, but the firms themselves are for real. Further, while some
such transactions serve the interests of the parent or otherwise dominant
firm – for example, the *shukko*-ing of surplus people to subcontractors to
avoid layoffs or the compensating balances main banks pressure clients
to maintain – others such as discounted purchases, debt-for-equity swaps,
and manipulated prices advantage the partner at the parent's expense.

The rash of U.S. corporate accounting scandals has evoked considerable
schadenfreude from European and Asian businesspeople, policy makers,
and journalists who see the humbling of U.S. business as payback for
the condescending criticism Americans had leveled at their overregulated,
network-ridden, styles of capitalism. A *Business Week* columnist aptly
captured the mood in Japan:

> After years of listening to triumphal U.S. executives, economists,
> and Clinton Administration bigwigs lecture about the importance

[170] *Financial Times* (2002:12).
[171] Dore (1983); Kerr (2001).

of shareholder values, sound risk management, and yada, yada, yada, the Japanese are breaking into a collective grin. And who can blame them ... given that the supposed guardians of U.S. financial probity – accountants, credit agencies, laser-focused independent board members, and skeptical journalists – screwed up on such a massive scale. ... What was that about the U.S. being the gold standard of global business practices?[172]

The impressive U.S. record of unemployment, entrepreneurial energy, and vibrant stock performance made it hard in the 1990s to resist U.S. claims to superiority. With the bursting of the dot-com bubble and the ensuing scandal epidemic, sentiment spread abroad that the United States should get its house in order before presuming to lecture the rest of the world on how to design an efficient and transparent economy. Certainly, the scope and systemic character of the U.S. scandals has hardened the opposition of conservatives in Asia and Europe to proposals to reform corporate governance systems in those regions and liberalize capital and labor markets. Japanese business leaders such as Canon CEO Fujio Mitarai and Hiroshi Okuda, Toyota Chairman and Keidanren chief, used the opportunity to defend traditional Japanese ways. Mitarai minced no words:

> At U.S. companies, chief executive officers often appoint as outside directors friends who are unfamiliar with the day-to-day operations of the firm, and so they follow the CEO's lead. The dictatorship of top management is much stronger in the U.S. than in Japan and enables malfeasance and opportunism such as the one [sic] involving Enron Corp. ... I don't think [a Japanese company needs outside board members]. ... Canon now has 21 board members, and I'm thinking of adding more because the company has grown. All the board members are corporate officers, and there will be no outsiders. ... Most Japanese CEOs are very loyal, thanks to the lifetime-employment system. The basis of corporate governance in Japan lies with the ethical standards of the CEO and a company's board members.[173]

However, nothing in the U.S. scandal wave gainsays the genuine structural weaknesses that abound in Japanese financial, corporate governance, and regulatory systems; the part they played in Japan's lost decade; and the still pressing need for reform. The *Financial Times*' opinion might be predictable but is no less valid for that:

---

[172] Bremner (2002).
[173] *Business Week*, 13 September 2002.

Japan's gleeful reaction to America's corporate scandals may be dangerous. Like it or not, moves by the US to encourage Japan to reproduce its corporate model have had an important effect in spurring much-needed corporate restructuring. A resurgent belief in "the Japanese way" threatens the momentum of reform. Much as the Japanese would love the U.S. corporate scandals to symbolize a validation for the Japanese way, the Japanese corporate model is itself far from flawless.[174]

Still, as much of the evidence for America's late-1990s financial performance turns out to be phony, the Asian and continental European ways look less bad and bear some reexamination. Canon CEO Mitarai's defense of large insider boards and the lifetime employment system may go a bit far but he makes a credible point. Executive decision making in large Japanese corporations has been more constrained than in the U.S. or even European executive suites. Japanese managers are thus, on the one hand, ill-equipped to carry out the aggressive and to date successful restructuring that a French executive, Carlos Ghosn, could impose on Nissan. On the other side of the ledger is that the team-based, consensus-oriented nature of Japanese corporate leadership rules out the kind of extreme self-serving and unaccountable cowboy shenanigans of which Andrew Fastow of Enron or Bernard Ebbers of WorldCom stand accused.[175]

Conclusion: The Future of the Network Economy

Since the collapse of the bubble economy in 1991, Japan's industrial architecture has been buffeted by an array of powerful forces. Not all would have deep or lasting impact, and some, such as the decline in stable shareholding, mask offsetting processes rarely addressed in the business press reports. However, in the aggregate, these trends capture the subtle, but often very real, changes Japan experienced over the decade. These represented broad macro-trends shaping the Japanese economy in important ways at the outset of the twenty-first century. What were these macro-trends, and what is their impact?

---

[174] *Financial Times* (2002).
[175] Even U.S. old-economy stalwarts such as AT&T, GM, or Kodak, long the whipping boys of business journalists, consultants, and professors for their hierarchical structures and stale cultures, have found new favor in the wake of the scandals. Why, the question was so often asked, could not AT&T reinvent itself as a competitor on a par with new economy telecom upstarts such as WorldCom? But with WorldCom's success exposed as so much smoke and mirrors, AT&T and its ilk looked less like dinosaurs and more like solid, reliable, and, above all, trustworthy firms.

We have evaluated Japanese restructuring in a number of areas, including finance and corporate governance, industrial production, and technological innovation. Some of the claimed changes do not live up to their billing in politicians' pronouncements and the press, but a distillation of trends and adjustments does reveal the contours of the new economy now emerging in Japan. It differs from the old in significant ways. In the language of network analysis, it is characterized by weaker, less concatenated, less expansive, less multiplex, and less embedded ties; more fleeting, fragmented, asymmetric, *and* numerous ties. The proposed reforms in Japanese corporate boards illustrate. A board with a larger percentage of bona fide outsiders means more links between the firm and its environment, but, absent the power of keiretsu to mold them, such ties will be less overlapping, interwoven, and otherwise ordered than in the past. Although our data show it proceeding in fits and starts depending on the period and the group, the slow and uneven dissolution of the keiretsu is an inescapable macro-trend. In their stead is materializing a looser, more flexibly structured amalgam of micro-network pairings and clusterings pegged closely to the strategic business goals of individual firms. However, much of the basis for the networks of the past persists: companies still make strategic and symbolic investments in one another and favor long-term, high-trust partnerships over short-term, arm's-length ties.

Attendant upon the fragmentation and thinning of keiretsu networks is the similarly discontinuous winding-down of keiretsu risk-sharing and redistribution. As our review suggests, neither the reform-minded Koizumi government, nor the beleaguered banks, nor even such lead manufacturers as Toyota are yet prepared wholly to relinquish the deep-rooted network economy practice of sustaining and rehabilitating ailing members of the community of firms, but there is less consensus on the legitimacy and efficacy of the practice than in the past. Bankruptcies, even of large firms and financial institutions, are now a familiar and accepted occurrence, and bailouts to salvage a sickened firm with dubious recovery prospects are increasingly met with overt opposition. Moreover, the government's effort to shift the burden of rescue and restructuring from the old behind-the-scenes coalitions of ministries, banks, and keiretsu partners to a new convoy apparatus – the Industrial Revitalization Corporation and its entourage of public agencies and private equity funds – represents a much more transparent and above-board policy-directed approach to the rehabilitation of distressed companies. It is also more market-oriented in that, if the IRC operates according to plan, for every company revived and rehabilitated, a number will be allowed to die.

Among other trends transforming the economy is the departure from its center stage of the large industrial and financial firms that have occupied the economy's core since the early post-war years. Notwithstanding the still formidable obstacles to venture creation in Japan, enterprise found-ings are proceeding apace. Some of these – the spin-offs and start-ups sponsored by established firms – have strong continuities with the prac-tices of the past. A significant subset exists merely to window-dress down-sizing programs and thus is not to be taken seriously as entrepreneurial attempts. Many others, however, are for real.[176] The highest profile model for aggressive and entrepreneurial firms remains Softbank, quick to seize advantage of market opportunities materializing in Japan's turbulent new economy to craft its own latter-day zaibatsu.

Another powerful force for restructuring is the speed and trajectory of technological change. Japan's newspapers spew forth stories on the "Internet tsunami" and high-tech products and services unimaginable a few years ago. Japanese banks are leveraging Internet technologies to broaden and integrate their financial service offerings. Trading compa-nies use them in creating electronic documents that speed resource and information transfers across their far-flung commercial empires. And blue chip industrials such as NEC and Fujitsu are working to transform them-selves from old-line mainframe and personal computer manufacturers to flexible Internet enterprises. Owing to problems of payment (low use of credit cards) and the tradition of strong customer service, "B2C" (busi-ness to customer) Internet retailing took off slowly in Japan. However, the popularity of NTT DoCoMo's mobile e-mail/Internet service and the fast diffusion of high-speed home connections (ADSL monthly charges being half current U.S. rates) have spurred a wave of online buying, propelling, on the strength of low prices and strong customer support, direct seller Dell Computer to the number five spot (ahead of IBM) in the Japanese PC market.

Will new information processing and communications technologies sweep away Japan's network-ridden business practices, bringing down market barriers, raising flexibility and efficiency, and paving the way for sustainable economic growth? How, in particular, will they alter lend-ing and trading relations, not to mention the industrial associations and technology tie-ups at the frontiers of innovation? The short-term signals are mixed. Online procurement, heralded by the press as a body blow to keiretsu sourcing, has spread fast among Japanese firms, propelled by

---

[176] A joint study by the *Nihon Keizai Shimbun* and Nikkei Research Institute of Industry and Markets of 790 new private ventures with proprietary technology show average sales in fiscal 2002 rising 10 percent and profits up by 40.1 percent. Such firms are suc-ceeding, says the *Nikkei*, "by using unique ideas and flexible management techniques that are rarely found in large, established companies." Like Lumica Corp., a manu-facturer of luminescent fishing floats using U.S. space program technology, they have highly focused strategies and stay lean by minimizing fixed investments in plant and equipment. *Nikkei Net Interactive*, 11 November 2002.

rising parts standardization, offshore production, and the globalization of supply chains.[177] Even so, stable and sticky bank–client and customer–supplier relations, as with long-term employment, remain by most accounts a core competency of the Japanese industrial firm, and our own interviews suggest that the new information technologies are for the most part an overlay on and assist to high-trust, face-to-face dealings, not a wholesale substitute for them.

The inward internationalization of Japanese industry is another network-destroying macro-trend. Until the 1990s, stories of foreign enterprises successfully entering the Japanese market mostly invoked the same short list: IBM and Texas Instruments in technology, Coca Cola and McDonald's in consumer food products, and the like. These names were reeled off whenever defenders of Japan's trading practices felt called upon to defend the openness of Japanese markets (although in fact the ritualized recitation of this time-worn list signaled the opposite). By the end of the 1990s, however, the list had been transformed. It included technology leaders such as Compaq, Cisco Systems, Apple, Oracle, and Yahoo!, not to mention foreign auto producers such as Ford, GM, and Renault that now have high profiles in Japan. More significant, perhaps, were the foreign players in financial services – the investment banks, equity funds, and occasional commercial lender such as Citicorp – an area that prior to the 1990s had no significant foreign participation. To be sure, foreign direct investment remains low in Japan by international standards, and healthy Japanese firms are still resistant to selling corporate assets to outsiders.[178] Nonetheless, the barriers to foreign involvement in the Japanese economy, once seemingly surmountable and still hanging on in some sectors, are falling away.

As for forces slowing down the rate of change, there is, once again, the bursting of the U.S. new economy bubble and the trashing, for now, of U.S. claims to a superior corporate governance paradigm. Of course, how much lasting significance the U.S. economy's embarrassing stumble will have for Japan and Europe depends on the speed of the U.S. recovery. If the United States is again going strong while Japan and Germany are stagnating, American ways will no doubt dominate again.

There is, too, the possibility, increasingly likely as we go to press, that the Japanese economy, whose real GDP grew -1.4 percent in 2001, 1.1 percent in 2002, and an estimated 2 percent in 2003 – will manage a sustained recovery. Just as the global upswing on the heels of the Asian financial crisis of 1997–98 slowed the impetus for change in Korea other Asian economies, a rapid reversal of Japan's fortunes, should it happen

---

[177] Sakakibara and Miki (1999).
[178] E. Lincoln (1990).

anytime soon, may undercut the momentum for reform. Direct foreign investment may slow as stock and real estate prices rise. A significant and sustained rally in those markets (the Nikkei index hit 11,000 in early 2004, more than 40 percent above the post-bubble low of 7,607) would also in short order transform the capital asset makeup of Japan's major banks, perhaps consigning the bad loan crisis which now has Japan transfixed to fast-receding memory.

Perhaps the broadest challenge facing Japan – and the most important as it frames all else we review here – is a resolution to the intellectual battles over what form Japanese capitalism will take in the twenty-first century. On the one side are the bearers of received modernization theory, the doctrine that Japanese distinctiveness, as Richard Katz put it, is not a different form of capitalism but merely the "holdover of a form better suited to its adolescence." For them, embracing U.S. "market individualism" is Japan's only hope for competitiveness and sustainable growth.

For now, however, serious voices on the other side are still being heard. Thoughtful observers such as Masahiko Aoki and Eisuke Sakakibara see the basic contours of the post-war Japanese business system as well-adapted still to the management of critical interdependencies that cannot and should not be abandoned. These holdouts for a distinctively Japanese path to economic growth see Japanese business practices offering important competitive advantages, such as (transaction) cost-reducing and flexibility-enhancing high-trust and high-cooperation partnerships; a more stable, better trained, and motivated workforce; and a commitment to the firm as a durable national asset. Radical reform to do away with these, they fear, may well destroy the Japanese competitive advantage in manufacturing. Indeed, Japan's own recent wave of corporate scandals – Mitsubishi Motors' cover-up of vehicle defects, the food poisoning fiasco at Snow Brand, the mislabeling of beef at Nippon Ham, and other recent quality and customer service snafus – are widely viewed in Japan as symptomatic of an erosion in commitment and discipline brought on by the crumbling of lifetime employment and other mainstays of the post-war network economy.[179]

---

[179] The *Keizai Doyukai* (Japan Association of Corporate Executives) has argued for the deregulation of the Japanese economy and creation of a more transparent system based on rules, shareholder rights, and the like. These reform, advocates argue, would create healthy competition among heretofore protected sectors of the economy, such as financial services, while also facilitating international harmonization. Similarly, the Corporate Governance Forum of Japan, a group of investors, scholars, and executives, favors a shift in Japanese corporate thinking toward greater accountability to shareholders, the implicit message being less focus on employees and other nonshareholder stakeholders. The Pension Fund Association for Local Government Officials, meanwhile, is endorsing the idea of companies appointing more directors with no ties to the firm (see Ahmadjian, 2003).

One of the most eloquent spokespersons for the preservation of Japan's distinctive economic institutions in contrast to the Anglo-American models of market-individualist shareholder capitalism is the dean of Japan sociologists, Ronald Dore. Three decades ago Dore championed the provocative hypothesis that Japan's network economy owed its origins, not to the preservation of feudal traditions or a failure to transcend economic adolescence, but to the country's status as a late developer. Its physical and social infrastructure demolished by the war, Japan rebuilt by scanning the world scene, copying and improving upon the leading edge in global economic practice. Dore's inverted modernization hypothesis – that early developers such as Britain are wedded to the past and late developers such Japan and Germany contain the economic institutions of the future – is consistent with the institutional theory claim that organizational forms carry the imprint of the era that spawned them.[180] Dore is not shy in acknowledging his preference for German and Japanese ways which, in his view, are distinguished by cooperation, equality, security, trust, and inclusiveness as opposed to the inequality, arm's-length dealings, hard competitiveness, and rampant job insecurity of what he calls the Anglo-Saxon economies. We confess to considerable sympathy with Dore's positive portrayal of Japan's network economy, although, as our review in this chapter suggests, we see much of it fading into history and perhaps inevitably so.

[180] Hannan and Freeman (1989); Stinchcombe (1965); Westney (1987).

Bibliography

Abegglen, James C. 1958. *The Japanese Factory: Aspects of Its Social Organization*. Glencoe, IL: Free Press.

Abegglen, James C. and George Stalk Jr. 1985. *Kaisha: The Japanese Corporation*. New York: Basic Books.

Ahmadjian, Christina L. 1996. "Japanese Supply Networks and the Governance of Interfirm Exchange." Presented at the Academy of Management, Cincinnati, August.

1997. "Network Affiliation and Supplier Performance in the Japanese Automotive Industry." Presented to the Academy of Management, Boston, August.

2003. "Changing Japanese Corporate Governance." In *Japan Changes: The New Political Economy of Structural Adjustment and Globalization*, edited by Ulrike Schaede and William Grimes. New York: M.E. Sharpe.

Ahmadjian, Christina L. and James R. Lincoln. 2001. "Keiretsu, Governance, and Learning: Case Studies in Change from the Japanese Automotive Industry." *Organization Science* 12:683–701.

Ahmadjian, Christina L. and Patricia Robinson. 2001. "Safety in Numbers: Downsizing and the Deinstitutionalization of Permanent Employment in Japan." *Administrative Science Quarterly* 46:622–54.

Akerlof, George A. 1982. "Labor Contracts as Partial Gift Exchange." *Quarterly Journal of Economics* 97:543–69.

Aldrich, Howard. 1979. *Organizations and Environments*. Englewood Cliffs, NJ: Prentice-Hall.

1999. *Organizations Evolving*. Thousand Oaks, CA: Sage Publications.

Anchordoguy, Marie. 1989. *Computers Inc: Japan's Challenge to IBM*. Cambridge, MA: Harvard University Press.

Aoki, Masahiko. 1984. "Risk-Sharing in the Corporate Group." Pp. 259–64 in *The Economic Analysis of the Japanese Firm*, edited by Masahiko Aoki. Amsterdam: North-Holland.

1988. *Information, Incentives, and Bargaining in the Japanese Economy*. New York: Cambridge University Press.

Aoki, Masahiko and Hugh T. Patrick. 1994. The *Japanese Main Bank System: Its Relevance for Developing and Transforming Economies*. New York: Oxford University Press.

Asahi Shimbun. 2003. *Japan Almanac*. Tokyo: Asahi Shimbun-sha.

Asanuma, Banri. 1985. "Transactional structure of parts supply in the Japanese automobile and electrical machinery industries." Technical Report No. 1, Socio-economic Systems Research Project, Kyoto University.

1989. "Manufacturer-Supplier Relationships in Japan and the Concept of Relation-Specific Skill." *Journal of the Japanese and International Economies* 3:1–30.

Asanuma, Banri and T. Kikutani. 1992. "Risk Absorption in Japanese Subcontracting – a Microeconometric Study of the Automobile-Industry." *Journal of the Japanese and International Economies* 6:1–29.

Associated Press. 2001. "Nissan Returns to Profitability." May 17.

Bacon, Jeremy and James K. Brown. 1978. The *Board of Directors: Perspectives and Practices in Nine Countries*. New York: Conference Board.

Baker, Wayne E. 1990. "Market Networks and Corporate Behavior." *American Journal of Sociology* 96:589–625.

Ballon, Robert J. and Iwao Tomita. 1976. *The Financial Behavior of Japanese Corporations*. Tokyo: Kodansha.

Baron, James N., Frank R. Dobbin, and P. D. Jennings. 1986. "War and Peace: The Evolution of Modern Personnel Administration in U.S. Industry." *American Journal of Sociology* 92:350–83.

Beer, Michael and B. A. Spector. 1981. "Matsushita Electric." Harvard Business School Case 9-481-146. Boston: Harvard Business School Press.

Berglof, Eric and Enrico Perotti. 1994. "The Governance Structure of the Japanese Financial Keiretsu." *Journal of Financial Economics* 36:259–84.

Berle, Adolf A. and Gardiner Means. 1932. *The Modern Corporation and Private Property*. New York: Macmillan.

Bertrand, Marianne, Paras Mehta, and Sendhil Mullainathan. 2002. "Ferreting out Tunneling: An Application to Indian Business Groups." *Quarterly Journal of Economics* 117:121–48.

Blau, Peter M. 1964. *Exchange and Power in Social Life*. New York: John Wiley.

Blinder, Alan S. 1991. "A Japanese Buddy System That Could Benefit U.S. Business." *Business Week*, October 14, p. 32.

Borgatti, S. P. and M. G. Everett. 1992. "Notions of position in social network analysis." *Sociological Methodology*, 22:1–35.

Branstetter, Lee. 2000. "Vertical Keiretsu and Knowledge Spillovers in Japanese Manufacturing: An Empirical Assessment." *Journal of the Japanese and International Economies* 14:73–104.

Brauchli, Marcus W. 1991. "Ousted Executive in Japan Accuses Nissan of Meddling." *Wall Street Journal*, May 15.

Bremner, Brian. 2002. "Misreading the Enron Scandal." *Business Week*, April 24.

Bremner, Brian and Emily Thornton. 1999. "Mitsubishi: Fall of a Keiretsu." *Business Week International Edition*, March 15.

Broadbridge, S. 1966. *Industrial Dualism in Japan: A Problem of Economic Growth and Structural Change.* London: Frank Cass & Co.

Burt, Ronald S. 1980. "Models of Network Structure." *Annual Review of Sociology* 6:79–141.

1983. *Corporate Profits and Cooptation.* New York: Academic Press.

1987. "Social Contagion and Innovation – Cohesion Versus Structural Equivalence." *American Journal of Sociology* 92:1287–1335.

1992. *Structural Holes.* Cambridge, MA: Harvard University Press.

Burt, R. S., K. P. Christman, and H. C. Kilburn. 1980. "Testing a Structural Theory of Corporate Cooptation." *American Sociological Review* 45:821–41.

Cable, John. 1983. "Hierarchies and Markets: An Empirical Test of the Multidivisional Hypothesis in West Germany." *International Journal of Industrial Organization* 1:43–62.

Cable, John and Hirohiko Yasuki. 1985. "Internal Organisation, Business Groups, and Corporate Performance: An Empirical Test of the Multidivisional Hypothesis in Japan." *International Journal of Industrial Organization* 3:401–20.

Calder, Kent E. 1993. *Strategic Capitalism: Private Business and Public Purpose in Japanese Industrial Finance.* Princeton, NJ: Princeton University Press.

Career Development Center (Kyarya Deberopmento Senta). 2002. *Kigyo gurupu to gyokai chizu* (Enterprise Groups and the Map of the Business World). Tokyo: Takabashi Shoten.

Cargill, Thomas F., Michael M. Hutchison, and Takatoshi Ito. 1997. *The Political Economy of Japanese Monetary Policy.* Cambridge, MA: MIT Press.

Caves, Richard and Masu Uekusa. 1976. *Industrial Organization in Japan.* Washington, DC: The Brookings Institution.

Chesbrough, Henry W. and David J. Teece. 1996. "When Is Virtual Virtuous? Organizing for Innovation." *Harvard Business Review* 74:65–73.

Clark, Rodney 1979. *The Japanese Company.* New Haven: Yale University Press.

Cole, Robert E. 1971. *Japanese Blue Collar: The Changing Tradition.* Berkeley, CA: University of California Press.

1989. *Strategies for Learning.* Berkeley, CA: University of California Press.

Coleman, James S. 1986. "Social Theory, Social Research, and a Theory of Action." *American Journal of Sociology* 16:1309–35.

Colignon, R. and C. Usui. 2001. "The Resilience of Japan's Iron Triangle – Amakudari." *Asian Survey* 41:865–95.

Cusumano, Michael A. 1985. *The Japanese Automobile Industry: Technology and Management at Nissan and Toyota.* Cambridge, MA: Harvard University Press.

1991. *Japan's Software Factories: A Challenge to U.S. Management.* New York: Oxford University Press.

Davis, Gerald F. and Mark S. Mizruchi. 1999. "The Money Center Cannot Hold: Commercial Banks in the US System of Corporate Governance." *Administrative Science Quarterly* 44:215–39.

Dechow, P. M., R. G. Sloan, and A. P. Sweeney. 1995. "Detecting Earnings Management." *Accounting Review* 70:193–225.

Dedrick, Jason and Kenneth L. Kraemer. 1998. *Asia's Computer Challenge: Threat or Opportunity for the United States & the World?* New York: Oxford University Press.

Dewatripont, M. and Gerard Roland. 1997. "Transition as a Process of Large Scale Institutional Change." Pp. 240–78 in *Advances in Economic Theory*, edited by D. Kreps and K. Wallis. New York: Cambridge University Press, vol. II.

DiMaggio, P. and W. W. Powell. 1983. "The Iron Cage Revisited: Institutional Isomorphism and Collective Rationality in Organizational Fields." *American Sociological Review* 48:147–60.

Dodwell Marketing Consultants. Various years. *Industrial Groupings in Japan.* Tokyo: Dodwell.

Dore, Ronald P. 1973. *British Factory, Japanese Factory.* Berkeley, CA: University of California Press.

1983. "Goodwill and the Spirit of Market Capitalism." *British Journal of Sociology* 34:459–82.

1986. *Flexible Rigidities: Industrial Policy and Structural Adjustment in the Japanese Economy 1970–80.* London: Athlone.

1987. *Taking Japan Seriously: A Confucian Perspective on Leading Economic Issues.* Stanford, CA: Stanford University Press.

2000. *Stock Market Capitalism: Welfare Capitalism.* Oxford, UK: Oxford University Press.

Dvorak, Phred, Robert A. Guth, Jason Singer, and Todd Zaun. 2001. "Recession Frays Japan Inc.'s Tradition of Loyal, Long-Term Corporate Alliances." *Wall Street Journal*, March 2.

Dyer, Jeffrey H. 1996a. "Does Governance Matter? Keiretsu Alliances and Asset Specificity as Sources of Japanese Competitive Advantage." *Organization Science* 7:649–66.

1996b. "Specialized Supplier Networks as a Source of Competitive Advantage: Evidence from the Auto Industry." *Strategic Management Journal* 17:271–91.

Dyer, Jeffrey H. and William G. Ouchi. 1993. "Japanese-Style Partnerships – Giving Companies a Competitive Edge." *Sloan Management Review* 35:51–63.

Economist. 2002. "Star Turn: What Distinguishes Companies That Have Bucked Japan's Corporate Downturn?" November 7.

Fair Trade Commission (*Kosei torihiki iinkai*). 1987. *Long-Term Relationships among Japanese Companies: A Report by the Study Group on Trade Frictions and Market Structure.* Tokyo: Fair Trade Commission. April.

1992. *The Outline of the Report on the Actual Conditions of the Six Major Corporate Groups.* Tokyo: Executive Office, Fair Trade Commission.

Faust, Karen and A. K. Romney. 1985. "Does Structure Find Structure? A Critique of Burt's Use of Distance as a Measure of Equivalence." *Social Networks* 7:77–103.

Feenstra, Robert C., Deng-Shing Huang, and Gary G. Hamilton. 1997. "Business Groups and Trade in East Asia: Part 1, Networked Equilibria." Cambridge, MA: National Bureau of Economic Research. January.

Financial Times. 2002. "Japanese Delight as Scandals Rock the 'American Model': But Reform May Be Hit by a New Belief in the Old Way." August 15, p. 12.

Flaherty, M. Therese and Hiroyuki Itami. 1984. "Finance." Pp. 134–76 in *The Competitive Edge*, edited by Daniel I. Okimoto, Takuo Sugano, and Franklin B. Weinstein. Stanford, CA: Stanford University Press.

Flath, David. 1993. "Shareholding in the Keiretsu, Japan's Financial Groups." *Review of Economics and Statistics* 75:249–57.

Fligstein, Neil. 1990. *The Transformation of Corporate Control.* Cambridge, MA: Harvard University Press.

Fransman, Martin. 1990. *Beyond the Market: Cooperation and Competition in the Creation of Advanced Computing and Electronics Technologies in the Japanese System.* New York: Cambridge University Press.

Freeland, Robert F. 2001. *The Struggle for Control of the Modern Corporation: Organizational Change at General Motors, 1924–1970.* New York: Cambridge University Press.

Freeman, John, Glenn R. Carroll, and Michael T. Hannan. 1983. "The Liability of Newness: Age Dependence in Organizational Death Rates." *American Sociological Review* 48:692–710.

French, Howard. 2001. "In Stagnant Japan, Economic and Social Ills Match." *New York Times*, February 6.

Friedman, David. 1988. *The Misunderstood Miracle: Industrial Development and Political Change in Japan.* Ithaca, NY: Cornell University Press.

Fruin, W. Mark. 1983. *Kikkoman: Company, Clan, and Community.* Cambridge, MA: Harvard University Press.

1992. *The Japanese Enterprise System.* New York: Oxford University Press.

1997. *Knowledge Works: Managing Intellectual Capital at Toshiba.* New York: Oxford University Press.

Fruin, W. Mark and Toshihiro Nishiguchi. 1992. "Supplying the Toyota Production System: How to Make a Molehill out of a Mountain." In *Country Competitiveness*, edited by Bruce Kogut. New York: Oxford University Press.

Fuji Electric Co. 1973. *Fuji Electric History.* Tokyo: Fuji Electric.

Fujitsu. 1964. *Company History.* Tokyo: Fujitsu Limited.

1976. *Company History II: 1961–1975.* Tokyo: Fujitsu Limited.

Fukuda, Masako. 1997. "Group Ties Get Builder Out of Fiscal Bind." *Nikkei Weekly*, August 8.

Gao, Bai. 2001. *Japan's Economic Dilemma: The Institutional Origins of Prosperity and Stagnation.* New York: Cambridge University Press.

Geertz, Clifford, Hildred Geertz, and Lawrence Rosen. 1979. *Meaning and Order in Moroccan Society.* Cambridge, UK: Cambridge University Press.

Gerlach, Michael L. 1991. "Twilight of the Keiretsu? A Critical Assessment." *Journal of Japanese Studies* 8:79–118.

1992a. *Alliance Capitalism: The Social Organization of Japanese Business.* Berkeley, CA: University of California Press.

1992b. "The Japanese Corporate Network: A Blockmodel Analysis." *Administrative Science Quarterly* 37:105–39.

1997. "Organizational Logic of Business Groups: Evidence from the Zaibatsu." In *Beyond the Firm*, edited by T. Shiba and M. Shimotani. New York: Oxford University Press.

Gerlach, Michael L. and James R. Lincoln. 1992. "The Organization of Business Networks in the U.S. and Japan." Pp. 491–520 in *Networks and Organizations: Structure, Form, and Action*, edited by N. Nohria and R. Eccles. Boston: Harvard Business School Press.

1998. "The Structural Analysis of Japanese Economic Organization: A Conceptual Framework." In W. Mark Fruin (ed.): *Networks and Markets: Pacific Rim Strategies*. New York: Oxford University Press.

2001. "Economic Organization and Innovation in Japan: Networks, Spinoffs, and the Creation of Enterprise." Pp. 151–98 in *Knowledge Creation: A New Source of Value*, edited by Ikujiro Nonaka, Georg von Krogh, and Toshihiro Nishiguchi. London: Macmillan.

Ghemawat, Pankaj and Tarun Khanna. 1998. "The Nature of Diversified Business Groups: A Research Design and Two Case Studies." *Journal of Industrial Economics* 46:35–61.

Gordon, Andrew. 1985. *The Evolution of Labor Relations in Japan*. Cambridge, MA: Harvard University Press.

Goto, Akira. 1981. "Statistical Evidence on the Diversification of Japanese Large Firms." *Journal of Industrial Economics* 29:271–78.

1982. "Business Groups in a Market Economy." *European Economic Review* 19:53–70.

Gould, Roger V. and Roberto M. Fernandez. 1989. "Structures of Mediation: A Formal Approach to Brokerage in Transaction Networks." *Sociological Methodology* 19:89–126.

Gouldner, Alvin W. 1960. "The Norm of Reciprocity: A Preliminary Statement." *American Sociological Review* 25:161–78.

Granovetter, Mark. 1973. "The Strength of Weak Ties." *American Journal of Sociology* 78:1360–81.

1985. "Economic Action and Social Structure: The Problem of Embeddedness." *American Journal of Sociology* 91:481–510.

2003. "Business Groups and Social Organization." In *Handbook of Economic Sociology*, edited by N. Smelser and R. Swedberg. Princeton, NJ: Princeton University Press, 2nd edition.

Greene, William H. 1997. *Econometric Analysis*. Upper Saddle River, NJ: Prentice Hall.

Greve, H. R. and A. Taylor. 2000. "Innovations as Catalysts for Organizational Change." *Administrative Science Quarterly* 45:54–80.

Guetzkow, Harold. 1965. "Communication in Organizations." Pp. 534–72 in *Handbook of Organizations*, edited by James G. March. Chicago: Rand McNally.

Guillen, Mauro F. 2000. "Business Groups in Emerging Economies: A Resource-Based View." *Academy of Management Journal* 43:362–80.

2001. *The Limits of Convergence: Globalization and Organizational Change in Argentina, South Korea, and Spain*. Princeton, NJ: Princeton University Press.

Guillot, Dider and James R. Lincoln. 2001. "The Permeability of Network Boundaries: Strategic Alliances in the Japanese Electronics Industry in the 1990s."
Presented to the American Sociological Association, Anaheim, CA, August.

———. 2003. "Dyad and Network: Models of Manufacturer-Supplier Collaboration
in the Japanese TV Manufacturing Industry." In *Advances in International
Management: Special Issue on Changing Japan*, edited by Allan Bird and
Thomas Roehl. Greenwich, CT: JAI Press.

Guillot, Didier, David Mowery, and William Spencer. 2000. "The Changing Structure of Government-Industry Research Partnerships in Japan." Presented to
the Administrative Science Association of Canada, Montreal, July 7–11.

Gulati, Ranjay. 1995. "Social Structure and Alliance Formation Patterns: A Longitudinal Analysis." *Administrative Science Quarterly* 40:619–52.

Gulati, Ranjay and M. Gargiulo. 1999. "Where Do Interorganizational Networks
Come From?" *American Journal of Sociology* 104:1439–93.

Hadley, Eleanor. 1970. *Antitrust in Japan*. Princeton, NJ: Princeton University
Press.

———. 1984. "Counterpoint on Business Groupings and Government-Industry Relations in Automobiles." Pp. 227–58 in *The Economic Analysis of the Japanese
Firm*, edited by M. Aoki. Amsterdam: North-Holland.

Hamilton, Gary and Nicole Biggart. 1988. "Market, Culture, and Authority: A
Comparative Analysis of Management and Organization in the Far East."
American Journal of Sociology 94 (supplement):S52–S94.

Hamao, Yasushi, Jianping Mei, and Yexiao Xu. 2002. "Idiosyncratic Risk and
Creative Destruction in Japan." NBER Working paper 9642, Cambridge,
MA. April.

Hannan, Michael and John Freeman. 1989. *Organizational Ecology*. Cambridge,
MA: Harvard University Press.

Harary, Frank, Dorwin Cartwright, and Robert Zane Norman. 1965. *Structural
Models*. New York: Wiley.

Harrison, Bennett 1994. *Lean and Mean: The Changing Landscape of Corporate
Power in the Age of Flexibility*. New York: Basic Books.

Haunschild, P. R. and C. M. Beckman. 1998. "When Do Interlocks Matter? Alter-
nate Sources of Information and Interlock Influence." *Administrative Science
Quarterly* 43:815–44.

Hauser, Robert M. 1970. "Context and Consex: A Cautionary Tale." *American
Journal of Sociology* 75:645–64.

Hausman, Jerry A. 1978. "Specification Tests in Econometrics." *Econometrica*
46:1251–71.

Hausman, Jerry A. and William E. Taylor. 1981. "Panel Data and Unobservable
Individual Effects." *Econometrica* 49:1377–98.

Heimer, Carol A. 1992. "Doing Your Job and Helping Your Friends: Universalistic
Norms About Obligations to Particular Others in Networks." In *Networks
and Organizations: Structure, Form, and Action*, edited by Nitin Nohria and
Robert G. Eccles. Boston: Harvard Business School Press.

Helper, Susan R. and Mari Sako. 1995. "Supplier Relations in Japan and the
United States: Are They Converging?" *Sloan Management Review* 36:77–
84.

Hirsch, Paul M. 1975. "Organizational Effectiveness and the Institutional Environment." *Administrative Science Quarterly* 20:327–44.

Hirschmeier, Johannes and Tsunehiko Yui. 1975. *The Development of Japanese Business, 1600–1973.* Cambridge, MA: Harvard University Press.

Holland, Paul W. and Samuel Leinhardt. 1981. "An Exponential Family of Probability Distributions for Directed Graphs." *Journal of the American Statistical Association* 76:33–50.

Horiuchi, Akiyoshi, Frank Packer, and Shin'ichi Fukuda. 1988. "What Role Has the 'Main Bank' Played in Japan." *Journal of the Japanese and International Economies* 2:159–80.

Hoshi, Takeo. 2002. "The Convoy System for Insolvent Banks: How It Originally Worked and Why It Failed in the 1990s." *Japan and the World Economy* 14:155–80.

Hoshi, Takeo and Takatoshi Ito. 1992. "*Kigyo grupu kessokudo no bunseki*" (Analysis of Coherence of Firm Groups)." Pp. 73–96 in *Gendai nihon no kinyu bunseki* (Financial Analysis of Contemporary Japan), edited by Akiyoshi Horiuchi and Naoyuki Yoshino. Tokyo: University of Tokyo Press.

Hoshi, Takeo and Anil Kashyap. 2000. "The Japanese Banking Crisis: Where Did It Come from and How Will It End?" Pp. 129–201 in *NBER Macroeconomics Annual 1999*, volume 14.

——— 2001. *Corporate Financing and Governance in Japan.* Cambridge, MA: MIT Press.

Hoshi, Takeo, A. K. Kashyap, and G. Loveman. 1994. "Lessons from the Japanese Main Bank System for Financial System Reform in Poland." In *The Japanese Main Bank System: Its Relevance for Developing and Transforming Economies*, edited by M. Aoki and H. Patrich. New York: Oxford University Press.

Hoshi, Takeo, Anil Kashyap, and David Scharfstein. 1991a. "The Role of Banks in Reducing the Costs of Financial Distress in Japan." *Journal of Financial Economics* 27:67–88.

——— 1991b. "Corporate Structure, Liquidity, and Investment: Evidence from Japanese Industrial Groups." *Quarterly Journal of Economics* 106:33–60.

Ibison, David. 2003a. "Banks Tire of Waiting for Sun to Rise on Japan." *Financial Times.* February 15.

——— 2003b. "Business Links Make a Return in Japan." *Financial Times*, January 21.

Imai, Ken-ichi. 1990. "Japanese Business Groups and the Structural Impediments Initiative." In *Japan's Economic Structure: Should It Change?* Edited by Kozo Yamamura. Seattle: Society for Japanese Studies.

Imai, Kenichi and Hiroyuki Itami. 1984. "Interpenetration of Organization and Market: Japan's Firm and Market in Comparison with the U.S." *International Journal of Industrial Organization* 2:285–310.

Imai, Ken-ichi, Ikujiro Nonaka, and Hirotaka Takeuchi. 1985. "Managing the New Product Development Process: How Japanese Companies Learn and Unlearn." Pp. 337–76 in *The Uneasy Alliance: Managing the Productivity-Technology Dilemma*, edited by Kim B. Clark and Christopher Lorenz. Boston: Harvard Business School Press.

Inkeles, Alex and David Horton Smith. 1974. *Becoming Modern: Individual Change in Six Developing Countries.* Cambridge: MA: Harvard University Press.

Itami, Hiroyuki and Thomas W. Roehl. 1987. *Mobilizing Invisible Assets.* Cambridge, MA: Harvard University Press.

Ito, Kiyohiko. 1995. "Japanese Spinoffs: Unexplored Survival Strategies," *Strategic Management Journal* 16:431–46.

Ito, Takatoshi. 1992. *The Japanese Economy.* Cambridge, MA: MIT Press.

Itoh, Hideshi. 2003. "Corporate Restructuring in Japan, Part I: Can M-Form Organization Manage Diverse Businesses?" *Japanese Economic Review* 54:49–73.

Jacoby, Sanford M. 1985. *Employing Bureaucracy.* New York: Columbia University Press.

Japan Development Bank. 2000. *Corporate Finance Data Bank.* Tokyo: Development Bank of Japan.

Japan Small Business Research Institute. 1999. "A Study of the Present Conditions and the Future Outlook of Industrial Districts in Japan." Tokyo: METI Japan Small Business Research Institute. March.

Jensen, Michael C. and William H. Meckling. 1976. "Theory of the Firm." *Journal of Financial Economics* 3:305–60.

Jinji koshin roku (Personnel Inquiry Record). Various years. Tokyo: Jinji Koshin Roku-Sho.

Johnson, Chalmers A. 1982. *MITI and the Japanese Miracle.* Stanford, CA: Stanford University Press.

Judd, Charles M. and David A. Kenny. 1981. *Estimating the Effects of Social Interventions.* New York: Cambridge University Press.

Kageyama, Yuri. 2003. "Shinsei Experience: Lattes in the Lobby, Free ATM Transactions." *Japan Times,* January 31.

Kaisha nenkan (Company Annual). Various years. Tokyo: Nihon Keizai Shimbun-sha.

Kang, J. K. and A. Shivdasani. 1995. "Firm Performance, Corporate Governance, and Top Executive Turnover in Japan." *Journal of Financial Economics* 38:29–58.

Kaplan, Steven N. and Bernadette A. Minton. 1994. "Appointment of Outsiders to Japanese Boards: Determinants and Implications for Managers." *Journal of Financial Economics* 36:225–58.

Katz, Richard. 1998. *Japan: The System That Soured.* New York: M. E. Sharpe.

Kawasaki, S. and John McMillan. 1987. "The Design of Contracts: Evidence from Japanese Subcontracting." *Journal of the Japanese and International Economies* 1:327–49.

Kawashima, Takeyoshi. 1963. "Dispute Resolution in Contemporary Japan," in *Law in Japan: The Legal Order in a Changing Society,* edited by A. T. von Mehren. Cambridge, MA: Harvard University Press.

Keiretsu no kenkyu (Keiretsu Research). Various years. Tokyo: Keizai Chosa Kyokai.

Keister, Lisa A. 2001. "Exchange Structures in Transition: Lending and Trade Relations in Chinese Business Groups." *American Sociological Review* 66:336–60.

Keizai Kikakucho (Economic Planning Agency). 1997. *Keizai hakusho* (White Paper on the Economy). Tokyo: Keizai Kikakucho.

Kelley, Maryellen R. and Harvey Brooks. 1991. "External Learning Opportunities and the Diffusion of Process Innovations to Small Firms: The Case of Programmable Automation." *Technological Forecasting and Economic Change* 39:103–25.

Kerr, Alex. 2001. *Dogs and Demons: Tales from the Dark Side of Japan.* New York: Hill and Wang.

Kerr, Clark. 1960. *Industrialism and Industrial Man: The Problems of Labor and Management in Economic Growth.* Cambridge, MA: Harvard University Press.

Kester, W. Carl. 1991. *Japanese Takeovers: The Global Contest for Corporate Control.* Boston: Harvard Business School Press.

——— 1997. "Governance, Contracting, and Investment Horizons: A Look at Japan and Germany." Pp. 227–42 in *Studies in International Corporate Finance and Governance Systems: A Comparison of the U.S., Japan, and Europe,* edited by Donald H. Chew. New York: Oxford University Press.

Khanna, Tarun and K. Pelepu. 2000. "Is Group Affiliation Profitable in Emerging Markets? An Analysis of Diversified Indian Business Groups." *Journal of Finance* 55:867–91.

Khanna, Tarun and Jane W. Rivkin. 2001. "Estimating the Performance Effects of Business Groups in Emerging Markets." *Strategic Management Journal* 22:45–74.

Knoke, David and James H. Kuklinski. 1982. *Network Analysis.* Beverly Hills, CA: Sage Publications.

Knoke, David, F. U. Pappi, J. Broadbent, and Y. Tsujinaka. 1996. *Comparing Policy Networks: Labor Politics in the U.S., Germany, and Japan.* New York: Cambridge University Press.

Kobayashi, Hiroshi, Yukihiko Endo, and Seiji Ogishima. 1993. "New Directions in Japanese Banking Relationships" *Nomura Research Institute Quarterly* 11:2–27.

Kogut, Bruce. 1989. "The Stability of Joint Ventures – Reciprocity and Competitive Rivalry." *Journal of Industrial Economics* 38:183–98.

——— 2000. "The Network as Knowledge: Generative Rules and the Emergence of Structure." *Strategic Management Journal* 21:405–25.

Komiya, Ryutaro, Masahiro Okuno, and Kotaro Suzumura. 1988. *Industrial Policy in Japan.* Tokyo: Academic Press Japan.

Kondo, Dorinne K. 1990. *Crafting Selves: Power, Gender, and Discourses of Identity in a Japanese Workplace.* Chicago: University of Chicago Press.

Kono, Clifford, Donald Palmer, Roger Friedland, and Matthew Zafonte. 1998. "Lost in Space: The Geography of Corporate Interlocking Directorates." *American Journal of Sociology* 103:863–911.

Krackhardt, David. 1988. "Predicting with Networks: Nonparametric Multiple Regression Analysis of Dyadic Data." *Social Networks* 10:359–81.

Kristof, Nicholas D. 1998. "Hubris and Humility as U.S. Waxes and Asia Wanes." *New York Times*, March 22.

Kuroki, Fumiaki. 2001. *The Present Status of Unwinding of Cross-Shareholding: The Fiscal 2000 Survey of Cross-Shareholding.* Tokyo: NLI (Nippon Life Insurance) Research Institute Financial Research Group.

Landers, Peter. 2000a. "Asian News: Shoei Faces a Hostile Bid in a Milestone for Japan." *Wall Street Journal Europe*, January 25, p. 13.

———. 2000b. "A Hostile Takeover Bid Elbows Its Way into Usually Polite Japan." *Wall Street Journal*, January 25, p. A13.

———. 2000c. "Murakami Expects Bid for Shoei to Fall Short." *Wall Street Journal*, February 11.

———. 2002. "Reformer Takes on Japan's System, Seeking Respect for Shareholders." *Wall Street Journal Interactive Edition*, May 12.

Lawrence, Robert Z. 1991. "Efficient or Exclusionist? The Import Behavior of Japanese Corporate Groups." Pp. 311–30 in *Brookings Papers on Economic Activity*, edited by W. C. Brainard and G. L. Perry. Washington, DC: Brookings Institution.

———. 1993. "Japan's Different Trade Regime: An Analysis with Particular Reference to Keiretsu." *Journal of Economic Perspectives* 7:3–19.

Lazear, E. P. 1979. "Why Is There Mandatory Retirement." *Journal of Political Economy* 87:1261–84.

Leff, Nathaniel H. 1978. "Industrial Organization and Entrepreneurship in the Developing Countries." *Economic Development and Cultural Change* 26:661–75.

Leifer, Eric and Harrison White. 1987. "A Structural Approach to Markets." In *Intercorporate Relations: The Structural Analysis of Business*, edited by Mark S. Mizruchi and Michael Schwartz. New York: Cambridge University Press.

Levine, Joel H. 1972. "The Sphere of Influence." *American Sociological Review* 37:14–27.

Light, Ivan H. 1972. *Ethnic Enterprise in America.* Berkeley, CA: University of California Press.

Liker, J. K., R. R. Kamath, S. N. Wasti, and M. Nagamachi. 1996. "Supplier Involvement in Automotive Component Design: Are There Really Large US Japan Differences?" *Research Policy* 25:59–89.

Lincoln, Edward J. 1990. *Japan's Unequal Trade.* Washington, DC: Brookings Institution.

Lincoln, James R. 1978. "Urban Distribution of Headquarters and Branch Plants in Manufacturing – Mechanisms of Metropolitan Dominance." *Demography* 15:213–22.

———. 1982. "Intra- (and Inter-) Organizational Networks." Pp. 1–39 in *Research in the Sociology of Organizations*, edited by S. B. Bacharach. Greenwich, CT: JAI Press, volume 1.

1984. "Analyzing Relations in Dyads – Problems, Models, and an Application to Interorganizational Research." *Sociological Methods & Research* 13:45–76.

Lincoln, James R. 1990. "Japanese Organization and Organization Theory." Pp. 255–94 in *Research in Organizational Behavior*, Volume 12, edited by Barry M. Staw and L. L. Cummings. Greenwich, CT: JAI Press.

Lincoln, James R. and Christina Ahmadjian. 2001. "*Shukko* (Employee Transfers) and Tacit Knowledge Exchange in Japanese Supply Networks: The Electronics Industry Case." Pp. 151–98 in *Knowledge Emergence: Social, Technical, and Evolutionary Dimensions of Knowledge Creation*, edited by I. Nonaka and T. Nishiguchi. New York: Oxford University Press.

Lincoln, James R., Christina L. Ahmadjian, and Eliot Mason. 1998. "Organizational Learning and Purchase-Supply Relations in Japan: Hitachi, Matsushita, and Toyota Compared." *California Management Review: Special Issue on Knowledge and the Firm* 24:241–64.

Lincoln, James R., Michael L. Gerlach, and Christina L. Ahmadjian. 1996. "Keiretsu Networks and Corporate Performance in Japan." *American Sociological Review* 61:67–88.

1998. "Evolving Patterns of Keiretsu Organization and Action in Japan." Pp. 307–43 in *Research in Organizational Behavior*, Volume 20, edited by B. M. Staw and L. L. Cummings. Greenwich, CT: JAI Press.

Lincoln, J. R., M. L. Gerlach, and P. Takahashi. 1992. "Keiretsu Networks in the Japanese Economy – a Dyad Analysis of Intercorporate Ties." *American Sociological Review* 57:561–85.

Lincoln, James R. and Arne L. Kalleberg. 1990. *Culture, Control, and Commitment: A Study of Work Organization and Work Attitudes in the United States and Japan*. Cambridge, UK: Cambridge University Press.

Lincoln, James R. and Kerry McBride. 1985. "Resources, Homophily, and Dependence – Organizational Attributes and Asymmetric Ties in Human-Service Networks." *Social Science Research* 14:1–30.

Lincoln, James R. and Yoshifumi Nakata. 1997. "The Transformation of the Japanese Employment System: Nature, Depth, and Origins." *Work and Occupations* 24:33–55.

Lincoln, James R., Jon Olson, and Mitsuyo Hanada. 1978. "Cultural Effects on Organizational Structure: The Case of Japanese Firms in the United States." *American Sociological Review* 43:829–47.

Loasby, Brian J. 1976. *Choice, Complexity and Ignorance*. Cambridge, UK: Cambridge University Press.

Lockwood, William W. 1968. *The Economic Development of Japan: Growth and Structural Change*. Princeton, NJ: Princeton University Press.

Mace, Myles L. 1971. *Directors: Myth and Reality*. Boston: Harvard Business School Press.

Marsh, Robert M. and Hiroshi Mannari. 1976. *Modernization and the Japanese Factory*. Princeton, NJ: Princeton University Press.

Mason, Mark. 1992. *American Multinationals and Japan: The Political Economy of Japanese Capital Controls, 1899–1980*. Cambridge, MA: Harvard University Press.

McCabe, Kevin A., Mary L. Rigdon, and Vernon L. Smith. 2003. "Positive Reciprocity and Intentions in Trust Games." *Journal of Economic Behavior & Organization.* 52:267–75.

Miles, Raymond E. and Charles C. Snow. 1987. "Organizations: New Concepts for New Forms." *California Management Review* 28:62–73.

Mintz, Beth, and Michael Schwartz. 1985. *The Power Structure of American Business.* Chicago: University of Chicago Press.

Mitchell, J. Clyde. 1974. "Social Networks." *Annual Review of Anthropology* 3:279–99.

MITI. 1999. *White Paper on Small and Medium Enterprises in Japan: Into an Age of Business Innovation and New Start-Ups.* Tokyo: Small and Medium Enterprise Agency, Ministry of International Trade and Industry.

Miwa, Yoshiro. 1996. *Firms and Industrial Organization in Japan.* London: MacMillan.

Miwa, Yoshiro and J. Mark Ramseyer. 2000. "Rethinking Relationship-Specific Investments: Subcontracting in the Japanese Automobile Industry." *Michigan Law Review* 98:2636–67.

2002. "The Fable of the Keiretsu." *Journal of Economics & Management Strategy* 11:169–224.

Miyajima, Hideaki. 1994. "The Transformation of Zaibatsu to Postwar Corporate Groups – from Hierarchically Integrated Groups to Horizontally Integrated Groups." *Journal of the Japanese and International Economies* 8:293–328.

1998. "The Impact of Deregulation on Corporate Governance and Finance." In *Is Japan Really Changing Its Ways? Regulatory Reform and the Japanese Economy*, edited by Lonny E. Carlyle and Mark C. Tilton. Washington: Brookings Institution Press.

Miyamoto, Mataji and Yotaro Sakudo. 1979. *Sumitomo no keieishiteki kenkyu* (Historical Research on Sumitomo). Tokyo: Jikkyo Shuppan.

Miyamoto, Mataji and Keiichino Nakagawa. 1976. *Nihon keieishi koza.* Tokyo: Nihon Keizai Shinbunsha.

Miyashita, Kenichi and David Russell. 1994. *Keiretsu: Inside the Hidden Japanese Conglomerates.* New York: McGraw-Hill.

Mizruchi, Mark S. 1993. "Cohesion, Equivalence, and Similarity of Social Behavior: A Theoretical and Empirical Assessment." *Social Networks* 15:275–307.

1996. "What Do Interlocks Do? An Analysis, Critique, and Assessment of Research on Interlocking Directorates." *Annual Review of Sociology* 22:271–98.

Moerke, Andreas. 1999. "Performance and Corporate Governance Structures of Japanese Keiretsu Groups." In *Information Processing as a Competitive Advantage of Japanese Firms*, edited by Horst Albach, Ulrike Goertzen, and Rita Zobel. Berlin: Sigma.

Morck, Randall and Masao Nakamura. 1999. "Banks and Corporate Control in Japan." *Journal of Finance* 54:319–39.

Morck, Randall, Masao Nakamura, and A. Shivdasani. 2000. "Banks, Ownership Structure, and Firm Value in Japan." *Journal of Business* 73:539–67.

Morikawa, Hidemasa. 1980. *Zaibatsu no keieishiteki kenkyu*. Tokyo: Keizai Shin-posha.

1993. *Zaibatsu: The Rise and Fall of Family Enterprise Groups in Japan*. Tokyo, Japan: University of Tokyo Press.

Murphy, R. Taggart. 1996. *The Weight of the Yen*. New York: W. W. Norton.

Murray, Alan. 1997. "New Economic Models Are Failing while America Inc. Keeps Rolling." *Wall Street Journal*, December 8.

Murray, Matt. 2001. "As Huge Firms Keep Growing, CEOs Struggle to Keep Pace." *Wall Street Journal*, February 8.

Nakamura, Takafusa. 1983. *Economic Growth in Prewar Japan*. New Haven, CT: Yale University Press.

Nakane, Chie. 1970. *Japanese Society*. London: Weidenfeld & Nicolson.

Nakatani, Iwao. 1984. "The Economic Role of Financial Corporate Group-ing." Pp. 227–8 in *The Economic Analysis of the Japanese Firm*, edited by Masahiko Aoki. Amsterdam: North-Holland.

NEC (Nippon Electric Company). 1958a. *NEC 60 Year History*. Tokyo: NEC Limited.

1958b. *NEC 40th Edition*. Tokyo: NEC Limited.

1969. *NEC 70 Year History (1899–1969)*. Tokyo: NEC Limited.

Nelson, Richard R. 1995. "Recent Evolutionary Theorizing About Economic Change." *Journal of Economic Literature* 33:48–90.

Nikkei Databank Bureau. 1989. *NEEDS – Corporate Data*. Tokyo: Nihon Keizai Shimbun.

Nishiguchi, Toshihiro. 1994. *Strategic Industrial Sourcing: The Japanese Advan-tage*. New York: Oxford University Press.

Nishiguchi, Toshihiro and Alexandre Beaudet. 1998. "Case Study – the Toyota Group and the Aisin Fire." *Sloan Management Review* 40:49–60.

Noguchi, Y. 1998. "The 1940 System: Japan under the Wartime Economy." *Amer-ican Economic Review* 88:404–7.

Norville, Elizabeth. 1998. "The Illiberal Roots of Japanese Financial Regulatory Reform," Pp. 111–41 in *Is Japan Really Changing Its Ways?* Edited by Lonny Carlile and Mark Tilton. Washington, DC: Brookings Institution.

Odagiri, Hiroyuki. 1975. "Kigyo-shudan no riron" (The Theory of Corporate Groups). *Kikan riron keizaigaku* (Economics Studies Quarterly), volume 26.

1992. *Growth through Competition, Competition through Growth: A Study of Japanese Management*. New York: Clarendon Press.

Odaka, Konosuke, Keinosuke Ono, and Fumihiko Adachi. 1988. *The Automo-bile Industry in Japan: A Study of Ancillary Firm Development*. Tokyo: Kinokuniya.

Ogawa, Joshua. 1995. "Corporations Embrace Company System: Structure Em-ulates Outlawed Holding Firms, Improves Agility." *Nikkei Weekly*, May 1.

Ohkawa, Kazushi and Henry Rosovsky. 1973. *Japanese Economic Growth: Trend Acceleration in the Twentieth Century*. Stanford, CA: Stanford University Press.

Okazaki, Tetsuji. 1993. "The Japanese Firm under the Wartime Planned-Economy." *Journal of the Japanese and International Economies* 7:175–203.

Okimoto, Daniel I. 1989. *Between MITI and the Market: Japanese Industrial Policy for High Technology*. Stanford, CA: Stanford University Press.

Okumura, Hiroshi. 1982. "Interfirm Relations in an Enterprise Group – the Case of Mitsubishi." *Japanese Economic Studies* 10:53–82.

——. 1983. *Shin nihon no rokudai kigyo shudan* (A New Look at Japan's Six Major Enterprise Groups). Tokyo: Daiyamondo-sha.

Okuno-Fujiwara, Masahiro. 1991. "Industrial Policy in Japan: A Political Economy View." In *The U.S. And Japan: Trade and Investment*, edited by Paul R. Krugman. Chicago: University of Chicago Press.

Olson, Mancur. 1982. *The Rise and Decline of Nations: Economic Growth, Stagflation, and Social Rigidities*. New Haven, CT: Yale University Press.

Ord, Keith. 1975. "Estimation Methods for Models of Spatial Interaction." *Journal of the American Statistical Association* 70:120–26.

Ornstein, Michael D. 1984. "Interlocking Directorates in Canada: Intercorporate or Class Allliance?" *Administrative Science Quarterly* 29:210–31.

Orru, Marco, Nicole Woolsey Biggart, and Gary G. Hamilton. 1997. *The Economic Organization of East Asian Capitalism*. Thousand Oaks, CA: Sage Publications.

Orru, Marco, Gary G. Hamilton, and Mariko Suzuki. 1989. "Patterns of Inter-Firm Control in Japanese Business." *Organization Studies* 10:549–74.

Ouchi, William G. 1981. *Theory Z: How American Business Can Meet the Japanese Challenge*. Reading, MA: Addison-Wesley.

——. 1986. *The M-Form Society*. New York: Avon.

Ozawa, Ichiro. 1994. *Blueprint for a New Japan: The Rethinking of a Nation*. Tokyo: Kodansha.

Palmer, Donald. 1983. "Broken Ties: Interlocking Directorates and Intercorporate Coordination." *Administrative Science Quarterly* 28:40–55.

Palmer, Donald T., Roger Friedland, and Jitendra V. Singh. 1986. "The Ties That Bind: Organizational and Class Bases of Stability in a Corporate Interlock Network" *American Sociological Review* 51:781–96.

Pascale, Richard T. and Thomas Rohlen. 1983. "The Mazda Turnaround" *Journal of Japanese Studies* 9:219–63.

Pempel, T. J. 1998. *Regime Shift: Comparative Dynamics of the Japanese Political Economy*. Ithaca, NY: Cornell University Press.

Pennings, Johannes. 1980. *Interlocking Directorates*. San Francisco: Jossey-Bass.

Perrow, Charles. 1992. "Small Firm Networks." Pp. 445–70 in *Networks and Organizations: Structure, Form, and Action*, edited by Nitin Nohria and Rorbert G. Eccles. Boston: Harvard Business School Press.

Pesek, William. 2003. "Commentary: Japan Relies on the 'Bank of Toyota' Model." *International Herald Tribune*, January 22.

Pfeffer, Jeffrey and Gerald R. Salancik. 1978. *The External Control of Organizations: A Resource Dependence Perspective*. New York: Harper and Row.

Pilling, David. 2002. "Nonperforming Loans: Piles of Debt with Nowhere to Go." *Financial Times*, November 14.

Piore, Michael J. and Charles F. Sabel. 1984. *The Second Industrial Divide: Possibilities for Prosperity*. New York: Basic Books.

Podolny, Joel M. 1993. "A Status-Based Model of Market Competition." *American Journal of Sociology* 98:829–72.

Podolny, Joel M. and Karen L. Page. 1998. "Network Forms of Organization." *Annual Review of Sociology* 24:57–76.

Polanyi, Karl. 1944. *The Great Transformation.* New York: Farrar & Rinehart.

Porter, Michael E. 1990. *The Competitive Advantage of Nations.* New York: Free Press.

Powell, W. W. 1990. "Neither Market nor Hierarchy: Network Forms of Organization." Pp. 295–336 in *Research in Organizational Behavior,* volume 12, edited by Barry M. Staw and L. L. Cummings. Greenwich, CT: JAI Press.

Pred, Alan. 1977. *City Systems in Advanced Economies.* London: Hutchison.

Prestowitz, Clyde V. 1989. *Trading Places: How We Are Giving Our Future to Japan and How to Reclaim It.* New York: Basic Books.

Ramseyer, J. Mark. 1994. "Explicit Reasons for Implicit Contracts: the Legal Logic to the Japanese Main Bank System." Pp. 231–57 in *The Japanese Main Bank System: Its Relevance for Developing and Transforming Economies,* edited by M. Aoki and H. Patrick. Oxford, UK: Clarendon Press.

Richardson, G. B. 1972. "The Organization of Industry." *Economic Journal* 82:883–96.

Roe, Mark J. 1994. *Strong Managers, Weak Owners.* Princeton, NJ: Princeton University Press.

Roehl, Thomas W. 1983a. *An Economic Analysis of Industrial Groupings in Post-War Japan.* Unpublished Ph.D. dissertation, University of Washington.

———. 1983b. "A Transactions Cost Approach to International Trading Structures: The Case of the Japanese General Trading Companies." *Hitotsubashi Journal of Economics* 24:119–35.

Rohlen, Thomas P. 1974. *For Harmony and Strength: Japanese White-Collar Organization in Anthropological Perspective.* Berkeley, CA: University of California Press.

Rosenbluth, Frances McCall. 1989. *Financial Politics in Contemporary Japan.* Ithaca: Cornell University Press.

Rtischev, Dmitry and Robert E. Cole. 2003. "The Role of Organizational Discontinuity in High Technology: Insights from a U.S.-Japan Comparison." In *Roadblocks on the Information Highway,* edited by Jane Bachnik. Lanham, MD: Rowman Littlefield.

Rumelt, Richard P. 1974. *Strategy, Structure, and Economic Performance.* Cambridge, MA: Harvard Business School.

Sakakibara, Kiyonori. 1993. "R&D Cooperation among Competitors: A Case Study of the VLSI Semiconductor Research Project in Japan." *Journal of Engineering and Technology Management* 10:393–407.

Sakakibara, Kiyonori and Kouji Miki. 1999. "The International Comparative Study of Companies' Procurement Activities Supported by Information Technology." Tokyo: National Institute of Science and Technology Policy (NISTEP).

Sakamoto, Kazuichi. 1991. "Enterprise Groups in Contemporary Japan." *Japanese Economic Studies* 19:56–88.

Sako, Mari 1992. *Prices, Quality, and Trust: Inter-Firm Relations in Britain and Japan.* New York: Cambridge University Press.

1996. "Suppliers' Associations in the Japanese Automobile Industry: Collective Action for Technology Diffusion." *Cambridge Journal of Economics* 20:651–71.

2004. *Shifting Boundaries of the Firm: Japanese Management – Japanese Labour.* Oxford, UK: Oxford University Press.

Sako, Mari and Susan Helper. 1998. "Determinants of Trust in Supplier Relations: Evidence from the Automotive Industry in Japan and the United States." *Journal of Economic Behavior & Organization* 34:387–417.

Samuels, Richard J. 1987. *The Business of the Japanese State.* Ithaca, NY: Cornell University Press.

Sanger, David E. 2003. "The Global Cost of Crony Capitalism." *New York Times,* July 21.

SAS Institute. 1990. *SAS/Stat User's Guide,* Version 6. Cary, NC: SAS Institute.

Sato, Makoto. 1999a. "Sanwa Bank Scrambles to Keep Up as Three-Bank Deal Reshuffles Industry." *Nikkei Net Interactive,* September 6.

1999b. "Bank Merger to Blur Old Zaibatsu Lines." *Nikkei Weekly,* October 18.

Saxenian, AnnaLee. 1996. *Regional Advantage.* Cambridge, MA: Harvard University Press.

1991. "The Origins and Dynamics of Production Networks in Silicon Valley." *Research Policy* 20:423–37.

Schaede, Ulrike. 1995. "The Old-Boy Network and Government-Business Relationships in Japan." *Journal of Japanese Studies* 21:293–317.

1996. "The 1995 Financial Crisis in Japan." Berkeley, CA: Berkeley Roundtable on the International Economy. February.

2000. *Cooperative Capitalism: Self-Regulation, Trade Associations, and the Antimonopoly Law in Japan.* New York: Oxford University Press.

2001. "The Japanese Financial System: From Postwar to the New Millennium." Harvard Business School HBS Case 9-700-049.

Schelling, Thomas C. 1978. *Micromotives and Macrobehavior.* New York: Norton.

Scher, Mark J. 1997. *Japanese Interfirm Networks and their Main Banks.* New York: St. Martin's Press.

Schleifer, Andre and Robert W. Vishy. 1986. "Large Shareholders and Corporate Control." *Journal of Political Economy* 94:461–88.

Schumpeter, Joseph A. 1955. *Capitalism, Socialism, and Democracy.* New York: Harper & Row.

Scott, John. 1986. *Capitalist Property and Financial Power.* Brighton, England: Wheatsheaf Books.

Scott, W. Richard and John W. Meyer. 1994. *Institutional Environments and Organizations.* Thousand Oaks, CA: Sage.

Selznick, Philip. 1949. *TVA and the Grass Roots.* Berkeley, CA: University of California Press.

396   *Bibliography*

Sevastopulo, Demetri. 2002. "US View: Great Ideas but No Timetable for Delivery." *Financial Times*, November 14.

Sheard, Paul 1986a. "Main Banks and Internal Capital Markets in Japan." *Shoken keizai* 157:255–85.

—— 1986b. "General Trading Companies and Structural Adjustment in Japan." Research Paper No. 132, Australia-Japan Research Centre, February 1986.

—— 1989a. "The Main Bank System and Corporate Monitoring and Control in Japan." *Journal of Economic Behavior and Organization* 11:399–422.

—— 1989b. "The Japanese General Trading Company as an Aspect of Interfirm Risk-Sharing." *Journal of the Japanese and International Economies* 3:308–22.

—— 1991a. "The Economics of Japanese Corporate Organization and the Structural Impediments Debate – a Critical Review." *Japanese Economic Studies* 19:30–78.

—— 1991b. "The Role of Firm Organization in the Adjustment of a Declining Industry in Japan – the Case of Aluminum." *Journal of the Japanese and International Economies* 5:14–40.

—— 1994a. "Main Banks and the Governance of Financial Distress." In *The Japanese Main Bank System: Its Relevancy for Developing and Transforming Economies*, edited by Masahiko Aoki and Hugh Patrick. New York: Oxford University Press.

—— 1994b. "Reciprocal Delegated Monitoring in the Japanese Main Bank System." *Journal of the Japanese and International Economies* 8:1–21.

—— 1997. "Keiretsu, Competition, and Market Access." Pp. 501–46 in *Global Competition Policy*, edited by Edward M. Graham and J. David Richardson. Washington, DC: Institute for International Economics.

Shimotani, Masahiro. 1996. *Mochikabu-gaisha kaikin* (The Lifting of the Holding Company Ban). Tokyo: Chuo Koronsha.

—— 1998. *Matsushita gurupu no rekishi to kozo* (The History and Structure of the Matsushita Group). Tokyo: Yūhikaku.

Shioji, Hiromi. 1995. "'Itaku' Automotive Production: An Aspect of the Development of Full-Line and Wide-Selection Production by Toyota in the 1960's." *Kyoto University Economic Review*, vol. 66.

Shirai, Taishiro. 1983. *Contemporary Industrial Relations in Japan*. Madison, WI: University of Wisconsin Press.

Shirouzu, Norhiko. 1999a. "Toyota Is Tightening Control of Key Suppliers in Bid to Block Encroachment by Foreign Firms." *Wall Street Journal*, August 3, p. A18.

—— 1999b. "Nissan's Revival Relies on Operating Chief's Agility: Ghosn Must Lead Tough Revamping Despite Obstacles." *Wall Street Journal*, October 18.

—— 1999c. "Nissan Overhaul May Entice Foreign Corporate Raids without Keiretsu Tie-Ins, Suppliers Become Vulnerable." *Wall Street Journal*, October 20, p. A20.

—— 2000. "Founding Clan Vies with Outsider for a Place at the Top of Toyota." *Wall Street Journal*, May 15.

Smith, Randall, Steven Lipin, and Amal Kumar. 1994. "Managing Profits; How General Electric Damps Fluctuations in Its Annual Earnings." *Wall Street Journal*, October 3.

Smitka, Michael J. 1991. *Competitive Ties: Subcontracting in the Japanese Automotive Industry*. New York: Columbia University Press.

Spiegel, Mark M. 2000. "Bank Charter Value and the Viability of the Japanese Convoy System." *Journal of the Japanese and International Economies* 14:149–68.

Spindle, Bill. 1998. "Sakura Bank Seeks Infusion of 2 Billion from Big Holders." *Wall Street Journal*, August 31.

Stata Corporation. 1999. *Stata User's Guide: Release 6*. College Station, TX: Stata Press.

Stinchcombe, Arthur M. 1965. "Social Structure and Organizations." In *Handbook of Organizations*, edited by James G. March. Chicago: Rand McNally.

Strom, S. 1999. "Toyota Picks Aide to Founding Family as President." *New York Times*, April 14.

Sugawara, Sandra. 1998. "In Japan Ties Meant to Bind Now Strangle: Powerful Keiretsu System Stalls Nation's Recovery." *Washington Post*, October 16.

Sugiyama, Yoshikuni. 2003. "Other Firms Should Copy Toyota's Largesse." *Daily Yomiuri Online*, January 23.

Sumitomo Bank. 1926. *30 Year History*. Osaka: Sumitomo Bank Limited.

   1955a. *Sumitomo Bank Short History*. Osaka: Sumitomo Bank Limited.

   1955b. *Sumitomo Bank History*. Osaka: Sumitomo Bank Limited.

   1955c. *History of 60 Years: 1859–1955*. Osaka: Sumitomo Bank Limited.

   1965. *Sumitomo Bank History (Continued)*. Osaka: Sumitomo Bank Limited.

   1979. *History of 80 Years*. Osaka: Sumitomo Bank Limited.

Suzuki, Yoshio. 1987. *The Japanese Financial System*. Oxford, England: Clarendon Press.

Suzuki, Yumiko. 2001. "Last of Six Failed Insurers Find Firms to Bail Them Out." *Nikkei Weekly*, February 26.

Taira, Koji and Solomon Levine. 1985. "Japan's Industrial Relations: A Social Compact Emerges." Pp. 247–300 in *Industrial Relations in a Decade of Economic Change*, edited by Harvey Juris, Mark Thompson, and Wilbur Daniels. Madison, WI: Industrial Relations Research Association Series.

Takahashi, Kamekichi. 1930. *Nihon zaibatsu no kaibo*. Tokyo: Chuo Koronsha.

Takahashi, Peggy K. 1995. *Strategic Spin-offs and Organizational Change in the Japanese Electric and Electronic Equipment Industry*. Unpublished Ph.D. dissertation, University of California, Berkeley.

Teece, David J. 1986. "Transactions Cost Economics and the Multinational-Enterprise – an Assessment." *Journal of Economic Behavior & Organization* 7:21–45.

Teece, David J. and Sidney Winter 1984. "The Limits of Neoclassical Theory in Management Education." *American Economic Review* 74:116–21.

Teikoku Databank America. 2003. *Bankruptcy Report*. Tokyo: Teikoku Databank.

Teranishi, J. 1986. "Economic-Growth and Regulation of Financial-Markets – Japanese Experience during Postwar High Growth Period." *Hitotsubashi Journal of Economics* 27:149–65.

Tett, Gillian. 1997. "Fuji Bank: A Commitment Problem." *Financial Times*, November 22.

Thompson, James D. 1967. *Organizations in Action*. New York: McGraw-Hill.

Thornton, Emily. 1999. "Mystery at Toyota's Top: An Executive Shuffle Doesn't Clear Anything Up." *Business Week Online*, April 26.

Thurow, Lester C. 1993. *Head to Head: The Coming Economic Battle among Japan, Europe, and America*. New York: Warner Books.

Tokyo Stock Exchange. 2002. *Shareownership Survey of the National Conference of Stock Exchanges*. Tokyo: Tokyo Stock Exchange.

Toyo Keizai. Various years. *Kigyo keiretsu soran* (Enterprise Keiretsu Survey). Tokyo: Toyo Keizai Ltd.

Treece, James B. 1998. "When Times Get Tough, Toyota Goes Shopping." *Automotive News*, November 30.

Tushman, Michael and Philip Anderson. 1986. "Technological Discontinuities and Organizational Environments." *Administrative Science Quarterly* 31:439–65.

Useem, Michael. 1984. *The Inner Circle*. New York: Oxford University Press.

    1996. *Investor Capitalism: How Money Managers Are Changing the Face of Corporate America*. New York: Basic Books/ HarperCollins.

Uzzi, Brian. 1996. "The Sources and Consequences of Embeddedness for the Economic Performance of Organizations: The Network Effect." *American Sociological Review* 61:674–98.

Uzzi, Brian and James J. Gillespie. 2002. "Knowledge Spillover in Corporate Financing Networks: Embeddedness and the Firm's Debt Performance." *Strategic Management Journal* 23:595–618.

van Wolferen, Karel. 1989. *The Enigma of Japanese Power*. London: Macmillan.

von Mehren, Arthur T. 1963. Law in Japan. Cambridge, MA: Harvard University Press.

Walker, Gordon, B., Bruce Kogut, and W. J. Shan. 1997. "Social Capital, Structural Holes and the Formation of an Industry Network." *Organization Science* 8:109–25.

Wallich, Henry C. and Mable I. Wallich. 1976. "Banking and Finance." In *Asia's New Giant: How the Japanese Economy Works*, edited by Hugh Patrick and Henry Rosovsky. Washington, DC: Brookings Institution.

Wasserman, Stanley and Joseph Galaskiewicz. 1994. *Advances in Social Network Analysis*. Thousand Oaks, CA: Sage Publications.

Weinstein, David E and Yishay Yafeh. 1995. "Japan's Corporate Groups: Collusive or Competitive? An Empirical Investigation of Keiretsu Behavior." *Journal of Industrial Economics* 43:359–76.

Wellman, Barry and S. D. Berkowitz. 1987. *Social Structures: A Network Approach*, edited by Barry Wellman and S. D. Berkowitz. Cambridge, MA: Cambridge University Press.

Westney, D. Eleanor. 1987. *Imitation and Innovation: The Transfer of Western Organizational Patterns to Meiji Japan*. Cambridge, MA: Harvard University Press.

White, Harrison C. 1992. *Identity and Control: A Structural Theory of Social Action*. Princeton, NJ: Princeton University Press.

White, Harrison C., S. A. Boorman, and R. L. Breiger. 1976. "Social-Structure from Multiple Networks.1. Blockmodels of Roles and Positions." *American Journal of Sociology* 81:730–80.

Whittaker, D. H. 1997. *Small Firms in the Japanese Economy*. Cambridge, UK: Cambridge University Press.

Williamson, O. E. 1970. *Corporate Control and Business Behavior*. Englewood Cliffs, NJ: Prentice Hall.

1975. *Markets and Hierarchies*. New York: Free Press.

1985. *The Economic Institutions of Capitalism*. New York: Free Press.

1991. "Comparative Economic Organization: The Analysis of Discrete Structural Alternatives." *Administrative Science Quarterly* 36:269–96.

1994. "Transaction Cost Economics and Organizational Theory." Pp. 77–107 in *Handbook of Organizational Sociology*, edited by Neil Smelser and Richard Swedberg. Princeton, NJ: Princeton University Press.

Wolff, Kurt H. 1950. *The Sociology of Georg Simmel*. Glencoe, IL: Free Press.

Womack, J. P, D. T. Jones, and D. Roos. 1990. *The Machine That Changed the World*. New York: Rawson Associates.

Wray, William D. 1984. *Mitsubishi and the N.Y.K., 1870–1914: Business Strategy in the Japanese Shipping Industry*. Cambridge, MA: Harvard University Press.

Yasui, Takahiro. 1999. "Corporate Governance in Japan." In *Corporate Governance in Asia: A Comparative Perspective*. Paris: OECD.

Yokei, Tatsuya and Kennichi Kanno. 1999. "Young Mazda President Comes with Strings Attached: Former Boss Wallace Likely to Call Shots from Ford Head Office." *Nikkei Weekly*, December 20.

Yoshihara, Hideki, Akimatsu Sakuma, Hiryoyuki Itami, and Tadao Kagono. 1981. *Nihon kigyo no takaku-ka senryaku* (The Diversification Strategy of Japanese Firms: A Managerial Resource Approach). Tokyo: Nihon Keizai Shinbunsha.

Yoshihara, Hideki and Shin-ichi Yonekawa. 1987. *Business History of General Trading Companies: Proceedings of the Fuji Conference*. Tokyo: University of Tokyo Press.

Yoshino, M. Y. and Thomas B. Lifson. 1986. *The Invisible Link: Japan's Sogo Shosha and the Organization of Trade*. Cambridge, MA: MIT Press.

Zajac, Edward J. 1988. "Interlocking Directorates as an Organizational Strategy: A Test of Critical Assumptions." *Academy of Management Journal* 31:428–38.

Zielinski, Robert and Nigel Holloway. 1992. *Unequal Equities: Power and Risk in Japan's Stock Market*. New York: McGraw-Hill.

Index

401

legal system, 42–43
Leifer, Eric, 34–35
lender-borrow network
  cohesion of, 112, 113, 142
  cross-shareholding within, 200
  density of, 141
  director dispatch within, 200
Lincoln, James, 12, 27, 185
linear decline hypothesis, 88–91, 111
Lockwood, William, 14
LTCB (Long-Term Credit Bank), 311

machinery industry analysis, 198, 199
madoguchi shido, 215
management incentives
  American, 368–369
  Japanese, 369–370
market transactions. *See* economic
    exchange
Matsushita, 138–139, 263
Mazda
  assistance from Sumitomo, 94
  Ford's alliance with, 336–337
  Ford's management of, 282, 283
  relations with suppliers, 263
Mei, Jianping, 288
Meiji through pre-war period, 53–68,
    84–85
mergers, American, 161–162
metals industry analysis, 195, 196
METI (Ministry of Economy, Trade, and
    Industry). *See* MITI
Mikitani, Hiroshi, 348–349
Mitarai, Fujio, 371
MITI (Ministry of International Trade and
    Industry)
  foci of attention, 15
  historical functions, 214
  interests of bureaucrats in, 213
  keiretsu's role in helping, 213–214
  nature and size of, 13
  post-Occupation rebuilding measures, 74
  power of, 14–15, 213
  rebirth as METI, 15
Mitsubishi
  assistance to Akai Electric, 219–220
  blockmodel results for, 129–130
  foreign investment in, 337–338
  post-Occupation power of, 74
  relative coherence, 118
  transparency of company affiliation
    with, 23–24
Mitsubishi Chemical, 227
Mitsui
  blockmodel results for, 130–131
  central control loosening by, 65
  group coherence of, 118

merger with Sumitomo, 125–126,
    314–315
Mitsui Construction bailout, 220
Mitsukoshi Incident, 218
Miyashita, Kenichi, 161, 232
Mizuho Bank, 312–313, 317
modernization theory, 88–91, 111
MOF (Ministry of Finance), 305–306
mokuhyo genka, 75
moral hazard, 5
Mothers market section, 350–351
multiplexity, 24
Murakami, Yoshiaki, 330–331
Murphy, R. Taggart, 11–12, 158, 208–209,
    210–211
Mycal bankruptcy, 307

Nakamae, Tadashi, 211
Nakatani, Iwao, 205, 209–210
NASDAQ Japan, 351
National Mobilization Act – Article 11,
    69–70
NEC
  challenges to dominance of, 342–343
  founding, 67
  growth pattern within, 58–63
  web of affiliations, 23
nenko joretsu, 210
'netbatsu,' 298, 347
network analysis
  cohesion trends, 111–117, 118–120
  data and sample, 97–111
  methods, 96–97
  see also blockmodeling; economic
    exchange, analysis
network idea
  general incidence of, 10
  in scholarship on Japan, 11–13
'networkness'
  decline of, 3–4
  variation in, 45
networks
  change models summarized, 88
  cyclical change hypothesis, 94–96,
    116–117
  developmental phases, 51–52
  differences per industry, 185–191
  diversification within, 54–58
  independence and flexibility within,
    64–66
  linear decline hypothesis, 88–91, 111
  persistence within
    institutional-based, 92–94
    post-1990s, 297–298
  satellite spinoffs, 64–68
  satellite strategic partnering, 66–67
  sectoral variations within, 58–63

Printed in the United States
By Bookmasters